The Bird Almanac

The Bird Almanac

THE ULTIMATE GUIDE TO ESSENTIAL FACTS AND FIGURES OF THE WORLD'S BIRDS

David M. Bird

KEY PORTER BOOKS

Canadian Cataloguing in Publication Data

Bird, David M.
        The bird almanac

ISBN 1-55263-003-X

1. Birds.   I. Title.

QL673.B572 1999   598   C98-932400-1

The Canada Council | Le Conseil des Arts
FOR THE ARTS | DU CANADA
SINCE 1957 | DEPUIS 1957

The publisher gratefully acknowledges the support of the Canada Council for the Arts and the Ontario Arts Council for its publishing program.

Key Porter Books Limited
70 The Esplanade
Toronto, Ontario
Canada M5E 1R2

www.keyporter.com

Design: Peter Maher
Electronic formatting: Heidi Palfrey, Heidy Lawrance Associates
Illustrations: Ian Sproule / Studio Mars

Printed and bound in Canada

99 00 01 02 6 5 4 3 2 1

To the memory of my father,
David Archibald Bird (1924–1975),
who knew long before I did that I would
become a writer about wildlife.
Seldom a day passes that I do not think of him.

Table of Contents

Illustrations

Preface

Why a bird almanac? The idea actually took root because of the phone calls. As a weekly columnist on birds for *The Gazette* of Montreal (for at least a dozen years), I get numerous phone calls from people with questions about birds. While many are desperately seeking solutions to problems with unwanted pigeons or are looking for a cheaper place to buy cracked corn to feed pigeons, others simply want to know more about the birds in their backyard. For instance, what's the incubation period for those robin's eggs sitting in the nest over the porch light? What kinds of flowers attract hummingbirds? What kinds of foods can one offer to the birds? Perhaps a caller's child is looking for information for a school project on birds: What is the rate of a bird's heartbeat? How fast does a bird fly? How long do they live? Or maybe someone's trying to settle a bet or answer a trivia question: What's the world's fastest-flying bird or the smallest bird's egg? How much weight can a bird carry? Maybe the caller is merely searching for names of ecotourism companies catering to bird-watchers or for some tips on buying binoculars.

Oh yes, there are many fine books and scientific journals out there that provide answers to these questions and more. But I longed to have just one resource book by my telephone or in my briefcase that could answer most of the kinds of questions I am often asked. In searching for a model for this book, I came across the "almanac," that is, a reasonably compact, user-friendly, relatively up-to-date, but, most important of all, fairly inexpensive book designed to provide quick, ready answers to commonly asked questions. The famous *Farmers' Almanac* and, in more recent years, *The Universal Almanac* published by Andrews and McMeel (Kansas and New York), come to mind as examples. There now exist almanacs for a variety of subjects, ranging from fishing to the Civil War. However, much to my surprise, there existed no such almanac for birds and bird lovers!

There is no shortage of bird lovers out there either, whether professional or amateur. Several professional organizations in both North America and the United Kingdom have grown from as little as a dozen founding members to several thousand in a century's time. For example, the American Ornithologists' Union, founded in 1884, now has more than 4,000 members from countries throughout the world, while the British Ornithologists' Union, established in 1858, has more than 2,000 members worldwide.

Birds, with their wide distribution around the world, their amazing mobility and powers of flight, and a fascinating array of species and colors, have clearly caught the attention of the public at large as well. One in every four North Americans now casually watches birds, and bird-watching is second only to gardening as the number one recreation worldwide. Yet, in a sad twist of irony, no fewer than 11 percent of the world's 9,000 bird species are at risk of global extinction!

According to the spring 1997 issue of *Bird Conservation*, a magazine from the

American Bird Conservancy, the 1994–95 National Recreation Survey in the United States showed that interest in bird-watching as a recreational activity has increased by 155 percent in the last decade. Recent demographic analyses show that bird-watching will be the fastest-growing activity in the world from 1996 to 2011. The closest rival was hiking, with 94 percent growth. Fishing, hunting, and tennis were down by 4, 12, and 19 percent, respectively. According to a recent survey in *Fortune* magazine, when asked how they unwind on vacation more Americans said they prefer birding over golf. In a 1991 survey of Americans by the U.S. Fish and Wildlife Service, no fewer than 63 million reported that they watch and feed birds at home, and more than 24.7 million said that they traveled to watch birds. In that year, birders spent an incredible $5.2 billion (U.S.) on goods and services related to bird feeding and watching! In the United States today there are more than 360 franchise stores specializing in birding supplies.

In 1985 the World Series of Birding had 13 teams, no corporate sponsors, and $13,000 (U.S.) in contributions. Ten years later there were 55 teams, 27 corporate sponsors, and more than $450,000 (U.S.) in contributions. The numbers of bird-watchers participating in yearly Christmas Bird Counts is up 200 percent since 1970, and up nearly 35 percent since 1980. In 1900 there were only 27 participants, and in 1990 there were 43,000! The American Birding Association doubled its membership to 20,000 in the last five years.

Another aspect of bird-watching showing phenomenal growth is the event known as the birding festival. In 1985 there were five birding festivals, and in 1998 there were well over one hundred all over North America. Here's an example of festival success. The 1994 Rio Grande Valley Birding Festival attracted about 1,000 people and generated about $266,000 (U.S.) over its three days. The 1995 and 1996 events, expanded by two days, each attracted 1,800 people and brought in $1.6 million (U.S.).

One of the best things about the upsurge of interest in birds is that, in general, bird-watchers comprise a gentle folk who are eager to open their wallets and are considerate of others. However, I have heard some horror stories about armies of bird-watchers trampling vegetation and flushing and stressing wild birds. That's why I felt compelled to include in this book not one but two codes of ethics, one from the American Birding Association and another from Britain's Royal Society for the Protection of Birds. With a little education, opening up of new areas in which to bird, and some common-sense people management, the pros of the birding industry can surely far outweigh the cons.

The love affair between the public and birds is by no means restricted to the United States. In Canada in 1988, serious birders numbered 1.2 million, and casual birders 3.6 million. A more recent survey showed that, in 1991, 7.1 million Canadians maintained plants, shrubs, or housing for birds, and 6.6 million bought special feed for them. In that year, almost 19 million Canadians (90 percent of the population) participated in wildlife-related activities, devoting a total of 1.3 billion days and 5.6 billion dollars to those activities. Roughly 85 percent of all Canadians watched wildlife films or television shows; read wildlife books or magazines; or visited zoos, aquariums, and natural history museums. Over two-thirds of all Canadians watched, photographed, or fed wildlife around their homes or cottages in 1991. Nearly one in five Canadians went on trips specifically to enjoy wildlife.

Bird-watching and bird-feeding are even more popular in the United Kingdom. The Royal Society for the Protection of Birds recruited its millionth member at the end of 1997. And in that same year a survey by MORI, one of the U.K.'s largest polling firms, showed that 67 percent of British adults now regularly feed their garden birds.

Naturally, with such a booming interest in birds and bird-watching, books on the subject are no longer in short supply. Visit any library, nature store, or book-order company on the Web and you'll quickly see that there are plenty of bird guides for beginners and experts; how-to books on bird feeding, bird-watching, and birdhouses; coffee-table books; specialty books on certain bird groups; large reference books and encyclopedias; and ornithology textbooks. In recent years, a number of writers have published expensive hard-cover and inexpensive soft-cover reference or resource books on birds to meet this burgeoning curiosity about birds. Was there room for yet one more? It is becoming increasingly difficult to offer something relatively new to the bird-crazy public. How could my book be different?

I wanted a book that would cater to the interests of anyone in the world who liked birds for whatever reason, for example, ornithologists, casual to serious bird-watchers, schoolchildren doing projects on birds, and those offering food to birds. I felt that such a book should offer a brief fossil history of birds, the old and the new taxonomy, and a list of all the species in the world, including the geographical region in which they were found and their status, that is, endangered, threatened, and so on. To keep the book compact and affordable, the illustrations would be restricted to labeled line drawings of various aspects of bird anatomy. Offered in a format that makes it readily accessible should be information on avian anatomy, physiology, reproduction, flight and mortality, recommended bird feed, and housing and plantings to attract birds, among other topics. And to settle those bets or answer trivia questions, why not a list of world records for birds—for example, the deepest dive, the biggest nest, the greatest age attained, the most valuable—and a list of birds honored as official state, provincial, or national mascots?

Speaking of records, what about the people who study or watch birds? Should not an almanac chronicle the achievements of such people? How about a listing of those who have made the effort to record the most species in various geographical areas? Past-presidents of well-known ornithological societies? Winners of ornithological awards, the U.S. Federal Duck Stamp competition, the Ward World Carving Championship, or the World Series of Birding? And any respectable almanac should offer short biographies of famous, deceased ornithologists as well as bird-watchers and conservationists devoted to birds.

An almanac can also be useful by providing the latest listings of bird magazines and journals; organizations that cater to bird-lovers and ornithologists; video, audio, and CD-ROM products; companies that sell products that aid ornithologists and bird-watchers; tour companies focusing on birding; and a relatively new phenomenon—birding festivals.

Finally, no almanac on birds would be complete without a substantial glossary of ornithological terms. By encouraging a common language, perhaps *The Bird Almanac* can help bridge the gap between professional and amateur ornithologists.

I hasten to acknowledge that the process of compiling the information for this book could have led to errors or omissions. It would be surprising, for example, if all of the longevity records were current. Also, while it was my hope to cater to the bird-loving audience throughout the world, I admit to a strong emphasis on information arising in North America and the United Kingdom. Similar data from other countries were not easy to find, perhaps due to language differences. I am aware too that there are other important ornithological awards out there that should be included and that I have likely omitted a number of famous, deceased ornithologists from the who's who list. Records for most species seen and addresses also change frequently with time. If I have inadvertently left out (and I am sure that I have) the name of a prominent organization, company, product, and so on, please do not hesitate to inform me.

Since Key Porter Books expects to update *The Bird Almanac* on a regular basis, we humbly ask you, the reader, to help us ensure that the contents of this book are factual, up-to-date, and useful to as wide a bird-loving audience as possible. Lastly, and most important, it was never my intention for *The Bird Almanac* to be quoted as a scientific reference text and I beseech anyone even considering doing this to refer instead to the many excellent ornithological textbooks and scientific journals available on the market and in libraries.

Whether *The Bird Almanac* successfully fills a niche, time will tell. But, as Pete Dunne, arguably one of North America's top birders, said when I informed him of this book's imminent publication, "There can never be too many books on birds in the world."

Acknowledgments

No book of this sort was ever published without a great deal of help. In no particular order of importance, I gratefully acknowledge the kind assistance of Eleanor MacLean and Ann Habbick of the Blacker-Wood Library at McGill University; Bruce Grainger of the library on McGill's Macdonald Campus; ornithological historians Marianne Ainley and Stuart Houston; Keith Bildstein of the Hawk Mountain Sanctuary Association; Pete Dunne and Sheila Lego of the Cape May Bird Observatory; Frank Gill of the National Audubon Society; David Nettleship of the Canadian Wildlife Service; James Rising of the University of Toronto; Larry Bryan of Savannah River Ecology Laboratory; Charles Duncan of the Institute of Field

Ornithology; Mary Victoria McDonald of the University of Central Arkansas; Gary Duke of the University of Minnesota; Richard Clark of York University; Ian Newton of the Terrestrial Institute of Ecology, U.K.; Pierre Langlois of McGill University; Gwen Bonham of The Natural History Museum, U.K.; Gregory Butcher and Blake Maybank of the American Birding Association; Fred Lohrer and Glen Woolfenden of the Archbold Biological Station; Kathy Merk of the Cooper Ornithological Society; Allen Fish of the Golden Gate Bird Observatory; Derek Turner of the UK400 Club; Alistair Gammell and Chris Martin of the Royal Society for the Protection of Birds (BirdLife Partner in the U.K.); David Stroud of the Joint Nature Conservation Committee, U.K.; author John K. Terres; Bill Thompson III, editor of *Bird Watchers' Digest*; Sheila Hardie, Josep del Hoyo, and Andy Elliott, editors of *Handbook of the Birds of the World*; and Judith Vickey, and Rodger and Elise Titman of Wildlifers.

I have saved the very special people to the end. I was fortunate enough to have two highly resourceful and hard-working research assistants. Melanie Simard was assigned the difficult task of seeking out biographical information on famous, deceased ornithologists from all over the world and distilling their myriad accomplishments into a handful of short phrases. *The Bird Almanac* would not have been possible without the services of Oliver Love, whose brain melded with mine to give me exactly what I asked of him and more. I cannot speak highly enough of this energetic young man whose unwavering enthusiasm for the project and amazing ability to surf the Web helped me bring the book to life. Oliver in turn would like to thank the Science College of Concordia University and the Semeniuks of Kirkland, Quebec, for their support.

Every book has its publication editor. I was incredibly lucky to be blessed with Michael Mouland, former Senior International Editor for Key Porter, who was understanding and laid back enough to leave me to the job, and yet continually, and even humorously, cheered on my efforts to make the book a reality. It was indeed a real pleasure working with him. Mary Ann McCutcheon did a superb job in the later stages of the book and I was impressed with the incredible copy-editing performed by Beverley Beetham Endersby. I am also especially grateful to Ian Sproull of Studio Mars in Pointe Claire, Quebec, for his great care and professionalism in producing quality drawings for the illustrations.

Finally, there are no words to express my gratitude to my life partner and loving wife, Toni. She shared each and every one of my high and low points while working on the almanac, not to mention typing the lion's share of its text. When it comes to her, there is no luckier man on earth!

DAVID M. BIRD
1998

World Checklist of Birds

Key to Numbers

1 Nearctic (incl. Mexico)
2 Neotropic (incl. Hawaiian islands)
3 Palearctic
4 Oriental
5 Ethiopian
6 Australasia

Red List Categories (1994) of the IUCN (International Union for Conservation of Nature and Natural Resources)

DD Data Deficient
CD Conservation Dependent
NT Near Threatened
VU Vulnerable
EN Endangered
CR Critical
EW Extinct in Wild
EX Extinct
SSP Subspecies Only

Order STRUTHIONIFORMES
Family STRUTHIONIDAE

COMMON OSTRICH or OSTRICH *Struthio camelus* (5)

SOMALI OSTRICH *Struthio molybdophanes* (5)

Family RHEIDAE

GREATER RHEA *Rhea americana* (6) [NT]

LESSER RHEA *Rhea pennata* (6) [NT]

Family CASUARIIDAE

SOUTHERN CASSOWARY *Casuarius casuarius* (6) [VU]

DWARF CASSOWARY *Casuarius bennetti* (6) [NT]

NORTHERN CASSOWARY *Casuarius unappendiculatus* (6) [VU]

EMU *Dromaius novaehollandiae* (6)

Family APTERYGIDAE

BROWN KIWI *Apteryx australis* (6) [VU]

LITTLE SPOTTED KIWI *Apteryx owenii* (6) [VU]

GREAT SPOTTED KIWI *Apteryx haastii* (6) [VU]

Order TINAMIFORMES
Family TINAMIDAE

GRAY TINAMOU *Tinamus tao* (2)

SOLITARY TINAMOU *Tinamus solitarius* (2) [NT]

BLACK TINAMOU *Tinamus osgoodi* (2) [DD]

GREAT TINAMOU *Tinamus major* (2)

WHITE-THROATED TINAMOU *Tinamus guttatus* (2)

HIGHLAND TINAMOU *Nothocercus bonapartei* (2)

TAWNY-BREASTED TINAMOU *Nothocercus julius* (2)

HOODED TINAMOU *Nothocercus nigrocapillus* (2) [NT]

CINEREOUS TINAMOU *Crypturellus cinereus* (2)

LITTLE TINAMOU *Crypturellus soui* (2)

TEPUI TINAMOU *Crypturellus ptaritepui* (2) [VU]

BROWN TINAMOU *Crypturellus obsoletus* (2)

THICKET TINAMOU *Crypturellus cinnamomeus* (2)

UNDULATED TINAMOU *Crypturellus undulatus* (2)

PALE-BROWED TINAMOU *Crypturellus transfasciatus* (2) [NT]

BRAZILIAN TINAMOU *Crypturellus strigulosus* (2)

SLATY-BREASTED TINAMOU *Crypturellus boucardi* (2)

CHOCO TINAMOU *Crypturellus kerriae* (2) [VU]

RED-LEGGED TINAMOU *Crypturellus erythropus* (2)

GRAY-LEGGED TINAMOU *Crypturellus duidae* (2)

YELLOW-LEGGED TINAMOU *Crypturellus noctivagus* (2) [NT]

BLACK-CAPPED TINAMOU *Crypturellus atrocapillus* (2)

VARIEGATED TINAMOU *Crypturellus variegatus* (2)

RUSTY TINAMOU *Crypturellus brevirostris* (2)

BARTLETT'S TINAMOU *Crypturellus bartletti* (2)

SMALL-BILLED TINAMOU *Crypturellus parvirostris* (2)

BARRED TINAMOU *Crypturellus casiquiare* (2)

TATAUPA TINAMOU *Crypturellus tataupa* (2)

RED-WINGED TINAMOU *Rhynchotus rufescens* (2)

HUAYCO TINAMOU *Rhynchotus maculicollis* (2)

TACZANOWSKI'S TINAMOU *Nothoprocta taczanowskii* (2) [VU]

KALINOWSKI'S TINAMOU *Nothoprocta kalinowskii* (2) [CR]

ORNATE TINAMOU *Nothoprocta ornata* (2)

ANDEAN TINAMOU *Nothoprocta pentlandii* (2)

BRUSHLAND TINAMOU *Nothoprocta cinerascens* (2)

CURVE-BILLED TINAMOU *Nothoprocta curvirostris* (2)

DARWIN'S NOTHURA *Nothura darwinii* (2)

CHACO NOTHURA *Nothura chacoensis* (2)

SPOTTED NOTHURA *Nothura maculosa* (2)

LESSER NOTHURA *Nothura minor* (2) [VU]

WHITE-BELLIED NOTHURA *Nothura boraquira* (2)

DWARF TINAMOU *Taoniscus nanus* (2) [VU]

ELEGANT CRESTED TINAMOU *Eudromia elegans* (2)

QUEBRACHO CRESTED TINAMOU *Eudromia formosa* (2)

PUNA TINAMOU *Tinamotis pentlandii* (2)

PATAGONIAN TINAMOU *Tinamotis ingoufi* (2)

Order CRACIFORMES
Family CRACIDAE

PLAIN CHACHALACA *Ortalis vetula* (1)

GRAY-HEADED CHACHALACA *Ortalis cinereiceps* (1, 2)

CHESTNUT-WINGED CHACHALACA *Ortalis garrula* (2)

RUFOUS-VENTED CHACHALACA *Ortalis ruficauda* (2)

RUFOUS-HEADED CHACHALACA *Ortalis erythroptera* (2) [VU]

RUFOUS-BELLIED CHACHALACA or WAGLER'S CHACHALACA *Ortalis wagleri* (1)

WEST MEXICAN CHACHALACA *Ortalis poliocephala* (1)

CHACO CHACHALACA *Ortalis canicollis* (1, 2)

WHITE-BELLIED CHACHALACA *Ortalis leucogastra* (1, 2)

SPECKLED CHACHALACA *Ortalis guttata* (2)

LITTLE CHACHALACA *Ortalis motmot* (2)

BUFF-BROWED CHACHALACA *Ortalis superciliaris* (2)

BAND-TAILED GUAN *Penelope argyrotis* (2)

BEARDED GUAN *Penelope barbata* (2) [VU]

BAUDO GUAN *Penelope ortoni* (2) [VU]

ANDEAN GUAN *Penelope montagnii* (2)

MARAIL GUAN *Penelope marail* (2)

RUSTY-MARGINED GUAN *Penelope superciliaris* (1, 2)

RED-FACED GUAN *Penelope dabbenei* (1, 2)

CRESTED GUAN *Penelope purpurascens* (1, 2)

CAUCA GUAN *Penelope perspicax* (2) [VU]

WHITE-WINGED GUAN *Penelope albipennis* (2) [CR]

SPIX'S GUAN *Penelope jacquacu* (2)

DUSKY-LEGGED GUAN *Penelope obscura* (1, 2)

WHITE-CRESTED GUAN *Penelope pileata* (2) [NT]

CHESTNUT-BELLIED GUAN *Penelope ochrogaster* (2) [VU]

WHITE-BROWED GUAN *Penelope jacucaca* (2) [NT]

TRINIDAD PIPING-GUAN *Pipile pipile* (2) [CR]

BLUE-THROATED PIPING-GUAN *Pipile cumanensis* (2)

RED-THROATED PIPING-GUAN *Pipile cujubi* (2)

BLACK-FRONTED PIPING-GUAN *Pipile jacutinga* (2) [VU]

WATTLED GUAN *Aburria aburri* (2) [NT]

BLACK GUAN *Chamaepetes unicolor* (2) [NT]

SICKLE-WINGED GUAN *Chamaepetes goudotii* (2)

HIGHLAND GUAN or BLACK PENELOPINA *Penelopina nigra* (2)

HORNED GUAN *Oreophasis derbianus* (2) [VU]

NOCTURNAL CURASSOW *Nothocrax urumutum* (2)

CRESTLESS CURASSOW *Mitu tomentosa* (2)

SALVIN'S CURASSOW *Mitu salvini* (2)

RAZOR-BILLED CURASSOW *Mitu tuberosa* (2)

ALAGOAS CURASSOW *Mitu mitu* (2) [EW]

HELMETED CURASSOW or NORTHERN HELMETED CURASSOW *Pauxi pauxi* (2) [EN]

HORNED CRASSOW or SOUTHERN HELMETED CURASSOW *Pauxi unicornis* (2) [EN]

GREAT CURASSOW *Crax rubra* (2)

BLUE-KNOBBED CURASSOW or BLUE-BILLED CURASSOW *Crax alberti* (2) [CR]

YELLOW-KNOBBED CURASSOW *Crax daubentoni* (2)

BLACK CURASSOW *Crax alector* (2)

WATTLED CURASSOW *Crax globulosa* (2) [VU]

BARE-FACED CURASSOW *Crax fasciolata* (2)

RED-BILLED CURASSOW *Crax blumenbachii* (2) [CR]

Family MEGAPODIIDAE

AUSTRALIAN BRUSH-TURKEY *Alectura lathami* (6)

WATTLED BRUSH-TURKEY *Aepypodius arfakianus* (6)

BRUIJN'S BRUSH-TURKEY *Aepypodius bruijnii* (6) [VU]

RED-BILLED BRUSH-TURKEY *Talegalla cuvieri* (6)

BLACK-BILLED BRUSH-TURKEY *Talegalla fuscirostris* (6)

BROWN-COLLARED BRUSH-TURKEY *Talegalla jobiensis* (6)

MALEO *Macrocephalon maleo* (4) [VU]

NICOBAR SCRUBFOWL *Megapodius nicobariensis* (4) [VU]

TABON SCRUBFOWL *Megapodius cumingii* (4) [NT]

SULA SCRUBFOWL *Megapodius bernsteinii* (4) [NT]

TANIMBAR MEGAPODE *Megapodius tenimberensis* (4)

ORANGE-FOOTED SCRUBFOWL *Megapodius reinwardt* (6)

DUSKY SCRUBFOWL *Megapodius freycinet* (6)

FORSTEN'S SCRUBFOWL *Megapodius forstenii* (4)

GEELVINK SCRUBFOWL or GEELVINK MEGAPODE *Megapodius geelvinkianus* (6)

NEW GUINEA SCRUBFOWL *Megapodius affinis* (6)

MELANESIAN SCRUBFOWL *Megapodius eremita* (6)

VANUATU SCRUBFOWL *Megapodius layardi* (6) [VU]

MICRONESIAN SCRUBFOWL *Megapodius laperouse* (4) [VU]

NIUAFOOU SCRUBFOWL *Megapodius pritchardii* (4) [EN]

MOLUCCAN SCRUBFOWL *Megapodius wallacei* (4, 6) [VU]

MALLEEFOWL *Leipoa ocellata* (6) [VU]

Order GALLIFORMES
Family PHASIANIDAE

SNOW PARTRIDGE *Lerwa lerwa* (3, 4)

SEE-SEE PARTRIDGE *Ammoperdix griseogularis* (3)

SAND PARTRIDGE *Ammoperdix heyi* (3, 5)

CAUCASIAN SNOWCOCK *Tetraogallus caucasicus* (3)

CASPIAN SNOWCOCK *Tetraogallus caspius* (3)

TIBETAN SNOWCOCK *Tetraogallus tibetanus* (3, 4)

ALTAI SNOWCOCK *Tetraogallus altaicus* (3, 4)

HIMALAYAN SNOWCOCK *Tetraogallus himalayensis* (1, 3, 4)

CHESTNUT-THROATED PARTRIDGE *Tetraogallus obscurus* (4) [NT]

BUFF-THROATED PARTRIDGE *Tetraophasis szechenyii* (4) [NT]

BARBARY PARTRIDGE *Alectoris barbara* (5)

ARABIAN PARTRIDGE *Alectoris melanocephala* (3)

CHUKAR *Alectoris chukar* (1, 2, 3, 4, 5, 6)

PHILBY'S PARTRIDGE *Alectoris philbyi* (3)

RUSTY-NECKLACED PARTRIDGE *Alectoris magna* (4) [NT]

ROCK PARTRIDGE *Alectoris graeca* (3)

RED-LEGGED PARTRIDGE *Alectoris rufa* (3, 5)

BLACK FRANCOLIN *Francolinus francolinus* (1, 2, 3, 4)

PAINTED FRANCOLIN *Francolinus pictus* (4)

CHINESE FRANCOLIN *Francolinus pintadeanus* (4)

GRAY FRANCOLIN *Francolinus pondicerianus* (2, 3, 4, 5)

SWAMP FRANCOLIN *Francolinus gularis* (4) [VU]

COQUI FRANCOLIN *Peliperdix coqui* (5)

WHITE-THROATED FRANCOLIN *Peliperdix albogularis* (5)

SCHLEGEL'S FRANCOLIN *Peliperdix schlegelii* (5)

FOREST FRANCOLIN *Peliperdix lathami* (5)

CRESTED FRANCOLIN *Peliperdix sephaena* (5)

KIRK'S FRANCOLIN *Peliperdix rovuma* (5)

RING-NECKED FRANCOLIN *Scleroptila streptophorus* (5)

FINSCH'S FRANCOLIN *Scleroptila finschi* (5)

GRAY-WINGED FRANCOLIN *Scleroptila africanus* (5)

RED-WINGED FRANCOLIN *Scleroptila levaillantii* (5)

MOORLAND FRANCOLIN *Scleroptila psilolaemus* (5)

SHELLEY'S FRANCOLIN *Scleroptila shelleyi* (5)

ORANGE RIVER FRANCOLIN *Scleroptila levaillantoides* (5)

NAHAN'S FRANCOLIN *Pternistis nahani* (5) [DD]

HARTLAUB'S FRANCOLIN *Pternistis hartlaubi* (5)

DOUBLE-SPURRED FRANCOLIN *Pternistis bicalcaratus* (5)

CLAPPERTON'S FRANCOLIN *Pternistis clappertoni* (5)

HEUGLIN'S FRANCOLIN *Pternistis icterorhynchus* (5)

HARWOOD'S FRANCOLIN *Pternistis harwoodi* (5) [VU]

RED-BILLED FRANCOLIN *Pternistis adspersus* (5)

CAPE FRANCOLIN *Pternistis capensis* (5)

HILDEBRANDT'S FRANCOLIN *Pternistis hildebrandti* (5)

NATAL FRANCOLIN *Pternistis natalensis* (5)

AHANTA FRANCOLIN *Pternistis ahantensis* (5)

SCALY FRANCOLIN *Pternistis squamatus* (5)

GRAY-STRIPED FRANCOLIN *Pternistis griseostriatus* (5) [VU]

YELLOW-NECKED SPURFOWL *Pternistis leucoscepus* (5)

GRAY-BREASTED SPURFOWL *Pternistis rufopictus* (5)

RED-NECKED SPURFOWL *Pternistis afer* (5)

SWAINSON'S SPURFOWL *Pternistis swainsonii* (5)

ERCKEL'S FRANCOLIN *Pternistis erckelii* (2, 5)

OCHER-BREASTED FRANCOLIN or DJIBOUTI FRANCOLIN *Pternistis ochropectus* (5) [CR]

CHESTNUT-NAPED FRANCOLIN *Pternistis castaneicollis* (5)

HANDSOME FRANCOLIN *Pternistis nobilis* (5)

JACKSON'S FRANCOLIN *Pternistis jacksoni* (5)

CAMEROON FRANCOLIN or MOUNT CAMEROON FRANCOLIN *Pternistis camerunensis* (5) [VU]

SWIERSTRA'S FRANCOLIN *Pternistis swierstrai* (5) [VU]

GRAY PARTRIDGE *Perdix perdix* (1, 3, 4)

DAURIAN PARTRIDGE *Perdix dauurica* (3, 4)

TIBETAN PARTRIDGE *Perdix hodgsoniae* (3, 4)

LONG-BILLED PARTRIDGE *Rhizothera longirostris* (4)

MADAGASCAR PARTRIDGE *Margaroperdix madagarensis* (5)

BLACK PARTRIDGE *Melanoperdix nigra* (4) [NT]

COMMON QUAIL *Coturnix coturnix* (3, 4, 5)

JAPANESE QUAIL *Coturnix japonica* (2, 3, 4)

STUBBLE QUAIL *Coturnix pectoralis* (6)

NEW ZEALAND QUAIL *Coturnix novaezelandiae* (6) [EX]

RAIN QUAIL *Coturnix coromandelica* (4)

HARLEQUIN QUAIL *Coturnix delegorguei* (5)

BROWN QUAIL *Coturnix ypsilophora* (4, 6)

BLUE QUAIL *Coturnix adansonii* (5)

BLUE-BREASTED QUAIL or KING QUAIL *Coturnix chinensis* (4, 6)

SNOW MOUNTAIN QUAIL *Anurophasis monorthonyx* (6) [NT]

JUNGLE BUSH-QUAIL *Perdicula asiatica* (4)

ROCK BUSH-QUAIL *Perdicula argoondah* (4)

PAINTED BUSH-QUAIL *Perdicula erythrorhyncha* (4)

MANIPUR BUSH-QUAIL *Perdicula manipurensis* (4) [VU]

UDZUNGWA FOREST PARTRIDGE *Xenoperdix udzungwensis* (5) [EN]

HILL PARTRIDGE *Arborophila torqueola* (3, 4)

RUFOUS-THROATED PARTRIDGE *Arborophila rufogularis* (4)

WHITE-CHEEKED PARTRIDGE *Arborophila atrogularis* (4) [NT]

FORMOSAN PARTRIDGE *Arborophila crudigularis* (4) [NT]

CHESTNUT-BREASTED PARTRIDGE *Arborophila mandellii* (4) [VU]

BAR-BACKED PARTRIDGE *Arborophila brunneopectus* (4)

SICHUAN PARTRIDGE *Arborophila rufipectus* (4) [CR]

GRAY-BREASTED PARTRIDGE *Arborophila orientalis* (4)

CHESTNUT-BELLIED PARTRIDGE *Arborophila javanica* (4)

RED-BREASTED PARTRIDGE *Arborophila hyperythra* (4)

WHITE-NECKLACED PARTRIDGE *Arborophila gingica* (4) [VU]

ORANGE-NECKED PARTRIDGE *Arborophila davidi* (4) [CR]

CHESTNUT-HEADED PARTRIDGE *Arborophila cambodiana* (4) [VU]

SIAMESE PARTRIDGE *Arborophila diversa* (4)

RED-BILLED PARTRIDGE *Arborophila rubrirostris* (4)

HAINAN PARTRIDGE *Arborophila ardens* (4) [EN]

SCALY-BREASTED PARTRIDGE *Arborophila chloropus* (4)

ANNAM PARTRIDGE *Arborophila merlini* (4) [EN]

CHESTNUT-NECKLACED PARTRIDGE *Arborophila charltonii* (4) [VU]

FERRUGINOUS PARTRIDGE *Caloperdix oculea* (4)

CRIMSON-HEADED PARTRIDGE *Haematortyx sanguiniceps* (4)

CRESTED PARTRIDGE *Rollulus rouloul* (4)

STONE PARTRIDGE *Ptilopachus petrosus* (5)

MOUNTAIN BAMBOO-PARTRIDGE *Bambusicola fytchii* (4)

CHINESE BAMBOO-PARTRIDGE *Bambusicola thoracica* (2, 3, 4)

RED SPURFOWL *Galloperdix spadicea* (4)

PAINTED SPURFOWL *Galloperdix lunulata* (4)

SRI LANKA SPURFOWL or CEYLON SPURFOWL *Galloperdix bicalcarata* (4)

HIMALAYAN QUAIL *Ophrysia superciliosa* (4) [CR]

BLOOD PHEASANT *Ithaginis cruentus* (3, 4)

WESTERN TRAGOPAN *Tragopan melanocephalus* (3, 4) [VU]

SATYR TRAGOPAN *Tragopan satyra* (3, 4) [NT]

BLYTH'S TRAGOPAN *Tragopan blythii* (4) [VU]

TEMMINCK'S TRAGOPAN *Tragopan temminckii* (4) [NT]

KOKLASS PHEASANT *Pucrasia macrolopha* (3, 4)

HIMALAYAN MONAL *Lophophorus impejanus* (3, 4)

SCLATER'S MONAL *Lophophorus sclateri* (3, 4) [VU]

CHINESE MONAL *Lophophorus lhuysii* (4) [VU]

RED JUNGLEFOWL *Gallus gallus* (4)

GRAY JUNGLEFOWL *Gallus sonneratii* (4) [NT]

SRI LANKA JUNGLEFOWL or CEYLON JUNGLEFOWL *Gallus lafayetii* (4)

GREEN JUNGLEFOWL *Gallus varius* (4)

KALIJ PHEASANT *Lophura leucomelanos* (2, 3, 4)

SILVER PHEASANT *Lophura nycthemera* (4)

IMPERIAL PHEASANT *Lophura imperialis* (4) [CR]

EDWARDS'S PHEASANT *Lophura edwardsi* (4) [CR]

VIETNAMESE PHEASANT or VIETNAMESE FIREBACK *Lophura hatinhensis* (4) [EN]

SWINHOE'S PHEASANT *Lophura swinhoii* (4) [NT]

HOOGERWERF'S PHEASANT or SUMATRAN PHEASANT *Lophura hoogerwerfi* (4) [VU]

SALVADORI'S PHEASANT *Lophura inornata* (4) [VU]

CRESTLESS FIREBACK *Lophura erythrophthalma* (4) [VU]

CRESTED FIREBACK *Lophura ignita* (4) [VU]

SIAMESE FIREBACK *Lophura diardi* (4) [VU]

BULWER'S PHEASANT or BULWER'S FIREBACK *Lophura bulweri* (4) [VU]

TIBETAN EARED-PHEASANT *Crossoptilon harmani* (4) [VU]

WHITE EARED-PHEASANT *Crossoptilon crossoptilon* (4) [VU]

BROWN EARED-PHEASANT *Crossoptilon mantchuricum* (4) [VU]

BLUE EARED-PHEASANT *Crossoptilon auritum* (4) [NT]

CHEER PHEASANT *Catreus wallichii* (3, 4) [VU]

ELLIOT'S PHEASANT *Syrmaticus ellioti* (4) [VU]

MRS. HUME'S PHEASANT or HUME'S PHEASANT *Syrmaticus humiae* (4) [VU]

MIKADO PHEASANT *Syrmaticus mikado* (4) [NT]

COPPER PHEASANT *Syrmaticus soemmerringii* (3) [NT]

REEVES'S PHEASANT *Syrmaticus reevesii* (4) [VU]

COMMON PHEASANT *Phasianus colchicus* (1, 2, 3, 4)

GOLDEN PHEASANT *Chrysolophus pictus* (3, 4) [NT]

LADY AMHERST'S PHEASANT *Chrysolophus amherstiae* (3, 4) [NT]

BRONZE-TAILED PEACOCK-PHEASANT *Polyplectron chalcurum* (4) [NT]

MOUNTAIN PEACOCK-PHEASANT *Polyplectron inopinatum* (4) [VU]

GERMAIN'S PEACOCK-PHEASANT *Polyplectron germaini* (4) [VU]

GRAY PEACOCK-PHEASANT *Polyplectron bicalcaratum* (4)

HAINAN PEACOCK-PHEASANT *Polyplectron katsumatae* (4)

MALAYAN PEACOCK-PHEASANT *Polyplectron malacense* (4) [VU]

BORNEAN PEACOCK-PHEASANT *Polyplectron schleiermacheri* (4) [CR]

PALAWAN PEACOCK-PHEASANT *Polyplectron emphanum* (4) [EN]

CRESTED ARGUS *Rheinardia ocellata* (4) [VU]

MALAYSIAN ARGUS *Rheinardia nigrescens* (4)

GREAT ARGUS *Argusianus argus* (4)

CONGO PEACOCK or CONGO PEAFOWL *Afropavo congensis* (5) [VU]

INDIAN PEAFOWL *Pavo cristatus* (1, 3, 6)

GREEN PEAFOWL *Pavo muticus* (4) [VU]

SIBERIAN GROUSE *Falcipennis falcipennis* (3, 4)

SPRUCE GROUSE *Falcipennis canadensis* (1)

BLUE GROUSE *Dendragapus obscurus* (1)

WILLOW PTARMIGAN *Lagopus lagopus* (1, 3, 4)

ROCK PTARMIGAN *Lagopus mutus* (1, 3, 4)

WHITE-TAILED PTARMIGAN *Lagopus leucurus* (1)

BLACK GROUSE *Tetrao tetrix* (3, 4)

CAUCASIAN GROUSE *Tetrao mlokosiewiczi* (3)

WESTERN CAPERCAILLIE *Tetrao urogallus* (3, 4)

BLACK-BILLED CAPERCAILLIE or SPOTTED CAPERCAILLIE *Tetrao parvirostris* (3, 4)

HAZEL GROUSE *Bonasa bonasia* (3, 4)

CHINESE GROUSE *Bonasa sewerzowi* (4)

RUFFED GROUSE *Bonasa umbellus* (1)

SAGE GROUSE *Centrocercus urophasianus* (1)

SHARP-TAILED GROUSE *Tympanuchus phasianellus* (1)

GREATER PRAIRIE-CHICKEN *Tympanuchus cupido* (1)

LESSER PRAIRIE-CHICKEN *Tympanuchus pallidicinctus* (1)

WILD TURKEY *Meleagris gallopavo* (1, 2, 3, 6)

OCELLATED TURKEY *Meleagris ocellata* (1, 2) [NT]

Family NUMIDIDAE

WHITE-BREASTED GUINEAFOWL *Agelastes meleagrides* (5) [VU]

BLACK GUINEAFOWL *Agelastes niger* (5)

HELMETED GUINEAFOWL *Numida meleagris* (4, 5)

PLUMED GUINEAFOWL *Guttera plumifera* (5)

CRESTED GUINEAFOWL *Guttera pucherani* (5)

VULTURINE GUINEAFOWL *Acryllium vulturinum* (5)

Family ODONTOPHORIDAE

BEARDED WOOD-PARTRIDGE or BEARDED TREE-QUAIL *Dendrortyx barbatus* (1) [CR]

LONG-TAILED WOOD-PARTRIDGE or LONG-TAILED TREE-QUAIL *Dendrortyx macroura* (1) [NT]

BUFFY-CROWNED WOOD-PARTRIDGE or
BUFFY-CROWNED TREE-QUAIL *Dendrortyx
leucophrys* (1)

MOUNTAIN QUAIL *Oreortyx pictus* (1)

SCALED QUAIL *Callipepla squamata* (1)

ELEGANT QUAIL *Callipepla douglasii* (1)

CALIFORNIA QUAIL *Callipepla californica*
(1, 2, 3, 6)

GAMBEL'S QUAIL *Callipepla gambelii* (1)

BANDED QUAIL or BARRED QUAIL *Philortyx
fasciatus* (1)

NORTHERN BOBWHITE *Colinus virginianus*
(1)

BLACK-THROATED BOBWHITE or YUCATÁN
BOBWHITE *Colinus nigrogularis* (1)

CRESTED BOBWHITE *Colinus cristatus* (1, 2)

MARBLED WOOD-QUAIL *Odontophorus gujanensis* (1, 2)

SPOT-WINGED WOOD-QUAIL *Odontophorus
capueira* (2)

BLACK-EARED WOOD-QUAIL *Odontophorus
melanotis* (1)

RUFOUS-FRONTED WOOD-QUAIL
Odontophorus erythrops (2)

BLACK-FRONTED WOOD-QUAIL *Odontophorus
atrifrons* (2) [NT]

CHESTNUT WOOD-QUAIL *Odontophorus
hyperythrus* (2) [NT]

DARK-BACKED WOOD-QUAIL *Odontophorus
melanonotus* (2) [NT]

RUFOUS-BREASTED WOOD-QUAIL
Odontophorus speciosus (2)

TACARCUNA WOOD-QUAIL *Odontophorus
dialeucos* (2) [NT]

GORGETED WOOD-QUAIL *Odontophorus
strophium* (2) [EN]

VENEZUELAN WOOD-QUAIL *Odontophorus
columbianus* (2) [NT]

BLACK-BREASTED WOOD-QUAIL
Odontophorus leucolaemus (1, 2) [NT]

STRIPE-FACED WOOD-QUAIL *Odontophorus
balliviani* (2)

STARRED WOOD-QUAIL *Odontophorus
stellatus* (2)

SPOTTED WOOD-QUAIL *Odontophorus
guttatus* (1)

SINGING QUAIL *Dactylortyx thoracicus* (1)

MONTEZUMA QUAIL *Cyrtonyx montezumae*
(1)

OCELLATED QUAIL *Cyrtonyx ocellatus*
(1) [NT]

TAWNY-FACED QUAIL *Rhynchortyx cinctus*
(1, 2)

Order ANSERIFORMES
Family ANHIMIDAE

HORNED SCREAMER *Anhima cornuta* (2)

NORTHERN SCREAMER *Chauna chavaria* (2)
[NT]

SOUTHERN SCREAMER *Chauna torquata* (2)

Family ANSERANATIDAE

MAGPIE GOOSE *Anseranas semipalmata* (6)

Family DENDROCYGNIDAE

SPOTTED WHISTLING-DUCK *Dendrocygna
guttata* (4, 6)

PLUMED WHISTLING-DUCK *Dendrocygna
eytoni* (6)

FULVOUS WHISTLING-DUCK *Dendrocygna
bicolor* (4, 5)

WANDERING WHISTLING-DUCK *Dendrocygna
arcuata* (4),6

LESSER WHISTLING-DUCK *Dendrocygna
javanica* (4)

WHITE-FACED WHISTLING-DUCK
Dendrocygna viduata (2, 5)

WEST INDIAN WHISTLING-DUCK
Dendrocygna arborea (1) [VU]

BLACK-BELLIED WHISTLING-DUCK
Dendrocygna autumnalis (1, 2)

WHITE-BACKED DUCK *Thalassornis leuconotus* (5)

Family ANATIDAE
Subfamily OXYURINAE

MASKED DUCK *Nomonyx dominica* (1, 2)

RUDDY DUCK *Oxyura jamaicensis* (1, 3, 4)

ANDEAN DUCK *Oxyura ferruginea* (2)

WHITE-HEADED DUCK *Oxyura leucocephala*
(3, 4, 5) [VU]

MACCOA DUCK *Oxyura maccoa* (5)

LAKE DUCK *Oxyura vittata* (2)

BLUE-BILLED DUCK *Oxyura ustralis* (6)

MUSK DUCK *Biziura lobata* (6)

BLACK-HEADED DUCK *Heteronetta
atricapilla* (2) [NT]

FRECKLED DUCK *Stictonetta naevosa* (6) [VU]

Subfamily ANSERINAE

MUTE SWAN *Cygnus olor* (1, 3, 4)

BLACK SWAN *Cygnus atratus* (6)

BLACK-NECKED SWAN *Cygnus
melanocorypha* (2)

WHOOPER SWAN *Cygnus cygnus* (3, 4, 5)

TRUMPETER SWAN *Cygnus buccinator* (1) [NT]

TUNDRA SWAN *Cygnus columbianus* (1, 3, 4)

COSCOROBA SWAN *Coscoroba coscoroba* (2)

SWAN GOOSE *Anser cygnoides* (3, 4) [VU]

PINK-FOOTED GOOSE *Anser brachyrhynchus*
(1, 3)

BEAN GOOSE *Anser fabalis* (3, 4, 5)

GREATER WHITE-FRONTED GOOSE *Anser
albifrons* (1, 2, 3, 4, 5)

TULE GOOSE *Anser a. elgasi* (1)

LESSER WHITE-FRONTED GOOSE *Anser
erythropus* (3, 4) [VU]

GRAYLAG GOOSE *Anser anser* (3, 4)

BAR-HEADED GOOSE *Anser indicus* (3, 4)

SNOW GOOSE *Anser caerulescens* (1, 3)

ROSS'S GOOSE *Anser rossii* (1)

EMPEROR GOOSE *Anser canagica* (1)

HAWAIIAN GOOSE or NENE *Branta
sandvicensis* (1) [VU]

CANADA GOOSE *Branta canadensis* (1, 3, 6)

TUNDRA GOOSE *Branta hutchinsii* (1)

BARNACLE GOOSE *Branta leucopsis* (1, 3, 4, 5)

BRENT GOOSE *Branta bernicla* (1, 3, 4)

RED-BREASTED GOOSE *Branta ruficollis*
(3, 4, 5) [VU]

CAPE BARREN GOOSE *Cereopsis
novaehollandiae* (6)

Subfamily PLECTROPTERINAE

SPUR-WINGED GOOSE *Plectropterus
gambensis* (5)

Subfamily TADORNINAE

COMB DUCK *Sarkidiornis melanotos* (2, 4, 5)

RUDDY SHELDUCK *Tadorna ferruginea*
(3, 4, 5)

SOUTH AFRICAN SHELDUCK *Tadorna cana* (5)

AUSTRALIAN SHELDUCK *Tadorna tadornoides*
(6)

PARADISE SHELDUCK *Tadorna variegata* (6)

CRESTED SHELDUCK *Tadorna cristata* (4) [CR]

COMMON SHELDUCK *Tadorna tadorna* (3, 4)

RADJAH SHELDUCK *Tadorna radjah* (6)

PINK-EARED DUCK *Malacorhynchus
membranaceus* (6)

EGYPTIAN GOOSE *Alopochen aegyptiacus* (5)

ORINOCO GOOSE *Neochen jubata* (2) [NT]

ANDEAN GOOSE *Chloephaga melanoptera* (2)

UPLAND GOOSE or MAGELLAN GOOSE
Chloephaga picta (2)

KELP GOOSE *Chloephaga hybrida* (2)

ASHY-HEADED GOOSE *Chloephaga
poliocephala* (2)

RUDDY-HEADED GOOSE *Chloephaga rubidiceps*
(2) [NT]

BLUE-WINGED GOOSE *Cyanochen cyanopterus*
(5)

BLUE DUCK *Hymenolaimus malacorhynchos*
(6) [VU]

TORRENT DUCK *Merganetta armata* (2)

FLIGHTLESS STEAMERDUCK *Tachyeres pteneres* (2)

CHUBUT STEAMERDUCK *Tachyeres leucocephalus* (2) [NT]

FALKLAND STEAMERDUCK *Tachyeres brachypterus* (2)

FLYING STEAMERDUCK *Tachyeres patachonicus* (2)

Subfamily ANATINAE

HARTLAUB'S DUCK *Pteronetta hartlaubii* (5)

MUSCOVY DUCK *Cairina moschata* (1, 2)

WHITE-WINGED DUCK *Cairina scutulata* (4) [EN]

WOOD DUCK *Aix sponsa* (1)

MANDARIN DUCK *Aix galericulata* (1, 3, 4) [NT]

CRESTED DUCK *Lophonetta specularioides* (2)

GREEN PYGMY-GOOSE *Nettapus pulchellus* (6)

COTTON PYGMY-GOOSE *Nettapus coromandelianus* (4, 6)

AFRICAN PYGMY-GOOSE *Nettapus auritus* (5)

RINGED TEAL *Callonetta leucophrys* (2)

MANED DUCK or AUSTRALIAN WOOD DUCK *Chenonetta jubata* (6)

BRAZILIAN TEAL *Amazonetta brasiliensis* (2)

SALVADORI'S TEAL *Salvadorina waigiuensis* (6) [VU]

SPECTACLED DUCK *Anas specularis* (2) [NT]

CAPE TEAL *Anas capensis* (5)

GADWALL *Anas strepera* (1, 3, 4, 5)

FALCATED TEAL or FALCATED DUCK *Anas falcata* (1, 3, 4)

EURASIAN WIGEON *Anas penelope* (1, 3, 4, 5)

AMERICAN WIGEON *Anas americana* (1)

CHILOE WIGEON *Anas sibilatrix* (2)

AFRICAN BLACK DUCK *Anas sparsa* (5)

AMERICAN BLACK DUCK *Anas rubripes* (1, 3, 4)

MOTTLED DUCK *Anas fulvigula* (1)

MALLARD *Anas platyrhynchos* (1, 3, 4, 5, 6)

HAWAIIAN DUCK KOLOA *Anas wyvilliana* (1) [VU]

LAYSAN DUCK *Anas laysanensis* (1) [VU]

SPOT-BILLED DUCK *Anas poecilorhyncha* (3, 4)

PACIFIC BLACK DUCK *Anas superciliosa* (4, 6)

PHILIPPINE DUCK *Anas luzonica* (4) [NT]

YELLOW-BILLED DUCK *Anas undulata* (5)

MELLER'S DUCK *Anas melleri* (5) [NT]

BLUE-WINGED TEAL *Anas discors* (1, 2)

CINNAMON TEAL *Anas cyanoptera* (1, 2)

CAPE SHOVELER *Anas smithii* (5)

RED SHOVELER *Anas platalea* (2)

AUSTRALIAN SHOVELER *Anas rhynchotis* (6)

NORTHERN SHOVELER *Anas clypeata* (1, 3, 4)

BERNIER'S TEAL or MADAGASCAR TEAL *Anas bernieri* (5) [EN]

INDONESIAN TEAL *Anas gibberifrons* (4)

GRAY TEAL *Anas gracilis* (6)

CHESTNUT TEAL *Anas castanea* (6)

BROWN TEAL *Anas chlorotis* (6)

FLIGHTLESS TEAL *Anas aucklandica* (6) [VU]

WHITE-CHEEKED PINTAIL *Anas bahamensis* (1, 2)

RED-BILLED DUCK *Anas erythrorhyncha* (5)

SPECKLED TEAL *Anas flavirostris* (2)

NORTHERN PINTAIL *Anas acuta* (1, 3, 4, 5, 6)

EATON'S PINTAIL *Anas eatoni* (4)

YELLOW-BILLED PINTAIL *Anas georgica* (2)

GARGANEY *Anas querquedula* (1, 3, 4, 6)

BAIKAL TEAL *Anas formosa* (3, 4) [VU]

COMMON TEAL *Anas crecca* (1, 3, 4)

PUNA TEAL *Anas puna* (2)

SILVER TEAL *Anas versicolor* (2)

HOTTENTOT TEAL *Anas hottentota* (5)

MARBLED TEAL *Marmaronetta angustirostris* (3, 4, 5) [VU]

PINK-HEADED DUCK *Rhodonessa caryophyllacea* (4) [CR]

RED-CRESTED POCHARD *Netta rufina* (3, 4, 5)

ROSY-BILLED POCHARD *Netta peposaca* (2)

SOUTHERN POCHARD *Netta erythrophthalma* (2, 5)

COMMON POCHARD *Aythya ferina* (1, 3, 4, 5)

CANVASBACK *Aythya valisineria* (1)

REDHEAD *Aythya americana* (1)

RING-NECKED DUCK *Aythya collaris* (1, 3)

FERRUGINOUS POCHARD or FERRUGINOUS DUCK *Aythya nyroca* (3, 4, 5) [VU]

MADAGASCAR POCHARD *Aythya innotata* (5) [CR]

BAER'S POCHARD *Aythya baeri* (3, 4) [VU]

HARDHEAD *Aythya australis* (6)

TUFTED DUCK *Aythya fuligula* (1, 3, 4, 5)

NEW ZEALAND SCAUP *Aythya novaeseelandiae* (6)

GREATER SCAUP *Aythya marila* (1, 3, 4)

LESSER SCAUP *Aythya affinis* (1, 2, 3)

COMMON EIDER *Somateria mollissima* (1, 3)

KING EIDER *Somateria spectabilis* (1, 3)

SPECTACLED EIDER *Somateria fischeri* (1, 3) [VU]

STELLER'S EIDER *Polysticta stelleri* (1, 3) [VU]

LABRADOR DUCK *Camptorhynchus labradorius* (1) [EX]

HARLEQUIN DUCK *Histrionicus histrionicus* (1, 3)

LONG-TAILED DUCK or OLDSQUAW *Clangula hyemalis* (1, 3, 4)

BLACK SCOTER *Melanitta nigra* (1, 3, 4)

SURF SCOTER *Melanitta perspicillata* (1)

WHITE-WINGED SCOTER *Melanitta fusca* (1, 3, 4)

COMMON GOLDENEYE *Bucephala clangula* (1, 3, 4)

BARROW'S GOLDENEYE *Bucephala islandica* (1)

BUFFLEHEAD *Bucephala albeola* (1)

SMEW *Mergellus albellus* (1, 3, 4)

HOODED MERGANSER *Lophodytes cucullatus* (1)

BRAZILIAN MERGANSER *Mergus octosetaceus* (2) [CR]

RED-BREASTED MERGANSER *Mergus serrator* (1, 3, 4)

SCALY-SIDED MERGANSER *Mergus squamatus* (3, 4) [VU]

COMMON MERGANSER *Mergus merganser* (1, 3, 4)

AUCKLAND ISLANDS MERGANSER *Mergus australis* (1) [EX]

Order TURNICIFORMES
Family TURNICIDAE

SMALL BUTTONQUAIL *Turnix sylvatica* (3, 4, 5)

RED-BACKED BUTTONQUAIL *Turnix maculosa* (3, 4, 6)

BLACK-RUMPED BUTTONQUAIL *Turnix nana* (5)

HOTTENTOT BUTTONQUAIL *Turnix hottentotta* (5)

YELLOW-LEGGED BUTTONQUAIL *Turnix tanki* (3, 4)

SPOTTED BUTTONQUAIL *Turnix ocellata* (3, 4) [NT]

BARRED BUTTONQUAIL *Turnix suscitator* (3, 4)

MADAGASCAR BUTTONQUAIL *Turnix nigricollis* (5)

BLACK-BREASTED BUTTONQUAIL *Turnix melanogaster* (6) [EN]

CHESTNUT-BACKED BUTTONQUAIL *Turnix castanota* (6) [VU]

BUFF-BREASTED BUTTONQUAIL *Turnix olivii* (6) [EN]

PAINTED BUTTONQUAIL *Turnix varia* (6)

WORCESTER'S BUTTONQUAIL *Turnix worcesteri* (3, 4) [VU]

SUMBA BUTTONQUAIL *Turnix everetti* (4) [VU]

RED-CHESTED BUTTONQUAIL *Turnix pyrrhothorax* (6)

LITTLE BUTTONQUAIL *Turnix velox* (6)

LARK BUTTONQUAIL *Ortyxelos meiffrenii* (5)

Order PICIFORMES
Family INDICATORIDAE

SPOTTED HONEYGUIDE *Indicator maculatus* (5)

SCALY-THROATED HONEYGUIDE *Indicator variegatus* (5)

GREATER HONEYGUIDE *Indicator indicator* (5)

MALAYSIAN HONEYGUIDE *Indicator archipelagicus* (4) [NT]

LESSER HONEYGUIDE *Indicator minor* (5)

THICK-BILLED HONEYGUIDE *Indicator conirostris* (5)

WILLCOCKS'S HONEYGUIDE *Indicator willcocksi* (5)

LEAST HONEYGUIDE *Indicator exilis* (5)

DWARF HONEYGUIDE *Indicator pumilio* (5) [NT]

PALLID HONEYGUIDE *Indicator meliphilus* (5)

YELLOW-RUMPED HONEYGUIDE *Indicator xanthonotus* (5) [NT]

LYRE-TAILED HONEYGUIDE *Melichneutes robustus* (5)

YELLOW-FOOTED HONEYGUIDE *Melignomon eisentrauti* (5) [VU]

ZENKER'S HONEYGUIDE *Melignomon zenkeri* (5)

CASSIN'S HONEYGUIDE *Prodotiscus insignis* (5)

GREEN-BACKED HONEYGUIDE *Prodotiscus zambesiae* (5)

WAHLBERG'S HONEYGUIDE *Prodotiscus regulus* (5)

Family PICIDAE
Subfamily JYNGINAE

EURASIAN WRYNECK *Jynx torquilla* (3, 4, 5)

RUFOUS-NECKED WRYNECK *Jynx ruficollis* (5)

Subfamily PICINAE

SPECKLED PICULET *Picumnus innominatus* (4)

BAR-BREASTED PICULET or GOLD-FRONTED PICULET *Picumnus aurifrons* (2)

ORINOCO PICULET *Picumnus pumilus* (2)

LAFRESNAYE'S PICULET *Picumnus lafresnayi* (2)

GOLDEN-SPANGLED PICULET *Picumnus exilis* (2)

RUSTY-NECKED PICULET *Picumnus fuscus* (2)

ECUADORIAN PICULET *Picumnus sclateri* (2)

SCALED PICULET *Picumnus squamulatus* (2)

WHITE-BELLIED PICULET *Picumnus spilogaster* (2)

GUIANAN PICULET *Picumnus minutissimus* (2)

SPOTTED PICULET *Picumnus pygmaeus* (2)

SPECKLE-CHESTED PICULET *Picumnus steindachneri* (2) [NT]

VARZEA PICULET *Picumnus varzeae* (2)

OCELLATED PICULET *Picumnus dorbygnianus* (2)

OCHER-COLLARED PICULET *Picumnus temminckii* (2)

WHITE-WEDGED PICULET *Picumnus albosquamatus* (2)

WHITE-BARRED PICULET *Picumnus cirratus* (2)

RUFOUS-BREASTED PICULET *Picumnus rufiventris* (2)

TAWNY PICULET *Picumnus fulvescens* (2) [VU]

OCHRACEOUS PICULET *Picumnus limae* (2) [VU]

MOTTLED PICULET *Picumnus nebulosus* (2) [NT]

PLAIN-BREASTED PICULET *Picumnus castelnau* (2)

FINE-BARRED PICULET *Picumnus subtilis* (2) [NT]

OLIVACEOUS PICULET *Picumnus olivaceus* (1, 2)

GRAYISH PICULET *Picumnus granadensis* (2)

CHESTNUT PICULET *Picumnus cinnamomeus* (2)

AFRICAN PICULET *Sasia africana* (5)

RUFOUS PICULET *Sasia abnormis* (4)

WHITE-BROWED PICULET *Sasia ochracea* (4)

ANTILLEAN PICULET *Nesoctites micromegas* (1) [NT]

WHITE WOODPECKER *Melanerpes candidus* (2)

LEWIS'S WOODPECKER *Melanerpes lewis* (1)

GUADELOUPE WOODPECKER *Melanerpes herminieri* (1) [NT]

PUERTO RICAN WOODPECKER *Melanerpes portoricensis* (1)

RED-HEADED WOODPECKER *Melanerpes erythrocephalus* (1)

ACORN WOODPECKER *Melanerpes formicivorus* (1)

BLACK-CHEEKED WOODPECKER *Melanerpes pucherani* (1, 2)

GOLDEN-NAPED WOODPECKER *Melanerpes chrysauchen* (1)

YELLOW-TUFTED WOODPECKER *Melanerpes cruentatus* (2)

YELLOW-FRONTED WOODPECKER *Melanerpes flavifrons* (2)

WHITE-FRONTED WOODPECKER *Melanerpes cactorum* (2)

HISPANIOLAN WOODPECKER *Melanerpes striatus* (1)

JAMAICAN WOODPECKER *Melanerpes radiolatus* (1)

GOLDEN-CHEEKED WOODPECKER *Melanerpes chrysogenys* (1)

GRAY-BREASTED WOODPECKER *Melanerpes hypopolius* (1)

YUCATÁN WOODPECKER *Melanerpes pygmaeus* (1)

RED-CROWNED WOODPECKER *Melanerpes rubricapillus* (1, 2)

GILA WOODPECKER *Melanerpes uropygialis* (1)

RED-BELLIED WOODPECKER *Melanerpes carolinus* (1)

WEST INDIAN WOODPECKER *Melanerpes superciliaris* (1)

GOLDEN-FRONTED WOODPECKER *Melanerpes aurifrons* (1)

HOFFMANN'S WOODPECKER *Melanerpes hoffmannii* (1)

YELLOW-BELLIED SAPSUCKER *Sphyrapicus varius* (1)

RED-NAPED SAPSUCKER *Sphyrapicus nuchalis* (1)

RED-BREASTED SAPSUCKER *Sphyrapicus ruber* (1)

WILLIAMSON'S SAPSUCKER *Sphyrapicus thyroideus* (1)

CUBAN GREEN WOODPECKER *Xiphidiopicus percussus* (1)

FINE-SPOTTED WOODPECKER *Campethera punctuligera* (5)

NUBIAN WOODPECKER *Campethera nubica* (5)

BENNETT'S WOODPECKER *Campethera bennettii* (5)

GOLDEN-TAILED WOODPECKER *Campethera abingoni* (5)

MOMBASA WOODPECKER *Campethera mombassica* (5)

KNYSNA WOODPECKER *Campethera notata* (5) [NT]

LITTLE GREEN WOODPECKER *Campethera maculosa* (5)

GREEN-BACKED WOODPECKER *Campethera cailliautii* (5)

TULLBERG'S WOODPECKER *Campethera tullbergi* (5)

BUFF-SPOTTED WOODPECKER *Campethera nivosa* (5)

BROWN-EARED WOODPECKER *Campethera caroli* (5)

GROUND WOODPECKER *Geocolaptes olivaceus* (5) [NT]

LITTLE GRAY WOODPECKER *Dendropicos elachus* (5)

SPECKLE-BREASTED WOODPECKER *Dendropicos poecilolaemus* (5)

ABYSSINIAN WOODPECKER *Dendropicos abyssinicus* (5)

CARDINAL WOODPECKER *Dendropicos fuscescens* (5)

GABON WOODPECKER *Dendropicos gabonensis* (5)

STIERLING'S WOODPECKER *Dendropicos stierlingi* (5) [NT]

BEARDED WOODPECKER *Dendropicos namaquus* (5)

FIRE-BELLIED WOODPECKER *Dendropicos pyrrhogaster* (5)

GOLDEN-CROWNED WOODPECKER *Dendropicos xantholophus* (5)

ELLIOT'S WOODPECKER *Dendropicos elliotii* (5)

GRAY WOODPECKER *Dendropicos goertae* (5)

GRAY-HEADED WOODPECKER *Dendropicos spodocephalus* (5)

OLIVE WOODPECKER *Dendropicos griseocephalus* (5)

BROWN-BACKED WOODPECKER *Dendropicos obsoletus* (5)

SULAWESI WOODPECKER *Dendrocopos temminckii* (5)

PHILIPPINE WOODPECKER *Dendrocopos maculatus* (4)

BROWN-CAPPED WOODPECKER *Dendrocopos nanus* (4)

SUNDA WOODPECKER *Dendrocopos moluccensis* (4)

GRAY-CAPPED WOODPECKER *Dendrocopos canicapillus* (3, 4)

PYGMY WOODPECKER *Dendrocopos kizuki* (3, 4)

LESSER SPOTTED WOODPECKER *Dendrocopos minor* (3, 4, 5)

BROWN-FRONTED WOODPECKER *Dendrocopos auriceps* (4)

FULVOUS-BREASTED WOODPECKER *Dendrocopos macei* (4)

STRIPE-BREASTED WOODPECKER *Dendrocopos atratus* (4)

YELLOW-CROWNED WOODPECKER *Dendrocopos mahrattensis* (4)

ARABIAN WOODPECKER *Dendrocopos dorae* (3) [NT]

RUFOUS-BELLIED WOODPECKER *Dendrocopos hyperythrus* (4)

CRIMSON-BREASTED WOODPECKER *Dendrocopos cathpharius* (4)

DARJEELING WOODPECKER *Dendrocopos darjellensis* (4)

MIDDLE SPOTTED WOODPECKER *Dendrocopos medius* (3, 4)

WHITE-BACKED WOODPECKER *Dendrocopos leucotos* (3)

GREAT SPOTTED WOODPECKER *Dendrocopos major* (3, 4)

SYRIAN WOODPECKER *Dendrocopos syriacus* (3)

WHITE-WINGED WOODPECKER *Dendrocopos leucopterus* (3, 4) [NT]

SIND WOODPECKER *Dendrocopos assimilis* (3, 4)

HIMALAYAN WOODPECKER *Dendrocopos himalayensis* (3, 4)

STRIPED WOODPECKER *Picoides lignarius* (2)

CHECKERED WOODPECKER *Picoides mixtus* (1, 2)

NUTTALL'S WOODPECKER *Picoides nuttallii* (1)

LADDER-BACKED WOODPECKER *Picoides scalaris* (1)

DOWNY WOODPECKER *Picoides pubescens* (1)

RED-COCKADED WOODPECKER *Picoides borealis* (1) [VU]

STRICKLAND'S WOODPECKER or ARIZONA WOODPECKER *Picoides stricklandi* (1)

HAIRY WOODPECKER *Picoides villosus* (1)

WHITE-HEADED WOODPECKER *Picoides albolarvatus* (1)

EURASIAN THREE-TOED WOODPECKER *Picoides tridactylus* (3, 4)

AMERICAN THREE-TOED WOODPECKER *Picoides dorsalis* (1)

BLACK-BACKED WOODPECKER *Picoides arcticus* (1)

SCARLET-BACKED WOODPECKER *Veniliornis callonotus* (2)

YELLOW-VENTED WOODPECKER *Veniliornis dignus* (2)

BAR-BELLIED WOODPECKER *Veniliornis nigriceps* (2)

SMOKY-BROWN WOODPECKER *Veniliornis fumigatus* (2)

LITTLE WOODPECKER *Veniliornis passerinus* (2)

DOT-FRONTED WOODPECKER *Veniliornis frontalis* (2)

WHITE-SPOTTED WOODPECKER *Veniliornis spilogaster* (2)

BLOOD-COLORED WOODPECKER *Veniliornis sanguineus* (2)

RED-RUMPED WOODPECKER *Veniliornis kirkii* (1, 2)

CHOCO WOODPECKER *Veniliornis chocoensis* (2) [NT]

GOLDEN-COLLARED WOODPECKER *Veniliornis cassini* (2)

RED-STAINED WOODPECKER *Veniliornis affinis* (2)

YELLOW-EARED WOODPECKER *Veniliornis maculifrons* (2)

RUFOUS-WINGED WOODPECKER *Piculus simplex* (1, 2)

STRIPE-CHEEKED WOODPECKER *Piculus callopterus* (1)

LITA WOODPECKER *Piculus litae* (2)

WHITE-THROATED WOODPECKER *Piculus leucolaemus* (2)

YELLOW-THROATED WOODPECKER *Piculus flavigula* (2)

GOLDEN-GREEN WOODPECKER *Piculus chrysochloros* (2)

YELLOW-BROWED WOODPECKER or WHITE-BROWED WOODPECKER *Piculus aurulentus* (2) [NT]

GRAY-CROWNED WOODPECKER *Piculus auricularis* (1)

GOLDEN-OLIVE WOODPECKER *Piculus rubiginosus* (1, 2)

BRONZE-WINGED WOODPECKER *Piculus aeruginosus* (1)

CRIMSON-MANTLED WOODPECKER *Piculus rivolii* (2)

BLACK-NECKED WOODPECKER *Colaptes atricollis* (2)

SPOT-BREASTED WOODPECKER *Colaptes punctigula* (2)

GREEN-BARRED WOODPECKER *Colaptes melanochloros* (2)

NORTHERN FLICKER *Colaptes auratus* (1)

GILDED FLICKER *Colaptes chrysoides* (1)

FERNANDINA'S FLICKER or CUBAN FLICKER *Colaptes fernandinae* (1) [EN]

CHILEAN FLICKER *Colaptes pitius* (2)

ANDEAN FLICKER *Colaptes rupicola* (2)

CAMPO FLICKER or FIELD FLICKER *Colaptes campestris* (2)

RUFOUS WOODPECKER *Celeus brachyurus* (4)

CINNAMON WOODPECKER *Celeus loricatus* (1, 2)

SCALY-BREASTED WOODPECKER *Celeus grammicus* (2)

WAVED WOODPECKER *Celeus undatus* (2)

CHESTNUT-COLORED WOODPECKER *Celeus castaneus* (1, 2)

CHESTNUT WOODPECKER *Celeus elegans* (2)

PALE-CRESTED WOODPECKER *Celeus lugubris* (2)

BLOND-CRESTED WOODPECKER *Celeus flavescens* (2)

CREAM-COLORED WOODPECKER *Celeus flavus* (2)

RUFOUS-HEADED WOODPECKER *Celeus spectabilis* (2)

RINGED WOODPECKER *Celeus torquatus* (2)

HELMETED WOODPECKER *Dryocopus galeatus* (2) [EN]

PILEATED WOODPECKER *Dryocopus pileatus* (1)

LINEATED WOODPECKER *Dryocopus lineatus* (1, 2)

BLACK-BODIED WOODPECKER *Dryocopus schulzi* (2) [NT]

WHITE-BELLIED WOODPECKER *Dryocopus javensis* (4)

ANDAMAN WOODPECKER *Dryocopus hodgei* (4) [NT]

BLACK WOODPECKER *Dryocopus martius* (3, 4)

POWERFUL WOODPECKER *Campephilus pollens* (2)

CRIMSON-BELLIED WOODPECKER *Campephilus haematogaster* (2)

RED-NECKED WOODPECKER *Campephilus rubricollis* (2)

ROBUST WOODPECKER *Campephilus robustus* (2)

PALE-BILLED WOODPECKER *Campephilus guatemalensis* (1)

CRIMSON-CRESTED WOODPECKER *Campephilus melanoleucos* (1, 2)

GUAYAQUIL WOODPECKER *Campephilus gayaquilensis* (2)

CREAM-BACKED WOODPECKER *Campephilus leucopogon* (2)

MAGELLANIC WOODPECKER *Campephilus magellanicus* (2)

IMPERIAL WOODPECKER *Campephilus imperialis* (1) [CR]

IVORY-BILLED WOODPECKER *Campephilus principalis* (1, 2) [EX]

BANDED WOODPECKER *Picus mineaceus* (4)

LESSER YELLOWNAPE *Picus chlorolophus* (4)

CRIMSON-WINGED WOODPECKER *Picus puniceus* (4)

GREATER YELLOWNAPE *Picus flavinucha* (4)

CHECKER-THROATED WOODPECKER *Picus mentalis* (4)

STREAK-BREASTED WOODPECKER *Picus viridanus* (4)

LACED WOODPECKER *Picus vittatus* (4)

STREAK-THROATED WOODPECKER *Picus Xanthopygaeus* (4)

SCALY-BELLIED WOODPECKER *Picus squamatus* (3, 4)

JAPANESE WOODPECKER *Picus awokera* (3)

EURASIAN GREEN WOODPECKER *Picus viridis* (3)

LEVAILLANT'S WOODPECKER *Picus vaillantii* (5)

RED-COLLARED WOODPECKER *Picus rabieri* (4) [VU]

BLACK-HEADED WOODPECKER *Picus rrythropygius* (4)

GRAY-FACED WOODPECKER or GRAY-HEADED WOODPECKER *Picus canus* (3, 4)

OLIVE-BACKED WOODPECKER *Dinopium rafflesii* (4)

HIMALAYAN FLAMEBACK *Dinopium shorii* (3, 4)

COMMON FLAMEBACK *Dinopium javanense* (4)

BLACK-RUMPED FLAMEBACK *Dinopium benghalense* (4)

GREATER FLAMEBACK *Chrysocolaptes lucidus* (4)

WHITE-NAPED WOODPECKER *Chrysocolaptes festivus* (4)

PALE-HEADED WOODPECKER *Gecinulus grantia* (4)

BAMBOO WOODPECKER *Gecinulus viridis* (4)

OKINAWA WOODPECKER *Sapheopipo noguchii* (3) [VU]

MAROON WOODPECKER *Blythipicus rubiginosus* (4)

BAY WOODPECKER *Blythipicus pyrrhotis* (4)

ORANGE-BACKED WOODPECKER *Reinwardtipicus validus* (4)

BUFF-RUMPED WOODPECKER *Meiglyptes tristis* (4)

BLACK-AND-BUFF WOODPECKER *Meiglyptes jugularis* (4)

BUFF-NECKED WOODPECKER *Meiglyptes tukki* (4)

GRAY-AND-BUFF WOODPECKER *Hemicircus concretus* (4)

HEART-SPOTTED WOODPECKER *Hemicircus canente* (4)

ASHY WOODPECKER *Mulleripicus fulvus* (4)

SOOTY WOODPECKER *Mulleripicus funebris* (4)

GREAT SLATY WOODPECKER *Mulleripicus pulverulentus* (4)

Family MEGALAIMIDAE

FIRE-TUFTED BARBET *Psilopogon pyrolophus* (4)

GREAT BARBET *Megalaima virens* (4)

RED-VENTED BARBET *Megalaima lagrandieri* (4)

BROWN-HEADED BARBET *Megalaima zeylanica* (4)

LINEATED BARBET *Megalaima lineata* (4)

WHITE-CHEEKED BARBET *Megalaima viridis* (4)

GREEN-EARED BARBET *Megalaima faiostricta* (4)

BROWN-THROATED BARBET *Megalaima corvina* (4) [NT]

GOLD-WHISKERED BARBET *Megalaima chrysopogon* (4)

RED-CROWNED BARBET *Megalaima rafflesii* (4) [NT]

RED-THROATED BARBET *Megalaima mystacophanos* (4)

BLACK-BANDED BARBET *Megalaima javensis* (4) [NT]

YELLOW-FRONTED BARBET *Megalaima flavifrons* (4)

GOLDEN-THROATED BARBET *Megalaima franklinii* (4)

BLACK-BROWED BARBET *Megalaima oorti* (4)

BLUE-THROATED BARBET *Megalaima asiatica* (4)

MOUNTAIN BARBET *Megalaima monticola* (4)

MUSTACHED BARBET *Megalaima incognita* (4)

YELLOW-CROWNED BARBET *Megalaima henricii* (4)

FLAME-FRONTED BARBET *Megalaima armillaris* (4)

GOLDEN-NAPED BARBET *Megalaima pulcherrima* (4)

BLUE-EARED BARBET *Megalaima australis* (4)

BORNEAN BARBET *Megalaima eximia* (4)

CRIMSON-FRONTED BARBET *Megalaima malabarica* (4)

CRIMSON-THROATED BARBET or CRIMSON-FRONTED BARBET *Megalaima rubricapilla* (4)

COPPERSMITH BARBET *Megalaima haemacephala* (4)

BROWN BARBET *Calorhamphus fuliginosus* (4)

Family LYBIIDAE

NAKED-FACED BARBET *Gymnobucco calvus* (5)

BRISTLE-NOSED BARBET *Gymnobucco peli* (5)

SLADEN'S BARBET *Gymnobucco sladeni* (5)

GRAY-THROATED BARBET *Gymnobucco bonapartei* (5)

WHITE-EARED BARBET *Stactolaema leucotis* (5)

ANCHIETA'S BARBET *Stactolaema anchietae* (5)

WHYTE'S BARBET *Stactolaema whytii* (5)

GREEN BARBET *Stactolaema olivacea* (5)

WOODWARD'S BARBET *Stactolaema woodwardi* (5)

SPECKLED TINKERBIRD *Pogoniulus scolopaceus* (5)

WESTERN TINKERBIRD *Pogoniulus coryphaeus* (5)

MUSTACHED TINKERBIRD *Pogoniulus leucomystax* (5)

GREEN TINKERBIRD *Pogoniulus simplex* (5)

RED-RUMPED TINKERBIRD *Pogoniulus atroflavus* (5)

YELLOW-THROATED TINKERBIRD *Pogoniulus subsulphureus* (5)

YELLOW-RUMPED TINKERBIRD *Pogoniulus bilineatus* (5) [VU, SSP]

YELLOW-FRONTED TINKERBIRD *Pogoniulus chrysoconus* (5)

RED-FRONTED TINKERBIRD *Pogoniulus pusillus* (5)

YELLOW-SPOTTED BARBET *Buccanodon duchaillui* (5)

HAIRY-BREASTED BARBET *Tricholaema hirsuta* (5)

RED-FRONTED BARBET *Tricholaema diademata* (5)

MIOMBO BARBET *Tricholaema frontata* (5)

PIED BARBET *Tricholaema leucomelas* (5)

SPOT-FLANKED BARBET *Tricholaema lacrymosa* (5)

BLACK-THROATED BARBET *Tricholaema melanocephala* (5)

BANDED BARBET *Lybius undatus* (5)

VIEILLOT'S BARBET *Lybius vieilloti* (5)

WHITE-HEADED BARBET *Lybius leucocephalus* (5)

CHAPLIN'S BARBET *Lybius chaplini* (5) [NT]

RED-FACED BARBET *Lybius rubrifacies* (5) [NT]

BLACK-BILLED BARBET *Lybius guifsobalito* (5)

BLACK-COLLARED BARBET *Lybius torquatus* (5)

BROWN-BREASTED BARBET *Lybius melanopterus* (5)

BLACK-BACKED BARBET *Lybius minor* (5)

DOUBLE-TOOTHED BARBET *Lybius bidentatus* (5)

BEARDED BARBET *Lybius dubius* (5)

BLACK-BREASTED BARBET *Lybius rolleti* (5)

YELLOW-BILLED BARBET *Trachyphonus purpuratus* (5)

CRESTED BARBET *Trachyphonus vaillantii* (5)

YELLOW-BREASTED BARBET *Trachyphonus margaritatus* (5)

RED-AND-YELLOW BARBET *Trachyphonus erythrocephalus* (5)

D'ARNAUD'S BARBET *Trachyphonus darnaudii* (5)

Family RAMPHASTIDAE
Subfamily CAPITONINAE

SCARLET-CROWNED BARBET *Capito aurovirens* (2)

SPOT-CROWNED BARBET *Capito maculicoronatus* (2)

ORANGE-FRONTED BARBET *Capito squamatus* (2) [NT]

WHITE-MANTLED BARBET *Capito hypoleucus* (2) [EN]

BLACK-GIRDLED BARBET *Capito dayi* (2)

FIVE-COLORED BARBET *Capito quinticolor* (2) [VU]

BLACK-SPOTTED BARBET *Capito niger* (2)

BROWN-CHESTED BARBET *Capito brunneipectus* (2)

LEMON-THROATED BARBET *Eubucco richardsoni* (2)

RED-HEADED BARBET *Eubucco bourcierii* (2)

SCARLET-HOODED BARBET *Eubucco tucinkae* (2) [NT]

VERSICOLORED BARBET *Eubucco versicolor* (2)

PRONG-BILLED BARBET *Semnornis frantzii* (1)

TOUCAN BARBET *Semnornis ramphastinus* (2) [NT]

Subfamily RAMPHASTINAE

EMERALD TOUCANET *Aulacorhynchus prasinus* (1, 2)

GROOVE-BILLED TOUCANET *Aulacorhynchus sulcatus* (2)

CHESTNUT-TIPPED TOUCANET *Aulacorhynchus derbianus* (2)

CRIMSON-RUMPED TOUCANET *Aulacorhynchus haematopygus* (2)

YELLOW-BROWED TOUCANET *Aulacorhynchus huallagae* (2) [NT]

BLUE-BANDED TOUCANET *Aulacorhynchus coeruleicinctis* (2)

LETTERED ARACARI *Pteroglossus inscriptus* (2)

GREEN ARACARI *Pteroglossus viridis* (2)

RED-NECKED ARACARI *Pteroglossus bitorquatus* (2)

IVORY-BILLED ARACARI *Pteroglossus azara* (2)

BROWN-MANDIBLED ARACARI *Pteroglossus mariae* (2)

CHESTNUT-EARED ARACARI *Pteroglossus castanotis* (2)

BLACK-NECKED ARACARI *Pteroglossus aracari* (2)

COLLARED ARACARI *Pteroglossus torquatus* (1, 2)

FIERY-BILLED ARACARI *Pteroglossus frantzii* (1, 2)

STRIPE-BILLED ARACARI *Pteroglossus sanguineus* (1, 2)

PALE-MANDIBLED ARACARI Pteroglossus erythropygius (2)

MANY-BANDED ARACARI *Pteroglossus pluricinctus* (2)

CURL-CRESTED ARACARI *Pteroglossus beauharnaesii* (2)

SAFFRON TOUCANET *Baillonius bailloni* (2) [NT]

PLATE-BILLED MOUNTAIN-TOUCAN *Andigena laminirostris* (2) [NT]

GRAY-BREASTED MOUNTAIN-TOUCAN *Andigena hypoglauca* (2) [NT]

HOODED MOUNTAIN-TOUCAN *Andigena cucullata* (2) [NT]

BLACK-BILLED MOUNTAIN-TOUCAN *Andigena nigrirostris* (2) [NT]

YELLOW-EARED TOUCANET *Selenidera spectabilis* (1, 2)

GOLDEN-COLLARED TOUCANET *Selenidera reinwardtii* (2)

TAWNY-TUFTED TOUCANET *Selenidera nattereri* (2)

GUIANAN TOUCANET *Selenidera culik* (2)

SPOT-BILLED TOUCANET *Selenidera maculirostris* (2)

GOULD'S TOUCANET *Selenidera gouldii* (2)

KEEL-BILLED TOUCAN *Ramphastos sulfuratus* (1, 2)

CHOCO TOUCAN *Ramphastos brevis* (2)

CITRON-THROATED TOUCAN *Ramphastos citreolaemus* (2)

YELLOW-RIDGED TOUCAN *Ramphastos culminatus* (2)

CHANNEL-BILLED TOUCAN *Ramphastos vitellinus* (2)

RED-BREASTED TOUCAN *Ramphastos dicolorus* (2)

CHESTNUT-MANDIBLED TOUCAN *Ramphastos swainsonii* (2)

BLACK-MANDIBLED TOUCAN *Ramphastos ambiguus* (2)

RED-BILLED TOUCAN *Ramphastos tucanus* (2)

CUVIER'S TOUCAN *Ramphastos cuvieri* (2)

TOCO TOUCAN *Ramphastos toco* (2)

Order GALBULIFORMES
Family GALBULIDAE

WHITE-EARED JACAMAR *Galbalcyrhynchus leucotis* (2)

CHESTNUT JACAMAR *Galbalcyrhynchus purusianus* (2)

DUSKY-BACKED JACAMAR *Brachygalba salmoni* (2)

PALE-HEADED JACAMAR *Brachygalba goeringi* (2)

BROWN JACAMAR *Brachygalba lugubris* (2)

WHITE-THROATED JACAMAR *Brachygalba albogularis* (2)

THREE-TOED JACAMAR *Jacamaralcyon tridactyla* (2) [EN]

YELLOW-BILLED JACAMAR *Galbula albirostris* (2)

BLUE-NECKED JACAMAR *Galbula cyanicollis* (2)

RUFOUS-TAILED JACAMAR *Galbula ruficauda* (1, 2)

GREEN-TAILED JACAMAR *Galbula galbula* (2)

COPPERY-CHESTED JACAMAR *Galbula pastazae* (2) [VU]

WHITE-CHINNED JACAMAR *Galbula tombacea* (2)

BLUISH-FRONTED JACAMAR *Galbula cyanescens* (2)

PURPLISH JACAMAR *Galbula chalcothorax* (2)

BRONZY JACAMAR *Galbula leucogastra* (2)

PARADISE JACAMAR *Galbula dea* (2)

GREAT JACAMAR *Jacamerops aureus* (2)

Family BUCCONIDAE

WHITE-NECKED PUFFBIRD *Notharchus macrorhynchos* (1, 2)

BUFF-BELLIED PUFFBIRD *Notharchus swainsoni* (2)

BLACK-BREASTED PUFFBIRD *Notharchus pectoralis* (2)

BROWN-BANDED PUFFBIRD *Notharchus ordii* (2)

PIED PUFFBIRD *Notharchus tectus* (2)

CHESTNUT-CAPPED PUFFBIRD *Bucco macrodactylus* (2)

SPOTTED PUFFBIRD *Bucco tamatia* (2)

SOOTY-CAPPED PUFFBIRD *Bucco noanamae* (2) [NT]

COLLARED PUFFBIRD *Bucco capensis* (2)

BARRED PUFFBIRD *Nystalus radiatus* (2)

WHITE-EARED PUFFBIRD *Nystalus chacuru* (2)

STRIOLATED PUFFBIRD *Nystalus striolatus* (2)

SPOT-BACKED PUFFBIRD *Nystalus maculatus* (2)

RUSSET-THROATED PUFFBIRD *Hypnelus ruficollis* (2)

WHITE-CHESTED PUFFBIRD *Malacoptila fusca* (2)

SEMICOLLARED PUFFBIRD *Malacoptila semicincta* (2)

CRESCENT-CHESTED PUFFBIRD *Malacoptila striata* (2)

BLACK-STREAKED PUFFBIRD *Malacoptila fulvogularis* (2)

RUFOUS-NECKED PUFFBIRD *Malacoptila rufa* (2)

WHITE-WHISKERED PUFFBIRD *Malacoptila panamensis* (1, 2)

MUSTACHED PUFFBIRD *Malacoptila mystacalis* (2)

LANCEOLATED MONKLET *Micromonacha lanceolata* (1, 2) [NT]

RUSTY-BREASTED NUNLET *Nonnula rubecula* (2)

FULVOUS-CHINNED NUNLET *Nonnula sclateri* (2)

BROWN NUNLET *Nonnula brunnea* (2)

GRAY-CHEEKED NUNLET *Nonnula frontalis* (2)

RUFOUS-CAPPED NUNLET *Nonnula ruficapilla* (2)

CHESTNUT-HEADED NUNLET *Nonnula amaurocephala* (2) [NT]

WHITE-FACED NUNBIRD *Hapaloptila castanea* (2)

BLACK NUNBIRD *Monasa atra* (2)

BLACK-FRONTED NUNBIRD *Monasa nigrifrons* (2)

WHITE-FRONTED NUNBIRD *Monasa morphoeus* (2)

YELLOW-BILLED NUNBIRD *Monasa flavirostris* (2)

SWALLOW-WING *Chelidoptera tenebrosa* (2)

Order BUCEROTIFORMES
Family BUCEROTIDAE

WHITE-CRESTED HORNBILL *Tropicranus albocristatus* (5)

BLACK DWARF HORNBILL *Tockus hartlaubi* (5)

RED-BILLED DWARF HORNBILL *Tockus camurus* (5)

MONTEIRO'S HORNBILL *Tockus monteiri* (5)

RED-BILLED HORNBILL *Tockus erythrorhynchus* (5)

EASTERN YELLOW-BILLED HORNBILL *Tockus flavirostris* (5)

SOUTHERN YELLOW-BILLED HORNBILL *Tockus leucomelas* (5)

JACKSON'S HORNBILL *Tockus jacksoni* (5)

VON DER DECKEN'S HORNBILL *Tockus deckeni* (5)

CROWNED HORNBILL *Tockus alboterminatus* (5)

BRADFIELD'S HORNBILL *Tockus bradfieldi* (5)

AFRICAN PIED HORNBILL *Tockus fasciatus* (5)

HEMPRICH'S HORNBILL *Tockus hemprichii* (5)

AFRICAN GRAY HORNBILL *Tockus nasutus* (5)

PALE-BILLED HORNBILL *Tockus pallidirostris* (5)

MALABAR GRAY-HORNBILL *Ocyceros griseus* (4) [NT]

SRI LANKA GRAY-HORNBILL or CEYLON GRAY-HORNBILL *Ocyceros gingalensis* (4)

INDIAN GRAY-HORNBILL *Ocyceros birostris* (4)

MALABAR PIED-HORNBILL *Anthracoceros coronatus* (4) [NT]

ORIENTAL PIED-HORNBILL *Anthracoceros albirostris* (4)

BLACK HORNBILL *Anthracoceros malayanus* (4) [NT]

PALAWAN HORNBILL *Anthracoceros marchei* (4)

SULU HORNBILL *Anthracoceros montani* (4) [CR]

RHINOCEROS HORNBILL *Buceros rhinoceros* (4)

GREAT HORNBILL *Buceros bicornis* (4)

RUFOUS HORNBILL *Buceros hydrocorax* (4) [NT]

HELMETED HORNBILL *Buceros vigil* (4) [NT]

BROWN HORNBILL or TICKELL'S BROWN HORNBILL *Anorrhinus tickelli* (4) [NT]

AUSTEN'S BROWN HORNBILL *Anorrhinus austeni* (4)

BUSHY-CRESTED HORNBILL *Anorrhinus galeritus* (4)

MINDANAO HORNBILL *Penelopides affinis* (4) [NT]

LUZON HORNBILL or LUZON TARICTIC HORNBILL *Penelopides manillae* (4) [NT]

MINDORO HORNBILL *Penelopides mindorensis* (4) [EN]

TARICTIC HORNBILL or VISAYAN HORNBILL *Penelopides panini* (4) [CR]

SULAWESI HORNBILL *Penelopides exarhatus* (4)

WHITE-CROWNED HORNBILL *Aceros comatus* (4)

RUFOUS-NECKED HORNBILL *Aceros nipalensis* (4) [VU]

WRINKLED HORNBILL *Aceros corrugatus* (4) [VU]

RUFOUS-HEADED HORNBILL or WRITHED-BILLED HORNBILL *Aceros waldeni* (4) [CR]

WHITE-HEADED HORNBILL or WRITHED HORNBILL *Aceros leucocephalus* (4) [EN]

KNOBBED HORNBILL *Aceros cassidix* (4)

WREATHED HORNBILL *Aceros undulatus* (4)

NARCONDAM HORNBILL *Aceros narcondami* (4) [VU]

SUMBA HORNBILL *Aceros everetti* (4) [VU]

PLAIN-POUCHED HORNBILL *Aceros subruficollis* (4) [VU]

PAPUAN HORNBILL or BLYTH'S HORNBILL *Aceros plicatus* (6)

TRUMPETER HORNBILL *Ceratogymna bucinator* (5)

PIPING HORNBILL *Ceratogymna fistulator* (5)

SILVERY-CHEEKED HORNBILL *Ceratogymna brevis* (5)

BLACK-AND-WHITE-CASQUED HORNBILL *Ceratogymna subcylindricus* (5)

BROWN-CHEEKED HORNBILL *Ceratogymna cylindricus* (5) [NT]

WHITE-THIGHED HORNBILL *Ceratogymna albotibialis* (5)

BLACK-CASQUED HORNBILL *Ceratogymna atrata* (5)

YELLOW-CASQUED HORNBILL *Ceratogymna elata* (5) [NT]

Family BUCORVIDAE

NORTHERN GROUND-HORNBILL or ABYSSINIAN GROUND-HORNBILL *Bucorvus abyssinicus* (5)

SOUTHERN GROUND-HORNBILL *Bucorvus leadbeateri* (5)

Order TROGONIFORMES
Family TROGONIDAE
Subfamily APALODERMATINAE

NARINA TROGON *Apaloderma narina* (5)

BARE-CHEEKED TROGON *Apaloderma aequatoriale* (5)

BAR-TAILED TROGON *Apaloderma vittatum* (5)

Subfamily TROGONINAE

RESPLENDENT QUETZAL *Pharomachrus mocinno* (1) [NT]

CRESTED QUETZAL *Pharomachrus antisianus* (2)

WHITE-TIPPED QUETZAL *Pharomachrus fulgidus* (2)

GOLDEN-HEADED QUETZAL *Pharomachrus auriceps* (2)

PAVONINE QUETZAL *Pharomachrus pavoninus* (2)

EARED TROGON or EARED QUETZAL *Euptilotis neoxenus* (1) [EN]

CUBAN TROGON *Priotelus temnurus* (1)

HISPANIOLAN TROGON *Priotelus roseigaster* (1) [NT]

SLATY-TAILED TROGON *Trogon massena* (1, 2)

BLACK-TAILED TROGON *Trogon melanurus* (1, 2)

LATTICE-TAILED TROGON *Trogon clathratus* (1)

WHITE-EYED TROGON *Trogon comptus* (2)

BAIRD'S TROGON *Trogon bairdii* (1) [NT]

WHITE-TAILED TROGON *Trogon viridis* (1, 2)

CITREOLINE TROGON *Trogon citreolus* (1)

BLACK-HEADED TROGON *Trogon melanocephalus* (1)

MOUNTAIN TROGON *Trogon mexicanus* (1)

ELEGANT TROGON *Trogon elegans* (1)

COLLARED TROGON *Trogon collaris* (1)

ORANGE-BELLIED TROGON *Trogon aurantiiventris* (1)

MASKED TROGON *Trogon personatus* (2)

BLACK-THROATED TROGON *Trogon rufus* (2)

SURUCUA TROGON *Trogon surrucura* (2)

BLUE-CROWNED TROGON *Trogon curucui* (2)

VIOLACEOUS TROGON *Trogon violaceus* (2)

BLUE-TAILED TROGON *Harpactes reinwardtii* (4)

MALABAR TROGON *Harpactes fasciatus* (4)

RED-NAPED TROGON *Harpactes kasumba* (4)

DIARD'S TROGON *Harpactes diardii* (4)

PHILIPPINE TROGON *Harpactes ardens* (4)

WHITEHEAD'S TROGON *Harpactes whiteheadi* (4)

CINNAMON-RUMPED TROGON *Harpactes orrhophaeus* (4)

SCARLET-RUMPED TROGON *Harpactes duvaucelii* (4)

ORANGE-BREASTED TROGON *Harpactes oreskios* (4)

RED-HEADED TROGON *Harpactes erythrocephalus* (4)

WARD'S TROGON *Harpactes wardi* (4) [VU]

Order CORACIIFORMES
Family CORACIIDAE

EUROPEAN ROLLER *Coracias garrulus* (3, 4, 5)

ABYSSINIAN ROLLER *Coracias abyssinica* (5)

LILAC-BREASTED ROLLER *Coracias caudata* (5)

RACKET-TAILED ROLLER *Coracias spatulata* (5)

RUFOUS-CROWNED ROLLER *Coracias naevia* (5)

INDIAN ROLLER *Coracias benghalensis* (4)

PURPLE-WINGED ROLLER *Coracias temminckii* (5)

BLUE-BELLIED ROLLER *Coracias cyanogaster* (5)

BROAD-BILLED ROLLER *Eurystomus glaucurus* (5)

BLUE-THROATED ROLLER *Eurystomus gularis* (5)

DOLLARBIRD *Eurystomus orientalis* (3, 4, 6)

PURPLE ROLLER *Eurystomus azureus* (4)

Family BRACHYPTERACIIDAE

SHORT-LEGGED GROUND-ROLLER *Brachypteracias leptosomus* (5) [VU]

SCALY GROUND-ROLLER *Brachypteracias squamigera* (5) [VU]

PITTA-LIKE GROUND-ROLLER *Atelornis pittoides* (5) [NT]

RUFOUS-HEADED GROUND-ROLLER *Atelornis crossleyi* (5) [VU]

LONG-TAILED GROUND-ROLLER *Uratelornis chimaera* (5) [VU]

Family LEPTOSOMIDAE

CUCKOO ROLLER or COUROL *Leptosomus discolor* (5)

Family MOMOTIDAE

TODY MOTMOT *Hylomanes momotula* (1, 2)

BLUE-THROATED MOTMOT *Aspatha gularis* (1)

BROAD-BILLED MOTMOT *Electron platyrhynchum* (1, 2)

KEEL-BILLED MOTMOT *Electron carinatum* (1) [NT]

TURQUOISE-BROWED MOTMOT *Eumomota superciliosa* (1)

RUFOUS MOTMOT *Baryphthengus martii* (1, 2)

RUFOUS-CAPPED MOTMOT *Baryphthengus ruficapillus* (2)

RUSSET-CROWNED MOTMOT *Momotus mexicanus* (1)

BLUE-CROWNED MOTMOT *Momotus momota* (1, 2)

HIGHLAND MOTMOT *Momotus aequatorialis* (2)

Family TODIDAE

CUBAN TODY *Todus multicolor* (1)

NARROW-BILLED TODY *Todus angustirostris* (1) [NT]

PUERTO RICAN TODY *Todus mexicanus* (1)

JAMAICAN TODY *Todus todus* (1)

BROAD-BILLED TODY *Todus subulatus* (1)

Family ALCEDINIDAE

BLYTH'S KINGFISHER *Alcedo hercules* (4) [VU]

COMMON KINGFISHER *Alcedo atthis* (3, 4, 5)

HALF-COLLARED KINGFISHER *Alcedo semitorquata* (5)

SHINING-BLUE KINGFISHER *Alcedo quadribrachys* (5)

BLUE-EARED KINGFISHER *Alcedo meninting* (4)

AZURE KINGFISHER *Alcedo azurea* (6)

BISMARCK KINGFISHER *Alcedo websteri* (6)

BLUE-BANDED KINGFISHER *Alcedo euryzona* (4)

INDIGO-BANDED KINGFISHER *Alcedo cyanopecta* (4) [NT]

SILVERY KINGFISHER *Alcedo argentata* (4) [EN]

MALACHITE KINGFISHER *Alcedo cristata* (5)

MALAGASY KINGFISHER *Alcedo vintsioides* (5)

SÃO TOMÉ KINGFISHER *Alcedo thomensis* (5)

PRINCIPE KINGFISHER *Alcedo nais* (5)

WHITE-BELLIED KINGFISHER *Alcedo leucogaster* (5)

CERULEAN KINGFISHER or SMALL BLUE KINGFISHER *Alcedo coerulescens* (4)

LITTLE KINGFISHER *Alcedo pusilla* (6)

VARIABLE DWARF KINGFISHER or VARIABLE KINGFISHER *Ceyx lepidus* (4, 6)

ORIENTAL DWARF KINGFISHER or BLACK-BACKED KINGFISHER *Ceyx erithacus* (4)

RUFOUS-BACKED KINGFISHER *Ceyx rufidorsa* (4)

PHILIPPINE DWARF KINGFISHER or PHILIPPINE KINGFISHER *Ceyx melanurus* (4) [VU]

SULAWESI DWARF KINGFISHER or SULAWESI KINGFISHER *Ceyx fallax* (5)

MADAGASCAR PYGMY-KINGFISHER *Ispidina madagascariensis* (5)

AFRICAN PYGMY-KINGFISHER *Ispidina picta* (5)

DWARF KINGFISHER *Ispidina lecontei* (5)

Family HALCYONIDAE

BANDED KINGFISHER *Lacedo pulchella* (4)

LAUGHING KOOKABURRA *Dacelo novaeguineae* (6)

BLUE-WINGED KOOKABURRA *Dacelo leachii* (6)

SPANGLED KOOKABURRA *Dacelo tyro* (6)

RUFOUS-BELLIED KOOKABURRA *Dacelo gaudichaud* (6)

SHOVEL-BILLED KOOKABURRA *Clytoceyx rex* (6) [DD]

LILAC-MARKED KINGFISHER or MASKED KINGFISHER *Cittura cyanotis* (4)

BROWN-WINGED KINGFISHER *Pelargopsis amauropterus* (4) [NT]

STORK-BILLED KINGFISHER *Pelargopsis capensis* (4)

BLACK-BILLED KINGFISHER *Pelargopsis melanorhyncha* (4)

RUDDY KINGFISHER *Halcyon coromanda* (3, 4)

CHOCOLATE-BACKED KINGFISHER *Halcyon badia* (5)

WHITE-THROATED KINGFISHER *Halcyon smyrnensis* (4, 5)

BLACK-CAPPED KINGFISHER *Halcyon pileata* (4)

JAVAN KINGFISHER *Halcyon cyanoventris* (4)

GRAY-HEADED KINGFISHER *Halcyon leucocephala* (5)

WOODLAND KINGFISHER *Halcyon senegalensis* (5)

MANGROVE KINGFISHER *Halcyon senegaloides* (5)

BLUE-BREASTED KINGFISHER *Halcyon malimbica* (5)

BROWN-HOODED KINGFISHER *Halcyon albiventris* (5)

STRIPED KINGFISHER *Halcyon chelicuti* (5)

BLUE-BLACK KINGFISHER *Todiramphus nigrocyaneus* (6) [NT]

RUFOUS-LORED KINGFISHER *Todiramphus winchelli* (4) [EN]

BLUE-AND-WHITE KINGFISHER *Todiramphus diops* (4)

LAZULI KINGFISHER *Todiramphus lazuli* (4) [VU]

FOREST KINGFISHER *Todiramphus macleayii* (6)

NEW BRITAIN KINGFISHER *Todiramphus albonotatus* (6)

ULTRAMARINE KINGFISHER *Todiramphus leucopygius* (6)

CHESTNUT-BELLIED KINGFISHER *Todiramphus farquhari* (4) [VU]

RED-BACKED KINGFISHER *Todiramphus pyrrhopygia* (6)

FLAT-BILLED KINGFISHER *Todiramphus recurvirostris* (4)

MICRONESIAN KINGFISHER *Todiramphus cinnamominus* (4)

SOMBER KINGFISHER *Todiramphus funebris* (2) [NT]

COLLARED KINGFISHER *Todiramphus chloris* (4, 6)

TALAUD KINGFISHER *Todiramphus enigma* (6) [NT]

BEACH KINGFISHER *Todiramphus saurophaga* (4, 6)

CINNAMON-BANDED KINGFISHER or CINNAMON-COLLARED KINGFISHER *Todiramphus australasia* (4) [NT]

SACRED KINGFISHER *Todiramphus sanctus* (4)

TAHITI KINGFISHER *Todiramphus veneratus* (4)

MANGAIA KINGFISHER or TANGA'EO *Todiramphus ruficollaris* (4) [VU]

CHATTERING KINGFISHER *Todiramphus tuta* (4)

MARQUESAN KINGFISHER *Todiramphus godeffroyi* (4) [EN]

TUAMOTU KINGFISHER *Todiramphus gambieri* (4) [VU]

WHITE-RUMPED KINGFISHER *Caridonax fulgidus* (4)

HOOK-BILLED KINGFISHER *Melidora macrorrhina* (4, 6)

MUSTACHED KINGFISHER *Actenoides bougainvillei* (4) [VU]

RUFOUS-COLLARED KINGFISHER *Actenoides concretus* (4)

SPOTTED KINGFISHER *Actenoides lindsayi* (4) [NT]

BLUE-CAPPED KINGFISHER *Actenoides hombroni* (4) [VU]

GREEN-BACKED KINGFISHER *Actenoides monachus* (4)

SCALY KINGFISHER *Actenoides princeps* (4)

YELLOW-BILLED KINGFISHER *Syma torotoro* (6)

MOUNTAIN KINGFISHER *Syma megarhyncha* (6)

LITTLE PARADISE-KINGFISHER *Tanysiptera hydrocharis* (6) [DD]

COMMON PARADISE-KINGFISHER *Tanysiptera galatea* (4, 6)

KOFIAU PARADISE-KINGFISHER *Tanysiptera ellioti* (4)

BIAK PARADISE-KINGFISHER *Tanysiptera riedelii* (6) [NT]

NUMFOR PARADISE-KINGFISHER *Tanysiptera carolinae* (6)

RED-BREASTED PARADISE-KINGFISHER *Tanysiptera nympha* (6)

BROWN-HEADED PARADISE-KINGFISHER *Tanysiptera danae* (6)

BUFF-BREASTED PARADISE-KINGFISHER *Tanysiptera sylvia* (6)

Family CERYLIDAE

GIANT KINGFISHER *Megaceryle maxima* (5)

CRESTED KINGFISHER *Megaceryle lugubris* (3, 4)

BELTED KINGFISHER *Megaceryle alcyon* (1, 2)

RINGED KINGFISHER *Megaceryle torquata* (1, 2)

PIED KINGFISHER *Ceryle rudis* (3, 4, 5)

AMAZON KINGFISHER *Chloroceryle amazona* (1, 2)

GREEN KINGFISHER *Chloroceryle americana* (1, 2)

GREEN-AND-RUFOUS KINGFISHER *Chloroceryle inda* (1, 2)

AMERICAN PYGMY KINGFISHER *Chloroceryle aenea* (1, 2)

Family NYCTYORNITHIDAE

RED-BEARDED BEE-EATER *Nyctyornis amictus* (4)

BLUE-BEARDED BEE-EATER *Nyctyornis athertoni* (4)

Family MEROPIDAE

PURPLE-BEARDED BEE-EATER *Meropogon forsteni* (4)

BLACK BEE-EATER *Merops gularis* (5)

BLUE-HEADED BEE-EATER *Merops muelleri* (5)

RED-THROATED BEE-EATER *Merops bulocki* (5)

WHITE-FRONTED BEE-EATER *Merops bullockoides* (5)

LITTLE BEE-EATER *Merops pusillus* (5)

BLUE-BREASTED BEE-EATER *Merops variegatus* (5)

CINNAMON-CHESTED BEE-EATER *Merops oreobates* (5)

SWALLOW-TAILED BEE-EATER *Merops hirundineus* (5)

BLACK-HEADED BEE-EATER *Merops breweri* (5)

SOMALI BEE-EATER *Merops revoilii* (5)

WHITE-THROATED BEE-EATER *Merops albicollis* (5)

GREEN BEE-EATER or LITTLE GREEN BEE-EATER *Merops orientalis* (4, 5)

BOEHM'S BEE-EATER *Merops boehmi* (5)

BLUE-THROATED BEE-EATER *Merops viridis* (4)

BLUE-CHEEKED BEE-EATER *Merops persicus* (5)

MADAGASCAR BEE-EATER *Merops superciliosus* (5)

BLUE-TAILED BEE-EATER *Merops philippinus* (4, 6)

RAINBOW BEE-EATER *Merops ornatus* (4, 6)

EUROPEAN BEE-EATER *Merops apiaster* (3, 4, 5)

CHESTNUT-HEADED BEE-EATER *Merops leschenaulti* (4)

ROSY BEE-EATER *Merops malimbicus* (5)

NORTHERN CARMINE BEE-EATER *Merops nubicus* (5)

SOUTHERN CARMINE BEE-EATER *Merops nubicoides* (5)

Order COLIIFORMES
Family COLIIDAE
Subfamily COLIINAE

SPECKLED MOUSEBIRD *Colius striatus* (5)

WHITE-HEADED MOUSEBIRD *Colius leucocephalus* (5)

RED-BACKED MOUSEBIRD *Colius castanotus* (5)

WHITE-BACKED MOUSEBIRD *Colius colius* (5)

Subfamily UROCOLIINAE

BLUE-NAPED MOUSEBIRD *Urocolius macrourus* (5)

RED-FACED MOUSEBIRD *Urocolius indicus* (5)

Order CUCULIFORMES
Suborder CUCULI
Family CUCULIDAE

PIED CUCKOO *Clamator jacobinus* (3, 4, 5)

LEVAILLANT'S CUCKOO *Clamator levaillantii* (5)

CHESTNUT-WINGED CUCKOO *Clamator coromandus* (3, 4)

GREAT SPOTTED CUCKOO *Clamator glandarius* (3, 4, 5)

THICK-BILLED CUCKOO *Pachycoccyx audeberti* (5)

SULAWESI HAWK-CUCKOO *Cuculus crassirostris* (4)

LARGE HAWK-CUCKOO *Cuculus sparverioides* (3, 4)

COMMON HAWK-CUCKOO *Cuculus varius* (4)

MUSTACHED HAWK-CUCKOO *Cuculus vagans* (4)

HODGSON'S HAWK-CUCKOO *Cuculus fugax* (4)

NORTHERN HAWK-CUCKOO *Cuculus hyperythrus* (3, 4)

PHILIPPINE HAWK-CUCKOO *Cuculus pectoralis* (4)

RED-CHESTED CUCKOO *Cuculus solitarius* (5)

BLACK CUCKOO *Cuculus clamosus* (5)

INDIAN CUCKOO *Cuculus micropterus* (3, 4)

COMMON CUCKOO or EURASIAN CUCKOO *Cuculus canorus* (3, 4, 5)

AFRICAN CUCKOO *Cuculus gularis* (5)

ORIENTAL CUCKOO *Cuculus saturatus* (3, 4, 6)

LESSER CUCKOO *Cuculus poliocephalus* (3, 4, 5)

MADAGASCAR CUCKOO *Cuculus rochii* (5)

PALLID CUCKOO *Cuculus pallidus* (6)

DUSKY LONG-TAILED CUCKOO *Cercococcyx mechowi* (5)

OLIVE LONG-TAILED CUCKOO *Cercococcyx olivinus* (5)

BARRED LONG-TAILED CUCKOO *Cercococcyx montanus* (5)

BANDED BAY CUCKOO *Cacomantis sonneratii* (4)

GRAY-BELLIED CUCKOO *Cacomantis passerinus* (4)

PLAINTIVE CUCKOO *Cacomantis merulinus* (4)

RUSTY-BREASTED CUCKOO *Cacomantis sepulcralis* (4)

BRUSH CUCKOO *Cacomantis variolosus* (4, 6)

CHESTNUT-BREASTED CUCKOO *Cacomantis castaneiventris* (6)

MOLUCCAN CUCKOO *Cacomantis heinrichi* (4) [DD]

FAN-TAILED CUCKOO *Cacomantis flabelliformis* (6)

LONG-BILLED CUCKOO *Rhamphomantis megarhynchus* (6)

LITTLE BRONZE-CUCKOO *Chrysococcyx minutillus* (4, 6)

GOULD'S BRONZE-CUCKOO *Chrysococcyx russatus* (4, 6)

GREEN-CHEEKED BRONZE-CUCKOO *Chrysococcyx rufomerus* (4) [DD]

PIED BRONZE-CUCKOO *Chrysococcyx crassirostris* (4, 6)

SHINING BRONZE-CUCKOO *Chrysococcyx lucidus* (6)

HORSFIELD'S BRONZE-CUCKOO *Chrysococcyx basalis* (6)

RUFOUS-THROATED BRONZE-CUCKOO *Chrysococcyx ruficollis* (6)

WHITE-EARED BRONZE-CUCKOO *Chrysococcyx meyeri* (6)

ASIAN EMERALD CUCKOO *Chrysococcyx maculatus* (4)

VIOLET CUCKOO *Chrysococcyx xanthorhynchus* (4)

BLACK-EARED CUCKOO *Chrysococcyx osculans* (6)

YELLOW-THROATED CUCKOO *Chrysococcyx flavigularis* (5)

KLAAS'S CUCKOO *Chrysococcyx klaas* (4, 5)

AFRICAN EMERALD CUCKOO *Chrysococcyx cupreus* (5)

DIDERIC CUCKOO *Chrysococcyx caprius* (5)

WHITE-CROWNED KOEL *Caliechthrus leucolophus* (6)

DRONGO CUCKOO *Surniculus lugubris* (4)

DWARF KOEL *Microdynamis parva* (6)

ASIAN KOEL or COMMON KOEL *Eudynamys scolopacea* (3, 4, 6)

BLACK-BILLED KOEL *Eudynamys melanorhyncha* (4)

AUSTRALIAN KOEL *Eudynamys cyanocephala* (4, 6)

LONG-TAILED KOEL or LONG-TAILED CUCKOO *Eudynamys taitensis* (4)

CHANNEL-BILLED CUCKOO *Scythrops novaehollandiae* (4, 6)

YELLOWBILL *Ceuthmochares aereus* (5)

BLACK-BELLIED MALKOHA *Phaenicophaeus diardi* (4)

CHESTNUT-BELLIED MALKOHA *Phaenicophaeus sumatranus* (4)

GREEN-BILLED MALKOHA *Phaenicophaeus tristis* (4)

BLUE-FACED MALKOHA *Phaenicophaeus viridirostris* (4)

SIRKEER MALKOHA *Phaenicophaeus leschenaultii* (4)

RAFFLES'S MALKOHA *Phaenicophaeus chlorophaeus* (4)

RED-BILLED MALKOHA *Phaenicophaeus javanicus* (4)

YELLOW-BILLED MALKOHA *Phaenicophaeus calyorhynchus* (4)

CHESTNUT-BREASTED MALKOHA *Phaenicophaeus curvirostris* (4)

RED-FACED MALKOHA *Phaenicophaeus pyrrhocephalus* (4) [VU]

RED-CRESTED MALKOHA *Phaenicophaeus superciliosus* (4)

SCALE-FEATHERED MALKOHA *Phaenicophaeus cumingi* (4)

BORNEAN GROUND-CUCKOO or SUNDA GROUND-CUCKOO *Carpococcyx radiatus* (4) [VU]

SUMATRAN GROUND-CUCKOO *Carpococcyx viridis* (4)

CORAL-BILLED GROUND-CUCKOO *Carpococcyx renauldi* (4) [NT]

SNAIL-EATING COUA *Coua delalandei* (5) [EX]

GIANT COUA *Coua gigas* (5)

COQUEREL'S COUA *Coua coquereli* (5)

RED-BREASTED COUA *Coua serriana* (5)

RED-FRONTED COUA *Coua reynaudii* (5)

RUNNING COUA *Coua cursor* (5)

RED-CAPPED COUA *Coua ruficeps* (5)

CRESTED COUA *Coua cristata* (5)

VERREAUX'S COUA *Coua verreauxi* (5) [NT]

BLUE COUA *Coua caerulea* (5)

Family CENTROPODIDAE

BUFF-HEADED COUCAL *Centropus milo* (6)

GOLIATH COUCAL *Centropus goliath* (4)

VIOLACEOUS COUCAL *Centropus violaceus* (6)

GREATER BLACK COUCAL *Centropus menbeki* (6)

PIED COUCAL *Centropus ateralbus* (6)

PHEASANT COUCAL *Centropus phasianinus* (6)

KAI COUCAL *Centropus spilopterus* (6) [NT]

LESSER BLACK COUCAL *Centropus bernsteini* (6)

BIAK COUCAL *Centropus chalybeus* (6) [NT]

SHORT-TOED COUCAL *Centropus rectunguis* (4) [NT]

BLACK-HOODED COUCAL *Centropus steerii* (4) [CR]

GREATER COUCAL *Centropus sinensis* (4)

BROWN COUCAL *Centropus andamanensis* (4) [NT]

JAVAN COUCAL or SUNDA COUCAL *Centropus nigrorufus* (4) [VU]

PHILIPPINE COUCAL *Centropus viridis* (4)

MADAGASCAR COUCAL *Centropus toulou* (5)

BLACK COUCAL *Centropus grillii* (5)

LESSER COUCAL *Centropus bengalensis* (4)

GREEN-BILLED COUCAL *Centropus chlororhynchus* (4) [EN]

Black-Throated Coucal *Centropus leuco-gaster* (5)

Neumann's Coucal *Centropus neumanni* (5)

Gabon Coucal *Centropus anselli* (5)

Blue-Headed Coucal *Centropus monachus* (5)

Coppery-Tailed Coucal *Centropus cupreicaudus* (5)

Senegal Coucal *Centropus senegalensis* (5)

White-Browed Coucal *Centropus superciliosus* (5)

Burchell's Coucal *Centropus burchelli* (5)

Black-Faced Coucal *Centropus melanops* (4)

Bay Coucal *Centropus celebensis* (4)

Rufous Coucal *Centropus unirufus* (4) [NT]

Family COCCYZIDAE

Dwarf Cuckoo *Coccyzus pumilus* (2)

Ash-Colored Cuckoo *Coccyzus cinereus* (2)

Black-Billed Cuckoo *Coccyzus erythropthalmus* (1, 2)

Yellow-Billed Cuckoo *Coccyzus americanus* (1, 2)

Pearly-Breasted Cuckoo *Coccyzus euleri* (2)

Mangrove Cuckoo *Coccyzus minor* (1, 2)

Cocos Cuckoo *Coccyzus ferrugineus* (1) [VU]

Dark-Billed Cuckoo *Coccyzus melacoryphus* (2)

Gray-Capped Cuckoo *Coccyzus lansbergi* (2)

Chestnut-Bellied Cuckoo *Hyetornis pluvialis* (1)

Bay-Breasted Cuckoo or Rufous-Breasted Cuckoo *Hyetornis rufigularis* (1) [VU]

Squirrel Cuckoo *Piaya cayana* (1, 2)

Black-Bellied Cuckoo *Piaya melanogaster* (2)

Little Cuckoo *Piaya minuta* (2)

Great Lizard-Cuckoo *Saurothera merlini* (1)

Jamaican Lizard-Cuckoo *Saurothera vetula* (1)

Hispaniolan Lizard-Cuckoo *Saurothera longirostris* (1)

Puerto Rican Lizard-Cuckoo *Saurothera vieilloti* (1)

Family CROTOPHAGIDAE

Greater Ani *Crotophaga major* (1, 2)

Smooth-Billed Ani *Crotophaga ani* (1, 2)

Groove-Billed Ani *Crotophaga sulcirostris* (1, 2)

Guira Cuckoo *Guira guira* (2)

Family NEOMORPHIDAE

Striped Cuckoo *Tapera naevia* (1, 2)

Lesser Ground-Cuckoo *Morococcyx erythropygus* (1)

Pheasant Cuckoo *Dromococcyx phasianellus* (1, 2)

Pavonine Cuckoo *Dromococcyx pavoninus* (1, 2)

Greater Roadrunner *Geococcyx californianus* (1)

Lesser Roadrunner *Geococcyx velox* (1)

Rufous-Vented Ground-Cuckoo *Neomorphus geoffroyi* (1, 2)

Scaled Ground-Cuckoo *Neomorphus squamiger* (2) [NT]

Banded Ground-Cuckoo *Neomorphus radiolosus* (2) [EN]

Rufous-Winged Ground-Cuckoo *Neomorphus rufipennis* (2)

Red-Billed Ground-Cuckoo *Neomorphus pucheranii* (2)

Suborder OPISTHOCOMI
Family OPISTHOCOMIDAE

Hoatzin *Opisthocomus hoazin* (2)

Order PSITTACIFORMES

Family CACATUIDAE

PALM COCKATOO *Probosciger aterrimus* (6) [NT]

LONG-BILLED BLACK-COCKATOO *Calyptorhynchus baudinii* (6) [VU]

SHORT-BILLED BLACK-COCKATOO *Calyptorhynchus latirostris* (6) [VU]

YELLOW-TAILED BLACK-COCKATOO *Calyptorhynchus funereus* (6)

RED-TAILED BLACK-COCKATOO *Calyptorhynchus banksii* (6)

GLOSSY BLACK-COCKATOO *Calyptorhynchus lathami* (6) [VU]

GANG-GANG COCKATOO *Callocephalon fimbriatum* (6)

GALAH *Cacatua roseicapilla* (6)

PINK COCKATOO or MAJOR MITCHELL'S COCKATOO *Cacatua leadbeateri* (6) [NT]

YELLOW-CRESTED COCKATOO *Cacatua sulphurea* (4) [EN]

SULFUR-CRESTED COCKATOO *Cacatua galerita* (6)

BLUE-EYED COCKATOO *Cacatua ophthalmica* (6)

SALMON-CRESTED COCKATOO *Cacatua moluccensis* (6) [VU]

WHITE COCKATOO *Cacatua alba* (4) [VU]

PHILIPPINE COCKATOO *Cacatua haematuropygia* (4) [CR]

TANIMBAR COCKATOO or TANIMBAR CORELLA *Cacatua goffini* (4) [NT]

LITTLE COCKATOO or LITTLE CORELLA *Cacatua sanguinea* (6)

WESTERN CORELLA *Cacatua pastinator* (6) [NT]

LONG-BILLED CORELLA *Cacatua tenuirostris* (6)

DUCORPS'S COCKATOO *Cacatua oucorpsii* (4)

COCKATIEL *Nymphicus hollandicus* (6)

Family PSITTACIDAE

BLACK LORY *Chalcopsitta atra* (6)

BROWN LORY *Chalcopsitta duivenbodei* (6)

YELLOW-STREAKED LORY *Chalcopsitta sintillata* (6)

CARDINAL LORY *Chalcopsitta cardinalis* (4)

RED-AND-BLUE LORY *Eos histrio* (4) [EN]

VIOLET-NECKED LORY *Eos squamata* (4, 6)

RED LORY *Eos bornea* (4)

BLUE-STREAKED LORY *Eos reticulata* (4) [NT]

BLACK-WINGED LORY *Eos cyanogenia* (6) [VU]

BLUE-EARED LORY *Eos semilarvata* (4) [NT]

DUSKY LORY *Pseudeos fuscata* (4, 6)

ORNATE LORIKEET *Trichoglossus ornatus* (4)

RAINBOW LORIKEET *Trichoglossus haematodus* (4, 6)

OLIVE-HEADED LORIKEET *Trichoglossus euteles* (4)

YELLOW-AND-GREEN LORIKEET *Trichoglossus flavoviridis* (4)

MINDANAO LORIKEET *Trichoglossus johnstoniae* (4) [VU]

POHNPEI LORIKEET *Trichoglossus rubiginosus* (6)

SCALY-BREASTED LORIKEET *Trichoglossus chlorolepidotus* (6)

VARIED LORIKEET *Psitteuteles versicolor* (6)

IRIS LORIKEET *Psitteuteles iris* (4) [VU]

GOLDIE'S LORIKEET *Psitteuteles goldiei* (6)

CHATTERING LORY *Lorius garrulus* (4) [VU]

PURPLE-NAPED LORY *Lorius domicella* (4) [VU]

BLACK-CAPPED LORY *Lorius lory* (6)

PURPLE-BELLIED LORY *Lorius hypoinochrous* (6)

WHITE-NAPED LORY *Lorius albidinuchus* (6) [NT]

YELLOW-BIBBED LORY *Lorius chlorocercus* (4)

COLLARED LORY *Phigys solitarius* (4)

BLUE-CROWNED LORIKEET *Vini australis* (4)

KUHL'S LORIKEET *Vini kuhlii* (4) [EN]

STEPHEN'S LORIKEET or HENDERSON LORIKEET *Vini stepheni* (6) [VU]

BLUE LORIKEET *Vini peruviana* (6) [VU]

ULTRAMARINE LORIKEET *Vini ultramarina* (6) [EN]

MUSK LORIKEET *Glossopsitta concinna* (6)

LITTLE LORIKEET *Glossopsitta pusilla* (6)

PURPLE-CROWNED LORIKEET *Glossopsitta porphyrocephala* (6)

PALM LORIKEET *Charmosyna palmarum* (4) [NT]

RED-CHINNED LORIKEET *Charmosyna rubrigularis* (6)

MEEK'S LORIKEET *Charmosyna meeki* (6)

BLUE-FRONTED LORIKEET *Charmosyna toxopei* (4) [VU]

STRIATED LORIKEET *Charmosyna multistriata* (6) [NT]

PYGMY LORIKEET *Charmosyna wilhelminae* (6)

RED-FRONTED LORIKEET *Charmosyna rubronotata* (6)

RED-FLANKED LORIKEET *Charmosyna placentis* (6)

NEW CALEDONIAN LORIKEET *Charmosyna diadema* (6) [VU]

RED-THROATED LORIKEET *Charmosyna amabilis* (6) [VU]

DUCHESS LORIKEET *Charmosyna margarethae* (6) [NT]

FAIRY LORIKEET *Charmosyna pulchella* (6)

JOSEPHINE'S LORIKEET *Charmosyna josefinae* (6)

PAPUAN LORIKEET *Charmosyna papou* (6)

PLUM-FACED LORIKEET *Oreopsittacus arfaki* (6)

YELLOW-BILLED LORIKEET *Neopsittacus musschenbroekii* (6)

ORANGE-BILLED LORIKEET *Neopsittacus pullicauda* (6)

KEA *Nestor notabilis* (6) [NT]

NORFOLK ISLAND KAKA *Nestor productus* (6) [EX]

NEW ZEALAND KAKA *Nestor meridionalis* (6) [VU]

YELLOW-CAPPED PYGMY-PARROT *Micropsitta keiensis* (6)

GEELVINK PYGMY-PARROT *Micropsitta geelvinkiana* (6) [NT]

BUFF-FACED PYGMY-PARROT *Micropsitta pusio* (6)

MEEK'S PYGMY-PARROT *Micropsitta meeki* (6)

FINSCH'S PYGMY-PARROT *Micropsitta finschii* (6)

RED-BREASTED PYGMY-PARROT *Micropsitta bruijnii* (6)

ORANGE-BREASTED FIG-PARROT *Cyclopsitta gulielmitertii* (6)

DOUBLE-EYED FIG-PARROT *Cyclopsitta diophthalma* (6)

LARGE FIG-PARROT *Psittaculirostris desmarestii* (6)

EDWARDS'S FIG-PARROT *Psittaculirostris edwardsii* (6)

SALVADORI'S FIG-PARROT *Psittaculirostris salvadorii* (6) [VU]

GUAIABERO *Bolbopsittacus lunulatus* (4)

BLUE-RUMPED PARROT *Psittinus cyanurus* (4) [NT]

BREHM'S TIGER-PARROT *Psittacella brehmii* (6)

PAINTED TIGER-PARROT *Psittacella picta* (6)

MODEST TIGER-PARROT *Psittacella modesta* (6)

MADARASZ'S TIGER-PARROT *Psittacella madaraszi* (6)

RED-CHEEKED PARROT *Geoffroyus geoffroyi* (4, 6)

BLUE-COLLARED PARROT *Geoffroyus simplex* (6)

SINGING PARROT *Geoffroyus heteroclitus* (6)

MONTANE RACQUET-TAIL or LUZON RACQUET-TAIL *Prioniturus montanus* (4) [VU]

MINDANAO RACQUET-TAIL *Prioniturus waterstradti* (4) [VU]

BLUE-HEADED RACQUET-TAIL *Prioniturus platenae* (4) [VU]

GREEN RACQUET-TAIL *Prioniturus luconensis* (4) [EN]

BLUE-CROWNED RACQUET-TAIL *Prioniturus discurus* (4) [NT]

BLUE-WINGED RACQUET-TAIL *Prioniturus verticalis* (4) [EN]

YELLOW-BREASTED RACQUET-TAIL *Prioniturus flavicans* (4) [NT]

GOLDEN-MANTLED RACQUET-TAIL *Prioniturus platurus* (4) [NT]

BURU RACQUET-TAIL *Prioniturus mada* (4) [NT]

GREAT-BILLED PARROT *Tanygnathus megalorynchos* (4, 6)

BLUE-NAPED PARROT *Tanygnathus lucionensis* (4) [EN]

AZURE-RUMPED PARROT or BLUE-BACKED PARROT *Tanygnathus sumatranus* (4) [NT]

BLACK-LORED PARROT *Tanygnathus gramineus* (4) [VU]

ECLECTUS PARROT *Eclectus roratus* (6)

PESQUET'S PARROT *Psittrichas fulgidus* (6) [VU]

CRIMSON SHINING-PARROT *Prosopeia splendens* (6) [NT]

MASKED SHINING-PARROT *Prosopeia personata* (6) [NT]

RED SHINING-PARROT *Prosopeia tabuensis* (6)

AUSTRALIAN KING-PARROT *Alisterus scapularis* (6)

MOLUCCAN KING-PARROT *Alisterus amboinensis* (6) [NT]

PAPUAN KING-PARROT *Alisterus chloropterus* (6)

OLIVE-SHOULDERED PARROT *Aprosmictus jonquillaceus* (4) [NT]

RED-WINGED PARROT *Aprosmictus erythropterus* (6)

SUPERB PARROT *Polytelis swainsonii* (6) [VU]

REGENT PARROT *Polytelis anthopeplus* (6)

ALEXANDRA'S PARROT or PRINCESS PARROT *Polytelis alexandrae* (6) [VU]

RED-CAPPED PARROT *Purpureicephalus spurius* (6)

AUSTRALIAN RINGNECK or PORT LINCOLN RINGNECK *Barnardius zonarius* (6)

GREEN ROSELLA *Platycercus caledonicus* (6)

CRIMSON ROSELLA *Platycercus elegans* (6)

NORTHERN ROSELLA *Platycercus venustus* (6)

PALE-HEADED ROSELLA *Platycercus adscitus* (6)

EASTERN ROSELLA *Platycercus eximius* (6)

WESTERN ROSELLA *Platycercus icterotis* (6)

BLUEBONNET *Northiella haematogaster* (6)

RED-RUMPED PARROT *Psephotus haematonotus* (6)

MULGA PARROT *Psephotus varius* (6)

HOODED PARROT *Psephotus dissimilis* (6) [NT]

GOLDEN-SHOULDERED PARROT *Psephotus chrysopterygius* (6) [EN]

PARADISE PARROT *Psephotus pulcherrimus* (6) [EX]

ANTIPODES PARAKEET *Cyanoramphus unicolor* (6) [VU]

NORFOLK ISLAND PARAKEET *Cyanoramphus cookii* (6) [CR]

RED-FRONTED PARAKEET or RED-CROWNED PARAKEET *Cyanoramphus novaezelandiae* (6)

YELLOW-FRONTED PARAKEET *Cyanoramphus auriceps* (6) [NT]

BLACK-FRONTED PARAKEET or TAHITI PARAKEET *Cyanoramphus zealandicus* (4) [EX]

RAIATEA PARAKEET *Cyanoramphus ulietanus* (6) [EX]

HORNED PARAKEET E*unymphicus cornutus* (6) [VU]

BOURKE'S PARROT *Neopsephotus bourkii* (6)

BLUE-WINGED PARROT *Neophema chrysostoma* (6)

ELEGANT PARROT *Neophema elegans* (6)

ROCK PARROT *Neophema petrophila* (6)

ORANGE-BELLIED PARROT *Neophema chrysogaster* (6) [EN]

TURQUOISE PARROT *Neophema pulchella* (6) [NT]

SCARLET-CHESTED PARROT *Neophema splendida* (6) [VU]

SWIFT PARROT *Lathamus discolor* (6) [VU]

BUDGERIGAR *Melopsittacus undulatus* (1, 6)

GROUND PARROT *Pezoporus wallicus* (6)

NIGHT PARROT *Pezoporus occidentalis* (6) [CR]

KAKAPO *Strigops habroptilus* (6) [EW]

MASCARENE PARROT *Mascarinus mascarinus* (5) [EX]

VASA PARROT *Coracopsis vasa* (5)

BLACK PARROT *Coracopsis nigra* (5)

GRAY PARROT *Psittacus erithacus* (5)

BROWN-NECKED PARROT P*oicephalus robustus* (5)

RED-FRONTED PARROT *Poicephalus gulielmi* (5)

SENEGAL PARROT *Poicephalus senegalus* (5)

NIAM-NIAM PARROT *Poicephalus crassus* (5)

MEYER'S PARROT *Poicephalus meyeri* (5)

YELLOW-FRONTED PARROT *Poicephalus flavifrons* (5)

RED-BELLIED PARROT *Poicephalus rufiventris* (5)

BROWN-HEADED PARROT *Poicephalus cryptoxanthus* (5)

RUEPPELL'S PARROT *Poicephalus rueppellii* (5)

GRAY-HEADED LOVEBIRD *Agapornis canus* (5)

RED-HEADED LOVEBIRD *Agapornis pullarius* (5)

BLACK-WINGED LOVEBIRD *Agapornis taranta* (5)

BLACK-COLLARED LOVEBIRD *Agapornis swindernianus* (5)

ROSY-FACED LOVEBIRD *Agapornis roseicollis* (5)

FISCHER'S LOVEBIRD *Agapornis fischeri* (5) [NT]

YELLOW-COLLARED LOVEBIRD *Agapornis personatus* (5)

LILIAN'S LOVEBIRD *Agapornis lilianae* (5)

BLACK-CHEEKED LOVEBIRD *Agapornis nigrigenis* (5) [EN]

VERNAL HANGING-PARROT *Loriculus vernalis* (4)

SRI LANKA HANGING-PARROT or CEYLON HANGING-PARROT *Loriculus beryllinus* (4)

COLASISI or PHILIPPINE HANGING-PARROT *Loriculus philippensis* (4)

BLUE-CROWNED HANGING-PARROT *Loriculus galgulus* (4)

SULAWESI HANGING-PARROT *Loriculus stigmatus* (4)

MOLUCCAN HANGING-PARROT *Loriculus amabilis* (4)

SANGIHE HANGING-PARROT *Loriculus catamene* (4) [EN]

ORANGE-FRONTED HANGING-PARROT *Loriculus aurantiifrons* (6)

GREEN-FRONTED HANGING-PARROT *Loriculus tener* (6) [NT]

RED-BILLED HANGING-PARROT or PYGMY HANGING-PARROT *Loriculus exilis* (4)

YELLOW-THROATED HANGING-PARROT *Loriculus pusillus* (4) [NT]

WALLACE'S HANGING-PARROT *Loriculus flosculus* (4) [VU]

ALEXANDRINE PARAKEET *Psittacula eupatria* (4)

SEYCHELLES PARAKEET *Psittacula wardi* (5) [EX]

ROSE-RINGED PARAKEET *Psittacula krameri* (1, 3, 4, 5)

MAURITIUS PARAKEET *Psittacula echo* (5) [CR]

NEWTON'S PARAKEET *Psittacula exsul* (4) [EX]

SLATY-HEADED PARAKEET *Psittacula himalayana* (3)

GRAY-HEADED PARAKEET *Psittacula finschi* (4)

INTERMEDIATE PARAKEET *Psittacula intermedia* (4) [VU]

PLUM-HEADED PARAKEET *Psittacula cyanocephala* (4)

BLOSSOM-HEADED PARAKEET *Psittacula roseata* (4)

MALABAR PARAKEET *PSITTACULA columboides* (4)

LAYARD'S PARAKEET *Psittacula calthropae* (4)

DERBYAN PARAKEET *Psittacula derbiana* (4) [NT]

RED-BREASTED PARAKEET *Psittacula alexandri* (4)

NICOBAR PARAKEET *Psittacula caniceps* (4) [NT]

LONG-TAILED PARAKEET or PINK-CHEEKED PARAKEET *Psittacula longicauda* (4)

HYACINTH MACAW *Anodorhynchus hyacinthinus* (2) [VU]

INDIGO MACAW or LEAR'S MACAW *Anodorhynchus leari* (2) [CR]

GLAUCOUS MACAW *Anodorhynchus glaucus* (2) [EX]

LITTLE BLUE MACAW or SPIX'S MACAW *Cyanopsitta spixii* (2) [CR]

BLUE-AND-YELLOW MACAW *Ara ararauna* (2)

BLUE-THROATED MACAW *Ara glaucogularis* (2) [EN]

MILITARY MACAW *Ara militaris* (1, 2) [VU]

GREAT GREEN MACAW *Ara ambigua* (2)

SCARLET MACAW *Ara macao* (1, 2)

RED-AND-GREEN MACAW *Ara chloropterus* (2)

CUBAN MACAW *Ara tricolor* (2) [EX]

JAMAICAN MACAW *Ara gossei* (2) [EX]

RED-FRONTED MACAW *Ara rubrogenys* (2) [EN]

CHESTNUT-FRONTED MACAW *Ara severa* (2)

RED-BELLIED MACAW *Ara manilata* (2)

BLUE-HEADED MACAW *Ara couloni* (2)

BLUE-WINGED MACAW *Ara maracana* (2) [VU]

YELLOW-COLLARED MACAW *Ara auricollis* (2)

RED-SHOULDERED MACAW *Ara nobilis* (2)

BLUE-CROWNED PARAKEET *Aratinga acuticaudata* (2)

GOLDEN PARAKEET *Aratinga guarouba* (2) [EN]

GREEN PARAKEET *Aratinga holochlora* (2)

SOCORRO PARAKEET *Aratinga brevipes* (2) [VU]

RED-THROATED PARAKEET *Aratinga rubritorques* (2)

SCARLET-FRONTED PARAKEET *Aratinga wagleri* (2)

MITRED PARAKEET *Aratinga mitrata* (2)

RED-MASKED PARAKEET *Aratinga erythrogenys* (2) [NT]

CRIMSON-FRONTED PARAKEET *Aratinga finschi* (2)

WHITE-EYED PARAKEET *Aratinga leucophthalmus* (2)

CUBAN PARAKEET *Aratinga euops* (2) [VU]

HISPANIOLAN PARAKEET *Aratinga chloroptera* (2) [VU]

SUN PARAKEET *Aratinga solstitialis* (2)

JANDAYA PARAKEET *Aratinga jandaya* (2)

GOLDEN-CAPPED PARAKEET *Aratinga auricapilla* (2) [VU]

DUSKY-HEADED PARAKEET *Aratinga weddellii* (2)

AZTEC PARAKEET *Aratinga astec* (2)

OLIVE-THROATED PARAKEET *Aratinga nana* (2)

ORANGE-FRONTED PARAKEET *Aratinga canicularis* (1, 2)

PEACH-FRONTED PARAKEET *Aratinga aurea* (2)

BROWN-THROATED PARAKEET *Aratinga pertinax* (2)

CAATINGA PARAKEET *Aratinga cactorum* (2)

NANDAY PARAKEET *Nandayus nenday* (1, 2)

GOLDEN-PLUMED PARAKEET *Leptosittaca branickii* (2) [VU]

YELLOW-EARED PARROT *Ognorhynchus icterotis* (2) [CR]

THICK-BILLED PARROT *Rhynchopsitta pachyrhyncha* (1) [VU]

MAROON-FRONTED PARROT *Rhynchopsitta terrisi* (1) [VU]

CAROLINA PARAKEET *Conuropsis carolinensis* (1) [EX]

BURROWING PARAKEET *Cyanoliseus patagonus* (2)

BLUE-THROATED PARAKEET or BLUE-CHESTED PARAKEET *Pyrrhura cruentata* (2) [VU]

BLAZE-WINGED PARAKEET *Pyrrhura devillei* (2)

MAROON-BELLIED PARAKEET *Pyrrhura frontalis* (2)

CRIMSON-BELLIED PARAKEET *Pyrrhura perlata* (2)

GREEN-CHEEKED PARAKEET *Pyrrhura molinae* (2)

PAINTED PARAKEET *Pyrrhura picta* (2)

WHITE-EARED PARAKEET *Pyrrhura leucotis* (2)

SANTA MARTA PARAKEET *Pyrrhura viridicata* (2) [VU]

FIERY-SHOULDERED PARAKEET *Pyrrhura egregia* (2)

MAROON-TAILED PARAKEET *Pyrrhura melanura* (2)

EL ORO PARAKEET *Pyrrhura orcesi* (2) [VU]

BLACK-CAPPED PARAKEET *Pyrrhura rupicola* (2)

WHITE-NECKED PARAKEET *Pyrrhura albipectus* (2) [VU]

BROWN-BREASTED PARAKEET or FLAME-WINGED PARAKEET *Pyrrhura calliptera* (2) [VU]

RED-EARED PARAKEET *Pyrrhura hoematotis* (2)

ROSE-HEADED PARAKEET *Pyrrhura rhodocephala* (2) [NT]

SULFUR-WINGED PARAKEET *Pyrrhura hoffmanni* (2)

AUSTRAL PARAKEET *Enicognathus errugineus* (2)

SLENDER-BILLED PARAKEET *Enicognathus leptorhynchus* (2) [NT]

MONK PARAKEET *Myiopsitta monachus* (1, 2)

GRAY-HOODED PARAKEET *Bolborhynchus aymara* (2)

MOUNTAIN PARAKEET *Bolborhynchus aurifrons* (2)

BARRED PARAKEET *Bolborhynchus lineola* (1, 2)

ANDEAN PARAKEET *Bolborhynchus orbygnesius* (2)

RUFOUS-FRONTED PARAKEET *Bolborhynchus ferrugineifrons* (2) [EN]

MEXICAN PARROTLET *Forpus cyanopygius* (1)

GREEN-RUMPED PARROTLET *Forpus passerinus* (2)

BLUE-WINGED PARROTLET *Forpus xanthopterygius* (2)

SPECTACLED PARROTLET *Forpus conspicillatus* (2)

DUSKY-BILLED PARROTLET *Forpus sclateri* (2)

PACIFIC PARROTLET *Forpus coelestis* (2)

YELLOW-FACED PARROTLET *Forpus xanthops* (2) [VU]

PLAIN PARAKEET *Brotogeris tirica* (2)

CANARY-WINGED PARAKEET *Brotogeris versicolurus* (2)

YELLOW-CHEVRONED PARAKEET *Brotogeris chiriri* (1, 2)

GRAY-CHEEKED PARAKEET *Brotogeris pyrrhopterus* (2) [NT]

ORANGE-CHINNED PARAKEET *Brotogeris jugularis* (1, 2)

COBALT-WINGED PARAKEET *Brotogeris cyanoptera* (2)

GOLDEN-WINGED PARAKEET *Brotogeris chrysopterus* (2)

TUI PARAKEET *Brotogeris sanctithomae* (2)

TEPUI PARROTLET *Nannopsittaca panychlora* (2)

AMAZONIAN PARROTLET *Nannopsittaca dachilleae* (2) [NT]

LILAC-TAILED PARROTLET *Touit batavica* (2)

SCARLET-SHOULDERED PARROTLET *Touit huetii* (2)

RED-FRONTED PARROTLET *Touit costaricensis* (2) [NT]

BLUE-FRONTED PARROTLET *Touit dilectissima* (2)

SAPPHIRE-RUMPED PARROTLET *Touit purpurata* (2)

BROWN-BACKED PARROTLET *Touit melanonotus* (2) [EN]

GOLDEN-TAILED PARROTLET *Touit surda* (2) [EN]

SPOT-WINGED PARROTLET *Touit stictoptera* (2) [VU]

BLACK-HEADED PARROT *Pionites melanocephala* (2)

WHITE-BELLIED PARROT *Pionites leucogaster* (2)

PILEATED PARROT *Pionopsitta pileata* (2) [NT]

BROWN-HOODED PARROT *Pionopsitta haematotis* (1, 2)

ROSE-FACED PARROT *Pionopsitta pulchra* (2)

ORANGE-CHEEKED PARROT *Pionopsitta barrabandi* (2)

SAFFRON-HEADED PARROT *Pionopsitta pyrilia* (2)

CAICA PARROT *Pionopsitta caica* (2)

VULTURINE PARROT *Gypopsitta vulturina* (2)

BLACK-WINGED PARROT *Hapalopsittaca melanotis* (2)

RUSTY-FACED PARROT *Hapalopsittaca amazonina* (2) [EN]

INDIGO-WINGED PARROT or FUERTES'S PARROT *Hapalopsittaca fuertesi* (2) [CR]

RED-FACED PARROT *Hapalopsittaca pyrrhops* (2) [EN]

SHORT-TAILED PARROT *Graydidascalus brachyurus* (2)

BLUE-HEADED PARROT *Pionus menstruus* (2)

RED-BILLED PARROT *Pionus sordidus* (2)

SCALY-HEADED PARROT *Pionus maximiliani* (2)

SPECKLE-FACED PARROT *Pionus tumultuosus* (2)

WHITE-CROWNED PARROT *Pionus senilis* (1, 2)

BRONZE-WINGED PARROT *Pionus chalcopterus* (2)

DUSKY PARROT *Pionus fuscus* (2)

CUBAN PARROT *Amazona leucocephala* (2) [NT]

YELLOW-BILLED PARROT *Amazona collaria* (2) [NT]

HISPANIOLAN PARROT *Amazona ventralis* (2) [NT]

WHITE-FRONTED PARROT *Amazona albifrons* (1, 2)

YELLOW-LORED PARROT or YUCATÁN PARROT *Amazona xantholora* (1, 2)

BLACK-BILLED PARROT or BLACK-BILLED AMAZON *Amazona agilis* (2) [VU]

PUERTO RICAN PARROT or PUERTO RICAN AMAZON *Amazona vittata* (2) [CR]

TUCUMAN PARROT *Amazona tucumana* (2)

RED-SPECTACLED PARROT or RED-SPECTACLED AMAZON *Amazona pretrei* (2) [EN]

RED-CROWNED PARROT or GREEN-CHEEKED AMAZON *Amazona viridigenalis* (1, 2) [EN]

LILAC-CROWNED PARROT *Amazona finschi* (1) [NT]

RED-LORED PARROT *Amazona autumnalis* (1, 2)

BLUE-CHEEKED PARROT *Amazona dufresniana* (2) [NT]

RED-BROWED PARROT or RED-BROWED AMAZON *Amazona rhodocorytha* (2) [EN]

RED-TAILED PARROT or RED-TAILED AMAZON *Amazona brasiliensis* (2) [EN]

FESTIVE PARROT *Amazona festiva* (2)

YELLOW-FACED PARROT or YELLOW-FACED AMAZON *Amazona xanthops* (2) [VU]

YELLOW-SHOULDERED PARROT or YELLOW-SHOULDERED AMAZON *Amazona barbadensis* (2) [VU]

BLUE-FRONTED PARROT *Amazona aestiva* (2)

YELLOW-HEADED PARROT or YELLOW-HEADED AMAZON *Amazona oratrix* (1, 2) [EN]

YELLOW-NAPED PARROT *Amazona auropalliata* (1, 2)

YELLOW-CROWNED PARROT *Amazona ochrocephala* (2)

ORANGE-WINGED PARROT *Amazona amazonica* (2)

SCALY-NAPED PARROT *Amazona mercenaria* (2)

MEALY PARROT *Amazona farinosa* (1, 2)

KAWALL'S PARROT *Amazona kawalli* (2)

VINACEOUS PARROT or VINACEOUS AMAZON *Amazona vinacea* (2) [EN]

ST. LUCIA PARROT or ST. LUCIA AMAZON *Amazona versicolor* (2) [VU]

RED-NECKED PARROT or RED-NECKED AMAZON *Amazona arausiaca* (2) [VU]

ST. VINCENT PARROT or ST. VINCENT AMAZON *Amazona guildingii* (2) [VU]

IMPERIAL PARROT or IMPERIAL AMAZON *Amazona imperialis* (2) [VU]

RED-FAN PARROT *Deroptyus accipitrinus* (2)

BLUE-BELLIED PARROT *Triclaria malachitacea* (2) [EN]

Order APODIFORMES
Family APODIDAE
Subfamily CYPSELOIDINAE

BLACK SWIFT *Cypseloides niger* (1, 2)

WHITE-CHESTED SWIFT *Cypseloides lemosi* (2) [VU]

ROTHSCHILD'S SWIFT or GIANT SWIFT *Cypseloides rothschildi* (2) [NT]

SOOTY SWIFT *Cypseloides fumigatus* (2)

SPOT-FRONTED SWIFT *Cypseloides cherriei* (2)

WHITE-FRONTED SWIFT *Cypseloides storeri* (1) [DD]

WHITE-CHINNED SWIFT *Cypseloides cryptus* (1, 2)

GREAT DUSKY SWIFT *Cypseloides senex* (2)

TEPUI SWIFT *Streptoprocne phelpsi* (2)

CHESTNUT-COLLARED SWIFT *Streptoprocne rutila* (1, 2)

WHITE-COLLARED SWIFT *Streptoprocne zonaris* (1, 2)

BISCUTATE SWIFT *Streptoprocne biscutata* (2)

WHITE-NAPED SWIFT *Streptoprocne semicollaris* (1)

Subfamily CHAETURINAE

WATERFALL SWIFT *Hydrochous gigas* (4) [NT]

GLOSSY SWIFTLET *Collocalia esculenta* (4, 6)

GRAY-RUMPED SWIFTLET *Collocalia marginata* (4)

CAVE SWIFTLET *Collocalia linchi* (4)

PYGMY SWIFTLET *Collocalia troglodytes* (4)

SEYCHELLES SWIFTLET *Aerodramus elaphrus* (5) [VU]

MASCARENE SWIFTLET *Aerodramus francicus* (5) [NT]

INDIAN SWIFTLET *Aerodramus unicolor* (4)

PHILIPPINE SWIFTLET *Aerodramus mearnsi* (4)

MOLUCCAN SWIFTLET *Aerodramus infuscata* (4)

MOUNTAIN SWIFTLET *Aerodramus hirundinacea* (6)

WHITE-RUMPED SWIFTLET *Aerodramus spodiopygius* (4, 6)

AUSTRALIAN SWIFTLET *Aerodramus terraereginae* (6)

CHILLAGOE SWIFTLET *Aerodramus chillagoensis* (6)

HIMALAYAN SWIFTLET *Aerodramus brevirostris* (4)

VOLCANO SWIFTLET *Aerodramus vulcanorum* (4) [VU]

INDOCHINESE SWIFTLET *Aerodramus rogersi* (4)

WHITEHEAD'S SWIFTLET *Aerodramus whiteheadi* (4) [VU]

BARE-LEGGED SWIFTLET *Aerodramus nuditarsus* (6)

MAYR'S SWIFTLET *Aerodramus orientalis* (4) [DD]

MOSSY-NEST SWIFTLET *Aerodramus salanganus* (4)

PALAWAN SWIFTLET *Aerodramus palawanensis* (4)

GRAY SWIFTLET *Aerodramus amelis* (4)

UNIFORM SWIFTLET *Aerodramus vanikorensis* (4, 6)

PALAU SWIFTLET *Aerodramus pelewensis* (4)

MICRONESIAN SWIFTLET *Aerodramus inquieta* (4)

ATIU SWIFTLET *Aerodramus sawtelli* (4) [VU]

GUAM SWIFTLET *Aerodramus bartschi* (1, 4)

TAHITI SWIFTLET *Aerodramus leucophaeus* (6) [VU]

MARQUESAN SWIFTLET *Aerodramus ocista* (4)

BLACK-NEST SWIFTLET *Aerodramus maximus* (4)

EDIBLE-NEST SWIFTLET *Aerodramus fuciphagus* (4)

GERMAN'S SWIFTLET *Aerodramus germani* (4)

PAPUAN SWIFTLET *Aerodramus papuensis* (6)

PHILIPPINE NEEDLETAIL *Mearnsia picina* (4)

PAPUAN NEEDLETAIL *Mearnsia novaeguineae* (6)

MALAGASY SPINETAIL *Zoonavena grandidieri* (5)

SÃO TOMÉ SPINETAIL *Zoonavena thomensis* (5)

WHITE-RUMPED SPINETAIL *Zoonavena sylvatica* (4)

MOTTLED SPINETAIL *Telacanthura ussheri* (5)

BLACK SPINETAIL *Telacanthura melanopygia* (5)

SILVER-RUMPED SPINETAIL *Rhaphidura leucopygialis* (4)

SABINE'S SPINETAIL *Rhaphidura sabini* (5)

CASSIN'S SPINETAIL *Neafrapus cassini* (5)

BAT-LIKE SPINETAIL *Neafrapus boehmi* (5)

WHITE-THROATED NEEDLETAIL *Hirundapus caudacutus* (4, 6)

SILVER-BACKED NEEDLETAIL *Hirundapus cochinchinensis* (3, 4)

BROWN-BACKED NEEDLETAIL *Hirundapus giganteus* (4)

PURPLE NEEDLETAIL *Hirundapus celebensis* (4)

BAND-RUMPED SWIFT *Chaetura spinicauda* (2)

PALE-RUMPED SWIFT *Chaetura egregia* (2)

LESSER ANTILLEAN SWIFT *Chaetura martinica* (2)

GRAY-RUMPED SWIFT *Chaetura cinereiventris* (2)

CHIMNEY SWIFT *Chaetura pelagica* (1)

VAUX'S SWIFT *Chaetura vauxi* (1, 2)

CHAPMAN'S SWIFT *Chaetura chapmani* (2)

SHORT-TAILED SWIFT *Chaetura brachyura* (2)

ASHY-TAILED SWIFT *Chaetura andrei* (2)

SCARCE SWIFT *Schoutedenapus myoptilus* (5)

SCHOUTEDEN'S SWIFT *Schoutedenapus schoutedeni* (5) [VU]

Subfamily APODINAE

WHITE-THROATED SWIFT *Aeronautes saxatalis* (1, 2)

WHITE-TIPPED SWIFT *Aeronautes montivagus* (2)

ANDEAN SWIFT *Aeronautes andecolus* (2)

ANTILLEAN PALM-SWIFT *Tachornis phoenicobia* (2)

PYGMY SWIFT *Tachornis furcata* (2)

FORK-TAILED PALM-SWIFT *Tachornis squamata* (2)

GREAT SWALLOW-TAILED SWIFT *Panyptila sanctihieronymi* (1, 2)

LESSER SWALLOW-TAILED SWIFT *Panyptila cayennensis* (1, 2)

AFRICAN PALM-SWIFT *Cypsiurus parvus* (5)

ASIAN PALM-SWIFT *Cypsiurus balasiensis* (4)

ALPINE SWIFT *Tachymarptis melba* (4, 5)

MOTTLED SWIFT *Tachymarptis aequatorialis* (5)

ALEXANDER'S SWIFT *Apus alexandri* (5)

COMMON SWIFT *Apus apus* (3, 4)

PLAIN SWIFT *Apus unicolor* (5)

NYANZA SWIFT *Apus niansae* (5)

PALLID SWIFT *Apus pallidus* (4, 5)

AFRICAN SWIFT *Apus barbatus* (5)

FORBES-WATSON'S SWIFT *Apus berliozi* (5)

FERNANDO PO SWIFT *Apus sladeniae* (5) [DD]

BRADFIELD'S SWIFT *Apus bradfieldi* (5)

MADAGASCAR SWIFT *Apus balstoni* (5)

FORK-TAILED SWIFT *Apus pacificus* (4, 6)

DARK-RUMPED SWIFT *Apus acuticauda* (4) [VU]

LITTLE SWIFT *Apus affinis* (4, 5)

HOUSE SWIFT *Apus nipalensis* (4)

HORUS SWIFT *Apus horus* (5)

WHITE-RUMPED SWIFT *Apus caffer* (3, 5)

BATES'S SWIFT *Apus batesi* (5)

Family HEMIPROCNIDAE

CRESTED TREESWIFT *Hemiprocne coronata* (4)

GRAY-RUMPED TREESWIFT *Hemiprocne longipennis* (4)

MUSTACHED TREESWIFT *Hemiprocne mystacea* (4, 6)

WHISKERED TREESWIFT *Hemiprocne comata* (4)

Order TROCHILIFORME
Family TROCHILIDAE
Subfamily PHAETHORNITHINAE

BRONZY HERMIT *Glaucis aenea* (2)

RUFOUS-BREASTED HERMIT *Glaucis hirsuta* (2)

SOOTY BARBTHROAT *Threnetes niger* (2)

BAND-TAILED BARBTHROAT *Threnetes ruckeri* (2)

PALE-TAILED BARBTHROAT *Threnetes leucurus* (2)

WHITE-WHISKERED HERMIT *Phaethornis yaruqui* (2)

GREEN HERMIT *Phaethornis guy* (2)

TAWNY-BELLIED HERMIT *Phaethornis syrmatophorus* (2)

MEXICAN HERMIT *Phaethornis mexicanus* (2)

LONG-TAILED HERMIT *Phaethornis superciliosus* (1, 2)

GREAT-BILLED HERMIT *Phaethornis malaris* (2)

SCALE-THROATED HERMIT *Phaethornis eurynome* (2)

WHITE-BEARDED HERMIT *Phaethornis hispidus* (2)

PALE-BELLIED HERMIT *Phaethornis anthophilus* (2)

STRAIGHT-BILLED HERMIT *Phaethornis bourcieri* (2)

KOEPCKE'S HERMIT *Phaethornis koepckeae* (2) [NT]

NEEDLE-BILLED HERMIT *Phaethornis philippii* (2)

DUSKY-THROATED HERMIT *Phaethornis squalidus* (2)

STREAK-THROATED HERMIT *Phaethornis rupurumii* (2)

SOOTY-CAPPED HERMIT *Phaethornis augusti* (2)

PLANALTO HERMIT *Phaethornis pretrei* (2)

BUFF-BELLIED HERMIT *Phaethornis subochraceus* (2)

CINNAMON-THROATED HERMIT *Phaethornis nattereri* (2)

BROAD-TIPPED HERMIT *Phaethornis gounellei* (2)

REDDISH HERMIT *Phaethornis ruber* (2)

WHITE-BROWED HERMIT *Phaethornis stuarti* (2)

GRAY-CHINNED HERMIT *Phaethornis griseogularis* (2)

LITTLE HERMIT *Phaethornis longuemareus* (2)

BOUCARD'S HERMIT or DUSKY HERMIT *Phaethornis adolphi* (1, 2)

STRIPE-THROATED HERMIT *Phaethornis strigularis* (2)

MINUTE HERMIT or OBSCURE HERMIT *Phaethornis idaliae* (2)

WHITE-TIPPED SICKLEBILL *Eutoxeres aquila* (2)

BUFF-TAILED SICKLEBILL *Eutoxeres condamini* (2)

Subfamily TROCHILINAE

TOOTH-BILLED HUMMINGBIRD *Androdon aequatorialis* (2)

SAW-BILLED HERMIT *Ramphodon naevius* (2) [NT]

HOOK-BILLED HERMIT *Ramphodon dohrnii* (2) [CR]

BLUE-FRONTED LANCEBILL *Doryfera johannae* (2)

GREEN-FRONTED LANCEBILL *Doryfera ludovicae* (2)

SCALY-BREASTED HUMMINGBIRD *Phaeochroa cuvierii* (1, 2)

WEDGE-TAILED SABREWING *Campylopterus curvipennis* (1, 2)

LONG-TAILED SABREWING *Campylopterus excellens* (1) [NT]

GRAY-BREASTED SABREWING *Campylopterus largipennis* (2)

RUFOUS SABREWING *Campylopterus rufus* (1, 2)

RUFOUS-BREASTED SABREWING *Campylopterus hyperythrus* (2)

BUFF-BREASTED SABREWING *Campylopterus duidae* (2)

VIOLET SABREWING *Campylopterus hemileucurus* (1, 2)

WHITE-TAILED SABREWING *Campylopterus ensipennis* (2) [VU]

LAZULINE SABREWING *Campylopterus falcatus* (2)

SANTA MARTA SABREWING *Campylopterus phainopeplus* (2) [NT]

NAPO SABREWING *Campylopterus villaviscensio* (2) [NT]

SWALLOW-TAILED HUMMINGBIRD *Eupetomena macroura* (2)

WHITE-NECKED JACOBIN *Florisuga mellivora* (2)

BLACK JACOBIN *Melanotrochilus fuscus* (2)

BROWN VIOLET-EAR *Colibri delphinae* (2)

GREEN VIOLET-EAR *Colibri thalassinus* (1, 2)

SPARKLING VIOLET-EAR *Colibri coruscans* (2)

WHITE-VENTED VIOLET-EAR *Colibri serrirostris* (2)

GREEN-THROATED MANGO *Anthracothorax viridigula* (2)

GREEN-BREASTED MANGO *Anthracothorax prevostii* (1, 2)

VERAGUAS MANGO *Anthracothorax veraguensis* (2)

BLACK-THROATED MANGO *Anthracothorax nigricollis* (2)

JAMAICAN MANGO *Anthracothorax mango* (2)

ANTILLEAN MANGO *Anthracothorax dominicus* (2)

GREEN MANGO *Anthracothorax viridis* (2)

FIERY-TAILED AWLBILL *Avocettula recurvirostris* (2) [NT]

PURPLE-THROATED CARIB *Eulampis jugularis* (2)

GREEN-THROATED CARIB *Eulampis holosericeus* (2)

RUBY-TOPAZ HUMMINGBIRD *Chrysolampis mosquitus* (2)

ANTILLEAN CRESTED HUMMINGBIRD *Orthorhyncus cristatus* (2)

VIOLET-HEADED HUMMINGBIRD *Klais guimeti* (2)

EMERALD-CHINNED HUMMINGBIRD *Abeillia abeillei* (1, 2)

PLOVERCREST *Stephanoxis lalandi* (2)

TUFTED COQUETTE *Lophornis ornatus* (2)

DOT-EARED COQUETTE *Lophornis gouldii* (2)

FRILLED COQUETTE *Lophornis magnificus* (2)

SHORT-CRESTED COQUETTE *Lophornis brachylopha* (2) [EN]

RUFOUS-CRESTED COQUETTE *Lophornis delattrei* (2)

SPANGLED COQUETTE *Lophornis stictolophus* (2) [NT]

FESTIVE COQUETTE *Lophornis chalybeus* (2)

PEACOCK COQUETTE *Lophornis pavoninus* (2)

BLACK-CRESTED COQUETTE *Lophornis helenae* (1, 2)

WHITE-CRESTED COQUETTE *Lophornis adorabilis* (2)

WIRE-CRESTED THORNTAIL *Popelairia popelairii* (2)

BLACK-BELLIED THORNTAIL *Popelairia langsdorffi* (2)

COPPERY THORNTAIL *Popelairia letitiae* (2) [DD]

GREEN THORNTAIL *Popelairia conversii* (2)

RACKET-TAILED COQUETTE *Discosura longicauda* (2)

BLUE-CHINNED SAPPHIRE *Chlorestes notatus* (2)

GOLDEN-CROWNED EMERALD *Chlorostilbon suriceps* (1)

COZUMEL EMERALD *Chlorostilbon forficatus* (1)

CANIVET'S EMERALD or FORK-TAILED EMERALD *Chlorostilbon canivetii* (1, 2)

SALVIN'S EMERALD *Chlorostilbon salvini* (1, 2)

GARDEN EMERALD *Chlorostilbon assimilis* (2)

WEST ANDEAN EMERALD *Chlorostilbon melanorhynchus* (2)

RED-BILLED EMERALD *Chlorostilbon gibsoni* (2)

CHIRIBIQUETE EMERALD *Chlorostilbon olivaresi* (2)

BLUE-TAILED EMERALD *Chlorostilbon mellisugus* (2)

GLITTERING-BELLIED EMERALD *Chlorostilbon aureoventris* (2)

CUBAN EMERALD *Chlorostilbon ricordii* (2)

BRACE'S EMERALD *Chlorostilbon bracei* (2)

HISPANIOLAN EMERALD *Chlorostilbon swainsonii* (2)

PUERTO RICAN EMERALD *Chlorostilbon maugaeus* (2)

COPPERY EMERALD *Chlorostilbon russatus* (2)

NARROW-TAILED EMERALD *Chlorostilbon stenura* (2)

GREEN-TAILED EMERALD *Chlorostilbon alice* (2)

SHORT-TAILED EMERALD *Chlorostilbon poortmani* (2)

DUSKY HUMMINGBIRD *Cynanthus sordidus* (1)

BROAD-BILLED HUMMINGBIRD *Cynanthus latirostris* (1)

DOUBLEDAY'S HUMMINGBIRD *Cynanthus doubledayi* (1)

BLUE-HEADED HUMMINGBIRD *Cyanophaia bicolor* (2)

MEXICAN WOODNYMPH *Thalurania ridgwayi* (1) [VU]

BLUE-CROWNED WOODNYMPH or VIOLET-CROWNED WOODNYMPH *Thalurania colombica* (2)

GREEN-CROWNED WOODNYMPH *Thalurania fannyi* (2)

EMERALD-BELLIED WOODNYMPH *Thalurania hypochlora* (2)

FORK-TAILED WOODNYMPH *Thalurania furcata* (2)

LONG-TAILED WOODNYMPH *Thalurania watertonii* (2)

VIOLET-CAPPED WOODNYMPH *Thalurania glaucopis* (2)

FIERY-THROATED HUMMINGBIRD *Panterpe insignis* (2)

VIOLET-BELLIED HUMMINGBIRD *Damophila julie* (2)

SAPPHIRE-THROATED HUMMINGBIRD *Lepidopyga coeruleogularis* (2)

SAPPHIRE-BELLIED HUMMINGBIRD *Lepidopyga lilliae* (2) [CR]

SHINING-GREEN HUMMINGBIRD *Lepidopyga goudoti* (2)

XANTUS'S HUMMINGBIRD *Hylocharis xantusii* (1)

WHITE-EARED HUMMINGBIRD *Hylocharis leucotis* (1, 2)

BLUE-THROATED GOLDENTAIL *Hylocharis eliciae* (1, 2)

RUFOUS-THROATED SAPPHIRE *Hylocharis sapphirina* (2)

WHITE-CHINNED SAPPHIRE *Hylocharis cyanus* (2)

FLAME-RUMPED SAPPHIRE *Hylocharis pyropygia* (2)

GILDED HUMMINGBIRD *Hylocharis chrysura* (2)

BLUE-HEADED SAPPHIRE *Hylocharis grayi* (2)

HUMBOLDT'S SAPPHIRE *Hylocharis humboldti* (2)

GOLDEN-TAILED SAPPHIRE *Chrysuronia oenone* (2)

VIOLET-CAPPED HUMMINGBIRD *Goldmania violiceps* (2)

RUFOUS-CHEEKED HUMMINGBIRD *Goethalsia bella* (2) [NT]

STREAMERTAIL *Trochilus polytmus* (2)

WHITE-THROATED HUMMINGBIRD *Leucochloris albicollis* (2)

WHITE-TAILED GOLDENTHROAT *Polytmus guainumbi* (2)

TEPUI GOLDENTHROAT *Polytmus milleri* (2)

GREEN-TAILED GOLDENTHROAT *Polytmus theresiae* (2)

BUFFY HUMMINGBIRD *Leucippus fallax* (2)

TUMBES HUMMINGBIRD *Leucippus baeri* (2)

SPOT-THROATED HUMMINGBIRD *Leucippus taczanowskii* (2)

OLIVE-SPOTTED HUMMINGBIRD *Leucippus chlorocercus* (2)

MANY-SPOTTED HUMMINGBIRD *Taphrospilus hypostictus* (2)

GREEN-AND-WHITE HUMMINGBIRD *Amazilia viridicauda* (2)

WHITE-BELLIED HUMMINGBIRD *Amazilia chionogaster* (2)

WHITE-BELLIED EMERALD *Amazilia candida* (1, 2)

WHITE-CHESTED EMERALD *Amazilia chionopectus* (2)

VERSICOLORED EMERALD *Amazilia versicolor* (2)

HONDURAN EMERALD *Amazilia luciae* (2) [CR]

GLITTERING-THROATED EMERALD *Amazilia fimbriata* (2)

TACHIRA EMERALD *Amazilia distans* (2) [EN]

SAPPHIRE-SPANGLED EMERALD *Amazilia lactea* (2)

BLUE-CHESTED HUMMINGBIRD *Amazilia amabilis* (2)

CHARMING HUMMINGBIRD *Amazilia decora* (2)

PURPLE-CHESTED HUMMINGBIRD *Amazilia rosenbergi* (2)

MANGROVE HUMMINGBIRD *Amazilia boucardi* (2) [VU]

ANDEAN EMERALD *Amazilia franciae* (2)

PLAIN-BELLIED EMERALD *Amazilia leucogaster* (2)

AZURE-CROWNED HUMMINGBIRD *Amazilia cyanocephala* (1, 2)

INDIGO-CAPPED HUMMINGBIRD *Amazilia cyanifrons* (2)

BERYLLINE HUMMINGBIRD *Amazilia beryllina* (1, 2)

BLUE-TAILED HUMMINGBIRD *Amazilia cyanura* (1, 2)

STEELY-VENTED HUMMINGBIRD *Amazilia saucerrottei* (2)

COPPER-RUMPED HUMMINGBIRD *Amazilia tobaci* (2)

GREEN-BELLIED HUMMINGBIRD *Amazilia viridigaster* (2)

SNOWY-BREASTED HUMMINGBIRD *Amazilia edward* (2)

CINNAMON HUMMINGBIRD *Amazilia rutila* (1, 2)

BUFF-BELLIED HUMMINGBIRD *Amazilia yucatanensis* (1, 2)

RUFOUS-TAILED HUMMINGBIRD *Amazilia tzacatl* (1, 2)

CHESTNUT-BELLIED HUMMINGBIRD *Amazilia castaneiventris* (2) [EN]

AMAZILIA HUMMINGBIRD *Amazilia amazilia* (2)

GREEN-FRONTED HUMMINGBIRD *Amazilia viridifrons* (2)

CINNAMON-SIDED HUMMINGBIRD *Amazilia wagneri* (1)

VIOLET-CROWNED HUMMINGBIRD *Amazilia violiceps* (1)

WHITE-TAILED HUMMINGBIRD *Eupherusa poliocerca* (1) [EN]

BLUE-CAPPED HUMMINGBIRD or OAXACA HUMMINGBIRD *Eupherusa cyanophrys* (1) [EN]

STRIPE-TAILED HUMMINGBIRD *Eupherusa eximia* (1, 2)

BLACK-BELLIED HUMMINGBIRD *Eupherusa nigriventris* (2)

WHITE-TAILED EMERALD *Elvira chionura* (2)

COPPERY-HEADED EMERALD *Elvira cupreiceps* (2)

SNOWCAP *Microchera albocoronata* (2)

WHITE-VENTED PLUMELETEER *Chalybura buffonii* (2)

BRONZE-TAILED PLUMELETEER *Chalybura urochrysia* (2)

SOMBER HUMMINGBIRD *Aphantochroa cirrochloris* (2)

BLUE-THROATED HUMMINGBIRD *Lampornis clemenciae* (1)

AMETHYST-THROATED HUMMINGBIRD *Lampornis amethystinus* (1, 2)

GREEN-THROATED MOUNTAIN-GEM *Lampornis viridipallens* (1, 2)

GREEN-BREASTED MOUNTAIN-GEM *Lampornis sybillae* (2)

WHITE-BELLIED MOUNTAIN-GEM *Lampornis hemileucus* (2)

GRAY-TAILED MOUNTAIN-GEM *Lampornis cinereicauda* (2)

WHITE-THROATED MOUNTAIN-GEM or CHESTNUT-BELLIED MOUNTAIN-GEM *Lampornis castaneoventris* (2)

PURPLE-THROATED MOUNTAIN-GEM *Lampornis calolaema* (2)

GARNET-THROATED HUMMINGBIRD *Lamprolaima rhami* (1, 2)

SPECKLED HUMMINGBIRD *Adelomyia melanogenys* (2)

BLOSSOMCROWN *Anthocephala floriceps* (2) [NT]

ECUADORIAN PIEDTAIL *Phlogophilus hemileucurus* (2) [NT]

PERUVIAN PIEDTAIL *Phlogophilus harterti* (2) [NT]

BRAZILIAN RUBY *Clytolaema rubricauda* (2)

EMPRESS BRILLIANT *Heliodoxa imperatrix* (2)

VELVET-BROWED BRILLIANT *Heliodoxa xanthogonys* (2)

PINK-THROATED BRILLIANT *Heliodoxa gularis* (2) [NT]

RUFOUS-WEBBED BRILLIANT *Heliodoxa branickii* (2)

BLACK-THROATED BRILLIANT *Heliodoxa schreibersii* (2)

GOULD'S JEWELFRONT *Heliodoxa aurescens* (2)

FAWN-BREASTED BRILLIANT *Heliodoxa rubinoides* (2)

GREEN-CROWNED BRILLIANT *Heliodoxa jacula* (2)

VIOLET-FRONTED BRILLIANT *Heliodoxa leadbeateri* (2)

MAGNIFICENT HUMMINGBIRD *Eugenes fulgens* (1, 2)

SCISSOR-TAILED HUMMINGBIRD *Hylonympha macrocerca* (2) [CR]

VIOLET-CHESTED HUMMINGBIRD *Sternoclyta cyanopectus* (2)

FIERY TOPAZ *Topaza pyra* (2)

CRIMSON TOPAZ *Topaza pella* (2)

ECUADORIAN HILLSTAR *Oreotrochilus chimborazo* (2)

ANDEAN HILLSTAR *Oreotrochilus estella* (2)

WHITE-SIDED HILLSTAR *Oreotrochilus leucopleurus* (2)

BLACK-BREASTED HILLSTAR *Oreotrochilus melanogaste* (2)

WEDGE-TAILED HILLSTAR *Oreotrochilus adela* (2) [NT]

WHITE-TAILED HILLSTAR *Urochroa bougueri* (2)

GIANT HUMMINGBIRD *Patagona gigas* (2)

SHINING SUNBEAM *Aglaeactis cupripennis* (2)

WHITE-TUFTED SUNBEAM *Aglaeactis castelnaudii* (2)

PURPLE-BACKED SUNBEAM *Aglaeactis aliciae* (2) [VU]

BLACK-HOODED SUNBEAM *Aglaeactis pamela* (2)

MOUNTAIN VELVETBREAST *Lafresnaya lafresnayi* (2)

GREAT SAPPHIREWING *Pterophanes cyanopterus* (2)

BRONZY INCA *Coeligena coeligena* (2)

BROWN INCA *Coeligena wilsoni* (2)

BLACK INCA *Coeligena prunellei* (2) [VU]

COLLARED INCA *Coeligena torquata* (2)

WHITE-TAILED STARFRONTLET *Coeligena phalerata* (2)

GOLDEN-BELLIED STARFRONTLET *Coeligena bonapartei* (2)

BLUE-THROATED STARFRONTLET *Coeligena helianthea* (2)

BUFF-WINGED STARFRONTLET *Coeligena lutetiae* (2)

VIOLET-THROATED STARFRONTLET *Coeligena violifer* (2)

RAINBOW STARFRONTLET *Coeligena iris* (2)

SWORD-BILLED HUMMINGBIRD *Ensifera ensifera* (2)

GREEN-BACKED FIRECROWN *Sephanoides sephaniodes* (2)

JUAN FERNANDEZ FIRECROWN *Sephanoides fernandensis* (2) [CR]

BUFF-TAILED CORONET *Boissonneaua flavescens* (2)

CHESTNUT-BREASTED CORONET *Boissonneaua matthewsii* (2)

VELVET-PURPLE CORONET *Boissonneaua jardini* (2)

ORANGE-THROATED SUNANGEL *Heliangelus mavors* (2)

MERIDA SUNANGEL *Heliangelus spencei* (2)

AMETHYST-THROATED SUNANGEL *Heliangelus amethysticollis* (2)

GORGETED SUNANGEL *Heliangelus strophianus* (2)

TOURMALINE SUNANGEL *Heliangelus exortis* (2)

PURPLE-THROATED SUNANGEL *Heliangelus viola* (2)

BOGOTÁ SUNANGEL *Heliangelus zusii* (2) [CR]

ROYAL SUNANGEL *Heliangelus regalis* (2) [VU]

BLACK-BREASTED PUFFLEG *Eriocnemis nigrivestis* (2) [CR]

GLOWING PUFFLEG *Eriocnemis vestitus* (2)

TURQUOISE-THROATED PUFFLEG *Eriocnemis godini* (2) [CR]

SAPPHIRE-VENTED PUFFLEG *Eriocnemis luciani* (2)

COPPERY-BELLIED PUFFLEG *Eriocnemis cupreoventris* (2)

GOLDEN-BREASTED PUFFLEG *Eriocnemis mosquera* (2)

BLUE-CAPPED PUFFLEG *Eriocnemis glaucopoides* (2)

COLORFUL PUFFLEG *Eriocnemis mirabilis* (2) [VU]

EMERALD-BELLIED PUFFLEG *Eriocnemis elinae* (2)

BLACK-THIGHED PUFFLEG *Eriocnemis derbyi* (2) [NT]

GREENISH PUFFLEG *Haplophaedia aureliae* (2)

HOARY PUFFLEG *Haplophaedia lugens* (2) [NT]

PURPLE-BIBBED WHITETIP *Urosticte benjamini* (2)

RUFOUS-VENTED WHITETIP *Urosticte ruficrissa* (2)

BOOTED RACKET-TAIL *Ocreatus underwoodii* (2)

BLACK-TAILED TRAINBEARER *Lesbia victoriae* (2)

GREEN-TAILED TRAINBEARER *Lesbia nuna* (2)

RED-TAILED COMET *Sappho sparganura* (2)

BRONZE-TAILED COMET *Polyonymus caroli* (2) [NT]

PURPLE-BACKED THORNBILL *Ramphomicron microrhynchum* (2)

BLACK-BACKED THORNBILL *Ramphomicron dorsale* (2)

VIRIDIAN METALTAIL *Metallura williami* (2)

VIOLET-THROATED METALTAIL *Metallura baroni* (2) [VU]

NEBLINA METALTAIL *Metallura odomae* (2) [NT]

COPPERY METALTAIL *Metallura theresiae* (2)

FIRE-THROATED METALTAIL *Metallura eupogon* (2)

SCALED METALTAIL *Metallura aeneocauda* (2)

BLACK METALTAIL *Metallura phoebe* (2)

TYRIAN METALTAIL *Metallura tyrianthina* (2)

PERIJA METALTAIL *Metallura iracunda* (2) [NT]

RUFOUS-CAPPED THORNBILL *Chalcostigma ruficeps* (2)

OLIVACEOUS THORNBILL *Chalcostigma olivaceum* (2)

BLUE-MANTLED THORNBILL *Chalcostigma stanleyi* (2)

BRONZE-TAILED THORNBILL *Chalcostigma heteropogon* (2)

RAINBOW-BEARDED THORNBILL *Chalcostigma herrani* (2)

BEARDED HELMETCREST *Oxypogon guerinii* (2)

MOUNTAIN AVOCETBILL *Opisthoprora euryptera* (2)

GRAY-BELLIED COMET *Taphrolesbia griseiventris* (2) [VU]

LONG-TAILED SYLPH *Aglaiocercus kingi* (2)

VENEZUELAN SYLPH *Aglaiocercus berlepschi* (2)

VIOLET-TAILED SYLPH *Aglaiocercus coelestis* (2)

BEARDED MOUNTAINEER *Oreonympha nobilis* (2)

HOODED VISORBEARER *Augastes lumachellus* (2) [NT]

HYACINTH VISORBEARER *Augastes scutatus* (2) [NT]

WEDGE-BILLED HUMMINGBIRD *Augastes geoffroyi* (2)

PURPLE-CROWNED FAIRY *Heliothryx barroti* (2)

BLACK-EARED FAIRY *Heliothryx aurita* (2)

HORNED SUNGEM *Heliactin bilophum* (2)

MARVELOUS SPATULETAIL *Loddigesia mirabilis* (2) [VU]

PLAIN-CAPPED STARTHROAT *Heliomaster constantii* (1, 2)

LONG-BILLED STARTHROAT *Heliomaster longirostris* (1, 2)

STRIPE-BREASTED STARTHROAT *Heliomaster squamosus* (2)

BLUE-TUFTED STARTHROAT *Heliomaster furcifer* (2)

OASIS HUMMINGBIRD *Rhodopis vesper* (2)

PERUVIAN SHEARTAIL *Thaumastura cora* (2)

MAGENTA-THROATED WOODSTAR *Philodice bryantae* (2) [NT]

PURPLE-THROATED WOODSTAR *Philodice mitchellii* (2)

SLENDER SHEARTAIL *Doricha enicura* (1, 2)

MEXICAN SHEARTAIL *Doricha eliza* (1)

SPARKLING-TAILED HUMMINGBIRD *Tilmatura dupontii* (1, 2)

SLENDER-TAILED WOODSTAR *Microstilbon burmeisteri* (1, 2)

LUCIFER HUMMINGBIRD *Calothorax lucifer* (1)

BEAUTIFUL HUMMINGBIRD *Calothorax pulcher* (1)

RUBY-THROATED HUMMINGBIRD *Archilochus colubris* (1)

BLACK-CHINNED HUMMINGBIRD *Archilochus alexandri* (1)

ANNA'S HUMMINGBIRD *Calypte anna* (1)

COSTA'S HUMMINGBIRD *Calypte costae* (1)

BAHAMA WOODSTAR *Calliphlox evelynae* (1)

AMETHYST WOODSTAR *Calliphlox amethystina* (2)

BEE HUMMINGBIRD *Mellisuga helenae* (2) [NT]

VERVAIN HUMMINGBIRD *Mellisuga minima* (2)

CALLIOPE HUMMINGBIRD *Stellula calliope* (1)

BUMBLEBEE HUMMINGBIRD *Atthis heloisa* (1)

WINE-THROATED HUMMINGBIRD *Atthis ellioti* (1, 2)

PURPLE-COLLARED WOODSTAR *Myrtis fanny* (2)

CHILEAN WOODSTAR *Eulidia yarrellii* (2) [VU]

SHORT-TAILED WOODSTAR *Myrmia micrura* (2)

WHITE-BELLIED WOODSTAR *Acestrura mulsant* (2)

LITTLE WOODSTAR *Acestrura bombus* (2) [EN]

GORGETED WOODSTAR *Acestrura heliodor* (2)

SANTA MARTA WOODSTAR *Acestrura astreans* (2)

ESMERALDAS WOODSTAR *Acestrura berlepschi* (2) [EN]

RUFOUS-SHAFTED WOODSTAR *Chaetocercus jourdanii* (2)

BROAD-TAILED HUMMINGBIRD *Selasphorus platycercus* (1, 2)

RUFOUS HUMMINGBIRD *Selasphorus rufus* (1)

ALLEN'S HUMMINGBIRD *Selasphorus sasin* (1)

VOLCANO HUMMINGBIRD *Selasphorus flammula* (2)

SCINTILLANT HUMMINGBIRD *Selasphorus scintilla* (2)

GLOW-THROATED HUMMINGBIRD *Selasphorus ardens* (2) [VU]

Order MUSOPHAGIFORMES
Family MUSOPHAGIDAE
Subfamily MUSOPHAGINAE

GUINEA TURACO *Tauraco persa* (5)

BLACK-BILLED TURACO *Tauraco schuettii* (5)

SCHALOW'S TURACO *Tauraco schalowi* (5)

FISCHER'S TURACO *Tauraco fischeri* (5) [NT]

LIVINGSTONE'S TURACO *Tauraco livingstonii* (5)

KNYSNA TURACO *Tauraco corythaix* (5)

BANNERMAN'S TURACO *Tauraco bannermani* (5) [VU]

RED-CRESTED TURACO *Tauraco erythrolophus* (5)

YELLOW-BILLED TURACO *Tauraco macrorhynchus* (5)

WHITE-CHEEKED TURACO *Tauraco leucotis* (5)

RUSPOLI'S TURACO or PRINCE RUSPOLI'S TURACO *Tauraco ruspolii* (5) [EN]

HARTLAUB'S TURACO *Tauraco hartlaubi* (5)

WHITE-CRESTED TURACO *Tauraco leucolophus* (5)

RUWENZORI TURACO *Musophaga johnstoni* (5)

PURPLE-CRESTED TURACO *Musophaga porphyreolopha* (5)

VIOLET TURACO *Musophaga violacea* (5)

ROSS'S TURACO *Musophaga rossae* (5)

Subfamily CRINIFERINAE

GRAY GO-AWAY-BIRD *Corythaixoides concolor* (5)

BARE-FACED GO-AWAY-BIRD *Corythaixoides personatus* (5)

WHITE-BELLIED GO-AWAY-BIRD *Corythaixoides leucogaster* (5)

WESTERN GRAY PLANTAIN-EATER *Crinifer piscator* (5)

EASTERN GRAY PLANTAIN-EATER *Crinifer zonurus* (5)

GREAT BLUE TURACO *Corythaeola cristata* (5)

Order STRIGIFORMES
Family TYTONIDAE

GREATER SOOTY-OWL or SOOTY OWL *Tyto tenebricosa* (6)

LESSER SOOTY-OWL *Tyto multipunctata* (6) [NT]

MINAHASSA MASKED-OWL or MINAHASSA OWL *Tyto inexspectata* (4) [DD]

TALIABU MASKED-OWL or TALIABU OWL *Tyto nigrobrunnea* (4) [VU]

LESSER MASKED-OWL *Tyto sororcula* (4) [DD]

MANUS MASKED-OWL *Tyto manusi* (6) [VU]

BISMARCK MASKED-OWL *Tyto aurantia* (6) [VU]

AUSTRALIAN MASKED-OWL or MASKED OWL *Tyto novaehollandiae* (6)

TASMANIAN MASKED-OWL *Tyto castanops* (6)

SULAWESI OWL *Tyto rosenbergii* (6)

MADAGASCAR RED OWL *Tyto soumagnei* (5) [EN]

Barn Owl *Tyto alba* (1, 2, 3, 4, 5, 6)

Cape Verde Barn Owl *Tyto detorta* (5)

Ashy-Faced Owl *Tyto glaucops* (2)

African Grass-Owl or Grass Owl *Tyto capensis* (5)

Eastern Grass-Owl *Tyto longimembris* (4, 6)

Congo Bay-Owl *Phodilus prigoginei* (5) [VU]

Oriental Bay-Owl *Phodilus badius* (4)

Family STRIGIDAE

White-Fronted Scops-Owl *Otus sagittatus* (4) [VU]

Reddish Scops-Owl *Otus rufescens* (4)

Sandy Scops-Owl *Otus icterorhynchus* (5)

Sokoke Scops-Owl *Otus ireneae* (5) [VU]

Andaman Scops-Owl *Otus balli* (4) [NT]

Mountain Scops-Owl *Otus spilocephalus* (4)

Simeulue Scops-Owl *Otus umbra* (4)

Javan Scops-Owl *Otus angelinae* (4) [VU]

Sulawesi Scops-Owl *Otus manadensis* (4)

Luzon Scops-Owl *Otus longicornis* (4) [VU]

Mindoro Scops-Owl *Otus mindorensis* (4) [VU]

Mindanao Scops-Owl *Otus mirus* (4) [VU]

São Tomé Scops-Owl *Otus hartlaubi* (5) [NT]

Pallid Scops-Owl *Otus brucei* (4, 5)

Flammulated Owl *Otus flammeolus* (1, 2)

Common Scops-Owl or Eurasian Scops-Owl *Otus scops* (3, 4, 5)

Oriental Scops-Owl *Otus sunia* (4)

African Scops-Owl *Otus senegalensis* (5)

Elegant Scops-Owl *Otus elegans* (4)

Mantanani Scops-Owl *Otus mantananensis* (4)

Moluccan Scops-Owl *Otus magicus* (4)

Beccari's Scops-Owl *Otus beccarii* (6)

Flores Scops-Owl *Otus alfredi* (4)

Enggano Scops-Owl *Otus enganensis* (4)

Seychelles Scops-Owl *Otus insularis* (5) [CR]

Malagasy Scops-Owl *Otus rutilus* (5)

Pemba Scops-Owl *Otus pembaensis* (5) [NT]

Anjouan Scops-Owl *Otus capnodes* (5) [CR]

Comoro Scops-Owl or Grand Comoro Scops-Owl *Otus pauliani* (5) [CR]

Rajah Scops-Owl *Otus brookii* (4)

Indian Scops-Owl *Otus bakkamoena* (4)

Collared Scops-Owl *Otus lettia* (3, 4)

Sunda Scops-Owl *Otus lempiji* (3, 4)

Japanese Scops-Owl *Otus semitorques* (4)

Mentawai Scops-Owl *Otus mentawi* (4)

Palawan Scops-Owl *Otus fuliginosus* (4) [VU]

Philippine Scops-Owl *Otus megalotis* (4)

Wallace's Scops-Owl *Otus silvicola* (4) [NT]

White-Faced Scops-Owl *Otus leucotis* (5)

Western Screech-Owl *Otus kennicottii* (1)

Balsas Screech-Owl *Otus seductus* (1)

Pacific Screech-Owl *Otus cooperi* (1, 2)

Oaxaca Screech-Owl *Otus lambi* (1)

Eastern Screech-Owl *Otus asio* (1)

Whiskered Screech-Owl *Otus trichopsis* (1, 2)

Tropical Screech-Owl *Otus choliba* (2)

Koepcke's Screech-Owl *Otus koepckeae* (2)

West Peruvian Screech-Owl *Otus roboratus* (2)

Bare-Shanked Screech-Owl *Otus clarkii* (2)

Bearded Screech-Owl or Santa Barbara Screech-Owl *Otus barbarus* (1, 2) [NT]

Rufescent Screech-Owl *Otus ingens* (2)

Cloud-Forest Screech-Owl *Otus huberi* (2)

Tawny-Bellied Screech-Owl *Otus watsonii* (2)

Austral Screech-Owl *Otus usta* (2)

Variable Screech-Owl *Otus atricapillus* (2)

MIDDLE AMERICAN SCREECH-OWL *Otus guatemalae* (1, 2)

HOY'S SCREECH-OWL *Otus hoyi* (2)

VERMICULATED SCREECH-OWL *Otus vermiculatus* (2)

LONG-TUFTED SCREECH-OWL *Otus sanctaecatarinae* (2)

BARE-LEGGED OWL or CUBAN SCREECH-OWL *Otus lawrencii* (2)

PUERTO RICAN SCREECH-OWL *Otus nudipes* (2)

PALAU OWL *Otus podarginus* (1)

WHITE-THROATED SCREECH-OWL *Otus albogularis* (2)

LESSER EAGLE-OWL or MINDANAO EAGLE-OWL *Mimizuku gurneyi* (4) [EN]

GREAT HORNED OWL *Bubo virginianus* (1, 2)

EURASIAN EAGLE-OWL *Bubo bubo* (3, 4)

ROCK EAGLE-OWL *Bubo bengalensis* (4)

PHARAOH EAGLE-OWL *Bubo ascalaphus* (5)

CAPE EAGLE-OWL *Bubo capensis* (5)

SPOTTED EAGLE-OWL *Bubo africanus* (5)

FRASER'S EAGLE-OWL *Bubo poensis* (5)

USAMBARA EAGLE-OWL *Bubo vosseleri* (5) [VU]

SPOT-BELLIED EAGLE-OWL *Bubo nipalensis* (4) [NT]

BARRED EAGLE-OWL *Bubo sumatranus* (4)

SHELLEY'S EAGLE-OWL *Bubo shelleyi* (5)

VERREAUX'S EAGLE-OWL *Bubo lacteus* (5)

DUSKY EAGLE-OWL *Bubo coromandus* (4)

AKUN EAGLE-OWL *Bubo leucostictus* (5)

PHILIPPINE EAGLE-OWL *Bubo philippensis* (4) [EN]

BLAKISTON'S FISH-OWL *Ketupa blakistoni* (3, 4) [EN]

BROWN FISH-OWL *Ketupa zeylonensis* (4)

TAWNY FISH-OWL *Ketupa flavipes* (4) [NT]

BUFFY FISH-OWL *Ketupa ketupu* (4)

SNOWY OWL *Nyctea scandiaca* (1, 3)

PEL'S FISHING-OWL *Scotopelia peli* (5)

RUFOUS FISHING-OWL *Scotopelia ussheri* (5) [EN]

VERMICULATED FISHING-OWL *Scotopelia bouvieri* (5)

SPOTTED WOOD-OWL *Strix seloputo* (4)

MOTTLED WOOD-OWL *Strix ocellata* (4)

BROWN WOOD-OWL *Strix leptogrammica* (4)

TAWNY OWL *Strix aluco* (3, 4)

HUME'S OWL *Strix butleri* (4, 5)

SPOTTED OWL *Strix occidentalis* (1) [NT]

BARRED OWL *Strix varia* (1)

FULVOUS OWL *Strix fulvescens* (1, 2)

RUSTY-BARRED OWL *Strix hylophila* (2)

RUFOUS-LEGGED OWL *Strix rufipes* (2)

URAL OWL *Strix uralensis* (3, 4)

SICHUAN WOOD-OWL *Strix davidi* (4) [VU]

GREAT GRAY OWL *Strix nebulosa* (1, 3, 4)

MOTTLED OWL *Strix virgata* (1, 2)

BLACK-AND-WHITE OWL *Strix nigrolineata* (1, 2)

BLACK-BANDED OWL *Strix huhula* (2)

RUFOUS-BANDED OWL *Strix albitarsus* (2)

AFRICAN WOOD-OWL *Strix woodfordii* (5)

MANED OWL *Jubula lettii* (5)

CRESTED OWL *Lophostrix cristata* (1, 2)

SPECTACLED OWL *Pulsatrix perspicillata* (1, 2)

TAWNY-BROWED OWL *Pulsatrix koeniswaldiana* (2)

BAND-BELLIED OWL *Pulsatrix melanota* (2)

NORTHERN HAWK OWL *Surnia ulula* (1, 2, 3, 4)

EURASIAN PYGMY-OWL *Glaucidium passerinum* (3, 4)

COLLARED OWLET *Glaucidium brodiei* (3, 4)

PEARL-SPOTTED OWLET *Glaucidium perlatum* (5)

NORTHERN PYGMY-OWL *Glaucidium californicum* (1)

MOUNTAIN PYGMY-OWL *Glaucidium gnoma* (1)

GUATEMALAN PYGMY-OWL *Glaucidium cobanense* (2)

CAPE PYGMY-OWL *Glaucidium hoskinsii* (1)

ANDEAN PYGMY-OWL *Glaucidium jardinii* (2)

YUNGAS PYGMY-OWL *Glaucidium bolivianum* (2)

COLIMA PYGMY-OWL *Glaucidium palmarum* (1)

TAMAULIPAS PYGMY-OWL *Glaucidium sanchezi* (1)

CENTRAL AMERICAN PYGMY-OWL *Glaucidium griseiceps* (1, 2)

SUBTROPICAL PYGMY-OWL *Glaucidium parkeri* (2)

HARDY'S PYGMY-OWL or AMAZONIAN PYGMY-OWL *Glaucidium hardyi* (2)

BRAZILIAN PYGMY-OWL *Glaucidium minutissimum* (2)

FERRUGINOUS PYGMY-OWL *Glaucidium brasilianum* (1, 2)

TUCUMAN PYGMY-OWL *Glaucidium tucumanum* (2)

PERUVIAN PYGMY-OWL or PACIFIC PYGMY-OWL *Glaucidium peruanum* (2)

AUSTRAL PYGMY-OWL *Glaucidium nanum* (2)

CUBAN PYGMY-OWL *Glaucidium siju* (2)

RED-CHESTED OWLET *Glaucidium tephronotum* (5)

SJOSTEDT'S OWLET *Glaucidium sjostedti* (5)

ASIAN BARRED OWLET *Glaucidium cuculoides* (3, 4)

JAVAN OWLET *Glaucidium castanopterum* (4)

JUNGLE OWLET *Glaucidium radiatum* (4)

CHESTNUT-BACKED OWLET *Glaucidium castanonotum* (4) [NT]

AFRICAN BARRED OWLET *Glaucidium capense* (5)

CHESTNUT OWLET *Glaucidium castaneum* (5)

NGAMI OWLET *Glaucidium ngamiense* (5)

SCHEFFLER'S OWLET *Glaucidium scheffleri* (5)

ALBERTINE OWLET *Glaucidium albertinum* (5) [VU]

LONG-WHISKERED OWLET *Xenoglaux loweryi* (2) [NT]

ELF OWL *Micrathene whitneyi* (1)

LITTLE OWL *Athene noctua* (3, 4, 5)

SPOTTED OWLET *Athene brama* (4)

FOREST OWLET *Athene blewitti* (4) [CR]

BURROWING OWL *Speotyto cunicularia* (1, 2)

BOREAL OWL *Aegolius funereus* (1, 3, 4)

SAW-WHET OWL or NORTHERN SAW-WHET OWL *Aegolius acadicus* (1)

UNSPOTTED SAW-WHET OWL *Aegolius ridgwayi* (1, 2) [NT]

BUFF-FRONTED OWL *Aegolius harrisii* (2) [NT]

RUFOUS OWL *Ninox rufa* (6)

POWERFUL OWL *Ninox strenua* (6) [VU]

BARKING OWL *Ninox connivens* (4, 6)

SUMBA BOOBOOK *Ninox rudolfi* (4) [VU]

SOUTHERN BOOBOOK *Ninox boobook* (6)

MOREPORK *Ninox novaeseelandiae* (6)

BROWN BOOBOOK or BROWN HAWK OWL *Ninox scutulata* (4, 6)

ANDAMAN BOOBOOK or ANDAMAN HAWK OWL *Ninox affinis* (4) [NT]

WHITE-BROWED BOOBOOK *Ninox superciliaris* (5)

PHILIPPINE BOOBOOK or PHILIPPINE HAWK OWL *Ninox philippensis* (4)

OCHER-BELLIED BOOBOOK or OCHER-BELLIED HAWK OWL *Ninox ochracea* (4)

MOLUCCAN BOOBOOK or MOLUCCAN HAWK OWL *Ninox squamipila* (4)

CHRISTMAS BOOBOOK *Ninox natalis* (4)

JUNGLE BOOBOOK *Ninox theomacha* (6)

MANUS BOOBOOK *Ninox meeki* (6)

SPECKLED BOOBOOK or SPECKLED HAWK OWL
Ninox punctulata (4)

BISMARCK BOOBOOK *Ninox variegata* (6)

RUSSET BOOBOOK *Ninox odiosa* (6)

SOLOMON ISLANDS BOOBOOK *Ninox jacquinoti*
(4, 6)

PAPUAN BOOBOOK *Uroglaux dimorpha* (6)
[DD]

LAUGHING OWL *Sceloglaux albifacies* (6)

JAMAICAN OWL *Pseudoscops grammicus* (2)

STYGIAN OWL *Asio stygius* (1, 2)

LONG-EARED OWL *Asio otus* (1, 3, 4, 5)

ABYSSINIAN OWL *Asio abyssinicus* (5)

MADAGASCAR OWL *Asio madagascariensis* (5)

STRIPED OWL *Asio clamator* (1, 2)

SHORT-EARED OWL *Asio flammeus* (1, 2, 3, 4)

MARSH OWL *Asio capensis* (5)

FEARFUL OWL *Nesasio solomonensis* (4) [VU]

Order STRIGIFORMES
Family AEGOTHELIDAE

LONG-WHISKERED OWLET-NIGHTJAR or
MOLUCCAN OWLET NIGHTJAR *Aegotheles crinifrons* (4)

FELINE OWLET-NIGHTJAR *Aegotheles insignis* (6)

AUSTRALIAN OWLET-NIGHTJAR *Aegotheles cristatus* (6)

NEW CALEDONIAN OWLET-NIGHTJAR
Aegotheles savesi (6) [EN]

BARRED OWLET-NIGHTJAR *Aegotheles bennettii* (6)

WALLACE'S OWLET-NIGHTJAR *Aegotheles wallacii* (6)

ARCHBOLD'S OWLET-NIGHTJAR *Aegotheles archboldi* (6)

MOUNTAIN OWLET-NIGHTJAR *Aegotheles albertisi* (6)

Suborder CAPRIMULGI
Infraorder PODARGIDES
Family PODARGIDAE

TAWNY FROGMOUTH *Podargus strigoides* (6)

PAPUAN FROGMOUTH *Podargus papuensis* (6)

MARBLED FROGMOUTH *Podargus ocellatus* (6)

Family BATRACHOSTOMIDAE

LARGE FROGMOUTH *Batrachostomus auritus* (4) [DD]

DULIT FROGMOUTH *Batrachostomus harterti* (4) [DD]

PHILIPPINE FROGMOUTH *Batrachostomus septimus* (4)

GOULD'S FROGMOUTH *Batrachostomus stellatus* (4)

SRI LANKA FROGMOUTH or CEYLON
FROGMOUTH *Batrachostomus moniliger* (4)
[NT]

HODGSON'S FROGMOUTH *Batrachostomus hodgsoni* (4)

SHORT-TAILED FROGMOUTH *Batrachostomus poliolophus* (4) [DD]

BORNEAN FROGMOUTH *Batrachostomus mixtus* (4) [DD]

BLYTH'S FROGMOUTH *Batrachostomus affinis* (4)

JAVAN FROGMOUTH *Batrachostomus javensis* (4) [NT]

SUNDA FROGMOUTH *Batrachostomus cornutus* (4)

Infraorder CAPRIMULGIDES
Family STEATORNITHIDAE

OILBIRD *Steatornis caripensis* (4)

Family NYCTIBIIDAE

GREAT POTOO *Nyctibius grandis* (1, 2)

LONG-TAILED POTOO *Nyctibius aethereus* (2)

NORTHERN POTOO *Nyctibius jamaicensis*
(1, 2)

COMMON POTOO *Nyctibius griseus* (2)

ANDEAN POTOO *Nyctibius maculosus* (2)

WHITE-WINGED POTOO *Nyctibius leucopterus* (2)

RUFOUS POTOO *Nyctibius bracteatus* (2)

Family EUROSTOPODIDAE

SPOTTED EARED-NIGHTJAR or SPOTTED NIGHTJAR *Eurostopodus argus* (6)

WHITE-THROATED EARED-NIGHTJAR or WHITE-THROATED NIGHTJAR *Eurostopodus mystacalis* (4, 6)

SATANIC EARED-NIGHTJAR or HEINRICH'S NIGHTJAR *Eurostopodus diabolicus* (4) [VU]

PAPUAN EARED-NIGHTJAR *Eurostopodus papuensis* (6)

MOUNTAIN EARED-NIGHTJAR *Eurostopodus archboldi* (6)

MALAYSIAN EARED-NIGHTJAR *Eurostopodus temminckii* (4)

GREAT EARED-NIGHTJAR *Eurostopodus macrotis* (4)

Family CAPRIMULGIDAE
Subfamily CHORDEILINAE

SHORT-TAILED NIGHTHAWK *Lurocalis semitorquatus* (1, 2)

RUFOUS-BELLIED NIGHTHAWK *Lurocalis rufiventris* (2)

LEAST NIGHTHAWK *Chordeiles pusillus* (2)

CAATINGA NIGHTHAWK *Chordeiles vielliardi* (2)

SAND-COLORED NIGHTHAWK *Chordeiles rupestris* (2)

LESSER NIGHTHAWK *Chordeiles acutipennis* (1, 2)

COMMON NIGHTHAWK *Chordeiles minor* (1, 2)

ANTILLEAN NIGHTHAWK *Chordeiles gundlachii* (1, 2)

BAND-TAILED NIGHTHAWK *Nyctiprogne leucopyga* (2)

NACUNDA NIGHTHAWK *Podager nacunda* (2)

Subfamily CAPRIMULGINAE

PAURAQUE *Nyctidromus albicollis* (1, 2)

COMMON POORWILL *Phalaenoptilus nuttallii* (1)

JAMAICAN POORWILL or JAMAICAN PAURAQUE *Siphonorhis americanus* (2) [EX]

LEAST POORWILL *Siphonorhis brewsteri* (2) [NT]

EARED POORWILL *Nyctiphrynus mcleodii* (1)

YUCATÁN POORWILL *Nyctiphrynus yucatanicus* (1, 2)

OCELLATED POORWILL *Nyctiphrynus ocellatus* (2)

CHOCO POORWILL *Nyctiphrynus rosenbergi* (2) [NT]

CHUCK-WILL'S-WIDOW *Caprimulgus carolinensis* (1, 2)

RUFOUS NIGHTJAR *Caprimulgus rufus* (2)

GREATER ANTILLEAN NIGHTJAR *Caprimulgus cubanensis* (2)

TAWNY-COLLARED NIGHTJAR *Caprimulgus salvini* (1, 2)

YUCATÁN NIGHTJAR *Caprimulgus badius* (1, 2)

SILKY-TAILED NIGHTJAR *Caprimulgus sericocaudatus* (2)

BUFF-COLLARED NIGHTJAR *Caprimulgus ridgwayi* (1, 2)

WHIP-POOR-WILL *Caprimulgus vociferus* (1, 2)

PUERTO RICAN NIGHTJAR *Caprimulgus noctitherus* (2) [CR]

DUSKY NIGHTJAR *Caprimulgus saturatus* (2)

BAND-WINGED NIGHTJAR *Caprimulgus longirostris* (2)

WHITE-TAILED NIGHTJAR *Caprimulgus cayennensis* (2)

WHITE-WINGED NIGHTJAR *Caprimulgus candicans* (2) [CR]

SPOT-TAILED NIGHTJAR *Caprimulgus maculicaudus* (1, 2)

LITTLE NIGHTJAR *Caprimulgus parvulus* (2)

SCRUB NIGHTJAR *Caprimulgus anthonyi* (2)

CAYENNE NIGHTJAR *Caprimulgus maculosus* (2) [DD]

BLACKISH NIGHTJAR *Caprimulgus nigrescens* (2)

RORAIMAN NIGHTJAR *Caprimulgus whitelyi* (2) [NT]

PYGMY NIGHTJAR *Caprimulgus hirundinaceus* (2) [NT]

BROWN NIGHTJAR *Caprimulgus binotatus* (5)

RED-NECKED NIGHTJAR *Caprimulgus ruficollis* (3, 5)

GRAY NIGHTJAR *Caprimulgus indicus* (3, 4)

EURASIAN NIGHTJAR *Caprimulgus europaeus* (3, 4, 5)

SOMBER NIGHTJAR *Caprimulgus fraenatus* (5)

RUFOUS-CHEEKED NIGHTJAR *Caprimulgus rufigena* (5)

EGYPTIAN NIGHTJAR *Caprimulgus aegyptius* (4, 5)

SYKES'S NIGHTJAR *Caprimulgus mahrattensis* (4)

VAURIE'S NIGHTJAR *Caprimulgus centralasicus* (4) [VU]

NUBIAN NIGHTJAR *Caprimulgus nubicus* (5)

GOLDEN NIGHTJAR *Caprimulgus eximius* (5)

MADAGASCAR NIGHTJAR *Caprimulgus madagascariensis* (5)

LARGE-TAILED NIGHTJAR *Caprimulgus macrurus* (4, 6)

JERDON'S NIGHTJAR *Caprimulgus atripennis* (4)

PHILIPPINE NIGHTJAR *Caprimulgus manillensis* (4)

SULAWESI NIGHTJAR *Caprimulgus celebensis* (4)

DONALDSON-SMITH'S NIGHTJAR *Caprimulgus donaldsoni* (5)

FIERY-NECKED NIGHTJAR *Caprimulgus pectoralis* (5)

ITOMBWE NIGHTJAR or PRIGOGINE'S NIGHTJAR *Caprimulgus prigoginei* (5) [VU]

MONTANE NIGHTJAR *Caprimulgus poliocephalus* (5)

INDIAN NIGHTJAR *Caprimulgus asiaticus* (4)

SWAMP NIGHTJAR *Caprimulgus natalensis* (5)

PLAIN NIGHTJAR *Caprimulgus inornatus* (4, 5)

STAR-SPOTTED NIGHTJAR *Caprimulgus stellatus* (5)

SAVANNA NIGHTJAR *Caprimulgus affinis* (4)

FRECKLED NIGHTJAR *Caprimulgus tristigma* (5)

BONAPARTE'S NIGHTJAR *Caprimulgus concretus* (4) [NT]

SALVADORI'S NIGHTJAR *Caprimulgus pulchellus* (4) [DD]

COLLARED NIGHTJAR *Caprimulgus enarratus* (5)

BATES'S NIGHTJAR *Caprimulgus batesi* (5)

LONG-TAILED NIGHTJAR *Caprimulgus climacurus* (5)

SLENDER-TAILED NIGHTJAR *Caprimulgus clarus* (5)

SQUARE-TAILED NIGHTJAR *Caprimulgus fossii* (5)

NECHISAR NIGHTJAR *Caprimulgus solala* (5)

STANDARD-WINGED NIGHTJAR *Macrodipteryx longipennis* (5)

PENNANT-WINGED NIGHTJAR *Macrodipteryx vexillarius* (5)

LADDER-TAILED NIGHTJAR *Hydropsalis climacocerca* (2)

SCISSOR-TAILED NIGHTJAR *Hydropsalis brasiliana* (2)

SWALLOW-TAILED NIGHTJAR *Uropsalis segmentata* (2)

LYRE-TAILED NIGHTJAR *Uropsalis lyra* (2)

LONG-TRAINED NIGHTJAR *Macropsalis creagra* (2) [NT]

SICKLE-WINGED NIGHTJAR *Eleothreptus anomalus* (2) [NT]

Order COLUMBIFORMES
Family RAPHIDAE

DODO *Raphus cucullatus* (5) [EX]

REUNION SOLITAIRE *Raphus solitarius* (5) [EX]

RODRIGUEZ SOLITAIRE *Pezophaps solitaria* (5) [EX]

Family COLUMBIDAE

ROCK DOVE or COMMON PIGEON *Columba livia* (1, 2, 3, 4, 5, 6)

HILL PIGEON *Columba rupestris* (3, 4)

SNOW PIGEON *Columba leuconota* (3, 4)

SPECKLED PIGEON *Columba guinea* (5)

WHITE-COLLARED PIGEON *Columba albitorques* (5)

STOCK PIGEON or STOCK DOVE *Columba oenas* (3, 4)

SOMALI PIGEON *Columba oliviae* (5) [VU]

PALE-BACKED PIGEON *Columba eversmanni* (4) [VU]

COMMON WOOD-PIGEON *Columba palumbus* (3, 4)

TROCAZ PIGEON *Columba trocaz* (5) [CD]

BOLLE'S PIGEON or DARK-TAILED LAUREL PIGEON *Columba bollii* (5) [VU]

LAUREL PIGEON or WHITE-TAILED LAUREL PIGEON *Columba junoniae* (5) [VU]

AFEP PIGEON *Columba unicincta* (5)

CAMEROON OLIVE-PIGEON *Columba sjostedti* (5)

SÃO TOMÉ OLIVE-PIGEON or MAROON PIGEON *Columba thomensis* (5) [VU]

AFRICAN OLIVE-PIGEON *Columba arquatrix* (5)

COMORO OLIVE-PIGEON *Columba pollenii* (5) [NT]

SPECKLED WOOD-PIGEON *Columba hodgsonii* (4)

WHITE-NAPED PIGEON *Columba albinucha* (5) [NT]

ASHY WOOD-PIGEON *Columba pulchricollis* (4)

NILGIRI WOOD-PIGEON *Columba elphinstonii* (4) [NT]

SRI LANKA WOOD-PIGEON or CEYLON WOOD-PIGEON *Columba torringtoni* (4) [VU]

PALE-CAPPED PIGEON *Columba punicea* (4) [VU]

SILVERY WOOD-PIGEON *Columba argentina* (4) [VU]

ANDAMAN WOOD-PIGEON *Columba palumboides* (4) [NT]

JAPANESE WOOD-PIGEON *Columba janthina* (4) [NT]

METALLIC PIGEON *Columba vitiensis* (4, 6)

WHITE-HEADED PIGEON *Columba leucomela* (6)

BONIN PIGEON *Columba versicolor* (6) [EX]

RYUKYU PIGEON *Columba jouyi* (4) [EX]

YELLOW-LEGGED PIGEON *Columba pallidiceps* (4, 6) [CR]

WHITE-CROWNED PIGEON *Columba leucocephala* (1, 2)

SCALED PIGEON *Columba speciosa* (1, 2)

SCALY-NAPED PIGEON *Columba squamosa* (2)

BARE-EYED PIGEON *Columba corensis* (2)

PICAZURO PIGEON *Columba picazuro* (2)

SPOT-WINGED PIGEON *Columba maculosa* (2)

BAND-TAILED PIGEON *Columba fasciata* (1, 2)

CHILEAN PIGEON *Columba araucana* (2) [NT]

RING-TAILED PIGEON *Columba caribaea* (2) [CR]

PALE-VENTED PIGEON *Columba cayennensis* (1, 2)

RED-BILLED PIGEON *Columba flavirostris* (1, 2)

PERUVIAN PIGEON *Columba oenops* (2) [VU]

PLAIN PIGEON *Columba inornata* (2) [EN]

PLUMBEOUS PIGEON *Columba plumbea* (2)

RUDDY PIGEON *Columba subvinacea* (2)

SHORT-BILLED PIGEON *Columba nigrirostris* (1, 2)

DUSKY PIGEON *Columba goodsoni* (2)

WESTERN BRONZE-NAPED PIGEON *Columba iriditorques* (5)

SÃO TOMÉ BRONZE-NAPED PIGEON *Columba malherbii* (5)

EASTERN BRONZE-NAPED PIGEON *Columba delegorguei* (5)

PINK PIGEON *Columba mayeri* (5) [CR]

LEMON DOVE or CINNAMON DOVE *Aplopelia larvata* (5)

MADAGASCAR TURTLE-DOVE *Streptopelia picturata* (5)

EUROPEAN TURTLE-DOVE *Streptopelia turtur* (1, 3, 4, 5)

ADAMAWA TURTLE-DOVE *Streptopelia hypopyrrha* (5)

DUSKY TURTLE-DOVE *Streptopelia lugens* (5)

ORIENTAL TURTLE-DOVE *Streptopelia orientalis* (3, 4)

LAUGHING DOVE *Streptopelia senegalensis* (4, 5)

SPOTTED DOVE *Streptopelia chinensis* (4, 6)

MOURNING COLLARED-DOVE *Streptopelia decipiens* (5)

VINACEOUS DOVE *Streptopelia vinacea* (5)

RING-NECKED DOVE *Streptopelia capicola* (5)

RED COLLARED-DOVE *Streptopelia tranquebarica* (4)

RED-EYED DOVE *Streptopelia semitorquata* (5)

EURASIAN COLLARED-DOVE *Streptopelia decaocto* (1, 3, 4, 5)

AFRICAN COLLARED-DOVE *Streptopelia roseogrisea* (4, 5)

WHITE-WINGED COLLARED-DOVE *Streptopelia reichenowi* (5) [NT]

ISLAND COLLARED-DOVE *Streptopelia bitorquata* (4)

BARRED CUCKOO-DOVE *Macropygia unchall* (4)

ANDAMAN CUCKOO-DOVE *Macropygia rufipennis* (4) [NT]

PHILIPPINE CUCKOO-DOVE *Macropygia tenuirostris* (4)

RUDDY CUCKOO-DOVE *Macropygia emiliana* (4)

SLENDER-BILLED CUCKOO-DOVE *Macropygia amboinensis* (6)

DUSKY CUCKOO-DOVE *Macropygia magna* (4)

BROWN CUCKOO-DOVE *Macropygia phasianella* (6)

LITTLE CUCKOO-DOVE *Macropygia ruficeps* (4)

BLACK-BILLED CUCKOO-DOVE *Macropygia nigrirostris* (6)

MACKINLAY'S CUCKOO-DOVE *Macropygia mackinlayi* (6)

GREAT CUCKOO-DOVE *Reinwardtoena reinwardtii* (4, 6)

PIED CUCKOO-DOVE *Reinwardtoena browni* (6)

CRESTED CUCKOO-DOVE *Reinwardtoena crassirostris* (4)

WHITE-FACED CUCKOO-DOVE *Turacoena manadensis* (4)

BLACK CUCKOO-DOVE *Turacoena modesta. Monsoon Forest* (4)

BLACK-BILLED WOOD-DOVE *Turtur abyssinicus* (5)

EMERALD-SPOTTED WOOD-DOVE *Turtur chalcospilos* (5)

BLUE-SPOTTED WOOD-DOVE *Turtur afer* (5)

TAMBOURINE DOVE *Turtur tympanistria* (5)

BLUE-HEADED WOOD-DOVE *Turtur brehmeri* (5)

NAMAQUA DOVE *Oena capensis* (5)

EMERALD DOVE *Chalcophaps indica* (4, 6)

STEPHAN'S DOVE *Chalcophaps stephani* (4, 6)

NEW GUINEA BRONZEWING *Henicophaps albifrons* (6) [NT]

NEW BRITAIN BRONZEWING *Henicophaps foersteri* (6) [NT]

COMMON BRONZEWING *Phaps chalcoptera* (6)

BRUSH BRONZEWING *Phaps elegans* (6)

FLOCK BRONZEWING *Phaps histrionica* (6) [NT]

CRESTED PIGEON *Geophaps lophotes* (6)

SPINIFEX PIGEON *Geophaps plumifera* (6)

PARTRIDGE PIGEON *Geophaps smithii* (6) [NT]

SQUATTER PIGEON *Geophaps scripta* (6)

WHITE-QUILLED ROCK-PIGEON *Petrophassa albipennis* (6)

CHESTNUT-QUILLED ROCK-PIGEON *Petrophassa rufipennis* (6)

DIAMOND DOVE *Geopelia cuneata* (6)

ZEBRA DOVE *Geopelia striata* (4, 5)

BARRED DOVE *Geopelia maugeus* (4)

PEACEFUL DOVE *Geopelia placida* (6)

BAR-SHOULDERED DOVE *Geopelia humeralis* (6)

WONGA PIGEON *Leucosarcia melanoleuca* (6)

PASSENGER PIGEON *Ectopistes migratorius* (1)

MOURNING DOVE *Zenaida macroura* (1, 2)

SOCORRO DOVE *Zenaida graysoni* (2) [EW]

EARED DOVE *Zenaida auriculata* (2)

ZENAIDA DOVE *Zenaida aurita* (1)

WHITE-WINGED DOVE *Zenaida asiatica* (1, 2)

PACIFIC DOVE *Zenaida meloda* (2)

GALAPAGOS DOVE *Zenaida galapagoensis* (5)

INCA DOVE *Columbina inca* (1, 2)

SCALED DOVE *Columbina squammata* (2)

COMMON GROUND-DOVE *Columbina passerina* (1, 2)

PLAIN-BREASTED GROUND-DOVE *Columbina minuta* (1, 2)

RUDDY GROUND-DOVE *Columbina talpacoti* (1, 2)

ECUADORIAN GROUND-DOVE *Columbina buckleyi* (2)

PICUI GROUND-DOVE *Columbina picui* (2)

CROAKING GROUND-DOVE *Columbina cruziana* (2)

BLUE-EYED GROUND-DOVE *Columbina cyanopis* (2) [CR]

BLUE GROUND-DOVE *Claravis pretiosa* (1, 2)

MAROON-CHESTED GROUND-DOVE *Claravis mondetoura* (1, 2)

PURPLE-WINGED GROUND-DOVE *Claravis godefrida* (2) [CR]

BARE-FACED GROUND-DOVE *Metriopelia ceciliae* (2)

BARE-EYED GROUND-DOVE or MORENO'S BARE-FACED GROUND-DOVE *Metriopelia morenoi* (2)

BLACK-WINGED GROUND-DOVE *Metriopelia melanoptera* (2)

GOLDEN-SPOTTED GROUND-DOVE *Metriopelia aymara* (2)

LONG-TAILED GROUND-DOVE *Uropelia campestris* (2)

WHITE-TIPPED DOVE *Leptotila verreauxi* (1, 2)

WHITE-FACED DOVE *Leptotila megalura* (2)

GRAY-HEADED DOVE *Leptotila plumbeiceps* (1, 2)

BROWN-BACKED DOVE *Leptotila battyi* (2) [NT]

GRENADA DOVE *Leptotila wellsi* (2) [CR]

GRAY-FRONTED DOVE *Leptotila rufaxilla* (2)

CARIBBEAN DOVE *Leptotila jamaicensis* (2)

PALLID DOVE *Leptotila pallida* (2)

GRAY-CHESTED DOVE *Leptotila cassini* (1, 2)

OCHER-BELLIED DOVE *Leptotila ochraceiventris* (2) [VU]

TOLIMA DOVE *Leptotila conoveri* (2) [EN]

PURPLISH-BACKED QUAIL-DOVE *Geotrygon lawrencii* (2)

VERACRUZ QUAIL-DOVE *Geotrygon carrikeri* (1) [EN]

BUFF-FRONTED QUAIL-DOVE *Geotrygon costaricensis* (2)

SAPPHIRE QUAIL-DOVE *Geotrygon saphirina* (2)

GRAY-HEADED QUAIL-DOVE *Geotrygon caniceps* (2) [NT]

CRESTED QUAIL-DOVE *Geotrygon versicolor* (2) [NT]

OLIVE-BACKED QUAIL-DOVE *Geotrygon veraguensis* (2)

WHITE-FACED QUAIL-DOVE *Geotrygon albifacies* (1, 2)

RUFOUS-BREASTED QUAIL-DOVE *Geotrygon chiriquensis* (2)

RUSSET-CROWNED QUAIL-DOVE *Geotrygon goldmani* (2) [NT]

LINED QUAIL-DOVE *Geotrygon linearis* (2)

WHITE-THROATED QUAIL-DOVE *Geotrygon frenata* (2)

KEY WEST QUAIL-DOVE *Geotrygon chrysia* (1, 2)

BRIDLED QUAIL-DOVE *Geotrygon mystacea* (2) [NT]

VIOLACEOUS QUAIL-DOVE *Geotrygon violacea* (2)

RUDDY QUAIL-DOVE *Geotrygon montana* (1, 2)

BLUE-HEADED QUAIL-DOVE *Starnoenas cyanocephala* (2) [EN]

NICOBAR PIGEON *Caloenas nicobarica* (4) [NT]

LUZON BLEEDING-HEART *Gallicolumba luzonica* (4) [NT]

MINDORO BLEEDING-HEART *allicolumba platenae* (4) [CR]

NEGROS BLEEDING-HEART *Gallicolumba keayi* (4) [CR]

MINDANAO BLEEDING-HEART *Gallicolumba criniger* (4) [VU]

SULU BLEEDING-HEART *Gallicolumba menagei* (4) [EN]

CINNAMON GROUND-DOVE *Gallicolumba rufigula* (6)

SULAWESI GROUND-DOVE *Gallicolumba tristigmata* (4)

WHITE-BIBBED GROUND-DOVE *Gallicolumba jobiensis* (6)

CAROLINE ISLANDS GROUND-DOVE *Gallicolumba kubaryi* (6) [EN]

POLYNESIAN GROUND-DOVE *Gallicolumba erythroptera* (6) [CR]

WHITE-THROATED GROUND-DOVE *Gallicolumba xanthonura* (6) [NT]

FRIENDLY GROUND-DOVE *Gallicolumba stairi* (6) [NT]

SANTA CRUZ GROUND-DOVE *Gallicolumba sanctaecrucis* (4) [VU]

TANNA GROUND-DOVE *Gallicolumba ferruginea* (4) [EX]

THICK-BILLED GROUND-DOVE *Gallicolumba salamonis* (4) [CR]

MARQUESAN GROUND-DOVE *Gallicolumba rubescens* (4) [EN]

BRONZE GROUND-DOVE *Gallicolumba beccarii* (6)

PALAU GROUND-DOVE *Gallicolumba canifrons* (6) [NT]

WETAR GROUND-DOVE *Gallicolumba hoedtii* (6) [VU]

THICK-BILLED GROUND-PIGEON *Trugon terrestris* (6) [NT]

CHOISEUL PIGEON *Microgoura meeki* (4) [EX]

PHEASANT PIGEON *Otidiphaps nobilis* (6)

WHITE-EARED BROWN-DOVE *Phapitreron leucotis* (4)

AMETHYST BROWN-DOVE *Phapitreron amethystina* (4)

DARK-EARED BROWN-DOVE *Phapitreron cinereiceps* (4) [VU]

CINNAMON-HEADED GREEN-PIGEON *Treron fulvicollis* (4) [NT]

LITTLE GREEN-PIGEON *Treron olax* (4)

PINK-NECKED GREEN-PIGEON *Treron vernans* (4)

ORANGE-BREASTED GREEN-PIGEON *Treron bicincta* (4)

POMPADOUR GREEN-PIGEON *Treron pompadora* (4)

THICK-BILLED GREEN-PIGEON *Treron curvirostra* (4)

GRAY-CHEEKED GREEN-PIGEON *Treron griseicauda* (4)

FLORES GREEN-PIGEON *Treron floris* (4) [NT]

SUMBA GREEN-PIGEON *Treron teysmannii* (4) [NT]

TIMOR GREEN-PIGEON *Treron psittacea* (4) [VU]

LARGE GREEN-PIGEON *Treron capellei* (4) [NT]

YELLOW-FOOTED GREEN-PIGEON *Treron phoenicoptera* (4)

BRUCE'S GREEN-PIGEON *Treron waalia* (5)

AFRICAN GREEN-PIGEON *Treron calva* (5)

SÃO TOMÉ GREEN-PIGEON *Treron sanctithomae* (5)

PEMBA GREEN-PIGEON *Treron pembaensis* (5) [NT]

MADAGASCAR GREEN-PIGEON *Treron australis* (5)

PIN-TAILED GREEN-PIGEON *Treron apicauda* (4)

SUMATRAN GREEN-PIGEON *Treron oxyura* (4) [NT]

YELLOW-VENTED GREEN-PIGEON *Treron seimundi* (4) [NT]

WEDGE-TAILED GREEN-PIGEON *Treron sphenura* (4)

WHITE-BELLIED GREEN-PIGEON *Treron sieboldii* (4) [NT]

WHISTLING GREEN-PIGEON *Treron formosae* (4) [NT]

PINK-HEADED FRUIT-DOVE *Ptilinopus porphyreus* (4)

BLACK-BACKED FRUIT-DOVE *Ptilinopus cinctus* (4) [NT]

RED-NAPED FRUIT-DOVE *Ptilinopus dohertyi* (4) [VU]

BLACK-BANDED FRUIT-DOVE *Ptilinopus alligator* (6)

FLAME-BREASTED FRUIT-DOVE *Ptilinopus marchei* (4) [VU]

CREAM-BELLIED FRUIT-DOVE *Ptilinopus merrilli* (4) [NT]

YELLOW-BREASTED FRUIT-DOVE *Ptilinopus occipitalis* (4)

RED-EARED FRUIT-DOVE *Ptilinopus fischeri* (4)

JAMBU FRUIT-DOVE *Ptilinopus jambu* (4)

BLACK-CHINNED FRUIT-DOVE *Ptilinopus leclancheri* (4)

MAROON-CHINNED FRUIT-DOVE *Ptilinopus subgularis* (4)

SCARLET-BREASTED FRUIT-DOVE *Ptilinopus bernsteinii* (4)

WOMPOO FRUIT-DOVE *Ptilinopus magnificus* (6)

PINK-SPOTTED FRUIT-DOVE *Ptilinopus perlatus* (6)

ORNATE FRUIT-DOVE *Ptilinopus ornatus* (6)

TANNA FRUIT-DOVE *Ptilinopus tannensis* (4) [NT]

ORANGE-FRONTED FRUIT-DOVE *Ptilinopus aurantiifrons* (6)

WALLACE'S FRUIT-DOVE *Ptilinopus wallacii* (4, 6)

SUPERB FRUIT-DOVE *Ptilinopus superbus*

MANY-COLORED FRUIT-DOVE *Ptilinopus perousii* (4)

BLUE-CAPPED FRUIT-DOVE *Ptilinopus monacha* (4) [NT]

CORONETED FRUIT-DOVE *Ptilinopus coronulatus* (6)

BEAUTIFUL FRUIT-DOVE *Ptilinopus pulchellus* (6)

ROSE-CROWNED FRUIT-DOVE *Ptilinopus regina* (4, 6)

MARIANA FRUIT-DOVE *Ptilinopus roseicapilla* (4) [NT]

RED-BELLIED FRUIT-DOVE *Ptilinopus grayii* (4, 6)

SILVER-CAPPED FRUIT-DOVE *Ptilinopus richardsii* (4)

CRIMSON-CROWNED FRUIT-DOVE *Ptilinopus porphyraceus* (6)

PALAU FRUIT-DOVE *Ptilinopus pelewensis* (6)

COOK ISLANDS FRUIT-DOVE *Ptilinopus rarotongensis* (6) [NT]

RAPA FRUIT-DOVE *Ptilinopus huttoni* (6) [VU]

GRAY-GREEN FRUIT-DOVE *Ptilinopus purpuratus* (6)

ATOLL FRUIT-DOVE *Ptilinopus coralensis* (6) [NT]

MAKATEA FRUIT-DOVE *Ptilinopus chalcurus* (6) [VU]

HENDERSON ISLAND FRUIT-DOVE *Ptilinopus insularis* (6) [VU]

RED-MUSTACHED FRUIT-DOVE *Ptilinopus mercierii* (6) [EX]

WHITE-CAPPED FRUIT-DOVE *Ptilinopus dupetithouarsii* (6)

WHITE-BIBBED FRUIT-DOVE *Ptilinopus rivoli* (4, 6)

YELLOW-BIBBED FRUIT-DOVE *Ptilinopus solomonensis* (4, 6)

CLARET-BREASTED FRUIT-DOVE *Ptilinopus viridis* (4, 6)

WHITE-HEADED FRUIT-DOVE *Ptilinopus eugeniae* (4) [NT]

GRAY-HEADED FRUIT-DOVE *Ptilinopus hyogastra* (4)

CARUNCULATED FRUIT-DOVE *Ptilinopus granulifrons* (4) [VU]

ORANGE-BELLIED FRUIT-DOVE *Ptilinopus iozonus* (6)

KNOB-BILLED FRUIT-DOVE *Ptilinopus insolitus* (6)

DWARF FRUIT-DOVE *Ptilinopus naina* (6)

BLACK-NAPED FRUIT-DOVE *Ptilinopus melanospila* (4)

NEGROS FRUIT-DOVE *Ptilinopus arcanus* (4) [CR]

ORANGE DOVE *Ptilinopus victor* (6)

GOLDEN DOVE *Ptilinopus luteovirens* (6)

WHISTLING DOVE *Ptilinopus layardi* (6) [NT]

CLOVEN-FEATHERED DOVE *Drepanoptila holosericea* (6) [VU]

MADAGASCAR BLUE-PIGEON *Alectroenas madagascariensis* (5)

COMORO BLUE-PIGEON *Alectroenas sganzini* (5)

MAURITIUS BLUE-PIGEON *Alectroenas nitidissima* (5) [EX]

SEYCHELLES BLUE-PIGEON *Alectroenas pulcherrima* (5)

PINK-BELLIED IMPERIAL-PIGEON *Ducula poliocephala* (4)

WHITE-BELLIED IMPERIAL-PIGEON *Ducula forsteni* (4)

MINDORO IMPERIAL-PIGEON *Ducula mindorensis* (4) [EN]

GRAY-HEADED IMPERIAL-PIGEON *Ducula radiata* (4)

SPOTTED IMPERIAL-PIGEON *Ducula carola* (4) [VU]

GREEN IMPERIAL-PIGEON *Ducula aenea* (4)

WHITE-EYED IMPERIAL-PIGEON or WHITE-SPECTACLED IMPERIAL PIGEON *Ducula perspicillata* (4)

ELEGANT IMPERIAL-PIGEON or BLUE-TAILED IMPERIAL PIGEON *Ducula concinna* (4, 6)

PACIFIC IMPERIAL-PIGEON *Ducula pacifica* (4, 6)

MICRONESIAN IMPERIAL-PIGEON *Ducula oceanica* (6)

POLYNESIAN IMPERIAL-PIGEON *Ducula aurorae* (6) [VU]

MARQUESAN IMPERIAL-PIGEON *Ducula galeata* (6) [CR]

RED-KNOBBED IMPERIAL-PIGEON *Ducula rubricera* (4, 6)

SPICE IMPERIAL-PIGEON *Ducula myristicivora* (6)

ISLAND IMPERIAL-PIGEON *Ducula pistrinaria* (6)

CHRISTMAS ISLAND IMPERIAL-PIGEON *Ducula whartoni* (4) [VU]

PINK-HEADED IMPERIAL-PIGEON *Ducula rosacea* (4)

GRAY IMPERIAL-PIGEON *Ducula pickeringii* (4) [VU]

CINNAMON-BELLIED IMPERIAL-PIGEON *Ducula basilica* (4)

PURPLE-TAILED IMPERIAL-PIGEON *Ducula rufigaster* (6)

FINSCH'S IMPERIAL-PIGEON *Ducula finschii* (6) [NT]

SHINING IMPERIAL-PIGEON *Ducula chalconota* (6)

PEALE'S IMPERIAL-PIGEON *Ducula latrans* (6)

CHESTNUT-BELLIED IMPERIAL-PIGEON *Ducula brenchleyi* (4) [EN]

BAKER'S IMPERIAL-PIGEON or VANUATU IMPERIAL-PIGEON *Ducula bakeri* (4) [VU]

NEW CALEDONIAN IMPERIAL-PIGEON *Ducula goliath* (6) [VU]

PINON IMPERIAL-PIGEON *Ducula pinon* (6)

BISMARCK IMPERIAL-PIGEON *Ducula melanochroa* (6) [NT]

COLLARED IMPERIAL-PIGEON *Ducula mullerii* (6)

BANDED IMPERIAL-PIGEON *Ducula zoeae* (6)

MOUNTAIN IMPERIAL-PIGEON *Ducula badia* (4)

DARK-BACKED IMPERIAL-PIGEON *Ducula lacernulata* (4)

TIMOR IMPERIAL-PIGEON *Ducula cineracea* (4) [VU]

PIED IMPERIAL-PIGEON *Ducula bicolor* (4)

SILVER-TIPPED IMPERIAL-PIGEON *Ducula luctuosa* (4)

TORRESIAN IMPERIAL-PIGEON *Ducula spilorrhoa* (6)

KIMBERLEY IMPERIAL-PIGEON *Ducula constans* (6)

YELLOW-TINTED IMPERIAL-PIGEON *Ducula subflavescens* (6)

TOPKNOT PIGEON *Lopholaimus antarcticus* (6)

NEW ZEALAND PIGEON *Hemiphaga novaeseelandiae* (6)

SOMBER PIGEON *Cryptophaps poecilorrhoa* (4) [NT]

PAPUAN MOUNTAIN-PIGEON *Gymnophaps albertisii* (6)

LONG-TAILED MOUNTAIN-PIGEON *Gymnophaps mada* (4) [NT]

PALE MOUNTAIN-PIGEON *Gymnophaps solomonensis* (4)

WESTERN CROWNED-PIGEON *Goura cristata* (6) [VU]

VICTORIA CROWNED-PIGEON *Goura victoria* (6) [VU]

SOUTHERN CROWNED-PIGEON *Goura scheepmakeri* (6) [VU]

TOOTH-BILLED PIGEON *Didunculus strigirostris* (6) [VU]

Order GRUIFORMES
Family EURYPYGIDAE

SUNBITTERN *Eurypyga helias* (1, 2)

Family OTIDIDAE

LITTLE BUSTARD *Tetrax tetrax* (3, 4) [NT]

GREAT BUSTARD *Otis tarda* (3, 4, 5) [VU]

STANLEY BUSTARD *Neotis denhami* (5)

LUDWIG'S BUSTARD *Neotis ludwigii* (5)

NUBIAN BUSTARD *Neotis nuba* (5) [NT]

HEUGLIN'S BUSTARD *Neotis heuglinii* (5)

ARABIAN BUSTARD *Ardeotis arabs* (4, 5)

KORI BUSTARD *Ardeotis kori* (4, 5)

INDIAN BUSTARD or GREAT INDIAN BUSTARD *Ardeotis nigriceps* (4) [EN]

AUSTRALIAN BUSTARD *Ardeotis australis* (6)

HOUBARA BUSTARD *Chlamydotis undulata* (5)

MACQUEEN'S BUSTARD *Chlamydotis macqueenii* (3, 4, 5)

SAVILE'S BUSTARD *Eupodotis savilei* (5)

BUFF-CRESTED BUSTARD *Eupodotis gindiana* (5)

RED-CRESTED BUSTARD *Eupodotis ruficrista* (5)

WHITE-QUILLED BUSTARD or WHITE-WINGED KORHAAN *Eupodotis afraoides* (5)

BLACK BUSTARD or BLACK KORHAAN *Eupodotis afra* (5)

RUEPPELL'S BUSTARD *Eupodotis rueppellii* (5)

KAROO BUSTARD *Eupodotis vigorsii* (5)

LITTLE BROWN BUSTARD *Eupodotis humilis* (5) [NT]

WHITE-BELLIED BUSTARD *Eupodotis senegalensis* (5)

BARROW'S BUSTARD *Eupodotis barrowii* (5)

BLUE BUSTARD *Eupodotis caerulescens* (5) [NT]

BLACK-BELLIED BUSTARD *Eupodotis melanogaster* (5)

HARTLAUB'S BUSTARD *Eupodotis hartlaubii* (5)

BENGAL FLORICAN *Eupodotis bengalensis* (4) [EN]

LESSER FLORICAN *Eupodotis indica* (4) [CR]

Family GRUIDAE
Subfamily BALEARICINAE

BLACK CROWNED-CRANE *Balearica pavonina* (5)

GRAY CROWNED-CRANE *Balearica regulorum* (5)

Subfamily GRUINAE

SIBERIAN CRANE *Grus leucogeranus* (4) [EN]

SARUS CRANE *Grus antigone* (4, 6) [NT]

BROLGA *Grus rubicunda* (6)

WHITE-NAPED CRANE *Grus vipio* (3, 4) [VU]

SANDHILL CRANE *Grus canadensis* (1, 2)

DEMOISELLE CRANE *Grus virgo* (3, 4, 5)

BLUE CRANE *Grus paradisea* (5) [VU]

WATTLED CRANE *Grus carunculatus* (5) [VU]

COMMON CRANE *Grus grus* (3, 4, 5)

HOODED CRANE *Grus monacha* (3, 4) [CD]

WHOOPING CRANE *Grus americana* (1) [EN]

BLACK-NECKED CRANE *Grus nigricollis* (4) [VU]

RED-CROWNED CRANE *Grus japonensis* (3, 4) [VU]

Family ARAMIDAE

LIMPKIN *Aramus guarauna* (1, 2)

Family HELIORNITHIDAE

AFRICAN FINFOOT *Podica senegalensis* (5)

MASKED FINFOOT *Heliopais personata* (4) [VU]

SUNGREBE *Heliornis fulica* (1, 2)

Family PSOPHIIDAE

GRAY-WINGED TRUMPETER *Psophia crepitans* (2)

PALE-WINGED TRUMPETER or WHITE-WINGED TRUMPETER *Psophia leucoptera* (2)

DARK-WINGED TRUMPETER *Psophia viridis* (2)

Family CARIAMIDAE

RED-LEGGED SERIEMA *Cariama cristata* (2)

BLACK-LEGGED SERIEMA *Chunga burmeisteri* (2)

Family RHYNOCHETIDAE

KAGU *Rhynochetos jubatus* (6) [EN]

Family RALLIDAE

NKULENGU RAIL *Himantornis haematopus* (5)

GRAY-THROATED RAIL *Canirallus oculeus* (5)

KIOLOIDES RAIL or MADAGASCAR FOREST-RAIL *Canirallus kioloides* (5)

WHITE-SPOTTED FLUFFTAIL *Sarothrura pulchra* (5)

BUFF-SPOTTED FLUFFTAIL *Sarothrura elegans* (5)

RED-CHESTED FLUFFTAIL *Sarothrura rufa* (5)

CHESTNUT-HEADED FLUFFTAIL *Sarothrura lugens* (5)

STREAKY-BREASTED FLUFFTAIL *Sarothrura boehmi* (5)

STRIPED FLUFFTAIL *Sarothrura affinis* (5)

MADAGASCAR FLUFFTAIL *Sarothrura insularis* (5)

WHITE-WINGED FLUFFTAIL *Sarothrura ayresi* (5) [EN]

SLENDER-BILLED FLUFFTAIL *Sarothrura watersi* (5) [EN]

SWINHOE'S RAIL or SWINHOE'S CRAKE *Coturnicops exquisitus* (3, 4) [VU]

YELLOW RAIL *Coturnicops noveboracensis* (1)

SPECKLED RAIL *Coturnicops notatus* (2) [DD]

OCELLATED CRAKE *Micropygia schomburgkii* (2) [NT]

CHESTNUT FOREST-RAIL *Rallina rubra* (6)

WHITE-STRIPED FOREST-RAIL *Rallina leucospila* (6) [DD]

FORBES'S FOREST-RAIL *Rallina forbesi* (6)

MAYR'S FOREST-RAIL *Rallina mayri* (6) [DD]

RED-NECKED CRAKE or RED-NECKED RAIL *Rallina tricolor* (6)

ANDAMAN CRAKE *Rallina canningi* (4) [VU]

RED-LEGGED CRAKE *Rallina fasciata* (4)

SLATY-LEGGED CRAKE *Rallina eurizonoides* (4)

CHESTNUT-HEADED CRAKE *Anurolimnas castaneiceps* (2)

RUSSET-CROWNED CRAKE *Anurolimnas viridis* (2)

BLACK-BANDED CRAKE *Anurolimnas fasciatus* (2)

RUFOUS-SIDED CRAKE *Laterallus melanophaius* (2)

RUSTY-FLANKED CRAKE *Laterallus levraudi* (2) [VU]

RUDDY CRAKE *Laterallus ruber* (2)

WHITE-THROATED CRAKE *Laterallus albigularis* (2)

GRAY-BREASTED CRAKE *Laterallus exilis* (2)

BLACK RAIL *Laterallus jamaicensis* (1, 2)

JUNIN RAIL *Laterallus tuerosi* (2) [EN]

GALAPAGÓS RAIL *Laterallus spilonotus* (2) [NT]

RED-AND-WHITE CRAKE *Laterallus leucopyrrhus* (2)

RUFOUS-FACED CRAKE *Laterallus xenopterus* (2) [VU]

WOODFORD'S RAIL *Nesoclopeus woodfordi* (4) [EN]

BAR-WINGED RAIL *Nesoclopeus poecilopterus* (6) [EX]

WEKA *Gallirallus australis* (6) [NT]

NEW CALEDONIAN RAIL *Gallirallus lafresnayanus* (6) [CR]

LORD HOWE ISLAND RAIL or LORD HOWE WOODHEN *Gallirallus sylvestris* (6) [EN]

GILBERT RAIL *Gallirallus conditicius* (6)

OKINAWA RAIL *Gallirallus okinawae* (4) [EN]

BARRED RAIL *Gallirallus torquatus* (4, 6)

NEW BRITAIN RAIL *Gallirallus insignis* (6)

BUFF-BANDED RAIL *Gallirallus philippensis* (4, 6)

ROVIANA RAIL *Gallirallus rovianae* (4) [NT]

GUAM RAIL *Gallirallus owstoni* (4) [EW]

WAKE ISLAND RAIL *Gallirallus wakensis* (4) [EX]

TAHITI RAIL *Gallirallus pacificus* (6) [EX]

DIEFFENBACH'S RAIL *Gallirallus dieffenbachii* (4) [EX]

CHATHAM ISLANDS RAIL *Gallirallus modestus* (4) [EX]

SHARPE'S RAIL *Gallirallus sharpei* (4) [EX]

SLATY-BREASTED RAIL *Gallirallus striatus* (4)

CLAPPER RAIL *Rallus longirostris* (1)

KING RAIL *Rallus elegans* (1)

PLAIN-FLANKED RAIL *Rallus wetmorei* (2) [EN]

VIRGINIA RAIL *Rallus limicola* (1)

BOGOTÁ RAIL *Rallus semiplumbeus* (2) [EN]

AUSTRAL RAIL *Rallus antarcticus* (2) [CR]

WATER RAIL *Rallus aquaticus* (3, 4, 5)

KAFFIR RAIL *Rallus caerulescens* (5)

MADAGASCAR RAIL *Rallus madagascariensis* (5)

BROWN-BANDED RAIL or LUZON RAIL *Lewinia mirificus* (4) [EN]

LEWIN'S RAIL *Lewinia pectoralis* (6)

AUCKLAND ISLANDS RAIL *Lewinia muelleri* (6) [VU]

WHITE-THROATED RAIL *Dryolimnas cuvieri* (5)

AFRICAN CRAKE *Crecopsis egregia* (5)

CORN CRAKE or CORNCRAKE *Crex crex* (3, 4, 5) [VU]

ROUGET'S RAIL *Rougetius rougetii* (5) [NT]

SNORING RAIL *Aramidopsis plateni* (4) [VU]

INACCESSIBLE ISLAND RAIL or INACCESSIBLE RAIL *Atlantisia rogersi* (5) [VU]

LITTLE WOOD-RAIL *Aramides mangle* (2)

RUFOUS-NECKED WOOD-RAIL *Aramides axillaris* (1, 2)

GRAY-NECKED WOOD-RAIL *Aramides cajanea* (1, 2)

BROWN WOOD-RAIL *Aramides wolfi* (2) [VU]

GIANT WOOD-RAIL *Aramides ypecaha* (2)

SLATY-BREASTED WOOD-RAIL *Aramides saracura* (2)

RED-WINGED WOOD-RAIL *Aramides calopterus* (2)

UNIFORM CRAKE *Amaurolimnas concolor* (1, 2)

BALD-FACED RAIL or BLUE-FACED RAIL *Gymnocrex rosenbergii* (4) [VU]

BARE-EYED RAIL *Gymnocrex plumbeiventris* (4, 6)

BROWN CRAKE *Amaurornis akool* (4)

BUSH-HEN or PLAIN BUSH-HEN *Amaurornis olivaceus* (4)

ISABELLINE WATERHEN or ISABELLINE BUSH-HEN *Amaurornis isabellinus* (4)

RUFOUS-TAILED WATERHEN *Amaurornis moluccanus* (4, 6)

WHITE-BREASTED WATERHEN *Amaurornis phoenicurus* (4)

BLACK CRAKE *Amaurornis flavirostra* (5)

SAKALAVA RAIL *Amaurornis olivieri* (5) [CR]

BLACK-TAILED CRAKE *Amaurornis bicolor* (4)

LITTLE CRAKE *Porzana parva* (3, 5)

BAILLON'S CRAKE *Porzana pusilla* (3, 4, 5, 6)

LAYSAN CRAKE *Porzana palmeri* (1) [EX]

SPOTTED CRAKE *Porzana porzana* (3, 4, 5)

AUSTRALIAN CRAKE or AUSTRALIAN SPOTTED CRAKE *Porzana fluminea* (1, 2, 3, 6)

DOT-WINGED CRAKE *Porzana spiloptera* (2) [VU]

ASH-THROATED CRAKE *Porzana albicollis* (2)

HAWAIIAN CRAKE *Porzana sandwichensis* (6) [EX]

RUDDY-BREASTED CRAKE *Porzana fusca* (4)

BAND-BELLIED CRAKE *Porzana paykullii* (4) [NT]

SPOTLESS CRAKE *Porzana tabuensis* (4, 6)

KOSRAE CRAKE *Porzana monasa* (6) [EX]

HENDERSON ISLAND CRAKE or HENDERSON CRAKE *Porzana atra* (6) [VU]

YELLOW-BREASTED CRAKE *Porzana flaviventer* (1, 2)

WHITE-BROWED CRAKE *Porzana cinerea*
(4, 6)

STRIPED CRAKE *Aenigmatolimnas marginalis*
(5)

ZAPATA RAIL *Cyanolimnas cerverai* (2) [CR]

COLOMBIAN CRAKE *Neocrex colombianus* (2)
[NT]

PAINT-BILLED CRAKE *Neocrex erythrops* (2)

SPOTTED RAIL *Pardirallus maculatus* (1, 2)

BLACKISH RAIL *Pardirallus nigricans* (2)

PLUMBEOUS RAIL *Pardirallus sanguinolentus*
(2)

CHESTNUT RAIL *Eulabeornis castaneoventris*
(6)

INVISIBLE RAIL or DRUMMER RAIL *Habroptila wallacii* (4) [VU]

NEW GUINEA FLIGHTLESS RAIL *Megacrex inepta* (6) [DD]

WATERCOCK *Gallicrex cinerea* (4)

PURPLE SWAMPHEN *Porphyrio porphyrio*
(4, 5, 6)

LORD HOWE ISLAND SWAMPHEN or WHITE GALLINULE *Porphyrio albus* (6) [EX]

TAKAHE *Porphyrio mantelli* (6) [EN]

ALLEN'S GALLINULE *Porphyrio alleni* (5)

PURPLE GALLINULE *Porphyrio martinicus*
(1, 2, 3)

AZURE GALLINULE *Porphyrio flavirostris* (2)

SAMOAN MOORHEN *Gallinula pacifica* (6)
[CR]

SAN CRISTÓBAL MOORHEN *Gallinula silvestris*
(4) [CR]

TRISTAN MOORHEN or GOUGH MOORHEN *Gallinula nesiotis* (5) [VU]

COMMON MOORHEN *Gallinula chloropus*
(1, 2, 3, 4, 5)

DUSKY MOORHEN *Gallinula tenebrosa* (4, 6)

LESSER MOORHEN *Gallinula angulata* (5)

SPOT-FLANKED GALLINULE *Gallinula melanops*
(2)

BLACK-TAILED NATIVE-HEN *Gallinula ventralis*
(6)

TASMANIAN NATIVE-HEN *Gallinula mortierii*
(6)

RED-KNOBBED COOT *Fulica cristata* (5)

COMMON COOT or EURASIAN COOT *Fulica atra* (3, 4, 5)

HAWAIIAN COOT *Fulica alai* (6) [VU]

AMERICAN COOT *Fulica americana* (1, 2, 3, 6)

CARIBBEAN COOT *Fulica caribaea* (2)

WHITE-WINGED COOT *Fulica leucoptera* (2)

SLATE-COLORED COOT *Fulica ardesiaca* (2)

RED-GARTERED COOT *Fulica armillata* (2)

RED-FRONTED COOT *Fulica rufifrons* (2)

GIANT COOT *Fulica gigantea* (2)

HORNED COOT *Fulica cornuta* (2) [VU]

Family MESITORNITHIDAE

WHITE-BREASTED MESITE *Mesitornis variegata*
(5) [VU]

BROWN MESITE *Mesitornis unicolor* (5) [VU]

SUBDESERT MESITE *Monias benschi* (5) [VU]

Order CICONIIFORMES
Suborder CHARADRII
Family PTEROCLIDAE

TIBETAN SANDGROUSE *Syrrhaptes tibetanus* (4)

PALLAS'S SANDGROUSE *Syrrhaptes paradoxus*
(3, 4)

PIN-TAILED SANDGROUSE *Pterocles alchata*
(3, 4, 5)

NAMAQUA SANDGROUSE *Pterocles namaqua* (5)

CHESTNUT-BELLIED SANDGROUSE *Pterocles exustus* (3, 4, 5)

SPOTTED SANDGROUSE *Pterocles senegallus*
(4, 5)

YELLOW-THROATED SANDGROUSE *Pterocles gutturalis* (5)

BLACK-BELLIED SANDGROUSE *Pterocles orientalis* (3, 4, 5)

CROWNED SANDGROUSE *Pterocles coronatus* (3, 5)

MADAGASCAR SANDGROUSE *Pterocles personatus* (5)

BLACK-FACED SANDGROUSE *Pterocles decoratus* (5)

DOUBLE-BANDED SANDGROUSE *Pterocles bicinctus* (5)

FOUR-BANDED SANDGROUSE *Pterocles quadricinctus* (5)

PAINTED SANDGROUSE *Pterocles indicus* (4)

LICHTENSTEIN'S SANDGROUSE *Pterocles lichtensteinii* (3, 5)

BURCHELL'S SANDGROUSE *Pterocles burchelli* (5)

Family THINOCORIDAE

RUFOUS-BELLIED SEEDSNIPE *Attagis gayi* (2)

WHITE-BELLIED SEEDSNIPE *Attagis malouinus* (2)

GRAY-BREASTED SEEDSNIPE *Thinocorus orbignyianus* (2)

LEAST SEEDSNIPE *Thinocorus rumicivorus* (2)

Family PEDIONOMIDAE

PLAINS-WANDERER *Pedionomus torquatus* (6) [VU]

Family SCOLOPACIDAE
Subfamily SCOLOPACINAE

EURASIAN WOODCOCK *Scolopax pusticola* (3, 4, 5)

AMAMI WOODCOCK *Scolopax mira* (4) [VU]

RUFOUS WOODCOCK or DUSKY WOODCOCK *Scolopax saturata* (4, 6)

SULAWESI WOODCOCK *Scolopax celebensis* (4) [NT]

MOLUCCAN WOODCOCK *Scolopax rochussenii* (4) [VU]

AMERICAN WOODCOCK *Scolopax minor* (1)

SOLITARY SNIPE *Gallinago solitaria* (3, 4)

LATHAM'S SNIPE or JAPANESE SNIPE *Gallinago hardwickii* (4, 6) [NT]

WOOD SNIPE *Gallinago nemoricola* (3, 4) [VU]

PINTAIL SNIPE or PIN-TAILED SNIPE *Gallinago stenura* (3, 4)

SWINHOE'S SNIPE *Gallinago megala* (3, 4)

GREAT SNIPE *Gallinago media* (3, 5) [NT]

COMMON SNIPE *Gallinago gallinago* (1, 2, 3, 4, 5)

AFRICAN SNIPE *Gallinago nigripennis* (5)

MADAGASCAR SNIPE *Gallinago macrodactyla* (5)

SOUTH AMERICAN SNIPE *Gallinago paraguaiae* (2)

PUNA SNIPE *Gallinago andina* (2)

NOBLE SNIPE *Gallinago nobilis* (2)

GIANT SNIPE *Gallinago undulata* (2)

ANDEAN SNIPE *Gallinago jamesoni* (2)

FUEGIAN SNIPE *Gallinago stricklandii* (2) [NT]

IMPERIAL SNIPE *Gallinago imperialis* (2) [NT]

JACK SNIPE *Lymnocryptes minimus* (3, 4)

CHATHAM ISLANDS SNIPE *Coenocorypha pusilla* (6) [VU]

SUBANTARCTIC SNIPE *Coenocorypha aucklandica* (6) [NT]

Subfamily TRINGINAE

BLACK-TAILED GODWIT *Limosa limosa* (3, 4, 5, 6)

HUDSONIAN GODWIT *Limosa haemastica* (1, 2, 3, 5) [NT]

BAR-TAILED GODWIT *Limosa lapponica* (1, 2, 3, 4, 6)

MARBLED GODWIT *Limosa fedoa* (1, 2)

LITTLE CURLEW *Numenius minutus* (1, 3, 4, 6)

ESKIMO CURLEW *Numenius borealis* (1, 2) [CR]

WHIMBREL *Numenius phaeopus* (3, 4, 5, 6)

HUDSONIAN CURLEW *Numenius hudsonicus* (1, 2)

BRISTLE-THIGHED CURLEW *Numenius tahitiensis* (1, 6) [VU]

SLENDER-BILLED CURLEW *Numenius tenuirostris* (3, 6) [CR]

EURASIAN CURLEW *Numenius arquata* (3, 4, 5)

LONG-BILLED CURLEW *Numenius americanus* (1, 2)

FAR EASTERN CURLEW or EASTERN CURLEW *Numenius madagascariensis* (3, 4, 6) [NT]

UPLAND SANDPIPER *Bartramia longicauda* (1, 2, 3)

SPOTTED REDSHANK *Tringa erythropus* (1, 3, 4, 5)

COMMON REDSHANK *Tringa totanus* (1, 3, 4, 5)

MARSH SANDPIPER *Tringa stagnatilis* (3, 4, 5, 6)

COMMON GREENSHANK *Tringa nebularia* (3, 4, 5, 6)

NORDMANN'S GREENSHANK *Tringa guttifer* (3, 4) [EN]

GREATER YELLOWLEGS *Tringa melanoleuca* (1, 2, 3)

LESSER YELLOWLEGS *Tringa flavipes* (1, 2, 3, 5, 6)

SOLITARY SANDPIPER *Tringa solitaria* (1, 2, 3)

GREEN SANDPIPER *Tringa ochropus* (3, 4, 5)

WOOD SANDPIPER *Tringa glareola* (3, 4, 5, 6)

TEREK SANDPIPER *Tringa cinerea* (3, 4, 5, 6)

COMMON SANDPIPER *Tringa hypoleucos* (3, 4, 5, 6)

SPOTTED SANDPIPER *Tringa macularia* (1, 2, 3)

GRAY-TAILED TATTLER *Tringa brevipes* (1, 3, 4, 6)

WANDERING TATTLER *Tringa incana* (1, 2, 3, 4, 6)

WILLET *Catoptrophorus semipalmatus* (1, 2)

TUAMOTU SANDPIPER *Prosobonia cancellata* (4) [EN]

TAHITIAN SANDPIPER *Prosobonia leucoptera* (6) [EX]

RUDDY TURNSTONE *Arenaria interpres* (1, 2, 3, 4, 5, 6)

BLACK TURNSTONE *Arenaria melanocephala* (1)

SHORT-BILLED DOWITCHER *Limnodromus griseus* (1, 2, 3)

LONG-BILLED DOWITCHER *Limnodromus scolopaceus* (1, 2, 3)

ASIAN DOWITCHER *Limnodromus semipalmatus* (3, 4, 6) [NT]

SURFBIRD *Aphriza virgata* (1, 2)

GREAT KNOT *Calidris tenuirostris* (1, 3, 4, 5, 6)

RED KNOT *Calidris canutus* (1, 3, 4, 5, 6)

SANDERLING *Calidris alba* (1, 3, 4, 5, 6)

SEMIPALMATED SANDPIPER *Calidris pusilla* (1, 2, 3)

WESTERN SANDPIPER *Calidris mauri* (1, 2, 3, 6)

LITTLE STINT *Calidris minuta* (1, 3, 4)

RED-NECKED STINT or RUFOUS-NECKED STINT *Calidris ruficollis* (1, 3, 4, 5, 6)

TEMMINCK'S STINT *Calidris temminckii* (1, 3, 4, 5)

LONG-TOED STINT *Calidris subminuta* (1, 3, 4, 6)

LEAST SANDPIPER *Calidris minutilla* (1, 2, 3)

WHITE-RUMPED SANDPIPER *Calidris fuscicollis* (1, 2, 3, 6)

BAIRD'S SANDPIPER *Calidris bairdii* (1, 2, 3, 5)

PECTORAL SANDPIPER *Calidris melanotos* (1, 2, 3, 5, 6)

SHARP-TAILED SANDPIPER *Calidris acuminata* (1, 3, 6)

PURPLE SANDPIPER *Calidris maritima* (1, 3)

ROCK SANDPIPER *Calidris ptilocnemis* (1, 3)

DUNLIN *Calidris alpina* (1, 3, 4, 5)

CURLEW SANDPIPER *Calidris ferruginea* (3, 4, 5, 6)

STILT SANDPIPER *Micropalama himantopus* (1, 2)

BUFF-BREASTED SANDPIPER *Tryngites subruficollis* (1, 2, 3, 5)

SPOONBILL SANDPIPER or SPOON-BILLED SANDPIPER *Eurynorhynchus pygmeus* (1, 3, 4) [VU]

BROAD-BILLED SANDPIPER *Limicola falcinellus* (3, 4, 5, 6)

RUFF *Philomachus pugnax* (1, 2, 3, 4, 5, 6)

WILSON'S PHALAROPE *Phalaropus tricolor* (1, 2, 3, 5)

RED-NECKED PHALAROPE or NORTHERN PHALAROPE *Phalaropus lobatus* (1, 2, 3, 4, 5)

RED PHALAROPE or GRAY PHALAROPE *Phalaropus fulicaria* (1, 3, 5, 6)

Family ROSTRATULIDAE

GREATER PAINTED-SNIPE *Rostratula benghalensis* (4, 5, 6)

AMERICAN PAINTED-SNIPE *Rostratula semicollaris* (2)

Family JACANIDAE

AFRICAN JACANA *Actophilornis africanus* (5)

MADAGASCAR JACANA *Actophilornis albinucha* (5)

LESSER JACANA *Microparra capensis* (5)

COMB-CRESTED JACANA *Irediparra gallinacea* (4, 6)

PHEASANT-TAILED JACANA *Hydrophasianus chirurgus* (3, 4)

BRONZE-WINGED JACANA *Metopidius indicus* (4)

NORTHERN JACANA *Jacana spinosa* (1, 2)

WATTLED JACANA *Jacana jacana* (2)

Family CHIONIDAE

SNOWY SHEATHBILL *Chionis alba* (2, 6)

BLACK-FACED SHEATHBILL *Chionis minor* (4)

Family PLUVIANELLIDAE

MAGELLANIC PLOVER *Pluvianellus socialis* (2) [NT]

Family BURHINIDAE

EURASIAN THICK-KNEE *Burhinus oedicnemus* (3, 4, 5)

SENEGAL THICK-KNEE *Burhinus senegalensis* (5)

WATER THICK-KNEE *Burhinus vermiculatus* (5)

SPOTTED THICK-KNEE *Burhinus capensis* (5)

DOUBLE-STRIPED THICK-KNEE *Burhinus bistriatus* (1, 2)

PERUVIAN THICK-KNEE *Burhinus superciliaris* (2)

BUSH THICK-KNEE or BUSH STONE-CURLEW *Burhinus grallarius* (6)

GREAT THICK-KNEE *Burhinus recurvirostris* (4)

BEACH THICK-KNEE or BEACH STONE-CURLEW *Esacus neglectus* (4, 6)

Family CHARADRIIDAE
Subfamily RECURVIROSTRINAE
Tribe HAEMATOPODINI

EURASIAN OYSTERCATCHER *Haematopus ostralegus* (3, 4, 5)

CANARY ISLANDS OYSTERCATCHER *Haematopus meadewaldoi* (5) [EX]

AFRICAN OYSTERCATCHER *Haematopus moquini* (5) [NT]

SOUTH ISLAND OYSTERCATCHER *Haematopus finschi* (6)

BLACK OYSTERCATCHER *Haematopus bachmani* (1)

AMERICAN OYSTERCATCHER *Haematopus palliatus* (1, 2)

PIED OYSTERCATCHER *Haematopus longirostris* (6)

VARIABLE OYSTERCATCHER *Haematopus unicolor* (6)

CHATHAM ISLANDS OYSTERCATCHER *Haematopus chathamensis* (6) [EN]

SOOTY OYSTERCATCHER *Haematopus fuliginosus* (6)

BLACKISH OYSTERCATCHER *Haematopus ater* (2)

MAGELLANIC OYSTERCATCHER *Haematopus leucopodus* (2)

Tribe RECURVIROSTRINI

IBISBILL *Ibidorhyncha struthersii* (3, 4)

BLACK-WINGED STILT *Himantopus himantopus* (3, 4, 5)

WHITE-HEADED STILT *Himantopus leucocephalus* (4, 6)

BLACK STILT *Himantopus novaezelandiae* (6) [CR]

BLACK-NECKED STILT *Himantopus mexicanus* (1, 2) [CR, SSP]

WHITE-BACKED STILT *Himantopus melanurus* (2)

BANDED STILT *Cladorhynchus leucocephalus* (6)

PIED AVOCET *Recurvirostra avosetta* (3, 4, 5)

AMERICAN AVOCET *Recurvirostra americana* (1, 2)

RED-NECKED AVOCET *Recurvirostra novaehollandiae* (6)

ANDEAN AVOCET *Recurvirostra andina* (2)

Subfamily CHARADRIINAE

EUROPEAN GOLDEN-PLOVER *Pluvialis apricaria* (3, 4)

PACIFIC GOLDEN-PLOVER *Pluvialis fulva* (1, 3, 5, 6)

AMERICAN GOLDEN-PLOVER *Pluvialis dominica* (1, 2, 3, 5)

GRAY PLOVER or BLACK-BELLIED PLOVER *Pluvialis squatarola* (1, 2, 3, 4, 5, 6)

RED-BREASTED PLOVER or NEW ZEALAND DOTTEREL *Charadrius obscurus* (6) [EN]

COMMON RINGED PLOVER *Charadrius hiaticula* (1, 3, 4, 5, 6)

SEMIPALMATED PLOVER *Charadrius semipalmatus* (1, 2)

LONG-BILLED PLOVER *Charadrius placidus* (3, 4) [NT]

LITTLE RINGED PLOVER *Charadrius dubius* (3, 4, 5, 6)

WILSON'S PLOVER *Charadrius wilsonia* (1, 2)

KILLDEER *Charadrius vociferus* (1, 2, 3)

MADAGASCAR PLOVER *Charadrius thoracicus* (5) [VU]

ST. HELENA PLOVER *Charadrius sanctaehelenae* (6) [EN]

KITTLITZ'S PLOVER *Charadrius pecuarius* (5)

THREE-BANDED PLOVER *Charadrius tricollaris* (5)

FORBES'S PLOVER *Charadrius forbesi* (5)

PIPING PLOVER *Charadrius melodus* (1, 2) [VU]

CHESTNUT-BANDED PLOVER *Charadrius pallidus* (5)

KENTISH PLOVER or SNOWY PLOVER *Charadrius alexandrinus* (1, 2, 3, 4, 5)

WHITE-FRONTED PLOVER *Charadrius marginatus* (5)

RED-CAPPED PLOVER *Charadrius ruficapillus* (6)

MALAYSIAN PLOVER *Charadrius peronii* (4) [NT]

JAVAN PLOVER *Charadrius javanicus* (4) [NT]

COLLARED PLOVER *Charadrius collaris* (1, 2)

DOUBLE-BANDED PLOVER *Charadrius bicinctus* (6)

TWO-BANDED PLOVER *Charadrius falklandicus* (2)

PUNA PLOVER *Charadrius alticola* (2)

MONGOLIAN PLOVER or LESSER SAND PLOVER *Charadrius mongolus* (1, 3, 4, 5, 6)

GREATER SAND PLOVER *Charadrius leschenaultii* (3, 4, 5, 6)

CASPIAN PLOVER *Charadrius asiaticus* (3, 4, 5)

ORIENTAL PLOVER *Charadrius veredus* (3, 4, 6)

MOUNTAIN PLOVER *Charadrius montanus* (1) [VU]

RUFOUS-CHESTED PLOVER *Charadrius modestus* (2)

INLAND DOTTEREL *Charadrius australis* (6)

HOODED PLOVER *Thinornis rubricollis* (6) [VU]

SHORE PLOVER *Thinornis novaeseelandiae* (6) [EN]

RED-KNEED DOTTEREL *Erythrogonys cinctus* (6)

EURASIAN DOTTEREL *Eudromias morinellus* (1, 3, 4, 5)

TAWNY-THROATED DOTTEREL *Oreopholus ruficollis* (2)

WRYBILL *Anarhynchus frontalis* (6) [VU]

DIADEMED SANDPIPER-PLOVER *Phegornis mitchellii* (2) [NT]

BLACK-FRONTED DOTTEREL *Elseyornis melanops* (6)

NORTHERN LAPWING *Vanellus vanellus* (3, 4, 5)

LONG-TOED LAPWING *Vanellus crassirostris* (5)

YELLOW-WATTLED LAPWING *Vanellus malabaricus* (4)

JAVANESE LAPWING *Vanellus macropterus* (4) [EX]

BANDED LAPWING *Vanellus tricolor* (6)

MASKED LAPWING *Vanellus miles* (6)

BLACKSMITH LAPWING *Vanellus armatus* (5)

SPUR-WINGED LAPWING *Vanellus spinosus* (5)

RIVER LAPWING *Vanellus duvaucelii* (4)

BLACK-HEADED LAPWING *Vanellus tectus* (5)

SPOT-BREASTED LAPWING *Vanellus melanocephalus* (5)

GRAY-HEADED LAPWING *Vanellus cinereus* (4) [NT]

RED-WATTLED LAPWING *Vanellus indicus* (4)

WHITE-HEADED LAPWING *Vanellus albiceps* (5)

WATTLED LAPWING *Vanellus senegallus* (5)

SENEGAL LAPWING *Vanellus lugubris* (5)

BLACK-WINGED LAPWING *Vanellus melanopterus* (5)

CROWNED LAPWING *Vanellus coronatus* (5)

BROWN-CHESTED LAPWING *Vanellus superciliosus* (5)

SOCIABLE LAPWING *Vanellus gregarius* (3, 4, 5) [VU]

WHITE-TAILED LAPWING *Vanellus leucurus* (3, 4, 5)

PIED LAPWING *Vanellus cayanus* (2)

SOUTHERN LAPWING *Vanellus chilensis* (2)

ANDEAN LAPWING *Vanellus resplendens* (2)

Family GLAREOLIDAE
Subfamily DROMADINAE

CRAB PLOVER *Dromas ardeola* (5)

Subfamily GLAREOLINAE

EGYPTIAN PLOVER or CROCODILE-BIRD *Pluvianus aegyptius* (5)

DOUBLE-BANDED COURSER *Rhinoptilus africanus* (5)

BRONZE-WINGED COURSER *Rhinoptilus chalcopterus* (5)

THREE-BANDED COURSER *Rhinoptilus cinctus* (5)

JERDON'S COURSER *Rhinoptilus bitorquatus* (4) [EN]

CREAM-COLORED COURSER *Cursorius cursor* (4, 5)

SOMALI COURSER *Cursorius somalensis* (5)

BURCHELL'S COURSER *Cursorius rufus* (5)

TEMMINCK'S COURSER *Cursorius temminckii* (5)

INDIAN COURSER *Cursorius coromandelicus* (4)

COLLARED PRATINCOLE *Glareola pratincola* (3, 5)

ORIENTAL PRATINCOLE *Glareola maldivarum* (3, 4, 6)

BLACK-WINGED PRATINCOLE *Glareola nordmanni* (3, 5) [NT]

MADAGASCAR PRATINCOLE *Glareola ocularis* (5)

ROCK PRATINCOLE *Glareola nuchalis* (5)

GRAY PRATINCOLE *Glareola cinerea* (5)

SMALL PRATINCOLE *Glareola lactea* (4)

AUSTRALIAN PRATINCOLE *Stiltia isabella* (6)

Family LARIDAE
Subfamily LARINAE
Tribe STERCORARIINI

LONG-TAILED JAEGER or LONG-TAILED SKUA *Stercorarius longicaudus* (1, 3)

PARASITIC JAEGER or ARCTIC JAEGER *Stercorarius parasiticus* (1, 3, 4, 5)

POMARINE JAEGER *Stercorarius pomarinus* (1, 3, 4)

GREAT SKUA *Stercorarius skua* (1, 2, 3, 5)

SOUTH POLAR SKUA *Stercorarius maccormicki* (1, 3, 4, 5)

CHILEAN SKUA *Stercorarius chilensis* (2)

SOUTHERN SKUA *Stercorarius antarctica* (2, 5, 6)

BROWN SKUA *Stercorarius lonnbergi* (4, 6)

Tribe RYNCHOPINI

BLACK SKIMMER *Rynchops niger* (1, 2)

AFRICAN SKIMMER *Rynchops flavirostris* (5)

INDIAN SKIMMER *Rynchops albicollis* (4) [VU]

Tribe LARINI

DOLPHIN GULL *Larus scoresbii* (2)

PACIFIC GULL *Larus pacificus* (6) [NT]

BAND-TAILED GULL *Larus belcheri* (1, 2)

OLROG'S GULL *Larus atlanticus* (2) [VU]

BLACK-TAILED GULL *Larus crassirostris* (1, 2, 3, 4)

GRAY GULL *Larus modestus* (2)

HEERMANN'S GULL *Larus heermanni* (1) [NT]

WHITE-EYED GULL *Larus leucophthalmus* (5) [VU]

SOOTY GULL *Larus hemprichii* (5)

COMMON GULL *Larus canus* (3, 4, 5)

MEW GULL or SHORT-BILLED GULL *Larus brachyrhynchus* (1)

RING-BILLED GULL *Larus delawarensis* (1, 2)

AUDOUIN'S GULL *Larus audouinii* (3, 5) [CD]

CALIFORNIA GULL *Larus californicus* (1)

GREAT BLACK-BACKED GULL *Larus marinus* (1, 2, 3)

KELP GULL *Larus dominicanus* (1, 2, 5, 6)

GLAUCOUS-WINGED GULL *Larus glaucescens* (1)

WESTERN GULL *Larus occidentalis* (1, 2)

YELLOW-FOOTED GULL *Larus livens* (1)

GLAUCOUS GULL *Larus hyperboreus* (1, 3, 4)

ICELAND GULL *Larus glaucoides* (1, 3)

HERRING GULL *Larus argentatus* (1, 2, 3, 4)

SLATY-BACKED GULL *Larus schistisagus* (1, 3, 4)

YELLOW-LEGGED GULL *Larus cachinnans* (1, 3, 5)

ARMENIAN GULL *Larus armenicus* (3)

LESSER BLACK-BACKED GULL *Larus fuscus* (1, 3)

GREAT BLACK-HEADED GULL or PALLAS'S GULL *Larus ichthyaetus* (3, 4)

BROWN-HEADED GULL *Larus brunnicephalus* (4)

GRAY-HEADED GULL *Larus cirrocephalus* (2, 5)

KING GULL *Larus hartlaubii* (5)

Silver Gull *Larus novaehollandiae* (6)

Red-Billed Gull *Larus scopulinus* (6)

Black-Billed Gull *Larus bulleri* (6)

Brown-Hooded Gull *Larus maculipennis* (2)

Black-Headed Gull or Common Black-Headed Gull *Larus ridibundus* (1, 2, 3, 4, 5)

Slender-Billed Gull *Larus genei* (3, 4, 5)

Bonaparte's Gull *Larus philadelphia* (1, 2, 3)

Saunders's Gull *Larus saundersi* (4) [EN]

Andean Gull *Larus serranus* (2)

Mediterranean Gull *Larus melanocephalus* (3, 5)

Relict Gull *Larus relictus* (4) [NT]

Lava Gull *Larus fuliginosus* (2) [VU]

Laughing Gull *Larus atricilla* (1, 2, 3, 5, 6)

Franklin's Gull *Larus pipixcan* (1, 2, 3, 5)

Little Gull *Larus minutus* (1, 3)

Ivory Gull *Pagophila eburnea* (1)

Ross's Gull *Rhodostethia rosea* (1, 3)

Sabine's Gull *Xema sabini* (1, 2, 3, 5)

Swallow-Tailed Gull *Creagrus furcatus* (2)

Black-Legged Kittiwake *Rissa tridactyla* (1, 3, 4, 5)

Red-Legged Kittiwake *Rissa brevirostris* (1) [VU]

Tribe STERNINI

Gull-Billed Tern *Sterna nilotica* (1, 2, 3, 4, 6)

Caspian Tern *Sterna caspia* (1, 2, 4, 5, 6)

Royal Tern *Sterna maxima* (1, 2, 5)

Great Crested-Tern or Crested Tern *Sterna bergii* (4, 5, 6)

Elegant Tern *Sterna elegans* (1, 2, 3) [NT]

Lesser Crested-Tern *Sterna bengalensis* (4, 5, 6)

Chinese Crested-Tern *Sterna bernsteini* (4) [CR]

Sandwich Tern *Sterna sandvicensis* (1, 2, 3, 4, 5)

River Tern *Sterna aurantia* (4)

Roseate Tern *Sterna dougallii* (1, 2, 4, 5)

White-Fronted Tern *Sterna striata* (6)

Black-Naped Tern *Sterna sumatrana* (4, 5, 6)

South American Tern *Sterna hirundinacea* (2)

Common Tern *Sterna hirundo* (1, 2, 3, 4, 5, 6)

Arctic Tern *Sterna paradisaea* (1, 2, 3, 5, 6)

Antarctic Tern *Sterna vittata* (2, 5, 6)

Kerguelen Tern *Sterna firgata* (4) [VU]

Forster's Tern *Sterna forsteri* (1, 2, 3)

Snowy-Crowned Tern *Sterna trudeaui* (2)

Little Tern *Sterna albifrons* (3, 4, 5, 6)

Saunders's Tern *Sterna saundersi* (4, 5)

Least Tern *Sterna antillarum* (1, 2)

Yellow-Billed Tern *Sterna superciliaris* (2)

Peruvian Tern *Sterna lorata* (2)

Fairy Tern *Sterna nereis* (6) [VU]

Damara Tern *Sterna balaenarum* (5) [NT]

White-Cheeked Tern *Sterna repressa* (4, 5)

Black-Bellied Tern *Sterna acuticauda* (4) [VU]

Aleutian Tern *Sterna aleutica* (1, 3)

Gray-Backed Tern *Sterna lunata* (4, 6)

Bridled Tern *Sterna anaethetus* (1, 4, 5, 6)

Sooty Tern *Sterna fuscata* (1, 2, 3, 4, 5, 6)

Black-Fronted Tern *Chlidonias albostriatus* (6) [VU]

Whiskered Tern *Chlidonias hybridus* (3, 4, 5, 6)

White-Winged Tern or White-Winged Black Tern *Chlidonias leucopterus* (1, 3, 4, 5, 6)

Black Tern *Chlidonias niger* (1, 2, 3, 4, 5)

Large-Billed Tern *Phaetusa simplex* (2)

BROWN NODDY or COMMON NODDY *Anous stolidus* (1, 2, 5, 6)

BLACK NODDY *Anous minutus* (2, 4, 5, 6)

LESSER NODDY *Anous tenuirostris* (5, 6)

BLUE-GRAY NODDY or GRAY TERNLET *Procelsterna cerulea* (2, 6)

COMMON WHITE-TERN or WHITE TERN *Gygis alba* (1, 2, 5, 6)

LITTLE WHITE-TERN *Gygis microrhyncha* (4)

INCA TERN *Larosterna inca* (2)

Subfamily ALCINAE

DOVEKIE or LITTLE AUK *Alle alle* (1, 2, 3)

COMMON MURRE *Uria aalge* (1, 3, 4)

THICK-BILLED MURRE *Uria lomvia* (1, 3, 4)

RAZORBILL or RAZOR-BILLED AUK *Alca torda* (1, 3, 5)

GREAT AUK *Pinguinus impennis* (1, 3) [EX]

BLACK GUILLEMOT *Cepphus grylle* (1, 3)

PIGEON GUILLEMOT *Cepphus columba* (1, 3, 4)

SPECTACLED GUILLEMOT *Cepphus carbo* (4)

MARBLED MURRELET *Brachyramphus marmoratus* (1) [NT]

LONG-BILLED MURRELET *Brachyramphus perdix* (1, 4)

KITTLITZ'S MURRELET *Brachyramphus brevirostris* (1, 3)

XANTUS'S MURRELET *Synthliboramphus hypoleucus* (1) [NT]

CRAVERI'S MURRELET *Synthliboramphus craveri* (1) [NT]

ANCIENT MURRELET *Synthliboramphus antiquus* (1, 3, 4)

JAPANESE MURRELET *Synthliboramphus wumizusume* (4) [VU]

CASSIN'S AUKLET *Ptychoramphus aleuticus* (1)

PARAKEET AUKLET *Cyclorrhynchus psittacula* (1, 3, 4)

CRESTED AUKLET *Aethia cristatella* (1, 3, 4)

WHISKERED AUKLET *Aethia pygmaea* (3, 4)

LEAST AUKLET *Aethia pusilla* (1, 3, 4)

RHINOCEROS AUKLET *Cerorhinca monocerata* (1, 4)

ATLANTIC PUFFIN *Fratercula arctica* (1, 3, 5)

HORNED PUFFIN *Fratercula corniculata* (1, 2, 3, 4)

TUFTED PUFFIN *Fratercula cirrhata* (1, 4)

Order CICONIIFORMES
Suborder CICONII
Infraorder FALCONIDES
Parvorder ACCIPITRIDA
Family ACCIPITRIDAE
Subfamily PANDIONINAE

OSPREY *Pandion haliaetus* (1, 2, 3, 4, 5, 6)

Subfamily ACCIPITRINAE

AFRICAN BAZA *Aviceda cuculoides* (5)

MADAGASCAR BAZA *Aviceda madagascariensis* (5)

JERDON'S BAZA *Aviceda jerdoni* (4) [NT]

PACIFIC BAZA *Aviceda subcristata* (4, 6)

BLACK BAZA *Aviceda leuphotes* (4, 6)

GRAY-HEADED KITE *Leptodon cayanensis* (1, 2)

WHITE-COLLARED KITE *Leptodon forbesi* (2)

HOOK-BILLED KITE *Chondrohierax uncinatus* (1, 2)

LONG-TAILED HONEY-BUZZARD *Henicopernis longicauda* (6)

BLACK HONEY-BUZZARD *Henicopernis infuscatus* (6) [NT]

EUROPEAN HONEY-BUZZARD *Pernis apivorus* (3, 5)

ORIENTAL HONEY-BUZZARD *Pernis ptilorhyncus* (4)

BARRED HONEY-BUZZARD *Pernis celebensis* (4)

SQUARE-TAILED KITE *Lophoictinia isura* (6) [VU]

BLACK-BREASTED BUZZARD *Hamirostra melanosternon* (6)

SWALLOW-TAILED KITE *Elanoides forficatus* (1, 2)

BAT HAWK *Macheiramphus alcinus* (4, 5, 6)

PEARL KITE *Gampsonyx swainsonii* (2)

BLACK-WINGED KITE or BLACK-SHOULDERED KITE *Elanus caeruleus* (3, 4, 5)

BLACK-SHOULDERED KITE *Elanus axillaris* (6)

WHITE-TAILED KITE *Elanus leucurus* (1, 2)

LETTER-WINGED KITE *Elanus scriptus* (6)

SCISSOR-TAILED KITE *Chelictinia riocourii* (5)

SNAIL KITE or EVERGLADE KITE *Rostrhamus sociabilis* (1, 2)

SLENDER-BILLED KITE *Rostrhamus hamatus* (2)

DOUBLE-TOOTHED KITE *Harpagus bidentatus* (2)

RUFOUS-THIGHED KITE *Harpagus diodon* (2)

MISSISSIPPI KITE *Ictinia mississippiensis* (1, 2)

PLUMBEOUS KITE *Ictinia plumbea* (1, 2)

RED KITE *Milvus milvus* (3, 5)

CAPE VERDE KITE *Milvus fasciicauda* (5) [CR]

BLACK KITE *Milvus migrans* (3, 4, 5, 6)

YELLOW-BILLED KITE *Milvus parasitus* (5)

BLACK-EARED KITE *Milvus lineatus* (3, 4)

WHISTLING KITE *Haliastur sphenurus* (6)

BRAHMINY KITE *Haliastur indus* (4, 6)

WHITE-BELLIED SEA-EAGLE or WHITE-BELLIED FISH-EAGLE *Haliaeetus leucogaster* (4, 6)

SANFORD'S FISH-EAGLE *Haliaeetus sanfordi* (4) [VU]

AFRICAN FISH-EAGLE *Haliaeetus vocifer* (5)

MADAGASCAR FISH-EAGLE *Haliaeetus vociferoides* (5) [CR]

PALLAS'S FISH-EAGLE or PALLAS'S SEA-EAGLE *Haliaeetus leucoryphus* (3, 4) [VU]

WHITE-TAILED EAGLE *Haliaeetus albicilla* (3, 4) [NT]

BALD EAGLE *Haliaeetus leucocephalus* (1, 3)

STELLER'S SEA-EAGLE *Haliaeetus pelagicus* (2, 3) [VU]

LESSER FISH-EAGLE *Ichthyophaga humilis* (4) [NT]

GRAY-HEADED FISH-EAGLE *Ichthyophaga ichthyaetus* (4) [NT]

PALM-NUT VULTURE *Gypohierax angolensis* (5)

LAMMERGEIER *Gypaetus barbatus* (3, 4, 5)

EGYPTIAN VULTURE *Neophron percnopterus* (3, 4, 5)

HOODED VULTURE *Necrosyrtes monachus* (5)

WHITE-BACKED VULTURE *Gyps africanus* (5)

WHITE-RUMPED VULTURE *Gyps bengalensis* (4) [NT]

LONG-BILLED VULTURE *Gyps indicus* (4) [NT]

RUEPPELL'S GRIFFON or RUEPPELL'S VULTURE *Gyps rueppellii* (5)

HIMALAYAN GRIFFON *Gyps himalayensis* (3, 4)

EURASIAN GRIFFON *Gyps fulvus* (3, 4, 5)

CAPE GRIFFON *Gyps coprotheres* (5) [VU]

CINEREOUS VULTURE *Aegypius monachus* (3, 4, 5) [NT]

LAPPET-FACED VULTURE *Torgos tracheliotus* (5)

WHITE-HEADED VULTURE *Trigonoceps occipitalis* (5)

RED-HEADED VULTURE *Sarcogyps calvus* (4) [NT]

SHORT-TOED SNAKE-EAGLE *Circaetus gallicus* (3, 4, 5)

BLACK-CHESTED SNAKE-EAGLE *Circaetus pectoralis* (5)

BROWN SNAKE-EAGLE *Circaetus cinereus* (5)

FASCIATED SNAKE-EAGLE *Circaetus fasciolatus* (5) [NT]

BANDED SNAKE-EAGLE *Circaetus cinerascens* (5)

BATELEUR *Terathopius ecaudatus* (5)

CRESTED SERPENT-EAGLE *Spilornis cheela* (4)

RYUKYU SERPENT-EAGLE *Spilornis perplexus* (4)

SIMEULUE SERPENT-EAGLE *Spilornis abbotti* (4)

NIAS SERPENT-EAGLE *Spilornis asturinus* (4)

BAWEAN SERPENT-EAGLE *Spilornis baweanus* (4)

MENTAWAI SERPENT-EAGLE *Spilornis sipora* (4)

NATUNA SERPENT-EAGLE *Spilornis natunensis* (4)

NICOBAR SERPENT-EAGLE *Spilornis minimus* (4) [NT]

MOUNTAIN SERPENT-EAGLE *Spilornis kina-baluensis* (4) [DD]

SULAWESI SERPENT-EAGLE *Spilornis rufipectus* (4)

PHILIPPINE SERPENT-EAGLE *Spilornis holospilu* (4)

ANDAMAN SERPENT-EAGLE *Spilornis elgini* (4) [NT]

CONGO SERPENT-EAGLE *Dryotriorchis spectabilis* (5)

MADAGASCAR SERPENT-EAGLE *Eutriorchis astur* (5) [CR]

WESTERN MARSH-HARRIER or EURASIAN MARSH-HARRIER *Circus aeruginosus* (3, 4, 5)

AFRICAN MARSH-HARRIER *Circus ranivorus* (5)

EASTERN MARSH-HARRIER *Circus spilonotus* (3, 4)

SWAMP HARRIER *Circus approximans* (6)

REUNION MARSH-HARRIER *Circus maillardi* (4, 5) [NT]

MADAGASCAR MARSH-HARRIER *Circus macrosceles* (5)

LONG-WINGED HARRIER *Circus buffoni* (2)

SPOTTED HARRIER *Circus assimilis* (6)

BLACK HARRIER *Circus maurus* (5) [NT]

NORTHERN HARRIER or HEN HARRIER *Circus cyaneus* (3, 4)

AMERICAN HARRIER or MARSH HAWK *Circus hudsonius* (1, 2)

CINEREOUS HARRIER *Circus cinereus* (2)

PALLID HARRIER *Circus macrourus* (3, 4, 5)

[NT]

PIED HARRIER *Circus melanoleucos* (3, 4)

MONTAGU'S HARRIER *Circus pygargus* (3, 4, 5)

AFRICAN HARRIER-HAWK or GYMNOGENE *Polyboroides typus* (5)

MADAGASCAR HARRIER-HAWK or MADAGASCAR GYMNOGENE *Polyboroides radiatus* (5)

LIZARD BUZZARD *Kaupifalco monogrammicus* (5)

DARK CHANTING-GOSHAWK *Melierax metabates* (5)

EASTERN CHANTING-GOSHAWK *Melierax poliopterus* (5)

PALE CHANTING-GOSHAWK *Melierax canorus* (5)

GABAR GOSHAWK *Melierax gabar* (5)

GRAY-BELLIED GOSHAWK *Accipiter poliogaster* (2) [NT]

CRESTED GOSHAWK *Accipiter trivirgatus* (4)

SULAWESI GOSHAWK *Accipiter griseiceps* (4)

AFRICAN GOSHAWK *Accipiter tachiro* (5)

CHESTNUT-FLANKED SPARROWHAWK *Accipiter castanilius* (5)

SHIKRA *Accipiter badius* (3, 4, 5)

NICOBAR SPARROWHAWK *Accipiter butleri* (5) [NT]

LEVANT SPARROWHAWK *Accipiter brevipes* (3, 5)

CHINESE GOSHAWK *Accipiter soloensis* (4)

FRANCES'S GOSHAWK *Accipiter francesiae* (5)

SPOT-TAILED GOSHAWK *Accipiter trinotatus* (4)

GRAY GOSHAWK *Accipiter novaehollandiae* (6)

VARIABLE GOSHAWK *Accipiter hiogaster* (4, 6)

BROWN GOSHAWK *Accipiter fasciatus* (4, 6)

BLACK-MANTLED GOSHAWK *Accipiter melanochlamys* (6)

PIED GOSHAWK *Accipiter albogularis* (4, 6)

WHITE-BELLIED GOSHAWK *Accipiter haplochrous* (6)

FIJI GOSHAWK *Accipiter rufitorques* (6)

MOLUCCAN GOSHAWK *Accipiter henicogrammus* (4)

SLATY-MANTLED SPARROWHAWK *Accipiter luteoschistaceus* (6) [NT]

IMITATOR SPARROWHAWK *Accipiter imitator* (4) [EN]

GRAY-HEADED GOSHAWK *Accipiter poliocephalus* (4, 6)

NEW BRITAIN GOSHAWK *Accipiter princeps* (6) [NT]

TINY HAWK *Accipiter superciliosus* (2)

SEMICOLLARED HAWK *Accipiter collaris* (2) [NT]

RED-THIGHED SPARROWHAWK *Accipiter erythropus* (5)

LITTLE SPARROWHAWK *Accipiter minullus* (5)

JAPANESE SPARROWHAWK *Accipiter gularis* (3, 4)

BESRA *Accipiter virgatus* (4)

SMALL SPARROWHAWK *Accipiter nanus* (4) [NT]

RUFOUS-NECKED SPARROWHAWK *Accipiter erythrauchen* (4)

COLLARED SPARROWHAWK *Accipiter cirrocephalus* (6)

NEW BRITAIN SPARROWHAWK *Accipiter brachyurus* (6) [VU]

VINOUS-BREASTED SPARROWHAWK *Accipiter rhodogaster* (4)

MADAGASCAR SPARROWHAWK *Accipiter madagascariensis* (5) [NT]

OVAMBO SPARROWHAWK *Accipiter ovampensis* (5)

EURASIAN SPARROWHAWK *Accipiter nisus* (3, 4, 5)

RUFOUS-CHESTED SPARROWHAWK *Accipiter rufiventris* (5)

SHARP-SHINNED HAWK *Accipiter striatus* (1, 2)

WHITE-BREASTED HAWK *Accipiter chionogaster* (2)

PLAIN-BREASTED HAWK *Accipiter ventralis* (2)

RUFOUS-THIGHED HAWK *Accipiter erythronemius* (2)

COOPER'S HAWK *Accipiter cooperii* (1, 2)

GUNDLACH'S HAWK *Accipiter gundlachi* (2) [EN]

BICOLORED HAWK *Accipiter bicolor* (1, 2)

CHILEAN HAWK *Accipiter chilensis* (1, 2)

BLACK GOSHAWK *Accipiter melanoleucus* (5)

HENST'S GOSHAWK *Accipiter henstii* (5) [NT]

NORTHERN GOSHAWK *Accipiter gentilis* (1, 3, 4)

MEYER'S GOSHAWK *Accipiter meyerianus* (4)

CHESTNUT-SHOULDERED GOSHAWK *Erythrotriorchis buergersi* (6) [DD]

RED GOSHAWK *Erythrotriorchis radiatus* (6) [EN]

DORIA'S GOSHAWK *Megatriorchis doriae* (6) [NT]

LONG-TAILED HAWK *Urotriorchis macrourus* (5)

GRASSHOPPER BUZZARD *Butastur rufipennis* (5)

WHITE-EYED BUZZARD *Butastur teesa* (5)

RUFOUS-WINGED BUZZARD *Butastur liventer* (4) [NT]

GRAY-FACED BUZZARD *Butastur indicus* (3, 4)

CRANE HAWK *Geranospiza caerulescens* (1, 2)

PLUMBEOUS HAWK *Leucopternis plumbea* (2) [NT]

SLATE-COLORED HAWK *Leucopternis schistacea* (2)

BARRED HAWK *Leucopternis princeps* (2)

BLACK-FACED HAWK *Leucopternis melanops* (2)

WHITE-BROWED HAWK *Leucopternis kuhli* (2)

WHITE-NECKED HAWK *Leucopternis lacernulata* (2) [VU]

SEMIPLUMBEOUS HAWK *Leucopternis semi-plumbea* (2) [NT]

WHITE HAWK *Leucopternis albicollis* (1, 2)

GRAY-BACKED HAWK *Leucopternis accidentalis* (2) [EN]

MANTLED HAWK *Leucopternis polionota* (2) [NT]

RUFOUS CRAB-HAWK *Buteogallus aequinoctialis* (2)

COMMON BLACK-HAWK *Buteogallus anthracinus* (1, 2)

MANGROVE BLACK-HAWK or PACIFIC BLACK-HAWK *Buteogallus subtilis* (1, 2)

GREAT BLACK-HAWK *Buteogallus urubitinga* (1, 2)

SAVANNA HAWK *Buteogallus meridionalis* (2)

HARRIS'S HAWK *Parabuteo unicinctus* (1, 2)

BLACK-COLLARED HAWK *Busarellus nigricollis* (1, 2)

BLACK-CHESTED BUZZARD-EAGLE *Geranoaetus melanoleucus* (2)

SOLITARY EAGLE *Harpyhaliaetus solitarius* (1, 2) [NT]

CROWNED EAGLE *Harpyhaliaetus coronatus* (2) [VU]

GRAY HAWK *Buteo plagiatus* (1, 2)

GRAY-LINED HAWK *Buteo nitidus* (2)

ROADSIDE HAWK *Buteo magnirostris* (1, 2)

RED-SHOULDERED HAWK *Buteo lineatus* (1)

RIDGWAY'S HAWK *Buteo ridgwayi* (2) [EN]

BROAD-WINGED HAWK *Buteo platypterus* (1, 2)

WHITE-RUMPED HAWK *Buteo leucorrhous* (2)

SHORT-TAILED HAWK *Buteo brachyurus* (1, 2)

WHITE-THROATED HAWK *Buteo albigula* (2)

SWAINSON'S HAWK *Buteo swainsoni* (1, 2)

GALAPAGÓS HAWK *Buteo galapagoensis* (2) [VU]

WHITE-TAILED HAWK *Buteo albicaudatus* (1, 2)

RED-BACKED HAWK *Buteo polyosoma* (2)

PUNA HAWK *Buteo poecilochrous* (2)

ZONE-TAILED HAWK *Buteo albonotatus* (1, 2)

HAWAIIAN HAWK *Buteo solitarius* (2) [NT]

RED-TAILED HAWK *Buteo jamaicensis* (1, 2)

RUFOUS-TAILED HAWK *Buteo ventralis* (2) [NT]

COMMON BUZZARD *Buteo buteo* (3, 4, 5)

CAPE VERDE BUZZARD *Buteo bannermani* (5) [CR]

FOREST BUZZARD *Buteo trizonatus* (5)

MOUNTAIN BUZZARD *Buteo oreophilus* (5)

MADAGASCAR BUZZARD *Buteo brachypterus* (5)

LONG-LEGGED BUZZARD *Buteo rufinus* (3, 4, 5)

UPLAND BUZZARD *Buteo hemilasius* (3, 4)

FERRUGINOUS HAWK *Buteo regalis* (1)

ROUGH-LEGGED HAWK *Buteo lagopus* (1, 3, 4)

RED-NECKED BUZZARD *Buteo auguralis* (5)

AUGUR BUZZARD *Buteo augur* (5)

ARCHER'S BUZZARD *Buteo archeri* (5)

JACKAL BUZZARD *Buteo rufofuscus* (5)

CRESTED EAGLE *Morphnus guianensis* (2) [NT]

HARPY EAGLE *Harpia harpyja* (2) [NT]

NEW GUINEA EAGLE or NEW GUINEA HARPY EAGLE *Harpyopsis novaeguineae* (6) [VU]

GREAT PHILIPPINE EAGLE or PHILIPPINE EAGLE *Pithecophaga jefferyi* (4) [CR]

BLACK EAGLE *Ictinaetus malayensis* (4)

LESSER SPOTTED EAGLE *Aquila pomarina* (3, 5)

INDIAN SPOTTED EAGLE *Aquila hastata* (4)

GREATER SPOTTED EAGLE *Aquila clanga* (3, 4) [VU]

TAWNY EAGLE *Aquila rapax* (4, 5)

STEPPE EAGLE *Aquila nipalensis* (3, 4, 5)

ADALBERT'S EAGLE or SPANISH IMPERIAL EAGLE *Aquila adalberti* (3) [VU]

IMPERIAL EAGLE *Aquila heliaca* (3, 4) [VU]

GURNEY'S EAGLE *Aquila gurneyi* (4, 6) [NT]

GOLDEN EAGLE *Aquila chrysaetos* (1, 3, 4, 5)

WEDGE-TAILED EAGLE *Aquila audax* (6)

VERREAUX'S EAGLE *Aquila verreauxii* (5)

WAHLBERG'S EAGLE *Aquila wahlbergi* (5)

BONELLI'S EAGLE *Hieraaetus fasciatus* (3, 4, 5)

AFRICAN HAWK-EAGLE *Hieraaetus spilogaster* (5)

BOOTED EAGLE *Hieraaetus pennatus* (3, 4, 5)

LITTLE EAGLE *Hieraaetus morphnoides* (6)

AYRES'S HAWK-EAGLE *Hieraaetus ayresii* (5)

RUFOUS-BELLIED EAGLE *Hieraaetus kienerii* (4)

MARTIAL EAGLE *Polemaetus bellicosus* (5)

BLACK-AND-WHITE HAWK-EAGLE *Spizastur melanoleucus* (1, 2) [NT]

LONG-CRESTED EAGLE *Lophaetus occipitalis* (5)

CASSIN'S HAWK-EAGLE *Spizaetus africanus* (5)

CHANGEABLE HAWK-EAGLE *Spizaetus cirrhatus* (4)

MOUNTAIN HAWK-EAGLE *Spizaetus nipalensis* (3, 4)

BLYTH'S HAWK-EAGLE *Spizaetus alboniger* (4)

JAVAN HAWK-EAGLE *Spizaetus bartelsi* (4) [EN]

SULAWESI HAWK-EAGLE *Spizaetus lanceolatus* (4) [NT]

PHILIPPINE HAWK-EAGLE *Spizaetus philippensis* (4) [VU]

WALLACE'S HAWK-EAGLE *Spizaetus nanus* (4) [VU]

BLACK HAWK-EAGLE *Spizaetus tyrannus* (1, 2)

ORNATE HAWK-EAGLE *Spizaetus ornatus* (2)

CROWNED HAWK-EAGLE *Stephanoaetus coronatus* (5)

BLACK-AND-CHESTNUT EAGLE *Oroaetus isidori* (2) [NT]

Family SAGITTARIIDAE

SECRETARY-BIRD *Sagittarius serpentarius* (5)

Parvorder FALCONIDA
Family FALCONIDAE
Subfamily HERPETOTHERINAE

LAUGHING FALCON *Herpetotheres cachinnans* (1, 2)

BARRED FOREST-FALCON *Micrastur ruficollis* (1, 2)

PLUMBEOUS FOREST-FALCON *Micrastur plumbeus* (2) [EN]

LINED FOREST-FALCON *Micrastur gilvicollis* (2)

SLATY-BACKED FOREST-FALCON *Micrastur mirandollei* (2)

COLLARED FOREST-FALCON *Micrastur semitorquatus* (2)

BUCKLEY'S FOREST-FALCON *Micrastur buckleyi* (2)

Subfamily FALCONINAE
Tribe CARACARINI

BLACK CARACARA *Daptrius ater* (2)

RED-THROATED CARACARA *Daptrius americanus* (1, 2)

CARUNCULATED CARACARA *Phalcoboenus carunculatus* (2)

MOUNTAIN CARACARA *Phalcoboenus megalopterus* (2)

WHITE-THROATED CARACARA *Phalcoboenus albogularis* (2)

STRIATED CARACARA *Phalcoboenus australis* (2) [NT]

GUADALUPE CARACARA *Caracara lutosus* (1) [EX]

SOUTHERN CARACARA *Caracara plancus* (2)

CRESTED CARACARA *Caracara cheriway* (1, 2)

YELLOW-HEADED CARACARA *Milvago chimachima* (2)

CHIMANGO CARACARA *Milvago chimango* (2)

Tribe FALCONINI

SPOT-WINGED FALCONET *Spiziapteryx circumcinctus* (2)

PYGMY FALCON *Polihierax semitorquatus* (5)

WHITE-RUMPED FALCON *Polihierax insignis* (4) [NT]

COLLARED FALCONET *Microhierax caerulescens* (3, 4)

BLACK-THIGHED FALCONET *Microhierax fringillarius* (4)

WHITE-FRONTED FALCONET *Microhierax latifrons* (4) [NT]

PHILIPPINE FALCONET *Microhierax erythrogenys* (4)

PIED FALCONET *Microhierax melanoleucus* (4) [NT]

BROWN FALCON *Falco berigora* (6)

LESSER KESTREL *Falco naumanni* (3, 4, 5) [VU]

COMMON KESTREL *Falco tinnunculus* (3, 4, 5)

LESSER CAPE VERDE KESTREL or NEGLECTED KESTREL *Falco neglectus* (5)

GREATER CAPE VERDE KESTREL or ALEXANDER'S KESTREL *Falco alexandri* (5)

MADAGASCAR KESTREL *Falco newtoni* (5)

MAURITIUS KESTREL *Falco punctatus* (5) [EN]

SEYCHELLES KESTREL *Falco araea* (5) [VU]

SPOTTED KESTREL *Falco moluccensis* (4)

AUSTRALIAN KESTREL or NANKEEN KESTREL *Falco cenchroides* (6)

AMERICAN KESTREL *Falco sparverius* (1, 2)

GREATER KESTREL *Falco rupicoloides* (5)

FOX KESTREL *Falco alopex* (5)

GRAY KESTREL *Falco ardosiaceus* (5)

DICKINSON'S KESTREL *Falco dickinsoni* (5)

BANDED KESTREL *Falco zoniventris* (5)

RED-NECKED FALCON *Falco chicquera* (3, 4, 5) [NT]

RED-FOOTED FALCON *Falco vespertinus* (3, 4, 5)

AMUR FALCON *Falco amurensis* (3, 4, 5)

ELEONORA'S FALCON *Falco eleonorae* (3, 5)

SOOTY FALCON *Falco concolor* (3, 5)

APLOMADO FALCON *Falco femoralis* (1, 2)

MERLIN *Falco columbarius* (1, 2, 3, 4)

BAT FALCON *Falco rufigularis* (1, 2)

ORANGE-BREASTED FALCON *Falco deiroleucus* (1, 2) [NT]

EURASIAN HOBBY *Falco subbuteo* (3, 4, 5)

AFRICAN HOBBY *Falco cuvierii* (5)

ORIENTAL HOBBY *Falco severus* (4, 6)

AUSTRALIAN HOBBY *Falco longipennis* (6)

NEW ZEALAND FALCON *Falco novaeseelandiae* (6) [NT]

GRAY FALCON *Falco hypoleucos* (6) [VU]

BLACK FALCON *Falco subniger* (6)

LANNER FALCON *Falco biarmicus* (3, 5)

LAGGAR FALCON *Falco jugger* (3, 4)

SAKER FALCON *Falco cherrug* (3, 4, 5)

GYRFALCON *Falco rusticolus* (1, 3)

PRAIRIE FALCON *Falco mexicanus* (1)

PEREGRINE FALCON *Falco peregrinus* (1, 2, 3, 4, 5, 6)

CAPE VERDE PEREGRINE FALCON or CAPE VERDE PEREGRINE *Falco madens* (5) [CR]

BARBARY FALCON *Falco pelegrinoides* (3, 4, 5)

TAITA FALCON *Falco fasciinucha* (5) [VU]

Order CICONIIFORMES
Family PODICIPEDIDAE

WHITE-TUFTED GREBE *Rollandia rolland* (2)

SHORT-WINGED GREBE or TITICACA FLIGHTLESS GREBE *Rollandia microptera* (2)

LITTLE GREBE *Tachybaptus ruficollis* (3, 4, 5)

AUSTRALASIAN GREBE *Tachybaptus novaehollandiae* (4, 6)

ALAOTRA GREBE *Tachybaptus rufolavatus* (5) [CR]

MADAGASCAR GREBE *Tachybaptus pelzelnii* (5) [VU]

LEAST GREBE *Tachybaptus dominicus* (1, 2)

PIED-BILLED GREBE *Podilymbus podiceps* (1, 2)

ATITLAN GREBE *Podilymbus gigas* (2) [EX]

HOARY-HEADED GREBE *Poliocephalus poliocephalus* (6)

NEW ZEALAND GREBE or NEW ZEALAND DABCHICK *Poliocephalus rufopectus* (6) [EN]

GREAT GREBE *Podiceps major* (2)

RED-NECKED GREBE *Podiceps grisegena* (1, 3, 4)

GREAT CRESTED GREBE *Podiceps cristatus* (3, 4, 5, 6)

HORNED GREBE or SLAVONIAN GREBE *Podiceps auritus* (1, 3, 4)

BLACK-NECKED GREBE or EARED GREBE *Podiceps nigricollis* (1, 2, 3, 4, 5)

COLOMBIAN GREBE *Podiceps andinus* (2) [EX]

SILVERY GREBE *Podiceps occipitalis* (2)

PUNA GREBE or JUNIN GREBE *Podiceps taczanowskii* (2) [CR]

HOODED GREBE *Podiceps gallardoi* (2) [NT]

WESTERN GREBE *Aechmophorus occidentalis* (1)

CLARK'S GREBE *Aechmophorus clarkii* (1)

Family PHAETHONTIDAE

RED-BILLED TROPICBIRD *Phaethon aethereus* (1, 2, 3, 4, 5)

RED-TAILED TROPICBIRD *Phaethon rubricauda* (2, 4, 5, 6)

WHITE-TAILED TROPICBIRD *Phaethon lepturus* (1, 2, 4, 5, 6)

Family SULIDAE

ABBOTT'S BOOBY *Papasula abbotti* (4, 5) [VU]

NORTHERN GANNET *Morus bassanus* (1, 3, 5)

CAPE GANNET *Morus capensis* (5) [NT]

AUSTRALASIAN GANNET *Morus serrator* (2, 4, 6)

BLUE-FOOTED BOOBY *Sula nebouxii* (1, 2)

PERUVIAN BOOBY *Sula variegata* (2)

MASKED BOOBY *Sula dactylatra* (1, 2, 4, 5, 6)

NAZCA BOOBY *Sula granti* (1, 2)

RED-FOOTED BOOBY *Sula sula* (2, 4, 5, 6)

BROWN BOOBY *Sula leucogaster* (1, 2, 4, 5, 6)

Family ANHINGIDAE

ANHINGA *Anhinga anhinga* (1, 2)

AFRICAN DARTER *Anhinga rufa* (5)

ORIENTAL DARTER *Anhinga melanogaster* (3, 4) [NT]

AUSTRALIAN DARTER *Anhinga novaehollandiae* (6)

Family PHALACROCORACIDAE

LONG-TAILED CORMORANT *Phalacrocorax africanus* (5)

CROWNED CORMORANT *Phalacrocorax coronatus* (5) [NT]

PYGMY CORMORANT *Phalacrocorax pygmeus* (3, 5) [NT]

LITTLE CORMORANT *Phalacrocorax niger* (3, 4)

LITTLE PIED CORMORANT *Phalacrocorax melanoleucos* (4, 6)

PALLAS'S CORMORANT *Phalacrocorax perspicillatus* (6) [EX]

BRANDT'S CORMORANT *Phalacrocorax penicillatus* (1)

FLIGHTLESS CORMORANT or GALAPAGÓS CORMORANT *Phalacrocorax harrisi* (2) [VU]

BANK CORMORANT *Phalacrocorax neglectus* (5) [NT]

BLACK-FACED CORMORANT *Phalacrocorax fuscescens* (6)

NEOTROPIC CORMORANT or OLIVACEOUS CORMORANT *Phalacrocorax brasilianus* (1, 2)

DOUBLE-CRESTED CORMORANT *Phalacrocorax auritus* (1, 2, 3)

INDIAN CORMORANT *Phalacrocorax fuscicollis* (3, 4)

PIED CORMORANT *Phalacrocorax varius* (6)

LITTLE BLACK CORMORANT *Phalacrocorax sulcirostris* (4, 6)

GREAT CORMORANT *Phalacrocorax carbo* (1, 3, 4, 5, 6)

JAPANESE CORMORANT *Phalacrocorax capillatus* (3, 4)

SOCOTRA CORMORANT *Phalacrocorax nigrogularis* (3) [NT]

CAPE CORMORANT *Phalacrocorax capensis* (5)

GUANAY CORMORANT *Phalacrocorax bougainvillii* (2)

KERGUELEN SHAG *Phalacrocorax verrucosus* (4)

IMPERIAL SHAG *Phalacrocorax atriceps* (6) [CR]

ANTARCTIC SHAG *Phalacrocorax bransfieldensis* (6)

SOUTH GEORGIA SHAG *Phalacrocorax georgianus* (6)

CROZET SHAG *Phalacrocorax melanogenis* (6)

CAMPBELL ISLAND SHAG *Phalacrocorax campbelli* (6) [VU]

ROUGH-FACED SHAG or NEW ZEALAND KING SHAG *Phalacrocorax carunculatus* (6) [VU]

BRONZE SHAG or STEWART ISLAND SHAG *Phalacrocorax chalconotus* (6) [VU]

CHATHAM ISLANDS SHAG *Phalacrocorax onslowi* (6) [VU]

AUCKLAND ISLANDS SHAG *Phalacrocorax colensoi* (6) [VU]

BOUNTY ISLANDS SHAG *Phalacrocorax ranfurlyi* (6) [VU]

ROCK SHAG *Phalacrocorax magellanicus* (2)

RED-FACED CORMORANT *Phalacrocorax urile* (1, 3, 4)

AMCHITKA CORMORANT *Phalacrocorax kenyoni* (1) [DD]

PELAGIC CORMORANT *Phalacrocorax pelagicus* (1, 3, 4)

EUROPEAN SHAG *Phalacrocorax aristotelis* (3, 5)

RED-LEGGED CORMORANT *Phalacrocorax gaimardi* (2) [NT]

SPOTTED SHAG *Phalacrocorax punctatus* (6)

PITT ISLAND SHAG *Phalacrocorax featherstoni* (6) [VU]

Family ARDEIDAE
Subfamily TIGRISOMATINAE

BARE-THROATED TIGER-HERON *Tigrisoma mexicanum* (2)

FASCIATED TIGER-HERON *Tigrisoma fasciatum* (2) [NT]

RUFESCENT TIGER-HERON *Tigrisoma lineatum* (1, 2)

WHITE-CRESTED TIGER-HERON *Tigriornis leucolophus* (5)

Subfamily COCHLEARIINAE

BOAT-BILLED HERON *Cochlearius cochlearia* (1, 2)

Subfamily BOTAURINAE

FOREST BITTERN *Zonerodius heliosylus* (6) [NT]

ZIGZAG HERON *Zebrilus undulatus* (2) [NT]

STRIPE-BACKED BITTERN *Ixobrychus involucris* (2)

LITTLE BITTERN *Ixobrychus minutus* (3, 4, 5, 6)

YELLOW BITTERN *Ixobrychus sinensis* (3, 4, 6)

BLACK-BACKED BITTERN *Ixobrychus novaezelandiae* (6) [EX]

LEAST BITTERN *Ixobrychus exilis* (1, 2)

SCHRENCK'S BITTERN *Ixobrychus eurhythmus* (4) [NT]

CINNAMON BITTERN *Ixobrychus cinnamomeus* (4)

DWARF BITTERN *Ixobrychus sturmii* (5)

BLACK BITTERN *Ixobrychus flavicollis* (4, 6)

AMERICAN BITTERN *Botaurus lentiginosus* (1, 2, 3)

PINNATED BITTERN *Botaurus pinnatus* (1, 2)

GREAT BITTERN *Botaurus stellaris* (3, 4, 5)

AUSTRALASIAN BITTERN *Botaurus poiciloptilus* (6) [EN]

Subfamily ARDEINAE

AGAMI HERON or CHESTNUT-BELLIED HERON *Agamia agami* (1, 2) [NT]

YELLOW-CROWNED NIGHT-HERON *Nyctanassa violacea* (1, 2)

BLACK-CROWNED NIGHT-HERON *Nycticorax nycticorax* (1, 2, 3, 4, 5)

RUFOUS NIGHT-HERON or NANKEEN NIGHT-HERON *Nycticorax caledonicus* (4, 6)

WHITE-BACKED NIGHT-HERON *Gorsachius leuconotus* (5)

WHITE-EARED NIGHT-HERON *Gorsachius magnificus* (4) [CR]

JAPANESE NIGHT-HERON *Gorsachius goisagi* (4) [VU]

MALAYAN NIGHT-HERON *Gorsachius melanolophus* (4)

WHISTLING HERON *Syrigma sibilatrix* (2)

REDDISH EGRET *Egretta rufescens* (1, 2)

SLATY EGRET *Egretta vinaceigula* (5) [VU]

BLACK HERON *Egretta ardesiaca* (5)

TRICOLORED HERON *Egretta tricolor* (1, 2)

WHITE-FACED HERON *Egretta novaehollandiae* (4, 6)

LITTLE BLUE HERON *Egretta caerulea* (1, 2)

LITTLE EGRET *Egretta garzetta* (3, 4, 5, 6)

WESTERN REEF-EGRET *Egretta gularis* (5)

DIMORPHIC EGRET *Egretta dimorpha* (5)

SNOWY EGRET *Egretta thula* (1, 2)

CHINESE EGRET *Egretta eulophotes* (3, 4) [EN]

PACIFIC REEF-EGRET or EASTERN REEF-EGRET *Egretta sacra* (4, 6)

CAPPED HERON *Pilherodius pileatus* (2)

GRAY HERON *Ardea cinerea* (3, 4, 5)

GREAT BLUE HERON *Ardea herodias* (1, 2)

COCOI HERON *Ardea cocoi* (2)

PACIFIC HERON or WHITE-NECKED HERON *Ardea pacifica* (6)

BLACK-HEADED HERON *Ardea melanocephala* (5)

HUMBLOT'S HERON or MADAGASCAR HERON *Ardea humbloti* (5) [VU]

GOLIATH HERON *Ardea goliath* (4, 5)

WHITE-BELLIED HERON *Ardea insignis* (4) [EN]

GREAT-BILLED HERON *Ardea sumatrana* (4, 6) [NT]

PURPLE HERON *Ardea purpurea* (3, 4, 5)

CAPE VERDE PURPLE HERON *Ardea bournei* (5) [CR]

PIED HERON *Ardea picata* (4, 6)

GREAT EGRET *Ardea alba* (1, 2, 3, 4, 5, 6)

INTERMEDIATE EGRET *Ardea intermedia* (4, 5, 6)

CATTLE EGRET *Bubulcus ibis* (1, 2, 3, 4, 5, 6)

SQUACCO HERON *Ardeola ralloides* (3, 5)

INDIAN POND-HERON *Ardeola grayii* (3, 4)

CHINESE POND-HERON *Ardeola bacchus* (4)

JAVAN POND-HERON *Ardeola speciosa* (4)

MADAGASCAR POND-HERON *Ardeola idea* (5) [NT]

RUFOUS-BELLIED HERON *Ardeola rufiventris* (5)

STRIATED HERON or LITTLE HERON *Butorides striatus* (2, 3, 4, 5, 6)

GREEN HERON *Butorides virescens* (1, 2)

GALAPAGÓS HERON *Butorides sundevalli* (2)

Family SCOPIDAE

HAMERKOP or HAMMERHEAD *Scopus umbretta* (5)

Family PHOENICOPTERIDAE

GREATER FLAMINGO *Phoenicopterus ruber* (1, 2, 3, 4, 5)

CHILEAN FLAMINGO *Phoenicopterus chilensis* (2)

LESSER FLAMINGO *Phoenicopterus minor* (4, 5) [NT]

ANDEAN FLAMINGO *Phoenicopterus andinus* (2) [VU]

PUNA FLAMINGO or JAMES'S FLAMINGO *Phoenicopterus jamesi* (2) [VU]

Family THRESKIORNITHIDAE

WHITE IBIS *Eudocimus albus* (1, 2)

SCARLET IBIS *Eudocimus ruber* (1, 2)

WHISPERING IBIS *Phimosus infuscatus* (2)

GLOSSY IBIS *Plegadis falcinellus* (1, 2, 3, 4, 5, 6)

WHITE-FACED IBIS *Plegadis chihi* (1, 2)

PUNA IBIS *Plegadis ridgwayi* (2)

SHARP-TAILED IBIS *Cercibis oxycerca* (2)

PLUMBEOUS IBIS *Theristicus caerulescens* (2)

BUFF-NECKED IBIS *Theristicus caudatus* (2)

ANDEAN IBIS *Theristicus branickii* (2)

BLACK-FACED IBIS *Theristicus melanopis* (2)

GREEN IBIS *Mesembrinibis cayennensis* (2)

HADADA IBIS *Bostrychia hagedash* (5)

WATTLED IBIS *Bostrychia carunculata* (5)

OLIVE IBIS *Bostrychia olivacea* (5)

DWARF OLIVE IBIS *Bostrychia bocagei* (5) [CR]

SPOT-BREASTED IBIS *Bostrychia rara* (5)

WALDRAPP or NORTHERN BALD IBIS *Geronticus eremita* (5) [CR]

BALD IBIS or SOUTHERN BALD IBIS *Geronticus calvus* (5) [VU]

WHITE-WINGED IBIS *Lophotibis cristata* (5) [NT]

SACRED IBIS *Threskiornis aethiopicus* (3, 5)

BLACK-HEADED IBIS *Threskiornis melanocephalus* (4) [NT]

AUSTRALIAN IBIS or AUSTRALIAN WHITE IBIS *Threskiornis molucca* (6)

STRAW-NECKED IBIS *Threskiornis spinicollis* (6)

RED-NAPED IBIS or BLACK IBIS *Pseudibis papillosa* (4) [NT]

WHITE-SHOULDERED IBIS *Pseudibis davisoni* (4) [EN]

GIANT IBIS *Pseudibis gigantea* (4) [CR]

CRESTED IBIS *Nipponia nippon* (4) [CR]

EURASIAN SPOONBILL *Platalea leucorodia* (3, 4, 5)

ROYAL SPOONBILL *Platalea regia* (6)

AFRICAN SPOONBILL *Platalea alba* (5)

BLACK-FACED SPOONBILL *Platalea minor* (4) [CR]

YELLOW-BILLED SPOONBILL *Platalea flavipes* (6)

ROSEATE SPOONBILL *Ajaia ajaja* (1, 2)

Family PELECANIDAE
Subfamily BALAENICIPITINAE

SHOEBILL *Balaeniceps rex* (5) [NT]

Subfamily PELECANINAE

GREAT WHITE PELICAN *Pelecanus onocrotalus* (3, 4, 5)

PINK-BACKED PELICAN *Pelecanus rufescens* (3, 5)

DALMATIAN PELICAN *Pelecanus crispus* (3, 4) [VU]

SPOT-BILLED PELICAN *Pelecanus philippensis* (4) [VU]

AUSTRALIAN PELICAN *Pelecanus conspicillatus* (4, 6)

AMERICAN WHITE PELICAN *Pelecanus erythrorhynchos* (1, 2)

BROWN PELICAN *Pelecanus occidentalis* (1, 2)

PERUVIAN PELICAN *Pelecanus thagus* (2)

Family CICONIIDAE
Subfamily CATHARTINAE

BLACK VULTURE *Coragyps atratus* (1, 2)

TURKEY VULTURE *Cathartes aura* (1, 2)

LESSER YELLOW-HEADED VULTURE *Cathartes burrovianus* (1, 2)

GREATER YELLOW-HEADED VULTURE *Cathartes melambrotus* (2)

CALIFORNIA CONDOR *Gymnogyps californianus* (1) [CR]

ANDEAN CONDOR *Vultur gryphus* (2)

KING VULTURE *Sarcoramphus papa* (1, 2)

Subfamily CICONIINAE

WOOD STORK *Mycteria americana* (1, 2)

MILKY STORK *Mycteria cinerea* (4) [VU]

YELLOW-BILLED STORK *Mycteria ibis* (5)

PAINTED STORK *Mycteria leucocephala* (4) [NT]

ASIAN OPENBILL *Anastomus oscitans* (4) [NT]

AFRICAN OPENBILL *Anastomus lamelligerus* (5)

BLACK STORK *Ciconia nigra* (3, 4, 5)

ABDIM'S STORK *Ciconia abdimii* (5)

WOOLY-NECKED STORK *Ciconia episcopus* (4, 5)

STORM'S STORK *Ciconia stormi* (4) [EN]

MAGUARI STORK *Ciconia maguari* (2)

WHITE STORK *Ciconia ciconia* (3, 5)

ORIENTAL STORK *Ciconia boyciana* (3, 4) [EN]

BLACK-NECKED STORK *Ephippiorhynchus asiaticus* (4, 6)

SADDLE-BILLED STORK *Ephippiorhynchus senegalensis* (5)

JABIRU *Jabiru mycteria* (1, 2)

LESSER ADJUTANT *Leptoptilos javanicus* (4) [VU]

MARABOU STORK *Leptoptilos crumeniferus* (5)

GREATER ADJUTANT *Leptoptilos dubius* (4) [EN]

Family FREGATIDAE

MAGNIFICENT FRIGATEBIRD *Fregata magnificens* (1, 2, 5)

ASCENSION FRIGATEBIRD *Fregata aquila* (2, 5) [CR]

GREAT FRIGATEBIRD *Fregata minor* (2, 4, 5, 6)

LESSER FRIGATEBIRD *Fregata ariel* (2, 4, 5, 6)

CHRISTMAS ISLAND FRIGATEBIRD *Fregata andrewsi* (4) [VU]

Family SPHENISCIDAE

KING PENGUIN *Aptenodytes patagonicus* (2, 5, 6)

EMPEROR PENGUIN *Aptenodytes forsteri* (6)

GENTOO PENGUIN *Pygoscelis papua* (2, 6)

ADÉLIE PENGUIN *Pygoscelis adeliae* (2, 6)

CHINSTRAP PENGUIN *Pygoscelis antarctica* (2, 6)

ROCKHOPPER PENGUIN *Eudyptes chrysocome* (2, 5, 6)

FIORDLAND PENGUIN *Eudyptes pachyrhynchus* (6) [VU]

SNARES PENGUIN or SNARES ISLANDS PENGUIN *Eudyptes robustus* (6) [VU]

ERECT-CRESTED PENGUIN *Eudyptes sclateri* (6) [VU]

MACARONI PENGUIN *Eudyptes chrysolophus* (2, 5, 6)

ROYAL PENGUIN *Eudyptes schlegeli* (6)

YELLOW-EYED PENGUIN *Megadyptes antipodes* (6) [VU]

LITTLE PENGUIN *Eudyptula minor* (6)

JACKASS PENGUIN *Spheniscus demersus* (5) [NT]

HUMBOLDT PENGUIN *Spheniscus humboldti* (2) [NT]

MAGELLANIC PENGUIN *Spheniscus magellanicus* (2, 6)

GALÁPAGOS PENGUIN *Spheniscus mendiculus* (2) [VU]

Family GAVIIDAE

RED-THROATED LOON *Gavia stellata* (1, 3, 4)

ARCTIC LOON *Gavia arctica* (1, 3, 4)

PACIFIC LOON *Gavia pacifica* (1, 3)

COMMON LOON *Gavia immer* (1, 3, 5)

YELLOW-BILLED LOON *Gavia adamsii* (1, 3)

Family PROCELLARIIDAE
Subfamily PROCELLARIINAE

ANTARCTIC GIANT-PETREL or SOUTHERN GIANT-PETREL *Macronectes giganteus* (2, 6)

HALL'S GIANT-PETREL or NORTHERN GIANT-PETREL *Macronectes halli* (2, 6) [NT]

NORTHERN FULMAR *Fulmarus glacialis* (1, 2, 3, 4)

SOUTHERN FULMAR *Fulmarus glacialoides* (2, 5, 6)

ANTARCTIC PETREL *Thalassoica antarctica* (2, 5, 6)

CAPE PETREL *Daption capense* (2, 6)

SNOW PETREL *Pagodroma nivea* (6)

KERGUELEN PETREL *Lugensa brevirostris* (4, 5, 6)

MASCARENE PETREL or MASCARENE BLACK PETREL *Pterodroma aterrima* (6) [CR]

BECK'S PETREL *Pterodroma becki* (6) [CR]

TAHITI PETREL *Pterodroma rostrata* (1, 6)

FIJI PETREL *Pterodroma macgillivrayi* (6) [CR]

CHATHAM ISLANDS PETREL *Pterodroma axillaris* (6) [CR]

BLACK-WINGED PETREL *Pterodroma nigripennis* (4, 6)

WHITE-NECKED PETREL *Pterodroma cervicalis* (2, 4) [VU]

MOTTLED PETREL *Pterodroma inexpectata* (1, 6)

BONIN PETREL *Pterodroma hypoleuca* (2, 6)

WHITE-WINGED PETREL or GOULD'S PETREL *Pterodroma leucoptera* (2, 4, 6)

COLLARED PETREL *Pterodroma brevipes* (5)

COOK'S PETREL *Pterodroma cookii* (1, 6) [VU]

DEFILLIPI'S PETREL or DEFILIPPE'S PETREL *Pterodroma defilippiana* (2) [VU]

PYCROFT'S PETREL *Pterodroma pycrofti* (6) [VU]

STEJNEGER'S PETREL *Pterodroma longirostris* (1, 2, 4)

PHOENIX PETREL *Pterodroma alba* (2, 6)

TRINDADE PETREL *Pterodroma arminjoniana* (1, 2, 4)

HERALD PETREL *Pterodroma heraldica* (2, 6)

HENDERSON PETREL *Pterodroma atrata* (6)

HAWAIIAN PETREL *Pterodroma sandwichensis* (2, 6) [VU]

GALAPAGÓS PETREL or DARK-RUMPED PETREL *Pterodroma phaeopygia* (1, 2) [CR]

KERMADEC PETREL *Pterodroma neglecta* (1, 2, 6)

JUAN FERNANDEZ PETREL *Pterodroma externa* (1, 2, 4, 6)

BARAU'S PETREL *Pterodroma baraui* (4, 6) [CR]

MURPHY'S PETREL *Pterodroma ultima* (1, 2, 6)

SOLANDER'S PETREL or PROVIDENCE PETREL *Pterodroma solandri* (2, 4, 6) [VU]

GREAT-WINGED PETREL *Pterodroma macroptera* (4, 5)

MAGENTA PETREL *Pterodroma magentae* (6) [CR]

WHITE-HEADED PETREL *Pterodroma lessonii* (6)

ZINO'S PETREL or MADEIRA PETREL *Pterodroma madeira* (2, 5) [CR]

FEA'S PETREL or CAPE VERDE PETREL *Pterodroma feae* (5) [VU]

SOFT-PLUMAGED PETREL *Pterodroma mollis* (4)

ATLANTIC PETREL *Pterodroma incerta* (2, 4, 5) [VU]

BERMUDA PETREL *Pterodroma cahow* (2) [EN]

BLACK-CAPPED PETREL *Pterodroma hasitata* (2) [EN]

JAMAICA PETREL or BLUE MOUNTAIN DUCK *Pterodroma caribbaea* (2) [CR]

BLUE PETREL *Halobaena caerulea* (2, 5, 6)

BROAD-BILLED PRION *Pachyptila vittata* (4, 5, 6)

MEDIUM-BILLED PRION *Pachyptila salvini* (4, 5, 6)

ANTARCTIC PRION *Pachyptila desolata* (2, 5, 6)

SLENDER-BILLED PRION *Pachyptila belcheri* (2, 5, 6)

FAIRY PRION *Pachyptila turtur* (6)

FULMAR PRION *Pachyptila crassirostris* (6)

BULWER'S PETREL *Bulweria bulwerii* (1, 2, 4, 5)

JOUANIN'S PETREL *Bulweria fallax* (2, 3, 4)

WHITE-CHINNED PETREL *Procellaria aequinoctialis* (2, 4, 6)

PARKINSON'S PETREL or BLACK PETREL *Procellaria parkinsoni* (1, 6) [VU]

WESTLAND PETREL *Procellaria westlandica* (6) [VU]

GRAY PETREL *Procellaria cinerea* (4, 6)

CORY'S SHEARWATER *Calonectris diomedea* (2, 3, 5)

CAPE VERDE SHEARWATER *Calonectris edwardsii* (5)

STREAKED SHEARWATER *Calonectris leucomelas* (4, 6)

WEDGE-TAILED SHEARWATER *Puffinus pacificus* (1, 2, 4, 5, 6)

BULLER'S SHEARWATER *Puffinus bulleri* (1, 2, 4, 6) [NT]

FLESH-FOOTED SHEARWATER *Puffinus carneipes* (1, 3, 4, 6)

PINK-FOOTED SHEARWATER *Puffinus creatopus* (1, 2, 6) [VU]

GREAT SHEARWATER or GREATER SHEARWATER *Puffinus gravis* (1, 2, 4)

SOOTY SHEARWATER *Puffinus griseus* (1, 2, 4, 5, 6)

SHORT-TAILED SHEARWATER *Puffinus tenuirostris* (1, 4, 6)

CHRISTMAS ISLAND SHEARWATER *Puffinus nativitatis* (1, 2, 4, 6)

MANX SHEARWATER *Puffinus puffinus* (1, 2, 3, 5)

MEDITERRANEAN SHEARWATER or YELKOUAN SHEARWATER *Puffinus yelkouan* (3)

BALEARIC SHEARWATER *Puffinus mauretanicus* (3, 5)

TOWNSEND'S SHEARWATER *Puffinus auricularis* (1, 2) [VU]

NEWELL'S SHEARWATER *Puffinus newelli* (2, 4, 6) [VU]

BLACK-VENTED SHEARWATER *Puffinus opisthomelas* (1) [VU]

FLUTTERING SHEARWATER *Puffinus gavia* (4, 6)

HUTTON'S SHEARWATER *Puffinus huttoni* (6) [EN]

MASCARENE SHEARWATER *Puffinus atrodorsalis* (5)

LITTLE SHEARWATER *Puffinus assimilis* (1, 2, 4, 5, 6)

CAPE VERDE LITTLE SHEARWATER *Puffinus boydi* (5)

AUDUBON'S SHEARWATER *Puffinus lherminieri* (1, 2, 4, 5, 6)

PERSIAN SHEARWATER *Puffinus persicus* (3)

BANNERMAN'S SHEARWATER *Puffinus bannermani* (2)

HEINROTH'S SHEARWATER *Puffinus heinrothi* (6) [EN]

PERUVIAN DIVING-PETREL *Pelecanoides garnotii* (2) [EN]

MAGELLANIC DIVING-PETREL *Pelecanoides magellani* (2)

SOUTH GEORGIA DIVING-PETREL *Pelecanoides georgicus* (6)

COMMON DIVING-PETREL *Pelecanoides urinatrix* (2, 4, 6)

Subfamily DIOMEDEINAE

WANDERING ALBATROSS *Diomedea exulans*
(1, 2, 4, 6) [VU]

AMSTERDAM ISLAND ALBATROSS or AMSTERDAM
ALBATROSS *Diomedea amsterdamensis* (6)
[CR]

ROYAL ALBATROSS *Diomedea epomophora*
(2, 6) [NT]

WAVED ALBATROSS *Diomedea irrorata* (2)
[NT]

SHORT-TAILED ALBATROSS *Diomedea albatrus*
(6) [EN]

BLACK-FOOTED ALBATROSS *Diomedea nigripes*
(2, 4)

LAYSAN ALBATROSS *Diomedea immutabilis*
(1, 2, 4)

BLACK-BROWED ALBATROSS *Diomedea
melanophris* (2, 3, 4, 6)

SHY ALBATROSS or WHITE-CAPPED ALBATROSS
Diomedea cauta (2, 5, 6) [CR, SPP]

GRAY-HEADED ALBATROSS *Diomedea chrysostoma* (4) [NT]

YELLOW-NOSED ALBATROSS *Diomedea
chlororhynchos* (4, 6)

BULLER'S ALBATROSS *Diomedea bulleri* (2, 6)
[NT]

SOOTY ALBATROSS *Phoebetria fusca* (4, 6)
[NT]

LIGHT-MANTLED ALBATROSS or LIGHT-
MANTLED SOOTY ALBATROSS *Phoebetria
palpebrata* (6)

Subfamily HYDROBATINAE

WILSON'S STORM-PETREL *Oceanites oceanicus*
(1, 2, 3, 4)

WHITE-VENTED STORM-PETREL or ELLIOT'S
STORM-PETREL *Oceanites gracilis* (2) [DD]

GRAY-BACKED STORM-PETREL *Garrodia nereis*
(2, 6)

WHITE-FACED STORM-PETREL *Pelagodroma
marina* (4, 5, 6)

BLACK-BELLIED STORM-PETREL *Fregetta tropica*
(4, 5, 6)

WHITE-BELLIED STORM-PETREL *Fregetta grallaria* (2, 4, 5, 6)

POLYNESIAN STORM-PETREL *Nesofregetta fuliginosa* (2, 6)

EUROPEAN STORM-PETREL *Hydrobates pelagicus* (3, 4, 5)

LEAST STORM-PETREL *Oceanodroma micro-
soma* (1, 2)

WEDGE-RUMPED STORM-PETREL or GALAPAGÓS
STORM-PETREL *Oceanodroma tethys* (2)
[NT]

BAND-RUMPED STORM-PETREL or HARCOURT'S
STORM-PETREL *Oceanodroma castro*
(1, 2, 3, 4, 5)

LEACH'S STORM-PETREL *Oceanodroma leu-
corhoa* (1, 2, 3, 4, 5)

SWINHOE'S STORM-PETREL *Oceanodroma
monorhis* (3, 4) [NT]

GUADALUPE STORM-PETREL *Oceanodroma
macrodactyla* (1) [CR]

TRISTRAM'S STORM-PETREL *Oceanodroma tristrami* (2) [NT]

MARKHAM'S STORM-PETREL *Oceanodroma
markhami* (2) [DD]

MATSUDAIRA'S STORM-PETREL *Oceanodroma
matsudairae* (2, 4, 5, 6) [DD]

BLACK STORM-PETREL *Oceanodroma melania*
(1, 2)

ASHY STORM-PETREL *Oceanodroma
homochroa* (1) [NT]

RINGED STORM-PETREL *Oceanodroma hornbyi*
(2) [DD]

FORK-TAILED STORM-PETREL *Oceanodroma
furcata* (1, 2, 3, 4)

Order PASSERIFORMES
Suborder TYRANNI
Infraorder ACANTHISITTIDES
Family ACANTHISITTIDAE

RIFLEMAN *Acanthisitta chloris* (6)

BUSH WREN *Xenicus longipes* (6) [EX]

SOUTH ISLAND WREN *Xenicus gilviventris* (6) [NT]

STEPHENS ISLAND WREN *Xenicus lyalli* (6) [EX]

Infraorder EURYLAIMIDES
Family PITTIDAE

EARED PITTA *Pitta phayrei* (4)

BLUE-NAPED PITTA *Pitta nipalensis* (4) [NT]

BLUE-RUMPED PITTA *Pitta soror* (4) [NT]

RUSTY-NAPED PITTA *Pitta oatesi* (4)

SCHNEIDER'S PITTA *Pitta schneideri* (4) [VU]

GIANT PITTA *Pitta caerulea* (4) [NT]

BLUE PITTA *Pitta cyanea* (4)

BANDED PITTA *Pitta guajana* (4)

BAR-BELLIED PITTA *Pitta elliotii* (4) [NT]

GURNEY'S PITTA *Pitta gurneyi* (4) [CR]

BLUE-HEADED PITTA *Pitta baudii* (4) [NT]

HOODED PITTA *Pitta sordida* (4, 6)

IVORY-BREASTED PITTA *Pitta maxima* (4)

SUPERB PITTA *Pitta superba* (6) [VU]

AZURE-BREASTED PITTA *Pitta steerii* (4) [VU]

WHISKERED PITTA *Pitta kochi* (4) [VU]

RED-BELLIED PITTA *Pitta erythrogaster* (4, 6)

SULA PITTA *Pitta dohertyi* (4) [NT]

BLUE-BANDED PITTA *Pitta arquata* (4)

GARNET PITTA *Pitta granatina* (4)

BLACK-AND-CRIMSON PITTA *Pitta ussheri* (4)

BLACK-CROWNED PITTA or GRACEFUL PITTA *Pitta venusta* (4)

AFRICAN PITTA *Pitta angolensis* (5)

GREEN-BREASTED PITTA *Pitta reichenowi* (5)

INDIAN PITTA *Pitta brachyura* (4)

FAIRY PITTA *Pitta nympha* (4) [VU]

BLUE-WINGED PITTA *Pitta moluccensis* (4, 6)

MANGROVE PITTA *Pitta megarhyncha* (4) [NT]

ELEGANT PITTA *Pitta elegans* (4)

RAINBOW PITTA *Pitta iris* (6)

NOISY PITTA *Pitta versicolor* (6)

BLACK-FACED PITTA *Pitta anerythra* (4) [VU]

Family EURYLAIMIDAE

AFRICAN BROADBILL *Smithornis capensis* (5)

GRAY-HEADED BROADBILL *Smithornis sharpei* (5)

RUFOUS-SIDED BROADBILL *Smithornis rufolateralis* (5)

GRAUER'S BROADBILL or AFRICAN GREEN BROADBILL *Pseudocalyptomena graueri* (5) [VU]

DUSKY BROADBILL *Corydon sumatranus* (4)

BLACK-AND-RED BROADBILL *Cymbirhynchus macrorhynchos* (4)

BANDED BROADBILL *Eurylaimus javanicus* (4)

BLACK-AND-YELLOW BROADBILL *Eurylaimus ochromalus* (4)

MINDANAO WATTLED BROADBILL *Eurylaimus steerii* (4) [VU]

VISAYAN WATTLED BROADBILL *Eurylaimus samarensis* (4) [VU]

SILVER-BREASTED BROADBILL *Serilophus lunatus* (4)

LONG-TAILED BROADBILL *Psarisomus dalhousiae* (3, 4)

GREEN BROADBILL *Calyptomena viridis* (4)

HOSE'S BROADBILL *Calyptomena hosii* (4)

WHITEHEAD'S BROADBILL *Calyptomena whiteheadi* (4)

Family PHILEPITTIDAE

VELVET ASITY *Philepitta castanea* (5)

SCHLEGEL'S ASITY *Philepitta schlegeli* (5) [NT]

SUNBIRD ASITY *Neodrepanis coruscans* (5)

YELLOW-BELLIED ASITY *Neodrepanis hypoxantha* (5) [EN]

Family TYRANNIDAE

BROAD-BILLED SAPAYOA *Sapayoa aenigma* (2)

Subfamily CORYTHOPIDINAE

STREAK-NECKED FLYCATCHER *Mionectes striaticollis* (2)

OLIVE-STRIPED FLYCATCHER *Mionectes olivaceus* (2)

OCHER-BELLIED FLYCATCHER *Mionectes oleagineus* (1, 2)

MACCONNELL'S FLYCATCHER *Mionectes macconnelli* (2)

GRAY-HOODED FLYCATCHER *Mionectes rufiventris* (2)

RUFOUS-BREASTED FLYCATCHER *Leptopogon rufipectus* (2)

INCA FLYCATCHER *Leptopogon taczanowskii* (2)

SEPIA-CAPPED FLYCATCHER *Leptopogon amaurocephalus* (1, 2)

SLATY-CAPPED FLYCATCHER *Leptopogon superciliaris* (2)

BRONZE-OLIVE PYGMY-TYRANT *Pseudotriccus pelzelni* (2)

HAZEL-FRONTED PYGMY-TYRANT *Pseudotriccus simplex* (2)

RUFOUS-HEADED PYGMY-TYRANT *Pseudotriccus ruficeps* (2)

RUFOUS-CROWNED TODY-TYRANT *Poecilotriccus ruficeps* (2)

BLACK-AND-WHITE TODY-TYRANT *Poecilotriccus capitalis* (2)

WHITE-CHEEKED TODY-TYRANT *Poecilotriccus albifacies* (2) [NT]

BLACK-CHESTED TYRANT *Taeniotriccus andrei* (2)

SNETHLAGE'S TODY-TYRANT *Hemitriccus minor* (2)

YUNGAS TODY-TYRANT *Hemitriccus spodiops* (2)

BOAT-BILLED TODY-TYRANT *Hemitriccus josephinae* (2) [NT]

FLAMMULATED BAMBOO-TYRANT *Hemitriccus flammulatus* (2)

DRAB-BREASTED BAMBOO-TYRANT *Hemitriccus diops* (2)

BROWN-BREASTED BAMBOO-TYRANT *Hemitriccus obsoletus* (2)

WHITE-EYED TODY-TYRANT *Hemitriccus zosterops* (2)

ZIMMER'S TODY-TYRANT *Hemitriccus minimus* (2) [NT]

EYE-RINGED TODY-TYRANT *Hemitriccus orbitatus* (2) [NT]

JOHANNES'S TODY-TYRANT *Hemitriccus iohannis* (2)

STRIPE-NECKED TODY-TYRANT *Hemitriccus striaticollis* (2)

HANGNEST TODY-TYRANT *Hemitriccus nidipendulus* (2) [NT]

PEARLY-VENTED TODY-TYRANT *Hemitriccus margaritaceiventer* (2)

PELZELN'S TODY-TYRANT *Hemitriccus inornatus* (2)

BLACK-THROATED TODY-TYRANT *Hemitriccus granadensis* (2)

BUFF-THROATED TODY-TYRANT *Hemitriccus rufigularis* (2) [NT]

CINNAMON-BREASTED TODY-TYRANT *Hemitriccus cinnamomeipectus* (2) [NT]

BUFF-BREASTED TODY-TYRANT *Hemitriccus mirandae* (2) [VU]

KAEMPFER'S TODY-TYRANT *Hemitriccus kaempferi* (2) [EN]

FORK-TAILED TODY-TYRANT *Hemitriccus furcatus* (2) [VU]

BUFF-CHEEKED TODY-FLYCATCHER *Todirostrum senex* (2)

RUDDY TODY-FLYCATCHER *Todirostrum russatum* (2)

OCHER-FACED TODY-FLYCATCHER *Todirostrum plumbeiceps* (2)

RUSTY-FRONTED TODY-FLYCATCHER *Todirostrum latirostre* (2)

SMOKY-FRONTED TODY-FLYCATCHER *Todirostrum fumifrons* (2)

SLATE-HEADED TODY-FLYCATCHER *Todirostrum sylvia* (1, 2)

SPOTTED TODY-FLYCATCHER *Todirostrum maculatum* (2)

YELLOW-LORED TODY-FLYCATCHER *Todirostrum poliocephalum* (2)

COMMON TODY-FLYCATCHER *Todirostrum cinereum* (1, 2)

MARACAIBO TODY-FLYCATCHER *Todirostrum viridanum* (2) [NT]

BLACK-HEADED TODY-FLYCATCHER *Todirostrum nigriceps* (2)

PAINTED TODY-FLYCATCHER *Todirostrum pictum* (2)

YELLOW-BROWED TODY-FLYCATCHER *Todirostrum chrysocrotaphum* (2)

GOLDEN-WINGED TODY-FLYCATCHER *Todirostrum calopterum* (2)

BLACK-BACKED TODY-FLYCATCHER *Todirostrum pulchellum* (2)

RINGED ANTPIPIT *Corythopis torquata* (2)

SOUTHERN ANTPIPIT *Corythopis delalandi* (2)

Subfamily TYRANNINAE

PLANALTO TYRANNULET *Phyllomyias fasciatus* (2)

WHITE-FRONTED TYRANNULET *Phyllomyias zeledoni* (2)

ROUGH-LEGGED TYRANNULET *Phyllomyias burmeisteri* (2)

REISER'S TYRANNULET *Phyllomyias reiseri* (2) [NT]

URICH'S TYRANNULET *Phyllomyias urichi* (2)

GREENISH TYRANNULET *Phyllomyias virescens* (2)

SCLATER'S TYRANNULET *Phyllomyias sclateri* (2)

GRAY-CAPPED TYRANNULET *Phyllomyias griseocapilla* (2) [NT]

SOOTY-HEADED TYRANNULET *Phyllomyias griseiceps* (2)

PLUMBEOUS-CROWNED TYRANNULET *Phyllomyias plumbeiceps* (2)

BLACK-CAPPED TYRANNULET *Phyllomyias nigrocapillus* (2)

ASHY-HEADED TYRANNULET *Phyllomyias cinereiceps* (2)

TAWNY-RUMPED TYRANNULET *Phyllomyias uropygialis* (2)

PALTRY TYRANNULET *Zimmerius vilissimus* (1, 2)

VENEZUELAN TYRANNULET *Zimmerius improbus* (2)

BOLIVIAN TYRANNULET *Zimmerius bolivianus* (2)

RED-BILLED TYRANNULET *Zimmerius cinereicapillus* (2)

SLENDER-FOOTED TYRANNULET *Zimmerius gracilipes* (2)

PERUVIAN TYRANNULET *Zimmerius viridiflavus* (2)

GOLDEN-FACED TYRANNULET *Zimmerius chrysops* (2)

WHITE-LORED TYRANNULET *Ornithion inerme* (2)

YELLOW-BELLIED TYRANNULET *Ornithion semiflavum* (1, 2)

BROWN-CAPPED TYRANNULET *Ornithion brunneicapillum* (2)

NORTHERN BEARDLESS-TYRANNULET *Camptostoma imberbe* (1, 2)

SOUTHERN BEARDLESS-TYRANNULET *Camptostoma obsoletum* (2)

MOUSE-COLORED TYRANNULET *Phaeomyias murina* (2)

COCOS FLYCATCHER *Nesotriccus ridgwayi* (2) [VU]

YELLOW TYRANNULET *Capsiempis flaveola* (2)

NORTHERN SCRUB-FLYCATCHER *Sublegatus arenarum* (2)

AMAZONIAN SCRUB-FLYCATCHER *Sublegatus obscurior* (2)

SOUTHERN SCRUB-FLYCATCHER *Sublegatus modestus* (2)

CAMPO SUIRIRI *Suiriri affinis* (2)

CHACO SUIRIRI or SUIRIRI FLYCATCHER *Suiriri suiriri* (2)

YELLOW-CROWNED TYRANNULET *Tyrannulus elatus* (2)

FOREST ELAENIA *Myiopagis gaimardii* (2)

GRAY ELAENIA *Myiopagis caniceps* (2)

PACIFIC ELAENIA *Myiopagis subplacens* (2)

YELLOW-CROWNED ELAENIA *Myiopagis flavivertex* (2)

JAMAICAN ELAENIA *Myiopagis cotta* (2)

GREENISH ELAENIA *Myiopagis viridicata* (1, 2)

GRAY-AND-WHITE TYRANNULET *Pseudelaenia leucospodia* (2)

CARIBBEAN ELAENIA *Elaenia martinica* (2)

YELLOW-BELLIED ELAENIA *Elaenia flavogaster* (1, 2)

LARGE ELAENIA *Elaenia spectabilis* (2)

NORONHA ELAENIA *Elaenia ridleyana* (2)

WHITE-CRESTED ELAENIA *Elaenia albiceps* (2)

SMALL-BILLED ELAENIA *Elaenia parvirostris* (2)

SLATY ELAENIA *Elaenia strepera* (2)

OLIVACEOUS ELAENIA *Elaenia mesoleuca* (2)

MOTTLE-BACKED ELAENIA *Elaenia gigas* (2)

BROWNISH ELAENIA *Elaenia pelzelni* (2)

PLAIN-CRESTED ELAENIA *Elaenia cristata* (2)

RUFOUS-CROWNED ELAENIA *Elaenia ruficeps* (2)

LESSER ELAENIA *Elaenia chiriquensis* (2)

MOUNTAIN ELAENIA *Elaenia frantzii* (2)

HIGHLAND ELAENIA *Elaenia obscura* (2)

GREAT ELAENIA *Elaenia dayi* (2)

SIERRAN ELAENIA *Elaenia pallatangae* (2)

GREATER ANTILLEAN ELAENIA *Elaenia fallax* (2)

WHITE-THROATED TYRANNULET *Mecocerculus leucophrys* (2)

WHITE-TAILED TYRANNULET *Mecocerculus poecilocercus* (2)

BUFF-BANDED TYRANNULET *Mecocerculus hellmayri* (2)

RUFOUS-WINGED TYRANNULET *Mecocerculus calopterus* (2)

SULFUR-BELLIED TYRANNULET *Mecocerculus mino* (2)

WHITE-BANDED TYRANNULET *Mecocerculus stictopterus* (2)

TORRENT TYRANNULET *Serpophaga cinerea* (2)

SOOTY TYRANNULET *Serpophaga nigricans* (2)

RIVER TYRANNULET *Serpophaga hypoleuca* (2)

WHITE-CRESTED TYRANNULET *Serpophaga subcristata* (2)

WHITE-BELLIED TYRANNULET *Serpophaga munda* (2)

SLENDER-BILLED TYRANNULET *Inezia tenuirostris* (2)

PLAIN TYRANNULET *Inezia inornata* (2)

PALE-TIPPED TYRANNULET *Inezia subflava* (2)

LESSER WAGTAIL-TYRANT *Stigmatura napensis* (2)

GREATER WAGTAIL-TYRANT *Stigmatura budytoides* (2)

AGILE TIT-TYRANT *Uromyias agilis* (2)

UNSTREAKED TIT-TYRANT *Uromyias agraphia* (2)

ASH-BREASTED TIT-TYRANT *Anairetes alpinus* (2) [EN]

MARANON TIT-TYRANT *Anairetes nigrocristatus* (2)

PIED-CRESTED TIT-TYRANT *Anairetes reguloides* (2)

YELLOW-BILLED TIT-TYRANT *Anairetes flavirostris* (2)

JUAN FERNANDEZ TIT-TYRANT *Anairetes fernandezianus* (2)

TUFTED TIT-TYRANT *Anairetes parulus* (2)

MANY-COLORED RUSH-TYRANT *Tachuris rubrigastra* (2)

SHARP-TAILED GRASS-TYRANT *Culicivora caudacuta* (2) [NT]

BEARDED TACHURI *Polystictus pectoralis* (2) [NT]

GRAY-BACKED TACHURI *Polystictus superciliaris* (2) [NT]

CRESTED DORADITO *Pseudocolopteryx sclateri* (2)

DINELLI'S DORADITO *Pseudocolopteryx dinellianus* (2) [VU]

SUBTROPICAL DORADITO *Pseudocolopteryx acutipennis* (2)

WARBLING DORADITO *Pseudocolopteryx flaviventris* (2)

TAWNY-CROWNED PYGMY-TYRANT *Euscarthmus meloryphus* (2)

RUFOUS-SIDED PYGMY-TYRANT *Euscarthmus rufomarginatus* (2) [VU]

MARBLE-FACED BRISTLE-TYRANT *Phylloscartes ophthalmicus* (2)

VENEZUELAN BRISTLE-TYRANT *Phylloscartes venezuelanus* (2) [NT]

ANTIOQUIA BRISTLE-TYRANT *Phylloscartes lanyoni* (2) [EN]

SPECTACLED BRISTLE-TYRANT *Phylloscartes orbitalis* (2)

VARIEGATED BRISTLE-TYRANT *Phylloscartes poecilotis* (2)

SOUTHERN BRISTLE-TYRANT *Phylloscartes eximius* (2) [NT]

BLACK-FRONTED TYRANNULET *Phylloscartes nigrifrons* (2)

CHAPMAN'S TYRANNULET *Phylloscartes chapmani* (2)

ECUADORIAN TYRANNULET *Phylloscartes gualaquizae* (2)

RUFOUS-LORED TYRANNULET *Phylloscartes flaviventris* (2)

MINAS GERAIS TYRANNULET *Phylloscartes roquettei* (2) [EN]

SÃO PAULO TYRANNULET *Phylloscartes paulistus* (2) [VU]

OUSTALET'S TYRANNULET *Phylloscartes oustaleti* (2) [NT]

SERRA DO MAR TYRANNULET *Phylloscartes difficilis* (2) [NT]

ALAGOAS TYRANNULET *Phylloscartes ceciliae* (2) [EN]

MOTTLE-CHEEKED TYRANNULET *Phylloscartes ventralis* (2)

RESTINGA TYRANNULET *Phylloscartes kronei* (2) [EN]

BAHIA TYRANNULET *Phylloscartes beckeri* (2)

YELLOW-GREEN TYRANNULET *Phylloscartes flavovirens* (2)

OLIVE-GREEN TYRANNULET *Phylloscartes virescens* (2)

RUFOUS-BROWED TYRANNULET *Phylloscartes superciliaris* (2)

BAY-RINGED TYRANNULET *Phylloscartes sylviolus* (2) [NT]

WHITE-BELLIED PYGMY-TYRANT *Myiornis albiventris* (2) [NT]

EARED PYGMY-TYRANT *Myiornis auricularis* (2)

BLACK-CAPPED PYGMY-TYRANT *Myiornis atricapillus* (2)

SHORT-TAILED PYGMY-TYRANT *Myiornis ecaudatus* (2)

SCALE-CRESTED PYGMY-TYRANT *Lophotriccus pileatus* (2)

DOUBLE-BANDED PYGMY-TYRANT *Lophotriccus vitiosus* (2)

LONG-CRESTED PYGMY-TYRANT *Lophotriccus eulophotes* (2)

HELMETED PYGMY-TYRANT *Lophotriccus galeatus* (2)

PALE-EYED PYGMY-TYRANT *Atalotriccus pilaris* (2)

NORTHERN BENTBILL *Oncostoma cinereigulare* (1, 2)

SOUTHERN BENTBILL *Oncostoma olivaceum* (2)

BROWNISH FLYCATCHER or BROWNISH TWISTWING *Cnipodectes subbrunneus* (2)

EYE-RINGED FLATBILL *Rhynchocyclus brevirostris* (1, 2)

OLIVACEOUS FLATBILL *Rhynchocyclus olivaceus* (2)

FULVOUS-BREASTED FLATBILL *Rhynchocyclus fulvipectus* (2)

PACIFIC FLATBILL *Rhynchocyclus pacificus* (2)

YELLOW-OLIVE FLYCATCHER *Tolmomyias sulphurescens* (1, 2)

YELLOW-MARGINED FLYCATCHER *Tolmomyias assimilis* (2)

GRAY-CROWNED FLYCATCHER *Tolmomyias poliocephalus* (2)

YELLOW-BREASTED FLYCATCHER *Tolmomyias flaviventris* (2)

CINNAMON-CRESTED SPADEBILL *Platyrinchus saturatus* (2)

STUB-TAILED SPADEBILL *Platyrinchus cancrominus* (1, 2)

WHITE-THROATED SPADEBILL *Platyrinchus mystaceus* (2)

GOLDEN-CROWNED SPADEBILL *Platyrinchus coronatus* (2)

YELLOW-THROATED SPADEBILL *Platyrinchus flavigularis* (2)

WHITE-CRESTED SPADEBILL *Platyrinchus platyrhynchos* (2)

RUSSET-WINGED SPADEBILL *Platyrinchus leucoryphus* (2) [VU]

ROYAL FLYCATCHER *Onychorhynchus coronatus* (1, 2)

PACIFIC ROYAL FLYCATCHER *Onychorhynchus occidentalis* (2) [VU]

ATLANTIC ROYAL FLYCATCHER *Onychorhynchus swainsoni* (2) [EN]

ORNATE FLYCATCHER *Myiotriccus ornatus* (2)

FLAVESCENT FLYCATCHER *Myiophobus flavicans* (2)

ORANGE-CRESTED FLYCATCHER *Myiophobus phoenicomitra* (2)

UNADORNED FLYCATCHER *Myiophobus inornatus* (2)

RORAIMAN FLYCATCHER *Myiophobus roraimae* (2)

HANDSOME FLYCATCHER *Myiophobus pulcher* (2)

ORANGE-BANDED FLYCATCHER *Myiophobus lintoni* (2) [NT]

OCHRACEOUS-BREASTED FLYCATCHER *Myiophobus ochraceiventris* (2)

BRAN-COLORED FLYCATCHER *Myiophobus fasciatus* (2)

OLIVE-CHESTED FLYCATCHER *Myiophobus cryptoxanthus* (2)

CINNAMON TYRANT or CINNAMON TYRANT-MANAKIN *Neopipo cinnamomea* (2)

RUDDY-TAILED FLYCATCHER *Myiobius erythrurus* (1, 2)

TAWNY-BREASTED FLYCATCHER *Myiobius villosus* (2)

SULFUR-RUMPED FLYCATCHER *Myiobius barbatus* (1, 2)

BLACK-TAILED FLYCATCHER *Myiobius atricaudus* (2)

CINNAMON FLYCATCHER *Pyrrhomyias cinnamomea* (2)

CLIFF FLYCATCHER or NORTHERN CLIFF-FLYCATCHER *Hirundinea ferruginea* (2)

SWALLOW FLYCATCHER or SOUTHERN CLIFF-FLYCATCHER *Hirundinea bellicosa* (2)

FUSCOUS FLYCATCHER *Cnemotriccus fuscatus* (2)

EULER'S FLYCATCHER *Lathrotriccus euleri* (2)

GRAY-BREASTED FLYCATCHER *Lathrotriccus griseipectus* (2) [VU]

TAWNY-CHESTED FLYCATCHER *Aphanotriccus capitalis* (2) [NT]

BLACK-BILLED FLYCATCHER *Aphanotriccus audax* (2) [NT]

BELTED FLYCATCHER *Xenotriccus callizonus* (1, 2) [NT]

PILEATED FLYCATCHER *Xenotriccus mexicanus* (1) [NT]

TUFTED FLYCATCHER *Mitrephanes phaeocercus* (1, 2)

OLIVE FLYCATCHER *Mitrephanes olivaceus* (2)

OLIVE-SIDED FLYCATCHER *Contopus cooperi* (1, 2)

GREATER PEWEE *Contopus pertinax* (1, 2)

DARK PEWEE *Contopus lugubris* (2)

SMOKE-COLORED PEWEE *Contopus fumigatus* (2)

OCHRACEOUS PEWEE *Contopus ochraceus* (2) [NT]

WESTERN WOOD-PEWEE *Contopus sordidulus* (1, 2)

EASTERN WOOD-PEWEE *Contopus virens* (1, 2)

TROPICAL PEWEE *Contopus cinereus* (1, 2)

BLACKISH PEWEE *Contopus nigrescens* (2)

WHITE-THROATED PEWEE *Contopus albogularis* (2)

CUBAN PEWEE *Contopus caribaeus* (2)

JAMAICAN PEWEE *Contopus pallidus* (2)

HISPANIOLAN PEWEE *Contopus hispaniolensis* (2)

LESSER ANTILLEAN PEWEE *Contopus latirostris* (2)

YELLOW-BELLIED FLYCATCHER *Empidonax flaviventris* (1, 2)

ACADIAN FLYCATCHER *Empidonax virescens* (1, 2)

ALDER FLYCATCHER *Empidonax alnorum* (1, 2)

WILLOW FLYCATCHER *Empidonax traillii* (1, 2)

WHITE-THROATED FLYCATCHER *Empidonax albigularis* (1, 2)

LEAST FLYCATCHER *Empidonax minimus* (1, 2)

HAMMOND'S FLYCATCHER *Empidonax hammondii* (1, 2)

GRAY FLYCATCHER *Empidonax wrightii* (1)

DUSKY FLYCATCHER *Empidonax oberholseri* (1)

PINE FLYCATCHER *Empidonax affinis* (1)

PACIFIC-SLOPE FLYCATCHER *Empidonax difficilis* (1)

CORDILLERAN FLYCATCHER *Empidonax occidentalis* (1)

YELLOWISH FLYCATCHER *Empidonax flavescens* (1, 2)

BUFF-BREASTED FLYCATCHER *Empidonax aulvifrons* (1, 2)

BLACK-CAPPED FLYCATCHER *Empidonax atriceps* (2)

EASTERN PHOEBE *Sayornis phoebe* (1)

SAY'S PHOEBE *Sayornis saya* (1)

BLACK PHOEBE *Sayornis nigricans* (1, 2)

VERMILION FLYCATCHER *Pyrocephalus rubinus* (1, 2)

CROWNED CHAT-TYRANT *Silvicultrix frontalis* (2)

JELSKI'S CHAT-TYRANT *Silvicultrix jelskii* (2)

YELLOW-BELLIED CHAT-TYRANT *Silvicultrix diadema* (2)

GOLDEN-BROWED CHAT-TYRANT *Silvicultrix pulchella* (2)

SLATY-BACKED CHAT-TYRANT *Ochthoeca cinnamomeiventris* (2)

RUFOUS-BREASTED CHAT-TYRANT *Ochthoeca rufipectoralis* (2)

BROWN-BACKED CHAT-TYRANT *Ochthoeca fumicolor* (2)

D'ORBIGNY'S CHAT-TYRANT *Ochthoeca oenanthoides* (2)

WHITE-BROWED CHAT-TYRANT *Ochthoeca leucophrys* (2)

PIURA CHAT-TYRANT *Ochthoeca piurae* (2) [NT]

TUMBES TYRANT *Ochthoeca salvini* (2) [NT]

PATAGONIAN TYRANT *Colorhamphus parvirostris* (2)

DRAB WATER-TYRANT *Ochthornis littoralis* (2)

RED-RUMPED BUSH-TYRANT *Cnemarchus erythropygius* (2)

STREAK-THROATED BUSH-TYRANT *Myiotheretes striaticollis* (2)

SANTA MARTA BUSH-TYRANT *Myiotheretes pernix* (2) [VU]

SMOKY BUSH-TYRANT *Myiotheretes fumigatus* (2)

RUFOUS-BELLIED BUSH-TYRANT *Myiotheretes fuscorufus* (2) [NT]

FIRE-EYED DIUCON *Xolmis pyrope* (2)

GRAY MONJITA *Xolmis cinerea* (2)

BLACK-CROWNED MONJITA *Xolmis coronata* (2)

WHITE-RUMPED MONJITA *Xolmis velata* (2)

WHITE MONJITA *Xolmis irupero* (2)

BLACK-AND-WHITE MONJITA *Xolmis dominicana* (2) [VU]

RUSTY-BACKED MONJITA *Xolmis rubetra* (2)

SALINAS MONJITA *Xolmis salinarum* (2) [NT]

CHOCOLATE-VENTED TYRANT *Xolmis rufiventris* (2)

BLACK-BILLED SHRIKE-TYRANT *Agriornis montana* (2)

WHITE-TAILED SHRIKE-TYRANT *Agriornis andicola* (2) [VU]

GREAT SHRIKE-TYRANT *Agriornis livida* (2)

GRAY-BELLIED SHRIKE-TYRANT *Agriornis microptera* (2)

LESSER SHRIKE-TYRANT *Agriornis murina* (2)

RUFOUS-WEBBED BUSH-TYRANT *Polioxolmis rufipennis* (2)

SPOT-BILLED GROUND-TYRANT *Muscisaxicola maculirostris* (2)

LITTLE GROUND-TYRANT *Muscisaxicola fluviatilis* (2)

DARK-FACED GROUND-TYRANT *Muscisaxicola macloviana* (2)

CINNAMON-BELLIED GROUND-TYRANT *Muscisaxicola capistrata* (2)

RUFOUS-NAPED GROUND-TYRANT *Muscisaxicola rufivertex* (2)

PUNA GROUND-TYRANT *Muscisaxicola juninensis* (2)

WHITE-BROWED GROUND-TYRANT *Muscisaxicola albilora* (2)

PLAIN-CAPPED GROUND-TYRANT *Muscisaxicola alpina* (2)

CINEREOUS GROUND-TYRANT *Muscisaxicola cinerea* (2)

WHITE-FRONTED GROUND-TYRANT *Muscisaxicola albifrons* (2)

OCHER-NAPED GROUND-TYRANT *Muscisaxicola flavinucha* (2)

BLACK-FRONTED GROUND-TYRANT *Muscisaxicola frontalis* (2)

SHORT-TAILED FIELD-TYRANT *Muscigralla brevicauda* (2)

ANDEAN NEGRITO *Lessonia oreas* (2)

PATAGONIAN NEGRITO or AUSTRAL NEGRITO *Lessonia rufa* (2)

CINEREOUS TYRANT *Knipolegus striaticeps* (2)

HUDSON'S BLACK-TYRANT *Knipolegus hudsoni* (2) [NT]

AMAZONIAN BLACK-TYRANT *Knipolegus poecilocercus* (2)

ANDEAN TYRANT *Knipolegus signatus* (2)

BLUE-BILLED BLACK-TYRANT *Knipolegus cyanirostris* (2)

RUFOUS-TAILED TYRANT *Knipolegus poecilurus* (2)

RIVERSIDE TYRANT *Knipolegus orenocensis* (2)

WHITE-WINGED BLACK-TYRANT *Knipolegus aterrimus* (2) [CR]

VELVETY BLACK-TYRANT *Knipolegus nigerrimus* (2)

CRESTED BLACK-TYRANT *Knipolegus lophotes* (2)

SPECTACLED TYRANT *Hymenops perspicillatus* (2)

PIED WATER-TYRANT *Fluvicola pica* (2)

BLACK-BACKED WATER-TYRANT *Fluvicola albiventer* (2)

MASKED WATER-TYRANT *Fluvicola nengeta* (2)

WHITE-HEADED MARSH-TYRANT *Arundinicola leucocephala* (2)

COCK-TAILED TYRANT *Alectrurus tricolor* (2) [NT]

STRANGE-TAILED TYRANT *Alectrurus risora* (2) [VU]

STREAMER-TAILED TYRANT *Gubernetes yetapa* (2)

YELLOW-BROWED TYRANT *Satrapa icterophrys* (2)

LONG-TAILED TYRANT *Colonia colonus* (2)

CATTLE TYRANT *Machetornis rixosus* (2)

SHEAR-TAILED GRAY TYRANT *Muscipipra vetula* (2) [NT]

RUFOUS-TAILED ATTILA *Attila phoenicurus* (2)

CINNAMON ATTILA *Attila cinnamomeus* (2)

OCHRACEOUS ATTILA *Attila torridus* (2) [VU]

CITRON-BELLIED ATTILA *Attila citriniventris* (2)

DULL-CAPPED ATTILA or WHITE-EYED ATTILA *Attila bolivianus* (2)

GRAY-HOODED ATTILA *Attila rufus* (2)

BRIGHT-RUMPED ATTILA *Attila spadiceus* (1, 2)

RUFOUS CASIORNIS *Casiornis rufa* (2)

ASH-THROATED CASIORNIS *Casiornis fusca* (2)

RUFOUS MOURNER *Rhytipterna holerythra* (1, 2)

GRAYISH MOURNER *Rhytipterna simplex* (2)

PALE-BELLIED MOURNER *Rhytipterna immunda* (2)

SPECKLED MOURNER *Laniocera rufescens* (1, 2)

CINEREOUS MOURNER *Laniocera hypopyrra* (2)

SIRYSTES *Sirystes sibilator* (2)

RUFOUS FLYCATCHER *Myiarchus semirufus* (2)

YUCATÁN FLYCATCHER *Myiarchus yucatanensis* (1, 2)

DUSKY-CAPPED FLYCATCHER *Myiarchus tuberculifer* (1, 2)

SAD FLYCATCHER *Myiarchus barbirostris* (2)

SWAINSON'S FLYCATCHER *Myiarchus swainsoni* (2)

VENEZUELAN FLYCATCHER *Myiarchus venezuelensis* (2)

PANAMA FLYCATCHER *Myiarchus panamensis* (2)

SHORT-CRESTED FLYCATCHER *Myiarchus ferox* (2)

PALE-EDGED FLYCATCHER *Myiarchus cephalotes* (2)

SOOTY-CROWNED FLYCATCHER *Myiarchus phaeocephalus* (2)

APICAL FLYCATCHER *Myiarchus apicalis* (2)

ASH-THROATED FLYCATCHER *Myiarchus cinerascens* (1, 2)

NUTTING'S FLYCATCHER *Myiarchus nuttingi* (1, 2)

GREAT CRESTED FLYCATCHER *Myiarchus crinitus* (1, 2)

BROWN-CRESTED FLYCATCHER *Myiarchus tyrannulus* (1, 2)

GRENADA FLYCATCHER *Myiarchus nugator* (2)

LARGE-BILLED FLYCATCHER *Myiarchus magnirostris* (2)

RUFOUS-TAILED FLYCATCHER *Myiarchus validus* (2)

LA SAGRA'S FLYCATCHER *Myiarchus sagrae* (2)

STOLID FLYCATCHER *Myiarchus stolidus* (2)

PUERTO RICAN FLYCATCHER *Myiarchus antillarum* (2)

LESSER ANTILLEAN FLYCATCHER *Myiarchus oberi* (2)

FLAMMULATED FLYCATCHER *Deltarhynchus flammulatus* (1)

LARGE-HEADED FLATBILL *Ramphotrigon megacephala* (2)

DUSKY-TAILED FLATBILL *Ramphotrigon fuscicauda* (2)

RUFOUS-TAILED FLATBILL *Ramphotrigon ruficauda* (2)

SNOWY-THROATED KINGBIRD *Tyrannus niveigularis* (2)

WHITE-THROATED KINGBIRD *Tyrannus albogularis* (2)

TROPICAL KINGBIRD *Tyrannus melancholicus* (1, 2)

COUCH'S KINGBIRD *Tyrannus couchii* (1, 2)

CASSIN'S KINGBIRD *Tyrannus vociferans* (1, 2)

THICK-BILLED KINGBIRD *Tyrannus crassirostris* (1)

WESTERN KINGBIRD *Tyrannus verticalis* (1, 2)

SCISSOR-TAILED FLYCATCHER *Tyrannus forficatus* (1)

FORK-TAILED FLYCATCHER *Tyrannus savana* (1, 2)

EASTERN KINGBIRD *Tyrannus tyrannus* (1, 2)

GRAY KINGBIRD *Tyrannus dominicensis* (1, 2)

LOGGERHEAD KINGBIRD *Tyrannus caudifasciatus* (2)

GIANT KINGBIRD *Tyrannus cubensis* (2) [EN]

VARIEGATED FLYCATCHER *Empidonomus varius* (1, 2)

CROWNED SLATY FLYCATCHER *Griseotyrannus aurantioatrocristatus* (2)

SULFURY FLYCATCHER *Tyrannopsis sulphurea* (2)

BOAT-BILLED FLYCATCHER *Megarynchus pitangua* (1, 2)

WHITE-RINGED FLYCATCHER *Conopias albovittata* (2)

YELLOW-THROATED FLYCATCHER *Conopias parva* (2)

THREE-STRIPED FLYCATCHER *Conopias trivirgata* (2)

LEMON-BROWED FLYCATCHER *Conopias cinchoneti* (2)

GOLDEN-BELLIED FLYCATCHER *Myiodynastes hemichrysus* (2)

GOLDEN-CROWNED FLYCATCHER *Myiodynastes chrysocephalus* (2)

BAIRD'S FLYCATCHER *Myiodynastes bairdii* (2)

STREAKED FLYCATCHER *Myiodynastes maculatus* (1, 2)

SULFUR-BELLIED FLYCATCHER *Myiodynastes luteiventris* (1, 2)

RUSTY-MARGINED FLYCATCHER *Myiozetetes cayanensis* (2)

SOCIAL FLYCATCHER *Myiozetetes similis* (1, 2)

GRAY-CAPPED FLYCATCHER *Myiozetetes granadensis* (2)

DUSKY-CHESTED FLYCATCHER *Myiozetetes luteiventris* (2)

PIRATIC FLYCATCHER *Legatus leucophaius* (1, 2)

LESSER KISKADEE *Philohydor lictor* (2)

GREAT KISKADEE *Pitangus sulphuratus* (1, 2)

WHITE-BEARDED FLYCATCHER *Phelpsia inornata* (2)

Subfamily TITYRINAE
Tribe SCHIFFORNITHINI

GREATER SCHIFFORNIS or VARZEA MOURNER *Schiffornis major* (2)

THRUSH-LIKE SCHIFFORNIS or THRUSH-LIKE MOURNER *Schiffornis turdinus* (1, 2)

GREENISH SCHIFFORNIS or GREENISH MOURNER *Schiffornis virescens* (2)

Tribe TITYRINI

WHITE-NAPED XENOPSARIS or XENOPSARIS *Xenopsaris albinucha* (2)

GREEN-BACKED BECARD *Pachyramphus viridis* (2)

YELLOW-CHEEKED BECARD *Pachyramphus xanthogenys* (2)

BARRED BECARD *Pachyramphus versicolor* (2)

CINNAMON BECARD *Pachyramphus cinnamomeus* (1, 2)

CHESTNUT-CROWNED BECARD *Pachyramphus castaneus* (2)

WHITE-WINGED BECARD *Pachyramphus polychopterus* (2)

GRAY-COLLARED BECARD *Pachyramphus major* (1, 2)

BLACK-AND-WHITE BECARD *Pachyramphus albogriseus* (2)

BLACK-CAPPED BECARD *Pachyramphus marginatus* (2)

GLOSSY-BACKED BECARD *Pachyramphus surinamus* (2)

CINEREOUS BECARD *Pachyramphus rufus* (2)

SLATY BECARD *Pachyramphus spodiurus* (2) [NT]

ROSE-THROATED BECARD *Pachyramphus aglaiae* (1, 2)

ONE-COLORED BECARD *Pachyramphus homochrous* (2)

PINK-THROATED BECARD *Pachyramphus mino* (2)

JAMAICAN BECARD *Pachyramphus niger* (2)

CRESTED BECARD *Pachyramphus validus* (2)

BLACK-TAILED TITYRA *Tityra cayana* (2)

MASKED TITYRA *Tityra semifasciata* (1, 2)

BLACK-CROWNED TITYRA *Tityra inquisitor* (1, 2)

Subfamily COTINGINAE

BLACK-NECKED RED-COTINGA *Phoenicircus nigricollis* (2)

GUIANAN RED-COTINGA *Phoenicircus carnifex* (2)

SHRIKE-LIKE COTINGA *Laniisoma elegans* (2) [VU]

SWALLOW-TAILED COTINGA *Phibalura flavirostris* (2) [NT]

BLACK-AND-GOLD COTINGA *Tijuca atra* (2) [NT]

GRAY-WINGED COTINGA *Tijuca condita* (2) [VU]

HOODED BERRYEATER *Carpornis cucullatus* (2) [NT]

BLACK-HEADED BERRYEATER *Carpornis melanocephalus* (2) [VU]

BAY-VENTED COTINGA *Doliornis sclateri* (2)

CHESTNUT-BELLIED COTINGA *Doliornis remseni* (2) [VU]

RED-CRESTED COTINGA *Ampelion rubrocristatus* (2)

CHESTNUT-CRESTED COTINGA *Ampelion rufaxilla* (2)

PERUVIAN PLANTCUTTER *Phytotoma raimondii* (2)

WHITE-TIPPED PLANTCUTTER *Phytotoma rutila* (2)

RUFOUS-TAILED PLANTCUTTER *Phytotoma rara* (2)

WHITE-CHEEKED COTINGA *Zaratornis stresemanni* (2) [VU]

GREEN-AND-BLACK FRUITEATER *Pipreola riefferii* (2)

BAND-TAILED FRUITEATER *Pipreola intermedia* (2)

BARRED FRUITEATER *Pipreola arcuata* (2)

GOLDEN-BREASTED FRUITEATER *Pipreola aureopectus* (2)

ORANGE-BREASTED FRUITEATER *Pipreola jucunda* (2)

BLACK-CHESTED FRUITEATER *Pipreola lubomirskii* (2) [NT]

MASKED FRUITEATER *Pipreola pulchra* (2)

FIERY-THROATED FRUITEATER *Pipreola chlorolepidota* (2) [NT]

SCARLET-BREASTED FRUITEATER *Pipreola frontalis* (2) [NT]

HANDSOME FRUITEATER *Pipreola formosa* (2)

RED-BANDED FRUITEATER *Pipreola whitelyi* (2)

SCALED FRUITEATER *Ampelioides tschudii* (2) [NT]

BUFF-THROATED PURPLETUFT *Iodopleura pipra* (2) [VU]

WHITE-BROWED PURPLETUFT *Iodopleura isabellae* (2)

DUSKY PURPLETUFT *Iodopleura fusca* (2)

KINGLET CALYPTURA *Calyptura cristata* (2) [CR]

GRAY-TAILED PIHA *Lipaugus subalaris* (2)

OLIVACEOUS PIHA *Lipaugus cryptolophus* (2)

DUSKY PIHA *Lipaugus fuscocinereus* (2)

SCIMITAR-WINGED PIHA *Lipaugus uropygialis* (2)

SCREAMING PIHA *Lipaugus vociferans* (2)

RUFOUS PIHA *Lipaugus unirufus* (1, 2)

CINNAMON-VENTED PIHA *Lipaugus lanioides* (2) [VU]

ROSE-COLLARED PIHA *Lipaugus streptophorus* (2)

PURPLE-THROATED COTINGA *Porphyrolaema porphyrolaema* (2) [NT]

LOVELY COTINGA *Cotinga amabilis* (1, 2)

TURQUOISE COTINGA *Cotinga ridgwayi* (2) [VU]

BLUE COTINGA *Cotinga nattererii* (2)

PLUM-THROATED COTINGA *Cotinga maynana* (2)

PURPLE-BREASTED COTINGA *Cotinga cotinga* (2)

BANDED COTINGA *Cotinga maculata* (2) [EN]

SPANGLED COTINGA *Cotinga cayana* (2)

POMPADOUR COTINGA *Xipholena punicea* (2)

WHITE-TAILED COTINGA *Xipholena lamellipennis* (2)

WHITE-WINGED COTINGA *Xipholena atropurpurea* (2) [VU]

SNOWY COTINGA *Carpodectes nitidus* (2)

YELLOW-BILLED COTINGA *Carpodectes antoniae* (2) [VU]

BLACK-TIPPED COTINGA *Carpodectes hopkei* (2) [NT]

BLACK-FACED COTINGA *Conioptilon mcilhennyi* (2) [NT]

BARE-NECKED FRUITCROW *Gymnoderus foetidus* (2)

CRIMSON FRUITCROW *Haematoderus militaris* (2)

PURPLE-THROATED FRUITCROW *Querula purpurata* (2)

RED-RUFFED FRUITCROW *Pyroderus scutatus* (2)

BARE-NECKED UMBRELLABIRD *Cephalopterus glabricollis* (2) [VU]

LONG-WATTLED UMBRELLABIRD *Cephalopterus penduliger* (2) [VU]

AMAZONIAN UMBRELLABIRD *Cephalopterus ornatus* (2)

CAPUCHINBIRD *Perissocephalus tricolor* (2)

THREE-WATTLED BELLBIRD *Procnias tricarunculata* (2) [VU]

WHITE BELLBIRD *Procnias alba* (2)

BEARDED BELLBIRD *Procnias averano* (2)

BARE-THROATED BELLBIRD *Procnias nudicollis* (2) [NT]

GUIANAN COCK-OF-THE-ROCK *Rupicola rupicola* (2)

ANDEAN COCK-OF-THE-ROCK *Rupicola peruviana* (2)

SHARPBILL *Oxyruncus cristatus* (2)

Subfamily PIPRINAE

CRIMSON-HOODED MANAKIN *Pipra aureola* (2)

BAND-TAILED MANAKIN *Pipra fasciicauda* (2)

WIRE-TAILED MANAKIN *Pipra filicauda* (2)

RED-CAPPED MANAKIN *Pipra mentalis* (1, 2)

GOLDEN-HEADED MANAKIN *Pipra erythrocephala* (2)

RED-HEADED MANAKIN *Pipra rubrocapilla* (2)

ROUND-TAILED MANAKIN *Pipra chloromeros* (2)

SCARLET-HORNED MANAKIN *Pipra cornuta* (2)

WHITE-CROWNED MANAKIN *Pipra pipra* (2)

BLUE-CROWNED MANAKIN *Lepidothrix coronata* (2)

WHITE-FRONTED MANAKIN *Lepidothrix serena* (2)

ORANGE-BELLIED MANAKIN *Lepidothrix suavissima* (2)

OPAL-CROWNED MANAKIN *Lepidothrix iris* (2) [NT]

GOLDEN-CROWNED MANAKIN *Lepidothrix vilasboasi* (2) [VU]

SNOW-CAPPED MANAKIN *Lepidothrix nattereri* (2)

BLUE-RUMPED MANAKIN *Lepidothrix isidorei* (2)

CERULEAN-CAPPED MANAKIN *Lepidothrix coeruleocapilla* (2)

HELMETED MANAKIN *Antilophia galeata* (2)

LONG-TAILED MANAKIN *Chiroxiphia linearis* (1, 2)

LANCE-TAILED MANAKIN *Chiroxiphia lanceolata* (2)

BLUE-BACKED MANAKIN *Chiroxiphia pareola* (2)

YUNGAS MANAKIN *Chiroxiphia boliviana* (2)

SWALLOW-TAILED MANAKIN or BLUE MANAKIN *Chiroxiphia caudata* (2)

GOLDEN-WINGED MANAKIN *Masius chrysopterus* (2)

PIN-TAILED MANAKIN *Ilicura militaris* (2)

WHITE-THROATED MANAKIN *Corapipo gutturalis* (2)

WHITE-RUFFED MANAKIN *Corapipo altera* (2)

WHITE-BIBBED MANAKIN *Corapipo leucorrhoa* (2)

WHITE-COLLARED MANAKIN *Manacus candei* (1, 2)

ORANGE-COLLARED MANAKIN *Manacus aurantiacus* (2)

GOLDEN-COLLARED MANAKIN *Manacus vitellinus* (2)

WHITE-BEARDED MANAKIN *Manacus manacus* (2)

FIERY-CAPPED MANAKIN *Machaeropterus pyrocephalus* (2)

STRIPED MANAKIN *Machaeropterus regulus* (2)

CLUB-WINGED MANAKIN *Machaeropterus deliciosus* (2)

BLACK MANAKIN *Xenopipo atronitens* (2)

JET MANAKIN *Chloropipo unicolor* (2)

OLIVE MANAKIN *Chloropipo uniformis* (2)

GREEN MANAKIN *Chloropipo holochlora* (2)

YELLOW-HEADED MANAKIN *Chloropipo flavicapilla* (2) [NT]

YELLOW-CRESTED MANAKIN *Heterocercus flavivertex* (2)

ORANGE-CRESTED MANAKIN *Heterocercus aurantiivertex* (2)

FLAME-CRESTED MANAKIN *Heterocercus linteatus* (2)

SAFFRON-CRESTED TYRANT-MANAKIN *Neopelma chrysocephalum* (2)

SULFUR-BELLIED TYRANT-MANAKIN *Neopelma sulphureiventer* (2)

PALE-BELLIED TYRANT-MANAKIN *Neopelma pallescens* (2)

WIED'S TYRANT-MANAKIN *Neopelma aurifrons* (2)

SERRA DO MAR TYRANT-MANAKIN *Neopelma chrysolophum* (2)

DWARF TYRANT-MANAKIN *Tyranneutes stolzmanni* (2)

TINY TYRANT-MANAKIN *Tyranneutes virescens* (2)

BLACK-CAPPED PIPRITES or BLACK-CAPPED MANAKIN *Piprites pileatus* (2) [VU]

GRAY-HEADED PIPRITES *Piprites griseiceps* (2) [NT]

WING-BARRED PIPRITES *Piprites chloris* (2)

Family THAMNOPHILIDAE

FASCIATED ANTSHRIKE *Cymbilaimus lineatus* (2)

BAMBOO ANTSHRIKE *Cymbilaimus sanctae-mariae* (2)

SPOT-BACKED ANTSHRIKE *Hypoedaleus guttatus* (2)

GIANT ANTSHRIKE *Batara cinerea* (2)

TUFTED ANTSHRIKE *Mackenziaena severa* (2)

LARGE-TAILED ANTSHRIKE *Mackenziaena leachii* (2)

BLACK-THROATED ANTSHRIKE *Frederickena viridis* (2)

UNDULATED ANTSHRIKE *Frederickena unduligera* (2)

GREAT ANTSHRIKE *Taraba major* (1, 2)

BLACK-CRESTED ANTSHRIKE *Sakesphorus canadensis* (2)

SILVERY-CHEEKED ANTSHRIKE *Sakesphorus cristatus* (2)

COLLARED ANTSHRIKE *Sakesphorus bernardi* (2)

BLACK-BACKED ANTSHRIKE *Sakesphorus melanonotus* (2)

BAND-TAILED ANTSHRIKE *Sakesphorus melanothorax* (2)

GLOSSY ANTSHRIKE *Sakesphorus luctuosus* (2)

WHITE-BEARDED ANTSHRIKE *Biatas nigropectus* (2) [VU]

BARRED ANTSHRIKE *Thamnophilus doliatus* (1, 2)

CHAPMAN'S ANTSHRIKE *Thamnophilus zarumae* (2)

BAR-CRESTED ANTSHRIKE *Thamnophilus multistriatus* (2)

CHESTNUT-BACKED ANTSHRIKE *Thamnophilus palliatus* (2)

LINED ANTSHRIKE *Thamnophilus tenuepunctatus* (2)

BLACK-HOODED ANTSHRIKE *Thamnophilus bridgesi* (2)

BLACK ANTSHRIKE *Thamnophilus nigriceps* (2)

COCHA ANTSHRIKE *Thamnophilus praecox* (2) [NT]

BLACKISH-GRAY ANTSHRIKE *Thamnophilus nigrocinereus* (2)

CASTELNAU'S ANTSHRIKE *Thamnophilus cryptoleucus* (2)

WHITE-SHOULDERED ANTSHRIKE *Thamnophilus aethiops* (2)

UNIFORM ANTSHRIKE *Thamnophilus unicolor* (2)

PLAIN-WINGED ANTSHRIKE *Thamnophilus schistaceus* (2)

MOUSE-COLORED ANTSHRIKE *Thamnophilus murinus* (2)

UPLAND ANTSHRIKE *Thamnophilus aroyae* (2)

EASTERN SLATY-ANTSHRIKE *Thamnophilus punctatus* (2)

WESTERN SLATY-ANTSHRIKE *Thamnophilus atrinucha* (2)

STREAK-BACKED ANTSHRIKE *Thamnophilus insignis* (2)

AMAZONIAN ANTSHRIKE *Thamnophilus amazonicus* (2)

VARIABLE ANTSHRIKE *Thamnophilus caerulescens* (2)

RUFOUS-WINGED ANTSHRIKE *Thamnophilus torquatus* (2)

RUFOUS-CAPPED ANTSHRIKE *Thamnophilus ruficapillus* (2)

SPOT-WINGED ANTSHRIKE *Pygiptila stellaris* (2)

PEARLY ANTSHRIKE *Megastictus margaritatus* (2)

BLACK BUSHBIRD *Neoctantes niger* (2)

RECURVE-BILLED BUSHBIRD *Clytoctantes alixii* (2) [EN]

RONDONIA BUSHBIRD or BLACK-THROATED BUSHBIRD *Clytoctantes atrogularis* (2) [DD]

SPECKLED ANTSHRIKE *Xenornis setifrons* (2) [VU]

RUSSET ANTSHRIKE *Thamnistes anabatinus* (1, 2)

SPOT-BREASTED ANTVIREO *Dysithamnus stictothorax* (2) [NT]

PLAIN ANTVIREO *Dysithamnus mentalis* (1, 2)

STREAK-CROWNED ANTVIREO *Dysithamnus striaticeps* (2)

SPOT-CROWNED ANTVIREO *Dysithamnus puncticeps* (2)

RUFOUS-BACKED ANTVIREO *Dysithamnus xanthopterus* (2)

WHITE-STREAKED ANTVIREO *Dysithamnus leucostictus* (2)

PLUMBEOUS ANTVIREO *Dysithamnus plumbeus* (2) [VU]

BICOLORED ANTVIREO *Dysithamnus occidentalis* (2) [VU]

SATURNINE ANTSHRIKE *Thamnomanes saturninus* (2)

DUSKY-THROATED ANTSHRIKE *Thamnomanes ardesiacus* (2)

CINEREOUS ANTSHRIKE *Thamnomanes caesius* (2)

BLUISH-SLATE ANTSHRIKE *Thamnomanes schistogynus* (2)

Subfamily MYRMOTHERULA

PYGMY ANTWREN *Myrmotherula brachyura* (2)

SHORT-BILLED ANTWREN *Myrmotherula obscura* (2)

SCLATER'S ANTWREN *Myrmotherula sclateri* (2)

KLAGES'S ANTWREN *Myrmotherula klagesi* (2) [NT]

YELLOW-THROATED ANTWREN *Myrmotherula ambigua* (2)

STREAKED ANTWREN *Myrmotherula surinamensis* (2)

CHERRIE'S ANTWREN *Myrmotherula cherriei* (2)

STRIPE-CHESTED ANTWREN *Myrmotherula longicauda* (2)

PLAIN-THROATED ANTWREN *Myrmotherula hauxwelli* (2)

RUFOUS-BELLIED ANTWREN *Myrmotherula guttata* (2)

STAR-THROATED ANTWREN *Myrmotherula gularis* (2)

BROWN-BELLIED ANTWREN *Myrmotherula gutturalis* (2)

CHECKER-THROATED ANTWREN *Myrmotherula fulviventris* (2)

WHITE-EYED ANTWREN *Myrmotherula leucophthalma* (2)

STIPPLE-THROATED ANTWREN *Myrmotherula haematonota* (2)

FOOTHILL ANTWREN *Myrmotherula spodionota* (2)

ORNATE ANTWREN *Myrmotherula ornata* (2)

RUFOUS-TAILED ANTWREN *Myrmotherula erythrura* (2)

WHITE-FLANKED ANTWREN *Myrmotherula axillaris* (2)

RIO DE JANEIRO ANTWREN *Myrmotherula fluminensis* (2) [VU]

SLATY ANTWREN *Myrmotherula schisticolor* (2)

RIO SUNO ANTWREN *Myrmotherula sunensis* (2)

LONG-WINGED ANTWREN *Myrmotherula longipennis* (2)

SALVADORI'S ANTWREN *Myrmotherula minor* (2) [VU]

IHERING'S ANTWREN *Myrmotherula iheringi* (2)

ASHY ANTWREN or YUNGAS ANTWREN *Myrmotherula grisea* (2) [VU]

UNICOLORED ANTWREN *Myrmotherula unicolor* (2) [VU]

ALAGOAS ANTWREN *Myrmotherula snowi* (2) [CR]

PLAIN-WINGED ANTWREN *Myrmotherula behni* (2)

BAND-TAILED ANTWREN *Myrmotherula urosticta* (2) [VU]

GRAY ANTWREN *Myrmotherula menetriesii* (2)

LEADEN ANTWREN *Myrmotherula assimilis* (2)

BANDED ANTBIRD *Dichrozona cincta* (2)

STRIPE-BACKED ANTBIRD *Myrmorchilus strigilatus* (2)

ASH-THROATED ANTWREN *Herpsilochmus parkeri* (2) [VU]

CREAMY-BELLIED ANTWREN *Herpsilochmus motacilloides* (2)

BLACK-CAPPED ANTWREN *Herpsilochmus atricapillus* (2) [NT]

BAHIA ANTWREN or PILEATED ANTWREN *Herpsilochmus pileatus* (2)

SPOT-TAILED ANTWREN *Herpsilochmus sticturus* (2)

DUGAND'S ANTWREN *Herpsilochmus dugandi* (2)

TODD'S ANTWREN *Herpsilochmus stictocephalus* (2)

SPOT-BACKED ANTWREN *Herpsilochmus dorsimaculatus* (2)

RORAIMAN ANTWREN *Herpsilochmus roraimae* (2)

PECTORAL ANTWREN *Herpsilochmus pectoralis* (2) [VU]

LARGE-BILLED ANTWREN *Herpsilochmus longirostris* (2)

YELLOW-BREASTED ANTWREN *Herpsilochmus axillaris* (2)

RUFOUS-WINGED ANTWREN *Herpsilochmus rufimarginatus* (2)

DOT-WINGED ANTWREN *Microrhopias quixensis* (1, 2)

NARROW-BILLED ANTWREN *Formicivora iheringi* (2) [VU]

WHITE-FRINGED ANTWREN *Formicivora grisea* (2)

BLACK-BELLIED ANTWREN *Formicivora melanogaster* (2)

SERRA ANTWREN *Formicivora serrana* (2) [NT]

RESTINGA ANTWREN *Formicivora littoralis* (2) [EN]

BLACK-HOODED ANTWREN *Formicivora erythronotos* (2) [CR]

RUSTY-BACKED ANTWREN *Formicivora rufa* (2)

LONG-BILLED ANTWREN *Stymphalornis acutirostris* (2)

FERRUGINOUS ANTBIRD *Drymophila ferruginea* (2)

BERTONI'S ANTBIRD *Drymophila rubricollis* (2)

RUFOUS-TAILED ANTBIRD *Drymophila genei* (2) [NT]

OCHER-RUMPED ANTBIRD *Drymophila ochropyga* (2) [NT]

STRIATED ANTBIRD *Drymophila devillei* (2)

LONG-TAILED ANTBIRD *Drymophila caudata* (2)

DUSKY-TAILED ANTBIRD *Drymophila malura* (2)

SCALED ANTBIRD *Drymophila squamata* (2)

STREAK-CAPPED ANTWREN *Terenura maculata* (2)

ORANGE-BELLIED ANTWREN *Terenura sicki* (2) [VU]

RUFOUS-RUMPED ANTWREN *Terenura callinota* (2)

CHESTNUT-SHOULDERED ANTWREN *Terenura humeralis* (2)

YELLOW-RUMPED ANTWREN *Terenura sharpei* (2) [VU]

ASH-WINGED ANTWREN *Terenura spodioptila* (2)

GRAY ANTBIRD *Cercomacra cinerascens* (2)

RIO DE JANEIRO ANTBIRD *Cercomacra brasiliana* (2) [NT]

DUSKY ANTBIRD *Cercomacra tyrannina* (1, 2)

BLACKISH ANTBIRD *Cercomacra nigrescens* (2)

BANANAL ANTBIRD *Cercomacra ferdinandi* (2)

BLACK ANTBIRD *Cercomacra serva* (2)

JET ANTBIRD *Cercomacra nigricans* (2)

RIO BRANCO ANTBIRD *Cercomacra carbonaria* (2) [VU]

MANU ANTBIRD *Cercomacra manu* (2)

MATO GROSSO ANTBIRD *Cercomacra melanaria* (2)

WHITE-BACKED FIRE-EYE *Pyriglena leuconota* (2)

WHITE-SHOULDERED FIRE-EYE *Pyriglena leucoptera* (2)

FRINGE-BACKED FIRE-EYE *Pyriglena atra* (2) [EN]

SLENDER ANTBIRD *Rhopornis ardesiaca* (2) [VU]

WHITE-BROWED ANTBIRD *Myrmoborus leucophrys* (2)

ASH-BREASTED ANTBIRD *Myrmoborus lugubris* (2)

BLACK-FACED ANTBIRD *Myrmoborus myotherinus* (2)

BLACK-TAILED ANTBIRD *Myrmoborus melanurus* (2) [VU]

WARBLING ANTBIRD *Hypocnemis cantator* (2)

YELLOW-BROWED ANTBIRD *Hypocnemis hypoxantha* (2)

BLACK-CHINNED ANTBIRD *Hypocnemoides melanopogon* (2)

BAND-TAILED ANTBIRD *Hypocnemoides maculicauda* (2)

BLACK-AND-WHITE ANTBIRD *Myrmochanes hemileucus* (2)

BARE-CROWNED ANTBIRD *Gymnocichla nudiceps* (2)

SILVERED ANTBIRD *Sclateria naevia* (2)

BLACK-HEADED ANTBIRD *Percnostola rufifrons* (2)

SLATE-COLORED ANTBIRD *Percnostola schistacea* (2)

SPOT-WINGED ANTBIRD *Percnostola leucostigma* (2)

CAURA ANTBIRD *Percnostola caurensis* (2)

WHITE-LINED ANTBIRD *Percnostola lophotes* (2)

STUB-TAILED ANTBIRD *Myrmeciza berlepschi* (2)

WHITE-BELLIED ANTBIRD *Myrmeciza longipes* (2)

CHESTNUT-BACKED ANTBIRD *Myrmeciza exsul* (2)

FERRUGINOUS-BACKED ANTBIRD *Myrmeciza ferruginea* (2)

SCALLOPED ANTBIRD *Myrmeciza ruficauda* (2) [VU]

WHITE-BIBBED ANTBIRD *Myrmeciza loricata* (2)

SQUAMATE ANTBIRD *Myrmeciza squamosa* (2)

DULL-MANTLED ANTBIRD *Myrmeciza laemosticta* (2)

ESMERALDAS ANTBIRD *Myrmeciza nigricauda* (2)

YAPACANA ANTBIRD *Myrmeciza disjuncta* (2)

GRAY-BELLIED ANTBIRD *Myrmeciza pelzelni* (2)

CHESTNUT-TAILED ANTBIRD *Myrmeciza hemimelaena* (2)

PLUMBEOUS ANTBIRD *Myrmeciza hyperythra* (2)

WHITE-SHOULDERED ANTBIRD *Myrmeciza melanoceps* (2)

GOELDI'S ANTBIRD *Myrmeciza goeldii* (2)

SOOTY ANTBIRD *Myrmeciza fortis* (2)

IMMACULATE ANTBIRD *Myrmeciza immaculata* (2)

GRAY-HEADED ANTBIRD *Myrmeciza griseiceps* (2) [EN]

BLACK-THROATED ANTBIRD *Myrmeciza atrothorax* (2)

WHITE-PLUMED ANTBIRD *Pithys albifrons* (2)

WHITE-MASKED ANTBIRD *Pithys castanea* (2) [DD]

RUFOUS-THROATED ANTBIRD *Gymnopithys rufigula* (2)

BICOLORED ANTBIRD *Gymnopithys bicolor* (2)

WHITE-CHEEKED ANTBIRD *Gymnopithys leucaspis* (2)

LUNULATED ANTBIRD *Gymnopithys lunulata* (2)

WHITE-THROATED ANTBIRD *Gymnopithys salvini* (2)

WING-BANDED ANTBIRD *Myrmornis torquata* (2)

HAIRY-CRESTED ANTBIRD *Rhegmatorhina melanosticta* (2)

CHESTNUT-CRESTED ANTBIRD *Rhegmatorhina cristata* (2)

WHITE-BREASTED ANTBIRD *Rhegmatorhina hoffmannsi* (2) [NT]

HARLEQUIN ANTBIRD *Rhegmatorhina berlepschi* (2)

SANTAREM ANTBIRD or BARE-EYED ANTBIRD *Rhegmatorhina gymnops* (2) [NT]

SPOTTED ANTBIRD *Hylophylax naevioides* (2)

SPOT-BACKED ANTBIRD *Hylophylax naevia* (2)

DOT-BACKED ANTBIRD *Hylophylax punctulata* (2)

SCALE-BACKED ANTBIRD *Hylophylax poecilinota* (2)

BLACK-SPOTTED BARE-EYE *Phlegopsis nigromaculata* (2)

REDDISH-WINGED BARE-EYE *Phlegopsis erythroptera* (2)

PALE-FACED BARE-EYE *Skutchia borbae* (2)

OCELLATED ANTBIRD *Phaenostictus mcleannani* (2)

Family FURNARIIDAE
Subfamily FURNARIINAE

CAMPO MINER *Geobates poecilopterus* (2)

COMMON MINER *Geositta cunicularia* (2)

GRAYISH MINER *Geositta maritima* (2)

COASTAL MINER *Geositta peruviana* (2)

PUNA MINER *Geositta punensis* (2)

DARK-WINGED MINER *Geositta saxicolina* (2)

CREAMY-RUMPED MINER *Geositta isabellina* (2)

SHORT-BILLED MINER *Geositta antarctica* (2)

RUFOUS-BANDED MINER *Geositta rufipennis* (2)

THICK-BILLED MINER *Geositta crassirostris* (2)

SLENDER-BILLED MINER *Geositta tenuirostris* (2)

BOLIVIAN EARTHCREEPER *Upucerthia harterti* (2) [NT]

CHACO EARTHCREEPER *Upucerthia certhioides* (2)

STRAIGHT-BILLED EARTHCREEPER *Upucerthia ruficauda* (2)

ROCK EARTHCREEPER *Upucerthia andaecola* (2)

STRIATED EARTHCREEPER *Upucerthia serrana* (2)

SCALE-THROATED EARTHCREEPER *Upucerthia dumetaria* (2)

WHITE-THROATED EARTHCREEPER *Upucerthia albigula* (2)

PLAIN-BREASTED EARTHCREEPER *Upucerthia jelskii* (2)

BUFF-BREASTED EARTHCREEPER *Upucerthia validirostris* (2)

BAR-WINGED CINCLODES *Cinclodes fuscus* (2)

CORDOBA CINCLODES *Cinclodes comechingonus* (2)

LONG-TAILED CINCLODES *Cinclodes pabsti* (2)

GRAY-FLANKED CINCLODES *Cinclodes oustaleti* (2)

OLROG'S CINCLODES *Cinclodes olrogi* (2)

STOUT-BILLED CINCLODES *Cinclodes excelsior* (2)

ROYAL CINCLODES *Cinclodes aricomae* (2) [CR]

DARK-BELLIED CINCLODES *Cinclodes patagonicus* (2)

SURF CINCLODES *Cinclodes taczanowskii* (2)

SEASIDE CINCLODES *Cinclodes nigrofumosus* (2)

BLACKISH CINCLODES *Cinclodes antarcticus* (2)

WHITE-WINGED CINCLODES *Cinclodes atacamensis* (2)

WHITE-BELLIED CINCLODES *Cinclodes palliatus* (2) [VU]

CRAG CHILIA *Chilia melanura* (2)

LESSER HORNERO *Furnarius minor* (2)

WING-BANDED HORNERO or BAND-TAILED HORNERO *Furnarius figulus* (2)

PALE-LEGGED HORNERO *Furnarius leucopus* (2)

PALE-BILLED HORNERO *Furnarius torridus* (2)

RUFOUS HORNERO *Furnarius rufus* (2)

CRESTED HORNERO *Furnarius cristatus* (2)

DES MURS'S WIRETAIL *Sylviorthorhynchus desmursii* (2)

THORN-TAILED RAYADITO *Aphrastura spinicauda* (2)

MAS AFUERA RAYADITO *Aphrastura masafuerae* (2) [VU]

BROWN-CAPPED TIT-SPINETAIL *Leptasthenura fuliginiceps* (2)

TAWNY TIT-SPINETAIL *Leptasthenura yanacensis* (2) [NT]

TUFTED TIT-SPINETAIL *Leptasthenura platensis* (2)

PLAIN-MANTLED TIT-SPINETAIL *Leptasthenura aegithaloides* (2)

STRIOLATED TIT-SPINETAIL *Leptasthenura striolata* (2)

RUSTY-CROWNED TIT-SPINETAIL *Leptasthenura pileata* (2)

WHITE-BROWED TIT-SPINETAIL *Leptasthenura xenothorax* (2) [CR]

STREAKED TIT-SPINETAIL *Leptasthenura striata* (2)

ANDEAN TIT-SPINETAIL *Leptasthenura andicola* (2)

ARAUCARIA TIT-SPINETAIL *Leptasthenura setaria* (2) [NT]

PERIJA THISTLETAIL *Schizoeaca perijana* (2) [NT]

OCHER-BROWED THISTLETAIL *Schizoeaca coryi* (2)

WHITE-CHINNED THISTLETAIL *Schizoeaca fuliginosa* (2)

MOUSE-COLORED THISTLETAIL *Schizoeaca griseomurina* (2)

EYE-RINGED THISTLETAIL *Schizoeaca palpebralis* (2)

VILCABAMBA THISTLETAIL *Schizoeaca vilcabambae* (2)

PUNA THISTLETAIL *Schizoeaca helleri* (2)

BLACK-THROATED THISTLETAIL *Schizoeaca harterti* (2)

ITATIAIA THISTLETAIL *Schizoeaca moreirae* (2)

CHOTOY SPINETAIL *Schoeniophylax phryganophila* (2)

PINTO'S SPINETAIL or PLAIN SPINETAIL *Synallaxis infuscata* (2) [EN]

RUFOUS-CAPPED SPINETAIL *Synallaxis ruficapilla* (2)

BAHIA SPINETAIL *Synallaxis whitneyi* (2)

SOOTY-FRONTED SPINETAIL *Synallaxis frontalis* (2)

AZARA'S SPINETAIL *Synallaxis azarae* (2)

APURIMAC SPINETAIL *Synallaxis courseni* (2) [VU]

PALE-BREASTED SPINETAIL S *ynallaxis albescens* (2)

CHICLI SPINETAIL or SPIX'S SPINETAIL *Synallaxis spixi* (2)

SLATY SPINETAIL *Synallaxis brachyura* (2)

DARK-BREASTED SPINETAIL *Synallaxis albigularis* (2)

CINEREOUS-BREASTED SPINETAIL *Synallaxis hypospodia* (2)

DUSKY SPINETAIL *Synallaxis moesta* (2)

MACCONNELL'S SPINETAIL *Synallaxis macconnelli* (2)

CABANIS'S SPINETAIL *Synallaxis cabanisi* (2)

SILVERY-THROATED SPINETAIL *Synallaxis subpudica* (2)

BLACKISH-HEADED SPINETAIL *Synallaxis tithys* (2) [VU]

GRAY-BELLIED SPINETAIL *Synallaxis cinerascens* (2)

WHITE-BELLIED SPINETAIL *Synallaxis propinqua* (2)

RED-SHOULDERED SPINETAIL *Synallaxis hellmayri* (2) [VU]

MARANON SPINETAIL *Synallaxis maranonica* (2)

PLAIN-CROWNED SPINETAIL *Synallaxis gujanensis* (2)

WHITE-LORED SPINETAIL *Synallaxis albilora* (2)

RUDDY SPINETAIL *Synallaxis rutilans* (2)

CHESTNUT-THROATED SPINETAIL *Synallaxis cherriei* (2) [NT]

RUFOUS SPINETAIL *Synallaxis unirufa* (2)

BLACK-THROATED SPINETAIL *Synallaxis castanea* (2)

RUSTY-HEADED SPINETAIL *Synallaxis fuscorufa* (2) [NT]

RUSSET-BELLIED SPINETAIL *Synallaxis zimmeri* (2) [EN]

RUFOUS-BREASTED SPINETAIL *Synallaxis erythrothorax* (1, 2)

STRIPE-BREASTED SPINETAIL *Synallaxis cinnamomea* (2)

NECKLACED SPINETAIL *Synallaxis stictothorax* (2)

CHINCHIPE SPINETAIL *Synallaxis chinchipensis* (2)

WHITE-WHISKERED SPINETAIL *Synallaxis candei* (2)

HOARY-THROATED SPINETAIL *Synallaxis kollari* (2) [VU]

OCHER-CHEEKED SPINETAIL *Synallaxis scutata* (2)

WHITE-BROWED SPINETAIL *Hellmayrea gularis* (2)

RED-FACED SPINETAIL *Cranioleuca erythrops* (2)

LINE-CHEEKED SPINETAIL *Cranioleuca antisiensis* (2)

BARON'S SPINETAIL *Cranioleuca baroni* (2)

PALLID SPINETAIL *Cranioleuca pallida* (2)

ASH-BROWED SPINETAIL *Cranioleuca curtata* (2)

TEPUI SPINETAIL *Cranioleuca demissa* (2)

STREAK-CAPPED SPINETAIL *Cranioleuca hellmayri* (2)

CRESTED SPINETAIL *Cranioleuca subcristata* (2)

STRIPE-CROWNED SPINETAIL *Cranioleuca pyrrhophia* (2)

INQUISIVI SPINETAIL *Cranioleuca henricae* (2)

OLIVE SPINETAIL *Cranioleuca obsoleta* (2)

MARCAPATA SPINETAIL *Cranioleuca marcapatae* (2)

LIGHT-CROWNED SPINETAIL *Cranioleuca albiceps* (2)

GRAY-HEADED SPINETAIL *Cranioleuca semicinerea* (2)

CREAMY-CRESTED SPINETAIL *Cranioleuca albicapilla* (2)

COIBA SPINETAIL *Cranioleuca dissita* (2) [NT]

RUSTY-BACKED SPINETAIL *Cranioleuca vulpina* (2)

SCALED SPINETAIL *Cranioleuca muelleri* (2)

SPECKLED SPINETAIL *Cranioleuca gutturata* (2)

SULFUR-BEARDED SPINETAIL *Cranioleuca sulphurifera* (2)

YELLOW-CHINNED SPINETAIL *Certhiaxis cinnamomea* (2)

RED-AND-WHITE SPINETAIL *Certhiaxis mustelina* (2)

LESSER CANASTERO or SHARP-BILLED CANASTERO *Asthenes pyrrholeuca* (2)

SHORT-BILLED CANASTERO *Asthenes baeri* (2)

CANYON CANASTERO *Asthenes pudibunda* (2)

RUSTY-FRONTED CANASTERO *Asthenes ottonis* (2)

MAQUIS CANASTERO *Asthenes heterura* (2) [VU]

CACTUS CANASTERO *Asthenes cactorum* (2) [NT]

CORDILLERAN CANASTERO *Asthenes modesta* (2)

CIPO CANASTERO *Asthenes luizae* (2) [EN]

CREAMY-BREASTED CANASTERO *Asthenes dorbignyi* (2)

DARK-WINGED CANASTERO *Asthenes arequipae* (2)

PALE-TAILED CANASTERO *Asthenes huancavelicae* (2) [VU]

BERLEPSCH'S CANASTERO *Asthenes berlepschi* (2) [VU]

STEINBACH'S CANASTERO or CHESTNUT CANASTERO *Asthenes steinbachi* (2) [VU]

DUSKY-TAILED CANASTERO *Asthenes humicola* (2)

PATAGONIAN CANASTERO *Asthenes patagonica* (2)

STREAK-THROATED CANASTERO *Asthenes humilis* (2)

STREAK-BACKED CANASTERO *Asthenes wyatti* (2)

PUNA CANASTERO *Asthenes sclateri* (2)

AUSTRAL CANASTERO *Asthenes anthoides* (2) [VU]

LINE-FRONTED CANASTERO *Asthenes urubambensis* (2) [NT]

MANY-STRIPED CANASTERO *Asthenes flammulata* (2)

JUNIN CANASTERO *Asthenes virgata* (2)

SCRIBBLE-TAILED CANASTERO *Asthenes maculicauda* (2)

HUDSON'S CANASTERO *Asthenes hudsoni* (2)

ORINOCO SOFTTAIL *Thripophaga cherriei* (2) [VU]

STRIATED SOFTTAIL *Thripophaga macroura* (2) [VU]

RUSSET-MANTLED SOFTTAIL *Thripophaga berlepschi* (2) [NT]

PLAIN SOFTTAIL *Thripophaga fusciceps* (2)

GREAT SPINETAIL *Siptornopsis hypochondriacus* (2) [NT]

RUFOUS-FRONTED THORNBIRD or COMMON THORNBIRD *Phacellodomus rufifrons* (2)

LITTLE THORNBIRD *Phacellodomus sibilatrix* (2)

STREAK-FRONTED THORNBIRD *Phacellodomus striaticeps* (2)

FRECKLE-BREASTED THORNBIRD *Phacellodomus striaticollis* (2)

SPOT-BREASTED THORNBIRD *Phacellodomus maculipectus* (2)

GREATER THORNBIRD *Phacellodomus ruber* (2)

CHESTNUT-BACKED THORNBIRD *Phacellodomus dorsalis* (2) [NT]

RED-EYED THORNBIRD *Phacellodomus erythrophthalmus* (2)

CANEBRAKE GROUNDCREEPER *Clibanornis dendrocolaptoides* (2) [NT]

BAY-CAPPED WREN-SPINETAIL *Spartonoica maluroides* (2) [NT]

WREN-LIKE RUSHBIRD *Phleocryptes melanops* (2)

CURVE-BILLED REEDHAUNTER *Limnornis curvirostris* (2)

STRAIGHT-BILLED REEDHAUNTER *Limnornis rectirostris* (2) [NT]

FIREWOOD-GATHERER *Anumbius annumbi* (2)

LARK-LIKE BRUSHRUNNER *Coryphistera alaudina* (2)

BAND-TAILED EARTHCREEPER *Eremobius phoenicurus* (2)

SPECTACLED PRICKLETAIL *Siptornis striaticollis* (2)

ORANGE-FRONTED PLUSHCROWN *Metopothrix aurantiacus* (2)

DOUBLE-BANDED GRAYTAIL *Xenerpestes minlosi* (2)

EQUATORIAL GRAYTAIL *Xenerpestes singularis* (2) [NT]

RORAIMAN BARBTAIL *Roraimia adusta* (2)

RUSTY-WINGED BARBTAIL *Premnornis guttuligera* (2)

SPOTTED BARBTAIL *Premnoplex brunnescens* (2)

WHITE-THROATED BARBTAIL *Premnoplex tatei* (2) [EN]

RUDDY TREERUNNER *Margarornis rubiginosus* (2)

FULVOUS-DOTTED TREERUNNER or STAR-CHESTED TREERUNNER *Margarornis stellatus* (2)

BEAUTIFUL TREERUNNER *Margarornis bellulus* (2) [NT]

PEARLED TREERUNNER *Margarornis squamiger* (2)

SHARP-TAILED STREAMCREEPER *Lochmias nematura* (2)

RUFOUS CACHOLOTE *Pseudoseisura cristata* (2)

BROWN CACHOLOTE *Pseudoseisura lophotes* (2)

WHITE-THROATED CACHOLOTE *Pseudoseisura gutturalis* (2)

BUFFY TUFTEDCHEEK *Pseudocolaptes lawrencii* (2)

PACIFIC TUFTEDCHEEK *Pseudocolaptes johnsoni* (2)

STREAKED TUFTEDCHEEK *Pseudocolaptes boissonneautii* (2)

POINT-TAILED PALMCREEPER *Berlepschia rikeri* (2)

CHESTNUT-WINGED HOOKBILL *Ancistrops strigilatus* (2)

PALE-BROWED TREEHUNTER *Cichlocolaptes leucophrus* (2)

STRIPED WOODHAUNTER *Hyloctistes subulatus* (2)

GUTTULATED FOLIAGE-GLEANER *Syndactyla guttulata* (2)

LINEATED FOLIAGE-GLEANER *Syndactyla subalaris* (2)

BUFF-BROWED FOLIAGE-GLEANER *Syndactyla rufosuperciliata* (2)

RUFOUS-NECKED FOLIAGE-GLEANER *Syndactyla ruficollis* (2) [VU]

SCALY-BREASTED FOLIAGE-GLEANER or SCALY-THROATED FOLIAGE-GLEANER *Anabacerthia variegaticeps* (1, 2)

MONTANE FOLIAGE-GLEANER *Anabacerthia striaticollis* (2)

RUFOUS-TAILED FOLIAGE-GLEANER *Philydor ruficaudatus* (2)

CINNAMON-RUMPED FOLIAGE-GLEANER *Philydor pyrrhodes* (2)

RUSSET-MANTLED FOLIAGE-GLEANER or PLANALTO FOLIAGE-GLEANER *Philydor dimidiatus* (2) [NT]

SLATY-WINGED FOLIAGE-GLEANER *Philydor fuscipennis* (2)

RUFOUS-RUMPED FOLIAGE-GLEANER *Philydor erythrocercus* (2)

OCHER-BELLIED FOLIAGE-GLEANER *Philydor ochrogaster* (2)

CHESTNUT-WINGED FOLIAGE-GLEANER *Philydor erythropterus* (2)

WHITE-BROWED FOLIAGE-GLEANER *Philydor amaurotis* (2) [NT]

OCHER-BREASTED FOLIAGE-GLEANER *Philydor lichtensteini* (2)

BUFF-FRONTED FOLIAGE-GLEANER *Philydor rufus* (2)

BLACK-CAPPED FOLIAGE-GLEANER *Philydor atricapillus* (2)

ALAGOAS FOLIAGE-GLEANER *Philydor novaesi* (2) [CR]

PERUVIAN RECURVEBILL *Simoxenops ucayalae* (2) [NT]

BOLIVIAN RECURVEBILL *Simoxenops striatus* (2) [VU]

WHITE-COLLARED FOLIAGE-GLEANER *Anabazenops fuscus* (2)

UNIFORM TREEHUNTER *Thripadectes ignobilis* (2)

STREAK-BREASTED TREEHUNTER *Thripadectes rufobrunneus* (2)

STREAK-CAPPED TREEHUNTER *Thripadectes virgaticeps* (2)

BLACK-BILLED TREEHUNTER *Thripadectes melanorhynchus* (2)

STRIPED TREEHUNTER *Thripadectes holostictus* (2)

FLAMMULATED TREEHUNTER *Thripadectes flammulatus* (2)

BUFF-THROATED TREEHUNTER or PERUVIAN TREEHUNTER *Thripadectes scrutator* (2)

BUFF-THROATED FOLIAGE-GLEANER *Automolus ochrolaemus* (2)

CRESTED FOLIAGE-GLEANER or DUSKY-CHEEKED FOLIAGE-GLEANER *Automolus dorsalis* (2)

OLIVE-BACKED FOLIAGE-GLEANER *Automolus infuscatus* (2)

WHITE-EYED FOLIAGE-GLEANER *Automolus leucophthalmus* (2)

WHITE-THROATED FOLIAGE-GLEANER *Automolus roraimae* (2)

BROWN-RUMPED FOLIAGE-GLEANER *Automolus melanopezus* (2)

RUDDY FOLIAGE-GLEANER *Automolus rubiginosus* (1, 2)

CHESTNUT-CROWNED FOLIAGE-GLEANER *Automolus rufipileatus* (2)

CHESTNUT-CAPPED FOLIAGE-GLEANER *Hylocryptus rectirostris* (2) [NT]

HENNA-HOODED FOLIAGE-GLEANER *Hylocryptus erythrocephalus* (2) [VU]

TAWNY-THROATED LEAFTOSSER *Sclerurus mexicanus* (1, 2)

SHORT-BILLED LEAFTOSSER *Sclerurus rufigularis* (2)

GRAY-THROATED LEAFTOSSER *Sclerurus albigularis* (2)

BLACK-TAILED LEAFTOSSER *Sclerurus caudacutus* (2)

RUFOUS-BREASTED LEAFTOSSER *Sclerurus scansor* (2)

SCALY-THROATED LEAFTOSSER *Sclerurus guatemalensis* (1, 2)

SHARP-BILLED TREEHUNTER *Heliobletus contaminatus* (2)

RUFOUS-TAILED XENOPS *Xenops milleri* (2)

SLENDER-BILLED XENOPS *Xenops renuirostris* (2)

PLAIN XENOPS *Xenops minutus* (1, 2)

STREAKED XENOPS *Xenops rutilans* (2)

GREAT XENOPS *Megaxenops parnaguae* (2) [VU]

WHITE-THROATED TREERUNNER *Pygarrhichas albogularis* (2)

Subfamily DENDROCOLAPTINAE

SCIMITAR-BILLED WOODCREEPER *Drymornis bridgesii* (2)

LONG-BILLED WOODCREEPER *Nasica longirostris* (2)

TYRANNINE WOODCREEPER *Dendrocincla tyrannina* (2)

PLAIN-BROWN WOODCREEPER *Dendrocincla fuliginosa* (2)

THRUSH-LIKE WOODCREEPER *Dendrocincla turdina* (2)

TAWNY-WINGED WOODCREEPER *Dendrocincla anabatina* (1, 2)

WHITE-CHINNED WOODCREEPER *Dendrocincla merula* (2)

RUDDY WOODCREEPER *Dendrocincla homochroa* (2)

LONG-TAILED WOODCREEPER *Deconychura longicauda* (2)

SPOT-THROATED WOODCREEPER *Deconychura stictolaema* (2)

OLIVACEOUS WOODCREEPER *Sittasomus griseicapillus* (2)

WEDGE-BILLED WOODCREEPER *Glyphorynchus spirurus* (1, 2)

BAR-BELLIED WOODCREEPER *Hylexetastes stresemanni* (2)

RED-BILLED WOODCREEPER *Hylexetastes perrotii* (2)

UNIFORM WOODCREEPER *Hylexetastes uniformis* (2)

BRIGIDA'S WOODCREEPER *Hylexetastes brigidai* (2)

STRONG-BILLED WOODCREEPER *Xiphocolaptes promeropirhynchus* (1, 2)

WHITE-THROATED WOODCREEPER *Xiphocolaptes albicollis* (2)

MUSTACHED WOODCREEPER *Xiphocolaptes falcirostris* (2) [VU]

GREAT RUFOUS WOODCREEPER *Xiphocolaptes major* (2)

BARRED WOODCREEPER *Dendrocolaptes certhia* (1, 2)

HOFFMANNS'S WOODCREEPER *Dendrocolaptes hoffmannsi* (2)

BLACK-BANDED WOODCREEPER *Dendrocolaptes picumnus* (1, 2)

PLANALTO WOODCREEPER *Dendrocolaptes platyrostris* (2)

STRAIGHT-BILLED WOODCREEPER *Xiphorhynchus picus* (2)

ZIMMER'S WOODCREEPER *Xiphorhynchus necopinus* (2)

STRIPED WOODCREEPER *Xiphorhynchus obsoletus* (2)

OCELLATED WOODCREEPER *Xiphorhynchus ocellatus* (2)

SPIX'S WOODCREEPER *Xiphorhynchus spixii* (2)

ELEGANT WOODCREEPER *Xiphorhynchus elegans* (2)

CHESTNUT-RUMPED WOODCREEPER *Xiphorhynchus pardalotus* (2)

BUFF-THROATED WOODCREEPER *Xiphorhynchus guttatus* (2)

COCOA WOODCREEPER *Xiphorhynchus susurrans* (2)

IVORY-BILLED WOODCREEPER *Xiphorhynchus flavigaster* (1, 2)

BLACK-STRIPED WOODCREEPER *Xiphorhynchus lachrymosus* (2)

SPOTTED WOODCREEPER *Xiphorhynchus erythropygius* (1, 2)

OLIVE-BACKED WOODCREEPER *Xiphorhynchus triangularis* (2)

WHITE-STRIPED WOODCREEPER *Lepidocolaptes leucogaster* (1)

STREAK-HEADED WOODCREEPER *Lepidocolaptes souleyetii* (1, 2)

NARROW-BILLED WOODCREEPER *Lepidocolaptes angustirostris* (2)

SPOT-CROWNED WOODCREEPER *Lepidocolaptes affinis* (1, 2)

MONTANE WOODCREEPER *Lepidocolaptes lacrymiger* (2)

SCALED WOODCREEPER *Lepidocolaptes squamatus* (2)

LESSER WOODCREEPER *Lepidocolaptes fuscus* (2)

LINEATED WOODCREEPER *Lepidocolaptes albolineatus* (2)

GREATER SCYTHEBILL *Campylorhamphus pucherani* (2) [NT]

RED-BILLED SCYTHEBILL *Campylorhamphus trochilirostris* (2)

BLACK-BILLED SCYTHEBILL *Campylorhamphus falcularius* (2)

BROWN-BILLED SCYTHEBILL *Campylorhamphus pusillus* (2)

CURVE-BILLED SCYTHEBILL *Campylorhamphus procurvoides* (2)

Superfamily FORMICARIOIDEA
Family FORMICARIIDAE

RUFOUS-CAPPED ANTTHRUSH *Formicarius colma* (2)

MEXICAN ANTTHRUSH *Formicarius moniliger* (1, 2)

BLACK-FACED ANTTHRUSH *Formicarius analis* (2)

RUFOUS-FRONTED ANTTHRUSH *Formicarius rufifrons* (2) [VU]

BLACK-HEADED ANTTHRUSH *Formicarius nigricapillus* (2)

RUFOUS-BREASTED ANTTHRUSH *Formicarius rufipectus* (2)

SHORT-TAILED ANTTHRUSH *Chamaeza campanisona* (2)

STRIATED ANTTHRUSH or NOBLE ANTTHRUSH *Chamaeza nobilis* (2)

SCHWARTZ'S ANTTHRUSH or SCALLOPED ANTTHRUSH *Chamaeza turdina* (2)

SUCH'S ANTTHRUSH or CRYPTIC ANTTHRUSH *Chamaeza meruloides* (2)

RUFOUS-TAILED ANTTHRUSH *Chamaeza ruficauda* (2)

BARRED ANTTHRUSH *Chamaeza mollissima* (2)

BLACK-CROWNED ANTPITTA *Pittasoma michleri* (2)

RUFOUS-CROWNED ANTPITTA *Pittasoma rufopileatum* (2)

UNDULATED ANTPITTA *Grallaria squamigera* (2)

GIANT ANTPITTA *Grallaria gigantea* (2) [VU]

GREAT ANTPITTA *Grallaria excelsa* (2) [NT]

VARIEGATED ANTPITTA *Grallaria varia* (2)

SCALED ANTPITTA *Grallaria guatimalensis* (1, 2)

MUSTACHED ANTPITTA *Grallaria alleni* (2) [EN]

TACHIRA ANTPITTA *Grallaria chthonia* (2) [VU]

PLAIN-BACKED ANTPITTA *Grallaria haplonota* (2)

OCHER-STRIPED ANTPITTA *Grallaria dignissima* (2)

ELUSIVE ANTPITTA *Grallaria eludens* (2) [NT]

CUNDINAMARCA ANTPITTA *Grallaria kaestneri* (2) [VU]

SANTA MARTA ANTPITTA *Grallaria bangsi* (2) [NT]

CHESTNUT-CROWNED ANTPITTA *Grallaria ruficapilla* (2)

SCRUB ANTPITTA *Grallaria watkinsi* (2)

STRIPE-HEADED ANTPITTA *Grallaria andicola* (2)

BICOLORED ANTPITTA *Grallaria rufocinerea* (2) [EN]

CHESTNUT-NAPED ANTPITTA *Grallaria nuchalis* (2)

PALE-BILLED ANTPITTA *Grallaria carrikeri* (2)

WHITE-THROATED ANTPITTA *Grallaria albigula* (2)

YELLOW-BREASTED ANTPITTA *Grallaria flavotincta* (2)

WHITE-BELLIED ANTPITTA *Grallaria hypoleuca* (2)

RUSTY-TINGED ANTPITTA *Grallaria przewalskii* (2)

BAY ANTPITTA *Grallaria capitalis* (2)

RED-AND-WHITE ANTPITTA *Grallaria erythroleuca* (2)

GRAY-NAPED ANTPITTA *Grallaria griseonucha* (2)

RUFOUS ANTPITTA *Grallaria rufula* (2)

CHESTNUT ANTPITTA *Grallaria blakei* (2) [NT]

RUFOUS-FACED ANTPITTA *Grallaria erythrotis* (2)

TAWNY ANTPITTA *Grallaria quitensis* (2)

BROWN-BANDED ANTPITTA *Grallaria milleri* (1, 2) [EN]

SPECTACLED ANTPITTA or STREAK-CHESTED ANTPITTA *Hylopezus perspicillatus* (2)

SPOTTED ANTPITTA *Hylopezus macularius* (2)

FULVOUS-BELLIED ANTPITTA *Hylopezus dives* (2)

WHITE-LORED ANTPITTA *Hylopezus fulviventris* (2)

AMAZONIAN ANTPITTA *Hylopezus berlepschi* (2)

WHITE-BROWED ANTPITTA *Hylopezus ochroleucus* (2) [NT]

SPECKLE-BREASTED ANTPITTA *Hylopezus nattereri* (2)

THRUSH-LIKE ANTPITTA *Myrmothera campanisona* (2)

BROWN-BREASTED ANTPITTA or TEPUI ANTPITTA *Myrmothera simplex* (2)

OCHER-BREASTED ANTPITTA *Grallaricula flavirostris* (2)

RUSTY-BREASTED ANTPITTA *Grallaricula ferrugineipectus* (2)

SLATE-CROWNED ANTPITTA *Grallaricula nana* (2)

SCALLOP-BREASTED ANTPITTA *Grallaricula loricata* (2) [NT]

PERUVIAN ANTPITTA *Grallaricula peruviana* (2) [NT]

OCHER-FRONTED ANTPITTA *Grallaricula ochraceifrons* (2) [NT]

CRESCENT-FACED ANTPITTA *Grallaricula lineifrons* (2) [NT]

HOODED ANTPITTA *Grallaricula cucullata* (2) [VU]

Family CONOPOPHAGIDAE

RUFOUS GNATEATER *Conopophaga lineata* (2)

CHESTNUT-BELTED GNATEATER *Conopophaga aurita* (2)

HOODED GNATEATER *Conopophaga roberti* (2) [NT]

ASH-THROATED GNATEATER *Conopophaga peruviana* (2)

SLATY GNATEATER *Conopophaga ardesiaca* (2)

CHESTNUT-CROWNED GNATEATER *Conopophaga castaneiceps* (2)

BLACK-CHEEKED GNATEATER *Conopophaga melanops* (2)

BLACK-BELLIED GNATEATER *Conopophaga melanogaster* (2)

Family RHINOCRYPTIDAE

BLACK-THROATED HUET-HUET *Pteroptochos tarnii* (2)

CHESTNUT-THROATED HUET-HUET *Pteroptochos castaneus* (2)

MUSTACHED TURCA *Pteroptochos megapodius* (2)

WHITE-THROATED TAPACULO *Scelorchilus albicollis* (2)

CHUCAO TAPACULO *Scelorchilus rubecula* (2)

CRESTED GALLITO *Rhinocrypta lanceolata* (2)

SANDY GALLITO *Teledromas fuscus* (2)

RUSTY-BELTED TAPACULO *Liosceles thoracicus* (2)

SPOTTED BAMBOOWREN *Psilorhamphus guttatus* (2)

SLATY BRISTLEFRONT *Merulaxis ater* (2)

STRESEMANN'S BRISTLEFRONT *Merulaxis stresemanni* (2) [CR]

OCHER-FLANKED TAPACULO *Eugralla paradoxa* (2)

ASH-COLORED TAPACULO *Myornis senilis* (2)

COLLARED CRESCENT-CHEST *Melanopareia torquata* (2)

OLIVE-CROWNED CRESCENT-CHEST *Melanopareia maximiliani* (2)

ELEGANT CRESCENT-CHEST *Melanopareia elegans* (2)

MARANON CRESCENT-CHEST *Melanopareia maranonica* (2) [NT]

UNICOLORED TAPACULO *Scytalopus unicolor* (2)

GRAY TAPACULO *Scytalopus parvirostris* (2)

LARGE-FOOTED TAPACULO *Scytalopus macropus* (2)

PERUVIAN RUFOUS-VENTED TAPACULO *Scytalopus femoralis* (2)

EQUATORIAL RUFOUS-VENTED TAPACULO *Scytalopus micropterus* (2)

SOUTHERN WHITE-CROWNED TAPACULO *Scytalopus bolivianus* (2)

NORTHERN WHITE-CROWNED TAPACULO *Scytalopus atratus* (2)

SANTA MARTA TAPACULO *Scytalopus sanctaemartae* (2)

TACARCUNA TAPACULO or PALE-THROATED TAPACULO *Scytalopus panamensis* (2)

NARINO TAPACULO *Scytalopus vicinior* (2)

SILVERY-FRONTED TAPACULO *Scytalopus argentifrons* (2)

BROWN-RUMPED TAPACULO *Scytalopus latebricola* (2)

MERIDA TAPACULO *Scytalopus meridanus* (2)

CARACAS TAPACULO *Scytalopus caracae* (2)

SPILLMAN'S TAPACULO *Scytalopus spillmani* (2)

ZIMMER'S TAPACULO *Scytalopus zimmeri* (2)

ANDEAN TAPACULO *Scytalopus simonsi* (2)

CUZCO TAPACULO *Scytalopus urubambae* (2)

ELFIN FOREST TAPACULO *Scytalopus altirostris* (2)

ANCASH TAPACULO *Scytalopus affinis* (2)

PARAMO TAPACULO *Scytalopus canus* (2)

MAGELLANIC TAPACULO *Scytalopus magellanicus* (2)

RUFOUS-RUMPED TAPACULO *Scytalopus griseicollis* (2)

WHITE-BROWED TAPACULO *Scytalopus superciliaris* (2)

DUSKY TAPACULO *Scytalopus fuscus* (2)

SHARP-BILLED TAPACULO *Scytalopus acutirostris* (2)

MOUSE-COLORED TAPACULO *Scytalopus speluncae* (2)

BRASILIA TAPACULO *Scytalopus novacapitalis* (2) [VU]

CHESTNUT-SIDED TAPACULO or BAHIA TAPACULO *Scytalopus psychopompus* (2) [EN]

WHITE-BREASTED TAPACULO *Scytalopus indigoticus* (2)

DIADEMED TAPACULO *Scytalopus schulenbergi* (2)

CHOCO TAPACULO *Scytalopus chocoensis* (2)

ECUADORIAN TAPACULO *Scytalopus robbinsi* (2)

CHUSQUEA TAPACULO *Scytalopus parkeri* (2)

OCELLATED TAPACULO *Acropternis orthonyx* (2)

Parvorder CORVIDA
Superfamily MENUROIDEA
Family CLIMACTERIDAE

PAPUAN TREECREEPER *Cormobates placens* (6)

WHITE-THROATED TREECREEPER *Cormobates leucophaeus* (6)

WHITE-BROWED TREECREEPER *Climacteris affinis* (6)

RED-BROWED TREECREEPER *Climacteris erythrops* (6)

BROWN TREECREEPER *Climacteris picumnus* (6)

BLACK-TAILED TREECREEPER *Climacteris melanura* (6)

RUFOUS TREECREEPER *Climacteris rufa* (6)

Family MENURIDAE
Subfamily MENURINAE

ALBERT'S LYREBIRD *Menura alberti* (6) [NT]

SUPERB LYREBIRD *Menura novaehollandiae* (6)

Subfamily ATRICHORNITHINAE

RUFOUS SCRUB-BIRD *Atrichornis rufescens* (6) [VU]

NOISY SCRUB-BIRD *Atrichornis clamosus* (6) [VU]

Family PTILONORHYNCHIDAE

WHITE-EARED CATBIRD *Ailuroedus buccoides* (6)

SPOTTED CATBIRD or BLACK-EARED CATBIRD *Ailuroedus melanotis* (6)

GREEN CATBIRD *Ailuroedus crassirostris* (6)

TOOTH-BILLED CATBIRD *Scenopooetes dentirostris* (6) [NT]

ARCHBOLD'S BOWERBIRD *Archboldia papuensis* (6) [VU]

SANFORD'S BOWERBIRD or TOMBA BOWERBIRD *Archboldia sanfordi* (6)

VOGELKOP BOWERBIRD *Amblyornis inornatus* (6)

MACGREGOR'S BOWERBIRD *Amblyornis macgregoriae* (6)

STREAKED BOWERBIRD *Amblyornis subalaris* (6)

GOLDEN-FRONTED BOWERBIRD *Amblyornis flavifrons* (6) [NT]

GOLDEN BOWERBIRD *Prionodura newtoniana* (6) [CD]

FLAME BOWERBIRD *Sericulus aureus* (6)

FIRE-MANED BOWERBIRD *Sericulus bakeri* (6) [VU]

REGENT BOWERBIRD *Sericulus chrysocephalus* (6)

SATIN BOWERBIRD *Ptilonorhynchus violaceus* (6)

WESTERN BOWERBIRD *Chlamydera guttata* (6)

SPOTTED BOWERBIRD *Chlamydera maculata* (6)

GREAT BOWERBIRD *Chlamydera nuchalis* (6)

YELLOW-BREASTED BOWERBIRD *Chlamydera lauterbachi* (6)

FAWN-BREASTED BOWERBIRD *Chlamydera cerviniventris* (6)

Family TURNAGRIDAE

PIOPIO *Turnagra capensis* (6) [EX]

Superfamily MELIPHAGOIDEA
Family MALURIDAE
Subfamily MALURINAE
Tribe MALURINI

ORANGE-CROWNED FAIRYWREN *Clytomyias insignis* (6)

WALLACE'S FAIRYWREN *Sipodotus wallacii* (6)

BROAD-BILLED FAIRYWREN *Malurus grayi* (6) [NT]

CAMPBELL'S FAIRYWREN *Malurus campbelli* (6) [DD]

WHITE-SHOULDERED FAIRYWREN *Malurus alboscapulatus* (6)

RED-BACKED FAIRYWREN *Malurus melanocephalus* (6)

WHITE-WINGED FAIRYWREN *Malurus leucopterus* (6)

SUPERB FAIRYWREN *Malurus cyaneus* (6)

SPLENDID FAIRYWREN *Malurus splendens* (6)

VARIEGATED FAIRYWREN *Malurus lamberti* (6)

LOVELY FAIRYWREN *Malurus amabilis* (6)

RED-WINGED FAIRYWREN *Malurus elegans* (6)

BLUE-BREASTED FAIRYWREN *Malurus pulcherrimus* (6)

PURPLE-CROWNED FAIRYWREN *Malurus coronatus* (6) [NT]

EMPEROR FAIRYWREN *Malurus cyanocephalus* (6)

Tribe STIPITURINI

RUFOUS-CROWNED EMUWREN *Stipiturus ruficeps* (6)

SOUTHERN EMUWREN *Stipiturus malachurus* (6)

MALLEE EMUWREN *Stipiturus mallee* (6) [CD]

Subfamily AMYTORNITHINAE

GRAY GRASSWREN *Amytornis barbatus* (6) [NT]

WHITE-THROATED GRASSWREN *Amytornis woodwardi* (6) [NT]

CARPENTARIAN GRASSWREN *Amytornis dorotheae* (6) [VU]

STRIATED GRASSWREN *Amytornis striatus* (6)

EYREAN GRASSWREN *Amytornis goyderi* (6)

THICK-BILLED GRASSWREN *Amytornis textilis* (6) [VU]

DUSKY GRASSWREN *Amytornis purnelli* (6)

BLACK GRASSWREN *Amytornis housei* (6) [NT]

Family MELIPHAGIDAE

DRAB MYZOMELA *Myzomela blasii* (4)

WHITE-CHINNED MYZOMELA *Myzomela albigula* (6) [DD]

RED-THROATED MYZOMELA *Myzomela eques* (6)

ASHY MYZOMELA *Myzomela cineracea* (6)

DUSKY MYZOMELA *Myzomela obscura* (6)

RED MYZOMELA *Myzomela cruentata* (6)

BLACK MYZOMELA *Myzomela nigrita* (6)

OLIVE-YELLOW MYZOMELA or NEW IRELAND HONEYEATER *Myzomela pulchella* (6)

MOUNTAIN MYZOMELA or MOUNTAIN RED-HEADED HONEYEATER *Myzomela adolphinae* (6)

CRIMSON-HOODED MYZOMELA *Myzomela kuehni* (6) [DD]

SUMBA MYZOMELA *Myzomela dammermani* (6)

RED-HEADED MYZOMELA *Myzomela erythrocephala* (6)

SULAWESI MYZOMELA *Myzomela chloroptera* (4)

WAKOLO MYZOMELA *Myzomela wakoloensis* (4)

BANDA MYZOMELA *Myzomela boiei* (6)

SCARLET MYZOMELA or SCARLET HONEYEATER *Myzomela sanguinolenta* (6)

NEW CALEDONIAN MYZOMELA *Myzomela caledonica* (6)

MICRONESIAN MYZOMELA *Myzomela rubratra* (6)

CARDINAL MYZOMELA *Myzomela cardinalis* (6)

ROTUMA MYZOMELA *Myzomela chermesina* (6) [VU]

SCARLET-BIBBED MYZOMELA *Myzomela sclateri* (6)

EBONY MYZOMELA *Myzomela pammelaena* (6)

SCARLET-NAPED MYZOMELA *Myzomela lafargei* (6)

YELLOW-VENTED MYZOMELA *Myzomela eichhorni* (6)

BLACK-HEADED MYZOMELA *Myzomela melanocephala* (4, 6)

RED-BELLIED MYZOMELA *Myzomela malaitae* (4)

SOOTY MYZOMELA *Myzomela tristrami* (4)

ORANGE-BREASTED MYZOMELA *Myzomela jugularis* (6)

BLACK-BELLIED MYZOMELA or NEW BRITAIN RED-HEADED HONEYEATER *Myzomela erythromelas* (6)

RED-RUMPED MYZOMELA *Myzomela vulnerata* (4) [NT]

RED-COLLARED MYZOMELA *Myzomela rosenbergii* (6)

BANDED HONEYEATER *Certhionyx pectoralis* (6)

BLACK HONEYEATER *Certhionyx niger* (6)

PIED HONEYEATER *Certhionyx variegatus* (6)

OLIVE STRAIGHTBILL *Timeliopsis fulvigula* (6)

TAWNY STRAIGHTBILL *Timeliopsis griseigula* (6)

LONG-BILLED HONEYEATER *Melilestes megarhynchus* (6)

BOUGAINVILLE HONEYEATER *Stresemannia bougainvillei* (4)

GREEN-BACKED HONEYEATER *Glycichaera fallax* (6)

SCALY-CROWNED HONEYEATER *Lichmera lombokia* (6)

OLIVE HONEYEATER *Lichmera argentauris* (4, 6)

INDONESIAN HONEYEATER *Lichmera limbata* (4)

BROWN HONEYEATER *Lichmera indistincta* (6)

DARK-BROWN HONEYEATER *Lichmera incana* (6)

WHITE-TUFTED HONEYEATER *Lichmera squamata* (4)

SILVER-EARED HONEYEATER *Lichmera alboauricularis* (6)

BURU HONEYEATER *Lichmera deningeri* (4) [NT]

SERAM HONEYEATER *Lichmera monticola* (4)

YELLOW-EARED HONEYEATER *Lichmera flavicans* (4)

BLACK-CHESTED HONEYEATER or BLACK-NECKLACED HONEYEATER *Lichmera notabilis* (4) [DD]

WHITE-STREAKED HONEYEATER *Trichodere cockerelli* (4)

FOREST HONEYEATER or FOREST WHITE-EARED HONEYEATER *Meliphaga montana* (4)

MOTTLE-BREASTED HONEYEATER or SPOT-BREASTED HONEYEATER *Meliphaga mimikae* (4)

HILL-FOREST HONEYEATER or MOUNTAIN YELLOW-EARED HONEYEATER *Meliphaga orientalis* (6)

SCRUB HONEYEATER *Meliphaga albonotata* (6)

PUFF-BACKED HONEYEATER *Meliphaga aruensis* (6)

MIMIC HONEYEATER or MIMETIC HONEYEATER *Meliphaga analoga* (6)

TAGULA HONEYEATER *Meliphaga vicina* (6) [DD]

GRACEFUL HONEYEATER *Meliphaga gracilis* (6)

YELLOW-SPOTTED HONEYEATER *Meliphaga notata* (6)

YELLOW-GAPED HONEYEATER *Meliphaga flavirictus* (6)

LEWIN'S HONEYEATER *Meliphaga lewinii* (6)

WHITE-LINED HONEYEATER *Meliphaga albilineata* (6)

STREAKY-BREASTED HONEYEATER *Meliphaga reticulata* (4) [NT]

GUADALCANAL HONEYEATER *Guadalcanaria inexpectata* (4)

WATTLED HONEYEATER *Foulehaio carunculata* (6)

BLACK-THROATED HONEYEATER *Lichenostomus subfrenatus* (6)

OBSCURE HONEYEATER *Lichenostomus obscurus* (6)

BRIDLED HONEYEATER *Lichenostomus frenatus* (6) [NT]

EUNGELLA HONEYEATER *Lichenostomus hindwoodi* (6) [CD]

YELLOW-FACED HONEYEATER *Lichenostomus chrysops* (6)

VARIED HONEYEATER *Lichenostomus versicolor* (6)

MANGROVE HONEYEATER *Lichenostomus fasciogularis* (6)

SINGING HONEYEATER *Lichenostomus cirescens* (6)

YELLOW HONEYEATER *Lichenostomus flavus* (6)

WHITE-GAPED HONEYEATER *Lichenostomus unicolor* (6)

WHITE-EARED HONEYEATER *Lichenostomus leucotis* (6)

YELLOW-THROATED HONEYEATER *Lichenostomus flavicollis* (6)

YELLOW-TUFTED HONEYEATER *Lichenostomus melanops* (6)

PURPLE-GAPED HONEYEATER *Lichenostomus cratitius* (6)

GRAY-HEADED HONEYEATER *Lichenostomus keartlandi* (6)

YELLOW-TINTED HONEYEATER *Lichenostomus flavescens* (6)

FUSCOUS HONEYEATER *Lichenostomus fuscus* (6)

GRAY-FRONTED HONEYEATER *Lichenostomus plumulus* (6)

YELLOW-PLUMED HONEYEATER *Lichenostomus ornatus* (6)

WHITE-PLUMED HONEYEATER *Lichenostomus penicillatus* (6)

TAWNY-BREASTED HONEYEATER *Xanthotis flaviventer* (6)

SPOTTED HONEYEATER *Xanthotis polygramma* (6)

MACLEAY'S HONEYEATER *Xanthotis macleayana* (6)

KADAVU HONEYEATER *Xanthotis provocator* (6) [NT]

ORANGE-CHEEKED HONEYEATER *Oreornis chrysogenys* (6)

WHITE-NAPED HONEYEATER *Melithreptus lunatus* (6)

BLACK-HEADED HONEYEATER *Melithreptus affinis* (6)

WHITE-THROATED HONEYEATER *Melithreptus albogularis* (6)

BLACK-CHINNED HONEYEATER *Melithreptus gularis* (6)

STRONG-BILLED HONEYEATER *Melithreptus validirostris* (6)

BROWN-HEADED HONEYEATER *Melithreptus brevirostris* (6)

STITCHBIRD *Notiomystis cincta* (6) [VU]

PLAIN HONEYEATER *Pycnopygius ixoides* (6)

MARBLED HONEYEATER *Pycnopygius cinereus* (6)

STREAK-HEADED HONEYEATER *Pycnopygius stictocephalus* (6)

WHITE-STREAKED FRIARBIRD *Melitograis gilolensis* (4)

MEYER'S FRIARBIRD *Philemon meyeri* (6)

PLAIN FRIARBIRD or TIMOR FRIARBIRD *Philemon inornatus* (4) [NT]

GRAY FRIARBIRD *Philemon kisserensis* (4) [DD]

BRASS'S FRIARBIRD *Philemon brassi* (6) [DD]

LITTLE FRIARBIRD *Philemon citreogularis* (6)

DUSKY FRIARBIRD *Philemon fuscicapillus* (4) [DD]

BLACK-FACED FRIARBIRD *Philemon moluccensis* (4)

GRAY-NECKED FRIARBIRD *Philemon subcorniculatus* (4)

HELMETED FRIARBIRD *Philemon buceroides* (4, 6)

NEW GUINEA FRIARBIRD *Philemon novaeguineae* (6)

WHITE-NAPED FRIARBIRD or MANUS FRIARBIRD *Philemon albitorques* (6)

NEW BRITAIN FRIARBIRD *Philemon cockerelli* (6)

NEW IRELAND FRIARBIRD *Philemon eichhorni* (6)

SILVER-CROWNED FRIARBIRD *Philemon argenticeps* (6)

NOISY FRIARBIRD *Philemon corniculatus. Lowland Savanna* (6)

NEW CALEDONIAN FRIARBIRD *Philemon diemenensis* (6)

LEADEN HONEYEATER *Ptiloprora plumbea* (6)

OLIVE-STREAKED HONEYEATER *Ptiloprora meekiana* (6)

RUFOUS-SIDED HONEYEATER *Ptiloprora erythropleura* (6)

MAYR'S HONEYEATER *Ptiloprora mayri* (6)

RUFOUS-BACKED HONEYEATER *Ptiloprora guisei* (6)

BLACK-BACKED HONEYEATER *Ptiloprora perstriata* (6)

SOOTY HONEYEATER or SOOTY MELIDECTES *Melidectes fuscus* (6)

BISMARCK HONEYEATER or BISMARCK MELIDECTES *Melidectes whitemanensis* (6)

SHORT-BEARDED HONEYEATER or SHORT-BEARDED MELIDECTES *Melidectes nouhuysi* (6)

LONG-BEARDED HONEYEATER or LONG-BEARDED MELIDECTES *Melidectes princeps* (6) [VU]

CINNAMON-BROWED HONEYEATER or CINNAMON-BROWED MELIDECTES *Melidectes ochromelas* (6)

VOGELKOP HONEYEATER or VOGELKOP MELIDECTES *Melidectes leucostephes* (6) [NT]

BELFORD'S HONEYEATER or BELFORD'S MELIDECTES *Melidectes belfordi* (6)

YELLOW-BROWED HONEYEATER or YELLOW-BROWED MELIDECTES *Melidectes rufocrissalis* (6)

HUON WATTLED HONEYEATER or HUON MELIDECTES *Melidectes foersteri* (6)

ORNATE HONEYEATER or ORNATE MELIDECTES *Melidectes torquatus* (6)

SAN CRISTÓBAL HONEYEATER or SAN CRISTÓBAL MELIDECTES *Melidectes sclateri* (6)

ARFAK HONEYEATER or WESTERN SMOKY HONEYEATER *Melipotes gymnops* (6)

SMOKY HONEYEATER *Melipotes fumigatus* (6)

SPANGLED HONEYEATER *Melipotes ater* (6)

DARK-EARED MYZA *Myza celebensis* (4)

WHITE-EARED MYZA *Myza sarasinorum* (4)

GIANT HONEYEATER *Gymnomyza viridis* (6)

MAO *Gymnomyza samoensis* (6) [VU]

CROW HONEYEATER *Gymnomyza aubryana* (6) [VU]

KAUAI OO *Moho braccatus* (2) [EX]

OAHU OO *Moho apicalis* (2) [EX]

BISHOP'S OO *Moho bishopi* (2) [EX]

HAWAII OO *Moho nobilis* (2) [EX]

KIOEA *Chaetoptila angustipluma* (2) [EX]

CRESCENT HONEYEATER *Phylidonyris pyrrhoptera* (6)

NEW HOLLAND HONEYEATER *Phylidonyris novaehollandiae* (6)

WHITE-CHEEKED HONEYEATEr *Phylidonyris nigra* (6)

WHITE-FRONTED HONEYEATER *Phylidonyris albifrons* (6)

BARRED HONEYEATER *Phylidonyris undulata* (6)

NEW HEBRIDES HONEYEATER *Phylidonyris notabilis* (6)

TAWNY-CROWNED HONEYEATER *Phylidonyris melanops* (6)

BROWN-BACKED HONEYEATER *Ramsayornis modestus* (6)

BAR-BREASTED HONEYEATER *Ramsayornis fasciatus* (6)

STRIPED HONEYEATER *Plectorhyncha lanceolata* (6)

RUFOUS-BANDED HONEYEATER *Conopophila albogularis* (6)

RUFOUS-THROATED HONEYEATER *Conopophila rufogularis* (6)

GRAY HONEYEATER *Conopophila whitei* (6)

PAINTED HONEYEATER *Grantiella picta* (6) [VU]

REGENT HONEYEATER *Xanthomyza phrygia* (6) [EN]

EASTERN SPINEBILl *Acanthorhynchus tenuirostris* (6)

WESTERN SPINEBILL *Acanthorhynchus superciliosus* (6)

BLUE-FACED HONEYEATER *Entomyzon cyanotis* (6)

BELL MINER *Manorina melanophrys* (6)

NOISY MINER *Manorina melanocephala* (6)

YELLOW-THROATED MINER *Manorina flavigula* (6)

BLACK-EARED MINER *Manorina melanotis* (6) [CR]

NEW ZEALAND BELLBIRD *Anthornis melanura* (6)

SPINY-CHEEKED HONEYEATER *Acanthagenys rufogularis* (6)

LITTLE WATTLEBIRD *Anthochaera lunulata* (6)

BRUSH WATTLEBIRD *Anthochaera chrysoptera* (6)

RED WATTLEBIRD *Anthochaera carunculata* (6)

YELLOW WATTLEBIRD *Anthochaera paradoxa* (6)

CRIMSON CHAT *Epthianura tricolor* (6)

ORANGE CHAT *Epthianura aurifrons* (6)

YELLOW CHAT *Epthianura crocea* (6) [NT]

WHITE-FRONTED CHAT *Epthianura albifrons* (6)

GIBBERBIRD *Ashbyia lovensis* (6)

BONIN ISLANDS WHITE-EYE *Apalopteron familiare* (6) [VU]

Family PARDALOTIDAE
Subfamily PARDALOTINAE

SPOTTED PARDALOTE *Pardalotus punctatus* (6)

FORTY-SPOTTED PARDALOTE *Pardalotus quadragintus* (6) [VU]

RED-BROWED PARDALOTE *Pardalotus rubricatus* (6)

STRIATED PARDALOTE *Pardalotus striatus* (6)

Subfamily DASYORNITHINAE

WESTERN BRISTLEBIRD *Dasyornis longirostris* (6) [EN]

EASTERN BRISTLEBIRD *Dasyornis brachypterus* (6) [VU]

RUFOUS BRISTLEBIRD *Dasyornis broadbenti* (6) [VU]

Subfamily ACANTHIZINAE
Tribe SERICORNITHINI

PILOTBIRD *Pycnoptilus floccosus* (6)

ROCKWARBLER or ORIGMA *Origma solitaria* (6)

FERNWREN *Oreoscopus gutturalis* (6)

RUSTY MOUSE-WARBLER *Crateroscelis murina* (6)

BICOLORED MOUSE-WARBLER *Crateroscelis nigrorufa* (6)

MOUNTAIN MOUSE-WARBLER *Crateroscelis robusta* (6)

YELLOW-THROATED SCRUBWREN *Sericornis citreogularis* (6)

WHITE-BROWED SCRUBWREN *Sericornis frontalis* (6)

BROWN SCRUBWREN or TASMANIAN SCRUBWREN *Sericornis humilis* (6)

ATHERTON SCRUBWREN *Sericornis keri* (6) [CD]

BECCARI'S SCRUBWREN or TROPICAL SCRUBWREN *Sericornis beccarii* (6)

PERPLEXING SCRUBWREN *Sericornis virgatus* (6)

LARGE SCRUBWREN *Sericornis nouhuysi* (6)

LARGE-BILLED SCRUBWREN *Sericornis magnirostris* (6)

VOGELKOP SCRUBWREN *Sericornis rufescens* (6)

BUFF-FACED SCRUBWREN *Sericornis perspicillatus* (6)

GRAY-GREEN SCRUBWREN *Sericornis arfakianus* (6)

PAPUAN SCRUBWREN *Sericornis papuensis* (6)

PALE-BILLED SCRUBWREN *Sericornis spilodera* (6)

SCRUBTIT *Acanthornis magnus* (6)

REDTHROAT *Pyrrholaemus brunneus* (6)

SPECKLED WARBLER *Chthonicola sagittatus* (6)

RUFOUS CALAMANTHUS or RUFOUS FIELDWREN *Calamanthus campestris* (6)

STRIATED CALAMANTHUS or STRIATED FIELDWREN *Calamanthus fuliginosus* (6)

CHESTNUT-RUMPED HYLACOLA or CHESTNUT-RUMPED HEATHWREN *Hylacola pyrrhopygia* (6)

SHY HYLACOLA or SHY HEATHWREN *Hylacola cautus* (6)

Tribe ACANTHIZINI

PAPUAN THORNBILL *Acanthiza murina* (6)

MOUNTAIN THORNBILL *Acanthiza katherina* (6) [CD]

BROWN THORNBILL *Acanthiza pusilla* (6)

TASMANIAN THORNBILL *Acanthiza ewingii* (6)

BUFF-RUMPED THORNBILL *Acanthiza reguloides* (6)

WESTERN THORNBILL *Acanthiza inornata* (6)

SLENDER-BILLED THORNBILL *Acanthiza iredalei* (6) [VU]

YELLOW-RUMPED THORNBILL *Acanthiza chrysorrhoa* (6)

CHESTNUT-RUMPED THORNBILL *Acanthiza uropygialis* (6)

YELLOW THORNBILL *Acanthiza nana* (6)

STRIATED THORNBILL *Acanthiza lineata* (6)

SLATY-BACKED THORNBILL *Acanthiza robustirostris* (6)

WEEBILL *Smicrornis brevirostris* (6)

MOUNTAIN GERYGONE *Gerygone cinerea* (6)

GREEN-BACKED GERYGONE *Gerygone chloronotus* (6)

FAIRY GERYGONE *Gerygone palpebrosa* (6)

WHITE-THROATED GERYGONE *Gerygone olivacea* (6)

YELLOW-BELLIED GERYGONE *Gerygone chrysogaster* (6)

LARGE-BILLED GERYGONE *Gerygone magnirostris* (6)

BIAK GERYGONE *Gerygone hypoxantha* (6) [EN]

DUSKY GERYGONE *Gerygone tenebrosa* (6)

GOLDEN-BELLIED GERYGONE *Gerygone sulphurea* (4)

PLAIN GERYGONE *Gerygone inornata* (4)

RUFOUS-SIDED GERYGONE *Gerygone dorsalis* (4)

BROWN-BREASTED GERYGONE *Gerygone ruficollis* (6)

MANGROVE GERYGONE *Gerygone levigaster* (6)

WESTERN GERYGONE *Gerygone fusca* (6)

LORD HOWE ISLAND GERYGONE *Gerygone insularis* (6) [EX]

BROWN GERYGONE *Gerygone mouki* (6)

NORFOLK ISLAND GERYGONE *Gerygone modesta* (6) [EN]

GRAY GERYGONE *Gerygone igata* (6)

CHATHAM ISLANDS GERYGONE *Gerygone albofrontata* (6)

FAN-TAILED GERYGONE *Gerygone flavolateralis* (4, 6)

SOUTHERN WHITEFACE *Aphelocephala leucopsis* (6)

CHESTNUT-BREASTED WHITEFACE *Aphelocephala pectoralis* (6) [VU]

BANDED WHITEFACE *Aphelocephala nigricincta* (6)

Superfamily CORVOIDEA
Family PETROICIDAE

GREATER GROUND-ROBIN *Amalocichla sclateriana* (6)

LESSER GROUND-ROBIN *Amalocichla incerta* (6)

TORRENT ROBIN *Monachella muelleriana* (6)

JACKY-WINTER *Microeca fascinans* (6)

GOLDEN-BELLIED FLYROBIN *Microeca hemixantha* (6) [NT]

LEMON-BELLIED FLYROBIN or LEMON-BELLIED FLYCATCHER *Microeca flavigaster* (6)

YELLOW-LEGGED FLYROBIN or YELLOW-LEGGED FLYCATCHER *Microeca griseoceps* (6)

OLIVE FLYROBIN *Microeca flavovirescens* (6)

CANARY FLYROBIN *Microeca papuana* (6)

GARNET ROBIN *Eugerygone rubra* (6)

ALPINE ROBIN *Petroica bivittata* (6)

SNOW MOUNTAIN ROBIN *Petroica archboldi* (6) [DD]

SCARLET ROBIN *Petroica multicolor* (6)

TOMTIT *Petroica macrocephala* (6)

RED-CAPPED ROBIN *Petroica goodenovii* (6)

FLAME ROBIN *Petroica phoenicea* (6)

ROSE ROBIN *Petroica rosea* (6)

PINK ROBIN *Petroica rodinogaster* (6)

NEW ZEALAND ROBIN *Petroica australis* (6)

CHATHAM ISLANDS ROBIN *Petroica traversi* (6) [EN]

HOODED ROBIN *Melanodryas cucullata* (6)

DUSKY ROBIN *Melanodryas vittata* (6)

PALE-YELLOW ROBIN *Tregellasia capito* (6)

WHITE-FACED ROBIN *Tregellasia leucops* (6)

YELLOW ROBIN or EASTERN YELLOW ROBIN *Eopsaltria australis* (6)

GRAY-BREASTED ROBIN or WESTERN YELLOW ROBIN *Eopsaltria griseogularis* (6)

YELLOW-BELLIED ROBIN *Eopsaltria flaviventris* (6)

WHITE-BREASTED ROBIN *Eopsaltria georgiana* (6)

MANGROVE ROBIN *Eopsaltria pulverulenta* (6)

BLACK-CHINNED ROBIN *Poecilodryas brachyura* (6)

BLACK-SIDED ROBIN *Poecilodryas hypoleuca* (6)

WHITE-BROWED ROBIN *Poecilodryas superciliosa* (6)

OLIVE-YELLOW ROBIN *Poecilodryas placens* (6) [DD]

BLACK-THROATED ROBIN *Poecilodryas albonotata* (6)

WHITE-WINGED ROBIN *Peneothello sigillatus* (6)

SMOKY ROBIN *Peneothello cryptoleucus* (6)

BLUE-GRAY ROBIN *Peneothello cyanus* (6)

WHITE-RUMPED ROBIN *Peneothello bimaculatus* (6)

ASHY ROBIN or BLACK-CHEEKED ROBIN *Heteromyias albispecularis* (6)

GRAY-HEADED ROBIN *Heteromyias cinereifrons* (6) [NT]

GREEN-BACKED ROBIN *Pachycephalopsis hattamensis* (6)

WHITE-EYED ROBIN *Pachycephalopsis poliosoma* (6)

NORTHERN SCRUB-ROBIN *Drymodes superciliaris* (6)

SOUTHERN SCRUB-ROBIN *Drymodes brunneopygia* (6)

Family IRENIDAE

ASIAN FAIRY-BLUEBIRD *Irena puella* (4)

PHILIPPINE FAIRY-BLUEBIRD *Irena cyanogaster* (4)

PHILIPPINE LEAFBIRD *Chloropsis flavipennis* (4) [EN]

YELLOW-THROATED LEAFBIRD *Chloropsis palawanensis* (4)

GREATER GREEN LEAFBIRD *Chloropsis sonnerati* (4)

LESSER GREEN LEAFBIRD *Chloropsis cyanopogon* (4)

BLUE-WINGED LEAFBIRD *Chloropsis cochinchinensis* (4)

GOLDEN-FRONTED LEAFBIRD *Chloropsis aurifrons* (4)

ORANGE-BELLIED LEAFBIRD *Chloropsis hardwickii* (4)

BLUE-MASKED LEAFBIRD *Chloropsis venusta* (4) [NT]

Family ORTHONYCHIDAE

LOGRUNNER *Orthonyx temminckii* (6)

CHOWCHILLA *Orthonyx spaldingii* (6)

Family POMATOSTOMIDAE

NEW GUINEA BABBLER *Pomatostomus isidorei* (6)

GRAY-CROWNED BABBLER *Pomatostomus temporalis* (6)

WHITE-BROWED BABBLER *Pomatostomus superciliosus* (6)

HALL'S BABBLER *Pomatostomus halli* (6)

CHESTNUT-CROWNED BABBLER *Pomatostomus ruficeps* (6)

Family LANIIDAE

TIGER SHRIKE *Lanius tigrinus* (3, 4)

BULL-HEADED SHRIKE *Lanius bucephalus* (3, 4)

RED-BACKED SHRIKE *Lanius collurio* (3, 4)

RUFOUS-TAILED SHRIKE *Lanius isabellinus* (3, 4, 5)

BROWN SHRIKE *Lanius cristatus* (1, 4, 6)

BURMESE SHRIKE *Lanius collurioides* (4)

EMIN'S SHRIKE *Lanius gubernator* (5)

SOUSA'S SHRIKE *Lanius souzae* (5)

BAY-BACKED SHRIKE *Lanius vittatus* (3)

LONG-TAILED SHRIKE *Lanius schach* (3, 4)

GRAY-BACKED SHRIKE *Lanius tephronotus* (3, 4)

MOUNTAIN SHRIKE *Lanius validirostris* (4)

LESSER GRAY SHRIKE *Lanius minor* (3, 5)

LOGGERHEAD SHRIKE *Lanius ludovicianus* (1)

NORTHERN SHRIKE or GREAT GRAY SHRIKE *Lanius excubitor* (1, 3, 4)

SOUTHERN GRAY SHRIKE *Lanius meridionalis* (3, 5)

CHINESE GRAY SHRIKE *Lanius sphenocercus* (4)

GRAY-BACKED FISCAL *Lanius excubitoroides* (5)

LONG-TAILED FISCAL *Lanius cabanisi* (5)

TAITA FISCAL *Lanius dorsalis* (5)

SOMALI FISCAL *Lanius somalicus* (5)

MACKINNON'S SHRIKE *Lanius mackinnoni* (5)

COMMON FISCAL *Lanius collaris* (5)

NEWTON'S FISCAL or SÃO TOMÉ FISCAL SHRIKE *Lanius newtoni* (5) [CR]

UHEHE FISCAL *Lanius marwitzi* (5)

WOODCHAT SHRIKE *Lanius senator* (3, 4, 5)

MASKED SHRIKE *Lanius nubicus* (3, 5)

YELLOW-BILLED SHRIKE *Corvinella corvina* (5)

MAGPIE SHRIKE *Corvinella melanoleuca* (5)

WHITE-RUMPED SHRIKE *Eurocephalus rueppelli* (5)

WHITE-CROWNED SHRIKE *Eurocephalus anguitimens* (5)

Family VIREONIDAE

RUFOUS-BROWED PEPPERSHRIKE *Cyclarhis gujanensis* (1, 2)

BLACK-BILLED PEPPERSHRIKE *Cyclarhis nigrirostris* (2)

CHESTNUT-SIDED SHRIKE-VIREO *Vireolanius melitophrys* (1, 2) [NT]

GREEN SHRIKE-VIREO *Vireolanius pulchellus* (1, 2)

YELLOW-BROWED SHRIKE-VIREO *Vireolanius eximius* (2)

SLATY-CAPPED SHRIKE-VIREO *Vireolanius leucotis* (2)

SLATY VIREO *Vireo brevipennis* (1) [NT]

BELL'S VIREO *Vireo bellii* (1, 2)

BLACK-CAPPED VIREO *Vireo atricapillus* (1) [EN]

DWARF VIREO *Vireo nelsoni* (1) [NT]

HUTTON'S VIREO *Vireo huttoni* (1, 2)

YELLOW-WINGED VIREO *Vireo carmioli* (2)

CHOCO VIREO *Vireo masteri* (2) [VU]

WHITE-EYED VIREO *Vireo griseus* (1, 2)

MANGROVE VIREO *Vireo pallens* (1, 2)

COZUMEL VIREO *Vireo bairdi* (1)

CUBAN VIREO *Vireo gundlachii* (2)

THICK-BILLED VIREO *Vireo crassirostris* (2)

ST. ANDREW VIREO or SAN ANDRES VIREO *Vireo caribaeus* (2) [CR]

GRAY VIREO *Vireo vicinior* (1)

GOLDEN VIREO *Vireo hypochryseus* (1)

JAMAICAN VIREO *Vireo modestus* (2)

FLAT-BILLED VIREO *Vireo nanus* (2)

PUERTO RICAN VIREO *Vireo latimeri* (2)

BLUE MOUNTAINS VIREO *Vireo osburni* (2) [NT]

CASSIN'S VIREO *Vireo cassinii* (1)

PLUMBEOUS VIREO *Vireo plumbeus* (1, 2)

BLUE-HEADED VIREO *Vireo solitarius* (1, 2)

YELLOW-THROATED VIREO *Vireo flavifrons* (1, 2)

PHILADELPHIA VIREO *Vireo philadelphicus* (1, 2, 3)

RED-EYED VIREO *Vireo olivaceus* (1, 2, 3)

YELLOW-GREEN VIREO *Vireo flavoviridis* (1, 2)

NORONHA VIREO *Vireo gracilirostris* (2) [VU]

BLACK-WHISKERED VIREO *Vireo altiloquus* (1, 2)

YUCATÁN VIREO *Vireo magister* (1, 2)

WESTERN WARBLING-VIREO *Vireo swainsonii* (1)

CAPE WARBLING-VIREO *Vireo victoriae* (1)

EASTERN WARBLING-VIREO *Vireo gilvus* (1, 2)

BROWN-CAPPED VIREO *Vireo leucophrys* (1, 2)

GRAY-EYED GREENLET *Hylophilus amaurocephalus* (2)

RUFOUS-CROWNED GREENLET *Hylophilus poicilotis* (2)

LEMON-CHESTED GREENLET *Hylophilus griseiventris* (2)

RIO DE JANEIRO GREENLET *Hylophilus thoracicus* (2)

GRAY-CHESTED GREENLET *Hylophilus semicinereus* (2)

ASHY-HEADED GREENLET *Hylophilus pectoralis* (2)

TEPUI GREENLET *Hylophilus sclateri* (2)

BUFF-CHEEKED GREENLET *Hylophilus muscicapinus* (2)

BROWN-HEADED GREENLET *Hylophilus brunneiceps* (2)

DUSKY-CAPPED GREENLET *Hylophilus hypoxanthus* (2)

RUFOUS-NAPED GREENLET *Hylophilus semibrunneus* (2)

GOLDEN-FRONTED GREENLET *Hylophilus aurantiifrons* (2)

SCRUB GREENLET *Hylophilus flavipes* (2)

OLIVACEOUS GREENLET *Hylophilus olivaceus* (2)

TAWNY-CROWNED GREENLET *Hylophilus ochraceiceps* (1, 2)

LESSER GREENLET *Hylophilus decurtatus* (1, 2)

Family CORVIDAE
Subfamily CINCLOSOMATINAE

PAPUAN WHIPBIRD *Androphobus viridis* (6) [DD]

EASTERN WHIPBIRD *Psophodes olivaceus* (6)

WESTERN WHIPBIRD *Psophodes nigrogularis* (6) [VU]

CHIMING WEDGEBILL *Psophodes occidentalis* (6)

CHIRRUPING WEDGEBILL *Psophodes cristatus* (6)

SPOTTED QUAIL-THRUSH *Cinclosoma punctatum* (6)

CHESTNUT QUAIL-THRUSH *Cinclosoma castanotus* (6)

CHESTNUT-BREASTED QUAIL-THRUSH (6)

CINNAMON QUAIL-THRUSH *Cinclosoma cinnamomeum* (6) [CR, SSP]

PAINTED QUAIL-THRUSH *Cinclosoma ajax* (6)

SPOTTED JEWEL-BABBLER *Ptilorrhoa leucosticta* (6)

BLUE JEWEL-BABBLER *Ptilorrhoa caerulescens* (6)

CHESTNUT-BACKED JEWEL-BABBLER *Ptilorrhoa castanonota* (6)

MALAYSIAN RAIL-BABBLER or RAIL-BABBLER *Eupetes macrocerus* (4)

IFRIT or BLUE-CAPPED *Ifrita Ifrita kowaldi* (6)

Subfamily CORCORACINAE

WHITE-WINGED CHOUGH *Corcorax melanorhamphos* (6)

APOSTLEBIRD *Struthidea cinerea* (6)

Subfamily PACHYCEPHALINAE
Tribe NEOSITTINI

VARIED SITTELLA *Daphoenositta chrysoptera* (6)

BLACK SITTELLA *Daphoenositta miranda* (6)

Tribe MOHOUINI

WHITEHEAD *Mohoua albicilla* (6)

YELLOWHEAD *Mohoua ochrocephala* (6) [VU]

PIPIPI *Mohoua novaeseelandiae* (6)

Tribe FALCUNCULINI

CRESTED SHRIKE-TIT *Falcunculus frontatus* (6)

CRESTED BELLBIRD *Oreoica gutturalis* (6)

MOTTLED WHISTLER *Rhagologus leucostigma* (6)

Tribe PACHYCEPHALINI

GOLDENFACE *Pachycare flavogrisea* (6)

OLIVE-FLANKED WHISTLER *Hylocitrea bonensis* (4)

RUFOUS-NAPED WHISTLER *Aleadryas rufinucha* (6)

MAROON-BACKED WHISTLER *Coracornis raveni* (4)

OLIVE WHISTLER *Pachycephala olivacea* (6)

RED-LORED WHISTLER *Pachycephala rufogularis* (6) [CD]

GILBERT'S WHISTLER *Pachycephala inornata* (6)

MANGROVE WHISTLER *Pachycephala grisola* (4)

GREEN-BACKED WHISTLER *Pachycephala albiventris* (4)

WHITE-VENTED WHISTLER *Pachycephala homeyeri* (4)

ISLAND WHISTLER *Pachycephala phaionotus* (4, 6)

RUSTY WHISTLER *Pachycephala hyperythra* (6)

BROWN-BACKED WHISTLER *Pachycephala modesta* (6)

BORNEAN WHISTLER *Pachycephala hypoxantha* (4)

SULFUR-BELLIED WHISTLER *Pachycephala sulfuriventer* (4)

YELLOW-BELLIED WHISTLER *Pachycephala philippinensis* (4)

VOGELKOP WHISTLER *Pachycephala meyeri* (6) [NT]

GRAY-HEADED WHISTLER *Pachycephala griseiceps* (6)

BROWN WHISTLER or GRAY WHISTLER *Pachycephala simplex* (6)

FAWN-BREASTED WHISTLER *Pachycephala orpheus* (4) [NT]

GOLDEN WHISTLER *Pachycephala pectoralis* (6)

SCLATER'S WHISTLER *Pachycephala soror* (6)

LORENTZ'S WHISTLER *Pachycephala lorentzi* (6)

BLACK-TAILED WHISTLER or MANGROVE GOLDEN WHISTLER *Pachycephala melanura* (6)

NEW CALEDONIAN WHISTLER *Pachycephala caledonica* (6)

SAMOAN WHISTLER *Pachycephala flavifrons* (6)

TONGAN WHISTLER *Pachycephala jacquinoti* (6) [NT]

REGENT WHISTLER *Pachycephala schlegelii* (6)

BARE-THROATED WHISTLER *Pachycephala nudigula* (4)

HOODED WHISTLER *Pachycephala implicata* (4) [NT]

GOLDEN-BACKED WHISTLER *Pachycephala aurea* (6)

DRAB WHISTLER *Pachycephala griseonota* (4)

WALLACEAN WHISTLER *Pachycephala arctitorquis* (4)

BLACK-HEADED WHISTLER *Pachycephala monacha* (6)

WHITE-BELLIED WHISTLER *Pachycephala leucogastra* (6)

RUFOUS WHISTLER *Pachycephala rufiventris* (6)

WHITE-BREASTED WHISTLER *Pachycephala lanioides* (6)

SOOTY SHRIKE-THRUSH *Colluricincla umbrina* (6)

LITTLE SHRIKE-THRUSH *Colluricincla megarhyncha* (6)

BOWER'S SHRIKE-THRUSH *Colluricincla boweri* (6) [NT]

SANDSTONE SHRIKE-THRUSH *Colluricincla woodwardi* (6)

GRAY SHRIKE-THRUSH *Colluricincla harmonica* (6)

MORNINGBIRD *Colluricincla tenebrosa* (6)

VARIABLE PITOHUI *Pitohui kirhocephalus* (6)

HOODED PITOHUI *Pitohui dichrous* (6)

WHITE-BELLIED PITOHUI *Pitohui incertus* (6)

RUSTY PITOHUI *Pitohui ferrugineus* (6)

CRESTED PITOHUI *Pitohui cristatus* (6)

BLACK PITOHUI *Pitohui nigrescens* (6)

WATTLED PLOUGHBILL *Eulacestoma nigropectus* (6)

Subfamily CORVINAE
Tribe CORVINI

CRESTED JAY *Platylophus galericulatus* (4)

BLACK MAGPIE *Platysmurus leucopterus* (4) [NT]

PINYON JAY *Gymnorhinus cyanocephalus* (1)

BLUE JAY *Cyanocitta cristata* (1)

STELLER'S JAY *Cyanocitta stelleri* (1, 2)

ISLAND SCRUB-JAY or SANTA CRUZ ISLAND SCRUB-JAY *Aphelocoma insularis* (1)

WESTERN SCRUB-JAY or CALIFORNIA JAY *Aphelocoma californica* (1)

FLORIDA SCRUB-JAY or FLORIDA JAY *Aphelocoma coerulescens* (1)

MEXICAN JAY or GRAY-BREASTED JAY *Aphelocoma ultramarina* (1)

UNICOLORED JAY *Aphelocoma unicolor* (1, 2)

BLACK-COLLARED JAY *Cyanolyca armillata* (2)

TURQUOISE JAY *Cyanolyca turcosa* (2)

WHITE-COLLARED JAY *Cyanolyca viridicyana* (2)

AZURE-HOODED JAY *Cyanolyca cucullata* (1, 2)

BEAUTIFUL JAY *Cyanolyca pulchra* (2) [NT]

BLACK-THROATED JAY *Cyanolyca pumilo* (1, 2)

DWARF JAY *Cyanolyca nana* (1) [EN]

WHITE-THROATED JAY *Cyanolyca mirabilis* (1) [EN]

SILVERY-THROATED JAY *Cyanolyca argentigula* (2)

BUSHY-CRESTED JAY *Cyanocorax melanocyaneus* (2)

SAN BLAS JAY *Cyanocorax sanblasianus* (1)

YUCATÁN JAY *Cyanocorax yucatanicus* (1, 2)

PURPLISH-BACKED JAY *Cyanocorax beecheii* (1)

PURPLISH JAY *Cyanocorax cyanomelas* (2)

AZURE JAY *Cyanocorax caeruleus* (2) [NT]

VIOLACEOUS JAY *Cyanocorax violaceus* (2)

CURL-CRESTED JAY *Cyanocorax cristatellus* (2)

AZURE-NAPED JAY *Cyanocorax heilprini* (2)

CAYENNE JAY *Cyanocorax cayanus* (2)

BLACK-CHESTED JAY *Cyanocorax affinis* (2)

TUFTED JAY *Cyanocorax dickeyi* (2) [NT]

PLUSH-CRESTED JAY *Cyanocorax chrysops* (2)

WHITE-NAPED JAY *Cyanocorax cyanopogon* (2)

WHITE-TAILED JAY *Cyanocorax mystacalis* (2)

GREEN JAY *Cyanocorax luxuosus* (1, 2)

INCA JAY *Cyanocorax yncas* (2)

BROWN JAY *Psilorhinus morio* (1, 2)

BLACK-THROATED MAGPIE-JAY *Calocitta collie* (1)

WHITE-THROATED MAGPIE-JAY *Calocitta formosa* (1, 2)

EURASIAN JAY *Garrulus glandarius* (3, 4)

BLACK-HEADED JAY *Garrulus lanceolatus* (3, 4)

LIDTH'S JAY *Garrulus lidthi* (4) [VU]

SIBERIAN JAY *Perisoreus infaustus* (3, 4)

SICHUAN JAY *Perisoreus internigrans* (4) [VU]

GRAY JAY *Perisoreus canadensis* (1)

SRI LANKA MAGPIE or CEYLON MAGPIE *Urocissa ornata* (4) [VU]

FORMOSAN MAGPIE or TAIWAN BLUE MAGPIE *Urocissa caerulea* (4)

GOLD-BILLED MAGPIE or YELLOW-BILLED BLUE MAGPIE *Urocissa flavirostris* (4)

BLUE MAGPIE or RED-BILLED BLUE MAGPIE *Urocissa erythrorhyncha* (4)

WHITE-WINGED MAGPIE *Urocissa whiteheadi* (4) [NT]

GREEN MAGPIE or COMMON GREEN MAGPIE *Cissa chinensis* (4)

YELLOW-BREASTED MAGPIE or INDOCHINESE GREEN MAGPIE *Cissa hypoleuca* (4) [NT]

SHORT-TAILED MAGPIE or SHORT-TAILED GREEN MAGPIE *Cissa thalassina* (4)

AZURE-WINGED MAGPIE *Cyanopica cyana* (3, 4)

RUFOUS TREEPIE *Dendrocitta vagabunda* (4)

GRAY TREEPIE *Dendrocitta formosae* (4)

SUNDA TREEPIE or SUMATRAN TREEPIE *Dendrocitta occipitalis* (4)

BORNEAN TREEPIE *Dendrocitta cinerascens* (4)

WHITE-BELLIED TREEPIE *Dendrocitta leucogastra* (4) [NT]

COLLARED TREEPIE *Dendrocitta frontalis* (3, 4)

ANDAMAN TREEPIE *Dendrocitta bayleyi* (4) [NT]

RACKET-TAILED TREEPIE *Crypsirina temia* (4)

HOODED TREEPIE *Crypsirina cucullata* (4) [VU]

RATCHET-TAILED TREEPIE *Temnurus temnurus* (4)

BLACK-BILLED MAGPIE *Pica pica* (1, 3, 4, 5)

YELLOW-BILLED MAGPIE *Pica nuttalli* (1)

STRESEMANN'S BUSH-CROW *Zavattariornis stresemanni* (5) [VU]

MONGOLIAN GROUND-JAY *Podoces hendersoni* (3, 4)

XINJIANG GROUND-JAY *Podoces biddulphi* (4) [VU]

TURKESTAN GROUND-JAY *Podoces panderi* (3)

IRANIAN GROUND-JAY *Podoces pleskei* (3)

TIBETAN GROUND-JAY or HUME'S GROUNDPECKER *Pseudopodoces humilis* (3)

CLARK'S NUTCRACKER *Nucifraga columbiana* (1, 2)

SPOTTED NUTCRACKER *Nucifraga caryocatactes* (3, 4)

RED-BILLED CHOUGH *Pyrrhocorax pyrrhocorax* (3, 4, 5)

YELLOW-BILLED CHOUGH *Pyrrhocorax graculus* (3, 4)

PIAPIAC *Ptilostomus afer* (5)

EURASIAN JACKDAW *Corvus monedula* (3, 4)

DAURIAN JACKDAW *Corvus dauuricus* (3, 4)

HOUSE CROW *Corvus splendens* (3, 4, 5)

NEW CALEDONIAN CROW *Corvus moneduloides* (7)

SLENDER-BILLED CROW *Corvus enca* (4)

PIPING CROW *Corvus typicus* (4)

BANGGAI CROW *Corvus unicolor* (4) [VU]

FLORES CROW *Corvus florensis* (4) [VU]

MARIANA CROW *Corvus kubaryi* (4) [CR]

LONG-BILLED CROW *Corvus validus* (4)

BOUGAINVILLE CROW *Corvus meeki* (4) [NT]

WHITE-BILLED CROW *Corvus woodfordi* (4) [NT]

BROWN-HEADED CROW *Corvus fuscicapillus* (6) [NT]

GRAY CROW *Corvus tristis* (4, 6)

CAPE CROW *Corvus capensis* (5)

ROOK *Corvus frugilegus* (3, 4, 5, 6)

NORTHWESTERN CROW *Corvus caurinus* (1)

AMERICAN CROW *Corvus brachyrhynchos* (1)

FISH CROW *Corvus ossifragus* (1)

TAMAULIPAS CROW or MEXICAN CROW *Corvus imparatus* (1, 2)

SINALOA CROW *Corvus sinaloae* (1)

PALM CROW *Corvus palmarum* (2) [NT]

JAMAICAN CROW *Corvus jamaicensis* (2)

CUBAN CROW *Corvus nasicus* (2)

WHITE-NECKED CROW *Corvus leucognaphalus* (2) [VU]

CARRION CROW *Corvus corone* (3, 4, 5)

LARGE-BILLED CROW *Corvus macrorhynchos* (3, 4)

TORRESIAN CROW *Corvus orru* (4, 6)

LITTLE CROW *Corvus bennetti* (6)

AUSTRALIAN RAVEN *Corvus coronoides* (6)

LITTLE RAVEN *Corvus mellori* (6)

RELICT RAVEN *Corvus boreus* (6)

FOREST RAVEN *Corvus tasmanicus* (6)

COLLARED CROW *Corvus torquatus* (4)

HAWAIIAN CROW *Corvus hawaiiensis* (2) [CR]

CHIHUAHUAN RAVEN *Corvus cryptoleucus* (1)

PIED CROW *Corvus albus* (3, 5)

BROWN-NECKED RAVEN *Corvus ruficollis* (3, 5)

COMMON RAVEN *Corvus corax* (1, 3, 4, 5)

FAN-TAILED RAVEN *Corvus rhipidurus* (3, 5)

WHITE-NECKED RAVEN *Corvus albicollis* (5)

THICK-BILLED RAVEN *Corvus crassirostris* (5)

Tribe PARADISAEINI

LESSER MELAMPITTA *Melampitta lugubris* (6)

GREATER MELAMPITTA *Melampitta gigantea* (6)

YELLOW-BREASTED BIRD-OF-PARADISE *Loboparadisea sericea* (6) [DD]

CRESTED BIRD-OF-PARADISE *Cnemophilus macgregorii* (6)

LORIA'S BIRD-OF-PARADISE *Cnemophilus loriae* (6)

MACGREGOR'S BIRD-OF-PARADISE *Macgregoria pulchra* (6) [VU]

PARADISE-CROW *Lycocorax pyrrhopterus* (4)

GLOSSY-MANTLED MANUCODE *Manucodia atra* (6)

CRINKLE-COLLARED MANUCODE *Manucodia chalybata* (6)

CURL-CRESTED MANUCODE *Manucodia comrii* (6)

JOBI MANUCODE *Manucodia jobiensis* (6)

TRUMPET MANUCODE *Manucodia keraudrenii* (6)

STANDARDWING or STANDARDWING BIRD-OF-PARADISE *Semioptera wallacii* (4) [NT]

LONG-TAILED PARADIGALLA *Paradigalla carunculata* (6) [NT]

SHORT-TAILED PARADIGALLA *Paradigalla brevicauda* (6)

BLACK SICKLEBILL *Epimachus fastuosus* (6) [VU]

BROWN SICKLEBILL *Epimachus meyeri* (6)

BLACK-BILLED SICKLEBILL *Epimachus albertisi* (6)

PALE-BILLED SICKLEBILL *Epimachus bruijnii* (6) [NT]

SUPERB BIRD-OF-PARADISE *Lophorina superba* (6)

WESTERN PAROTIA *Parotia sefilata* (6)

CAROLA'S PAROTIA *Parotia carolae* (6)

LAWES'S PAROTIA *Parotia lawesii* (6)

EASTERN PAROTIA *Parotia helenae* (6)

WAHNES'S PAROTIA *Parotia wahnesi* (6) [VU]

MAGNIFICENT RIFLEBIRD *Ptiloris magnificus* (6)

EASTERN RIFLEBIRD *Ptiloris intercedens* (6)

VICTORIA'S RIFLEBIRD *Ptiloris victoriae* (6)

PARADISE RIFLEBIRD *Ptiloris paradiseus* (6) [NT]

MAGNIFICENT BIRD-OF-PARADISE *Cicinnurus magnificus* (6)

WILSON'S BIRD-OF-PARADISE *Cicinnurus respublica* (6) [NT]

KING BIRD-OF-PARADISE *Cicinnurus regius* (6)

ARFAK ASTRAPIA *Astrapia nigra* (6) [NT]

SPLENDID ASTRAPIA *Astrapia splendidissima* (6)

RIBBON-TAILED ASTRAPIA *Astrapia mayeri* (6) [VU]

STEPHANIE'S ASTRAPIA *Astrapia stephaniae* (6)

HUON ASTRAPIA *Astrapia rothschildi* (6)

KING-OF-SAXONY BIRD-OF-PARADISE *Pteridophora alberti* (6)

TWELVE-WIRED BIRD-OF-PARADISE *Seleucidis melanoleuca* (6)

RED BIRD-OF-PARADISE *Paradisaea rubra* (6) [NT]

LESSER BIRD-OF-PARADISE *Paradisaea minor* (6)

GREATER BIRD-OF-PARADISE *Paradisaea apoda* (6)

RAGGIANA BIRD-OF-PARADISE *Paradisaea raggiana* (6)

GOLDIE'S BIRD-OF-PARADISE *Paradisaea decora* (6) [VU]

EMPEROR BIRD-OF-PARADISE *Paradisaea guilielmi* (6)

BLUE BIRD-OF-PARADISE *Paradisaea rudolphi* (6) [VU]

Tribe ARTAMINI

BLACK-BACKED BUTCHERBIRD *Cracticus mentalis* (6)

GRAY BUTCHERBIRD *Cracticus torquatus* (6)

HOODED BUTCHERBIRD *Cracticus cassicus* (6)

TAGULA BUTCHERBIRD *Cracticus louisiadensis* (6) [DD]

PIED BUTCHERBIRD *Cracticus nigrogularis* (6)

BLACK BUTCHERBIRD *Cracticus quoyi* (6)

AUSTRALIAN MAGPIE *Gymnorhina tibicen* (6)

PIED CURRAWONG *Strepera graculina* (6)

BLACK CURRAWONG *Strepera fuliginosa* (6)

GRAY CURRAWONG *Strepera versicolor* (6)

ASHY WOODSWALLOW *Artamus fuscus* (4)

WHITE-BREASTED WOODSWALLOW *Artamus leucorynchus* (4, 6)

IVORY-BACKED WOODSWALLOW *Artamus monachus* (4)

GREAT WOODSWALLOW *Artamus maximus* (6)

BISMARCK WOODSWALLOW *Artamus insignis* (6)

FIJI WOODSWALLOW *Artamus mentalis* (6)

MASKED WOODSWALLOW *Artamus personatus* (6)

WHITE-BROWED WOODSWALLOW *Artamus superciliosus* (6)

BLACK-FACED WOODSWALLOW *Artamus cinereus* (4, 6)

DUSKY WOODSWALLOW *Artamus cyanopterus* (6)

LITTLE WOODSWALLOW *Artamus minor* (6)

BORNEAN BRISTLEHEAD *Pityriasis gymnocephala* (4) [NT]

LOWLAND PELTOPS *Peltops blainvillii* (6)

MOUNTAIN PELTOPS *Peltops montanus* (6)

Tribe ORIOLINI

OLIVE-BROWN ORIOLE *Oriolus melanotis* (6)

BLACK-EARED ORIOLE *Oriolus bouroensis* (4)

GRAY-COLLARED ORIOLE *Oriolus forsteni* (4)

DUSKY-BROWN ORIOLE *Oriolus phaeochromus* (4)

BROWN ORIOLE *Oriolus szalayi* (6)

OLIVE-BACKED ORIOLE *Oriolus sagittatus* (6)

GREEN ORIOLE or YELLOW ORIOLE *Oriolus flavocinctus* (6)

DARK-THROATED ORIOLE *Oriolus xanthonotus* (4)

PHILIPPINE ORIOLE *Oriolus steerii* (4)

WHITE-LORED ORIOLE *Oriolus albiloris* (4)

ISABELA ORIOLE *Oriolus isabellae* (4) [CR]

EURASIAN GOLDEN-ORIOLE *Oriolus oriolus* (3, 4, 5)

AFRICAN GOLDEN-ORIOLE *Oriolus auratus* (5)

BLACK-NAPED ORIOLE *Oriolus chinensis* (3, 4)

SLENDER-BILLED ORIOLE *Oriolus tenuirostris* (4)

GREEN-HEADED ORIOLE *Oriolus chlorocephalus* (5)

SÃO TOMÉ ORIOLE *Oriolus crassirostris* (5) [VU]

WESTERN BLACK-HEADED ORIOLE *Oriolus brachyrhynchus*

DARK-HEADED ORIOLE *Oriolus monacha* (5)

AFRICAN BLACK-HEADED ORIOLE *Oriolus larvatus* (5)

BLACK-TAILED ORIOLE *Oriolus percivali* (5)

BLACK-WINGED ORIOLE *Oriolus nigripennis* (5)

BLACK-HOODED ORIOLE *Oriolus xanthornus* (4)

BLACK ORIOLE *Oriolus hosii* (4) [NT]

BLACK-AND-CRIMSON ORIOLE *Oriolus cruentus* (4)

MAROON ORIOLE *Oriolus traillii* (3, 4)

SILVER ORIOLE *Oriolus mellianus* (4) [VU]

WETAR FIGBIRD *Sphecotheres hypoleucus* (4) [DD]

TIMOR FIGBIRD *Sphecotheres viridis* (4)

GREEN FIGBIRD *Sphecotheres vieilloti* (6)

GROUND CUCKOOSHRIKE *Coracina maxima* (6)

SUNDA CUCKOOSHRIKE *Coracina larvata* (4)

LARGE CUCKOOSHRIKE *Coracina macei* (4)

JAVAN CUCKOOSHRIKE *Coracina javensis* (4)

SLATY CUCKOOSHRIKE *Coracina schistacea* (4)

WALLACEAN CUCKOOSHRIKE *Coracina personata* (4)

MOLUCCAN CUCKOOSHRIKE *Coracina atriceps* (4)

BURU CUCKOOSHRIKE *Coracina fortis* (4) [VU]

MELANESIAN CUCKOOSHRIKE *Coracina caledonica* (6)

BLACK-FACED CUCKOOSHRIKE *Coracina novaehollandiae* (6)

STOUT-BILLED CUCKOOSHRIKE *Coracina caeruleogrisea* (6)

CERULEAN CUCKOOSHRIKE *Coracina temminckii* (4)

BAR-BELLIED CUCKOOSHRIKE *Coracina striata* (4)

PIED CUCKOOSHRIKE *Coracina bicolor* (4) [NT]

BARRED CUCKOOSHRIKE or YELLOW-EYED CUCKOOSHRIKE *Coracina lineata* (6)

BOYER'S CUCKOOSHRIKE *Coracina boyeri* (6)

WHITE-RUMPED CUCKOOSHRIKE *Coracina leucopygia* (4)

WHITE-BELLIED CUCKOOSHRIKE *Coracina papuensis* (4, 6)

HOODED CUCKOOSHRIKE *Coracina longicauda* (6)

HALMAHERA CUCKOOSHRIKE *Coracina parvula* (4)

PYGMY CUCKOOSHRIKE *Coracina abbotti* (4)

NEW CALEDONIAN CUCKOOSHRIKE *Coracina analis* (6)

WHITE-BREASTED CUCKOOSHRIKE *Coracina pectoralis* (5)

GRAY CUCKOOSHRIKE *Coracina caesia* (5)

BLUE CUCKOOSHRIKE *Coracina azurea* (5)

GRAUER'S CUCKOOSHRIKE *Coracina graueri* (5) [NT]

ASHY CUCKOOSHRIKE *Coracina cinerea* (5)

MAURITIUS CUCKOOSHRIKE *Coracina typica* (5) [VU]

REUNION CUCKOOSHRIKE *Coracina newtoni* (4) [EN]

BLACKISH CUCKOOSHRIKE *Coracina coerulescens* (4) [NT]

SLENDER-BILLED CICADABIRD or CICADABIRD *Coracina tenuirostris* (4, 6) [CR]

SUMBA CICADABIRD *Coracina dohertyi* (4) [NT]

SULA CICADABIRD *Coracina sula* (4)

KAI CICADABIRD *Coracina dispar* (6) [NT]

BLACK-BIBBED CICADABIRD *Coracina mindanensis* (4) [VU]

SULAWESI CICADABIRD *Coracina morio* (4)

PALE CICADABIRD *Coracina ceramensis* (4)

BLACK-SHOULDERED CICADABIRD *Coracina incerta* (6)

GRAY-HEADED CUCKOOSHRIKE *Coracina schisticeps* (6)

NEW GUINEA CUCKOOSHRIKE *Coracina melas* (6)

BLACK-BELLIED CUCKOOSHRIKE *Coracina montana* (6)

SOLOMON ISLANDS CUCKOOSHRIKE *Coracina holopolia* (4)

MCGREGOR'S CUCKOOSHRIKE *Coracina mcgregori* (4) [VU]

WHITE-WINGED CUCKOOSHRIKE *Coracina ostenta* (4) [VU]

INDOCHINESE CUCKOOSHRIKE *Coracina polioptera* (4)

BLACK-WINGED CUCKOOSHRIKE *Coracina melaschistos* (4)

LESSER CUCKOOSHRIKE *Coracina fimbriata* (4)

BLACK-HEADED CUCKOOSHRIKE *Coracina melanoptera* (4)

GOLDEN CUCKOOSHRIKE *Campochaera sloetii* (6)

BLACK-AND-WHITE TRILLER *Lalage melanoleuca* (4)

PIED TRILLER *Lalage nigra* (4)

WHITE-RUMPED TRILLER *Lalage leucopygialis* (4)

WHITE-SHOULDERED TRILLER *Lalage sueurii* (4)

WHITE-WINGED TRILLER *Lalage tricolor* (6)

RUFOUS-BELLIED TRILLER *Lalage aurea* (4)

WHITE-BROWED TRILLER *Lalage moesta* (4)

BLACK-BROWED TRILLER *Lalage atrovirens* (6)

VARIED TRILLER *Lalage leucomela* (6)

POLYNESIAN TRILLER *Lalage maculosa* (6)

SAMOAN TRILLER *Lalage sharpei* (6) [NT]

LONG-TAILED TRILLER *Lalage leucopyga* (6)

PETIT'S CUCKOOSHRIKE *Campephaga petiti* (5)

BLACK CUCKOOSHRIKE *Campephaga flava* (5)

RED-SHOULDERED CUCKOOSHRIKE *Campephaga phoenicea* (5)

PURPLE-THROATED CUCKOOSHRIKE *Campephaga quiscalina* (5)

GHANA CUCKOOSHRIKE or WESTERN WATTLED CUCKOOSHRIKE *Campephaga lobata* (5) [VU]

ORIOLE CUCKOOSHRIKE *Campephaga oriolina* (5)

ROSY MINIVET *Pericrocotus roseus* (4)

BROWN-RUMPED MINIVET or SWINHOE'S MINIVET *Pericrocotus cantonensis* (4) [NT]

ASHY MINIVET *Pericrocotus divaricatus* (4)

RYUKYU MINIVET *Pericrocotus tegimae* (4)

SMALL MINIVET *Pericrocotus cinnamomeus* (4)

FIERY MINIVET *Pericrocotus igneus* (4)

FLORES MINIVET *Pericrocotus lansbergei* (6)

WHITE-BELLIED MINIVET *Pericrocotus erythropygius* (4) [NT]

GRAY-CHINNED MINIVET *Pericrocotus solaris* (4)

LONG-TAILED MINIVET *Pericrocotus ethologus* (4)

SHORT-BILLED MINIVET *Pericrocotus brevirostris* (4)

SUNDA MINIVET *Pericrocotus miniatus* (4)

SCARLET MINIVET *Pericrocotus flammeus* (4)

BAR-WINGED FLYCATCHER-SHRIKE *Hemipus picatus* (4)

BLACK-WINGED FLYCATCHER-SHRIKE *Hemipus hirundinaceus* (4)

Subfamily DICRURINAE
Tribe RHIPIDURINI

YELLOW-BELLIED FANTAIL *Rhipidura hypoxantha* (3, 4)

BLUE FANTAIL *Rhipidura superciliaris* (4)

BLUE-HEADED FANTAIL *Rhipidura cyaniceps* (4)

RUFOUS-TAILED FANTAIL *Rhipidura phoenicura* (4)

BLACK-AND-CINNAMON FANTAIL *Rhipidura nigrocinnamomea* (4)

WHITE-THROATED FANTAIL *Rhipidura albicollis* (3, 4)

SPOT-BREASTED FANTAIL *Rhipidura albogularis* (4)

WHITE-BELLIED FANTAIL *Rhipidura euryura* (4) [NT]

WHITE-BROWED FANTAIL *Rhipidura aureola* (4)

PIED FANTAIL *Rhipidura javanica* (4)

SPOTTED FANTAIL *Rhipidura perlata* (4)

WILLIE-WAGTAIL *Rhipidura leucophrys* (4, 6)

BROWN-CAPPED FANTAIL *Rhipidura diluta* (6)

NORTHERN FANTAIL *Rhipidura rufiventris* (4, 6)

CINNAMON-TAILED FANTAIL *Rhipidura fuscorufa* (4) [NT]

WHITE-WINGED FANTAIL *Rhipidura cockerelli* (4)

SOOTY THICKET-FANTAIL *Rhipidura threnothorax* (6)

BLACK THICKET-FANTAIL *Rhipidura maculipectus* (6)

WHITE-BELLIED THICKET-FANTAIL *Rhipidura leucothorax* (6)

BLACK FANTAIL *Rhipidura atra* (6)

CHESTNUT-BELLIED FANTAIL *Rhipidura hyperythra* (6)

FRIENDLY FANTAIL *Rhipidura albolimbata* (6)

MANGROVE FANTAIL *Rhipidura phasiana* (6)

GRAY FANTAIL *Rhipidura fuliginosa* (6)

BROWN FANTAIL *Rhipidura drownei* (4)

DUSKY FANTAIL *Rhipidura tenebrosa* (4) [NT]

RENNELL FANTAIL *Rhipidura rennelliana* (4)

STREAKED FANTAIL *Rhipidura spilodera* (6)

KADAVU FANTAIL *Rhipidura personata* (6) [NT]

SAMOAN FANTAIL *Rhipidura nebulosa* (6)

DIMORPHIC FANTAIL *Rhipidura brachyrhyncha* (6)

RUSTY-BELLIED FANTAIL *Rhipidura teysmanni* (4)

TAWNY-BACKED FANTAIL *Rhipidura superflua* (4) [NT]

STREAKY-BREASTED FANTAIL *Rhipidura dedemi* (4)

LONG-TAILED FANTAIL *Rhipidura opistherythra* (4) [NT]

PALAU FANTAIL *Rhipidura lepida* (6)

RUFOUS-BACKED FANTAIL *Rhipidura rufidorsa* (6)

BISMARCK FANTAIL *Rhipidura dahli* (6)

MATTHIAS FANTAIL *Rhipidura matthiae* (6) [DD]

MALAITA FANTAIL *Rhipidura malaitae* (4) [VU]

POHNPEI FANTAIL *Rhipidura kubaryi* (4)

RUFOUS FANTAIL *Rhipidura rufifrons* (4, 6)

MANUS FANTAIL *Rhipidura semirubra* (6) [VU]

Tribe DICRURINI

PYGMY DRONGO *Chaetorhynchus papuensis* (6)

SQUARE-TAILED DRONGO *Dicrurus ludwigii* (5)

SHINING DRONGO *Dicrurus atripennis* (5)

FORK-TAILED DRONGO *Dicrurus adsimilis* (5)

VELVET-MANTLED DRONGO *Dicrurus modestus* (5) [NT]

ALDABRA DRONGO *Dicrurus aldabranus* (5) [NT]

COMORO DRONGO or GRAND COMORO DRONGO *Dicrurus fuscipennis* (5) [CR]

CRESTED DRONGO *Dicrurus forficatus* (5)

MAYOTTE DRONGO *Dicrurus waldenii* (5) [CR]

BLACK DRONGO *Dicrurus macrocercus* (3, 4)

ASHY DRONGO *Dicrurus leucophaeus* (3, 4)

WHITE-BELLIED DRONGO *Dicrurus caerulescens* (3, 4)

CROW-BILLED DRONGO *Dicrurus annectans* (4)

BRONZED DRONGO *Dicrurus aeneus* (4)

LESSER RACKET-TAILED DRONGO *Dicrurus remifer* (4)

HAIR-CRESTED DRONGO or SPANGLED DRONGO *Dicrurus hottentottus* (4)

BALICASSIAO or PHILIPPINE DRONGO *Dicrurus balicassius* (4)

SULAWESI DRONGO *Dicrurus montanus* (4)

SUMATRAN DRONGO *Dicrurus sumatranus* (4) [NT]

WALLACEAN DRONGO *Dicrurus densus* (4)

RIBBON-TAILED DRONGO *Dicrurus megarhynchus* (6)

SPANGLED DRONGO *Dicrurus bracteatus* (4, 6)

ANDAMAN DRONGO *Dicrurus andamanensis* (4) [NT]

GREATER RACKET-TAILED DRONGO *Dicrurus paradiseus* (4)

Tribe MONARCHINI

FAIRY FLYCATCHER *Stenostira scita* (5)

CHESTNUT-CAPPED FLYCATCHER *Erythrocercus mccallii* (5)

YELLOW FLYCATCHER *Erythrocercus holochlorus* (5)

LIVINGSTONE'S FLYCATCHER *Erythrocercus livingstonei* (5)

AFRICAN BLUE-FLYCATCHER *Elminia longicauda* (5)

WHITE-TAILED BLUE-FLYCATCHER *Elminia albicauda* (5)

DUSKY CRESTED-FLYCATCHER *Elminia nigromitrata* (5)

WHITE-BELLIED CRESTED-FLYCATCHER *Elminia albiventris* (5)

WHITE-TAILED CRESTED-FLYCATCHER *Elminia albonotata* (5)

BLUE-HEADED CRESTED-FLYCATCHER *Trochocercus nitens* (5)

AFRICAN CRESTED-FLYCATCHER *Trochocercus cyanomelas* (5)

SHORT-CRESTED MONARCH *Hypothymis helenae* (4) [NT]

CELESTIAL MONARCH *Hypothymis coelestis* (4) [EN]

BLACK-NAPED MONARCH *Hypothymis azurea* (4)

CERULEAN PARADISE-FLYCATCHER *Eutrichomyias rowleyi* (4) [CR]

BLACK-HEADED PARADISE-FLYCATCHER *Terpsiphone rufiventer* (5)

BEDFORD'S PARADISE-FLYCATCHER *Terpsiphone bedfordi* (5) [NT]

ANNOBON PARADISE-FLYCATCHER *Terpsiphone smithii* (5) [VU]

RUFOUS-VENTED PARADISE-FLYCATCHER *Terpsiphone rufocinerea* (5)

AFRICAN PARADISE-FLYCATCHER *Terpsiphone viridis* (5)

SÃO TOMÉ PARADISE-FLYCATCHER *Terpsiphone atrochalybeia* (5)

MADAGASCAR PARADISE-FLYCATCHER *Terpsiphone mutata* (5)

SEYCHELLES PARADISE-FLYCATCHER *Terpsiphone corvina* (5) [CR]

MASCARENE PARADISE-FLYCATCHER *Terpsiphone bourbonnensis* (5)

ASIAN PARADISE-FLYCATCHER *Terpsiphone paradisi* (3, 4)

JAPANESE PARADISE-FLYCATCHER *Terpsiphone atrocaudata* (4) [NT]

RUFOUS PARADISE-FLYCATCHER *Terpsiphone cinnamomea* (4) [NT]

BLUE PARADISE-FLYCATCHER *Terpsiphone cyanescens* (4) [NT]

ELEPAIO or HAWAIIAN MONARCH *Chasiempis sandwichensis* (2)

RAROTONGA MONARCH *Pomarea dimidiata* (6) [CR]

TAHITI MONARCH *Pomarea nigra* (6) [CR]

IPHIS MONARCH *Pomarea iphis* (6) [VU]

MARQUESAN MONARCH *Pomarea mendozae* (6) [EN]

FATUHIVA MONARCH *Pomarea whitneyi* (6) [VU]

OGEA MONARCH *Mayrornis versicolor* (6) [VU]

SLATY MONARCH *Mayrornis lessoni* (6)

VANIKORO MONARCH *Mayrornis schistaceus* (6) [NT]

BUFF-BELLIED MONARCH *Neolalage banksiana* (4)

SOUTHERN SHRIKEBILL *Clytorhynchus pachycephaloides* (6)

FIJI SHRIKEBILL *Clytorhynchus vitiensis* (6) [CR]

BLACK-THROATED SHRIKEBILL *Clytorhynchus nigrogularis* (4) [NT]

RENNELL SHRIKEBILL *Clytorhynchus hamlini* (4) [NT]

TRUK MONARCH *Metabolus rugensis* (4) [EN]

BLACK MONARCH *Monarcha axillaris* (6)

RUFOUS MONARCH *Monarcha rubiensis* (6)

ISLAND MONARCH *Monarcha cinerascens* (4, 6)

BLACK-WINGED MONARCH *Monarcha frater* (6)

BLACK-FACED MONARCH *Monarcha melanopsis* (6)

BOUGAINVILLE MONARCH *Monarcha erythrostictus* (4)

CHESTNUT-BELLIED MONARCH *Monarcha castaneiventris* (4)

WHITE-CAPPED MONARCH *Monarcha richardsii* (4)

WHITE-NAPED MONARCH *Monarcha pileatus* (4)

LOETOE MONARCH *Monarcha castus* (4) [NT]

WHITE-EARED MONARCH *Monarcha leucotis* (6)

SPOT-WINGED MONARCH *Monarcha guttulus* (6)

BLACK-BIBBED MONARCH *Monarcha mundus* (4) [NT]

SPECTACLED MONARCH *Monarcha trivirgatus* (4, 6)

FLORES MONARCH *Monarcha sacerdotum* (4) [EN]

WHITE-TIPPED MONARCH *Monarcha everetti* (4) [VU]

BLACK-TIPPED MONARCH *Monarcha loricatus* (4) [NT]

BLACK-CHINNED MONARCH *Monarcha boanensis* (4) [EN]

WHITE-TAILED MONARCH *Monarcha leucurus* (4) [NT]

BLACK-BACKED MONARCH *Monarcha julianae* (6)

HOODED MONARCH *Monarcha manadensis* (6)

BIAK MONARCH *Monarcha brehmii* (6) [EN]

MANUS MONARCH *Monarcha infelix* (4) [NT]

WHITE-BREASTED MONARCH *Monarcha menckei* (6) [DD]

BLACK-TAILED MONARCH *Monarcha verticalis* (6)

BLACK-AND-WHITE MONARCH *Monarcha barbatus* (4)

KULAMBANGRA MONARCH *Monarcha browni* (4) [NT]

WHITE-COLLARED MONARCH *Monarcha viduus* (4)

YAP MONARCH *Monarcha godeffroyi* (4) [NT]

TINIAN MONARCH *Monarcha takatsukasae* (4) [VU]

GOLDEN MONARCH *Monarcha chrysomela* (6) [CR]

FRILLED MONARCH *Arses telescophthalmus* (6)

RUFOUS-COLLARED MONARCH *Arses insularis* (6)

PIED MONARCH *Arses kaupi* (6)

GUAM FLYCATCHER *Myiagra freycineti* (4) [EX]

MANGROVE FLYCATCHER *Myiagra erythrops* (6)

OCEANIC FLYCATCHER *Myiagra oceanica* (4)

POHNPEI FLYCATCHER *Myiagra pluto* (4)

BIAK FLYCATCHER *Myiagra atra* (6) [NT]

DARK-GRAY FLYCATCHER or SLATY MONARCH *Myiagra galeata* (4)

LEADEN FLYCATCHER *Myiagra rubecula* (6)

STEEL-BLUE FLYCATCHER *Myiagra ferrocyanea* (4)

OCHER-HEADED FLYCATCHER *Myiagra cervinicauda* (4) [NT]

MELANESIAN FLYCATCHER *Myiagra caledonica* (4, 6)

VANIKORO FLYCATCHER *Myiagra vanikorensis* (6)

SAMOAN FLYCATCHER *Myiagra albiventris* (6) [VU]

BLUE-CRESTED FLYCATCHER *Myiagra azureocapilla* (6)

BROAD-BILLED FLYCATCHER *Myiagra ruficollis* (4, 6)

SATIN FLYCATCHER *Myiagra cyanoleuca* (6)

RESTLESS FLYCATCHER *Myiagra inquieta* (6)

SHINING FLYCATCHER *Myiagra alecto* (4, 6)

DULL FLYCATCHER *Myiagra hebetior* (6)

SILKTAIL *Lamprolia victoriae* (6) [VU]

YELLOW-BREASTED BOATBILL *Machaerirhynchus flaviventer* (6)

BLACK-BREASTED BOATBILL *Machaerirhynchus nigripectus* (6)

MAGPIE-LARK *Grallina cyanoleuca* (4, 6)

TORRENT-LARK *Grallina bruijni* (6)

Subfamily AEGITHININAE

COMMON IORA *Aegithina tiphia* (4)

WHITE-TAILED IORA or MARSHALL'S IORA *Aegithina nigrolutea* (4)

GREEN IORA *Aegithina viridissima* (4)

GREAT IORA *Aegithina lafresnayei* (4)

Subfamily MALACONOTINAE
Tribe MALACONOTINI

CHATSHRIKE *Lanioturdus torquatus* (5)

BRUBRU *Nilaus afer* (5)

NORTHERN PUFFBACK *Dryoscopus gambensis* (5)

PRINGLE'S PUFFBACK *Dryoscopus pringlii* (5)

BLACK-BACKED PUFFBACK *Dryoscopus cubla* (5)

RED-EYED PUFFBACK *Dryoscopus senegalensis* (5)

PINK-FOOTED PUFFBACK *Dryoscopus angolensis* (5)

LARGE-BILLED PUFFBACK *Dryoscopus sabin* (5)

MARSH TCHAGRA *Tchagra minuta* (5)

BLACK-CROWNED TCHAGRA *Tchagra senegala* (5)

BROWN-CROWNED TCHAGRA *Tchagra australis* (5)

THREE-STREAKED TCHAGRA *Tchagra jamesi* (5)

SOUTHERN TCHAGRA *Tchagra tchagra* (5)

RED-NAPED BUSHSHRIKE *Laniarius ruficeps* (5)

LUEHDER'S BUSHSHRIKE *Laniarius luehderi* (5) [EN, SPP]

BULO BURTI BOUBOU or BULO BURTI BUSHSHRIKE *Laniarius liberatus* (5) [CR]

TURATI'S BOUBOU *Laniarius turatii* (5) [NT]

TROPICAL BOUBOU *Laniarius aethiopicus* (5)

GABON BOUBOU *Laniarius bicolor* (5)

SOUTHERN BOUBOU *Laniarius ferrugineus* (5)

COMMON GONOLEK *Laniarius barbarus* (5)

BLACK-HEADED GONOLEK *Laniarius erythrogaster* (5)

CRIMSON-BREASTED GONOLEK *Laniarius atrococcineus* (5)

PAPYRUS GONOLEK *Laniarius mufumbiri* (5) [NT]

YELLOW-BREASTED BOUBOU *Laniarius atroflavus* (5)

SLATE-COLORED BOUBOU *Laniarius funebris* (5)

SOOTY BOUBOU *Laniarius leucorhynchus* (5)

MOUNTAIN BOUBOU *Laniarius poensis* (5)

FUELLEBORN'S BOUBOU *Laniarius fuelleborni* (5)

ROSY-PATCHED BUSHSHRIKE *Rhodophoneus cruentus* (5)

BOKMAKIERIE *Telophorus zeylonus* (5)

GRAY-GREEN BUSHSHRIKE *Telophorus bocagei* (5)

SULFUR-BREASTED BUSHSHRIKE *Telophorus sulfureopectus* (5)

OLIVE BUSHSHRIKE *Telophorus olivaceus* (5)

MANY-COLORED BUSHSHRIKE *Telophorus multicolor* (5)

BLACK-FRONTED BUSHSHRIKE *Telophorus nigrifrons* (5)

SERLE'S BUSHSHRIKE or MT. KUPE BUSHSHRIKE *Telophorus kupeensis* (5) [CR]

PERRIN'S BUSHSHRIKE *Telophorus viridis* (5)

DOHERTY'S BUSHSHRIKE *Telophorus dohertyi* (5)

FOUR-COLORED BUSHSHRIKE *Telophorus quadricolor* (5)

FIERY-BREASTED BUSHSHRIKE *Malaconotus cruentus* (5)

LAGDEN'S BUSHSHRIKE *Malaconotus lagdeni* (5) [NT]

GREEN-BREASTED BUSHSHRIKE *Malaconotus gladiator* (5) [VU]

GRAY-HEADED BUSHSHRIKE *Malaconotus blanchoti* (5)

MONTEIRO'S BUSHSHRIKE *Malaconotus monteiri* (5) [EN]

ULUGURU BUSHSHRIKE *Malaconotus alius* (5) [CR]

Tribe VANGINI

WHITE HELMETSHRIKE *Prionops plumatus* (5)

GRAY-CRESTED HELMETSHRIKE *Prionops poliolophus* (5) [VU]

YELLOW-CRESTED HELMETSHRIKE *Prionops alberti* (5) [VU]

CHESTNUT-BELLIED HELMETSHRIKE *Prionops caniceps* (5)

RETZ'S HELMETSHRIKE or RED-BILLED HELMETSHRIKE *Prionops retzii* (5)

ANGOLA HELMETSHRIKE or GABELA HELMETSHRIKE *Prionops gabela* (5) [EN]

CHESTNUT-FRONTED HELMETSHRIKE *Prionops scopifrons* (5)

AFRICAN SHRIKE-FLYCATCHER *Bias flammulatus* (5)

BLACK-AND-WHITE SHRIKE-FLYCATCHER *Bias musicus* (5)

WARD'S SHRIKE-FLYCATCHER *Pseudobias wardi* (5)

RUWENZORI BATIS *Batis diops* (5)

BOULTON'S BATIS *Batis margaritae* (5)

SHORT-TAILED BATIS *Batis mixta* (5)

REICHENOW'S BATIS *Batis reichenowi* (5)

MALAWI BATIS *Batis dimorpha* (5)

CAPE BATIS *Batis capensis* (5)

WOODWARD'S BATIS *Batis fratrum* (5)

CHINSPOT BATIS *Batis molitor* (5)

PALE BATIS *Batis soror* (5)

PRIRIT BATIS *Batis pririt* (5)

SENEGAL BATIS *Batis senegalensis* (5)

GRAY-HEADED BATIS *Batis orientalis* (5)

BLACK-HEADED BATIS *Batis minor* (5)

PYGMY BATIS *Batis perkeo* (5)

VERREAUX'S BATIS *Batis minima* (5) [DD]

ITURI BATIS *Batis ituriensis* (5)

WEST AFRICAN BATIS *Batis occulta* (5)

FERNANDO PO BATIS *Batis poensis* (5)

ANGOLA BATIS *Batis minulla* (5)

BROWN-THROATED WATTLE-EYE *Platysteira cyanea* (5)

BLACK-THROATED WATTLE-EYE *Platysteira peltata* (5)

BANDED WATTLE-EYE *Platysteira laticincta* (5) [VU]

WHITE-FRONTED WATTLE-EYE *Platysteira albifrons* (5) [NT]

CHESTNUT WATTLE-EYE *Platysteira castanea* (5)

WHITE-SPOTTED WATTLE-EYE *Platysteira tonsa* (5)

RED-CHEEKED WATTLE-EYE *Platysteira blissetti* (5)

BLACK-NECKED WATTLE-EYE *Platysteira chalybea* (5)

JAMESON'S WATTLE-EYE *Platysteira jamesoni* (5)

YELLOW-BELLIED WATTLE-EYE *Platysteira concreta* (5)

RUFOUS-WINGED PHILENTOMA *Philentoma pyrhopterum* (4)

MAROON-BREASTED PHILENTOMA *Philentoma velatum* (4)

LARGE WOODSHRIKE *Tephrodornis gularis* (4)

COMMON WOODSHRIKE *Tephrodornis pondicerianus* (4)

RED-TAILED VANGA *Calicalicus madagascariensis* (5)

RUFOUS VANGA *Schetba rufa* (5)

HOOK-BILLED VANGA *Vanga curvirostris* (5)

LAFRESNAYE'S VANGA *Xenopirostris xenopirostris* (5)

VAN DAM'S VANGA *Xenopirostris damii* (5) [VU]

POLLEN'S VANGA *Xenopirostris polleni* (5) [VU]

SICKLE-BILLED VANGA *Falculea palliata* (5)

WHITE-HEADED VANGA *Artamella viridis* (5)

CHABERT'S VANGA *Leptopterus chabert* (5)

BLUE VANGA *Cyanolanius madagascarinus* (5)

BERNIER'S VANGA *Oriolia bernieri* (5) [VU]

HELMETBIRD *Euryceros prevostii* (5) [NT]

TYLAS VANGA or KINKIMAVO *Tylas eduardi* (5)

CORAL-BILLED NUTHATCH or NUTHATCH VANGA *Hypositta corallirostris* (5)

Family CALLAEATIDAE

KOKAKO *Callaeas cinerea* (6) [EN]

SADDLEBACK *Philesturnus carunculatus* (6) [CD]

HUIA *Heteralocha acutirostris* (6) [EX]

Family PICATHARTIDAE

RUFOUS ROCK-JUMPER *Chaetops frenatus* (5) [NT]

ORANGE-BREASTED ROCK-JUMPER *Chaetops aurantius* (5) [NT]

WHITE-NECKED ROCKFOWL *Picathartes gymnocephalus* (5) [VU]

GRAY-NECKED ROCKFOWL *Picathartes oreas* (5) [VU]

Family BOMBYCILLIDAE
Tribe DULINI

PALMCHAT *Dulus dominicus* (2)

Tribe PTILOGONATINI

GRAY SILKY-FLYCATCHER *Ptilogonys cinereus* (1, 2)

LONG-TAILED SILKY-FLYCATCHER *Ptilogonys caudatus* (2)

PHAINOPEPLA *Phainopepla nitens* (1)

BLACK-AND-YELLOW SILKY-FLYCATCHER *Phainoptila melanoxantha* (2)

Tribe BOMBYCILLINI

BOHEMIAN WAXWING *Bombycilla garrulus* (1, 3)

JAPANESE WAXWING *Bombycilla japonica* (3, 4) [NT]

CEDAR WAXWING *Bombycilla cedrorum* (1, 2)

Family CINCLIDAE

WHITE-THROATED DIPPER *Cinclus cinclus* (3, 4, 5)

BROWN DIPPER *Cinclus pallasii* (3, 4)

AMERICAN DIPPER *Cinclus mexicanus* (1, 2)

WHITE-CAPPED DIPPER *Cinclus leucocephalus* (2)

RUFOUS-THROATED DIPPER *Cinclus schulzi* (2) [VU]

Subfamily TURDINAE

FINSCH'S FLYCATCHER-THRUSH *Neocossyphus finschii* (5)

RUFOUS FLYCATCHER-THRUSH *Neocossyphus fraseri* (5)

RED-TAILED ANT-THRUSH *Neocossyphus rufus* (5)

WHITE-TAILED ANT-THRUSH *Neocossyphus poensis* (5)

FOREST ROCK-THRUSH *Pseudocossyphus sharpei* (5) [NT]

BENSON'S ROCK-THRUSH *Pseudocossyphus bensoni* (5) [VU]

LITTORAL ROCK-THRUSH *Pseudocossyphus imerinus* (5)

CAPE ROCK-THRUSH *Monticola rupestris* (5)

SENTINEL ROCK-THRUSH *Monticola explorator* (5)

SHORT-TOED ROCK-THRUSH *Monticola brevipes* (5)

TRANSVAAL ROCK-THRUSH *Monticola pretoriae* (5)

MIOMBO ROCK-THRUSH *Monticola angolensis* (5)

RUFOUS-TAILED ROCK-THRUSH *Monticola saxatilis* (3, 4, 5)

LITTLE ROCK-THRUSH *Monticola rufocinereus* (3, 5)

BLUE-CAPPED ROCK-THRUSH *Monticola cinclorhynchus* (3, 4)

WHITE-THROATED ROCK-THRUSH *Monticola gularis* (4)

CHESTNUT-BELLIED ROCK-THRUSH *Monticola rufiventris* (3, 4)

BLUE ROCK-THRUSH *Monticola solitarius* (3, 4, 5)

SRI LANKA WHISTLING-THRUSH or CEYLON WHISTLING-THRUSH *Myophonus blighior* (4) [EN]

SHINY WHISTLING-THRUSH *Myophonus melanurus* (4)

SUNDA WHISTLING-THRUSH *Myophonus glaucinus* (4)

MALAYAN WHISTLING-THRUSH *Myophonus robinsoni* (4) [NT]

MALABAR WHISTLING-THRUSH *Myophonus horsfieldii* (4)

BLUE WHISTLING-THRUSH *Myophonus caeruleus* (3, 4)

FORMOSAN WHISTLING-THRUSH or TAIWAN WHISTLING-THRUSH *Myophonus insularis* (4)

GEOMALIA *Geomalia heinrichi* (4) [NT]

SLATY-BACKED THRUSH *Zoothera schistacea* (4) [NT]

MOLUCCAN THRUSH *Zoothera dumasi* (4) [DD]

CHESTNUT-CAPPED THRUSH *Zoothera interpres* (4)

RED-BACKED THRUSH *Zoothera erythronota* (4) [NT]

CHESTNUT-BACKED THRUSH *Zoothera dohertyi* (4)

PIED THRUSH *Zoothera wardii* (4) [NT]

ASHY THRUSH *Zoothera cinerea* (4) [VU]

ORANGE-BANDED THRUSH or ORANGE-SIDED THRUSH *Zoothera peronii* (4) [NT]

ORANGE-HEADED THRUSH *Zoothera citrina* (4)

EVERETT'S THRUSH *Zoothera everetti* (4) [NT]

SIBERIAN THRUSH *Zoothera sibirica* (3, 4)

VARIED THRUSH *Zoothera naevia* (1, 3)

AZTEC THRUSH *Zoothera pinicola* (1)

ABYSSINIAN GROUND-THRUSH *Zoothera piaggiae* (5)

KIVU GROUND-THRUSH *Zoothera tanganjicae* (5) [NT]

CROSSLEY'S GROUND-THRUSH *Zoothera crossleyi* (5) [NT]

ORANGE GROUND-THRUSH *Zoothera gurneyi* (5)

OBERLAENDER'S GROUND-THRUSH *Zoothera oberlaenderi* (5) [NT]

BLACK-EARED GROUND-THRUSH *Zoothera cameronensis* (5)

GRAY GROUND-THRUSH *Zoothera princei* (5)

SPOTTED GROUND-THRUSH *Zoothera guttata* (5) [EN]

SPOT-WINGED THRUSH *Zoothera spiloptera* (4) [NT]

SUNDA THRUSH *Zoothera andromedae* (4)

PLAIN-BACKED THRUSH *Zoothera mollissima* (4)

LONG-TAILED THRUSH *Zoothera dixoni* (4)

SCALY THRUSH or WHITE'S THRUSH *Zoothera dauma* (3, 4)

AMAMI THRUSH *Zoothera major* (4) [CR]

FAWN-BREASTED THRUSH *Zoothera machiki* (4) [NT]

OLIVE-TAILED THRUSH or BASSIAN THRUSH *Zoothera lunulata* (6)

RUSSET-TAILED THRUSH *Zoothera heinei* (6)

NEW BRITAIN THRUSH *Zoothera talaseae* (4, 6) [NT]

SAN CRISTÓBAL THRUSH *Zoothera margaretae* (4) [NT]

LONG-BILLED THRUSH *Zoothera monticola* (3, 4) [NT]

DARK-SIDED THRUSH *Zoothera marginata* (3, 4)

BONIN THRUSH *Zoothera terrestris* (4) [EX]

SULAWESI THRUSH *Cataponera turdoides* (4)

TRISTAN THRUSH *Nesocichla eremita* (4) [NT]

FOREST THRUSH *Cichlherminia lherminieri* (4) [NT]

EASTERN BLUEBIRD *Sialia sialis* (1, 2)

WESTERN BLUEBIRD *Sialia mexicana* (1)

MOUNTAIN BLUEBIRD *Sialia currucoides* (1)

KAMAO *Myadestes myadestinus* (2) [CR]

AMAUI *Myadestes oahensis* (2) [EX]

OLOMAO *Myadestes lanaiensis* (2) [CR]

OMAO *Myadestes obscurus* (2)

PUAIOHI *Myadestes palmeri* (2) [CR]

TOWNSEND'S SOLITAIRE *Myadestes townsendi* (1)

BROWN-BACKED SOLITAIRE *Myadestes occidentalis* (1, 2)

CUBAN SOLITAIRE *Myadestes elisabeth* (2) [NT]

RUFOUS-THROATED SOLITAIRE *Myadestes genibarbis* (2)

BLACK-FACED SOLITAIRE *Myadestes melanops* (2)

VARIED SOLITAIRE *Myadestes coloratus* (2)

ANDEAN SOLITAIRE *Myadestes ralloides* (2)

SLATE-COLORED SOLITAIRE *Myadestes unicolor* (1, 2)

RUFOUS-BROWN SOLITAIRE *Cichlopsis leucogenys* (2) [NT]

WHITE-EARED SOLITAIRE *Entomodestes leucotis* (2)

BLACK SOLITAIRE *Entomodestes coracinus* (2)

BLACK-BILLED NIGHTINGALE-THRUSH *Catharus gracilirostris* (2)

ORANGE-BILLED NIGHTINGALE-THRUSH *Catharus aurantiirostris* (1, 2)

SLATY-BACKED NIGHTINGALE-THRUSH *Catharus fuscater* (2)

RUSSET NIGHTINGALE-THRUSH *Catharus occidentalis* (1)

RUDDY-CAPPED NIGHTINGALE-THRUSH *Catharus frantzii* (1, 2)

BLACK-HEADED NIGHTINGALE-THRUSH *Catharus mexicanus* (1, 2)

SPOTTED NIGHTINGALE-THRUSH *Catharus dryas* (1, 2)

VEERY *Catharus fuscescens* (1, 2)

GRAY-CHEEKED THRUSH *Catharus minimus* (1, 2, 3)

BICKNELL'S THRUSH *Catharus bicknelli* (1, 2)

SWAINSON'S THRUSH *Catharus ustulatus* (1, 2)

HERMIT THRUSH *Catharus guttatus* (1, 2, 3)

WOOD THRUSH *Catharus mustelinus* (1, 2, 3)

YELLOW-LEGGED THRUSH *Platycichla flavipes* (2)

PALE-EYED THRUSH *Platycichla leucops* (2)

GROUNDSCRAPER THRUSH *Psophocichla litsipsirupa* (5)

AFRICAN THRUSH *Turdus pelios* (5)

BARE-EYED THRUSH *Turdus tephronotus* (5)

KURRICHANE THRUSH *Turdus libonyanus* (5)

OLIVACEOUS THRUSH *Turdus olivaceofuscus* (5) [NT]

OLIVE THRUSH *Turdus olivaceus* (5)

SOMALI THRUSH *Turdus ludoviciae* (5) [EN]

TAITA THRUSH *Turdus helleri* (5) [CR]

YEMEN THRUSH *Turdus menachensis* (3) [VU]

COMORO THRUSH *Turdus bewsheri* (5)

GRAY-BACKED THRUSH *Turdus hortulorum* (3, 4)

TICKELL'S THRUSH *Turdus unicolor* (3, 4)

BLACK-BREASTED THRUSH *Turdus dissimilis* (4) [NT]

JAPANESE THRUSH *Turdus cardis* (4)

WHITE-COLLARED BLACKBIRD *Turdus albocinctus* (3, 4)

RING OUZEL *Turdus torquatus* (3, 5)

GRAY-WINGED BLACKBIRD *Turdus boulboul* (3, 4)

EURASIAN BLACKBIRD or COMMON BLACKBIRD *Turdus merula* (3, 4, 5, 6)

ISLAND THRUSH *Turdus poliocephalus* (4, 6)

CHESTNUT THRUSH *Turdus rubrocanus* (3, 4)

WHITE-BACKED THRUSH or KESSLER'S THRUSH *Turdus kessleri* (3, 4)

GRAY-SIDED THRUSH *Turdus feae* (4) [VU]

EYEBROWED THRUSH *Turdus obscurus* (3, 4)

PALE THRUSH *Turdus pallidus* (4)

BROWN-HEADED THRUSH *Turdus chrysolaus* (4)

IZU THRUSH *Turdus celaenops* (4) [VU]

DARK-THROATED THRUSH *Turdus ruficollis* (3, 4)

DUSKY THRUSH *Turdus naumanni* (3, 4)

FIELDFARE *Turdus pilaris* (3, 5)

REDWING *Turdus iliacus* (3, 4)

SONG THRUSH *Turdus philomelos* (3, 4, 6)

CHINESE THRUSH *Turdus mupinensis* (4) [NT]

MISTLE THRUSH *Turdus viscivorus* (3, 4)

WHITE-CHINNED THRUSH *Turdus aurantius* (2)

GRAND CAYMAN THRUSH *Turdus ravidus* (2) [EX]

RED-LEGGED THRUSH *Turdus plumbeus* (2)

CHIGUANCO THRUSH *Turdus chiguanco* (2)

SOOTY THRUSH *Turdus nigrescens* (2)

GREAT THRUSH *Turdus fuscater* (2)

BLACK THRUSH *Turdus infuscatus* (2)

GLOSSY-BLACK *Thrush Turdus serranus* (2)

ANDEAN SLATY-THRUSH *Turdus nigriceps* (2)

EASTERN SLATY-THRUSH *Turdus subalaris* (2)

PLUMBEOUS-BACKED THRUSH *Turdus reevei* (2)

BLACK-HOODED THRUSH *Turdus olivater* (2)

MARANON THRUSH *Turdus maranonicus* (2)

CHESTNUT-BELLIED THRUSH *Turdus fulviventris* (2)

RUFOUS-BELLIED THRUSH *Turdus rufiventris* (2)

AUSTRAL THRUSH *Turdus falcklandii* (2)

PALE-BREASTED THRUSH *Turdus leucomelas* (2)

CREAMY-BELLIED THRUSH *Turdus amaurochalinus* (2)

AMERICAN MOUNTAIN THRUSH *Turdus plebejus* (1, 2)

BLACK-BILLED THRUSH *Turdus ignobilis* (2)

LAWRENCE'S THRUSH *Turdus lawrencii* (2)

PALE-VENTED THRUSH *Turdus obsoletus* (2)

COCOA THRUSH *Turdus fumigatus* (2)

HAUXWELL'S THRUSH *Turdus hauxwelli* (2)

CLAY-COLORED THRUSH *Turdus grayi* (1, 2)

YELLOW-EYED THRUSH *Turdus nudigenis* (2)

ECUADORIAN THRUSH *Turdus maculirostris* (2)

UNICOLORED THRUSH *Turdus haplochrous* (2) [NT]

WHITE-EYED THRUSH *Turdus jamaicensis* (2)

WHITE-THROATED THRUSH *Turdus assimilis* (1, 2)

WHITE-NECKED THRUSH *Turdus albicollis* (2)

RUFOUS-BACKED THRUSH *Turdus rufopallia-tus* (1)

GRAYSON'S THRUSH *Turdus graysoni* (1) [NT]

LA SELLE THRUSH *Turdus swalesi* (2) [VU]

AMERICAN ROBIN *Turdus migratorius* (1, 2, 3)

RUFOUS-COLLARED ROBIN *Turdus rufitorques* (2)

BLACK-BREASTED FRUIT-HUNTER *Chlamydochaera jefferyi* (4)

GOULD'S SHORTWING *Brachypteryx stellata* (3, 4) [NT]

RUSTY-BELLIED SHORTWING *Brachypteryx hyperythra* (3, 4) [VU]

WHITE-BELLIED SHORTWING *Brachypteryx major* (4) [NT]

LESSER SHORTWING *Brachypteryx leucophrys* (3, 4)

WHITE-BROWED SHORTWING *Brachypteryx montana* (3, 4)

GREAT SHORTWING *Heinrichia calligyna* (4)

BROWN-CHESTED ALETHE *Alethe poliocephala* (5)

RED-THROATED ALETHE *Alethe poliophrys* (5)

WHITE-CHESTED ALETHE *Alethe fuelleborni* (5)

CHOLO ALETHE or THYOLO ALETHE *Alethe choloensis* (5) [VU]

WHITE-TAILED ALETHE *Alethe diademata* (5)

Tribe MUSCICAPINI

SILVERBIRD *Empidornis semipartitus* (5)

PALE FLYCATCHER *Bradornis pallidus* (5)

CHAT FLYCATCHER *Bradornis infuscatus* (5)

MARIQUA FLYCATCHER *Bradornis mariquensis* (5)

LARGE FLYCATCHER *Bradornis microrhynchus* (5)

ABYSSINIAN SLATY-FLYCATCHER *Dioptrornis chocolatinus* (5)

ANGOLA SLATY-FLYCATCHER *Dioptrornis brunneus* (5)

NORTHERN BLACK-FLYCATCHER *Melaenornis edolioides* (5)

SOUTHERN BLACK-FLYCATCHER *Melaenornis pammelaina* (5)

YELLOW-EYED BLACK-FLYCATCHER *Melaenornis ardesiacus* (5)

WEST AFRICAN BLACK-FLYCATCHER or NIMBA FLYCATCHER *Melaenornis annamarulae* (5) [VU]

AFRICAN FOREST-FLYCATCHER *Fraseria ocreata* (5)

WHITE-BROWED FOREST-FLYCATCHER *Fraseria cinerascens* (5)

FISCAL FLYCATCHER *Sigelus silens* (5)

STREAKY-BREASTED JUNGLE-FLYCATCHER *Rhinomyias addita* (4) [VU]

RUSSET-BACKED JUNGLE-FLYCATCHER *Rhinomyias oscillans* (4) [NT]

BROWN-CHESTED JUNGLE-FLYCATCHER *Rhinomyias brunneata* (4) [VU]

FULVOUS-CHESTED JUNGLE-FLYCATCHER *Rhinomyias olivacea* (4)

GRAY-CHESTED JUNGLE-FLYCATCHER *Rhinomyias umbratilis* (4)

RUFOUS-TAILED JUNGLE-FLYCATCHER *Rhinomyias ruficauda* (4)

HENNA-TAILED JUNGLE-FLYCATCHER *Rhinomyias colonus* (4) [NT]

EYEBROWED JUNGLE-FLYCATCHER *Rhinomyias gularis* (4)

WHITE-BROWED JUNGLE-FLYCATCHER *Rhinomyias insignis* (4) [EN]

WHITE-THROATED JUNGLE-FLYCATCHER *Rhinomyias albigularis* (4) [CR]

SLATY-BACKED JUNGLE-FLYCATCHER *Rhinomyias goodfellowi* (4) [VU]

SPOTTED FLYCATCHER *Muscicapa striata* (3, 4, 5)

GAMBAGA FLYCATCHER *Muscicapa gambagae* (5)

GRAY-STREAKED FLYCATCHER *Muscicapa griseisticta* (4, 6)

DARK-SIDED FLYCATCHER *Muscicapa sibirica* (3, 4)

ASIAN BROWN FLYCATCHER *Muscicapa daurica* (3, 4)

BROWN-STREAKED FLYCATCHER *Muscicapa williamsoni* (4)

ASHY-BREASTED FLYCATCHER *Muscicapa randi* (4) [EN]

SUMBA BROWN FLYCATCHER *Muscicapa segregata* (4) [DD]

RUSTY-TAILED FLYCATCHER *Muscicapa ruficauda* (3, 4)

BROWN-BREASTED FLYCATCHER *Muscicapa muttui* (4) [NT]

FERRUGINOUS FLYCATCHER *Muscicapa ferruginea* (3, 4)

USSHER'S FLYCATCHER *Muscicapa ussheri* (5)

SOOTY FLYCATCHER *Muscicapa infuscata* (5)

BOEHM'S FLYCATCHER *Muscicapa boehmi* (5)

SWAMP FLYCATCHER *Muscicapa aquatica* (5)

OLIVACEOUS FLYCATCHER *Muscicapa olivascens* (5)

CHAPIN'S FLYCATCHER *Muscicapa lendu* (5) [VU]

ITOMBWE FLYCATCHER *Muscicapa itombwensis* (5)

AFRICAN DUSKY FLYCATCHER *Muscicapa adusta* (5)

LITTLE GRAY FLYCATCHER *Muscicapa epulata* (5)

YELLOW-FOOTED FLYCATCHER *Muscicapa sethsmithi* (5)

DUSKY-BLUE FLYCATCHER *Muscicapa comitata* (5)

TESSMANN'S FLYCATCHER *Muscicapa tessmanni* (5)

CASSIN'S FLYCATCHER *Muscicapa cassini* (5)

ASHY FLYCATCHER *Muscicapa caerulescens* (5)

GRAY-THROATED TIT-FLYCATCHER *Myioparus griseigularis* (5)

GRAY TIT-FLYCATCHER *Myioparus plumbeus* (5)

HUMBLOT'S FLYCATCHER or GRAND COMORO FLYCATCHER *Humblotia flavirostris* (5) [VU]

EUROPEAN PIED FLYCATCHER *Ficedula hypoleuca* (3, 5)

COLLARED FLYCATCHER *Ficedula albicollis* (3, 5)

SEMICOLLARED FLYCATCHER *Ficedula semitorquata* (3, 5)

YELLOW-RUMPED FLYCATCHER *Ficedula zanthopygia* (3, 4)

NARCISSUS FLYCATCHER *Ficedula narcissina* (3, 4)

CHINESE FLYCATCHER *Ficedula elisae* (4)

MUGIMAKI FLYCATCHER *Ficedula mugimaki* (4)

SLATY-BACKED FLYCATCHER *Ficedula hodgsonii* (4)

RUFOUS-GORGETED FLYCATCHER *Ficedula strophiata* (3, 4)

RED-BREASTED FLYCATCHER or RED-THROATED FLYCATCHER *Ficedula parva* (3)

KASHMIR FLYCATCHER *Ficedula subrubra* (3, 4) [VU]

WHITE-GORGETED FLYCATCHER *Ficedula monileger* (3, 4)

RUFOUS-BROWED FLYCATCHER *Ficedula solitaris* (4)

SNOWY-BROWED FLYCATCHER *Ficedula hyperythra* (4)

RUFOUS-CHESTED FLYCATCHER *Ficedula dumetoria* (4)

RUFOUS-THROATED FLYCATCHER *Ficedula rufigula* (4) [NT]

CINNAMON-CHESTED FLYCATCHER *Ficedula buruensis* (4)

LITTLE SLATY FLYCATCHER *Ficedula basilanica* (4) [VU]

DAMAR FLYCATCHER *Ficedula henrici* (4) [VU]

SUMBA FLYCATCHER *Ficedula harterti* (4) [NT]

PALAWAN FLYCATCHER *Ficedula platenae* (4) [EN]

CRYPTIC FLYCATCHER *Ficedula crypta* (4) [VU]

FURTIVE FLYCATCHER *Ficedula disposita* (4) [EN]

LOMPOBATTANG FLYCATCHER *Ficedula bonthaina* (4) [EN]

LITTLE PIED FLYCATCHER *Ficedula westermanni* (4)

ULTRAMARINE FLYCATCHER *Ficedula superciliaris* (4)

SLATY-BLUE FLYCATCHER *Ficedula tricolor* (3, 4)

SAPPHIRE FLYCATCHER *Ficedula sapphira* (4)

BLACK-AND-RUFOUS FLYCATCHER or BLACK-AND-ORANGE Flycatcher *Ficedula nigrorufa* (4) [NT]

BLACK-BANDED FLYCATCHER *Ficedula timorensis* (4) [NT]

BLUE-AND-WHITE FLYCATCHER *Cyanoptila cyanomelana* (3, 4)

VERDITER FLYCATCHER *Eumyias thalassina* (3, 4)

DULL-BLUE FLYCATCHER *Eumyias sordida* (4) [NT]

ISLAND FLYCATCHER *Eumyias panayensis* (4)

NILGIRI FLYCATCHER *Eumyias albicaudata* (4) [NT]

INDIGO FLYCATCHER *Eumyias indigo* (4)

LARGE NILTAVA *Niltava grandis* (4)

SMALL NILTAVA *Niltava macgrigoriae* (4)

FUJIAN NILTAVA *Niltava davidi* (4) [NT]

RUFOUS-BELLIED *Niltava Niltava sundara* (4)

RUFOUS-VENTED *Niltava Niltava sumatrana* (4)

VIVID NILTAVA *Niltava vivida* (4)

MATINAN FLYCATCHER *Cyornis sanfordi* (4) [VU]

BLUE-FRONTED FLYCATCHER *Cyornis hoevelli* (4)

TIMOR BLUE-FLYCATCHER *Cyornis hyacinthinus* (4)

WHITE-TAILED FLYCATCHER *Cyornis concretus* (4)

RUECK'S BLUE-FLYCATCHER *Cyornis ruckii* (4) [VU]

BLUE-BREASTED FLYCATCHER *Cyornis herioti* (4) [NT]

HAINAN BLUE-FLYCATCHER *Cyornis hainanus* (4)

WHITE-BELLIED BLUE-FLYCATCHER *Cyornis pallipes* (4)

PALE-CHINNED FLYCATCHER *Cyornis poliogenys* (4)

PALE BLUE-FLYCATCHER *Cyornis unicolor* (4)

BLUE-THROATED FLYCATCHER *Cyornis rubeculoides* (4)

HILL BLUE-FLYCATCHER *Cyornis banyumas* (4)

PALAWAN BLUE-FLYCATCHER *Cyornis lemprieri* (4)

BORNEAN BLUE-FLYCATCHER *Cyornis superbus* (4)

LARGE-BILLED BLUE-FLYCATCHER *Cyornis caerulatus* (4)

MALAYSIAN BLUE-FLYCATCHER *Cyornis turcosus* (4)

TICKELL'S BLUE-FLYCATCHER *Cyornis tickelliae* (4)

MANGROVE BLUE-FLYCATCHER *Cyornis rufigastra* (4)

SULAWESI BLUE-FLYCATCHER *Cyornis omissus* (4)

PYGMY BLUE-FLYCATCHER *Muscicapella hodgsoni* (4)

GRAY-HEADED CANARY-FLYCATCHER *Culicicapa ceylonensis* (4)

CITRINE CANARY-FLYCATCHER *Culicicapa helianthea* (4)

DOHRN'S FLYCATCHER *Horizorhinus dohrni* (5)

Tribe SAXICOLINI

WHITE-STARRED ROBIN *Pogonocichla stellata* (5)

SWYNNERTON'S ROBIN *Swynnertonia swynnertoni* (5) [VU]

FOREST ROBIN *Stiphrornis erythrothorax* (5)

ALEXANDER'S AKALAT *Sheppardia poensis* (5)

BOCAGE'S AKALAT *Sheppardia bocagei* (5)

LOWLAND AKALAT *Sheppardia cyornithopsis* (5)

EQUATORIAL AKALAT *Sheppardia aequatorialis* (5)

SHARPE'S AKALAT *Sheppardia sharpei* (5)

EAST COAST AKALAT *Sheppardia gunningi* (5) [VU]

GABELA AKALAT *Sheppardia gabela* (5) [EN]

USAMBARA AKALAT *Sheppardia montana* (5) [VU]

IRINGA AKALAT *Sheppardia lowei* (5) [VU]

EUROPEAN ROBIN *Erithacus rubecula* (3, 5)

JAPANESE ROBIN *Erithacus akahige* (3, 4)

RYUKYU ROBIN *Erithacus komadori* (3) [NT]

RUFOUS-TAILED ROBIN *Luscinia sibilans* (3, 4)

THRUSH NIGHTINGALE *Luscinia luscinia* (3, 5)

COMMON NIGHTINGALE *Luscinia megarhynchos* (3, 5)

SIBERIAN RUBYTHROAT *Luscinia calliope* (3, 4)

WHITE-TAILED RUBYTHROAT *Luscinia pectoralis* (3, 4)

BLUETHROAT *Luscinia svecica* (1, 3, 4, 5)

RUFOUS-HEADED ROBIN *Luscinia ruficeps* (4) [VU]

BLACK-THROATED BLUE ROBIN or BLACKTHROAT *Luscinia obscura* (4) [VU]

FIRETHROAT *Luscinia pectardens* (4) [NT]

INDIAN BLUE ROBIN *Luscinia brunnea* (3, 4)

SIBERIAN BLUE ROBIN *Luscinia cyane* (4)

RED-FLANKED BLUETAIL or ORANGE-FLANKED BUSH ROBIN *Tarsiger cyanurus* (1, 3, 4)

GOLDEN BUSH-ROBIN *Tarsiger chrysaeus* (3, 4)

WHITE-BROWED BUSH-ROBIN *Tarsiger indicus* (3, 4)

RUFOUS-BREASTED BUSH-ROBIN *Tarsiger hyperythrus* (3, 4) [NT]

COLLARED BUSH-ROBIN *Tarsiger johnstoniae* (4)

WHITE-THROATED ROBIN *Irania gutturalis* (3, 5)

WHITE-BELLIED ROBIN-CHAT *Cossyphicula roberti* (5)

MOUNTAIN ROBIN-CHAT *Cossypha isabellae* (5)

ARCHER'S ROBIN-CHAT *Cossypha archeri* (5)

OLIVE-FLANKED ROBIN-CHAT *Cossypha anomala* (5)

CAPE ROBIN-CHAT *Cossypha caffra* (5)

WHITE-THROATED ROBIN-CHAT *Cossypha humeralis* (5)

BLUE-SHOULDERED ROBIN-CHAT *Cossypha cyanocampter* (5)

GRAY-WINGED ROBIN-CHAT *Cossypha polioptera* (5)

RUEPPELL'S ROBIN-CHAT *Cossypha semirufa* (5)

WHITE-BROWED ROBIN-CHAT *Cossypha heuglini* (5)

RED-CAPPED ROBIN-CHAT *Cossypha natalensis* (5)

CHORISTER ROBIN-CHAT *Cossypha dichroa* (5)

WHITE-HEADED ROBIN-CHAT *Cossypha heinrichi* (5) [VU]

SNOWY-CROWNED ROBIN-CHAT *Cossypha niveicapilla* (5)

WHITE-CROWNED ROBIN-CHAT *Cossypha albicapilla* (5)

ANGOLA CAVE-CHAT *Xenocopsychus ansorgei* (5) [NT]

COLLARED PALM-THRUSH *Cichladusa arquata* (5)

RUFOUS-TAILED PALM-THRUSH *Cichladusa ruficauda* (5)

SPOTTED MORNING-THRUSH *Cichladusa guttata* (5)

FOREST SCRUB-ROBIN *Cercotrichas leucosticta* (5)

BEARDED SCRUB-ROBIN *Cercotrichas quadrivirgata* (5)

MIOMBO SCRUB-ROBIN *Cercotrichas barbata* (5)

BROWN SCRUB-ROBIN *Cercotrichas signata* (5)

BROWN-BACKED SCRUB-ROBIN *Cercotrichas hartlaubi* (5)

RED-BACKED SCRUB-ROBIN *Cercotrichas leucophrys* (5)

RUFOUS-TAILED SCRUB ROBIN *Cercotrichas galactotes* (5)

KALAHARI SCRUB-ROBIN *Cercotrichas paena* (5)

KAROO SCRUB-ROBIN *Cercotrichas coryphaeus* (5)

BLACK SCRUB-ROBIN *Cercotrichas podobe* (4, 5)

HERERO CHAT *Namibornis herero* (4) [NT]

SEYCHELLES MAGPIE-ROBIN *Copsychus sechellarum* (5) [CR]

MADAGASCAR MAGPIE-ROBIN *Copsychus albospecularis* (5)

ORIENTAL MAGPIE-ROBIN *Copsychus saularis* (4)

WHITE-RUMPED SHAMA *Copsychus malabaricus* (4)

WHITE-CROWNED SHAMA *Copsychus stricklandii* (4)

WHITE-BROWED SHAMA *Copsychus luzoniensis* (4)

WHITE-VENTED SHAMA *Copsychus niger* (4)

BLACK SHAMA *Copsychus cebuensis* (4) [EN]

RUFOUS-TAILED SHAMA *Trichixos pyrropyga* (4)

INDIAN ROBIN *Saxicoloides fulicata* (4)

ALA SHAN REDSTART *Phoenicurus alaschanicus* (4) [NT]

RUFOUS-BACKED REDSTART *Phoenicurus erythronota* (3, 4)

BLUE-CAPPED REDSTART *Phoenicurus caeruleocephalus* (3, 4)

BLACK REDSTART *Phoenicurus ochruros* (3, 4, 5)

COMMON REDSTART *Phoenicurus phoenicurus* (3, 5)

HODGSON'S REDSTART *Phoenicurus hodgsoni* (3, 4)

WHITE-THROATED REDSTART *Phoenicurus schisticeps* (4)

DAURIAN REDSTART *Phoenicurus auroreus* (3, 4)

MOUSSIER'S REDSTART *Phoenicurus moussieri* (5)

WHITE-WINGED REDSTART *Phoenicurus erythrogaster* (3, 4)

BLUE-FRONTED REDSTART *Phoenicurus frontalis* (3, 4)

WHITE-CAPPED WATER-REDSTART *Chaimarrornis leucocephalus* (3, 4)

PLUMBEOUS WATER-REDSTART *Rhyacornis fuliginosus* (3, 4)

LUZON WATER-REDSTART *Rhyacornis bicolor* (4) [EN]

WHITE-BELLIED REDSTART *Hodgsonius phaenicuroides* (3, 4)

WHITE-TAILED ROBIN *Cinclidium leucurum* (4)

SUNDA ROBIN *Cinclidium diana* (4)

BLUE-FRONTED ROBIN *Cinclidium frontale* (4) [NT]

GRANDALA *Grandala coelicolor* (4)

LITTLE FORKTAIL *Enicurus scouleri* (3, 4)

SUNDA FORKTAIL *Enicurus velatus* (4)

CHESTNUT-NAPED FORKTAIL *Enicurus ruficapillus* (4)

BLACK-BACKED FORKTAIL *Enicurus immaculatus* (4)

SLATY-BACKED FORKTAIL *Enicurus cchistaceus* (4)

WHITE-CROWNED FORKTAIL *Enicurus leschenaulti* (4)

SPOTTED FORKTAIL *Enicurus maculatus* (4)

PURPLE COCHOA *Cochoa purpurea* (4) [NT]

GREEN COCHOA *Cochoa viridis* (4) [NT]

SUMATRAN COCHOA *Cochoa beccarii* (4) [VU]

JAVAN COCHOA *Cochoa azurea* (4) [VU]

WHINCHAT *Saxicola rubetra* (3, 5)

WHITE-BROWED BUSHCHAT or STOLICZKA'S BUSHCHAT *Saxicola macrorhyncha* (3) [VU]

WHITE-THROATED BUSHCHAT or HODGSON'S BUSHCHAT *Saxicola insignis* (3, 4) [VU]

CANARY ISLANDS CHAT *Saxicola dacotiae* (5) [NT]

COMMON STONECHAT *Saxicola torquata* (3, 5)

AFRICAN STONECHAT *Saxicola axillaris* (5)

SIBERIAN STONECHAT *Saxicola maura* (3, 4, 5)

REUNION STONECHAT *Saxicola tectes* (5)

WHITE-TAILED STONECHAT *Saxicola leucura* (4)

PIED BUSHCHAT *Saxicola caprata* (3, 4)

BLACK BUSHCHAT *Saxicola aethiops* (6)

JERDON'S BUSHCHAT *Saxicola jerdoni* (4) [NT]

GRAY BUSHCHAT *Saxicola ferrea* (3, 4)

WHITE-BELLIED BUSHCHAT *Saxicola gutturalis* (4) [NT]

BUFF-STREAKED WHEATEAR *Oenanthe bifasciata* (5) [NT]

WHITE-TAILED WHEATEAR *Oenanthe leucopyga* (3, 5)

HOODED WHEATEAR *Oenanthe monacha* (3, 5)

HUME'S WHEATEAR *Oenanthe alboniger* (3, 4)

BLACK WHEATEAR *Oenanthe leucura* (3, 5)

MOUNTAIN WHEATEAR *Oenanthe monticola* (5)

SOMALI WHEATEAR *Oenanthe phillipsi* (5)

NORTHERN WHEATEAR *Oenanthe oenanthe* (1, 3, 4, 5)

MOURNING WHEATEAR *Oenanthe lugens* (3, 5)

ARABIAN WHEATEAR *Oenanthe lugentoides* (3)

SCHALOW'S WHEATEAR *Oenanthe lugubris* (5)

FINSCH'S WHEATEAR *Oenanthe finschii* (3, 5)

VARIABLE WHEATEAR *Oenanthe picata* (3, 4)

RED-RUMPED WHEATEAR *Oenanthe moesta* (3, 5)

BLACK-EARED WHEATEAR *Oenanthe hispanica* (3, 5)

PIED WHEATEAR *Oenanthe pleschanka* (3, 4, 5)

CYPRUS WHEATEAR *Oenanthe cypriaca* (5)

RUFOUS-TAILED WHEATEAR *Oenanthe xanthoprymna* (3, 4, 5)

DESERT WHEATEAR *Oenanthe deserti* (3, 4, 5)

CAPPED WHEATEAR *Oenanthe pileata* (5)

ISABELLINE WHEATEAR *Oenanthe isabellina* (3, 4, 5)

BOTTA'S WHEATEAR *Oenanthe bottae* (3, 5)

HEUGLIN'S WHEATEAR *Oenanthe heuglini* (5)

SICKLEWING CHAT *Cercomela sinuata* (5)

KAROO CHAT *Cercomela schlegelii* (5)

TRACTRAC CHAT *Cercomela tractrac* (5)

FAMILIAR CHAT *Cercomela familiaris* (5)

BROWN-TAILED CHAT *Cercomela scotocerca* (5)

INDIAN CHATOR BROWN ROCK-CHAT *Cercomela fusca* (4)

SOMBRE CHAT *Cercomela dubia* (5) [NT]

BLACKSTART *Cercomela melanura* (3, 5)

MOORLAND CHAT *Cercomela sordida* (5)

CONGO MOOR-CHAT *Myrmecocichla tholloni* (5)

NORTHERN ANTEATER-CHAT *Myrmecocichla aethiops* (5)

SOUTHERN ANTEATER-CHAT *Myrmecocichla formicivora* (5)

SOOTY CHAT *Myrmecocichla nigra* (5)

RUEPPELL'S CHAT *Myrmecocichla melaena* (5)

WHITE-FRONTED BLACK-CHAT *Myrmecocichla albifrons* (5)

WHITE-HEADED BLACK-CHAT *Myrmecocichla arnotti* (5)

MOCKING CLIFF-CHAT *Thamnolaea cinnamomeiventris* (5)

WHITE-CROWNED CLIFF-CHAT *Thamnolaea coronata* (5)

WHITE-WINGED CLIFF-CHAT *Thamnolaea semirufa* (5)

BOULDER CHAT *Pinarornis plumosus* (5)

Family STURNIDAE
Tribe STURNINI

RUSTY-WINGED STARLING *Aplonis zelandica* (4) [NT]

MOUNTAIN STARLING or SANTO MOUNTAIN STARLING *Aplonis santovestris* (4) [VU]

POHNPEI STARLING or POHNPEI MOUNTAIN STARLING *Aplonis pelzelni* (4) [CR]

SAMOAN STARLING *Aplonis atrifusca* (4)

KOSRAE STARLING *Aplonis corvina* (4) [EX]

MYSTERIOUS STARLING *Aplonis mavornata* (6) [EX]

RAROTONGA STARLING *Aplonis cinerascens* (6) [VU]

POLYNESIAN STARLING *Aplonis tabuensis* (6)

STRIATED STARLING *Aplonis striata* (6)

NORFOLK STARLING or TASMAN STARLING *Aplonis fusca* (6) [EX]

MICRONESIAN STARLING *Aplonis opaca* (6)

TANIMBAR STARLING *Aplonis crassa* (4) [NT]

SINGING STARLING *Aplonis cantoroides* (4, 6)

ATOLL STARLING *Aplonis feadensis* (4)

RENNELL STARLING *Aplonis insularis* (4) [NT]

BROWN-WINGED STARLING *Aplonis grandis* (4)

SAN CRISTÓBAL STARLING *Aplonis dichroa* (4)

MOLUCCAN STARLING or ISLAND STARLING *Aplonis mysolensis* (4)

SHORT-TAILED STARLING *Aplonis minor* (4)

ASIAN GLOSSY STARLING *Aplonis panayensis* (4)

METALLIC STARLING or SHINING STARLING *Aplonis metallica* (4, 6)

LONG-TAILED STARLING *Aplonis magna* (6)

YELLOW-EYED STARLING *Aplonis mystacea* (6) [NT]

WHITE-EYED STARLING *Aplonis brunne-icapilla* (4) [EN]

STUHLMANN'S STARLING *Poeoptera stuhlmanni* (5)

KENRICK'S STARLING *Poeoptera kenricki* (5)

NARROW-TAILED STARLING *Poeoptera lugubris* (5)

WHITE-COLLARED STARLING *Grafisia torquata* (5)

WALLER'S STARLING *Onychognathus walleri* (5)

PALE-WINGED STARLING *Onychognathus nabouroup* (5)

TRISTRAM'S STARLING *Onychognathus tristramii* (3, 5)

RED-WINGED STARLING *Onychognathus morio* (5)

SOMALI STARLING *Onychognathus blythii* (5)

SOCOTRA STARLING *Onychognathus frater* (3) [VU]

CHESTNUT-WINGED STARLING *Onychognathus fulgidus* (5)

SLENDER-BILLED STARLING *Onychognathus tenuirostris* (5)

WHITE-BILLED STARLING *Onychognathus albirostris* (5)

BRISTLE-CROWNED STARLING *Onychognathus salvadorii* (5)

IRIS GLOSSY-STARLING or EMERALD STARLING *Coccycolius iris* (5)

COPPER-TAILED GLOSSY-STARLING *Lamprotornis cupreocauda* (5) [NT]

PURPLE-HEADED GLOSSY-STARLING *Lamprotornis purpureiceps* (5)

BLACK-BELLIED GLOSSY-STARLING *Lamprotornis corruscus* (5)

PURPLE GLOSSY-STARLING *Lamprotornis purpureus* (5)

RED-SHOULDERED GLOSSY-STARLING *Lamprotornis nitens* (5)

BRONZE-TAILED GLOSSY-STARLING *Lamprotornis chalcurus* (5)

GREATER BLUE-EARED GLOSSY-STARLING *Lamprotornis chalybaeus* (5)

LESSER BLUE-EARED GLOSSY-STARLING *Lamprotornis chloropterus* (5)

SHARP-TAILED GLOSSY-STARLING *Lamprotornis acuticaudus* (5)

SPLENDID GLOSSY-STARLING *Lamprotornis splendidus* (5)

PRINCIPE GLOSSY-STARLING *Lamprotornis ornatus* (5)

BURCHELL'S GLOSSY-STARLING *Lamprotornis australis* (5)

MEVES'S GLOSSY-STARLING *Lamprotornis mevesii* (5)

LONG-TAILED GLOSSY-STARLING *Lamprotornis caudatus* (5)

RUEPPELL'S GLOSSY-STARLING *Lamprotornis purpuropterus* (5)

SUPERB STARLING *Lamprotornis superbus* (5)

CHESTNUT-BELLIED STARLING *Lamprotornis pulcher* (5)

SHELLEY'S STARLING *Lamprotornis shelleyi* (5)

HILDEBRANDT'S STARLING *Lamprotornis hildebrandti* (5)

SHARPE'S STARLING *Cinnyricinclus sharpii* (5)

ABBOTT'S STARLING *Cinnyricinclus femoralis* (5) [VU]

VIOLET-BACKED STARLING *Cinnyricinclus leucogaster* (5)

MAGPIE STARLING *Speculipastor bicolor* (5)

BABBLING STARLING *Neocichla gutturalis* (5)

FISCHER'S STARLING *Spreo fischeri* (5)

AFRICAN PIED STARLING *Spreo bicolor* (5)

WHITE-CROWNED STARLING *Spreo albicapillus* (5)

GOLDEN-BREASTED STARLING *Cosmopsarus regius* (5)

ASHY STARLING *Cosmopsarus unicolor* (5)

MADAGASCAR STARLING *Saroglossa aurata* (5)

SPOT-WINGED STARLING *Saroglossa spiloptera* (4) [NT]

WATTLED STARLING *Creatophora cinerea* (5)

RODRIGUEZ STARLING *Necropsar rodericanus* (5) [EX]

REUNION STARLING *Fregilupus varius* (5) [EX]

WHITE-FACED STARLING *Sturnus senex* (4) [NT]

CHESTNUT-TAILED STARLING *Sturnus malabaricus* (4)

WHITE-HEADED STARLING *Sturnus erythropygius* (4) [NT]

BRAHMINY STARLING *Sturnus pagodarum* (4)

RED-BILLED STARLING *Sturnus sericeus* (4) [NT]

PURPLE-BACKED STARLING *Sturnus sturninus* (3, 4)

CHESTNUT-CHEEKED STARLING *Sturnus philippensis* (3, 4) [NT]

WHITE-SHOULDERED STARLING *Sturnus sinensis* (3, 4)

COMMON STARLING *Sturnus vulgaris* (1, 2, 3, 4, 5, 6)

SPOTLESS STARLING *Sturnus unicolor* (3, 5)

WHITE-CHEEKED STARLING *Sturnus cineraceus* (3, 4)

ASIAN PIED STARLING *Sturnus contra* (4)

BLACK-COLLARED STARLING *Sturnus nigricollis* (4)

VINOUS-BREASTED STARLING *Sturnus burmannicus* (4)

BLACK-WINGED STARLING *Sturnus melanopterus* (4) [NT]

BALI MYNA or BALI STARLING *Leucopsar rothschildi* (4) [CR]

COMMON MYNA *Acridotheres tristis* (2, 3, 4, 5, 6)

BANK MYNA *Acridotheres ginginianus* (3, 4)

JUNGLE MYNA *Acridotheres fuscus* (4)

WHITE-VENTED MYNA *Acridotheres grandis* (4)

PALE-BELLIED MYNA or WHITE-VENTED STARLING *Acridotheres cinereus* (4)

COLLARED MYNA *Acridotheres albocinctus* (4) [NT]

CRESTED MYNA *Acridotheres cristatellus* (1, 4)

GOLDEN-CRESTED MYNA *Ampeliceps coronatus* (4)

GOLDEN MYNA *Mino anais* (6)

YELLOW-FACED MYNA *Mino dumontii* (6)

SULAWESI MYNA *Basilornis celebensis* (4)

HELMETED MYNA *Basilornis galeatus* (4) [NT]

LONG-CRESTED MYNA *Basilornis corythaix* (4)

APO MYNA *Basilornis miranda* (4) [NT]

WHITE-NECKED MYNA *Streptocitta albicollis* (4)

BARE-EYED MYNA *Streptocitta albertinae* (4) [NT]

COLETO *Sarcops calvus* (4)

SRI LANKA MYNA or CEYLON MYNA *Gracula ptilogenys* (4)

HILL MYNA *Gracula religiosa* (2, 4)

FIERY-BROWED MYNA *Enodes erythrophris* (4)

FINCH-BILLED MYNA *Scissirostrum dubium* (4)

YELLOW-BILLED OXPECKER *Buphagus africanus* (5)

RED-BILLED OXPECKER *Buphagus erythrorhynchus* (5)

Tribe MIMINI

GRAY CATBIRD *Dumetella carolinensis* (1, 2)

BLACK CATBIRD *Melanoptila glabrirostris* (1, 2) [NT]

BLUE MOCKINGBIRD *Melanotis caerulescens* (1)

BLUE-AND-WHITE MOCKINGBIRD *Melanotis hypoleucus* (1, 2)

NORTHERN MOCKINGBIRD *Mimus polyglottos* (1, 2)

TROPICAL MOCKINGBIRD *Mimus gilvus* (1, 2)

BAHAMA MOCKINGBIRD *Mimus gundlachii* (1, 2)

CHALK-BROWED MOCKINGBIRD *Mimus saturninus* (2)

PATAGONIAN MOCKINGBIRD *Mimus patagonicus* (2)

BROWN-BACKED MOCKINGBIRD *Mimus dorsalis* (2)

WHITE-BANDED MOCKINGBIRD *Mimus triurus* (2)

LONG-TAILED MOCKINGBIRD *Mimus longicaudatus* (2)

CHILEAN MOCKINGBIRD *Mimus thenca* (2)

GALAPAGÓS MOCKINGBIRD *Nesomimus parvulus* (2)

CHARLES MOCKINGBIRD or FLOREANA MOCKINGBIRD *Nesomimus trifasciatus* (2) [EN]

HOOD MOCKINGBIRD *Nesomimus macdonaldi* (2)

SAN CRISTÓBAL MOCKINGBIRD *Nesomimus melanotis* (2)

SOCORRO MOCKINGBIRD *Mimodes graysoni* (1) [EN]

SAGE THRASHER *Oreoscoptes montanus* (1)

BROWN THRASHER *Toxostoma rufum* (1)

LONG-BILLED THRASHER *Toxostoma longirostre* (1)

COZUMEL THRASHER *Toxostoma guttatum* (1) [NT]

BENDIRE'S THRASHER *Toxostoma bendirei* (1)

GRAY THRASHER *Toxostoma cinereum* (1)

CURVE-BILLED THRASHER *Toxostoma curvirostre* (1)

OCELLATED THRASHER *Toxostoma ocellatum* (1)

LE CONTE'S THRASHER *Toxostoma lecontei* (1)

VIZCAINO THRASHER *Toxostoma arenicola* (1)

CALIFORNIA THRASHER *Toxostoma redivivum* (1)

CRISSAL THRASHER *Toxostoma crissale* (1)

BROWN TREMBLER *Cinclocerthia ruficauda* (2)

GRAY TREMBLER *Cinclocerthia gutturalis* (2)

WHITE-BREASTED THRASHER *Ramphocinclus brachyurus* (2) [EN]

SCALY-BREASTED THRASHER *Margarops fuscus* (2)

PEARLY-EYED THRASHER *Margarops fuscatus* (2)

Superfamily SYLVIOIDEA
Family SITTIDAE
Subfamily Sittinae

WOOD NUTHATCH or EURASIAN NUTHATCH *Sitta europaea* (3, 4, 5)

CHESTNUT-VENTED NUTHATCH *Sitta nagaensis* (4)

KASHMIR NUTHATCH *Sitta cashmirensis* (4)

CHESTNUT-BELLIED NUTHATCH *Sitta castanea* (4)

WHITE-TAILED NUTHATCH *Sitta himalayensis* (3, 4)

WHITE-BROWED NUTHATCH *Sitta victoriae* (3) [VU]

PYGMY NUTHATCH *Sitta pygmaea* (1)

BROWN-HEADED NUTHATCH *Sitta pusilla* (1)

CORSICAN NUTHATCH *Sitta whiteheadi* (3) [NT]

KABYLIE NUTHATCH or ALGERIAN NUTHATCH *Sitta ledanti* (5) [EN]

KRUEPER'S NUTHATCH *Sitta krueperi* (3)

SNOWY-BROWED NUTHATCH or CHINESE NUTHATCH *Sitta villosa* (4) [NT]

YUNNAN NUTHATCH *Sitta yunnanensis* (4) [VU]

RED-BREASTED NUTHATCH *Sitta canadensis* (1, 3)

WHITE-CHEEKED NUTHATCH *Sitta leucopsis* (4)

WHITE-BREASTED NUTHATCH *Sitta carolinensis* (1)

WESTERN ROCK-NUTHATCH *Sitta neumayer* (3)

EASTERN ROCK-NUTHATCH *Sitta tephronota* (3)

VELVET-FRONTED NUTHATCH *Sitta frontalis* (4)

YELLOW-BILLED NUTHATCH *Sitta solangiae* (4) [VU]

SULFUR-BILLED NUTHATCH *Sitta oenochlamys* (4)

BLUE NUTHATCH *Sitta azurea* (4)

GIANT NUTHATCH *Sitta magna* (4) [VU]

BEAUTIFUL NUTHATCH *Sitta formosa* (3, 4) [VU]

Subfamily TICHODROMINAE
WALLCREEPER *Tichodroma muraria* (3, 4)

Family CERTHIIDAE
Subfamily CERTHIINAE
Tribe CERTHIINI
EURASIAN TREE-CREEPER *Certhia familiaris* (3, 4)

BROWN CREEPER or AMERICAN TREE-CREEPER *Certhia americana* (1, 2)

SHORT-TOED TREE-CREEPER *Certhia brachydactyla* (3, 5)

BAR-TAILED TREE-CREEPER *Certhia himalayana* (4)

RUSTY-FLANKED TREE-CREEPER *Certhia nipalensis* (4)

BROWN-THROATED TREE-CREEPER *Certhia discolor* (4)

Tribe SALPORNITHINI
SPOTTED CREEPER *Salpornis spilonotus* (4, 5)

Subfamily TROGLODYTINAE
BLACK-CAPPED DONACOBIUS *Donacobius atricapillus* (2)

SPOTTED WREN *Campylorhynchus gularis* (1)

CACTUS WREN *Campylorhynchus brunneicapillus* (1)

BOUCARD'S WREN *Campylorhynchus jocosus* (1)

YUCATÁN WREN *Campylorhynchus yucatanicus* (1)

GIANT WREN *Campylorhynchus chiapensis* (1)

BICOLORED WREN *Campylorhynchus griseus* (2)

RUFOUS-NAPED WREN *Campylorhynchus rufinucha* (1, 2)

THRUSH-LIKE WREN *Campylorhynchus turdinus* (2)

GRAY-BARRED WREN *Campylorhynchus megalopterus* (1)

BAND-BACKED WREN *Campylorhynchus zonatus* (1, 2)

WHITE-HEADED WREN *Campylorhynchus albobrunneus* (2)

STRIPE-BACKED WREN *Campylorhynchus nuchalis* (2)

FASCIATED WREN *Campylorhynchus fasciatus* (2)

GRAY-MANTLED WREN *Odontorchilus branickii* (2)

TOOTH-BILLED WREN *Odontorchilus cinereus* (2)

ROCK WREN *Salpinctes obsoletus* (1, 2)

CANYON WREN *Catherpes mexicanus* (1, 2)

SLENDER-BILLED WREN or SUMICHRAST'S WREN *Hylorchilus sumichrasti* (1) [VU]

NAVA'S WREN *Hylorchilus navai* (1) [VU]

RUFOUS WREN *Cinnycerthia unirufa* (2)

SHARPE'S WREN *Cinnycerthia olivascens* (2)

PERUVIAN WREN or SEPIA-BROWN WREN *Cinnycerthia peruana* (2)

FULVOUS WREN or SUPERCILIATED WREN *Cinnycerthia fulva* (2)

SEDGE WREN *Cistothorus platensis* (1, 2)

APOLINAR'S WREN *Cistothorus apolinari* (2) [EN]

MERIDA WREN *Cistothorus meridae* (2)

MARSH WREN *Cistothorus palustris* (1)

BEWICK'S WREN *Thryomanes bewickii* (1)

ZAPATA WREN *Ferminia cerverai* (2) [CR]

BLACK-THROATED WREN *Thryothorus atrogularis* (2)

SOOTY-HEADED WREN *Thryothorus spadix* (2)

BLACK-BELLIED WREN *Thryothorus fasciatoventris* (2)

PLAIN-TAILED WREN *Thryothorus euophrys* (2)

INCA WREN *Thryothorus eisenmanni* (2)

WHISKERED WREN *Thryothorus mystacalis* (2)

MUSTACHED WREN *Thryothorus genibarbis* (2)

CORAYA WREN *Thryothorus coraya* (2)

HAPPY WREN *Thryothorus felix* (1)

SPOT-BREASTED WREN *Thryothorus maculipectus* (1, 2)

RUFOUS-BREASTED WREN *Thryothorus rutilus* (2)

SPECKLE-BREASTED WREN *Thryothorus sclateri* (2)

RIVERSIDE WREN *Thryothorus semibadius* (2)

BAY WREN *Thryothorus nigricapillus* (2)

STRIPE-BREASTED WREN *Thryothorus thoracicus* (2)

STRIPE-THROATED WREN *Thryothorus leucopogon* (2)

BANDED WREN *Thryothorus pleurostictus* (2)

CAROLINA WREN *Thryothorus ludovicianus* (1)

WHITE-BROWED WREN *Thryothorus albinucha* (1, 2)

RUFOUS-AND-WHITE WREN *Thryothorus rufalbus* (2)

NICEFORO'S WREN *Thryothorus nicefori* (2) [CR]

SINALOA WREN *Thryothorus sinaloa* (1)

PLAIN WREN *Thryothorus modestus* (1, 2)

BUFF-BREASTED WREN *Thryothorus leucotis* (2)

SUPERCILIATED WREN *Thryothorus superciliaris* (2)

FAWN-BREASTED WREN *Thryothorus guarayanus* (2)

LONG-BILLED WREN *Thryothorus longirostris* (2)

GRAY WREN *Thryothorus griseus* (2)

WINTER WREN *Troglodytes troglodytes* (1, 3, 4)

HOUSE WREN *Troglodytes aedon* (1, 2)

ANTILLEAN WREN *Troglodytes martinicensis* (2)

COBB'S WREN *Troglodytes cobbi* (2) [VU]

CLARION WREN *Troglodytes tanneri* (1) [VU]

SOCORRO WREN *Troglodytes sissonii* (1) [NT]

RUFOUS-BROWED WREN *Troglodytes rufociliatus* (2)

OCHRACEOUS WREN *Troglodytes ochraceus* (2)

SANTA MARTA WREN *Troglodytes monticola* (2)

MOUNTAIN WREN *Troglodytes solstitialis* (2)

TEPUI WREN *Troglodytes rufulus* (2)

TIMBERLINE WREN *Thryorchilus browni* (2)

WHITE-BELLIED WREN *Uropsila leucogastra* (1, 2)

WHITE-BREASTED WOOD-WREN *Henicorhina leucosticta* (1, 2)

GRAY-BREASTED WOOD-WREN *Henicorhina leucophrys* (1, 2)

BAR-WINGED WOOD-WREN *Henicorhina leucoptera* (2) [NT]

NORTHERN NIGHTINGALE-WREN *Microcerculus philomela* (1, 2)

SOUTHERN NIGHTINGALE-WREN *Microcerculus marginatus* (2)

FLUTIST WREN *Microcerculus ustulatus* (2)

WING-BANDED WREN *Microcerculus bambla* (2)

SONG WREN *Cyphorhinus phaeocephalus* (2)

CHESTNUT-BREASTED WREN *Cyphorhinus thoracicus* (2)

MUSICIAN WREN *Cyphorhinus aradus* (2)

Subfamily POLIOPTILINAE

VERDIN *Auriparus flaviceps* (1)

COLLARED GNATWREN *Microbates collaris* (2)

TAWNY-FACED GNATWREN *Microbates cinereiventris* (2)

LONG-BILLED GNATWREN *Ramphocaenus melanurus* (1, 2)

BLUE-GRAY GNATCATCHER *Polioptila caerulea* (1, 2)

CALIFORNIA GNATCATCHER *Polioptila californica* (1)

BLACK-TAILED GNATCATCHER *Polioptila melanura* (1)

CUBAN GNATCATCHER *Polioptila lembeyei* (2) [NT]

BLACK-CAPPED GNATCATCHER *Polioptila nigriceps* (1)

WHITE-LORED GNATCATCHER *Polioptila albiloris* (1, 2)

TROPICAL GNATCATCHER *Polioptila plumbea* (2)

WHITE-FACED GNATCATCHER *Polioptila bilineata* (1, 2)

MARANON GNATCATCHER *Polioptila maranonica* (2)

CREAMY-BELLIED GNATCATCHER *Polioptila lactea* (2) [NT]

GUIANAN GNATCATCHER *Polioptila guianensis* (2)

SLATE-THROATED GNATCATCHER *Polioptila schistaceigula* (2)

MASKED GNATCATCHER *Polioptila dumicola* (2)

Family PARIDAE
Subfamily REMIZINAE

EURASIAN PENDULINE-TIT *Remiz pendulinus* (3)

BLACK-HEADED PENDULINE-TIT *Remiz macronyx* (3)

WHITE-CROWNED PENDULINE-TIT *Remiz coronatus* (3, 4)

CHINESE PENDULINE-TIT *Remiz consobrinus* (3, 4)

SENNAR PENDULINE-TIT *Anthoscopus punctifrons* (5)

YELLOW PENDULINE-TIT *Anthoscopus parvulus* (5)

MOUSE-COLORED PENDULINE-TIT *Anthoscopus musculus* (5)

FOREST PENDULINE-TIT *Anthoscopus flavifrons* (5)

AFRICAN PENDULINE-TIT *Anthoscopus caroli* (5)

SOUTHERN PENDULINE-TIT *Anthoscopus minutus* (5)

FIRE-CAPPED TIT *Cephalopyrus flammiceps* (3, 4)

TIT-HYLIA *Pholidornis rushiae* (5)

Subfamily PARINAE

MARSH TIT *Parus palustris* (3, 4)

BLACK-BIBBED MARSH TIT *Parus hypermelaena* (4)

SOMBRE TIT *Parus lugubris* (3)

CASPIAN TIT or ELBURZ TIT *Parus hyrcanus* (3)

WILLOW TIT *Parus montanus* (3, 4)

SONGAR TIT *Parus songarus* (4)

CAROLINA CHICKADEE *Parus carolinensis* (1)

BLACK-CAPPED CHICKADEE *Parus atricapillus* (1)

MOUNTAIN CHICKADEE *Parus gambeli* (1)

MEXICAN CHICKADEE *Parus sclateri* (1)

WHITE-BROWED TIT *Parus superciliosus* (4)

RUSTY-BREASTED TIT *Parus davidi* (3, 4)

SIBERIAN TIT *Parus cinctus* (1, 3, 4)

BOREAL CHICKADEE *Parus hudsonicus* (1)

CHESTNUT-BACKED CHICKADEE *Parus rufescens* (1)

DARK-GRAY TIT or RUFOUS-NAPED TIT *Parus rufonuchalis* (3, 4)

RUFOUS-VENTED TIT *Parus rubidiventris* (3, 4)

BLACK-CRESTED TIT or SPOT-WINGED TIT *Parus melanolophus* (3, 4)

COAL TIT *Parus ater* (3, 4, 5)

YELLOW-BELLIED TIT *Parus venustulus* (4)

ELEGANT TIT *Parus elegans* (4)

PALAWAN TIT *Parus amabilis* (4)

CRESTED TIT *Parus cristatus* (3)

GRAY-CRESTED TIT *Parus dichrous* (3, 4)

WHITE-WINGED TIT *Parus leucomelas* (5)

CARP'S TIT *Parus carp* (5)

BLACK TIT *Parus niger* (5)

WHITE-BELLIED TIT *Parus albiventris* (5)

WHITE-BACKED TIT *Parus leuconotus* (5)

DUSKY TIT *Parus funereus* (5)

RUFOUS-BELLIED TIT *Parus rufiventris* (5)

RED-THROATED TIT *Parus fringillinus* (5) [NT]

STRIPE-BREASTED TIT *Parus fasciiventer* (5)

SOMALI TIT *Parus thruppi* (5)

MIOMBO TIT *Parus griseiventris* (5)

ASHY TIT *Parus cinerascens* (5)

GRAY TIT *Parus afer* (5)

GREAT TIT *Parus major* (3, 4)

TURKESTAN TIT *Parus bokharensis* (3, 4)

GREEN-BACKED TIT *Parus monticolus* (3, 4)

WHITE-NAPED TIT *Parus nuchalis* (4) [VU]

BLACK-LORED TIT *Parus xanthogenys* (4)

YELLOW-CHEEKED TIT *Parus spilonotus* (4)

YELLOW TIT *Parus holsti* (4) [NT]

EUROPEAN BLUE TIT *Parus caeruleus* (3)

AFRICAN BLUE TIT *Parus ultramarinus* (3, 5)

FUERTEVENTURA BLUE TIT *Parus degener* (5)

TENERIFE BLUE TIT *Parus teneriffae* (5)

HIERRO BLUE TIT *Parus ombriosus* (5)

PALMA BLUE TIT *Parus palmensis* (5)

AZURE TIT *Parus cyanus* (3, 4)

YELLOW-BREASTED TIT *Parus flavipectus* (3, 4)

VARIED TIT *Parus varius* (3, 4)

WHITE-FRONTED TIT *Parus semilarvatus* (4) [NT]

BRIDLED TITMOUSE *Parus wollweberi* (1)

PLAIN TITMOUSE or OAK TITMOUSE *Parus inornatus* (1)

RIDGWAY'S TITMOUSE or JUNIPER TITMOUSE *Parus ridgway* (1)

CAPE TITMOUSE *Parus cineraceus* (1)

TUFTED TITMOUSE *Parus bicolor* (1)

BLACK-CRESTED TITMOUSE *Parus atricristatus* (1)

YELLOW-BROWED TIT *Sylviparus modestus* (3, 4)

SULTAN TIT *Melanochlora sultanea* (4)

Family AEGITHALIDAE

LONG-TAILED TIT *Aegithalos caudatus* (3, 4)

WHITE-CHEEKED TIT *Aegithalos leucogenys* (3)

BLACK-THROATED TIT *Aegithalos concinnus* (4)

WHITE-THROATED TIT *Aegithalos niveogularis* (3, 4) [NT]

RUFOUS-FRONTED TIT *Aegithalos iouschistos* (3, 4)

BLACK-BROWED TIT *Aegithalos bonvaloti* (4)

WHITE-NECKLACED TIT or SOOTY TIT *Aegithalos fuliginosus* (4) [NT]

BUSHTIT *Psaltriparus minimus* (1)

PYGMY TIT *Psaltria exilis* (4)

Family HIRUNDINIDAE
Subfamily PSEUDOCHELIDONINAE

AFRICAN RIVER-MARTIN *Pseudochelidon eurystomina* (5)

WHITE-EYED RIVER-MARTIN *Pseudochelidon sirintarae* (4) [CR]

Subfamily HIRUNDININAE

TREE SWALLOW *Tachycineta bicolor* (1, 2)

MANGROVE SWALLOW *Tachycineta albilinea* (1, 2)

TUMBES SWALLOW *Tachycineta stolzmanni* (2)

WHITE-WINGED SWALLOW *Tachycineta albiventer* (2)

WHITE-RUMPED SWALLOW *Tachycineta leucorrhoa* (2)

CHILEAN SWALLOW *Tachycineta meyeni* (2)

VIOLET-GREEN SWALLOW *Tachycineta thalassina* (1, 2)

BAHAMA SWALLOW *Tachycineta cyaneoviridis* (2) [NT]

GOLDEN SWALLOW *Tachycineta euchrysea* (2) [NT]

PURPLE MARTIN *Progne subis* (1, 2)

CUBAN MARTIN *Progne cryptoleuca* (2)

CARIBBEAN MARTIN *Progne dominicensis* (2)

SINALOA MARTIN *Progne sinaloae* (1, 2) [DD]

GRAY-BREASTED MARTIN *Progne chalybea* (1, 2)

SOUTHERN MARTIN *Progne modesta* (2)

BROWN-CHESTED MARTIN *Progne tapera* (2)

BROWN-BELLIED SWALLOW *Notiochelidon murina* (2)

BLUE-AND-WHITE SWALLOW *Notiochelidon cyanoleuca* (2)

PALE-FOOTED SWALLOW *Notiochelidon flavipes* (2)

BLACK-CAPPED SWALLOW *Notiochelidon pileata* (2)

WHITE-BANDED SWALLOW *Atticora fasciata* (2)

BLACK-COLLARED SWALLOW *Atticora melanoleuca* (2)

WHITE-THIGHED SWALLOW *Neochelidon tibialis* (2)

TAWNY-HEADED SWALLOW *Stelgidopteryx fucata* (2)

ANDEAN SWALLOW *Stelgidopteryx andecola* (2)

NORTHERN ROUGH-WINGED SWALLOW *Stelgidopteryx serripennis* (1, 2)

RIDGWAY'S ROUGH-WINGED SWALLOW *Stelgidopteryx ridgwayi* (1, 2)

SOUTHERN ROUGH-WINGED SWALLOW *Stelgidopteryx ruficollis* (2)

WHITE-BACKED SWALLOW *Cheramoeca leucosternus* (6)

GRAY-RUMPED SWALLOW *Pseudhirundo griseopyga* (5)

SAND MARTIN or BANK SWALLOW *Riparia riparia* (1, 2, 3, 4, 5)

PLAIN MARTIN *Riparia paludicola* (4, 5)

CONGO MARTIN *Riparia congica* (5)

BANDED MARTIN *Riparia cincta* (5)

MASCARENE MARTIN *Phedina borbonica* (5)

BRAZZA'S MARTIN *Phedina brazzae* (5)

EURASIAN CRAG-MARTIN *Hirundo rupestris* (3, 4, 5)

PALE CRAG-MARTIN *Hirundo obsoleta* (3, 5)

ROCK MARTIN *Hirundo fuligula* (5)

DUSKY CRAG-MARTIN *Hirundo concolor* (4)

BARN SWALLOW *Hirundo rustica*
(1, 2, 3, 4, 5, 6)

RED-CHESTED SWALLOW *Hirundo lucida* (5)

ETHIOPIAN SWALLOW *Hirundo aethiopica* (5)

ANGOLA SWALLOW *Hirundo angolensis* (5)

WHITE-THROATED SWALLOW *Hirundo albigularis* (5)

HILL SWALLOW *Hirundo domicola* (4)

PACIFIC SWALLOW *Hirundo tahitica* (4, 6)

WELCOME SWALLOW *Hirundo neoxena* (6)

WIRE-TAILED SWALLOW *Hirundo smithii*
(3, 4, 5)

WHITE-THROATED BLUE SWALLOW *Hirundo nigrita* (5)

BLACK-AND-RUFOUS SWALLOW *Hirundo nigrorufa* (5)

BLUE SWALLOW *Hirundo atrocaerulea* (5)
[VU]

PIED-WINGED SWALLOW *Hirundo leucosoma* (5)

WHITE-TAILED SWALLOW *Hirundo megaensis* (5) [VU]

PEARL-BREASTED SWALLOW *Hirundo dimidiata* (5)

GREATER STRIPED-SWALLOW *Hirundo cucullata* (5)

LESSER STRIPED-SWALLOW *Hirundo abyssinica* (5)

RUFOUS-CHESTED SWALLOW *Hirundo semirufa* (5)

MOSQUE SWALLOW *Hirundo senegalensis* (5)

RED-RUMPED SWALLOW *Hirundo daurica*
(3, 4, 5, 6)

WEST AFRICAN SWALLOW *Hirundo domicella* (5)

STRIATED SWALLOW *Hirundo striolata* (4)

RED SEA SWALLOW *Hirundo perdita* (5) [VU]

PREUSS'S SWALLOW *Hirundo preussi* (5)

RED-THROATED SWALLOW *Hirundo rufigula* (5)

SOUTH AFRICAN SWALLOW *Hirundo spilodera* (5)

CLIFF SWALLOW *Hirundo pyrrhonota* (1, 2)

CAVE SWALLOW *Hirundo fulva* (1, 2)

CHESTNUT-COLLARED SWALLOW *Hirundo rufocollaris* (2)

TREE MARTIN *Hirundo nigricans* (4, 6)

STREAK-THROATED SWALLOW or INDIAN CLIFF SWALLOW *Hirundo fluvicola* (3, 4)

FAIRY MARTIN *Hirundo ariel* (4, 6)

FOREST SWALLOW *Hirundo fuliginosa* (5)

NORTHERN HOUSE-MARTIN *Delichon urbica*
(3, 4, 5)

ASIAN HOUSE-MARTIN *Delichon dasypus*
(3, 4)

NEPAL HOUSE-MARTIN *Delichon nipalensis*
(4)

SQUARE-TAILED SAWWING *Psalidoprocne nitens* (5)

MOUNTAIN SAWWING *Psalidoprocne fuliginosa* (5) [NT]

WHITE-HEADED SAWWING *Psalidoprocne albiceps* (5)

SHARI SAWWING *Psalidoprocne chalybea* (5)

PETIT'S SAWWING *Psalidoprocne petiti* (5)

MANGBETTU SAWWING *Psalidoprocne mangbettorum* (5)

ETHIOPIAN SAWWING *Psalidoprocne oleaginea* (5)

BLUE SAWWING *Psalidoprocne pristoptera* (5)

BROWN SAWWING *Psalidoprocne antinorii* (5)

EASTERN SAWWING *Psalidoprocne orientalis*
(5)

BLACK SAWWING *Psalidoprocne holomelas* (5)

FANTI SAWWING *Psalidoprocne obscura* (5)

Family REGULIDAE

RUBY-CROWNED KINGLET *Regulus calendula*
(1, 2)

GOLDCREST *Regulus regulus* (3, 4)

CANARY ISLANDS KINGLET *Regulus teneriffae* (5)

FLAMECREST *Regulus goodfellowi* (4)

FIRECREST *Regulus ignicapillus* (3)

GOLDEN-CROWNED KINGLET *Regulus satrapa* (1)

Family PYCNONOTIDAE

CRESTED FINCHBILL *Spizixos canifrons* (4)

COLLARED FINCHBILL *Spizixos semitorques* (4)

STRAW-HEADED BULBUL *Pycnonotus zeylanicus* (4) [VU]

STRIATED BULBUL or STRIPED BULBUL *Pycnonotus striatus* (4)

CREAM-STRIPED BULBUL *Pycnonotus leucogrammicus* (4)

SPOT-NECKED BULBUL *Pycnonotus tympanistrigus* (4) [VU]

BLACK-AND-WHITE BULBUL *Pycnonotus melanoleucos* (4)

GRAY-HEADED BULBUL *Pycnonotus priocephalus* (4) [NT]

BLACK-HEADED BULBUL *Pycnonotus atriceps* (4)

BLACK-CRESTED BULBUL *Pycnonotus melanicterus* (4)

SCALY-BREASTED BULBUL *Pycnonotus squamatus* (4)

GRAY-BELLIED BULBUL *Pycnonotus cyaniventris* (4)

RED-WHISKERED BULBUL *Pycnonotus jocosus* (1, 2, 4, 5, 6)

BROWN-BREASTED BULBUL *Pycnonotus xanthorrhous* (4)

LIGHT-VENTED BULBUL *Pycnonotus sinensis* (4)

STYAN'S BULBUL *Pycnonotus taivanus* (4) [NT]

GARDEN BULBUL *Pycnonotus barbatus* (5)

SOMALI BULBUL *Pycnonotus somaliensis* (5)

DODSON'S BULBUL *Pycnonotus dodsoni* (5)

DARK-CAPPED BULBUL *Pycnonotus tricolor* (5)

BLACK-FRONTED BULBUL or RED-EYED BULBUL *Pycnonotus nigricans* (5)

CAPE BULBUL *Pycnonotus capensis* (5)

WHITE-SPECTACLED BULBUL *Pycnonotus xanthopygos* (3, 5)

WHITE-EARED BULBUL *Pycnonotus leucotis* (3, 4)

HIMALAYAN BULBUL *Pycnonotus leucogenys* (3, 4)

RED-VENTED BULBUL *Pycnonotus cafer* (4, 6)

SOOTY-HEADED BULBUL *Pycnonotus aurigaster* (4)

PUFF-BACKED BULBUL *Pycnonotus eutilotus* (4)

BLUE-WATTLED BULBUL *Pycnonotus nieuwenhuisii* (4) [DD]

YELLOW-WATTLED BULBUL *Pycnonotus urostictus* (4)

ORANGE-SPOTTED BULBUL *Pycnonotus bimaculatus* (4)

STRIPE-THROATED BULBUL *Pycnonotus finlaysoni* (4)

YELLOW-THROATED BULBUL *Pycnonotus xantholaemus* (4) [NT]

YELLOW-EARED BULBUL *Pycnonotus penicillatus* (4) [NT]

FLAVESCENT BULBUL *Pycnonotus flavescens* (4)

WHITE-BROWED BULBUL *Pycnonotus luteolus* (4)

YELLOW-VENTED BULBUL *Pycnonotus goiavier* (4)

OLIVE-WINGED BULBUL *Pycnonotus plumosus* (4)

STREAK-EARED BULBUL *Pycnonotus blanfordi* (4)

CREAM-VENTED BULBUL *Pycnonotus simplex* (4)

RED-EYED BULBUL *Pycnonotus brunneus* (4)

SPECTACLED BULBUL *Pycnonotus erythropthalmos* (4)

CAMEROON GREENBUL *Andropadus montanus* (5) [NT]

SHELLEY'S GREENBUL *Andropadus masukuensis* (5)

KAKAMEGA GREENBUL *Andropadus kakamegae* (5)

LITTLE GREENBUL *Andropadus virens* (5)

HALL'S GREENBUL *Andropadus hallae* (5)

GRAY GREENBUL *Andropadus gracilis* (5)

ANSORGE'S GREENBUL *Andropadus ansorgei* (5)

PLAIN GREENBUL *Andropadus curvirostris* (5)

SLENDER-BILLED GREENBUL *Andropadus gracilirostris* (5)

SOMBER GREENBUL *Andropadus importunus* (5)

YELLOW-WHISKERED GREENBUL *Andropadus latirostris* (5)

GRAY-THROATED GREENBUL *Andropadus tephrolaemus* (5)

MOUNTAIN GREENBUL *Andropadus nigriceps* (5)

ULUGURU MOUNTAIN GREENBUL *Andropadus neumanni* (5)

SOUTHERN MOUNTAIN GREENBUL *Andropadus chlorigula* (5)

NORTHERN MOUNTAIN GREENBUL *Andropadus fusciceps* (5)

STRIPE-CHEEKED GREENBUL *Andropadus milanjensis* (5)

GOLDEN GREENBUL *Calyptocichla serina* (5)

HONEYGUIDE GREENBUL *Baeopogon indicator* (5)

WHITE-TAILED GREENBUL *Baeopogon clamans* (5)

SPOTTED GREENBUL *Ixonotus guttatus* (5)

SIMPLE GREENBUL *Chlorocichla simplex* (5)

YELLOW-THROATED GREENBUL *Chlorocichla flavicollis* (5)

YELLOW-NECKED GREENBUL *Chlorocichla falkensteini* (5)

YELLOW-BELLIED GREENBUL *Chlorocichla flaviventris* (5)

JOYFUL GREENBUL *Chlorocichla laetissima* (5)

PRIGOGINE'S GREENBUL *Chlorocichla prigoginei* (5) [VU]

SWAMP GREENBUL *Thescelocichla leucopleura* (5)

LEAF-LOVE *Pyrrhurus scandens* (5)

CABANIS'S GREENBUL *Phyllastrephus cabanisi* (5)

FISCHER'S GREENBUL *Phyllastrephus fischeri* (5)

PLACID GREENBUL *Phyllastrephus placidus* (5)

TERRESTRIAL BROWNBUL *Phyllastrephus terrestris* (5)

NORTHERN BROWNBUL *Phyllastrephus strepitans* (5)

PALE-OLIVE GREENBUL *Phyllastrephus fulviventris* (5)

GRAY-OLIVE GREENBUL *Phyllastrephus cerviniventris* (5)

BAUMANN'S OLIVE-GREENBUL *Phyllastrephus baumanni* (5) [NT]

CAMEROON OLIVE-GREENBUL *Phyllastrephus poensis* (5)

TORO OLIVE-GREENBUL *Phyllastrephus hypochloris* (5)

SASSI'S GREENBUL *Phyllastrephus lorenzi* (5) [NT]

GRAY-HEADED GREENBUL *Phyllastrephus poliocephalus* (5) [NT]

YELLOW-STREAKED GREENBUL *Phyllastrephus flavostriatus* (5)

SHARPE'S GREENBUL *Phyllastrephus alfredi* (5)

TINY GREENBUL *Phyllastrephus debilis* (5)

WHITE-THROATED GREENBUL *Phyllastrephus albigularis* (5)

ICTERINE GREENBUL *Phyllastrephus icterinus* (5)

LIBERIAN GREENBUL *Phyllastrephus leucolepis* (5) [CR]

XAVIER'S GREENBUL *Phyllastrephus xavieri* (5)

LONG-BILLED GREENBUL *Phyllastrephus madagascariensis* (5)

SPECTACLED GREENBUL *Phyllastrephus zosterops* (5)

APPERT'S GREENBUL *Phyllastrephus apperti* (5) [VU]

DUSKY GREENBUL *Phyllastrephus tenebrosus* (5) [EN]

GRAY-CROWNED GREENBUL *Phyllastrephus cinereiceps* (5) [VU]

COMMON BRISTLEBILL *Bleda syndactyla* (5)

GREEN-TAILED BRISTLEBILL *Bleda eximia* (5) [VU]

LESSER BRISTLEBILL *Bleda notata* (5)

GRAY-HEADED BRISTLEBILL *Bleda canicapilla* (5)

YELLOW-SPOTTED NICATOR *Nicator chloris* (5)

EASTERN NICATOR *Nicator gularis* (5)

YELLOW-THROATED NICATOR *Nicator vireo* (5)

BEARDED BULBUL *Criniger barbatus* (5)

GREEN-BACKED BULBUL *Criniger chloronotus* (5)

RED-TAILED BULBUL *Criniger calurus* (5)

YELLOW-BEARDED BULBUL or YELLOW-THROATED OLIVE GREENBUL *Criniger olivaceus* (5) [VU]

WHITE-BEARDED BULBUL *Criniger ndussumensis* (5)

FINSCH'S BULBUL *Alophoixus finschii* (4)

WHITE-THROATED BULBUL *Alophoixus flaveolus* (4)

PUFF-THROATED BULBUL *Alophoixus pallidus* (4)

OCHRACEOUS BULBUL *Alophoixus ochraceus* (4)

GRAY-CHEEKED BULBUL *Alophoixus bres* (4)

YELLOW-BELLIED BULBUL *Alophoixus phaeocephalus* (4)

GOLDEN BULBUL *Alophoixus affinis* (4)

HOOK-BILLED BULBUL *Setornis criniger* (4) [NT]

HAIRY-BACKED BULBUL *Tricholestes criniger* (4)

OLIVE BULBUL *Iole virescens* (4)

GRAY-EYED BULBUL *Iole propinqua* (4)

BUFF-VENTED BULBUL *Iole olivacea* (4)

YELLOW-BROWED BULBUL *Iole indica* (4)

SULFUR-BELLIED BULBUL *Ixos palawanensis* (4)

PHILIPPINE BULBUL *Ixos philippinus* (4)

ZAMBOANGA BULBUL *Ixos rufigularis* (4)

STREAK-BREASTED BULBUL *Ixos siquijorensis* (4) [EN]

BROWN-EARED BULBUL *Ixos amaurotis* (3, 4)

YELLOWISH BULBUL *Ixos everetti* (4) [NT]

STREAKED BULBUL *Ixos malaccensis* (4)

ASHY BULBUL *Hemixos flavala* (4)

CHESTNUT BULBUL *Hemixos castanonotus* (4)

MOUNTAIN BULBUL *Hypsipetes mcclellandii* (4)

SUNDA BULBUL *Hypsipetes virescens* (4)

MADAGASCAR BULBUL *Hypsipetes madagascariensis* (5)

SEYCHELLES BULBUL *Hypsipetes crassirostris* (5)

COMORO BULBUL *Hypsipetes parvirostris* (5)

REUNION BLACK BULBUL or OLIVACEOUS BULBUL *Hypsipetes borbonicus* (5)

MAURITIUS BLACK BULBUL *Hypsipetes olivaceus* (5) [VU]

BLACK BULBUL *Hypsipetes leucocephalus* (4)

NICOBAR BULBUL *Hypsipetes nicobariensis* (5) [VU]

WHITE-HEADED BULBUL *Hypsipetes thompsoni* (4)

BLACK-COLLARED BULBUL *Neolestes torquatus* (5)

MALIA *Malia grata* (4)

Family INC. SEDIS HYPOCOLIIDAE

GRAY HYPOCOLIUS *Hypocolius ampelinus* (3, 5)

Family PRINIIDAE

CRYPTIC WARBLER *Cryptosylvicola randrianasoloi* (5)

RED-FACED CISTICOLA *Cisticola erythrops* (5)

LEPE CISTICOLA *Cisticola lepe* (5)

SINGING CISTICOLA *Cisticola cantans* (5)

WHISTLING CISTICOLA *Cisticola lateralis* (5)

CHATTERING CISTICOLA *Cisticola anonymus* (5)

TRILLING CISTICOLA *Cisticola woosnami* (5)

BUBBLING CISTICOLA *Cisticola bulliens* (5)

BROWN-BACKED CISTICOLA *Cisticola discolor* (5)

CHUBB'S CISTICOLA *Cisticola chubbi* (5)

HUNTER'S CISTICOLA *Cisticola hunteri* (5)

BLACK-LORED CISTICOLA *Cisticola nigriloris* (5)

ROCK-LOVING CISTICOLA *Cisticola emini* (5)

LAZY CISTICOLA *Cisticola aberrans* (5)

BORAN CISTICOLA *Cisticola bodessa* (5)

RATTLING CISTICOLA *Cisticola chiniana* (5)

ASHY CISTICOLA *Cisticola cinereolus* (5)

RED-PATE CISTICOLA *Cisticola ruficeps* (5)

DORST'S CISTICOLA *Cisticola dorsti* (5)

GRAY CISTICOLA *Cisticola rufilatus* (5)

RED-HEADED CISTICOLA *Cisticola subruficapillus* (5)

WAILING CISTICOLA *Cisticola lais* (5)

LYNES'S CISTICOLA *Cisticola distinctus* (5)

TANA RIVER CISTICOLA *Cisticola restrictus* (5) [DD]

CHURRING CISTICOLA *Cisticola njombe* (5) [NT]

WINDING CISTICOLA *Cisticola galactotes* (5)

CHIRPING CISTICOLA *Cisticola pipiens* (5)

CARRUTHERS'S CISTICOLA *Cisticola carruthersi* (5)

TINKLING CISTICOLA *Cisticola tinniens* (5)

ANGOLA CISTICOLA *Cisticola angolensis* (5)

STOUT CISTICOLA *Cisticola robustus* (5)

ABERDARE CISTICOLA *Cisticola aberdare* (5)

CROAKING CISTICOLA *Cisticola natalensis* (5)

PIPING CISTICOLA *Cisticola fulvicapillus* (5)

TABORA CISTICOLA *Cisticola angusticauda* (5)

SLENDER-TAILED CISTICOLA *Cisticola melanura* (5)

SIFFLING CISTICOLA *Cisticola brachypterus* (5)

RUFOUS CISTICOLA *Cisticola rufus* (5)

FOXY CISTICOLA *Cisticola troglodytes* (5)

TINY CISTICOLA *Cisticola nanus* (5)

ZITTING CISTICOLA *Cisticola juncidis* (3, 4, 5)

ISLAND CISTICOLA or SOCOTRA CISTICOLA *Cisticola haesitatus* (5) [VU]

MADAGASCAR CISTICOLA *Cisticola cherinus* (5)

DESERT CISTICOLA *Cisticola aridulus* (5)

TINK-TINK CISTICOLA *Cisticola trextrix* (5)

BLACK-NECKED CISTICOLA *Cisticola eximius* (5)

CLOUD-SCRAPING CISTICOLA *Cisticola dambo* (5)

PECTORAL-PATCH CISTICOLA *Cisticola brunnescens* (5)

WING-SNAPPING CISTICOLA *Cisticola ayresii* (5)

GOLDEN-HEADED CISTICOLA or BRIGHT-HEADED CISTICOLA *Cisticola exilis* (4, 6)

SOCOTRA WARBLER *Incana incana* (4)

STREAKED SCRUB-WARBLER *Scotocerca inquieta* (3, 5)

WHITE-BROWED CHINESE WARBLER *Rhopophilus pekinensis* (4)

RUFOUS-VENTED PRINIA *Prinia burnesii* (3, 4) [VU]

SWAMP PRINIA *Prinia cinerascens* (4)

STRIATED PRINIA *Prinia criniger* (4)

BROWN PRINIA *Prinia polychroa* (4)

HILL PRINIA *Prinia atrogularis* (4)

GRAY-CROWNED PRINIA *Prinia cinereocapilla* (4) [NT]

RUFOUS-FRONTED PRINIA *Prinia buchanani* (3, 4)

RUFESCENT PRINIA *Prinia rufescens* (4)

GRAY-BREASTED PRINIA *Prinia hodgsonii* (3, 4)

GRACEFUL PRINIA *Prinia gracilis* (3, 4, 5)

JUNGLE PRINIA *Prinia sylvatica* (3, 4)

BAR-WINGED PRINIA *Prinia familiaris* (4)

YELLOW-BELLIED PRINIA *Prinia flaviventris* (3, 4)

ASHY PRINIA *Prinia socialis* (4)

TAWNY-FLANKED PRINIA *Prinia subflava* (5)

PALE PRINIA *Prinia somalica* (5)

PLAIN PRINIA *Prinia inornata* (4)

RIVER PRINIA *Prinia fluviatilis* (5) [DD]

BLACK-CHESTED PRINIA *Prinia flavicans* (5)

SAFFRON-BREASTED PRINIA or DRAKENSBERG PRINIA *Prinia hypoxantha* (5)

KAROO PRINIA *Prinia maculosa* (5)

SÃO TOMÉ PRINIA *Prinia molleri* (5)

BRIAR WARBLER *Prinia robertsi* (5)

SIERRA LEONE PRINIA or WHITE-EYED PRINIA *Prinia leontica* (5) [VU]

WHITE-CHINNED PRINIA *Prinia leucopogon* (5)

BANDED PRINIA *Prinia bairdii* (5)

NAMAQUA WARBLER *Phragmacia substriata* (5)

RED-WINGED WARBLER *Heliolais erythroptera* (5)

RUFOUS-EARED WARBLER *Malcorus pectoralis* (5)

RED-WINGED GRAY WARBLER *Drymocichla incana* (5)

GREEN LONGTAIL *Urolais epichlora* (5)

CRICKET LONGTAIL or SCALY-FRONTED WARBLER *Spiloptila clamans* (5)

RED-FRONTED WARBLER *Spiloptila rufifrons* (5)

BUFF-BELLIED WARBLER *Phyllolais pulchella* (5)

BLACK-COLLARED APALIS *Apalis pulchra* (5)

COLLARED APALIS *Apalis ruwenzorii* (5)

BAR-THROATED APALIS *Apalis thoracica* (5)

TAITA APALIS *Apalis fuscigularis* (5) [CR]

NAMULI APALIS *Apalis lynesi* (5) [VU]

BLACK-CAPPED APALIS *Apalis nigriceps* (5)

BLACK-THROATED APALIS *Apalis jacksoni* (5)

WHITE-WINGED APALIS *Apalis chariessa* (5) [VU]

MASKED APALIS *Apalis binotata* (5)

BLACK-FACED APALIS *Apalis personata* (5)

YELLOW-BREASTED APALIS *Apalis flavida* (5)

BROWN-TAILED APALIS *Apalis viridiceps* (5)

RUDD'S APALIS *Apalis ruddi* (5)

SHARPE'S APALIS *Apalis sharpii* (5)

BUFF-THROATED APALIS *Apalis rufogularis* (5)

KUNGWE APALIS *Apalis argentea* (5) [VU]

BAMENDA APALIS *Apalis bamendae* (5) [VU]

GOSLING'S APALIS *Apalis goslingi* (5)

CHESTNUT-THROATED APALIS *Apalis porphyrolaema* (5)

KABOBO APALIS *Apalis kaboboensis* (5) [DD]

CHAPIN'S APALIS *Apalis chapini* (5)

BLACK-HEADED APALIS *Apalis melanocephala* (5)

CHIRINDA APALIS *Apalis chirindensis* (5)

LONG-BILLED APALIS or LONG-BILLED TAILORBIRD *Apalis moreaui* (5) [CR]

GRAY APALIS *Apalis cinerea* (5)

BROWN-HEADED APALIS *Apalis alticola* (5)

KARAMOJA APALIS *Apalis karamojae* (5) [VU]

ORIOLE WARBLER *Hypergerus atriceps* (5)

GRAY-CAPPED WARBLER *Eminia lepida* (5)

GREEN-BACKED CAMAROPTERA *Camaroptera brachyura* (5)

YELLOW-BROWED CAMAROPTERA *Camaroptera superciliaris* (5)

OLIVE-GREEN CAMAROPTERA *Camaroptera chloronota* (5)

GRAY WREN-WARBLER *Calamonastes simplex* (5)

PALE WREN-WARBLER *Calamonastes undosus* (5)

BARRED WREN-WARBLER *Calamonastes fasciolatus* (5)

WHITE-TAILED WARBLER *Poliolais lopezi* (5)

GRAUER'S WARBLER *Graueria vittata* (5)

KOPJE WARBLER *Euryptila subcinnamomea* (5)

Family ZOSTEROPIDAE

CAMEROON SPEIROPS or MOUNT CAMEROON SPEIROPS *Speirops melanocephalus* (5) [VU]

BLACK-CAPPED SPEIROPS *Speirops lugubris* (5)

FERNANDO PO SPEIROPS *Speirops brunneus* (5) [VU]

PRINCIPE SPEIROPS *Speirops leucophoeus* (5) [VU]

AFRICAN YELLOW WHITE-EYE *Zosterops senegalensis* (5)

PEMBA WHITE-EYE *Zosterops vaughani* (5) [NT]

CHESTNUT-SIDED WHITE-EYE *Zosterops mayottensis* (5)

BROAD-RINGED WHITE-EYE *Zosterops poliogaster* (5)

TAITA WHITE-EYE *Zosterops silvanus* (5) [CR]

KULAL WHITE-EYE *Zosterops kulalensis* (5) [CR]

SOUTH PARE WHITE-EYE *Zosterops winifredae* (5) [VU]

WHITE-BREASTED WHITE-EYE *Zosterops abyssinicus* (5)

PALE WHITE-EYE *Zosterops pallidus* (5)

MALAGASY WHITE-EYE *Zosterops maderaspatanus* (5)

COMORO WHITE-EYE or MOUNT KARTHALA WHITE-EYE *Zosterops mouroniensis* (5)

PRINCIPE WHITE-EYE or SÃO TOMÉ WHITE-EYE *Zosterops ficedulinus* (5) [VU]

ANNOBON WHITE-EYE *Zosterops griseovirescens* (5) [VU]

MASCARENE GRAY WHITE-EYE *Zosterops borbonicus* (5)

REUNION OLIVE WHITE-EYE *Zosterops olivaceus* (5)

MAURITIUS OLIVE WHITE-EYE *Zosterops chloronothos* (5) [CR]

SEYCHELLES GRAY WHITE-EYE or SEYCHELLES WHITE-EYE *Zosterops modestus* (5) [CR]

SRI LANKA WHITE-EYE or CEYLON WHITE-EYE *Zosterops ceylonensis* (4)

CHESTNUT-FLANKED WHITE-EYE *Zosterops erythropleurus* (3)

ORIENTAL WHITE-EYE *Zosterops palpebrosus* (3, 4)

JAPANESE WHITE-EYE *Zosterops japonicus* (3, 4)

LOWLAND WHITE-EYE *Zosterops meyeni* (4)

ENGGANO WHITE-EYE *Zosterops salvadorii* (4)

BRIDLED WHITE-EYE *Zosterops conspicillatus* (4) [NT, SSP]

ROTA WHITE-EYE *Zosterops rotensis* (4) [CR]

PLAIN WHITE-EYE *Zosterops hypolais* (4) [NT]

CAROLINE ISLANDS WHITE-EYE *Zosterops semperi* (4)

BLACK-CAPPED WHITE-EYE *Zosterops atricapillus*

EVERETT'S WHITE-EYE *Zosterops everetti* (4)

GOLDEN-GREEN WHITE-EYE *Zosterops nigrorum* (4)

MOUNTAIN WHITE-EYE *Zosterops montanus* (4)

CHRISTMAS ISLAND WHITE-EYE *Zosterops natalis* (4) [NT]

JAVAN WHITE-EYE *Zosterops flavus* (4) [NT]

LEMON-BELLIED WHITE-EYE *Zosterops chloris* (4)

ASHY-BELLIED WHITE-EYE or PALE WHITE-EYE *Zosterops citrinellus* (4)

PEARL-BELLIED WHITE-EYE *Zosterops grayi* (6) [NT]

GOLDEN-BELLIED WHITE-EYE *Zosterops uropygialis* (6) [NT]

PALE-BELLIED WHITE-EYE *Zosterops consobrinorum* (4) [NT]

LEMON-THROATED WHITE-EYE or BLACK-RINGED WHITE-EYE *Zosterops anomalus* (4) [NT]

YELLOW-SPECTACLED WHITE-EYE *Zosterops wallacei* (4)

BLACK-CROWNED WHITE-EYE *Zosterops atrifrons* (4)

CREAMY-THROATED WHITE-EYE *Zosterops atriceps* (4)

BLACK-FRONTED WHITE-EYE *Zosterops minor* (6)

WHITE-THROATED WHITE-EYE *Zosterops meeki* (6) [DD]

BLACK-HEADED WHITE-EYE *Zosterops hypoxanthus* (6)

BIAK WHITE-EYE *Zosterops mysorensis* (6) [NT]

CAPPED WHITE-EYE *Zosterops fuscicapillus* (6)

BURU YELLOW WHITE-EYE or BURU WHITE-EYE *Zosterops buruensis* (4)

AMBON YELLOW WHITE-EYE *Zosterops kuehni* (4) [NT]

NEW GUINEA WHITE-EYE *Zosterops novaeguineae* (6)

AUSTRALIAN YELLOW WHITE-EYE or YELLOW WHITE-EYE *Zosterops luteus* (6)

LOUISIADE WHITE-EYE *Zosterops griseotinctus* (6)

RENNELL WHITE-EYE *Zosterops rennellianus* (4) [NT]

BANDED WHITE-EYE *Zosterops vellalavella* (4)

GANONGGA WHITE-EYE *Zosterops splendidus* (4)

SPLENDID WHITE-EYE or GHIZO WHITE-EYE *Zosterops luteirostris* (4) [VU]

SOLOMON ISLANDS WHITE-EYE *Zosterops kulambangrae* (4)

HERMIT WHITE-EYE *Zosterops murphyi* (4)

YELLOW-THROATED WHITE-EYE *Zosterops metcalfii* (4)

GRAY-THROATED WHITE-EYE *Zosterops rendovae* (4)

MALAITA WHITE-EYE *Zosterops stresemanni* (4)

SANTA CRUZ WHITE-EYE *Zosterops sanctaecrucis* (4)

SILVEREYE *Zosterops lateralis* (6)

LORD HOWE ISLAND WHITE-EYE *Zosterops tephropleurus* (6) [VU]

ROBUST WHITE-EYE *Zosterops strenuus* (6) [EX]

SLENDER-BILLED WHITE-EYE *Zosterops tenuirostris* (6) [VU]

WHITE-CHESTED WHITE-EYE *Zosterops albogularis* (6) [CR]

LARGE LIFOU WHITE-EYE *Zosterops inornatus* (6)

LAYARD'S WHITE-EYE *Zosterops explorator* (6)

YELLOW-FRONTED WHITE-EYE *Zosterops flavifrons* (4)

GREEN-BACKED WHITE-EYE *Zosterops xanthochrous* (6)

SMALL LIFOU WHITE-EYE *Zosterops minutus* (6)

SAMOAN WHITE-EYE *Zosterops samoensis* (6) [VU]

DUSKY WHITE-EYE *Zosterops finschii* (4)

GRAY-BROWN WHITE-EYE *Zosterops cinereus* (4)

YAP OLIVE WHITE-EYE *Zosterops oleagineus* (4) [VU]

LONG-BILLED WHITE-EYE *Rukia longirostra* (4) [NT]

TRUK WHITE-EYE or FAICHUK WHITE-EYE *Rukia ruki* (4) [EN]

GOLDEN WHITE-EYE *Cleptornis marchei* (4) [VU]

BONIN WHITE-EYE or BONIN ISLANDS WHITE-EYE *Apalopteron familiare* (3)

BICOLORED WHITE-EYE *Tephrozosterops stalkeri* (4)

RUFOUS-THROATED WHITE-EYE *Madanga ruficollis* (4) [VU]

JAVAN GRAY-THROATED WHITE-EYE *Lophozosterops javanicus* (4)

STREAKY-HEADED WHITE-EYE *Lophozosterops squamiceps* (4)

BLACK-MASKED WHITE-EYE *Lophozosterops goodfellowi* (4)

YELLOW-BROWED WHITE-EYE *Lophozosterops superciliaris* (4)

GRAY-HOODED WHITE-EYE *Lophozosterops pinaiae* (4)

CRESTED WHITE-EYE *Lophozosterops dohertyi* (4) [NT]

PYGMY WHITE-EYE *Oculocincta squamifrons* (4)

THICK-BILLED WHITE-EYE *Heleia crassirostris* (4)

SPOT-BREASTED WHITE-EYE *Heleia muelleri* (4) [NT]

MOUNTAIN BLACKEYE *Chlorocharis emiliae* (4)

BARE-EYED WHITE-EYE *Woodfordia superciliosa* (4)

SANFORD'S WHITE-EYE *Woodfordia lacertosa* (4) [NT]

GIANT WHITE-EYE *Megazosterops palauensis* (4)

CINNAMON IBON *Hypocryptadius cinnamomeus* (4)

Family SYLVIIDAE
Subfamily ACROCEPHALINAE

CHESTNUT-HEADED TESIA *Tesia castaneocoronata* (4)

SLATY-BELLIED TESIA *Tesia olivea* (4)

GRAY-BELLIED TESIA *Tesia cyaniventer* (4)

JAVAN TESIA *Tesia superciliaris* (4)

RUSSET-CAPPED TESIA *Tesia everetti* (4)

TIMOR STUBTAIL *Urosphena subulata* (4) [NT]

BORNEAN STUBTAIL *Urosphena whiteheadi* (4)

ASIAN STUBTAIL *Urosphena squameiceps* (3, 4)

PALE-FOOTED BUSH-WARBLER *Cettia pallidipes* (4)

MANCHURIAN BUSH-WARBLER *Cettia canturians* (3, 4)

JAPANESE BUSH-WARBLER *Cettia diphone* (3, 4)

PHILIPPINE BUSH-WARBLER *Cettia seebohmi* (4)

PALAU BUSH-WARBLER *Cettia annae* (4)

SHADE WARBLER *Cettia parens* (4) [NT]

FIJI BUSH-WARBLER *Cettia ruficapilla* (6)

BROWNISH-FLANKED BUSH-WARBLER *Cettia fortipes* (3, 4)

SUNDA BUSH-WARBLER *Cettia vulcania* (4)

TANIMBAR BUSH-WARBLER *Cettia carolinae* (4) [NT]

CHESTNUT-CROWNED BUSH-WARBLER *Cettia major* (3, 4)

ABERRANT BUSH-WARBLER *Cettia flavolivacea* (4)

YELLOWISH-BELLIED BUSH-WARBLER *Cettia acanthizoides* (3, 4)

GRAY-SIDED BUSH-WARBLER *Cettia brunnifrons* (3, 4)

CETTI'S WARBLER *Cettia cetti* (3, 4, 5)

AFRICAN BUSH-WARBLER *Bradypterus baboecala* (5)

DJA RIVER SCRUB-WARBLER *Bradypterus grandis* (5) [DD]

WHITE-WINGED SCRUB-WARBLER *Bradypterus carpalis* (5)

GRAUER'S SCRUB-WARBLER *Bradypterus graueri* (5) [VU]

BAMBOO SCRUB-WARBLER *Bradypterus alfredi* (5)

KNYSNA SCRUB-WARBLER *Bradypterus sylvaticus* (5)

BANGWA FOREST-WARBLER *Bradypterus bangwaensis* (5) [NT]

EVERGREEN FOREST-WARBLER *Bradypterus lopezi* (5)

AFRICAN SCRUB-WARBLER *Bradypterus barratti* (5)

CINNAMON BRACKEN-WARBLER *Bradypterus cinnamomeus* (5)

VICTORIN'S SCRUB-WARBLER *Bradypterus victorini* (5)

SPOTTED BUSH-WARBLER *Bradypterus thoracicus* (3, 4)

DAVID'S BUSH-WARBLER *Bradypterus davidi* (3, 4)

LONG-BILLED BUSH-WARBLER *Bradypterus major* (3, 4) [VU]

CHINESE BUSH-WARBLER *Bradypterus tacsanowskius* (3, 4)

BROWN BUSH-WARBLER *Bradypterus luteoventris* (3, 4)

RUSSET BUSH-WARBLER *Bradypterus seebohmi* (3, 4)

JAVAN BUSH-WARBLER *Bradypterus montis* (4)

TIMOR BUSH-WARBLER *Bradypterus timoriensis* (4)

SRI LANKA BUSH-WARBLER or CEYLON BUSH-WARBLER *Bradypterus palliseri* (4) [NT]

LONG-TAILED BUSH-WARBLER *Bradypterus caudatus* (4) [NT]

FRIENDLY BUSH-WARBLER *Bradypterus accentor* (4)

CHESTNUT-BACKED BUSH-WARBLER *Bradypterus castaneus* (4)

BROWN EMU-TAIL *Dromaeocercus brunneus* (5) [NT]

GRAY EMU-TAIL *Dromaeocercus seebohmi* (5)

BLACK-CAPPED RUFOUS WARBLER *Bathmocercus cerviniventris* (5) [VU]

BLACK-FACED RUFOUS WARBLER *Bathmocercus rufus* (5)

MRS. MOREAU'S WARBLER *Bathmocercus winifredae* (5) [VU]

ALDABRA BRUSH-WARBLER *Nesillas aldabrana* (5) [EX]

ANJOUAN BRUSH-WARBLER *Nesillas longicaudata* (5)

MALAGASY BRUSH-WARBLER *Nesillas typica* (5)

MOHELI BRUSH-WARBLER *Nesillas moheliensis* (5) [NT]

GRAND COMORO BRUSH-WARBLER *Nesillas brevicaudata* (5)

MRS. BENSON'S BRUSH-WARBLER *Nesillas mariae* (5)

THAMNORNIS WARBLER *Thamnornis chloropetoides* (5)

MUSTACHED GRASS-WARBLER *Melocichla mentalis* (5)

DAMARA ROCK-JUMPER *Achaetops pycnopygius* (5)

CAPE GRASS-WARBLER *Sphenoeacus afer* (5)

LANCEOLATED WARBLER *Locustella lanceolata* (3, 4)

COMMON GRASSHOPPER-WARBLER *locustella Naevia* (3, 4)

PALLAS'S GRASSHOPPER-WARBLER or RUSTY-RUMPED WARBLER *Locustella certhiola* (3, 4)

MIDDENDORFF'S GRASSHOPPER-WARBLER *Locustella ochotensis* (3, 4)

PLESKE'S GRASSHOPPER-WARBLER or STYAN'S GRASSHOPPER-WARBLER *Locustella pleskei* (3, 4)

EURASIAN RIVER WARBLER *Locustella fluviatilis* (3, 5)

SAVI'S WARBLER *Locustella luscinioides* (3, 5)

GRAY'S GRASSHOPPER-WARBLER *Locustella fasciolata* (3, 4, 6)

JAPANESE SWAMP WARBLER or MARSH GRASSBIRD *Locustella pryeri* (3, 4) [VU]

MUSTACHED WARBLER *Acrocephalus melanopogon* (3, 4)

AQUATIC WARBLER *Acrocephalus paludicola* (3, 5) [VU]

SEDGE WARBLER *Acrocephalus schoenobaenus* (3, 4, 5)

STREAKED REED-WARBLER *Acrocephalus sorghophilus* (4) [VU]

BLACK-BROWED REED-WARBLER *Acrocephalus bistrigiceps* (3, 4)

PADDYFIELD WARBLER *Acrocephalus agricola* (3, 4)

MANCHURIAN PADDYFIELD WARBLER *Acrocephalus tangorum* (3)

BLUNT-WINGED WARBLER *Acrocephalus concinens* (3, 4)

EURASIAN REED-WARBLER *Acrocephalus scirpaceus* (3, 5)

AFRICAN REED-WARBLER *Acrocephalus baeticatus* (5)

BLYTH'S REED-WARBLER *Acrocephalus dumetorum* (3)

MARSH WARBLER *Acrocephalus palustris* (3, 5)

GREAT REED-WARBLER *Acrocephalus arundinaceus* (3, 4, 5)

ORIENTAL REED-WARBLER *Acrocephalus orientalis* (3, 4)

CLAMOROUS REED-WARBLER *Acrocephalus stentoreus* (3, 4, 5, 6)

BASRA REED-WARBLER *Acrocephalus griseldis* (3, 5) [NT]

AUSTRALIAN REED-WARBLER *Acrocephalus australis* (6)

NIGHTINGALE REED-WARBLER *Acrocephalus luscinia* (4) [VU]

CAROLINE ISLANDS REED-WARBLER *Acrocephalus syrinx* (4)

NAURU REED-WARBLER *Acrocephalus rehsei* (4) [VU]

MILLERBIRD *Acrocephalus familiaris* (2) [VU]

BOKIKOKIKO *Acrocephalus aequinoctialis* (4)

TAHITI REED-WARBLER *Acrocephalus caffer* (6) [VU]

MARQUESAN REED-WARBLER *Acrocephalus mendanae* (6)

TUAMOTU REED-WARBLER *Acrocephalus atyphus* (6)

COOK ISLANDS REED-WARBLER *Acrocephalus kerearako* (6)

RIMATARA REED-WARBLER *Acrocephalus rimatarae* (6)

PITCAIRN REED-WARBLER *Acrocephalus vaughani* (6) [VU]

HENDERSON ISLAND REED-WARBLER *Acrocephalus taiti* (6)

GREATER SWAMP-WARBLER *Acrocephalus rufescens* (5)

CAPE VERDE SWAMP-WARBLER or CAPE VERDE WARBLER *Acrocephalus brevipennis* (5) [VU]

LESSER SWAMP-WARBLER *Acrocephalus gracilirostris* (5)

MADAGASCAR SWAMP-WARBLER *Acrocephalus newtoni* (5)

THICK-BILLED WARBLER *Acrocephalus aedon* (3, 4)

RODRIGUEZ BRUSH-WARBLER or RODRIGUES WARBLER *Acrocephalus rodericanus* (5) [CR]

SEYCHELLES BRUSH-WARBLER or SEYCHELLES WARBLER *Acrocephalus sechellensis* (5) [VU]

BOOTED WARBLER *Hippolais caligata* (3, 4)

SYKES'S WARBLER *Hippolais rama* (3, 4)

OLIVACEOUS WARBLER *Hippolais pallida* (3, 5)

UPCHER'S WARBLER *Hippolais languida* (3, 5)

OLIVE-TREE WARBLER *Hippolais olivetorum* (3, 5)

MELODIOUS WARBLER *Hippolais polyglotta* (3, 5)

ICTERINE WARBLER *Hippolais icterina* (3, 5)

YELLOW FLYCATCHER-WARBLER *Chloropeta natalensis* (5)

MOUNTAIN FLYCATCHER-WARBLER *Chloropeta similis* (5)

THIN-BILLED FLYCATCHER-WARBLER or PAPYRUS YELLOW WARBLER *Chloropeta gracilirostris* (5) [VU]

AFRICAN TAILORBIRD *Orthotomus metopias* (5)

MOUNTAIN TAILORBIRD *Orthotomus cuculatus* (4)

RUFOUS-HEADED TAILORBIRD *Orthotomus heterolaemus* (4)

COMMON TAILORBIRD *Orthotomus sutorius* (4)

DARK-NECKED TAILORBIRD *Orthotomus atrogularis* (4)

PHILIPPINE TAILORBIRD *Orthotomus castaneiceps* (4)

RUFOUS-FRONTED TAILORBIRD *Orthotomus frontalis* (4)

GRAY-BACKED TAILORBIRD *Orthotomus derbianus* (4)

RUFOUS-TAILED TAILORBIRD *Orthotomus sericeus* (4)

ASHY TAILORBIRD *Orthotomus ruficeps* (4)

OLIVE-BACKED TAILORBIRD *Orthotomus sepium* (4)

YELLOW-BREASTED TAILORBIRD *Orthotomus samarensis* (4) [NT]

BLACK-HEADED TAILORBIRD *Orthotomus nigriceps* (4) [NT]

WHITE-EARED TAILORBIRD *Orthotomus cinereiceps* (4)

YELLOW-BELLIED EREMOMELA *Eremomela icteropygialis* (5)

SALVADORI'S EREMOMELA *Eremomela salvadorii* (5)

YELLOW-VENTED EREMOMELA *Eremomela flavicrissalis* (5)

SENEGAL EREMOMELA *Eremomela pusilla* (5)

GREEN-BACKED EREMOMELA *Eremomela canescens* (5)

GREENCAP EREMOMELA *Eremomela scotops* (5)

YELLOW-RUMPED EREMOMELA *Eremomela gregalis* (5)

RUFOUS-CROWNED EREMOMELA *Eremomela badiceps* (5)

TURNER'S EREMOMELA *Eremomela turneri* (5) [VU]

BLACK-NECKED EREMOMELA *Eremomela atricollis* (5)

BURNT-NECK EREMOMELA *Eremomela usticollis* (5)

RAND'S WARBLER *Randia pseudozosterops* (5)

Dark Newtonia *Newtonia amphichroa* (5)

Common Newtonia *Newtonia brunne-icauda* (5)

Archbold's Newtonia *Newtonia archboldi* (5)

Red-Tailed Newtonia *Newtonia fanovanae* (5) [VU]

Green Crombec *Sylvietta virens* (5)

Lemon-Bellied Crombec *Sylvietta denti* (5)

Chapin's Crombec *Sylvietta chapini* (5)

White-Browed Crombec *Sylvietta leucophrys* (5)

Northern Crombec *Sylvietta brachyura* (5)

Short-Billed Crombec *Sylvietta philippae* (5) [NT]

Red-Capped Crombec *Sylvietta ruficapilla* (5)

Red-Faced Crombec *Sylvietta whytii* (5)

Somali Crombec *Sylvietta isabellina* (5)

Cape Crombec *Sylvietta rufescens* (5)

Neumann's Warbler *Hemitesia neumanni* (5)

Kemp's Longbill *Macrosphenus kempi* (5)

Yellow Longbill *Macrosphenus flavicans* (5)

Gray Longbill *Macrosphenus concolor* (5)

Pulitzer's Longbill *Macrosphenus pulitzeri* (5) [EN]

Kretschmer's Longbill *Macrosphenus kretschmeri* (5)

Bocage's Longbill or São Tomé Short-Tail *Amaurocichla bocagii* (5) [VU]

Green Hylia *Hylia prasina* (5)

White-Browed Tit-Warbler *Leptopoecile sophiae* (4)

Crested Tit-Warbler *Leptopoecile elegans* (3, 4) [NT]

Red-Faced Woodland-Warbler *Phylloscopus laetus* (5)

Laura's Woodland-Warbler *Phylloscopus laurae* (5)

Yellow-Throated Woodland-Warbler *Phylloscopus ruficapillus* (5)

Black-Capped Woodland-Warbler *Phylloscopus herberti* (5)

Uganda Woodland-Warbler *Phylloscopus budongoensis* (5)

Brown Woodland-Warbler *Phylloscopus umbrovirens* (5)

Willow Warbler *Phylloscopus trochilus* (3, 5)

Eurasian Chiffchaff or Common Chiffchaff *Phylloscopus collybita* (3, 4, 5)

Siberian Chiffchaff *Phylloscopus tristis* (3)

Canary Islands Chiffchaff *Phylloscopus canariensis* (5)

Mountain Chiffchaff *Phylloscopus sindianus* (4)

Iberian Chiffchaff *Phylloscopus brehmii* (3, 5)

Plain Leaf-Warbler *Phylloscopus neglectus* (3, 4)

Western Bonelli's Warbler *Phylloscopus bonelli* (3, 4)

Eastern Bonelli's Warbler *Phylloscopus orientalis* (3)

Wood Warbler *Phylloscopus sibilatrix* (3, 5)

Dusky Warbler *Phylloscopus fuscatus* (1, 3, 4)

Smokey Warbler *Phylloscopus fuliginventer* (3, 4)

Tickell's Leaf-Warbler *Phylloscopus affinis* (3, 4)

Buff-Throated Warbler *Phylloscopus subaffinis* (4)

Sulfur-Bellied Warbler *Phylloscopus griseolus* (3, 4)

Yellow-Streaked Warbler *Phylloscopus armandii* (4)

Radde's Warbler *Phylloscopus schwarzi* (3, 4)

BUFF-BARRED WARBLER *Phylloscopus pulcher* (3, 4)

ASH-THROATED WARBLER *Phylloscopus maculipennis* (3, 4)

PALLAS'S LEAF-WARBLER *Phylloscopus proregulus* (3, 4)

GANSU LEAF-WARBLER *Phylloscopus kansuensis* (4)

LEMON-RUMPED WARBLER or PALE-RUMPED WARBLER *Phylloscopus chloronotus* (3, 4)

SICHUAN WARBLER or CHINESE LEAF-WARBLER *Phylloscopus sichuanensis* (4)

BROOKS'S LEAF-WARBLER *Phylloscopus subviridis* (3, 4)

INORNATE WARBLER or YELLOW-BROWED WARBLER *Phylloscopus inornatus* (3, 4)

BUFF-BROWED WARBLER or HUME'S WARBLER *Phylloscopus humei* (3, 4)

ARCTIC WARBLER *Phylloscopus borealis* (1, 3, 4, 6)

GREENISH WARBLER *Phylloscopus trochiloides* (3, 4)

BRIGHT-GREEN WARBLER *Phylloscopus nitidus* (3, 4)

PALE-LEGGED LEAF-WARBLER *Phylloscopus tenellipes* (3, 4)

SAKHALIN LEAF-WARBLER *Phylloscopus borealoides* (3)

LARGE-BILLED LEAF-WARBLER *Phylloscopus magnirostris* (3, 4)

TYTLER'S LEAF-WARBLER *Phylloscopus tytleri* (3, 4) [NT]

WESTERN CROWNED-WARBLER *Phylloscopus occipitalis* (3, 4)

EASTERN CROWNED-WARBLER *Phylloscopus coronatus* (3, 4)

IJIMA'S LEAF-WARBLER *Phylloscopus ijimae* (3, 4) [VU]

BLYTH'S LEAF-WARBLER *Phylloscopus reguloides* (3, 4)

HAINAN LEAF-WARBLER *Phylloscopus hainanus* (4) [VU]

EMEI LEAF-WARBLER *Phylloscopus emeiensis* (4)

WHITE-TAILED LEAF-WARBLER *Phylloscopus davisoni* (3, 4)

YELLOW-VENTED WARBLER *Phylloscopus cantator* (4) [NT]

SULFUR-BREASTED WARBLER *Phylloscopus ricketti* (4)

PHILIPPINE LEAF-WARBLER *Phylloscopus olivaceus* (4)

LEMON-THROATED LEAF-WARBLER *Phylloscopus cebuensis* (4)

MOUNTAIN LEAF-WARBLER *Phylloscopus trivirgatus* (4)

SULAWESI LEAF-WARBLER *Phylloscopus sarasinorum* (4)

TIMOR LEAF-WARBLER *Phylloscopus presbytes* (4)

ISLAND LEAF-WARBLER *Phylloscopus poliocephalus* (4, 6)

SAN CRISTÓBAL LEAF-WARBLER *Phylloscopus makirensis* (4) [NT]

SOMBER LEAF-WARBLER *Phylloscopus amoenus* (4) [VU]

GOLDEN-SPECTACLED WARBLER *Seicercus burkii* (3)

GRAY-HOODED WARBLER *Seicercus xanthoschistos* (3)

WHITE-SPECTACLED WARBLER *Seicercus affinis* (3, 4)

GRAY-CHEEKED WARBLER *Seicercus poliogenys* (3, 4)

CHESTNUT-CROWNED WARBLER *Seicercus castaniceps* (3, 4)

YELLOW-BREASTED WARBLER *Seicercus montis* (4)

SUNDA WARBLER *Seicercus grammiceps* (4)

BROAD-BILLED WARBLER *Tickellia hodgsoni* (3, 4) [NT]

RUFOUS-FACED WARBLER *Abroscopus albogularis* (3, 4)

BLACK-FACED WARBLER *Abroscopus schisti-ceps* (3, 4)

YELLOW-BELLIED WARBLER *Abroscopus super-ciliaris* (3, 4)

YELLOW-BELLIED HYLIOTA *Hyliota flavigaster* (5)

SOUTHERN HYLIOTA *Hyliota australis* (5)

VIOLET-BACKED HYLIOTA *Hyliota violacea* (5)

Subfamily MEGALURINAE

TAWNY GRASSBIRD *Megalurus timoriensis* (4, 6)

STRIATED GRASSBIRD *Megalurus palustris* (4)

FLY RIVER GRASSBIRD *Megalurus albolim-batus* (6) [VU]

LITTLE GRASSBIRD *Megalurus gramineus* (6)

NEW ZEALAND FERNBIRD *Megalurus puncta-tus* (6)

CHATHAM ISLANDS FERNBIRD *Megalurus rufescens* (6)

BROWN SONGLARK *Cincloramphus cruralis* (6)

RUFOUS SONGLARK *Cincloramphus mathewsi* (6)

SPINIFEX-BIRD *Eremiornis carteri* (6)

BUFF-BANDED GRASSBIRD *Buettikoferella bivittata* (4) [NT]

NEW CALEDONIAN GRASSBIRD *Megalurulus mariei* (6)

BISMARCK THICKETBIRD *Megalurulus grosvenori* (6) [DD]

BOUGAINVILLE THICKETBIRD *Megalurulus llaneae* (4) [DD]

GUADALCANAL THICKETBIRD *Megalurulus whitneyi* (4) [NT]

RUSTY THICKETBIRD *Megalurulus rubigi-nosus* (6)

LONG-LEGGED THICKETBIRD *Trichocichla rufa* (6) [CR]

BRISTLED GRASSBIRD or BRISTLED GRASS-WARBLER *Chaetornis striatus* (4) [VU]

RUFOUS-RUMPED GRASSBIRD *Graminicola bengalensis* (4)

FAN-TAILED GRASSBIRD *Schoenicola brevi-rostris* (5)

BROAD-TAILED GRASSBIRD *Schoenicola platyura* (4) [NT]

Subfamily GARRULACINAE

MALIA *Malia grata* (4)

ASHY-HEADED LAUGHINGTHRUSH *Garrulax cinereifrons* (4) [VU]

SUNDA LAUGHINGTHRUSH *Garrulax palliatus* (4)

RUFOUS-FRONTED LAUGHINGTHRUSH *Garrulax rufifrons* (4) [NT]

MASKED LAUGHINGTHRUSH *Garrulax perspic-illatus* (4)

WHITE-THROATED LAUGHINGTHRUSH *Garrulax albogularis* (4)

WHITE-CRESTED LAUGHINGTHRUSH *Garrulax leucolophus* (4)

LESSER NECKLACED LAUGHINGTHRUSH *Garrulax monileger* (4)

GREATER NECKLACED LAUGHINGTHRUSH *Garrulax pectoralis* (2, 4)

BLACK LAUGHINGTHRUSH *Garrulax lugubris* (4)

BARE-HEADED LAUGHINGTHRUSH *Garrulax calvus* (4)

STRIATED LAUGHINGTHRUSH *Garrulax striatus* (3, 4)

WHITE-NECKED LAUGHINGTHRUSH *Garrulax strepitans* (4)

BLACK-HOODED LAUGHINGTHRUSH *Garrulax milleti* (4) [VU]

GRAY LAUGHINGTHRUSH *Garrulax maesi* (4) [NT]

RUFOUS-NECKED LAUGHINGTHRUSH *Garrulax ruficollis* (4)

CHESTNUT-BACKED LAUGHINGTHRUSH *Garrulax nuchalis* (4) [NT]

BLACK-THROATED LAUGHINGTHRUSH *Garrulax chinensis* (4)

WHITE-CHEEKED LAUGHINGTHRUSH *Garrulax vassali* (4)

YELLOW-THROATED LAUGHINGTHRUSH *Garrulax galbanus* (4) [NT]

WYNAAD LAUGHINGTHRUSH *Garrulax delesserti* (4) [NT]

RUFOUS-VENTED LAUGHINGTHRUSH *Garrulax gularis* (4)

PLAIN LAUGHINGTHRUSH *Garrulax davidi* (4)

SNOWY-CHEEKED LAUGHINGTHRUSH *Garrulax sukatschewi* (4) [VU]

MUSTACHED LAUGHINGTHRUSH *Garrulax cineraceus* (3, 4)

RUFOUS-CHINNED LAUGHINGTHRUSH *Garrulax rufogularis* (3, 4)

BARRED LAUGHINGTHRUSH *Garrulax lunulatus* (3, 4) [NT]

WHITE-SPECKLED LAUGHINGTHRUSH *Garrulax bieti* (3, 4) [VU]

GIANT LAUGHINGTHRUSH *Garrulax maximus* (4)

SPOTTED LAUGHINGTHRUSH *Garrulax ocellatus* (3, 4)

GRAY-SIDED LAUGHINGTHRUSH *Garrulax caerulatus* (2, 4)

RUSTY LAUGHINGTHRUSH *Garrulax poecilorhynchus* (4)

CHESTNUT-CAPPED LAUGHINGTHRUSH *Garrulax mitratus* (4)

SPOT-BREASTED LAUGHINGTHRUSH *Garrulax merulinus* (3, 4) [NT]

HWAMEI *Garrulax canorus* (2, 4)

WHITE-BROWED LAUGHINGTHRUSH *Garrulax sannio* (4)

RUFOUS-BREASTED LAUGHINGTHRUSH or NILGIRI LAUGHINGTHRUSH *Garrulax cachinnans* (4) [NT]

GRAY-BREASTED LAUGHINGTHRUSH *Garrulax jerdoni* (4) [NT]

STREAKED LAUGHINGTHRUSH *Garrulax lineatus* (3)

STRIPED LAUGHINGTHRUSH *Garrulax virgatus* (4) [NT]

BROWN-CAPPED LAUGHINGTHRUSH *Garrulax austeni* (4) [DD]

BLUE-WINGED LAUGHINGTHRUSH *Garrulax squamatus* (3, 4)

SCALY LAUGHINGTHRUSH *Garrulax subunicolor* (3, 4)

ELLIOT'S LAUGHINGTHRUSH *Garrulax elliotii* (3, 4)

VARIEGATED LAUGHINGTHRUSH *Garrulax variegatus* (3, 4)

BROWN-CHEEKED LAUGHINGTHRUSH *Garrulax henrici* (3)

BLACK-FACED LAUGHINGTHRUSH *Garrulax affinis* (3, 4)

WHITE-WHISKERED LAUGHINGTHRUSH *Garrulax morrisonianus* (4)

CHESTNUT-CROWNED LAUGHINGTHRUSH *Garrulax erythrocephalus* (4)

COLLARED LAUGHINGTHRUSH *Garrulax yersini* (4) [VU]

RED-WINGED LAUGHINGTHRUSH *Garrulax formosus* (3, 4) [NT]

RED-TAILED LAUGHINGTHRUSH *Garrulax milnei* (3, 4) [NT]

RED-FACED LIOCICHLA *Liocichla phoenicea* (3, 4)

OMEI SHAN LIOCICHLA *Liocichla omeiensis* (4) [VU]

STEERE'S LIOCICHLA *Liocichla steerii* (4)

Subfamily SYLVIINAE
Tribe TIMALIINI

SPOT-THROAT *Modulatrix stictigula* (5)

DAPPLE-THROAT or DAPPLED MOUNTAIN-ROBIN *Arcanator orostruthus* (5) [VU]

WHITE-CHESTED BABBLER *Trichastoma rostratum* (4) [NT]

SULAWESI BABBLER *Trichastoma celebense* (4)

FERRUGINOUS BABBLER *Trichastoma bicolor* (4) [NT]

BAGOBO BABBLER *Leonardina woodi* (4) [VU]

ABBOTT'S BABBLER *Malacocincla abbotti* (4)

HORSFIELD'S BABBLER *Malacocincla sepiarium* (4)

VANDERBILT'S BABBLER *Malacocincla vanderbilti* (4) [VU]

BLACK-BROWED BABBLER *Malacocincla perspicillata* (4) [VU]

SHORT-TAILED BABBLER *Malacocincla malaccensis* (4)

ASHY-HEADED BABBLER *Malacocincla cinereiceps* (4)

BUFF-BREASTED BABBLER *Pellorneum tickelli* (4)

TEMMINCK'S BABBLER *Pellorneum pyrrogenys* (4)

SPOT-THROATED BABBLER *Pellorneum albiventre* (4)

MARSH BABBLER *Pellorneum palustre* (4) [VU]

PUFF-THROATED BABBLER *Pellorneum ruficeps* (4)

BROWN-CAPPED BABBLER *Pellorneum fuscocapillum* (4)

BLACK-CAPPED BABBLER *Pellorneum capistratum* (4)

MUSTACHED BABBLER *Malacopteron magnirostre* (4)

SOOTY-CAPPED BABBLER *Malacopteron affine* (4)

SCALY-CROWNED BABBLER *Malacopteron cinereum* (4)

RUFOUS-CROWNED BABBLER *Malacopteron magnum* (4)

MELODIOUS BABBLER *Malacopteron palawanense* (4) [EN]

GRAY-BREASTED BABBLER *Malacopteron albogulare* (4) [NT]

BLACKCAP ILLADOPSIS *Illadopsis cleaveri* (5)

SCALY-BREASTED ILLADOPSIS *Illadopsis albipectus* (5)

RUFOUS-WINGED ILLADOPSIS *Illadopsis rufescens* (5) [NT]

PUVEL'S ILLADOPSIS *Illadopsis puveli* (5)

PALE-BREASTED ILLADOPSIS *Illadopsis rufipennis* (5)

BROWN ILLADOPSIS *Illadopsis fulvescens* (5)

MOUNTAIN ILLADOPSIS *Illadopsis pyrrhoptera* (5)

RUWENZORI HILL-BABBLER *Pseudoalcippe atriceps* (5)

ABYSSINIAN HILL-BABBLER *Pseudoalcippe abyssinica* (5)

GRAY-CHESTED ILLADOPSIS *Kakamega poliothorax* (5)

THRUSH BABBLER *Ptyrticus turdinus* (5)

LARGE SCIMITAR-BABBLER *Pomatorhinus hypoleucos* (4)

SPOT-BREASTED SCIMITAR-BABBLER *Pomatorhinus erythrocnemis* (3, 4)

RUSTY-COKED SCIMITAR-BABBLER *Pomatorhinus erythrogenys* (3, 4)

INDIAN SCIMITAR-BABBLER or WHITE-BROWED SCIMITAR-BABBLER *Pomatorhinus horsfieldii* (4)

SLATY-HEADED SCIMITAR-BABBLER *Pomatorhinus schisticeps* (4)

CHESTNUT-BACKED SCIMITAR-BABBLER *Pomatorhinus montanus* (4)

STREAK-BREASTED SCIMITAR-BABBLER *Pomatorhinus ruficollis* (4)

RED-BILLED SCIMITAR-BABBLER *Pomatorhinus ochraceiceps* (4)

CORAL-BILLED SCIMITAR-BABBLER *Pomatorhinus ferruginosus* (4)

SLENDER-BILLED SCIMITAR-BABBLER *Xiphirhynchus superciliaris* (4) [NT]

SHORT-TAILED SCIMITAR-BABBLER *Jabouilleia danjoui* (4) [VU]

LONG-BILLED WREN-BABBLER *Rimator malacoptilus* (4) [NT]

BORNEAN WREN-BABBLER *Ptilocichla leucogrammica* (4) [NT]

STRIATED WREN-BABBLER *Ptilocichla mindanensis* (4) [NT]

FALCATED WREN-BABBLER *Ptilocichla falcata* (4) [EN]

STRIPED WREN-BABBLER *Kenopia striata* (4)

LARGE WREN-BABBLER *Napothera macrodactyla* (4) [NT]

RUSTY-BREASTED WREN-BABBLER *Napothera rufipectus* (4)

BLACK-THROATED WREN-BABBLER *Napothera atrigularis* (4)

MARBLED WREN-BABBLER *Napothera marmorata* (4) [NT]

LIMESTONE WREN-BABBLER *Napothera crispifrons* (4)

STREAKED WREN-BABBLER *Napothera brevicaudata* (4)

MOUNTAIN WREN-BABBLER *Napothera crassa* (4)

RABOR'S WREN-BABBLER *Napothera rabori* (4) [VU]

EYEBROWED WREN-BABBLER *Napothera epilepidota* (4)

SCALY-BREASTED WREN-BABBLER *Pnoepyga albiventer* (3, 4)

NEPAL WREN-BABBLER *Pnoepyga immaculata* (4) [NT]

PYGMY WREN-BABBLER *Pnoepyga pusilla* (4)

RUFOUS-THROATED WREN-BABBLER *Spelaeornis saudatus* (3, 4) [VU]

RUSTY-THROATED WREN-BABBLER *Spelaeornis badeigularis* (4) [VU]

BAR-WINGED WREN-BABBLER *Spelaeornis troglodytoides* (3, 4)

SPOTTED WREN-BABBLER *Spelaeornis formosus* (3, 4) [NT]

LONG-TAILED WREN-BABBLER *Spelaeornis chocolatinus* (3, 4)

TAWNY-BREASTED WREN-BABBLER *Spelaeornis longicaudatus* (3) [VU]

WEDGE-BILLED WREN-BABBLER *Sphenocichla humei* (3, 4) [NT]

COMMON JERY *Neomixis tenella* (5)

GREEN JERY *Neomixis viridis* (5)

STRIPE-THROATED JERY *Neomixis striatigula* (5)

WEDGE-TAILED JERY *Neomixis flavoviridis* (5) [NT]

BUFF-CHESTED BABBLER *Stachyris ambigua* (4)

DEIGNAN'S BABBLER *Stachyris rodolphei* (3, 4) [VU]

RUFOUS-FRONTED BABBLER *Stachyris rufifrons* (4)

RUFOUS-CAPPED BABBLER *Stachyris ruficeps* (3, 4)

BLACK-CHINNED BABBLER *Stachyris pyrrhops* (3, 4)

GOLDEN BABBLER *Stachyris chrysaea* (4)

PYGMY BABBLER *Stachyris plateni* (4) [NT]

GOLDEN-CROWNED BABBLER *Stachyris dennistouni* (4) [NT]

BLACK-CROWNED BABBLER *Stachyris nigrocapitata* (4)

RUSTY-CROWNED BABBLER *Stachyris capitalis* (4) [NT]

FLAME-TEMPLED BABBLER *Stachyris speciosa* (4) [EN]

CHESTNUT-FACED BABBLER *Stachyris whiteheadi* (4) [NT]

LUZON STRIPED-BABBLER *Stachyris striata* (4) [VU]

PANAY STRIPED-BABBLER *Stachyris latistriata* (4) [VU]

NEGROS STRIPED-BABBLER *Stachyris nigrorum* (4) [EN]

PALAWAN STRIPED-BABBLER *Stachyris hypogrammica* (4) [VU]

WHITE-BREASTED BABBLER *Stachyris grammiceps* (4) [VU]

SOOTY BABBLER *Stachyris herberti* (4) [VU]

GRAY-THROATED BABBLER *Stachyris nigriceps* (4)

GRAY-HEADED BABBLER *Stachyris poliocephala* (4)

SNOWY-THROATED BABBLER *Stachyris oglei* (4) [VU]

SPOT-NECKED BABBLER *Stachyris striolata* (4)

WHITE-NECKED BABBLER *Stachyris leucotis* (4)

BLACK-THROATED BABBLER *Stachyris nigricollis* (4)

WHITE-BIBBED BABBLER *Stachyris thoracica* (4)

CHESTNUT-RUMPED BABBLER *Stachyris maculata* (4)

CHESTNUT-WINGED BABBLER *Stachyris erythroptera* (4)

CRESCENT-CHESTED BABBLER *Stachyris melanothorax* (4)

TAWNY-BELLIED BABBLER *Dumetia hyperythra* (4)

DARK-FRONTED BABBLER *Rhopocichla atriceps* (4)

STRIPED TIT-BABBLER *Macronous gularis* (4)

GRAY-CHEEKED TIT-BABBLER *Macronous flavicollis* (4)

GRAY-FACED TIT-BABBLER *Macronous kelleyi* (4) [NT]

BROWN TIT-BABBLER *Macronous striaticeps* (4)

FLUFFY-BACKED TIT-BABBLER *Macronous ptilosus* (4)

MINIATURE TIT-BABBLER *Micromacronus leytensis* (4) [VU]

CHESTNUT-CAPPED BABBLER *Timalia pileata* (4)

YELLOW-EYED BABBLER *Chrysomma sinense* (3, 4)

JERDON'S BABBLER *Chrysomma altirostre* (3, 4) [VU]

RUFOUS-TAILED BABBLER *Chrysomma poecilotis* (3, 4) [NT]

SPINY BABBLER *Turdoides nipalensis* (4)

IRAQ BABBLER *Turdoides altirostris* (3) [NT]

COMMON BABBLER *Turdoides caudatus* (3, 4)

STRIATED BABBLER *Turdoides earlei* (3, 4)

WHITE-THROATED BABBLER *Turdoides gularis* (3)

SLENDER-BILLED BABBLER *Turdoides longirostris* (3, 4) [NT]

LARGE GRAY BABBLER *Turdoides malcolmi* (4)

ARABIAN BABBLER *Turdoides squamiceps* (3)

FULVOUS BABBLER or FULVOUS CHATTERER *Turdoides fulvus* (5)

SCALY CHATTERER *Turdoides aylmeri* (5)

RUFOUS CHATTERER *Turdoides rubiginosus* (5)

RUFOUS BABBLER *Turdoides subrufus* (4)

JUNGLE BABBLER *Turdoides striatus* (3, 4)

ORANGE-BILLED BABBLER *Turdoides rufescens* (4)

YELLOW-BILLED BABBLER *Turdoides affinis* (4)

BLACKCAP BABBLER *Turdoides reinwardii* (5)

DUSKY BABBLER *Turdoides tenebrosus* (5)

BLACK-LORED BABBLER *Turdoides melanops* (5)

SCALY BABBLER *Turdoides squamulatus* (5)

WHITE-RUMPED BABBLER *Turdoides leucopygius* (5)

ANGOLA BABBLER *Turdoides hartlaubii* (5)

SOUTHERN PIED-BABBLER *Turdoides bicolor* (5)

SHARPE'S PIED-BABBLER *Turdoides sharpei* (5)

NORTHERN PIED-BABBLER *Turdoides hypoleucus* (5)

HINDE'S PIED-BABBLER *Turdoides hindei* (5) [EN]

BROWN BABBLER *Turdoides plebejus* (5)

WHITE-HEADED BABBLER or CRETSCHMAR'S BABBLER *Turdoides leucocephalus* (5)

ARROW-MARKED BABBLER *Turdoides jardineii* (5)

BARE-CHEEKED BABBLER *Turdoides gymnogenys* (5)

CHINESE BABAX *Babax lanceolatus* (4)

GIANT BABAX *Babax waddelli* (4) [NT]

TIBETAN BABAX *Babax koslowi* (3, 4) [NT]

SILVER-EARED MESIA *Leiothrix argentauris* (4)

RED-BILLED MESIA *Leiothrix lutea* (3, 4)

CUTIA *Cutia nipalensis* (4)

BLACK-HEADED SHRIKE-BABBLER *Pteruthius rufiventer* (3, 4) [NT]

WHITE-BROWED SHRIKE-BABBLER *Pteruthius flaviscapis* (4)

GREEN SHRIKE-BABBLER *Pteruthius xanthochlorus* (3, 4)

BLACK-EARED SHRIKE-BABBLER *Pteruthius melanotis* (4)

CHESTNUT-FRONTED SHRIKE-BABBLER *Pteruthius aenobarbus* (4)

WHITE-HOODED BABBLER *Gampsorhynchus rufulus* (4)

RUSTY-FRONTED BARWING *Actinodura egertoni* (3, 4)

SPECTACLED BARWING *Actinodura ramsayi* (3, 4)

HOARY-THROATED BARWING *Actinodura nipalensis* (3, 4)

STREAK-THROATED BARWING *Actinodura waldeni* (3, 4)

STREAKED BARWING *Actinodura souliei* (3, 4) [NT]

TAIWAN BARWING or FORMOSAN BARWING *Actinodura morrisoniana* (4)

BLUE-WINGED MINLA *Minla cyanouroptera* (4)

CHESTNUT-TAILED MINLA *Minla strigula* (4)

RED-TAILED MINLA *Minla ignotincta* (4)

GOLDEN-BREASTED FULVETTA *Alcippe chrysotis* (3, 4)

GOLDEN-FRONTED FULVETTA *Alcippe variegaticeps* (4) [VU]

YELLOW-THROATED FULVETTA *Alcippe cinerea* (3, 4) [NT]

RUFOUS-WINGED FULVETTA *Alcippe castaneceps* (3, 4)

WHITE-BROWED FULVETTA *Alcippe vinipectus* (3, 4)

CHINESE FULVETTA *Alcippe striaticollis* (3, 4)

SPECTACLED FULVETTA *Alcippe ruficapilla* (3, 4) [NT]

STREAK-THROATED FULVETTA *Alcippe cinereiceps* (3, 4)

LUDLOW'S FULVETTA or BROWN-THROATED FULVETTA *Alcippe ludlowi* (3, 4)

RUFOUS-THROATED FULVETTA *Alcippe rufogularis* (4) [NT]

DUSKY FULVETTA *Alcippe brunnea* (3, 4)

RUSTY-CAPPED FULVETTA *Alcippe dubia* (3)

BROWN FULVETTA *Alcippe brunneicauda* (4)

BROWN-CHEEKED FULVETTA *Alcippe poioicephala* (4)

JAVAN FULVETTA *Alcippe pyrrhoptera* (4)

MOUNTAIN FULVETTA *Alcippe peracensis* (4)

GRAY-CHEEKED FULVETTA *Alcippe morrisonia* (4)

NEPAL FULVETTA *Alcippe nipalensis* (3, 4)

BLACKCAP MOUNTAIN-BABBLER *Lioptilus nigricapillus* (5) [NT]

WHITE-THROATED MOUNTAIN-BABBLER *Kupeornis gilberti* (5) [VU]

RED-COLLARED MOUNTAIN-BABBLER *Kupeornis rufocinctus* (5) [NT]

CHAPIN'S MOUNTAIN-BABBLER *Kupeornis chapini* (5) [NT]

ABYSSINIAN CATBIRD *Parophasma galinieri* (5)

CAPUCHIN BABBLER *Phyllanthus atripennis* (5)

GRAY-CROWNED CROCIAS *Crocias langbianis* (4) [CR]

SPOTTED CROCIAS *Crocias albonotatus* (4) [NT]

RUFOUS-BACKED SIBIA *Heterophasia annectens* (3, 4)

RUFOUS SIBIA *Heterophasia capistrata* (3, 4)

GRAY SIBIA *Heterophasia gracilis* (3, 4) [NT]

BLACK-BACKED SIBIA *Heterophasia melanoleuca* (3, 4)

BLACK-HEADED SIBIA *Heterophasia desgodinsi* (3, 4)

WHITE-EARED SIBIA *Heterophasia auricularis* (4)

BEAUTIFUL SIBIA *Heterophasia pulchella* (3, 4)

LONG-TAILED SIBIA *Heterophasia picaoides* (4)

STRIATED YUHINA *Yuhina castaniceps* (4)

CHESTNUT-CRESTED YUHINA *Yuhina everetti* (4)

WHITE-NAPED YUHINA *Yuhina bakeri* (3, 4)

WHISKERED YUHINA *Yuhina flavicollis* (3, 4)

BURMESE YUHINA *Yuhina humilis* (3, 4) [NT]

STRIPE-THROATED YUHINA *Yuhina gularis* (3, 4)

WHITE-COLLARED YUHINA *Yuhina diademata* (3, 4)

RUFOUS-VENTED YUHINA *Yuhina occipitalis* (3, 4)

TAIWAN YUHINA or FORMOSAN YUHINA *Yuhina brunneiceps* (4)

BLACK-CHINNED YUHINA *Yuhina nigrimenta* (3, 4)

WHITE-BELLIED YUHINA *Yuhina zantholeuca* (4)

FIRE-TAILED MYZORNIS *Myzornis pyrrhoura* (3, 4)

WHITE-THROATED OXYLABES *Oxylabes madagascariensis* (5)

YELLOW-BROWED OXYLABES or MADAGASCAR YELLOWBROW *Crossleyia xanthophrys* (5) [VU]

CROSSLEY'S BABBLER *Mystacornis crossleyi* (5)

BEARDED PARROTBILL or BEARDED REEDLING *Panurus biarmicus* (3, 4)

GREAT PARROTBILL *Conostoma oemodium* (3, 4)

THREE-TOED PARROTBILL *Paradoxornis paradoxus* (3, 4)

BROWN PARROTBILL *Paradoxornis unicolor* (3, 4)

GRAY-HEADED PARROTBILL *Paradoxornis gularis* (4)

BLACK-BREASTED PARROTBILL *Paradoxornis flavirostris* (4) [VU]

SPOT-BREASTED PARROTBILL *Paradoxornis guttaticollis* (3, 4)

SPECTACLED PARROTBILL *Paradoxornis conspicillatus* (3, 4) [NT]

VINOUS-THROATED PARROTBILL *Paradoxornis webbianus* (3, 4)

BROWN-WINGED PARROTBILL *Paradoxornis brunneus* (3, 4) [NT]

ASHY-THROATED PARROTBILL *Paradoxornis alphonsianus* (3, 4)

GRAY-HOODED PARROTBILL *Paradoxornis zappeyi* (4) [VU]

RUSTY-THROATED PARROTBILL *Paradoxornis przewalskii* (3, 4) [VU]

FULVOUS PARROTBILL *Paradoxornis fulvifrons* (3, 4)

BLACK-THROATED PARROTBILL *Paradoxornis nipalensis* (3, 4)

GOLDEN PARROTBILL *Paradoxornis verreauxi* (3, 4)

SHORT-TAILED PARROTBILL *Paradoxornis davidianus* (3, 4) [VU]

BLACK-BROWED PARROTBILL or LESSER RUFOUS-HEADED PARROTBILL *Paradoxornis atrosuperciliaris* (3, 4) [NT]

RUFOUS-HEADED PARROTBILL or GREATER RUFOUS-HEADED PARROTBILL *Paradoxornis ruficeps* (3, 4) [NT]

REED PARROTBILL *Paradoxornis heudei* (3, 4) [NT]

STRIPE-SIDED RHABDORNIS *Rhabdornis mystacalis* (4)

LONG-BILLED RHABDORNIS *Rhabdornis grandis* (4)

STRIPE-BREASTED RHABDORNIS *Rhabdornis inornatus* (4)

Tribe CHAMAEINI

WRENTIT *Chamaea fasciata* (1)

Tribe SYLVIINI

YEMEN WARBLER *Sylvia buryi* (3) [VU]

BROWN WARBLER *Sylvia lugens* (5)

BANDED WARBLER *Sylvia boehmi* (5)

LAYARD'S WARBLER *Sylvia layardi* (5)

RUFOUS-VENTED WARBLER *Sylvia subcaeruleum* (5)

BLACKCAP *Sylvia atricapilla* (3, 5)

GARDEN WARBLER *Sylvia borin* (3, 5)

GREATER WHITETHROAT *Sylvia communis* (3, 4, 5)

LESSER WHITETHROAT *Sylvia curruca* (3, 4, 5)

SMALL WHITETHROAT *Sylvia minula* (4)

HUME'S WHITETHROAT *Sylvia althaea* (3, 4)

DESERT WARBLER *Sylvia nana* (3, 4, 5)

BARRED WARBLER *Sylvia nisoria* (3, 4, 5)

ORPHEAN WARBLER *Sylvia hortensis* (3, 4, 5)

RED SEA WARBLER or ARABIAN WARBLER *Sylvia leucomelaena* (3, 5)

RUEPPELL'S WARBLER *Sylvia rueppelli* (3, 5)

SARDINIAN WARBLER *Sylvia melanocephala* (3, 5)

CYPRUS WARBLER *Sylvia melanothorax* (3, 5)

SUBALPINE WARBLER *Sylvia cantillans* (3, 5)

MENETRIES'S WARBLER *Sylvia mystacea* (3, 5)

SPECTACLED WARBLER *Sylvia conspicillata* (3, 5)

TRISTRAM'S WARBLER *Sylvia deserticola* (5)

DARTFORD WARBLER *Sylvia undata* (3, 5)

MARMORA'S WARBLER *Sylvia sarda* (3, 5)

Family ALAUDIDAE

MONOTONOUS LARK *Mirafra passerina* (5)

SINGING LARK or SINGING BUSHLARK *Mirafra cantillans* (5)

AUSTRALASIAN LARK or AUSTRALASIAN BUSHLARK *Mirafra javanica* (4, 6)

MELODIOUS LARK or LATAKOO LARK *Mirafra cheniana* (5)

WHITE-TAILED LARK *Mirafra albicauda* (5)

MADAGASCAR LARK *Mirafra hova* (5)

KORDOFAN LARK *Mirafra cordofanica* (5)

WILLIAMS'S LARK *Mirafra williamsi* (5) [NT]

FRIEDMANN'S LARK *Mirafra pulpa* (5) [NT]

RED-WINGED LARK *Mirafra hypermetra* (5)

SOMALI LONG-BILLED LARK *Mirafra somalica* (5)

ASH'S LARK *Mirafra ashi* (5) [EN]

RUFOUS-NAPED LARK *Mirafra africana* (5)

SOMALI LARK *Mirafra sharpii* (5)

ANGOLA LARK *Mirafra angolensis* (5)

FLAPPET LARK *Mirafra rufocinnamomea* (5)

CLAPPER LARK *Mirafra apiata* (5)

COLLARED LARK *Mirafra collaris* (5)

FAWN-COLORED LARK *Mirafra africanoides* (5)

ABYSSINIAN LARK *Mirafra alopex* (5)

INDIAN LARK or INDIAN BUSHLARK *Mirafra erythroptera* (4)

RUFOUS-WINGED LARK *Mirafra assamica* (3, 4)

RUSTY LARK *Mirafra rufa* (5)

GILLETT'S LARK *Mirafra gilletti* (5)

DEGODI LARK *Mirafra degodiensis* (5) [VU]

PINK-BREASTED LARK *Mirafra poecilosterna* (5)

BRADFIELD'S LARK *Mirafra naevia* (5)

SABOTA LARK *Mirafra sabota* (5)

RUFOUS-RUMPED LARK *Pinarocorys erythropygia* (5)

DUSKY LARK *Pinarocorys nigricans* (5)

ARCHER'S LARK *Heteromirafra archeri* (5) [EN]

SIDAMO LARK *Heteromirafra sidamoensis* (5) [EN]

RUDD'S LARK *Heteromirafra ruddi* (5) [CR]

LONG-BILLED LARK *Certhilauda curvirostris* (5)

SHORT-CLAWED LARK *Certhilauda chuana* (5) [NT]

DUNE LARK *Certhilauda erythrochlamys* (5)

KAROO LARK *Certhilauda albescens* (5)

CAVE'S LARK *Certhilauda cavei* (5)

FERRUGINOUS LARK or RED LARK *Certhilauda burra* (5) [VU]

SPIKE-HEELED LARK *Chersomanes albofasciata* (5)

CHESTNUT-BACKED SPARROW-LARK *Eremopterix leucotis* (5)

BLACK-EARED SPARROW-LARK *Eremopterix australis* (5)

GRAY-BACKED SPARROW-LARK *Eremopterix verticalis* (5)

FISCHER'S SPARROW-LARK *Eremopterix leucopareia* (5)

CHESTNUT-HEADED SPARROW-LARK *Eremopterix signata* (5)

BLACK-CROWNED SPARROW-LARK *Eremopterix nigriceps* (3, 4, 5)

ASHY-CROWNED SPARROW-LARK *Eremopterix grisea* (3, 4)

BAR-TAILED DESERT LARK *Ammomanes cincturus* (3, 5)

RUFOUS-TAILED LARK *Ammomanes phoenicurus* (4)

DESERT LARK *Ammomanes deserti* (3, 4, 5)

GRAY'S LARK *Ammomanes grayi* (5)

GREATER HOOPOE-LARK *Alaemon alaudipes* (5)

LESSER HOOPOE-LARK *Alaemon hamertoni* (5)

THICK-BILLED LARK *Ramphocoris clotbey* (3, 5)

CALANDRA LARK *Melanocorypha calandra* (3, 5)

BIMACULATED LARK *Melanocorypha bimaculata* (3, 4, 5)

TIBETAN LARK *Melanocorypha maxima* (4)

MONGOLIAN LARK *Melanocorypha mongolica* (4)

WHITE-WINGED LARK *Melanocorypha leucoptera* (3, 4)

BLACK LARK *Melanocorypha yeltoniensis* (3)

GREATER SHORT-TOED LARK *Calandrella brachydactyla* (3, 4, 5)

BLANFORD'S LARK *Calandrella blanfordi* (3, 5)

ERLANGER'S LARK *Calandrella erlangeri* (5)

RED-CAPPED LARK *Calandrella cinerea* (5)

HUME'S LARK *Calandrella acutirostris* (3, 4)

LESSER SHORT-TOED LARK *Calandrella rufescens* (3, 5)

ASIAN SHORT-TOED LARK *Calandrella cheleensis* (3, 4)

INDIAN SHORT-TOED LARK or SAND LARK *Calandrella raytal* (3, 4)

RUFOUS SHORT-TOED LARK *Calandrella somalica* (5)

ATHI SHORT-TOED LARK *Calandrella athensis* (5)

PINK-BILLED LARK *Spizocorys conirostris* (5)

SCLATER'S LARK *Spizocorys sclateri* (5) [NT]

OBBIA LARK *Spizocorys obbiensis* (5) [NT]

MASKED LARK *Spizocorys personata* (5)

BOTHA'S LARK *Spizocorys fringillaris* (5) [VU]

STARK'S LARK *Eremalauda starki* (5)

DUNN'S LARK *Eremalauda dunni* (3, 5)

DUPONT'S LARK *Chersophilus duponti* (5)

CRESTED LARK *Galerida cristata* (3, 4, 5)

THEKLA LARK *Galerida theklae* (3, 5)

MALABAR LARK *Galerida malabarica* (4)

TAWNY LARK or SYKES'S LARK *Galerida deva* (4)

SUN LARK *Galerida modesta* (5)

LARGE-BILLED LARK *Galerida magnirostris* (5)

SHORT-TAILED LARK *Pseudalaemon fremantlii* (5)

WOOD LARK *Lullula arborea* (3)

SKY LARK or SKYLARK or EURASIAN SKYLARK *Alauda arvensis* (1, 2, 3, 4, 5, 6)

JAPANESE SKY LARK *Alauda japonica* (3)

ORIENTAL SKY LARK *Alauda gulgula* (3, 4)

RAZO LARK or RASO LARK *Alauda razae* (5) [EN]

HORNED LARK or SHORE LARK *Eremophila alpestris* (1, 2, 3, 4, 5)

TEMMINCK'S LARK *Eremophila bilopha* (3, 5)

Family NECTARINIIDAE
Subfamily PROMEROPINAE

GURNEY'S SUGARBIRD *Promerops gurneyi* (5)

CAPE SUGARBIRD *Promerops cafer* (5)

Subfamily NECTARINIINAE
Tribe DICAEINI

OLIVE-BACKED FLOWERPECKER *Prionochilus olivaceus* (4)

YELLOW-BREASTED FLOWERPECKER *Prionochilus maculatus* (4)

CRIMSON-BREASTED FLOWERPECKER *Prionochilus percussus* (4)

PALAWAN FLOWERPECKER *Prionochilus plateni* (4)

YELLOW-RUMPED FLOWERPECKER *Prionochilus xanthopygius* (4)

SCARLET-BREASTED FLOWERPECKER *Prionochilus thoracicus* (4)

GOLDEN-RUMPED FLOWERPECKER *Dicaeum annae* (4)

THICK-BILLED FLOWERPECKER *Dicaeum agile* (4)

STRIPED FLOWERPECKER *Dicaeum aeruginosum* (4)

BROWN-BACKED FLOWERPECKER *Dicaeum everetti* (4) [NT]

WHISKERED FLOWERPECKER *Dicaeum proprium* (4) [VU]

YELLOW-VENTED FLOWERPECKER *Dicaeum chrysorrheum* (4)

YELLOW-BELLIED FLOWERPECKER *Dicaeum melanoxanthum* (4)

WHITE-THROATED FLOWERPECKER or LEGGE'S FLOWERPECKER *Dicaeum vincens* (4) [NT]

YELLOW-SIDED FLOWERPECKER *Dicaeum aureolimbatum* (4)

OLIVE-CAPPED FLOWERPECKER *Dicaeum nigrilore* (4)

FLAME-CROWNED FLOWERPECKER *Dicaeum anthonyi* (4) [NT]

BICOLORED FLOWERPECKER *Dicaeum bicolor* (4)

CEBU FLOWERPECKER *Dicaeum quadricolor* (4) [CR]

VISAYAN FLOWERPECKER *Dicaeum haematostictum* (4) [EN]

RED-STRIPED FLOWERPECKER *Dicaeum australe* (4)

SCARLET-COLLARED FLOWERPECKER *Dicaeum retrocinctum* (4) [CR]

ORANGE-BELLIED FLOWERPECKER *Dicaeum trigonostigma* (4)

BUZZING FLOWERPECKER *Dicaeum hypoleucum* (4)

PALE-BILLED FLOWERPECKER *Dicaeum erythrorhynchos* (4)

PLAIN FLOWERPECKER *Dicaeum concolor* (4)

PYGMY FLOWERPECKER *Dicaeum pygmaeum* (4)

CRIMSON-CROWNED FLOWERPECKER *Dicaeum nehrkorni* (4)

FLAME-BREASTED FLOWERPECKER *Dicaeum erythrothorax* (4)

ASHY FLOWERPECKER *Dicaeum vulneratum* (4)

OLIVE-CROWNED FLOWERPECKER *Dicaeum pectorale* (6)

RED-CAPPED FLOWERPECKER *Dicaeum geelvinkianum* (6)

LOUISIADE FLOWERPECKER *Dicaeum nitidum* (6)

RED-BANDED FLOWERPECKER *Dicaeum eximium* (6)

MIDGET FLOWERPECKER *Dicaeum aeneum* (4)

MOTTLED FLOWERPECKER *Dicaeum tristrami* (4)

BLACK-FRONTED FLOWERPECKER *Dicaeum igniferum* (4)

RED-CHESTED FLOWERPECKER *Dicaeum maugei* (4)

FIRE-BREASTED FLOWERPECKER *Dicaeum ignipectus* (4)

BLACK-SIDED FLOWERPECKER *Dicaeum monticolum* (4)

GRAY-SIDED FLOWERPECKER *Dicaeum celebicum* (4)

BLOOD-BREASTED FLOWERPECKER *Dicaeum sanguinolentum* (4)

MISTLETOEBIRD *Dicaeum hirundinaceum* (4, 6)

SCARLET-BACKED FLOWERPECKER *Dicaeum cruentatum* (4)

SCARLET-HEADED FLOWERPECKER *Dicaeum trochileum* (4)

Tribe NECTARINIINI

SCARLET-TUFTED SUNBIRD *Anthreptes fraseri* (5)

GRAY-HEADED SUNBIRD *Anthreptes axillaris* (5)

PLAIN-BACKED SUNBIRD *Anthreptes reichenowi* (5) [NT]

ANCHIETA'S SUNBIRD *Anthreptes anchietae* (5)

PLAIN SUNBIRD *Anthreptes simplex* (4)

PLAIN-THROATED SUNBIRD or BROWN-THROATED SUNBIRD *Anthreptes malacensis* (4)

RED-THROATED SUNBIRD *Anthreptes rhodolaema* (4)

RUBY-CHEEKED SUNBIRD *Anthreptes singalensis* (4)

MOUSE-BROWN SUNBIRD *Anthreptes gabonicus* (5)

WESTERN VIOLET-BACKED SUNBIRD *Anthreptes longuemarei* (5)

KENYA VIOLET-BACKED SUNBIRD *Anthreptes orientalis* (5)

ULUGURU VIOLET-BACKED SUNBIRD *Anthreptes neglectus* (5)

VIOLET-TAILED SUNBIRD *Anthreptes aurantium* (5)

AMANI SUNBIRD *Anthreptes pallidigaster* (5) [VU]

GREEN SUNBIRD *Anthreptes rectirostris* (5)

BANDED SUNBIRD *Anthreptes rubritorques* (5) [VU]

COLLARED SUNBIRD *Anthreptes collaris* (5)

PYGMY SUNBIRD *Anthreptes platurus* (5)

NILE VALLEY SUNBIRD *Anthreptes metallicus* (5)

PURPLE-NAPED SUNBIRD *Hypogramma hypogrammicum* (4)

SÃO TOMÉ SUNBIRD or GIANT SUNBIRD *Dreptes thomensis* (5) [VU]

LITTLE GREEN SUNBIRD *Nectarinia seimundi* (5)

BATES'S SUNBIRD *Nectarinia batesi* (5)

OLIVE SUNBIRD *Nectarinia olivacea* (5)

ORANGE-BREASTED SUNBIRD *Nectarinia violacea* (5)

MOUSE-COLORED SUNBIRD *Nectarinia veroxii* (5)

REICHENBACH'S SUNBIRD *Nectarinia reichenbachii* (5)

PRINCIPE SUNBIRD *Nectarinia hartlaubii* (5)

NEWTON'S SUNBIRD *Nectarinia newtonii* (5)

CAMEROON SUNBIRD *Nectarinia oritis* (5)

BLUE-HEADED SUNBIRD *Nectarinia alinae* (5)

GREEN-HEADED SUNBIRD *Nectarinia verticalis* (5)

BANNERMAN'S SUNBIRD *Nectarinia bannermani* (5)

BLUE-THROATED BROWN SUNBIRD *Nectarinia cyanolaema* (5)

SOCOTRA SUNBIRD *Nectarinia balfouri* (5)

SEYCHELLES SUNBIRD *Nectarinia dussumieri* (5)

CARMELITE SUNBIRD *Nectarinia fuliginosa* (5)

AMETHYST SUNBIRD *Nectarinia amethystina* (5)

GREEN-THROATED SUNBIRD *Nectarinia rubescens* (5)

SCARLET-CHESTED SUNBIRD *Nectarinia senegalensis* (5)

HUNTER'S SUNBIRD *Nectarinia hunteri* (5)

BUFF-THROATED SUNBIRD *Nectarinia adelberti* (5)

PURPLE-RUMPED SUNBIRD *Nectarinia zeylonica* (4)

CRIMSON-BACKED SUNBIRD *Nectarinia minima* (4)

PURPLE-THROATED SUNBIRD *Nectarinia sperata* (4)

BLACK SUNBIRD *Nectarinia aspasia* (4, 6)

COPPER-THROATED SUNBIRD *Nectarinia calcostetha* (4)

OLIVE-BACKED SUNBIRD or YELLOW-BELLIED SUNBIRD *Nectarinia jugularis* (4, 6)

APRICOT-BREASTED SUNBIRD *Nectarinia buettikoferi* (4)

FLAME-BREASTED SUNBIRD *Nectarinia solaris* (4)

SOUIMANGA SUNBIRD *Nectarinia sovimanga* (5)

HUMBLOT'S SUNBIRD *Nectarinia humbloti* (5)

ANJOUAN SUNBIRD *Nectarinia comorensis* (5)

MAYOTTE SUNBIRD *Nectarinia coquerellii* (5)

VARIABLE SUNBIRD *Nectarinia venusta* (5)

URSULA'S SUNBIRD *Nectarinia ursulae* (5) [NT]

WHITE-BREASTED SUNBIRD *Nectarinia talatala* (5)

OUSTALET'S SUNBIRD *Nectarinia oustaleti* (5)

ORANGE-TUFTED SUNBIRD *Nectarinia bouvieri* (5)

PALESTINE SUNBIRD *Nectarinia osea* (3, 5)

PURPLE SUNBIRD *Nectarinia asiatica* (3, 4)

SHINING SUNBIRD *Nectarinia habessinica* (5)

LONG-BILLED SUNBIRD or LOTEN'S SUNBIRD *Nectarinia lotenia* (4)

MIOMBO DOUBLE-COLLARED SUNBIRD *Nectarinia manoensis* (5)

SOUTHERN DOUBLE-COLLARED SUNBIRD *Nectarinia chalybea* (5)

GREATER DOUBLE-COLLARED SUNBIRD *Nectarinia afra* (5)

MONTANE DOUBLE-COLLARED SUNBIRD *Nectarinia ludovicensis* (5)

PRIGOGINE'S DOUBLE-COLLARED SUNBIRD *Nectarinia prigoginei* (5)

STUHLMANN'S DOUBLE-COLLARED SUNBIRD *Nectarinia stuhlmanni* (5)

NORTHERN DOUBLE-COLLARED SUNBIRD *Nectarinia preussi* (5)

EASTERN DOUBLE-COLLARED SUNBIRD *Nectarinia mediocris* (5)

NEERGAARD'S SUNBIRD *Nectarinia neergaardi* (5) [NT]

OLIVE-BELLIED SUNBIRD *Nectarinia chloropygia* (5)

TINY SUNBIRD *Nectarinia minulla* (5)

REGAL SUNBIRD *Nectarinia regia* (5)

LOVERIDGE'S SUNBIRD *Nectarinia loveridgei* (5) [NT]

MOREAU'S SUNBIRD *Nectarinia moreaui* (5) [NT]

ROCKEFELLER'S SUNBIRD *Nectarinia rockefelleri* (5) [VU]

COPPER SUNBIRD *Nectarinia cuprea* (5)

DUSKY SUNBIRD *Nectarinia fusca* (5)

RUFOUS-WINGED SUNBIRD *Nectarinia rufipennis* (5) [VU]

TACAZZE SUNBIRD *Nectarinia tacazze* (5)

PURPLE-BREASTED SUNBIRD *Nectarinia purpureiventris* (5)

BOCAGE'S SUNBIRD *Nectarinia bocagii* (5)

BRONZE SUNBIRD *Nectarinia kilimensis* (5)

GOLDEN-WINGED SUNBIRD *Nectarinia reichenowi* (5)

MALACHITE SUNBIRD *Nectarinia famosa* (5)

RED-TUFTED SUNBIRD *Nectarinia johnstoni* (5)

SHELLEY'S SUNBIRD *Nectarinia shelleyi* (5)

RED-CHESTED SUNBIRD *Nectarinia erythrocerca* (5)

CONGO SUNBIRD *Nectarinia congensis* (5)

MARICO SUNBIRD or MARIQUA SUNBIRD *Nectarinia mariquensis* (5)

PURPLE-BANDED SUNBIRD *Nectarinia bifasciata* (5)

PEMBA SUNBIRD *Nectarinia pembae* (5) [NT]

VIOLET-BREASTED SUNBIRD *Nectarinia chalcomelas* (5)

LONG-BILLED GREEN SUNBIRD *Nectarinia notata* (5)

SPLENDID SUNBIRD *Nectarinia coccinigaster* (5)

JOHANNA'S SUNBIRD *Nectarinia johannae* (5)

SUPERB SUNBIRD *Nectarinia superba* (5)

BEAUTIFUL SUNBIRD *Nectarinia pulchella* (5)

BLACK-BELLIED SUNBIRD *Nectarinia nectarinioides* (5)

GRAY-HOODED SUNBIRD *Aethopyga primigenius* (4)

APO SUNBIRD *Aethopyga boltoni* (4) [NT]

FLAMING SUNBIRD *Aethopyga flagrans* (4)

METALLIC-WINGED SUNBIRD *Aethopyga pulcherrima* (4)

ELEGANT SUNBIRD *Aethopyga duyvenbodei* (4) [EN]

LOVELY SUNBIRD *Aethopyga shelleyi* (4)

GOULD'S SUNBIRD or MRS. GOULD'S SUNBIRD *Aethopyga gouldiae* (3, 4)

GREEN-TAILED SUNBIRD *Aethopyga nipalensis* (3, 4)

WHITE-FLANKED SUNBIRD *Aethopyga eximia* (4)

FORK-TAILED SUNBIRD *Aethopyga christinae* (4)

BLACK-THROATED SUNBIRD *Aethopyga saturata* (4)

CRIMSON SUNBIRD *Aethopyga siparaja* (4)

SCARLET SUNBIRD or JAVAN SUNBIRD *Aethopyga mystacalis* (4)

TEMMINCK'S SUNBIRD *Aethopyga temminckii* (4)

FIRE-TAILED SUNBIRD *Aethopyga ignicauda* (4)

LITTLE SPIDERHUNTER *Arachnothera longirostra* (4)

THICK-BILLED SPIDERHUNTER *Arachnothera crassirostris* (4)

LONG-BILLED SPIDERHUNTER *Arachnothera robusta* (4)

SPECTACLED SPIDERHUNTER *Arachnothera flavigaster* (4)

YELLOW-EARED SPIDERHUNTER *Arachnothera chrysogenys* (4)

NAKED-FACED SPIDERHUNTER *Arachnothera clarae* (4) [NT]

GRAY-BREASTED SPIDERHUNTER *Arachnothera affinis* (4)

BORNEAN SPIDERHUNTER *Arachnothera everetti* (4)

STREAKED SPIDERHUNTER *Arachnothera magna* (4)

WHITEHEAD'S SPIDERHUNTER *Arachnothera juliae* (4)

Family MELANOCHARITIDAE
Tribe MELANOCHARITINI

OBSCURE BERRYPECKER *Melanocharis arfakiana* (6) [DD]

BLACK BERRYPECKER *Melanocharis nigra* (6)

LEMON-BREASTED BERRYPECKER *Melanocharis longicauda* (6)

FAN-TAILED BERRYPECKER *Melanocharis versteri* (6)

STREAKED BERRYPECKER *Melanocharis striativentris* (6)

SPOTTED BERRYPECKER *Melanocharis crassirostris* (6)

Tribe TOXORHAMPHINI

GREEN-CROWNED LONGBILL *Toxorhamphus novaeguineae* (6)

GRAY-WINGED LONGBILL *Toxorhamphus poliopterus* (6)

PLUMED LONGBILL *Toxorhamphus iliolophus* (6)

PYGMY LONGBILL *Oedistoma pygmaeum* (6)

Family PARAMYTHIIDAE

TIT BERRYPECKER *Oreocharis arfaki* (6)

CRESTED BERRYPECKER *Paramythia montium* (6)

Family PASSERIDAE
Subfamily PASSERINAE

SAXAUL SPARROW *Passer ammodendri* (3, 4)

HOUSE SPARROW *Passer domesticus* (1, 2, 3, 4, 5, 6)

SPANISH SPARROW or WILLOW SPARROW *Passer hispaniolensis* (3, 4, 5)

SIND SPARROW *Passer pyrrhonotus* (4)

SOMALI SPARROW *Passer castanopterus* (5)

RUSSET SPARROW *Passer rutilans* (3, 4)

PLAIN-BACKED SPARROW *Passer flaveolus* (4)

DEAD SEA SPARROW *Passer moabiticus* (3, 4)

IAGO SPARROW *Passer iagoensis* (5)

KENYA RUFOUS-SPARROW *Passer rufocinctus* (5)

SOCOTRA SPARROW *Passer insularis* (5)

SOUTHERN RUFOUS-SPARROW *Passer motitensis* (5)

CAPE SPARROW *Passer melanurus* (5)

GRAY-HEADED SPARROW *Passer griseus* (5)

SWAINSON'S SPARROW *Passer swainsonii* (5)

PARROT-BILLED SPARROW *Passer gongonensis* (5)

SWAHILI SPARROW *Passer suahelicus* (5)

SOUTHERN GRAY-HEADED SPARROW *Passer diffusus* (5)

DESERT SPARROW *Passer simplex* (5)

ASIAN DESERT SPARROW *Passer zarudnyi* (3)

EURASIAN TREE SPARROW *Passer montanus* (1, 3, 4, 5, 6)

SUDAN GOLDEN-SPARROW *Passer luteus* (5)

ARABIAN GOLDEN-SPARROW *Passer euchlorus* (5)

CHESTNUT SPARROW *Passer eminibey* (5)

YELLOW-SPOTTED PETRONIA *Petronia pyrgita* (5)

CHESTNUT-SHOULDERED PETRONIA *Petronia xanthocollis* (3, 4)

YELLOW-THROATED PETRONIA *Petronia superciliaris* (5)

BUSH PETRONIA *Petronia dentata* (5)

ROCK SPARROW PETRONIA *petronia* (3, 4, 5)

PALE ROCKFINCH *Carpospiza brachydactyla* (3, 5)

WHITE-WINGED SNOWFINCH *Montifringilla nivalis* (3, 4)

BLACK-WINGED SNOWFINCH or TIBETAN SNOWFINCH *Montifringilla adamsi* (3, 4)

WHITE-RUMPED SNOWFINCH *Montifringilla taczanowskii* (3, 4)

SMALL SNOWFINCH *Montifringilla davidiana* (3, 4)

RUFOUS-NECKED SNOWFINCH *Montifringilla ruficollis* (3, 4)

PLAIN-BACKED SNOWFINCH *Montifringilla blanfordi* (3, 4)

AFGHAN SNOWFINCH *Montifringilla theresae* (3)

Subfamily MOTACILLINAE

FOREST WAGTAIL *Dendronanthus indicus* (3, 4)

WHITE WAGTAIL *Motacilla alba* (1, 3, 4, 5, 6)

BLACK-BACKED WAGTAIL *Motacilla lugens* (1, 3, 4, 6)

JAPANESE WAGTAIL *Motacilla grandis* (3)

WHITE-BROWED WAGTAIL *Motacilla madaraspatensis* (3, 4)

AFRICAN PIED WAGTAIL *Motacilla aguimp* (5)

CAPE WAGTAIL *Motacilla capensis* (5)

MADAGASCAR WAGTAIL *Motacilla flaviventris* (5)

CITRINE WAGTAIL *Motacilla citreola* (3, 4)

YELLOW WAGTAIL *Motacilla flava* (1, 3, 4, 5, 6)

GRAY WAGTAIL *Motacilla cinerea* (3, 4, 5, 6)

MOUNTAIN WAGTAIL *Motacilla clara* (5)

GOLDEN PIPIT *Tmetothylacus tenellus* (5)

YELLOW-THROATED LONGCLAW *Macronyx croceus* (5)

FUELLEBORN'S LONGCLAW *Macronyx fuellebornii* (5)

CAPE LONGCLAW *Macronyx capensis* (5)

ABYSSINIAN LONGCLAW *Macronyx flavicollis* (5) [NT]

SHARPE'S PIPIT *Macronyx sharpei* (5) [NT]

ROSY-THROATED LONGCLAW *Macronyx ameliae* (5)

PANGANI LONGCLAW *Macronyx aurantiigula* (5)

GRIMWOOD'S LONGCLAW *Macronyx grimwoodi* (5) [NT]

LONG-TAILED PIPIT *Anthus longicaudatus* (5)

YELLOW-BREASTED PIPIT *Anthus chloris* (5) [VU]

STRIPED PIPIT *Anthus lineiventris* (5)

YELLOW-TUFTED PIPIT *Anthus crenatus* (5)

AFRICAN PIPIT *Anthus cinnamomeus* (5)

CAMEROON PIPIT *Anthus camaroonensis* (5)

MOUNTAIN PIPIT *Anthus hoeschi* (5) [NT]

RICHARD'S PIPIT *Anthus richardi* (3, 4, 5)

PADDYFIELD PIPIT *Anthus rufulus* (3, 4)

AUSTRALASIAN PIPIT *Anthus novaeseelandiae* (6)

PLAIN-BACKED PIPIT *Anthus leucophrys* (5)

BUFFY PIPIT *Anthus vaalensis* (5)

LONG-LEGGED PIPIT *Anthus pallidiventris* (5)

MALINDI PIPIT *Anthus melindae* (5) [NT]

TAWNY PIPIT *Anthus campestris* (3, 4, 5)

BERTHELOT'S PIPIT *Anthus berthelotii* (5)

BLYTH'S PIPIT *Anthus godlewskii* (3, 4)

BANNERMAN'S PIPIT *Anthus bannermani* (5)

JACKSON'S PIPIT *Anthus latistriatus* (5)

LONG-BILLED PIPIT *Anthus similis* (3, 4, 5)

WOODLAND PIPIT *Anthus nyassae* (5)

SHORT-TAILED PIPIT *Anthus brachyurus* (5)

BUSH PIPIT *Anthus caffer* (5)

SOKOKE PIPIT *Anthus sokokensis* (5) [VU]

TREE PIPIT *Anthus trivialis* (3, 4, 5)

Olive-Backed Pipit *Anthus hodgsoni* (3, 4)

Pechora Pipit *Anthus gustavi* (3, 4)

Meadow Pipit *Anthus pratensis* (3, 5)

Red-Throated Pipit *Anthus cervinus* (1, 3, 4, 5)

Rosy Pipit *Anthus roseatus* (3, 4)

Rock Pipit *Anthus petrosus* (3)

Water Pipit *Anthus spinoletta* (3, 4, 5)

American Pipit or Buff-Bellied Pipit *Anthus rubescens* (1, 2, 3)

Upland Pipit *Anthus sylvanus* (3, 4)

Nilgiri Pipit *Anthus nilghiriensis* (4)

Correndera Pipit *Anthus correndera* (2)

South Georgia Pipit *Anthus antarcticus* (2)

Sprague's Pipit *Anthus spragueii* (1)

Short-Billed Pipit *Anthus furcatus* (2)

Hellmayr's Pipit *Anthus hellmayri* (2)

Paramo Pipit *Anthus bogotensis* (2)

Yellowish Pipit *Anthus lutescens* (2)

Chaco Pipit *Anthus chacoensis* (2) [NT]

Ocher-Breasted Pipit *Anthus nattereri* (2) [EN]

Alpine Pipit *Anthus gutturalis* (6)

Subfamily PRUNELLINAE

Alpine Accentor *Prunella collaris* (3, 4)

Rufous-Streaked Accentor or Altai Accentor *Prunella himalayana* (3, 4)

Robin Accentor *Prunella rubeculoides* (3, 4)

Rufous-Breasted Accentor *Prunella strophiata* (3, 4)

Siberian Accentor *Prunella montanella* (3, 4)

Radde's Accentor *Prunella ocularis* (3)

Yemen Accentor *Prunella fagani* (3) [NT]

Brown Accentor *Prunella fulvescens* (3, 4)

Black-Throated Accentor *Prunella atrogularis* (3)

Mongolian Accentor *Prunella koslowi* (4)

Hedge Accentor *Prunella modularis* (3, 4)

Japanese Accentor *Prunella rubida* (3)

Maroon-Backed Accentor *Prunella immaculata* (3, 4)

Subfamily PLOCEINAE

White-Billed Buffalo-Weaver *Bubalornis albirostris* (5)

Red-Billed Buffalo-Weaver *Bubalornis niger* (5)

White-Headed Buffalo-Weaver *Dinemellia dinemelli* (5)

Speckle-Fronted Weaver *Sporopipes frontalis* (5)

Scaly Weaver *Sporopipes squamifrons* (5)

White-Browed Sparrow-Weaver *Plocepasser mahali* (5)

Chestnut-Crowned Sparrow-Weaver *Plocepasser superciliosus* (5)

Chestnut-Backed Sparrow-Weaver *Plocepasser rufoscapulatus* (5)

Donaldson-Smith's Sparrow-Weaver *Plocepasser donaldsoni* (5)

Rufous-Tailed Weaver *Histurgops ruficauda* (5)

Gray-Headed Social-Weaver *Pseudonigrita arnaudi* (5)

Black-Capped Social-Weaver *Pseudonigrita cabanisi* (5)

Social Weaver *Philetairus socius* (5)

Bannerman's Weaver *Ploceus bannermani* (5) [VU]

Bates's Weaver *Ploceus batesi* (5) [VU]

Black-Chinned Weaver *Ploceus nigrimentum* (5) [VU]

Baglafecht Weaver *Ploceus baglafecht* (5)

Bertrand's Weaver *Ploceus bertrandi* (5)

Slender-Billed Weaver *Ploceus pelzelni* (5)

Loango Weaver *Ploceus subpersonatus* (5) [VU]

LITTLE WEAVER *Ploceus luteolus* (5)

LESSER MASKED WEAVER *Ploceus intermedius* (5)

SPECTACLED WEAVER *Ploceus ocularis* (5)

BLACK-NECKED WEAVER *Ploceus nigricollis* (5)

BLACK-BILLED WEAVER *Ploceus melanogaster* (5)

STRANGE WEAVER *Ploceus alienus* (5)

BOCAGE'S WEAVER *Ploceus temporalis* (5)

CAPE WEAVER *Ploceus capensis* (5)

AFRICAN GOLDEN-WEAVER *Ploceus subaureus* (5)

HOLUB'S GOLDEN-WEAVER *Ploceus xanthops* (5)

PRINCIPE GOLDEN-WEAVER *Ploceus princeps* (5)

ORANGE WEAVER *Ploceus aurantius* (5)

GOLDEN PALM WEAVER *Ploceus bojeri* (5)

TAVETA GOLDEN-WEAVER *Ploceus castanei-ceps* (5)

SOUTHERN BROWN-THROATED WEAVER *Ploceus xanthopterus* (5)

NORTHERN BROWN-THROATED WEAVER *Ploceus castanops* (5)

KILOMBERO WEAVER *Ploceus burnieri* (5) [VU]

RUEPPELL'S WEAVER *Ploceus galbula* (5)

HEUGLIN'S MASKED-WEAVER *Ploceus heuglini* (5)

NORTHERN MASKED-WEAVER *Ploceus tae-niopterus* (5)

VITELLINE MASKED-WEAVER *Ploceus vitellinus* (5)

SOUTHERN MASKED-WEAVER *Ploceus velatus* (5)

KATANGA MASKED-WEAVER *Ploceus katangae* (5)

RUWET'S MASKED-WEAVER or LAKE LUFIRA WEAVER *Ploceus ruweti* (5) [VU]

TANZANIA MASKED-WEAVER *Ploceus reichardi* (5)

VILLAGE WEAVER *Ploceus cucullatus* (2, 5)

GIANT WEAVER *Ploceus grandis* (5)

SPEKE'S WEAVER *Ploceus spekei* (5)

FOX'S WEAVER *Ploceus spekeoides* (5) [NT]

VIEILLOT'S BLACK WEAVER *Ploceus nigerrimus* (5)

WEYNS'S WEAVER *Ploceus weynsi* (5)

CLARKE'S WEAVER *Ploceus golandi* (5) [VU]

BLACK-HEADED WEAVER *Ploceus melanocephalus* (5)

VICTORIA MASKED-WEAVER *Ploceus victoriae* (5) [DD]

JUBA WEAVER or SALVADORI'S WEAVER *Ploceus dicrocephalus* (5)

GOLDEN-BACKED WEAVER *Ploceus jacksoni* (5)

CINNAMON WEAVER *Ploceus badius* (5)

CHESTNUT WEAVER *Ploceus rubiginosus* (5)

GOLDEN-NAPED WEAVER *Ploceus aureonucha* (5) [VU]

YELLOW-MANTLED WEAVER *Ploceus tricolor* (5)

MAXWELL'S BLACK WEAVER *Ploceus albinucha* (5)

NELICOURVI WEAVER *Ploceus nelicourvi* (5)

SAKALAVA WEAVER *Ploceus sakalava* (5)

BLACK-BREASTED WEAVER *Ploceus benghalen-sis* (4)

STREAKED WEAVER *Ploceus manyar* (3, 4)

BAYA WEAVER *Ploceus philippinus* (3, 4)

ASIAN GOLDEN-WEAVER *Ploceus hypoxanthus* (4) [NT]

YELLOW WEAVER or FINN'S WEAVER *Ploceus megarhynchus* (3) [VU]

FOREST WEAVER *Ploceus bicolor* (5)

PREUSS'S WEAVER *Ploceus preussi* (5)

YELLOW-CAPPED WEAVER *Ploceus dorsomacu-latus* (5)

USAMBARA WEAVER or TANZANIAN MOUNTAIN WEAVER *Ploceus nicolli* (5) [VU]

OLIVE-HEADED WEAVER *Ploceus olivaceiceps* (5)

BROWN-CAPPED WEAVER *Ploceus insignis* (5)

BAR-WINGED WEAVER *Ploceus angolensis* (5)

SÃO TOMÉ WEAVER *Ploceus sanctithomae* (5)

COMPACT WEAVER *Pachyphantes superciliosus* (5)

YELLOW-LEGGED MALIMBE or YELLOW-LEGGED WEAVER *Malimbus flavipes* (5) [VU]

RED-CROWNED MALIMBE *Malimbus coronatus* (5)

BLACK-THROATED MALIMBE *Malimbus cassini* (5)

BALLMANN'S MALIMBE or GOLA MALIMBE *Malimbus ballmanni* (5) [EN]

RACHEL'S MALIMBE *Malimbus racheliae* (5)

RED-VENTED MALIMBE *Malimbus scutatus* (5)

IBADAN MALIMBE *Malimbus ibadanensis* (5) [CR]

RED-BELLIED MALIMBE *Malimbus erythrogaster* (5)

GRAY'S MALIMBE *Malimbus nitens* (5)

CRESTED MALIMBE *Malimbus malimbicus* (5)

RED-HEADED MALIMBE *Malimbus rubricollis* (5)

RED-HEADED WEAVER *Anaplectes rubriceps* (5)

BOB-TAILED WEAVER *Brachycope anomala* (5)

CARDINAL QUELEA *Quelea cardinalis* (5)

RED-HEADED QUELEA *Quelea erythrops* (5)

RED-BILLED QUELEA *Quelea quelea* (5)

MADAGASCAR RED FODY *Foudia madagascariensis* (5)

RED-HEADED FODY *Foudia eminentissima* (5)

FOREST FODY *Foudia omissa* (5)

MAURITIUS FODY *Foudia rubra* (5) [CR]

SEYCHELLES FODY *Foudia sechellarum* (5) [VU]

YELLOW FODY or RODRIGUES FODY *Foudia flavicans* (5) [VU]

YELLOW-CROWNED BISHOP *Euplectes afer* (2, 5)

FIRE-FRONTED BISHOP *Euplectes diadematus* (5)

BLACK BISHOP *Euplectes gierowii* (5)

BLACK-WINGED BISHOP *Euplectes hordeaceus* (5)

ORANGE BISHOP *Euplectes franciscanus* (2, 5)

RED BISHOP *Euplectes orix* (5)

ZANZIBAR BISHOP *Euplectes nigroventris* (5)

GOLDEN-BACKED BISHOP *Euplectes aureus* (5) [NT]

YELLOW BISHOP *Euplectes capensis* (5)

FAN-TAILED WIDOWBIRD *Euplectes axillaris* (5)

YELLOW-SHOULDERED WIDOWBIRD *Euplectes macrourus* (5)

WHITE-WINGED WIDOWBIRD *Euplectes albonotatus* (5)

RED-COLLARED WIDOWBIRD *Euplectes ardens* (5)

MARSH WIDOWBIRD *Euplectes hartlaubi* (5)

BUFF-SHOULDERED WIDOWBIRD *Euplectes psammocromius* (5)

LONG-TAILED WIDOWBIRD *Euplectes progne* (5)

JACKSON'S WIDOWBIRD *Euplectes jacksoni* (5) [NT]

PARASITIC WEAVER *Anomalospiza imberbis* (5)

GROSBEAK WEAVER *Amblyospiza albifrons* (5)

Subfamily ESTRILDINAE
Tribe ESTRILDINI

RED-FRONTED ANTPECKER *Parmoptila rubrifrons* (5)

WOODHOUSE'S ANTPECKER or RED-HEADED ANTPECKER *Parmoptila woodhousei* (5)

WHITE-BREASTED NEGROFINCH *Nigrita fusconota* (5)

CHESTNUT-BREASTED NEGROFINCH *Nigrita bicolor* (5)

PALE-FRONTED NEGROFINCH *Nigrita luteifrons* (5)

GRAY-HEADED NEGROFINCH *Nigrita canicapilla* (5)

FERNANDO PO OLIVEBACK *Nesocharis shelleyi* (5)

WHITE-COLLARED OLIVEBACK *Nesocharis ansorgei* (5)

GRAY-HEADED OLIVEBACK *Nesocharis capistrata* (5)

RED-WINGED PYTILIA *Pytilia phoenicoptera* (5)

LINEATED PYTILIA *Pytilia lineata* (5)

ORANGE-WINGED PYTILIA *Pytilia afra* (5)

GREEN-WINGED PYTILIA *Pytilia melba* (5)

RED-FACED PYTILIA *Pytilia hypogrammica* (5)

GREEN-BACKED TWINSPOT *Mandingoa nitidula* (5)

RED-FACED CRIMSON-WING *Cryptospiza reichenovii* (5)

ABYSSINIAN CRIMSON-WING *Cryptospiza salvadorii* (5)

DUSKY CRIMSON-WING *Cryptospiza jacksoni* (5)

SHELLEY'S CRIMSON-WING *Cryptospiza shelleyi* (5) [VU]

CRIMSON SEEDCRACKER *Pyrenestes sanguineus* (5)

BLACK-BELLIED SEEDCRACKER *Pyrenestes ostrinus* (5)

LESSER SEEDCRACKER *Pyrenestes minor* (5)

GRANT'S BLUEBILL *Spermophaga poliogenys* (5)

WESTERN BLUEBILL *Spermophaga haematina* (5)

RED-HEADED BLUEBILL *Spermophaga ruficapilla* (5)

BROWN TWINSPOT *Clytospiza monteiri* (5)

PETERS'S TWINSPOT *Hypargos niveoguttatus* (5)

PINK-THROATED TWINSPOT *Hypargos margaritatus* (5)

DYBOWSKI'S TWINSPOT *Euschistospiza dybowskii* (5)

DUSKY TWINSPOT *Euschistospiza cinereovinacea* (5)

BROWN FIREFINCH *Lagonosticta rufopicta* (5)

RED-BILLED FIREFINCH *Lagonosticta senegala* (5)

BLACK-BELLIED FIREFINCH *Lagonosticta rara* (5)

AFRICAN FIREFINCH *Lagonosticta rubricata* (5)

PALE-BILLED FIREFINCH *Lagonosticta landanae* (5)

MALI FIREFINCH *Lagonosticta virata* (5) [NT]

REICHENOW'S FIREFINCH *Lagonosticta umbrinodorsalis* (5)

JAMESON'S FIREFINCH *Lagonosticta rhodopareia* (5)

BLACK-THROATED FIREFINCH *Lagonosticta larvata* (5)

BLUE-BREASTED CORDONBLEU *Uraeginthus angolensis* (5)

RED-CHEEKED CORDONBLEU *Uraeginthus bengalus* (2, 5)

BLUE-CAPPED CORDONBLEU *Uraeginthus cyanocephalus* (5)

PURPLE GRENADIER *Uraeginthus ianthinogaster* (5)

COMMON GRENADIER *Uraeginthus granatina* (5)

LAVENDER WAXBILL *Estrilda caerulescens* (2, 5)

BLACK-TAILED WAXBILL *Estrilda perreini* (5)

CINDERELLA WAXBILL *Estrilda thomensis* (5) [NT]

YELLOW-BELLIED WAXBILL *Estrilda quartinia* (5)

SWEE WAXBILL *Estrilda melanotis* (5)

ANAMBRA WAXBILL *Estrilda poliopareia* (5) [VU]

FAWN-BREASTED WAXBILL *Estrilda paludicola* (5)

ABYSSINIAN WAXBILL *Estrilda ochrogaster* (5)

ORANGE-CHEEKED WAXBILL *Estrilda melpoda* (2, 3, 5)

CRIMSON-RUMPED WAXBILL *Estrilda rhodopyga* (5)

ARABIAN WAXBILL *Estrilda rufibarba* (3)

BLACK-RUMPED WAXBILL *Estrilda troglodytes* (2, 5)

COMMON WAXBILL *Estrilda astrild* (2, 4, 5, 6)

BLACK-FACED WAXBILL or BLACK-LORED WAXBILL *Estrilda nigriloris* (5) [VU]

BLACK-CROWNED WAXBILL *Estrilda nonnula* (5)

BLACK-HEADED WAXBILL *Estrilda atricapilla* (5)

KANDT'S WAXBILL *Estrilda kandti* (5)

RED-RUMPED WAXBILL *Estrilda charmosyna* (5)

BLACK-CHEEKED WAXBILL *Estrilda erythronotos* (5)

RED AVADAVAT *Amandava amandava* (2, 3, 4)

GREEN AVADAVAT *Amandava formosa* (4) [VU]

ZEBRA WAXBILL *Amandava subflava* (3, 5)

AFRICAN QUAILFINCH *Ortygospiza atricollis* (5)

RED-BILLED QUAILFINCH *Ortygospiza gabonensis* (5)

LOCUSTFINCH *Ortygospiza locustella* (5)

PAINTED FIRETAIL or PAINTED FINCH *Emblema pictum* (6)

BEAUTIFUL FIRETAIL *Stagonopleura bella* (6)

RED-EARED FIRETAIL *Stagonopleura oculata* (6) [NT]

DIAMOND FIRETAIL *Stagonopleura guttata* (6)

MOUNTAIN FIRETAIL *Oreostruthus fuliginosus* (6)

RED-BROWED FIRETAIL *Neochmia temporalis* (4, 6)

CRIMSON FINCH *Neochmia phaeton* (6)

STAR FINCH *Neochmia ruficauda* (6) [VU]

PLUM-HEADED FINCH *Neochmia modesta* (6)

ZEBRA FINCH *Taeniopygia guttata* (4)

CHESTNUT-EARED FINCH *Taeniopygia castanotis* (6)

DOUBLE-BARRED FINCH *Taeniopygia bichenovii* (6)

MASKED FINCH *Poephila personata* (6)

LONG-TAILED FINCH *Poephila acuticauda* (6)

BLACK-THROATED FINCH *Poephila cincta* (6)

TAWNY-BREASTED PARROTFINCH *Erythrura hyperythra* (4)

PIN-TAILED PARROTFINCH *Erythrura prasina* (4)

GREEN-FACED PARROTFINCH *Erythrura viridifacies* (4) [EN]

TRICOLORED PARROTFINCH *Erythrura tricolor* (4)

BLUE-FACED PARROTFINCH *Erythrura trichroa* (4, 6)

RED-EARED PARROTFINCH *Erythrura coloria* (4) [VU]

PAPUAN PARROTFINCH *Erythrura papuana* (6)

RED-THROATED PARROTFINCH *Erythrura psittacea* (6)

FIJI PARROTFINCH *Erythrura pealii* (4)

RED-HEADED PARROTFINCH *Erythrura cyaneovirens* (6)

ROYAL PARROTFINCH *Erythrura regia* (4) [VU]

PINK-BILLED PARROTFINCH *Erythrura kleinschmidti* (6) [EN]

GOULDIAN FINCH *Erythrura gouldiae* (6) [EN]

MADAGASCAR MUNIA *Lemuresthes nana* (5)

GRAY-HEADED SILVERBILL *Spermestes caniceps* (5)

BRONZE MUNIA *Spermestes cucullatus* (2, 5)

BLACK-AND-WHITE MUNIA *Spermestes bicolor* (5)

MAGPIE MUNIA *Spermestes fringilloides* (5)

AFRICAN SILVERBILL *Lonchura cantans* (2, 5)

WHITE-THROATED SILVERBILL or INDIAN SILVERBILL *Lonchura malabarica* (3, 4)

WHITE-RUMPED MUNIA *Lonchura striata* (3, 4)

JAVAN MUNIA *Lonchura leucogastroides* (4)

DUSKY MUNIA *Lonchura fuscans* (4)

BLACK-FACED MUNIA *Lonchura molucca* (4)

BLACK-THROATED MUNIA *Lonchura kelaarti* (4)

SCALY-BREASTED MUNIA or NUTMEG MANNIKIN *Lonchura punctulata* (2, 4, 5, 6)

WHITE-BELLIED MUNIA *Lonchura leucogastra* (4)

STREAK-HEADED MUNIA *Lonchura tristissima* (6)

WHITE-SPOTTED MUNIA *Lonchura leucosticta* (6)

INDIAN BLACK-HEADED MUNIA *Lonchura malacca* (4)

SOUTHERN BLACK-HEADED MUNIA *Lonchura atricapilla* (2, 4, 6)

WHITE-CAPPED MUNIA *Lonchura ferruginosa* (4)

FIVE-COLORED MUNIA *Lonchura quinticolor* (4)

WHITE-HEADED MUNIA *Lonchura maja* (4)

PALE-HEADED MUNIA *Lonchura pallida* (4)

GRAND MUNIA *Lonchura grandis* (6)

GRAY-BANDED MUNIA *Lonchura vana* (6) [VU]

GRAY-HEADED MUNIA *Lonchura caniceps* (6)

GRAY-CROWNED MUNIA *Lonchura nevermanni* (6) [NT]

HOODED MUNIA *Lonchura spectabilis* (6)

MOTTLED MUNIA *Lonchura hunsteini* (6)

NEW IRELAND MUNIA *Lonchura forbesi* (6)

NEW HANOVER MUNIA *Lonchura nigerrima* (6)

YELLOW-RUMPED MUNIA or YELLOW-RUMPED MANNIKIN *Lonchura flaviprymna* (6) [NT]

CHESTNUT-BREASTED MUNIA or CHESTNUT-BREASTED MANNIKIN *Lonchura castaneothorax* (6)

BLACK MUNIA *Lonchura stygia* (6) [NT]

BLACK-BREASTED MUNIA *Lonchura teerinki* (6)

SNOW MOUNTAIN MUNIA *Lonchura montana* (6)

ALPINE MUNIA *Lonchura monticola* (6)

BISMARCK MUNIA *Lonchura melaena* (6)

JAVA SPARROW *Lonchura oryzivora* (2, 3, 4) [VU]

TIMOR SPARROW *Lonchura fuscata* (4) [NT]

PICTORELLA MUNIA or PICTORELLA MANNIKIN *Heteromunia pectoralis* (6) [NT]

CUT-THROAT *Amadina fasciata* (5)

RED-HEADED FINCH *Amadina erythrocephala* (5)

Tribe VIDUINI

VILLAGE INDIGOBIRD *Vidua chalybeata* (5)

CAMEROON INDIGOBIRD *Vidua camerunensis* (5)

BLACK-FACED FIREFINCH INDIGOBIRD *Vidua larvaticola* (5)

VARIABLE INDIGOBIRD *Vidua funerea* (5)

JOS PLATEAU INDIGOBIRD *Vidua maryae* (5)

QUAILFINCH INDIGOBIRD *Vidua nigeriae* (5)

GOLDBREAST INDIGOBIRD *Vidua raricola* (5)

GREEN INDIGOBIRD or PETER'S TWINSPOT INDIGOBIRD *Vidua codringtoni* (5)

DUSKY INDIGOBIRD *Vidua purpurascens* (5)

PALE-WINGED INDIGOBIRD or BAR-BREASTED FIREFINCH INDIGOBIRD *Vidua wilsoni* (5)

STEEL-BLUE WHYDAH *Vidua hypocherina* (5)

STRAW-TAILED WHYDAH *Vidua fischeri* (5)

QUEEN WHYDAH or SHAFT-TAILED WHYDAH *Vidua regia* (5)

PIN-TAILED WHYDAH *Vidua macroura* (5)

NORTHERN PARADISE-WHYDAH *Vidua orientalis* (5)

TOGO PARADISE-WHYDAH *Vidua togoensis* (5)

LONG-TAILED PARADISE-WHYDAH *Vidua interjecta* (5)

EASTERN PARADISE-WHYDAH *Vidua paradisaea* (5)

BROAD-TAILED PARADISE-WHYDAH *Vidua obtusa* (5)

Family FRINGILLIDAE
Subfamily PEUCEDRAMINAE

OLIVE WARBLER *Peucedramus taeniatus* (1, 2)

Subfamily FRINGILLINAE
Tribe FRINGILLINI

CHAFFINCH *Fringilla coelebs* (3, 4, 5, 6)

BLUE CHAFFINCH *Fringilla teydea* (5) [CD]

BRAMBLING *Fringilla montifringilla* (1, 3, 4)

Tribe CARDUELINI

FIRE-FRONTED SERIN *Serinus pusillus* (4)

EUROPEAN SERIN *Serinus serinus* (3, 5)

SYRIAN SERIN *Serinus syriacus* (3, 5)

ISLAND CANARY *Serinus canaria* (2, 5)

CITRIL FINCH *Serinus citrinella* (3)

TIBETAN SERIN *Serinus thibetanus* (3, 4)

CAPE CANARY *Serinus canicollis* (5)

ABYSSINIAN SISKIN *Serinus nigriceps* (5)

WESTERN CITRIL *Serinus frontalis* (5)

AFRICAN CITRIL *Serinus citrinelloides* (5)

EAST AFRICAN CITRIL *Serinus hypostictus* (5)

BLACK-FACED CANARY *Serinus capistratus* (5)

PAPYRUS CANARY *Serinus koliensis* (5)

FOREST CANARY *Serinus scotops* (5)

WHITE-RUMPED SEEDEATER *Serinus leucopygius* (5)

OLIVE-RUMPED SERIN *Serinus rothschildi* (3)

YELLOW-THROATED SEEDEATER or YELLOW-THROATED SERIN *Serinus flavigula* (5) [EN]

SALVADORI'S SEEDEATER *Serinus xantholaemus* (5) [VU]

ABYSSINIAN YELLOW-RUMPED SEEDEATER *Serinus xanthopygius* (5)

BLACK-THROATED CANARY *Serinus atrogularis* (5)

KENYA YELLOW-RUMPED SEEDEATER *Serinus reichenowi* (5)

LEMON-BREASTED SEEDEATER *Serinus citrinipectus* (5)

YELLOW-FRONTED CANARY *Serinus mozambicus* (2, 5)

ABYSSINIAN GROSBEAK-CANARY *Serinus donaldsoni* (5)

KENYA GROSBEAK-CANARY *Serinus buchanani* (5)

WHITE-BELLIED CANARY *Serinus dorsostriatus* (5)

YELLOW CANARY *Serinus flaviventris* (5)

BRIMSTONE CANARY or BULLY CANARY *Serinus sulphuratus* (5)

WHITE-THROATED CANARY *Serinus albogularis* (5)

WEST AFRICAN SEEDEATER *Serinus canicapillus* (5)

REICHARD'S SEEDEATER *Serinus reichardi* (5)

STREAKY-HEADED SEEDEATER *Serinus gularis* (5)

BLACK-EARED SEEDEATER *Serinus mennelli* (5)

BROWN-RUMPED SEEDEATER *Serinus tristriatus* (5)

YEMEN SERIN *Serinus menachensis* (3)

ANKOBER SERIN *Serinus ankoberensis* (5) [EN]

STREAKY SEEDEATER *Serinus striolatus* (5)

THICK-BILLED SEEDEATER *Serinus burtoni* (5)

PRINCIPE SEEDEATER *Serinus rufobrunneus* (5)

KIPENGERE SEEDEATER *Serinus melanochrous* (5) [NT]

PROTEA SEEDEATER or WHITE-WINGED SEEDEATER *Serinus leucopterus* (5) [NT]

CAPE SISKIN *Serinus totta* (5) [NT]

DRAKENSBERG SISKIN *Serinus symonsi* (5) [NT]

BLACK-HEADED CANARY *Serinus alario* (5)

MOUNTAIN SERIN *Serinus estherae* (4)

SÃO TOMÉ GROSBEAK *Neospiza concolor* (5) [CR]

ORIOLE FINCH *Linurgus olivaceus* (5)

GOLDEN-WINGED GROSBEAK *Rhynchostruthus socotranus* (3)

EUROPEAN GREENFINCH *Carduelis chloris* (3, 5, 6)

GRAY-CAPPED GREENFINCH *Carduelis sinica* (1, 3, 4)

YELLOW-BREASTED GREENFINCH *Carduelis spinoides* (4)

BLACK-HEADED GREENFINCH *Carduelis ambigua* (4)

VIETNAMESE GREENFINCH *Carduelis monguilloti* (4) [NT]

EURASIAN SISKIN *Carduelis spinus* (1, 3, 4)

PINE SISKIN *Carduelis pinus* (1, 2)

BLACK-CAPPED SISKIN *Carduelis atriceps* (1, 2) [NT]

ANDEAN SISKIN *Carduelis spinescens* (2)

YELLOW-FACED SISKIN *Carduelis yarrellii* (2) [VU]

RED SISKIN *Carduelis cucullata* (2) [EN]

THICK-BILLED SISKIN *Carduelis crassirostris* (2)

HOODED SISKIN *Carduelis magellanica* (2)

SAFFRON SISKIN *Carduelis siemiradzkii* (2) [VU]

OLIVACEOUS SISKIN *Carduelis olivacea* (2)

BLACK-HEADED SISKIN *Carduelis notata* (1, 2)

BLACK-CHINNED SISKIN *Carduelis barbata* (2)

YELLOW-BELLIED SISKIN *Carduelis xanthogastra* (2)

BLACK SISKIN *Carduelis atrata* (2)

YELLOW-RUMPED SISKIN *Carduelis uropygialis* (2)

AMERICAN GOLDFINCH *Carduelis tristis* (1)

LESSER GOLDFINCH *Carduelis psaltria* (1, 2)

LAWRENCE'S GOLDFINCH *Carduelis lawrencei* (1)

ANTILLEAN SISKIN *Carduelis dominicensis* (2)

EUROPEAN GOLDFINCH *Carduelis carduelis* (2, 3, 4, 5)

HOARY REDPOLL *Carduelis hornemanni* (1, 3)

COMMON REDPOLL *Carduelis flammea* (1, 3, 6)

TWITE *Carduelis flavirostris* (3, 4)

EURASIAN LINNET *Carduelis xannabina* (3, 4, 5)

YEMEN LINNET *Carduelis yemenensis* (3)

WARSANGLI LINNET *Carduelis johannis* (5) [EN]

PLAIN MOUNTAIN-FINCH *Leucosticte nemoricola* (3, 4)

BLACK-HEADED MOUNTAIN-FINCH or BRANDT'S MOUNTAIN-FINCH *Leucosticte brandti* (3, 4)

SILLEM'S MOUNTAIN-FINCH *Leucosticte sillemi* (4) [DD]

ASIAN ROSY-FINCH *Leucosticte arctoa* (3, 4)

GRAY-CROWNED ROSY-FINCH *Leucosticte tephrocotis* (1)

BLACK ROSY-FINCH *Leucosticte atrata* (1)

BROWN-CAPPED ROSY-FINCH *Leucosticte australis* (1)

SPECTACLED FINCH *Callacanthis burtoni* (3)

CRIMSON-WINGED FINCH *Rhodopechys sanguinea* (3)

TRUMPETER FINCH *Rhodopechys githaginea* (3, 4, 5)

MONGOLIAN FINCH *Rhodopechys mongolica* (3, 4)

DESERT FINCH *Rhodopechys obsoleta* (3, 4)

LONG-TAILED ROSEFINCH *Uragus sibiricus* (3, 4)

CRIMSON ROSEFINCH or BLANFORD'S ROSEFINCH *Carpodacus rubescens* (3, 4)

DARK-BREASTED ROSEFINCH *Carpodacus nipalensis* (3, 4)

COMMON ROSEFINCH *Carpodacus erythrinus* (3, 4, 5)

PURPLE FINCH *Carpodacus purpureus* (1)

CASSIN'S FINCH *Carpodacus cassinii* (1)

HOUSE FINCH *Carpodacus mexicanus* (1, 2)

BEAUTIFUL ROSEFINCH *Carpodacus pulcherrimus* (3, 4)

PINK-RUMPED ROSEFINCH *Carpodacus eos* (3, 4)

PINK-BROWED ROSEFINCH *Carpodacus rodochrous* (3)

VINACEOUS ROSEFINCH *Carpodacus vinaceus* (3, 4)

DARK-RUMPED ROSEFINCH *Carpodacus edwardsii* (3, 4)

PALE ROSEFINCH *Carpodacus synoicus* (3, 4)

PALLAS'S ROSEFINCH *Carpodacus roseus* (3, 4)

THREE-BANDED ROSEFINCH *Carpodacus trifasciatus* (3, 4)

SPOT-WINGED ROSEFINCH *Carpodacus rodopeplus* (3, 4)

WHITE-BROWED ROSEFINCH *Carpodacus thura* (3, 4)

RED-MANTLED ROSEFINCH *Carpodacus rhodochlamys* (3, 4)

STREAKED ROSEFINCH *Carpodacus rubicilloides* (3, 4)

GREAT ROSEFINCH *Carpodacus rubicilla* (3, 4)

RED-FRONTED ROSEFINCH *Carpodacus puniceus* (3, 4)

TIBETAN ROSEFINCH *Carpodacus roborowskii* (3) [DD]

BONIN GROSBEAK *Chaunoproctus ferreorostris* (3) [EX]

PINE GROSBEAK *Pinicola enucleator* (1, 3, 4)

CRIMSON-BROWED FINCH *Pinicola subhimachalus* (3, 4)

SCARLET FINCH *Haematospiza sipahi* (3, 4)

PARROT CROSSBILL *Loxia pytyopsittacus* (3)

SCOTTISH CROSSBILL *Loxia scotica* (3) [DD]

RED CROSSBILL *Loxia curvirostra* (1, 2, 3, 4)

WHITE-WINGED CROSSBILL *Loxia leucoptera* (1, 3, 4)

BROWN BULLFINCH *Pyrrhula nipalensis* (3, 4)

WHITE-CHEEKED BULLFINCH *Pyrrhula leucogenis* (4) [NT]

ORANGE BULLFINCH *Pyrrhula aurantiaca* (4) [NT]

RED-HEADED BULLFINCH *Pyrrhula erythrocephala* (3, 4)

GRAY-HEADED BULLFINCH *Pyrrhula erythaca* (3, 4)

EURASIAN BULLFINCH *Pyrrhula pyrrhula* (3, 4)

AZORES BULLFINCH *Pyrrhula murina* (5)

HAWFINCH *Coccothraustes coccothraustes* (3, 4, 5)

YELLOW-BILLED GROSBEAK *Eophona migratoria* (3, 4)

JAPANESE GROSBEAK *Eophona personata* (3, 4)

BLACK-AND-YELLOW GROSBEAK *Mycerobas icterioides* (3, 4)

COLLARED GROSBEAK *Mycerobas affinis* (3, 4)

SPOT-WINGED GROSBEAK *Mycerobas melanozanthos* (3, 4)

WHITE-WINGED GROSBEAK *Mycerobas carnipes* (3, 4)

EVENING GROSBEAK *Hesperiphona vespertina* (1)

HOODED GROSBEAK *Hesperiphona abeillei* (1, 2)

GOLD-NAPED FINCH *Pyrrhoplectes epauletta* (3, 4)

Tribe DREPANIDINI

NIHOA FINCH *Telespiza ultima* (2) [VU]

LAYSAN FINCH *Telespiza cantans* (2) [VU]

OU *Psittirostra psittacea* (2) [CR]

LANAI HOOKBILL *Dysmorodrepanis munroi* (2) [EX]

PALILA *Loxioides bailleui* (2) [EN]

LESSER KOA-FINCH *Rhodacanthis flaviceps* (2) [EX]

GREATER KOA-FINCH *Rhodacanthis palmeri* (2) [EX]

KONA GROSBEAK *Chloridops kona* (2) [EX]

MAUI PARROTBILL *Pseudonestor xanthophrys* (2) [VU]

KAUAI AMAKIHI *Hemignathus kauaiensis* (2) [VU]

HAWAII AMAKIHI *Hemignathus virens* (2)

OAHU AMAKIHI *Hemignathus chloris* (2) [EN]

ANIANIAU *Hemignathus parvus* (2) [VU]

GREATER AMAKIHI *Hemignathus sagittirostris* (2) [EX]

AKIALOA *Hemignathus obscurus* (2) [EX]

NUKUPUU *Hemignathus lucidus* (2) [CR]

AKIAPOLAAU *Hemignathus munroi* (2) [EN]

AKIKIKI or KAUAI CREEPER *Oreomystis bairdi* (2) [EN]

HAWAII CREEPER *Oreomystis mana* (2) [EN]

MAUI ALAUAHIO or MAUI CREEPER *Paroreomyza montana* (2) [NT]

KAKAWAHIE or MOLOKAI CREEPER *Paroreomyza flammea* (2) [EX]

OAHU ALAUAHIO or OAHU CREEPER *Paroreomyza maculata* (2) [CR]

AKEKEE *Loxops caeruleirostris* (2) [EN]

AKEPA *Loxops coccineus* (2) [EN]

ULA-AI-HAWANE *Ciridops anna* (2) [EX]

IIWI *Vestiaria coccinea* (2)

HAWAII MAMO *Drepanis pacifica* (2) [EX]

BLACK MAMO *Drepanis funerea* (2) [EX]

AKOHEKOHE *Palmeria dolei* (2) [VU]

APAPANE *Himatione sanguinea* (2)

POO-ULI *Melamprosops phaeosoma* (2) [CR]

Subfamily EMBERIZINAE
Tribe EMBERIZINI

PINK-TAILED BUNTING *Urocynchramus pylzowi* (3, 4)

CRESTED BUNTING *Melophus lathami* (4)

SLATY BUNTING *Latoucheornis siemsseni* (4) [NT]

YELLOWHAMMER *Emberiza citrinella* (3, 5)

PINE BUNTING *Emberiza leucocephalos* (3, 4)

CHESTNUT-BREASTED BUNTING or WHITE-CAPPED BUNTING *Emberiza stewarti* (3)

CIRL BUNTING *Emberiza cirlus* (3, 5, 6)

TIBETAN BUNTING or KOZLOV'S BUNTING *Emberiza koslowi* (3) [NT]

ROCK BUNTING *Emberiza cia* (3, 4)

GODLEWSKI'S BUNTING *Emberiza godlewskii* (3, 4)

MEADOW BUNTING *Emberiza cioides* (3, 4)

RUFOUS-BACKED BUNTING or JANKOWSKI'S BUNTING *Emberiza jankowskii* (3, 4) [VU]

GRAY-NECKED BUNTING *Emberiza buchanani* (3, 4)

CINEREOUS BUNTING *Emberiza cineracea* (3, 5) [NT]

ORTOLAN BUNTING *Emberiza hortulana* (3, 5)

CRETZSCHMAR'S BUNTING *Emberiza caesia* (3, 5)

HOUSE BUNTING *Emberiza striolata* (3, 4, 5)

LARK-LIKE BUNTING *Emberiza impetuani* (5)

CINNAMON-BREASTED BUNTING *Emberiza tahapisi* (5)

SOCOTRA BUNTING *Emberiza socotrana* (5) [VU]

CAPE BUNTING *Emberiza capensis* (5)

TRISTRAM'S BUNTING *Emberiza tristrami* (3, 4)

CHESTNUT-EARED BUNTING *Emberiza fucata* (3, 4)

LITTLE BUNTING *Emberiza pusilla* (1, 3, 4)

YELLOW-BROWED BUNTING *Emberiza chrysophrys* (3, 4)

RUSTIC BUNTING *Emberiza rustica* (1, 3, 4)

YELLOW-THROATED BUNTING *Emberiza elegans* (3, 4)

YELLOW-BREASTED BUNTING *Emberiza aureola* (3, 4)

CHESTNUT BUNTING *Emberiza rutila* (3, 4)

AFRICAN GOLDEN-BREASTED BUNTING *Emberiza flaviventris* (5)

SOMALI GOLDEN-BREASTED BUNTING *Emberiza poliopleura* (5)

BROWN-RUMPED BUNTING *Emberiza affinis* (5)

CABANIS'S BUNTING *Emberiza cabanisi* (5)

BLACK-HEADED BUNTING *Emberiza melanocephala* (3, 4)

RED-HEADED BUNTING *Emberiza bruniceps* (3, 4)

YELLOW BUNTING *Emberiza sulphurata* (3, 4) [VU]

BLACK-FACED BUNTING *Emberiza spodocephala* (3, 4)

GRAY BUNTING *Emberiza variabilis* (3)

PALLAS'S BUNTING *Emberiza pallasi* (3, 4)

REED BUNTING *Emberiza schoeniclus* (3, 4, 5)

OCHER-RUMPED BUNTING *Emberiza yessoensis* (3, 4) [NT]

CORN BUNTING *Emberiza calandra* (3, 4, 5)

MCCOWN'S LONGSPUR *Calcarius mccownii* (1)

LAPLAND LONGSPUR *Calcarius lapponicus* (1, 3, 4)

SMITH'S LONGSPUR *Calcarius pictus* (1)

CHESTNUT-COLLARED LONGSPUR *Calcarius ornatus* (1)

SNOW BUNTING *Plectrophenax nivalis* (1, 3, 4)

MCKAY'S BUNTING *Plectrophenax hyperboreus* (1)

LARK BUNTING *Calamospiza melanocorys* (1)

Fox Sparrow *Passerella iliaca* (1)

Song Sparrow *Melospiza melodia* (1)

Lincoln's Sparrow *Melospiza lincolnii* (1, 2)

Swamp Sparrow *Melospiza georgiana* (1)

Rufous-Collared Sparrow *Zonotrichia capensis* (1, 2)

Harris's Sparrow *Zonotrichia querula* (1)

White-Throated Sparrow *Zonotrichia albicollis* (1)

White-Crowned Sparrow *Zonotrichia leucophrys* (1, 2)

Golden-Crowned Sparrow *Zonotrichia atricapilla* (1)

Volcano Junco *Junco vulcani* (2)

Dark-Eyed Junco *Junco hyemalis* (1)

Guadalupe Junco *Junco insularis* (1) [CR]

Yellow-Eyed Junco *Junco phaeonotus* (1)

Baird's Junco *Junco bairdi* (1)

Savannah Sparrow *Passerculus sandwichensis* (1, 2)

Large-Billed Sparrow *Passerculus rostratus* (1)

Seaside Sparrow *Ammodramus maritimus* (1)

Nelson's Sharp-Tailed Sparrow *Ammodramus nelsoni* (1)

Saltmarsh Sharp-Tailed Sparrow *Ammodramus caudacutus* (1)

Le Conte's Sparrow *Ammodramus leconteii* (1)

Henslow's Sparrow *Ammodramus henslowii* (1) [NT]

Baird's Sparrow *Ammodramus bairdii* (1)

Grasshopper Sparrow *Ammodramus savannarum* (1, 2)

Grassland Sparrow *Ammodramus humeralis* (2)

Yellow-Browed Sparrow *Ammodramus aurifrons* (2)

Sierra Madre Sparrow *Xenospiza baileyi* (1) [EN]

American Tree Sparrow *Spizella arborea* (1)

Chipping Sparrow *Spizella passerina* (1, 2)

Clay-Colored Sparrow *Spizella pallida* (1, 2)

Timberline Sparrow *Spizella taverneri* (1)

Brewer's Sparrow *Spizella breweri* (1)

Field Sparrow *Spizella pusilla* (1)

Worthen's Sparrow *Spizella wortheni* (1) [EN]

Black-Chinned Sparrow *Spizella atrogularis* (1)

Vesper Sparrow *Pooecetes gramineus* (1)

Lark Sparrow *Chondestes grammacus* (1, 2)

Black-Throated Sparrow *Amphispiza bilineata* (1)

Sage Sparrow *Amphispiza belli* (1)

Five-Striped Sparrow *Aimophila quinquestriata* (1)

Bridled Sparrow *Aimophila mystacalis* (1)

Black-Chested Sparrow *Aimophila humeralis* (1)

Stripe-Headed Sparrow *Aimophila ruficauda* (1, 2)

Cinnamon-Tailed Sparrow *Aimophila sumichrasti* (1) [NT]

Stripe-Capped Sparrow *Aimophila strigiceps* (2)

Tumbes Sparrow *Aimophila stolzmanni* (2)

Bachman's Sparrow *Aimophila aestivalis* (1)

Botteri's Sparrow *Aimophila botterii* (1, 2)

Cassin's Sparrow *Aimophila cassinii* (1)

Rufous-Winged Sparrow *Aimophila carpalis* (1)

RUFOUS-CROWNED SPARROW *Aimophila ruficeps* (1)

OAXACA SPARROW *Aimophila notosticta* (1) [NT]

RUSTY SPARROW *Aimophila rufescens* (1, 2)

ZAPATA SPARROW or CUBAN SPARROW *Torreornis inexpectata* (2) [EN]

STRIPED SPARROW *Oriturus superciliosus* (1)

GREEN-TAILED TOWHEE *Pipilo chlorurus* (1)

COLLARED TOWHEE *Pipilo ocai* (1)

SPOTTED TOWHEE *Pipilo maculatus* (1)

EASTERN TOWHEE *Pipilo erythrophthalmus* (1)

WHITE-THROATED TOWHEE *Pipilo albicollis* (1)

CANYON TOWHEE *Pipilo fuscus* (1)

CALIFORNIA TOWHEE *Pipilo crissalis* (1)

ABERT'S TOWHEE *Pipilo aberti* (1)

RUSTY-CROWNED GROUND-SPARROW *Melozone kieneri* (1)

PREVOST'S GROUND-SPARROW *Melozone biarcuatum* (1, 2)

WHITE-EARED GROUND-SPARROW *Melozone leucotis* (1, 2)

ORANGE-BILLED SPARROW *Arremon aurantiirostris* (1, 2)

GOLDEN-WINGED SPARROW *Arremon schlegeli* (2)

PECTORAL SPARROW *Arremon taciturnus* (2)

BLACK-CAPPED SPARROW *Arremon abeillei* (2)

SAFFRON-BILLED SPARROW *Arremon flavirostris* (2)

OLIVE SPARROW *Arremonops rufivirgatus* (1, 2)

TOCUYO SPARROW *Arremonops tocuyensis* (2)

GREEN-BACKED SPARROW *Arremonops chloronotus* (1, 2)

BLACK-STRIPED SPARROW *Arremonops conirostris* (2)

WHITE-NAPED BRUSH-FINCH *Atlapetes albinucha* (1)

YELLOW-THROATED BRUSH-FINCH *Atlapetes gutturalis* (1, 2)

PALE-NAPED BRUSH-FINCH *Atlapetes pallidinucha* (2)

RUFOUS-NAPED BRUSH-FINCH *Atlapetes rufinucha* (2)

WHITE-RIMMED BRUSH-FINCH *Atlapetes leucopis* (2) [NT]

RUFOUS-CAPPED BRUSH-FINCH *Atlapetes pileatus* (1)

SANTA MARTA BRUSH-FINCH *Atlapetes melanocephalus* (2)

OLIVE-HEADED BRUSH-FINCH or YELLOW-HEADED BRUSH-FINCH *Atlapetes flaviceps* (2) [EN]

DUSKY-HEADED BRUSH-FINCH *Atlapetes fuscoolivaceus* (2) [NT]

TRICOLORED BRUSH-FINCH *Atlapetes tricolor* (2)

MUSTACHED BRUSH-FINCH *Atlapetes albofrenatus* (2)

SLATY BRUSH-FINCH *Atlapetes schistaceus* (2)

BAY-CROWNED BRUSH-FINCH *Atlapetes seebohmi* (2)

RUSTY-BELLIED BRUSH-FINCH *Atlapetes nationi* (2)

WHITE-WINGED BRUSH-FINCH *Atlapetes leucopterus* (2)

WHITE-HEADED BRUSH-FINCH *Atlapetes albiceps* (2)

PALE-HEADED BRUSH-FINCH *Atlapetes pallidiceps* (2) [CR]

RUFOUS-EARED BRUSH-FINCH *Atlapetes rufigenis* (2) [NT]

OCHER-BREASTED BRUSH-FINCH *Atlapetes semirufus* (2)

TEPUI BRUSH-FINCH *Atlapetes personatus* (2)

FULVOUS-HEADED BRUSH-FINCH *Atlapetes fulviceps* (2)

YELLOW-STRIPED BRUSH-FINCH *Atlapetes citrinellus* (2)

CHESTNUT-CAPPED BRUSH-FINCH *Atlapetes brunneinucha* (1, 2)

GREEN-STRIPED BRUSH-FINCH *Atlapetes virenticeps* (1)

BLACK-HEADED BRUSH-FINCH *Atlapetes atricapillus* (2)

STRIPE-HEADED BRUSH-FINCH *Atlapetes torquatus*

LARGE-FOOTED FINCH *Pezopetes capitalis* (2)

YELLOW-THIGHED FINCH *Pselliophorus tibialis* (2)

YELLOW-GREEN FINCH *Pselliophorus luteoviridis* (2) [VU]

SOOTY-FACED FINCH *Lysurus crassirostris* (2)

OLIVE FINCH *Lysurus castaneiceps* (2)

YELLOW CARDINAL *Gubernatrix cristata* (2) [EN]

RED-CRESTED CARDINAL *Paroaria coronata* (2)

RED-COWLED CARDINAL *Paroaria dominicana* (2)

RED-CAPPED CARDINAL *Paroaria gularis* (2)

CRIMSON-FRONTED CARDINAL *Paroaria baeri* (2)

YELLOW-BILLED CARDINAL *Paroaria capitata* (2)

Tribe PARULINI

BACHMAN'S WARBLER *Vermivora bachmanii* (1, 2) [CR]

BLUE-WINGED WARBLER *Vermivora pinus* (1, 2)

GOLDEN-WINGED WARBLER *Vermivora chrysoptera* (1, 2, 3)

TENNESSEE WARBLER *Vermivora peregrina* (1, 2, 3)

ORANGE-CROWNED WARBLER *Vermivora celata* (1, 2)

NASHVILLE WARBLER *Vermivora ruficapilla* (1, 2)

VIRGINIA'S WARBLER *Vermivora virginiae* (1)

COLIMA WARBLER *Vermivora crissalis* (1) [NT]

LUCY'S WARBLER *Vermivora luciae* (1)

NORTHERN PARULA *Parula americana* (1, 2, 3)

TROPICAL PARULA *Parula pitiayumi* (1, 2)

CRESCENT-CHESTED WARBLER *Parula superciliosa* (1, 2)

FLAME-THROATED WARBLER *Parula gutturalis* (2)

YELLOW WARBLER *Dendroica petechia* (1, 2)

CHESTNUT-SIDED WARBLER *Dendroica pensylvanica* (1, 2)

MAGNOLIA WARBLER *Dendroica magnolia* (1, 2)

CAPE MAY WARBLER *Dendroica tigrina* (1, 2, 3)

BLACK-THROATED BLUE WARBLER *Dendroica caerulescens* (1, 2)

YELLOW-RUMPED WARBLER *Dendroica coronata* (1, 2)

BLACK-THROATED GRAY WARBLER *Dendroica nigrescens* (1)

TOWNSEND'S WARBLER *Dendroica townsendi* (1, 2)

HERMIT WARBLER *Dendroica occidentalis* (1, 2)

BLACK-THROATED GREEN WARBLER *Dendroica virens* (1, 2)

GOLDEN-CHEEKED WARBLER *Dendroica chrysoparia* (1, 2) [EN]

BLACKBURNIAN WARBLER *Dendroica fusca* (1, 2, 3)

YELLOW-THROATED WARBLER *Dendroica dominica* (1, 2)

GRACE'S WARBLER *Dendroica graciae* (1, 2)

ADELAIDE'S WARBLER *Dendroica adelaidae* (2)

OLIVE-CAPPED WARBLER *Dendroica pityophila* (2)

PINE WARBLER *Dendroica pinus* (1, 2)

KIRTLAND'S WARBLER *Dendroica kirtlandii* (1, 2) [VU]

PRAIRIE WARBLER *Dendroica discolor* (1, 2)

VITELLINE WARBLER *Dendroica vitellina* (2) [NT]

PALM WARBLER *Dendroica palmarum* (1, 2)

BAY-BREASTED WARBLER *Dendroica castanea* (1, 2)

BLACKPOLL WARBLER *Dendroica striata* (1, 2, 3)

CERULEAN WARBLER *Dendroica cerulea* (1, 2, 3)

PLUMBEOUS WARBLER *Dendroica plumbea* (2)

ARROWHEAD WARBLER *Dendroica pharetra* (2)

ELFIN-WOODS WARBLER *Dendroica angelae* (2) [NT]

WHISTLING WARBLER *Catharopeza bishopi* (2) [VU]

BLACK-AND-WHITE WARBLER *Mniotilta varia* (1, 2, 3)

AMERICAN REDSTART *Setophaga ruticilla* (1, 2, 3)

PROTHONOTARY WARBLER *Protonotaria citrea* (1, 2)

WORM-EATING WARBLER *Helmitheros vermivorus* (1, 2)

SWAINSON'S WARBLER *Limnothlypis swainsonii* (1, 2)

OVENBIRD *Seiurus aurocapillus* (1, 2, 3)

NORTHERN WATERTHRUSH *Seiurus noveboracensis* (1, 2, 3)

LOUISIANA WATERTHRUSH *Seiurus motacilla* (1, 2)

KENTUCKY WARBLER *Oporornis formosus* (1, 2)

CONNECTICUT WARBLER *Oporornis agilis* (1, 2)

MOURNING WARBLER *Oporornis philadelphia* (1, 2)

MACGILLIVRAY'S WARBLER *Oporornis tolmiei* (1, 2)

COMMON YELLOWTHROAT *Geothlypis trichas* (1, 2)

BELDING'S YELLOWTHROAT *Geothlypis beldingi* (1) [VU]

ALTAMIRA YELLOWTHROAT *Geothlypis flavovelata* (1, 2) [NT]

BAHAMA YELLOWTHROAT *Geothlypis rostrata* (2)

OLIVE-CROWNED YELLOWTHROAT *Geothlypis semiflava* (2)

BLACK-POLLED YELLOWTHROAT *Geothlypis speciosa* (1) [VU]

HOODED YELLOWTHROAT *Geothlypis nelsoni* (1)

MASKED YELLOWTHROAT *Geothlypis aequinoctialis* (2)

CHIRIQUI YELLOWTHROAT *Geothlypis chiriquensis* (2)

BLACK-LORED YELLOWTHROAT *Geothlypis auricularis* (2)

SOUTHERN YELLOWTHROAT *Geothlypis velata* (2)

GRAY-CROWNED YELLOWTHROAT *Geothlypis poliocephala* (1, 2)

GREEN-TAILED GROUND WARBLER *Microligea palustris* (2)

YELLOW-HEADED WARBLER *Teretistris fernandinae* (2)

ORIENTE WARBLER *Teretistris fornsi* (2)

SEMPER'S WARBLER *Leucopeza semperi* (2) [CR]

HOODED WARBLER *Wilsonia citrina* (1, 2, 3)

WILSON'S WARBLER *Wilsonia pusilla* (1, 2)

CANADA WARBLER *Wilsonia canadensis* (1, 2)

RED-FACED WARBLER *Cardellina rubrifrons* (1, 2)

RED WARBLER *Ergaticus ruber* (1)

PINK-HEADED WARBLER *Ergaticus versicolor* (1, 2) [NT]

PAINTED REDSTART or PAINTED WHITESTART *Myioborus pictus* (1, 2)

SLATE-THROATED REDSTART or SLATE-THROATED WHITESTART *Myioborus miniatus* (1, 2)

TEPUI REDSTART or TEPUI WHITESTART *Myioborus castaneocapillus* (2)

YELLOW-FACED REDSTART or PARIA WHITESTART *Myioborus pariae* (2) [CR]

BROWN-CAPPED REDSTART or BROWN-CAPPED WHITESTART *Myioborus brunniceps* (2)

WHITE-FACED REDSTART or WHITE-FACED WHITESTART *Myioborus albifacies* (2) [NT]

SAFFRON-BREASTED REDSTART or GUAIQUINIMA WHITESTART *Myioborus cardonai* (2) [VU]

COLLARED REDSTART or COLLARED WHITESTART *Myioborus torquatus* (2)

SPECTACLED REDSTART or SPECTACLED WHITESTART *Myioborus melanocephalus* (2)

GOLDEN-FRONTED REDSTART or GOLDEN-FRONTED WHITESTART *Myioborus ornatus* (2)

WHITE-FRONTED REDSTART or WHITE-FRONTED WHITESTART *Myioborus albifrons* (2)

YELLOW-CROWNED REDSTART or YELLOW-CROWNED WHITESTART *Myioborus flavivertex* (2)

FAN-TAILED WARBLER *Euthlypis lachrymosa* (1, 2)

GRAY-AND-GOLD WARBLER *Basileuterus fraseri* (2)

TWO-BANDED WARBLER *Basileuterus bivittatus* (2)

GOLDEN-BELLIED WARBLER or CUZCO WARBLER *Basileuterus chrysogaster* (2)

CHOCO WARBLER *Basileuterus chlorophrys* (2)

PALE-LEGGED WARBLER *Basileuterus signatus* (2)

CITRINE WARBLER *Basileuterus luteoviridis* (2)

BLACK-CRESTED WARBLER *Basileuterus nigrocristatus* (2)

GRAY-HEADED WARBLER *Basileuterus criseiceps* (2) [CR]

SANTA MARTA WARBLER *Basileuterus casilicus* (2) [NT]

GRAY-THROATED WARBLER *Basileuterus cinereicollis* (2) [NT]

WHITE-LORED WARBLER *Basileuterus conspicillatus* (2) [NT]

RUSSET-CROWNED WARBLER *Basileuterus coronatus* (2)

GOLDEN-CROWNED WARBLER *Basileuterus culicivorus* (1, 2)

THREE-BANDED WARBLER *Basileuterus trifasciatus* (2)

WHITE-BELLIED WARBLER *Basileuterus hypoleucus* (2)

RUFOUS-CAPPED WARBLER *Basileuterus rufifrons* (1, 2)

CHESTNUT-CAPPED WARBLER *Basileuterus delattrii* (1, 2)

GOLDEN-BROWED WARBLER *Basileuterus belli* (1, 2)

BLACK-CHEEKED WARBLER *Basileuterus melanogenys* (2)

PIRRE WARBLER *Basileuterus ignotus* (2) [NT]

THREE-STRIPED WARBLER *Basileuterus tristriatus* (2)

WHITE-BROWED WARBLER *Basileuterus leucoblepharus* (2)

WHITE-STRIPED WARBLER *Basileuterus leucophrys* (2)

FLAVESCENT WARBLER *Basileuterus flaveolus* (2)

BUFF-RUMPED WARBLER *Basileuterus fulvicauda* (2)

NEOTROPICAL RIVER WARBLER or STREAMSIDE WARBLER *Basileuterus rivularis* (2)

WRENTHRUSH *Zeledonia coronata* (2)

YELLOW-BREASTED CHAT *Icteria virens* (1, 2)

RED-BREASTED CHAT *Granatellus venustus* (1)

GRAY-THROATED CHAT *Granatellus sallaei* (1, 2)

ROSE-BREASTED CHAT *Granatellus pelzelni* (2)

WHITE-WINGED WARBLER *Xenoligea montana* (2) [VU]

Tribe THRAUPINI

BANANAQUIT *Coereba flaveola* (2)

CHESTNUT-VENTED CONEBILL *Conirostrum speciosum* (2)

WHITE-EARED CONEBILL *Conirostrum leucogenys* (2)

BICOLORED CONEBILL *Conirostrum bicolor* (2)

PEARLY-BREASTED CONEBILL *Conirostrum margaritae* (2) [NT]

CINEREOUS CONEBILL *Conirostrum cinereum* (2)

TAMARUGO CONEBILL *Conirostrum tamarugense* (2) [VU]

WHITE-BROWED CONEBILL *Conirostrum ferrugineiventre* (2)

RUFOUS-BROWED CONEBILL *Conirostrum rufum* (2)

BLUE-BACKED CONEBILL *Conirostrum sitticolor* (2)

CAPPED CONEBILL *Conirostrum albifrons* (2)

BROWN TANAGER *Orchesticus abeillei* (2) [NT]

CINNAMON TANAGER *Schistochlamys ruficapillus* (2)

BLACK-FACED TANAGER *Schistochlamys melanopis* (2)

WHITE-BANDED TANAGER *Neothraupis fasciata* (2) [NT]

WHITE-RUMPED TANAGER *Cypsnagra hirundinacea* (2) [NT]

BLACK-AND-WHITE TANAGER *Conothraupis speculigera* (2) [NT]

CONE-BILLED TANAGER *Conothraupis mesoleuca* (2) [VU]

RED-BILLED PIED TANAGER *Lamprospiza melanoleuca* (2)

MAGPIE TANAGER *Cissopis leveriana* (2)

GRASS-GREEN TANAGER *Chlorornis riefferii* (2)

SCARLET-THROATED TANAGER *Compsothraupis loricata* (2)

WHITE-CAPPED TANAGER *Sericossypha albocristata* (2)

PUERTO RICAN TANAGER *Nesospingus speculiferus* (2)

COMMON BUSH-TANAGER *Chlorospingus ophthalmicus* (1, 2)

TACARCUNA BUSH-TANAGER *Chlorospingus tacarcunae* (2)

PIRRE BUSH-TANAGER *Chlorospingus inornatus* (2)

DUSKY BUSH-TANAGER or DUSKY-BELLIED BUSH-TANAGER *Chlorospingus semifuscus* (2)

SOOTY-CAPPED BUSH-TANAGER *Chlorospingus pileatus* (2)

YELLOW-WHISKERED BUSH-TANAGER or SHORT-BILLED BUSH-TANAGER *Chlorospingus parvirostris* (2)

YELLOW-THROATED BUSH-TANAGER *Chlorospingus flavigularis* (2)

YELLOW-GREEN BUSH-TANAGER *Chlorospingus flavovirens* (2) [VU]

ASHY-THROATED BUSH-TANAGER *Chlorospingus canigularis* (2)

GRAY-HOODED BUSH-TANAGER *Cnemoscopus rubrirostris* (2)

BLACK-CAPPED HEMISPINGUS *Hemispingus atropileus* (2)

ORANGE-BROWED HEMISPINGUS *Hemispingus calophrys* (2)

PARODI'S HEMISPINGUS *Hemispingus parodii* (2)

SUPERCILIARIED HEMISPINGUS *Hemispingus superciliaris* (2)

GRAY-CAPPED HEMISPINGUS *Hemispingus reyi* (2)

OLEAGINOUS HEMISPINGUS *Hemispingus frontalis* (2)

BLACK-EARED HEMISPINGUS *Hemispingus melanotis* (2)

SLATY-BACKED HEMISPINGUS *Hemispingus goeringi* (2) [VU]

RUFOUS-BROWED HEMISPINGUS *Hemispingus rufosuperciliaris* (2) [NT]

BLACK-HEADED HEMISPINGUS *Hemispingus verticalis* (2)

DRAB HEMISPINGUS *Hemispingus xanthophthalmus* (2)

THREE-STRIPED HEMISPINGUS *Hemispingus trifasciatus* (2)

CHESTNUT-HEADED TANAGER *Pyrrhocoma ruficeps* (2)

FULVOUS-HEADED TANAGER *Thlypopsis fulviceps* (2)

RUFOUS-CHESTED TANAGER *Thlypopsis ornata* (2)

BROWN-FLANKED TANAGER *Thlypopsis pectoralis* (2)

ORANGE-HEADED TANAGER *Thlypopsis sordida* (2)

BUFF-BELLIED TANAGER *Thlypopsis inornata* (2)

RUST-AND-YELLOW TANAGER *Thlypopsis ruficeps* (2)

GUIRA TANAGER *Hemithraupis guira* (2)

RUFOUS-HEADED TANAGER *Hemithraupis ruficapilla* (2)

YELLOW-BACKED TANAGER *Hemithraupis flavicollis* (2)

BLACK-AND-YELLOW TANAGER *Chrysothlypis chrysomelas* (2)

SCARLET-AND-WHITE TANAGER *Chrysothlypis salmoni* (2)

HOODED TANAGER *Nemosia pileata* (2)

CHERRY-THROATED TANAGER *Nemosia rourei* (2) [CR]

BLACK-CROWNED PALM-TANAGER *Phaenicophilus palmarum* (2)

GRAY-CROWNED PALM-TANAGER *Phaenicophilus poliocephalus* (2)

CHAT TANAGER *Calyptophilus frugivorus* (2) [VU]

ROSY THRUSH-TANAGER *Rhodinocichla rosea* (1, 2)

DUSKY-FACED TANAGER *Mitrospingus cassinii* (2)

OLIVE-BACKED TANAGER *Mitrospingus oleagineus* (2)

CARMIOL'S TANAGER or OLIVE TANAGER *Chlorothraupis carmioli* (2)

OLIVE TANAGER *Chlorothraupis frenata* (2)

LEMON-SPECTACLED TANAGER *Chlorothraupis olivacea* (2)

OCHER-BREASTED TANAGER *Chlorothraupis stolzmanni* (2)

OLIVE-GREEN TANAGER *Orthogonys chloricterus* (2)

GRAY-HEADED TANAGER *Eucometis penicillata* (1, 2)

FULVOUS SHRIKE-TANAGER *Lanio fulvus* (2)

WHITE-WINGED SHRIKE-TANAGER *Lanio versicolor* (2)

BLACK-THROATED SHRIKE-TANAGER *Lanio aurantius* (1, 2)

WHITE-THROATED SHRIKE-TANAGER *Lanio leucothorax* (2)

RUFOUS-CRESTED TANAGER *Creurgops verticalis* (2)

SLATY TANAGER *Creurgops dentata* (2)

SULFUR-RUMPED TANAGER *Heterospingus rubrifrons* (2)

SCARLET-BROWED TANAGER *Heterospingus xanthopygius* (2)

FLAME-CRESTED TANAGER *Tachyphonus cristatus* (2)

YELLOW-CRESTED TANAGER *Tachyphonus rufiventer* (2)

FULVOUS-CRESTED TANAGER *Tachyphonus surinamus* (2)

WHITE-SHOULDERED TANAGER *Tachyphonus luctuosus* (2)

TAWNY-CRESTED TANAGER *Tachyphonus delatrii* (2)

RUBY-CROWNED TANAGER *Tachyphonus coronatus* (2)

WHITE-LINED TANAGER *Tachyphonus rufus* (2)

RED-SHOULDERED TANAGER *Tachyphonus phoenicius* (2)

BLACK-GOGGLED TANAGER *Trichothraupis melanops* (2)

RED-CROWNED ANT-TANAGER *Habia rubica* (1, 2)

RED-THROATED ANT-TANAGER *Habia fuscicauda* (1, 2)

SOOTY ANT-TANAGER *Habia gutturalis* (2) [NT]

BLACK-CHEEKED ANT-TANAGER *Habia atrimaxillaris* (2) [VU]

CRESTED ANT-TANAGER *Habia cristata* (2)

FLAME-COLORED TANAGER *Piranga bidentata* (1, 2)

HEPATIC TANAGER *Piranga flava* (1, 2)

SUMMER TANAGER *Piranga rubra* (1, 2)

ROSE-THROATED TANAGER *Piranga roseogularis* (1, 2)

SCARLET TANAGER *Piranga olivacea* (1, 2)

WESTERN TANAGER *Piranga ludoviciana* (1, 2)

WHITE-WINGED TANAGER *Piranga leucoptera* (1, 2)

RED-HEADED TANAGER *Piranga erythrocephala* (1, 2)

VERMILION TANAGER *Calochaetes coccineus* (2)

CRIMSON-COLLARED TANAGER *Phlogothraupis sanguinolenta* (1, 2)

MASKED CRIMSON TANAGER *Ramphocelus nigrogularis* (2)

CRIMSON-BACKED TANAGER *Ramphocelus dimidiatus* (2)

HUALLAGA TANAGER *Ramphocelus melanogaster* (2)

SILVER-BEAKED TANAGER *Ramphocelus carbo* (2)

BRAZILIAN TANAGER *Ramphocelus bresilius* (2)

SCARLET-RUMPED TANAGER *Ramphocelus passerinii* (1, 2)

FLAME-RUMPED TANAGER or BRIGHT-RUMPED TANAGER *Ramphocelus flammigerus* (2)

STRIPE-HEADED TANAGER *Spindalis zena* (2)

BLUE-GRAY TANAGER *Thraupis episcopus* (1, 2)

GLAUCOUS TANAGER *Thraupis glaucocolpa* (2)

SAYACA TANAGER *Thraupis sayaca* (2)

AZURE-SHOULDERED TANAGER *Thraupis cyanoptera* (2) [NT]

GOLDEN-CHEVRONED TANAGER *Thraupis ornata* (2)

YELLOW-WINGED TANAGER *Thraupis abbas* (1, 2)

PALM TANAGER *Thraupis palmarum* (2)

BLUE-CAPPED TANAGER *Thraupis cyanocephala* (2)

BLUE-AND-YELLOW TANAGER *Thraupis bonariensis* (2)

BLUE-BACKED TANAGER *Cyanicterus cyanicterus* (2)

BLUE-AND-GOLD TANAGER *Bangsia arcaei* (2) [NT]

BLACK-AND-GOLD TANAGER *Bangsia melanochlamys* (2) [EN]

GOLDEN-CHESTED TANAGER *Bangsia rothschildi* (2)

MOSS-BACKED TANAGER *Bangsia edwardsi* (2)

GOLD-RINGED TANAGER *Bangsia aureocincta* (2) [VU]

HOODED MOUNTAIN-TANAGER *Buthraupis montana* (2)

BLACK-CHESTED MOUNTAIN-TANAGER *Buthraupis eximia* (2)

GOLDEN-BACKED MOUNTAIN-TANAGER *Buthraupis aureodorsalis* (2) [VU]

MASKED MOUNTAIN-TANAGER *Buthraupis wetmorei* (2) [VU]

ORANGE-THROATED TANAGER *Wetmorethraupis sterrhopteron* (2) [EN]

SANTA MARTA MOUNTAIN-TANAGER or BLACK-CHEEKED MOUNTAIN-TANAGER *Anisognathus melanogenys* (2)

LACRIMOSE MOUNTAIN-TANAGER *Anisognathus lacrymosus* (2)

SCARLET-BELLIED MOUNTAIN-TANAGER *Anisognathus igniventris* (2)

BLUE-WINGED MOUNTAIN-TANAGER *Anisognathus somptuosus* (2)

BLACK-CHINNED MOUNTAIN-TANAGER *Anisognathus notabilis* (2)

DIADEMED TANAGER *Stephanophorus diadematus* (2)

PURPLISH-MANTLED TANAGER *Iridosornis porphyrocephala* (2) [NT]

YELLOW-THROATED TANAGER *Iridosornis analis* (2)

GOLDEN-COLLARED TANAGER *Iridosornis jelskii* (2)

GOLDEN-CROWNED TANAGER *Iridosornis rufivertex* (2)

YELLOW-SCARFED TANAGER *Iridosornis reinhardti* (2)

BUFF-BREASTED MOUNTAIN-TANAGER *Dubusia taeniata* (2)

CHESTNUT-BELLIED MOUNTAIN-TANAGER *Delothraupis castaneoventris* (2)

FAWN-BREASTED TANAGER *Pipraeidea melanonota* (2)

JAMAICAN EUPHONIA *Euphonia jamaica* (2)

PLUMBEOUS EUPHONIA *Euphonia plumbea* (2)

SCRUB EUPHONIA *Euphonia affinis* (1, 2)

YELLOW-CROWNED EUPHONIA *Euphonia luteicapilla* (2)

PURPLE-THROATED EUPHONIA *Euphonia chlorotica* (2)

TRINIDAD EUPHONIA *Euphonia trinitatis* (2)

VELVET-FRONTED EUPHONIA *Euphonia concinna* (2)

ORANGE-CROWNED EUPHONIA *Euphonia saturata* (2)

FINSCH'S EUPHONIA *Euphonia finschi* (2)

VIOLACEOUS EUPHONIA *Euphonia violacea* (2)

THICK-BILLED EUPHONIA *Euphonia lanirostris* (2)

YELLOW-THROATED EUPHONIA *Euphonia hirundinacea* (1, 2)

GREEN-CHINNED EUPHONIA *Euphonia chalybea* (2) [NT]

BLUE-RUMPED EUPHONIA or BLUE-HOODED EUPHONIA *Euphonia elegantissima* (1, 2)

ANTILLEAN EUPHONIA *Euphonia musica* (2)

GOLDEN-RUMPED EUPHONIA *Euphonia cyanocephala* (2)

SPOT-CROWNED EUPHONIA *Euphonia imitans* (2)

FULVOUS-VENTED EUPHONIA *Euphonia fulvicrissa* (2)

OLIVE-BACKED EUPHONIA *Euphonia gouldi* (1, 2)

WHITE-LORED EUPHONIA *Euphonia chrysopasta* (2)

BRONZE-GREEN EUPHONIA *Euphonia mesochrysa* (2)

WHITE-VENTED EUPHONIA *Euphonia minuta* (1, 2)

TAWNY-CAPPED EUPHONIA *Euphonia anneae* (2)

ORANGE-BELLIED EUPHONIA *Euphonia xanthogaster* (2)

RUFOUS-BELLIED EUPHONIA *Euphonia rufiventris* (2)

GOLDEN-SIDED EUPHONIA *Euphonia cayennensis* (2)

CHESTNUT-BELLIED EUPHONIA *Euphonia pectoralis* (2)

YELLOW-COLLARED CHLOROPHONIA *Chlorophonia flavirostris* (2)

BLUE-NAPED CHLOROPHONIA *Chlorophonia cyanea* (2)

CHESTNUT-BREASTED CHLOROPHONIA *Chlorophonia pyrrhophrys* (2)

BLUE-CROWNED CHLOROPHONIA *Chlorophonia occipitalis* (1, 2)

GOLDEN-BROWED CHLOROPHONIA *Chlorophonia callophrys* (2)

GLISTENING-GREEN TANAGER *Chlorochrysa phoenicotis* (2)

ORANGE-EARED TANAGER *Chlorochrysa calliparaea* (2)

MULTICOLORED TANAGER *Chlorochrysa nitidissima* (2) [VU]

PLAIN-COLORED TANAGER *Tangara inornata* (2)

TURQUOISE TANAGER *Tangara mexicana* (2)

WHITE-BELLIED TANAGER *Tangara brasiliensis* (2)

AZURE-RUMPED TANAGER *Tangara cabanisi* (1, 2) [VU]

GRAY-AND-GOLD TANAGER *Tangara palmeri* (2)

PARADISE TANAGER *Tangara chilensis* (2)

SEVEN-COLORED TANAGER *Tangara fastuosa* (2) [EN]

GREEN-HEADED TANAGER *Tangara seledon* (2)

RED-NECKED TANAGER *Tangara cyanocephala* (2)

BRASSY-BREASTED TANAGER *Tangara desmaresti* (2)

GILT-EDGED TANAGER *Tangara cyanoventris* (2)

BLUE-WHISKERED TANAGER *Tangara johannae* (2) [NT]

GREEN-AND-GOLD TANAGER *Tangara schrankii* (2)

EMERALD TANAGER *Tangara florida* (2)

GOLDEN TANAGER *Tangara arthus* (2)

SILVER-THROATED TANAGER *Tangara icterocephala* (2)

SAFFRON-CROWNED TANAGER *Tangara xanthocephala* (2)

GOLDEN-EARED TANAGER *Tangara chrysotis* (2)

FLAME-FACED TANAGER *Tangara parzudakii* (2)

YELLOW-BELLIED TANAGER *Tangara xanthogastra* (2)

SPOTTED TANAGER *Tangara punctata* (2)

SPECKLED TANAGER *Tangara guttata* (2)

DOTTED TANAGER *Tangara varia* (2) [NT]

RUFOUS-THROATED TANAGER *Tangara rufigula* (2)

BAY-HEADED TANAGER *Tangara gyrola* (2)

RUFOUS-WINGED TANAGER *Tangara lavinia* (2)

BURNISHED-BUFF TANAGER *Tangara cayana* (2)

LESSER ANTILLEAN TANAGER *Tangara cucullata* (2)

BLACK-BACKED TANAGER *Tangara peruviana* (2) [EN]

CHESTNUT-BACKED TANAGER *Tangara preciosa* (2)

SCRUB TANAGER *Tangara vitriolina* (2)

GREEN-CAPPED TANAGER *Tangara meyerdeschauenseei* (2) [VU]

RUFOUS-CHEEKED TANAGER *Tangara rufigenis* (2)

GOLDEN-NAPED TANAGER *Tangara ruficervix* (2)

METALLIC-GREEN TANAGER *Tangara labradorides* (2)

BLUE-BROWED TANAGER *Tangara cyanotis* (2)

BLUE-NECKED TANAGER *Tangara cyanicollis* (2)

GOLDEN-HOODED TANAGER *Tangara larvata* (1, 2)

MASKED TANAGER *Tangara nigrocincta* (2)

SPANGLE-CHEEKED TANAGER *Tangara dowii* (2)

GREEN-NAPED TANAGER *Tangara fucosa* (2) [NT]

BERYL-SPANGLED TANAGER *Tangara nigroviridis* (2)

BLUE-AND-BLACK TANAGER *Tangara vassorii* (2)

BLACK-CAPPED TANAGER *Tangara heinei* (2)

SIRA TANAGER *Tangara phillipsi* (2) [NT]

SILVER-BACKED TANAGER *Tangara viridicollis* (2)

STRAW-BACKED TANAGER *Tangara argyrofenges* (2)

BLACK-HEADED TANAGER *Tangara cyanoptera* (2)

OPAL-RUMPED TANAGER *Tangara velia* (2)

SILVER-BREASTED TANAGER *Tangara cyanomelaena* (2)

OPAL-CROWNED TANAGER *Tangara callophrys* (2)

GOLDEN-COLLARED HONEYCREEPER *Iridophanes pulcherrima* (2)

TURQUOISE DACNIS-TANAGER or TURQUOISE DACNIS *Pseudodacnis hartlaubi* (2) [VU]

WHITE-BELLIED DACNIS *Dacnis albiventris* (2) [NT]

BLACK-FACED DACNIS *Dacnis lineata* (2)

YELLOW-TUFTED DACNIS *Dacnis egregia* (2)

YELLOW-BELLIED DACNIS *Dacnis flaviventer* (2)

BLACK-LEGGED DACNIS *Dacnis nigripes* (2) [VU]

SCARLET-THIGHED DACNIS *Dacnis venusta* (2)

BLUE DACNIS *Dacnis cayana* (2)

VIRIDIAN DACNIS *Dacnis viguieri* (2) [NT]

SCARLET-BREASTED DACNIS *Dacnis berlepschi* (2) [VU]

GREEN HONEYCREEPER *Chlorophanes spiza* (1, 2)

SHORT-BILLED HONEYCREEPER *Cyanerpes nitidus* (2)

SHINING HONEYCREEPER *Cyanerpes lucidus* (2)

PURPLE HONEYCREEPER *Cyanerpes caeruleus* (2)

RED-LEGGED HONEYCREEPER *Cyanerpes cyaneus* (1, 2)

TIT-LIKE DACNIS *Xenodacnis parina* (2) [NT]

SWALLOW TANAGER *Tersina viridis* (2)

PLUSHCAP *Catamblyrhynchus diadema* (2)

TANAGER FINCH *Oreothraupis arremonops* (2) [VU]

BLACK-BACKED BUSH-TANAGER *Urothraupis stolzmanni* (2)

PARDUSCO *Nephelornis oneilli* (2)

COAL-CRESTED FINCH *Charitospiza eucosma* (2) [NT]

BLACK-MASKED FINCH *Coryphaspiza melanotis* (2) [VU]

MANY-COLORED CHACO-FINCH *Saltatricula multicolor* (2)

PILEATED FINCH *Coryphospingus pileatus* (2)

RED-CRESTED FINCH *Coryphospingus cucullatus* (2)

CRIMSON-BREASTED FINCH or CRIMSON FINCH-TANAGER *Rhodospingus cruentus* (2)

BLACK-HOODED SIERRA-FINCH *Phrygilus atriceps* (2)

PERUVIAN SIERRA-FINCH *Phrygilus punensis* (2)

GRAY-HOODED SIERRA-FINCH *Phrygilus gayi* (2)

PATAGONIAN SIERRA-FINCH *Phrygilus patagonicus* (2)

MOURNING SIERRA-FINCH *Phrygilus fruticeti* (2)

PLUMBEOUS SIERRA-FINCH *Phrygilus unicolor* (2)

RED-BACKED SIERRA-FINCH *Phrygilus dorsalis* (2)

WHITE-THROATED SIERRA-FINCH *Phrygilus erythronotus* (2)

ASH-BREASTED SIERRA-FINCH *Phrygilus plebejus* (2)

CARBONATED SIERRA-FINCH *Phrygilus carbonarius* (2)

BAND-TAILED SIERRA-FINCH *Phrygilus alaudinus* (2)

CANARY-WINGED FINCH or BLACK-THROATED FINCH *Melanodera melanodera* (2) [NT]

YELLOW-BRIDLED FINCH *Melanodera xanthogramma* (2)

SLATY FINCH *Haplospiza rustica* (1, 2)

UNIFORM FINCH *Haplospiza unicolor* (2)

PEG-BILLED FINCH *Acanthidops bairdii* (2) [NT]

BLACK-CRESTED FINCH *Lophospingus pusillus* (2)

GRAY-CRESTED FINCH *Lophospingus griseocristatus* (2)

LONG-TAILED REED-FINCH *Donacospiza albifrons* (2)

GOUGH FINCH *Rowettia goughensis* (2) [VU]

NIGHTINGALE FINCH or TRISTAN BUNTING *Nesospiza acunhae* (2) [VU]

WILKINS'S FINCH or GROSBEAK BUNTING *Nesospiza wilkinsi* (2) [VU]

WHITE-WINGED DIUCA-FINCH *Diuca speculifera* (2)

COMMON DIUCA-FINCH *Diuca diuca* (2)

SHORT-TAILED FINCH *Idiopsar brachyurus* (2)

CINEREOUS FINCH *Piezorhina cinerea* (2)

SLENDER-BILLED FINCH *Xenospingus concolor* (2) [VU]

GREAT INCA-FINCH *Incaspiza pulchra* (2)

RUFOUS-BACKED INCA-FINCH *Incaspiza personata* (2)

GRAY-WINGED INCA-FINCH *Incaspiza ortizi* (2) [NT]

BUFF-BRIDLED INCA-FINCH *Incaspiza laeta* (2)

LITTLE INCA-FINCH *Incaspiza watkinsi* (2) [NT]

BAY-CHESTED WARBLING-FINCH *Poospiza thoracica* (2)

BOLIVIAN WARBLING-FINCH *Poospiza boliviana* (2)

PLAIN-TAILED WARBLING-FINCH *Poospiza alticola* (2) [EN]

RUFOUS-SIDED WARBLING-FINCH *Poospiza hypochondria* (2)

CINNAMON WARBLING-FINCH *Poospiza ornata* (2)

RUSTY-BROWED WARBLING-FINCH *Poospiza erythrophrys* (2)

BLACK-AND-CHESTNUT WARBLING-FINCH *Poospiza whitii* (2)

BLACK-AND-RUFOUS WARBLING-FINCH *Poospiza nigrorufa* (2)

RED-RUMPED WARBLING-FINCH *Poospiza lateralis* (2)

RUFOUS-BREASTED WARBLING-FINCH *Poospiza rubecula* (2) [EN]

COCHABAMBA MOUNTAIN-FINCH *Poospiza garleppi* (2) [EN]

TUCUMAN MOUNTAIN-FINCH *Poospiza baeri* (2) [VU]

CHESTNUT-BREASTED MOUNTAIN-FINCH *Poospiza caesar* (2)

COLLARED WARBLING-FINCH *Poospiza hispaniolensis* (2)

RINGED WARBLING-FINCH *Poospiza torquata* (2)

BLACK-CAPPED WARBLING-FINCH *Poospiza melanoleuca* (2)

CINEREOUS WARBLING-FINCH *Poospiza cinerea* (2) [NT]

STRIPE-TAILED YELLOW-FINCH *Sicalis citrina* (2)

PUNA YELLOW-FINCH *Sicalis lutea* (2)

BRIGHT-RUMPED YELLOW-FINCH *Sicalis uropygialis* (2)

CITRON-HEADED YELLOW-FINCH *Sicalis luteocephala* (2) [NT]

GREATER YELLOW-FINCH *Sicalis auriventris* (2)

GREENISH YELLOW-FINCH *Sicalis olivascens* (2)

PATAGONIAN YELLOW-FINCH *Sicalis lebruni* (2)

ORANGE-FRONTED YELLOW-FINCH *Sicalis columbiana* (2)

SAFFRON FINCH *Sicalis flaveola* (2)

GRASSLAND YELLOW-FINCH *Sicalis luteola* (1, 2)

MISTO YELLOW-FINCH *Sicalis luteiventris* (2)

RAIMONDI'S YELLOW-FINCH *Sicalis raimondii* (2)

SULFUR-THROATED FINCH *Sicalis taczanowskii* (2)

WEDGE-TAILED GRASS-FINCH *Emberizoides herbicola* (2)

DUIDA GRASS-FINCH *Emberizoides duidae* (2)

GRAY-CHEEKED GRASS-FINCH or LESSER GRASS-FINCH *Emberizoides ypiranganus* (2) [NT]

GREAT PAMPA-FINCH *Embernagra platensis* (2)

PALE-THROATED PAMPA-FINCH *Embernagra longicauda* (2) [NT]

BLUE-BLACK GRASSQUIT *Volatinia jacarina* (1, 2)

BUFFY-FRONTED SEEDEATER *Sporophila frontalis* (2) [EN]

TEMMINCK'S SEEDEATER *Sporophila falcirostris* (2) [EN]

SLATE-COLORED SEEDEATER *Sporophila schistacea* (2)

GRAY SEEDEATER *Sporophila intermedia* (2)

PLUMBEOUS SEEDEATER *Sporophila plumbea* (2)

VARIABLE SEEDEATER *Sporophila corvina* (1, 2)

WING-BARRED SEEDEATER *Sporophila americana* (2)

CAQUETA SEEDEATER *Sporophila murallae* (2)

WHITE-COLLARED SEEDEATER *Sporophila torqueola* (1, 2)

RUSTY-COLLARED SEEDEATER *Sporophila collaris* (2)

LESSON'S SEEDEATER *Sporophila bouvronides* (2)

LINED SEEDEATER *Sporophila lineola* (2)

BLACK-AND-WHITE SEEDEATER *Sporophila luctuosa* (2)

YELLOW-BELLIED SEEDEATER *Sporophila nigricollis* (2)

HOODED SEEDEATER *Sporophila melanops* (2) [VU]

DOUBLE-COLLARED SEEDEATER *Sporophila caerulescens* (2)

WHITE-THROATED SEEDEATER *Sporophila albogularis* (2)

WHITE-BELLIED SEEDEATER *Sporophila leucoptera* (2)

PARROT-BILLED SEEDEATER *Sporophila peruviana* (2)

DRAB SEEDEATER *Sporophila simplex* (2)

BLACK-AND-TAWNY SEEDEATER *Sporophila nigrorufa* (2) [EN]

CAPPED SEEDEATER *Sporophila bouvreuil* (2)

RUDDY-BREASTED SEEDEATER *Sporophila minuta* (1, 2)

TAWNY-BELLIED SEEDEATER *Sporophila hypoxantha* (2)

DARK-THROATED SEEDEATER *Sporophila ruficollis* (2) [NT]

MARSH SEEDEATER *Sporophila palustris* (2) [EN]

CHESTNUT-BELLIED SEEDEATER *Sporophila castaneiventris* (2)

GRAY-AND-CHESTNUT SEEDEATER or RUFOUS-RUMPED SEEDEATEr *Sporophila hypochroma* (2) [NT]

CHESTNUT SEEDEATER *Sporophila cinnamomea* (2) [NT]

NAROSKY'S SEEDEATER or ENTRE RIOS SEEDEATER *Sporophila zelichi* 2 [CR]

BLACK-BELLIED SEEDEATER *Sporophila melanogaster* (2) [NT]

CHESTNUT-THROATED SEEDEATER *Sporophila telasco* (2)

TUMACO SEEDEATER *Sporophila insulata* (2) [CR]

NICARAGUAN SEED-FINCH *Oryzoborus nuttingi* (2)

LARGE-BILLED SEED-FINCH *Oryzoborus crassirostris* (2) [NT]

BLACK-BILLED SEED-FINCH *Oryzoborus atrirostris* (2)

GREAT-BILLED SEED-FINCH *Oryzoborus maximiliani* (2) [NT]

LESSER SEED-FINCH *Oryzoborus angolensis* (1, 2)

BLUE SEEDEATER *Amaurospiza concolor* (1, 2)

SLATE-BLUE SEEDEATER *Amaurospiza relicta* (1) [NT]

BLACKISH-BLUE SEEDEATER *Amaurospiza moesta* (2) [NT]

CUBAN BULLFINCH *Melopyrrha nigra* (2)

WHITE-NAPED SEEDEATER *Dolospingus fringilloides* (2)

BAND-TAILED SEEDEATER *Catamenia analis* (2)

PLAIN-COLORED SEEDEATER *Catamenia inornata* (2)

PARAMO SEEDEATER *Catamenia homochroa* (2)

DULL-COLORED GRASSQUIT *Tiaris obscura* (2)

CUBAN GRASSQUIT *Tiaris canora* (2)

YELLOW-FACED GRASSQUIT *Tiaris olivacea* (1, 2)

BLACK-FACED GRASSQUIT *Tiaris bicolor* (2)

SOOTY GRASSQUIT *Tiaris fuliginosa* (2)

YELLOW-SHOULDERED GRASSQUIT *Loxipasser anoxanthus* (2)

PUERTO RICAN BULLFINCH *Loxigilla portoricensis* (2)

GREATER ANTILLEAN BULLFINCH *Loxigilla violacea* (2)

LESSER ANTILLEAN BULLFINCH *Loxigilla noctis* (2)

CINNAMON-BELLIED FLOWER-PIERCER *Diglossa baritula* (1, 2)

SLATY FLOWER-PIERCER *Diglossa plumbea* (2)

RUSTY FLOWER-PIERCER *Diglossa sittoides* (2)

VENEZUELAN FLOWER-PIERCER *Diglossa venezuelensis* (2) [CR]

WHITE-SIDED FLOWER-PIERCER *Diglossa albilatera* (2)

CHESTNUT-BELLIED FLOWER-PIERCER *Diglossa gloriosissima* (2)

GLOSSY FLOWER-PIERCER *Diglossa lafresnayii* (2)

MUSTACHED FLOWER-PIERCER *Diglossa mystacalis* (2)

MERIDA FLOWER-PIERCER *Diglossa gloriosa* (2)

BLACK FLOWER-PIERCER *Diglossa humeralis* (2)

BLACK-THROATED FLOWER-PIERCER *Diglossa brunneiventris* (2)

GRAY-BELLIED FLOWER-PIERCER *Diglossa carbonaria* (2)

SCALED FLOWER-PIERCER *Diglossa duidae* (2)

GREATER FLOWER-PIERCER *Diglossa major* (2)

INDIGO FLOWER-PIERCER *Diglossopis indigotica* (2)

DEEP-BLUE FLOWER-PIERCER or GOLDEN-EYED FLOWER-PIERCER *Diglossopis glauca* (2)

BLUISH FLOWER-PIERCER *Diglossopis caerulescens* (2)

MASKED FLOWER-PIERCER *Diglossopis cyanea* (2)

ORANGEQUIT *Euneornis campestris* (2)

ST. LUCIA BLACK FINCH *Melanospiza richardsoni* (2) [NT]

LARGE GROUND-FINCH *Geospiza magnirostris* (2)

MEDIUM GROUND-FINCH *Geospiza fortis* (2)

SMALL GROUND-FINCH *Geospiza fuliginosa* (2)

SHARP-BEAKED GROUND-FINCH *Geospiza difficilis* (2)

COMMON CACTUS-FINCH *Geospiza scandens* (2)

LARGE CACTUS-FINCH *Geospiza conirostris* (2)

VEGETARIAN FINCH *Camarhynchus crassirostris* (2)

LARGE TREE-FINCH *Camarhynchus psittacula* (2)

MEDIUM TREE-FINCH *Camarhynchus pauper* (2) [NT]

SMALL TREE-FINCH *Camarhynchus parvulus* (2)

WOODPECKER FINCH *Camarhynchus pallidus* (2)

MANGROVE FINCH *Camarhynchus heliobates* (2) [EN]

WARBLER FINCH *Certhidea olivacea* (2)

COCOS FINCH *Pinaroloxias inornata* (2) [VU]

Tribe CARDINALINI

DICKCISSEL *Spiza americana* (1, 2)

YELLOW GROSBEAK *Pheucticus chrysopeplus* (1)

GOLDEN-BELLIED GROSBEAK or SOUTHERN YELLOW-GROSBEAK *Pheucticus chrysogaster* (2)

BLACK-THIGHED GROSBEAK *Pheucticus tibialis* (2)

BLACK-BACKED GROSBEAK *Pheucticus aureoventris* (2)

ROSE-BREASTED GROSBEAK *Pheucticus ludovicianus* (1, 2)

BLACK-HEADED GROSBEAK *Pheucticus melanocephalus* (1)

NORTHERN CARDINAL *Cardinalis cardinalis* (1, 2)

VERMILION CARDINAL *Cardinalis phoeniceus* (2)

PYRRHULOXIA *Cardinalis sinuatus* (1)

BLACK-FACED GROSBEAK *Caryothraustes poliogaster* (1, 2)

YELLOW-GREEN GROSBEAK *Caryothraustes canadensis* (2)

YELLOW-SHOULDERED GROSBEAK *Caryothraustes humeralis* (2)

CRIMSON-COLLARED GROSBEAK *Rhodothraupis celaeno* (1)

RED-AND-BLACK GROSBEAK *Periporphyrus erythromelas* (2)

SLATE-COLORED GROSBEAK *Saltator grossus* (2)

BLACK-THROATED GROSBEAK *Saltator fuliginosus* (2)

BLACK-HEADED SALTATOR *Saltator atriceps* (1, 2)

BUFF-THROATED SALTATOR *Saltator maximus* (1, 2)

BLACK-WINGED SALTATOR *Saltator atripennis* (2)

GRAYISH SALTATOR *Saltator coerulescens* (1, 2)

GREEN-WINGED SALTATOR *Saltator similis* (2)

ORINOCAN SALTATOR *Saltator orenocensis* (2)

BLACK-COWLED SALTATOR *Saltator nigriceps* (2)

GOLDEN-BILLED SALTATOR *Saltator aurantiirostris* (2)

THICK-BILLED SALTATOR *Saltator maxillosus* (2) [NT]

MASKED SALTATOR *Saltator cinctus* (2) [NT]

BLACK-THROATED SALTATOR *Saltator atricollis* (2)

RUFOUS-BELLIED SALTATOR *Saltator rufiventris* (2) [VU]

LESSER ANTILLEAN SALTATOR *Saltator albicollis* (2)

STREAKED SALTATOR *Saltator striatipectus* (2)

INDIGO GROSBEAK or GLAUCOUS-BLUE GROSBEAK *Cyanoloxia glaucocaerulea* (2)

BLUE-BLACK GROSBEAK *Cyanocompsa cyanoides* (1, 2)

BLUE BUNTING *Cyanocompsa parellina* (1, 2)

ULTRAMARINE GROSBEAK *Cyanocompsa brissonii* (2)

BLUE GROSBEAK *Guiraca caerulea* (1, 2)

LAZULI BUNTING *Passerina amoena* (1)

INDIGO BUNTING *Passerina cyanea* (1, 2)

VARIED BUNTING *Passerina versicolor* (1)

PAINTED BUNTING *Passerina ciris* (1)

ROSE-BELLIED BUNTING *Passerina rositae* (1) [NT]

ORANGE-BREASTED BUNTING *Passerina leclancherii* (1)

YELLOW-BILLED BLUE FINCH *Porphyrospiza caerulescens* (2) [NT]

Tribe ICTERINI

CASQUED OROPENDOLA *Psarocolius oseryi* (2)

CRESTED OROPENDOLA *Psarocolius decumanus* (2)

GREEN OROPENDOLA *Psarocolius viridis* (2)

DUSKY-GREEN OROPENDOLA *Psarocolius atrovirens* (2)

RUSSET-BACKED OROPENDOLA *Psarocolius angustifrons* (2)

CHESTNUT-HEADED OROPENDOLA *Psarocolius wagleri* (1, 2)

BAND-TAILED OROPENDOLA *Ocyalus latirostris* (2)

MONTEZUMA OROPENDOLA *Gymnostinops montezuma* (1, 2)

BAUDO OROPENDOLA *Gymnostinops cassini* (2) [EN]

AMAZONIAN OROPENDOLA *Gymnostinops bifasciatus* (2)

BLACK OROPENDOLA *Gymnostinops guatimozinus* (2)

YELLOW-RUMPED CACIQUE *Cacicus cela* (2)

RED-RUMPED CACIQUE *Cacicus haemorrhous* (2)

SCARLET-RUMPED CACIQUE *Cacicus uropygialis* (2)

SELVA CACIQUE *Cacicus koepckeae* (2) [VU]

GOLDEN-WINGED CACIQUE *Cacicus chrysopterus* (2)

MOUNTAIN CACIQUE *Cacicus chrysonotus* (2)

ECUADORIAN CACIQUE *Cacicus sclateri* (2)

SOLITARY CACIQUE *Cacicus solitarius* (2)

YELLOW-WINGED CACIQUE *Cacicus melanicterus* (1, 2)

YELLOW-BILLED CACIQUE *Amblycercus holosericeus* (1, 2)

MORICHE ORIOLE *Icterus chrysocephalus* (2)

EPAULET ORIOLE *Icterus cayanensis* (2)

AUDUBON'S ORIOLE *Icterus graduacauda* (1)

YELLOW-BACKED ORIOLE *Icterus chrysater* (1, 2)

YELLOW ORIOLE *Icterus nigrogularis* (2)

JAMAICAN ORIOLE *Icterus leucopteryx* (2)

ORANGE ORIOLE *Icterus auratus* (2)

YELLOW-TAILED ORIOLE *Icterus mesomelas* (1, 2)

ORANGE-CROWNED ORIOLE *Icterus auricapillus* (2)

WHITE-EDGED ORIOLE *cterus graceannae* (2)

SPOT-BREASTED ORIOLE *Icterus pectoralis* (1, 2)

ALTAMIRA ORIOLE *Icterus gularis* (1, 2)

STREAK-BACKED ORIOLE *Icterus pustulatus* (1, 2)

TROUPIAL *Icterus icterus* (2)

CAMPO ORIOLE *Icterus jamacaii* (2)

BALTIMORE ORIOLE *Icterus galbula* (1, 2)

BULLOCK'S ORIOLE *Icterus bullockii* (1, 2)

BLACK-BACKED ORIOLE or ABEILLE'S ORIOLE *Icterus abeillei* (1)

HOODED ORIOLE *Icterus cucullatus* (1, 2)

ORCHARD ORIOLE *Icterus spurius* (1, 2)

BLACK-VENTED ORIOLE *Icterus wagleri* (1, 2)

BLACK-COWLED ORIOLE *Icterus dominicensis* (1, 2)

MONTSERRAT ORIOLE *Icterus oberi* (2) [NT]

MARTINIQUE ORIOLE *Icterus bonana* (2) [EN]

ST. LUCIA ORIOLE *Icterus laudabilis* (2) [NT]

BAR-WINGED ORIOLE *Icterus maculialatus* (1, 2)

SCOTT'S ORIOLE *Icterus parisorum* (1)

JAMAICAN BLACKBIRD *Nesopsar nigerrimus* (2) [NT]

ORIOLE BLACKBIRD *Gymnomystax mexicanus* (2)

YELLOW-HEADED BLACKBIRD *Xanthocephalus xanthocephalus* (1)

SAFFRON-COWLED BLACKBIRD *Agelaius flavus* (2) [EN]

PALE-EYED BLACKBIRD *Agelaius xanthophthalmus* (2)

YELLOW-WINGED BLACKBIRD *Agelaius thilius* (2)

UNICOLORED BLACKBIRD *Agelaius cyanopus* (2)

RED-WINGED BLACKBIRD *Agelaius phoeniceus* (1, 2)

RED-SHOULDERED BLACKBIRD or CUBAN RED-WINGED BLACKBIRD *Agelaius assimilis* (2)

TRICOLORED BLACKBIRD *Agelaius tricolor* (1)

YELLOW-HOODED BLACKBIRD *Agelaius icterocephalus* (2)

TAWNY-SHOULDERED BLACKBIRD *Agelaius humeralis* (2)

YELLOW-SHOULDERED BLACKBIRD *Agelaius xanthomus* (2) [EN]

CHESTNUT-CAPPED BLACKBIRD *Agelaius ruficapillus* (2)

RED-BREASTED BLACKBIRD *Leistes militaris* (2)

WHITE-BROWED BLACKBIRD *Leistes superciliaris* (2)

PERUVIAN MEADOWLARK *Sturnella bellicosa* (2)

PAMPAS MEADOWLARK *Sturnella militaris* (2) [EN]

LONG-TAILED MEADOWLARK *Sturnella loyca* (2)

EASTERN MEADOWLARK *Sturnella magna* (1, 2)

LILIAN'S MEADOWLARK *Sturnella lilianae* (1, 2)

WESTERN MEADOWLARK *Sturnella neglecta* (1, 2)

YELLOW-RUMPED MARSHBIRD *Pseudoleistes guirahuro* (2)

BROWN-AND-YELLOW MARSHBIRD *Pseudoleistes virescens* (2)

SCARLET-HEADED BLACKBIRD *Amblyramphus holosericeus* (2)

RED-BELLIED GRACKLE *Hypopyrrhus pyrohypogaster* (2) [EN]

AUSTRAL BLACKBIRD *Curaeus curaeus* (2)

FORBES'S BLACKBIRD *Curaeus forbesi* (2) [CR]

CHOPI BLACKBIRD *Gnorimopsar chopi* (2)

BOLIVIAN BLACKBIRD *Oreopsar bolivianus* (2)

VELVET-FRONTED GRACKLE *Lampropsar tanagrinus* (2)

GOLDEN-TUFTED GRACKLE *Macroagelaius imthurni* (2)

MOUNTAIN GRACKLE *Macroagelaius subalaris* (2) [NT]

CUBAN BLACKBIRD *Dives atroviolacea* (2)

MELODIOUS BLACKBIRD *Dives dives* (1, 2)

SCRUB BLACKBIRD *Dives warszewiczi* (2)

GREAT-TAILED GRACKLE *Quiscalus mexicanus* (1, 2)

BOAT-TAILED GRACKLE *Quiscalus major* (1)

SLENDER-BILLED GRACKLE *Quiscalus palustris* (1) [EX]

NICARAGUAN GRACKLE *Quiscalus nicaraguensis* (2) [NT]

COMMON GRACKLE *Quiscalus quiscula* (1)

GREATER ANTILLEAN GRACKLE *Quiscalus niger* (2)

CARIB GRACKLE *Quiscalus lugubris* (2)

RUSTY BLACKBIRD *Euphagus carolinus* (1)

BREWER'S BLACKBIRD *Euphagus cyanocephalus* (1)

BAY-WINGED COWBIRD *Molothrus badius* (2)

SCREAMING COWBIRD *Molothrus rufoaxillaris* (2)

SHINY COWBIRD *Molothrus bonariensis* (2)

BRONZED COWBIRD *Molothrus aeneus* (1, 2)

BROWN-HEADED COWBIRD *Molothrus ater* (3)

GIANT COWBIRD *Molothrus oryzivora* (1, 2)

BOBOLINK *Dolichonyx oryzivorus* (1, 2)

Source: adapted from C. Sibley and B. Monroe. *Distribution and Taxonomy of Birds of the World* (New Haven: Yale University Press, 1992), *Sibley's Birds of the World 2.0* (Cincinnati: Thayer Birding Software, 1994); J.F. Clements, *Birds of the World: A Checklist* (Vista, CA: Ibis Publishing Co., 1991); C.M. Perrins, *The Illustrated Encyclopedia of Birds* (New York: Prentice Hall Press, 1990); N.J. Collar, M.C. Crosby and A.J. Stattersfield, *Birds to Watch 2: The World List of Threatened Birds* (Cambridge, U.K.: BirdLife International 1994); and the International Union for Conservation of Nature and Natural Resources. (For ongoing changes, see the World List of Avian Names at http://www.zoonomen.net)

American and British Equivalencies in Names of Birds

American	Latin	British
Arctic loon	*Gavia arctica*	Black-throated diver
Atlantic puffin	*Fratercula arctica*	Puffin
Bank swallow	*Riparia riparia*	Sand martin
Barn swallow	*Hirundo rustica*	Swallow
Black scoter	*Melanitta nigra*	Common scoter
Black-bellied plover	*Pluvialis squatarola*	Grey plover
Black-billed magpie	*Pica pica*	Magpie
Black-crowned night heron	*Nycticorax nycticorax*	Night heron
Black-legged kittiwake	*Rissa tridactyla*	Kittiwake
Bohemian waxwing	*Bombycilla garrulus*	Waxwing
Boreal owl	*Aegolius funereus*	Tengmalm's owl
Brant	*Branta bernicla*	Brent Goose
Chickadees	*Parus spp.*	Tits
Common goldeneye	*Bucephala clangula*	Goldeneye
Common loon	*Gavia immer*	Great northern diver
Common merganser	*Mergus merganser*	Goosander
Common murre	*Uria aalge*	Guillemot
Common raven	*Corvus corax*	Raven
Dovekie	*Alle alle*	Little auk
Eared grebe	*Podiceps nigricollis*	Black-necked grebe
Great cormorant	*Phalacrocorax carbo*	Cormorant
Greater scaup	*Aythya marila*	Scaup
Green-winged teal	*Anas crecca*	Teal
Hawks	*Buteo spp.*	Buzzard
Horned grebe	*Podiceps auritus*	Slavonian grebe
Horned lark	*Eremophila alpestris*	Shore lark
Kinglets	*Regulus spp.*	Goldcrest, Firecrest
Lapland longspur	*Calcarius lapponicus*	Lapland bunting
Long-tailed jaeger	*Stercorarius longicaudus*	Long-tailed skua
Mew gull	*Larus canus*	Common gull
Northern harrier	*Circus cyaneus*	Hen harrier
Northern shoveler	*Anas clypeata*	Shoveler
Northern shrike	*Lanius excubitor*	Great grey shrike
Oldsquaw	*Clangula hyemalis*	Long-tailed duck
Parasitic jaeger	*Stercorarius parasiticus*	Arctic skua
Pomarine jaeger	*Stercorarius pomarinus*	Pomarine skua
Red crossbill	*Loxia curvirostra*	Crossbill
Red phalarope	*Phalaropus fulicaria*	Grey phalarope
Red-throated loon	*Gavia stellata*	Red-throated diver
Rock ptarmigan	*Lagopus mutus*	Ptarmigan
Ruddy turnstone	*Arenaria interpres*	Turnstone
Snowy plover	*Charadrius alexandrinus*	Kentish plover
Thick-billed murre	*Uria lomia*	Brünnich's guillemot
White-winged scoter	*Melanitta fusca*	Velvet scoter
White-winged crossbill	*Loxia leucoptera*	Two-barred crossbill
Willow ptarmigan	*Lagopus lagopus*	Red/Willow grouse
Winter wren	*Troglodytes troglodytes*	Wren
Yellow-billed loon	*Gavia adamsii*	White-billed diver

Classification of the Class Aves

Traditional

Order	Family	(No. of species)
STRUTHIONIFORMES	STRUTHIONIDAE	Ostrich (1)
	RHEIDAE	rheas (2)
	CASUARIIDAE	cassowaries (3)
	DROMAIIDAE	Emu (1)
	APTERYGIDAE	kiwis (3)
TINAMIFORMES	TINAMIDAE	tinamous (47)
SPHENISCIFORMES	SPHENISCIDAE	penguins (17)
GAVIIFORMES	GAVIIDAE	divers or loons (4)
PODICIPEDIFORMES	PODICIPEDIDAE	grebes (22)
PROCELLARIIFORMES	DIOMEDEIDAE	albatrosses (14)
	PROCELLARIIDAE	petrels, shearwaters (70)
	HYDROBATIDAE	storm-petrels (20)
	PELECANOIIDIDAE	diving-petrels (4)
PELECANIFORMES	PHAETHONTIDAE	tropicbirds (3)
	PELECANIDAE	pelicans (7)
	SULIDAE	gannets, boobies (9)
	PHALACROCORACIDAE	cormorants (39)
	ANHINGIDAE	darters (2)
	FREGATIDAE	frigatebirds (5)
CICONIFORMES	ARDEIDAE	herons (60)
	SCOPIDAE	Hamerkop (1)
	CICONIIDAE	storks (19)
	BALAENCIPITIDAE	Shoebill (1)
	THRESKIORNITHIDAE	ibises, spoonbills (32)
PHOENICOPTERIFORMES	PHOENICOPTERIDAE	flamingos (5)
ANSERIFORMES	ANHIMIDAE	screamers (3)
	ANATIDAE	ducks, geese, swans (147)
FALCONIFORMES	CATHARTIDAE	New World vultures and vultures (7)
	PANDIONIDAE	Osprey (1)
	ACCIPITRIDAE	hawks, eagles (217)
	SAGITTARIIDAE	Secretary Bird (1)
	FALCONIDAE	caracaras, falcons (61)
GALLIFORMES	MEGAPODIIDAE	megapodes (12)
	CRACIDAE	guans, chachalacas, curassows (44)
	PHASIANDIAE	pheasants, grouse (213)
	OPISTHOCOMIDAE	Hoatzin (1)

Order	Family	(No. of species)
GRUIFORMES	MESITORNITHIDAE	mesites (3)
	TURNICIDAE	buttonquails (14)
	PEDIONOMIDAE	Plains-wanderer (1)
	GRUIDAE	cranes (15)
	ARAMIDAE	Limpkin (1)
	PSOPHIIDAE	trumpeters (3)
	RALLIDAE	rails, coots (133)
	HELIORNITHIDAE	finfoots (3)
	RHYNOCHETIDAE	Kagu (1)
	EURYPYGIDAE	Sunbittern (1)
	CARIAMIDAE	seriemas (2)
	OTIDIDAE	bustards (24)
CHARADRIIFORMES	JACANIDAE	jacanas (8)
	ROSTRATULIDAE	painted-snipe (2)
	DROMADIDAE	Crab Plover (1)
	HAEMATOPODIDAE	oystercatchers (7)
	IBIDORHYNCHIDAE	Ibisbill (1)
	RECURVIROSTRIDAE	avocets, stilts (13)
	BURHINIDAE	thick-knees (9)
	GLAREOLIDAE	coursers, pratincoles (16)
	CHARADRIIDAE	plovers (64)
	SCOLOPACIDAE	sandpipers, snipe (86)
	THINOCORIDAE	seedsnipe (4)
	CHIONIDIDAE	sheathbills (2)
	STERCORARIIDAE	skuas (5)
	LARIDAE	gulls, terns (90)
	RYNCHOPIDAE	skimmers (3)
	ALCIDAE	auks (23)
COLUMBIFORMES	PTEROCLIDIDAE	sandgrouse (16)
	COLUMBIDAE	pigeons, doves (283)
PSITTACIFORMES	LORIIDAE	lories (55)
	CACATUIDAE	cockatoos (18)
	PSITTACIDAE	parrots (271)
CULCULIFORMES	MUSOPHAGIDAE	turacos (19)
	CUCULIDAE	cuckoos (130)
STRIGIFORMES	TYTONIDAE	barn owls (12)
	STRIGIDAE	typical owls (134)
CAPRIMULGIFORMES	STEATORNITHIDAE	Oilbird (1)
	PODARGIDAE	frogmouths (13)
	NYCTIBIIDAE	potoos (5)
	AEGOTHELIDAE	owlet-nightjars (8)
	CAPRIMULGIDAE	nightjars (76)
APODIFORMES	APODIDAE	swifts (82)
	HEMIPROCNIDAE	tree-swifts (4)
	TROCHILIDAE	hummingbirds (338)

Order	Family	(No. of species)
COLIFORMES	COLIIDAE	mousebirds (6)
TROGONIFORMES	TROGONIDAE	trogons (37)
CORACIIFORMES	ALCEDINIDAE	kingfishers (90)
	TODIDAE	todies (5)
	MOMOTIDAE	motmots (9)
	MEROPIDAE	bee-eaters (21)
	CORACIIDAE	rollers (11)
	BRACHYPTERACIIDAE	ground-rollers (5)
	LEPTOSOMATIDAE	Cuckoo-roller (1)
	UPUPIDAE	Hoopoe (1)
	PHOENICULIDAE	woodhoopoes (8)
	BUCEROTIDAE	hornbills (44)
PICIFORMES	GALBULIDAE	jacamars (17)
	BUCCONIDAE	puffbirds (34)
	CAPITONIDAE	barbets (81)
	INDICATORIDAE	honeyguides (14)
	RAMPHASTIDAE	toucans (33)
	PICIDAE	woodpeckers (204)
PASSERIFORMES	EURYLAIMIDAE	broadbills (14)
	DENDROCOCLAPTIDAE	woodcreepers (52)
	FURNARIIDAE	ovenbirds (218)
	FORMICARIIDAE	antbirds (228)
	CONOPOPHAGIDAE	gnateaters (11)
	RHINOCRYPTIDAE	tapaculos (30)
	COTINGIDAE	cotingas (79)
	PIPRIDAE	manakins (57)
	TYRANNIDAE	tyrant flycatchers (374)
	OXYRUNCIDAE	Sharpbill (1)
	PHYTOTOMIDAE	plantcutters (3)
	PITTIDAE	pittas (24)
	XENICIDAE	New Zealand wrens (4)
	PHILEPITTIDAE	asities (4)
	MENURIDAE	lyrebirds (2)
	ATRICHORNITHIDAE	scrub-birds (2)
	ALAUDIDAE	larks (77)
	HIRUNDINIDAE	swallows, martins (80)
	MOTACILLIDAE	wagtails, pipits (54)
	CAMPEPHAGIDAE	cuckooshrikes (70)
	PYCNONOTIDAE	bulbuls (123)
	IRENIDAE	leafbirds, ioras, fairy-bluebirds (14)
	LANIIDAE	shrikes (74)
	VANGIDAE	vanga shrikes (13)
	BOMBYCILLIDAE	waxwings (8)
	DULIDAE	Palmchat (1)

Order	Family	(No. of species)
	CINCLIDAE	dippers (5)
	TROGLODYTIDAE	wrens (59)
	MIMIDAE	mockingbirds, thrashers (31)
	PRUNELLIDAE	accentors (12)
	MUSCICAPIDAE	thrushes, chats, log-runners, babblers, parrotbills, rock-fowl, gnatwrens, Owl World warblers, Australasian wrens, Old World flycatchers, wattle-eyes, batises, monarchs, fantails, whistlers (1,423)
	AEGITHALIDAE	long-tailed tits (8)
	REMIZIDAE	penduline tits (10)
	PARIDAE	tits, chickadees (47)
	SITTIDAE	nuthatches (25)
	CERTHIIDAE	treecreepers (6)
	RHABDORNITHIDAE	Philippine creepers (2)
	CLIMACTERIDAE	Australian creepers (6)
	DICAEIDAE	flowerpeckers (58)
	NECTARINIIDAE	sunbirds (116)
	ZOSTEROPIDAE	white-eyes (83)
	MELIPHAGIDAE	honeyeaters (171)
	EMBERIZIDAE	buntings, cardinals, tanagers (558)
	PARULIDAE	New World warblers (126)
	DREPANIDIDAE	Hawaiian honeycreepers (23)
	VIREONIDAE	vireos (43)
	ICTERIDAE	New World blackbirds (95)
	FRINGILLIDAE	finches (122)
	ESTRILDIDAE	waxbills (127)
	PLOCEIDAE	weavers, sparrows (143)
	STURNIDAE	starlings (111)
	ORIOLIDAE	orioles (28)
	DICRURIDAE	drongos (20)
	CALLAEIDAE	wattlebirds (3)
	GRALLINIDAE	magpie-larks (4)
	ARTAMIDAE	woodswallows (10)
	CRACTICIDAE	butcherbirds (8)
	PTILONORHYNCHIDAE	bowerbirds (18)
	PARADISAEIDAE	birds of paradise (42)
	CORVIDAE	crows, jays (105)

SOURCE: J. del Hoyo, A. Elliott, and J. Sargatal, eds., *Handbook of the Birds of the World*, Vol. 1 (Barcelona: Lynx Edicions, 1992).

DNA–DNA Hybridization

Order	Family	(No. of species)
STRUTHIONIFORMES	STRUTHIONIDAE	Ostrich (1)
	RHEIDAE	rheas (2)
	CASUARIIDAE	cassowaries/Emu (4)
	APTERYGIDAE	kiwis (3)
TINAMIFORMES	TINAMIDAE	tinamous (47)
CRACIFORMES	CRACIDAE	guans, chachalacas, curassows (50)
	MEGAPODIIDAE	megapodes (19)
GALLIFORMES	PHASIANIDAE	grouse, turkeys, pheasants, partridges, etc. (177)
	NUMIDIDAE	guineafowl (6)
	ODONTOPHORIDAE	New World quails (31)
ANSERIFORMES	ANHIMIDAE	screamers (3)
	ANSERANATIDAE	Magpie Goose (1)
	DENDROCYGNIDAE	whistling-ducks (9)
	ANATIDAE	stiff-tailed ducks/Freckled Duck/swans/geese/typical ducks (148)
TURNICIFORMES	TURNICIDAE	buttonquails (17)
PICIFORMES	INDICATORIDAE	honeyguides (17)
	PICIDAE	woodpeckers, wrynecks (215)
	MEGALAIMIDAE	Asian barbets (26)
	LYBIIDAE	African barbets (42)
	RAMPHASTIDAE	New World barbets/toucans (55)
GALBULIFORMES	GALBULIDAE	jacamars (18)
	BUCCONIDAE	puffbirds (33)
BUCEROTIFORMES	BUCEROTIDAE	typical hornbills (54)
	BUCORVIDAE	ground-hornbills (2)
UPUPIFORMES	UPUPIDAE	hoopoes (2)
	PHOENICULIDAE	woodhoopoes (5)
	RHINOPOMASTIDAE	scimitarbills (3)
TROGONIFORMES	TROGONIDAE	African trogons/New World trogons/Asian trogons (39)
CORACIIFORMES	CORACIIDAE	typical rollers (12)
	BRACHYPTERACIIDAE	ground-rollers (5)
	LEPTOSOMIDAE	Cuckoo-roller (1)
	MOMOTIDAE	motmots (9)
	TODIDAE	todies (5)

Order	Family	(No. of species)
	ALCEDINIDAE	alcedinid kingfishers (24)
	DACELONIDAE	dacelonid kingfishers (61)
	CERYLIDAE	cerylid kingfishers (9)
	MEROPIDAE	bee-eaters (26)
COLIIFORMES	COLIIDAE	typical mousebirds/ long-tailed mousebirds (6)
CUCULIFORMES	CUCULIDAE	Old World cuckoos (79)
	CENTROPODIDAE	coucals (30)
	COCCYZIDAE	American cuckoos (18)
	OPISTHOCOMIDAE	Hoatzin (1)
	CROTOPHAGIDAE	anis/Guira Cuckoo (4)
	NEOMORPHIDAE	roadrunners, ground-cuckoos (11)
PSITTACIFORMES	PSITTACIDAE	parrots and allies (358)
APODIFORMES	APODIDAE	typical swifts (99)
	HEMIPROCNIDAE	tree-swifts (4)
TROCHILIFORMES	TROCHILIDAE	hermits/typical hummingbirds (319)
MUSOPHAGIFORMES	MUSOPHAGIDAE	turacos/plantain-eaters (23)
STRIGIFORMES	TYTONIDAE	barn and grass owls (17)
	STRIGIDAE	typical owls (161)
	AEGOTHELIDAE	owlet-nightjars (8)
	PODARGIDAE	Australian frogmouths (3)
	BATRACHOSTOMIDAE	Asian frogmouths (11)
	STEATORNITHIDAE	Oilbird (1)
	NYCTIBIIDAE	potoos (7)
	EUROSTOPODIDAE	eared-nightjars (7)
	CAPRIMULGIDAE	nighthawks/nightjars (76)
COLUMBIFORMES	COLUMBIDAE	pigeons, doves (310)
GRUIFORMES	EURYPYGIDAE	Sunbittern (1)
	OTIDIDAE	bustards (25)
	GRUIDAE	crowned-cranes/ typical cranes (15)
	HELIORNITHIDAE	Limpkin/finfoots (4)
	PSOPHIIDAE	trumpeters (3)
	CARIAMIDAE	seriemas (2)
	RHYNOCHETIDAE	Kagu (1)
	RALLIDAE	rails, gallinules, coots (142)
	MESITORNITHIDAE	mesites (3)
CICONIIFORMES	PTEROCLIDAE	sandgrouse (16)
	THINOCORIDAE	seedsnipe (4)
	PEDIONOMIDAE	Plains-wanderer (1)

Order	Family	(No. of species)
	SCOLOPACIDAE	woodcock, snipe/sandpipers, curlews, phalaropes (88)
	ROSTRATULIDAE	painted-snipe (2)
	JACANIDAE	jacanas (8)
	CHIOPMODODAE	sheathbills (2)
	BIRHIOMODAE	thick-knees (9)
	CHARADRIIDAE	oystercatchers/avocets, stilts/plovers, lapwings (89)
	GLAREOLIDAE	Crab Plover/pratincoles, coursers (18)
	LARIDAE	skuas, jaegers/skimmers/ gulls/terns/auks, murres, puffins (129)
	ACCIPITRIDAE	Osprey/hawks, eagles (240)
	SAGITTARIIDAE	Secretary Bird (1)
	FALCONIDAE	caracaras, falcons (63)
	PODICIPEDIDAE	grebes (21)
	PHAETHONTIDAE	tropicbirds (3)
	SULIDAE	gannets, boobies (9)
	ANHINGIDAE	darters (4)
	PHALACROCORACIDAE	cormorants (38)
	ARDEIDAE	herons (65)
	SCOPIDAE	Hamerkop (1)
	PHOENICOPTERIDAE	flamingos (5)
	THRESKIORNITHIDAE	ibises, spoonbills (34)
	PELECANIDAE	Shoebill/pelicans (9)
	CICONIIDAE	New World vultures/ storks (26)
	FREGATIDAE	frigatebirds (5)
	SPHENISCIDAE	penguins (17)
	GAVIIDAE	divers (5)
	PROCELLARIIDAE	petrels, shearwaters, diving-petrels/albatrosses/ storm-petrels (115)
PASSERIFORMES	ACANTHISITTIDAE	New Zealand wrens (4)
	PITTIDAE	pittas (31)
	EURYLAIMIDAE	broadbills (14)
	PHILEPITTIDAE	asities (4)
	INCERTAE SEDIS	Broad-billed Sapayoa (1)
	TYRANNIDAE	mionectine flycatchers, antpipits/tyrant flycatchers/ schiffornises/tityras, becards/ cotingas, plantcutters, Sharpbill/manakins (537)
	THAMNOPHILIDAE	typical antbirds (188)
	FURNARIIDAE	ovenbirds/woodcreepers (280)
	FORMICARIIDAE	ground antbirds (56)

Order	Family	(No. of species)
	CONOPOPHAGIDAE	gnateaters (8)
	RHINOCRYPTIDAE	tapaculos (28)
	CLIMACTERIDAE	Australo-Papuan treecreepers (7)
	MENURIDAE	lyrebirds/scrub-birds (4)
	PTILONORHYNCHIDAE	bowerbirds (20)
	MALURIDAE	fairywrens/emuwrens/grasswrens (26)
	MELIPHAGIDAE	honeyeaters, Australian chats (182)
	PARDALOTIDAE	pardalotes/bristlebirds/scrubwrens/thornbills, whitefaces, etc. (68)
	EOPSALTRIIDAE	Australo-Papuan robins, scrub-robins (46)
	IRENIDAE	fairy-bluebirds, leafbirds (10)
	ORTHONYCHIDAE	logrunners, chowchillas (2)
	POMATOSTOMIDAE	Australo-Papuan babblers (5)
	LANIIDAE	true shrikes (30)
	VIREONIDAE	vireos, peppershrikes, etc. (51)
	CORVIDAE	quail-thrushes, whipbirds/Australian Chough, Apostlebird/sittellas/*Mohoua*/shrike-tits, Crested Bellbird, Mottled Whistler/whistlers, shrike-thrushes/crows, magpies, jays, nutcrackers/birds of paradise, melampittas/currawongs, woodswallows, Peltops, Bornean Bristlehead/orioles, cuckooshrikes/fantails/drongos/monarchs, magpie-larks/ioras/bush-shrikes/helmet-shrikes, vangas, batises, wattle-eyes (647)
	CALLAEATIDAE	New Zealand wattlebirds (3)
	PICATHARTIDAE	rock-jumpers, rockfowl (4)
	BOMBYCILLIDAE	Palmchat/silky-flycatchers/waxwings (8)
	CINCLIDAE	dippers (5)
	MUSCICAPIDAE	true thrushes, Black-breasted Fruit-hunter, shortwings, alethes/Old World flycatchers/ chats (449)

Order	Family	(No. of species)
	STURNIDAE	starlings, mynas/mocking-birds, thrashers, catbirds (148)
	SITTIDAE	nuthatches/Wallcreeper (25)
	CERTHIIDAE	northern creepers/Spotted Creeper/wrens/gnatcatchers, Verdin, gnatwrens (97)
	PARIDAE	penduline tits/tits, chickadees (65)
	AEGITHALIDAE	long-tailed tits, bushtits (8)
	HIRUNDINIDAE	river martins/swallows, martins (89)
	REGULIDAE	kinglets (6)
	PYCNONOTIDAE	bulbuls (137)
	HYPOCOLIIDAE	Grey Hypocolius (1)
	CISTICOLIDAE	African warblers (119)
	ZOSTEROPIDAE	white-eyes (96)
	SYLVIIDAE	leaf-warblers/grass-warblers/laughingthrushes/babblers/rhabdornises/Wrentit/*Sylvia* warblers (552)
	ALAUDIDAE	larks (91)
	NECTARINIIDAE	sugarbirds/flowerpeckers/sunbirds, spiderhunters (169)
	MELANOCHARITIDAE	*Melanocharis* berrypeckers/longbills (10)
	PARAMYTHIIDAE	Tit Berrypecker, Crested Berrypecker (2)
	PASSERIDAE	sparrows, rock-sparrows, etc./wagtails, pipits/accentors/weavers/estrildine finches/whydahs (386)
	FRINGILLIDAE	Olive Warbler/chaffinches, Brambling/goldfinches, crossbills, etc./Hawaiian honeycreepers/buntings, longspurs, towhees/wood-warblers/tanagers, Neotropical honeycreepers, seedeaters, flower-piercers, etc./cardinals/troupials, meadowlarks, New World blackbirds, etc. (993)

SOURCE: J. del Hoyo, A. Elliott, and J. Sargatal, eds., *Handbook of the Birds of the World*, Vol. 1 (Barcelona: Lynx Edicions, 1992).

Suggested Fossil History of Birds

Geological Era	Geological Period	Epoch	Millions of Years Ago	Appearance of Modern Orders and Families	Some Extinct Birds Known from Fossils from This Period (MYA)
		Recent	0.011	Modern birds; Passeriformes are dominant order.	*Moas*, such as *Dinornis maximus*, extinct.
	Quaternary	Pleistocene	2	All modern orders and families represented; 50% of modern species appear during this time.	
		Pliocene	7	Species numbers reach maximum; larks, buntings, thrushes, swallows, fringillid sparrows, nuthatches appear.	
			13	Moas and tinamous appear.	*Argentavis magnificens* (Teratorn) (10 mya)
		Miocene	25	Most modern families and genera are present. Falcons, nighthawks, mouse-birds, shrikes North American Wood Warblers.	*Osteodontornis* (giant seabird)
			37	Families present: petrels, shearwaters, boobies, gannets, pigeons, goatsuckers, turkey, kingfishers, swifts, parrots, Old World warblers, sparrows, dabbling ducks, New World vultures.	
		Eocene	53	More than 20 modern orders now present. Penguins, ostriches, rheas, albatrosses, herons, storks, avocets, ducks, hawks, eagles, kites.	*Phororhacos* (giant flightless predatory bird) (40 mya) *Aepyornis Diatryma gigantea* (45–55 mya) *Presbyornis* (50 mya)

Geological Era	Geological Period	Epoch	Millions of Years Ago	Appearance of Modern Orders and Families	Some Extinct Birds Known from Fossils from This Period (MYA)
Cenozoic	Tertiary	Paleocene	65	Grouse, crane, pheasants, bustards, gulls and terns, auks, cuckoos, true owls, woodpeckers, rollers, hornbills, kingfishers, trog-ons, starlings, titmice.	
		Cretaceous	150	The earliest fossils resemble loons, cormorants, pelicans, grebes, ibises, sandpipers, flamingos, and rails.	Emergence and extinction of toothed birds: *Baptornis advenus*, *Neogaeornis*, *Hesperonis regalis* and *Ichthyornis dispar*. *Avimimus portentosus* (80 mya). *Gobipteryx minuta* (80 mya). *Ileropteryx* (125 mya). *Archaeopteryx lithographica*
		Jurassic	180		
Mesozoic	Triassic		220		Pseudosuchia, possible ancestor of *Archaeopteryx*.
	Permian		270	Emergence of dinosaurs.	*Protoavis (?)* (225 mya)
Paleozoic	Cambrian		600	Appearance of most kinds of invertebrates.	

BASED ON: C. Leahy, *The Birdwatcher's Companion: An Encyclopedic Handbook of North American Birdlife* (New York: Bonanza Books, 1984); N.S. Proctor and P.J. Lynch, *Manual of Ornithology: Avian Structure and Function* (New Haven, CT: Yale University Press, 1993); J.C. Welty and L. Baptista, *The Life of Birds*, 4th ed. (Orlando, FL: Harcourt Brace Jovanovich College Publishers, 1990).

Anatomy

Terms for Anatomical Characteristics of Birds

BILL

acute: bill tapering to sharp point, e.g., warbler

bent: bill deflected at an angle, e.g., flamingo, wrybill

chisel-like: bill tip beveled, e.g., woodpecker

compressed: bill mostly higher than wide, e.g., puffin

conical: bill cone-shaped, e.g., redpoll

crossed: mandible tips crossing over each other, e.g., crossbill

decurved: bill curving downward, e.g., curlew

depressed: bill wider than high, e.g., duck

gibbous: bill with a pronounced hump, e.g., scoter

hooked: upper mandible longer than lower, and with its tip bent over the tip of the lower, e.g., falcon

lamellate: mandibles with transverse, tooth-like ridges on tomia, e.g., geese

long: bill longer than head, e.g., heron

notched: bill with a slight nick in tomia of one or both mandibles, e.g., thrush

recurved: bill curving upward, e.g., godwit

serrate: bill with saw-like tomia, e.g., merganser

short: bill shorter than head, e.g., redpoll

spatulate: bill widened toward the tip, e.g., spoonbill

stout: bill high and wide, e.g., grouse

straight: line along which mandibles close following axis of head, e.g., heron

swollen: mandible sides convex, e.g., finch

terete: bill circular in cross-section, e.g., hummingbird

toothed: upper mandible tomium with one tooth, e.g., falcon, or several teeth, e.g., trogon

TAIL

double-rounded: central and outermost pairs of tail feathers are shorter than the intermediate ones producing a double-convex profile

emarginate: retrices increasing in length from the middle to the outermost pair, e.g., finch

forked: retrices increasing in length successively and in gradation from middle pair to outside pair, e.g., tern

graduated: retrices shorten successively from outside to inside, e.g., cuckoo

lanceolate: lance-shaped tail feather, i.e. two sides evenly graduated to a point

pointed: middle retrices longer than the others, e.g., pheasant

rounded: retrices shorten successively from inside to outside, e.g., crow

square: retrices all same length, e.g., sharp-shinned hawk

WING

broad: both primaries and secondaries long throughout the wing, e.g., red-tailed hawk

concave: extreme curvature of spread wing convex above and concave below, e.g., grouse

flat: slight curvature of spread wing, e.g., swift

long: distance from the bend to the tip longer than the trunk, e.g., falcon

narrow: primaries and secondaries short throughout the wing, e.g., gull

pointed: outermost primaries longest, e.g., gull

rounded: middle primaries longest and remainder graduated, e.g., sparrowhawk

short: distance from the bend to the tip is the same length as or shorter than the trunk, e.g., grebe

spurred: bend of wing with a horny structure like a spur, e.g., jacana

LEGS AND FEET

acute: nails extremely curved and sharp-pointed, e.g., woodpecker

anisodactyl: digits 2, 3, and 4 pointing forward, 1 backward; e.g., most songbirds

booted: tarsus covered by several long continuous platelike scales instead of small overlapping ones, e.g., thrush

elevated: hind toe or hallux inserted high on metatarsus such that its tip does not reach ground, e.g., rail

flattened: nails extremely flattened and broadened, e.g., grebe

heterodactyl: digits 3 and 4 forward, 1 and 2 backward; e.g., trogon

incumbent: hind toe or hallux inserted on metatarsus at same level as other three toes, e.g., meadowlark

lengthened: nails straight, elongated, and sharp-pointed, e.g., horned lark

lobate: anisodactyl with digits 2, 3, and 4 edged with lobes of skin that expand or contract during swimming; e.g., grebe

obtuse: nails less curved and blunt, e.g., grouse

palmate: anisodactyl with digits 2, 3, and 4 fully webbed; e.g., most waterfowl

pamprodactyl: zygodactyl with digits 1 and

4 pivoting freely forward and backward, e.g., swift

pectinate: nails with serrated edges, e.g., heron

raptorial: anisodactyl with strong digits armed with sharp claws or talons, e.g., hawk

reticulate: tarsus and foot covered with a fine, net-like patchwork of small, irregularly shaped plates, e.g., falcon

scutellate: tarsus and foot covered with layer of overlapping or imbricated horny keratin scales, e.g., songbirds

scutellate-booted: upper part of tarsus and foot scutellate and bottom of tarsus booted, e.g., catbird

scutellate–reticulate: upper part of tarsus and foot scutellate and bottom part reticulate, e.g., pigeon

semipalmate: anisodactyl with digits 2, 3, and 4 partially webbed; e.g., grouse

spurred: back side of tarsus modified to form a spur, e.g., pheasant

syndactyl: anisodactyl with digits 2 and 3 partly fused, e.g., kingfisher

totipalmate: anisodactyl with all four digits webbed, e.g., gannet

zygodactyl: digits 2 and 3 forward, 1 and 4 backward; e.g., owl

GENERAL ANATOMICAL REFERENCES

abdominal: region between thorax and pelvis

abductor: muscles drawing away from the body's midline

adductor: muscles drawing toward the body's midline

alar: area of the wing

antebrachium: forearm, composed of radius and ulna

anterior: toward the head

axillary: armpit area

brachial: upper arm composed of humerus

buccal: cheek area

carpal: wrist area

caudad: toward the tail

celiac: stomach area

cephalad: toward the head

cervical: neck area

costal: rib area

cranial: head area

cranially: toward the head

crural: leg area

digital: finger remnants in wing

distal: farther from the body's midline or point of attachment

dorsal: top or back side

dorsum: back surface

extensor: muscles that extend a part away from the body's midline

flexor: muscles that pull a part toward the body's midline

inferior: lower or ventral

interscapular: upper back between the shoulders

lateral: farther from the body's midline

medial: closer to the body's midline

mesial: see medial

nasal: area of nares or nostrils

nuchal: area of the nape

occipital: nape area where spine meets the skull

orbital: area of eye sockets

pectoral: chest and breast area between sternum and shoulder

plantar: sole of the feet

posterior: toward the tail

pronator: muscles that rotate wing bones forward and ventrally

proximal: closer to the body's midline or point of attachment

rostral: toward the head

sacral: pelvic area

sternal: breastbone area

superior: upper or dorsal

supinator: muscles that rotate wing bones backward and dorsally

tarsal: lower part of leg

terminally: toward the tail

ventral: lower or abdominal side

vertebral: spinal column

Skeleton

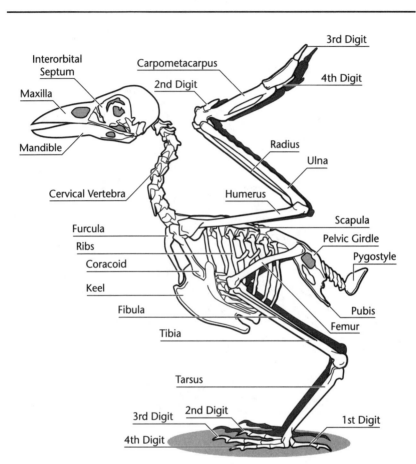

Topography

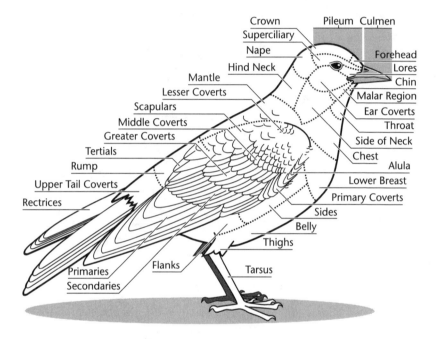

Crown
Superciliary
Nape
Hind Neck
Mantle
Lesser Coverts
Scapulars
Middle Coverts
Greater Coverts
Tertials
Rump
Upper Tail Coverts
Rectrices
Primaries
Secondaries
Flanks
Tarsus
Thighs
Belly
Sides
Lower Breast
Primary Coverts
Alula
Chest
Side of Neck
Throat
Ear Coverts
Malar Region
Chin
Lores
Forehead
Pileum Culmen

Measurements

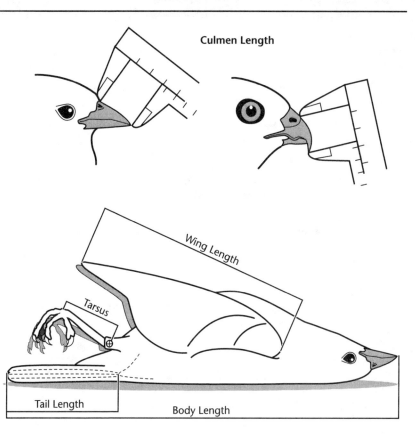

Culmen Length

Wing Length

Tarsus

Tail Length

Body Length

Circulatory System

Heart

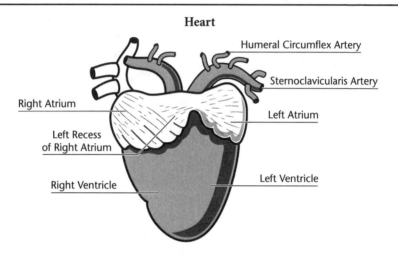

HEART WEIGHT OF SELECTED BIRD SPECIES RELATIVE TO BODY WEIGHT

	Body Weight (g)	Heart Weight (g)	% Body Weight
Ostrich	123,000	120	0.1
Emu	37,500	319	0.8
Goose	6,900	37	0.5
Chicken	3,120	14	0.4
Peking duck	2,900	23	0.8
Vulture	2,040	17	0.8
Duck	1,685	12	0.7
Pheasant	1,200	6	0.5
Common raven	1,200	12	1.0
Pigeon	297	4	1.3
Ptarmigan	258	3	1.2
Turtle dove	153	1.3	0.8
Budgerigar	35	0.45	1.3
Bluebird	29	0.5	1.7
Mango hummingbird	7.7	0.2	2.6

SOURCES: P.D. Sturkie, ed., *Avian Physiology*, 4th ed. (New York: Springer-Verlag, 1986); J.C. Welty and L. Baptista, *The Life of Birds*, 4th ed. (Orlando, FL: Harcourt Brace Jovanovich College Publishers, 1990).

APPROXIMATE HEARTBEAT RATES OF
SELECTED ADULT BIRDS AT REST

	Body Weight (g)	Heartbeat (per min)
Turkey	8,750	93
Brown pelican	7,500	150
Anser sp. (geese)	3,420	113
Mallard	2,670	118
Turkey vulture	2,000	132
Herring gull	930	218
Domestic pigeon	382	166
Crow	337	342
California quail	138	250
Mourning dove	130	135
Blue jay	77	307
Robin	69	328–384
Brown thrasher	59	303–465
Wood thrush	47	303
Cardinal	40	375
Catbird	28	307–427
House sparrow	28	350
Song sparrow	20	450
Black-capped chickadee	12	480
House wren	11	450
Ruby-throated hummingbird	4	615

SOURCES: W.A. Calder, *Condor* 70 (1968): 358–65; J.R. Simons, 1969. In *Biology and Comparative Physiology of Birds*, ed. A.J. Marshall (New York: Academic Press, 1969); A.R. Lewis, *Auk* 84 (1967): 131.

APPROXIMATE BLOOD VOLUMES FOR SELECTED BIRD SPECIES

	Body Weight (g)	Total Blood Volume (ml/100g)	Plasma Volume (ml/100g)
Great horned owl	1,495	6.4	3.4
Pheasant	1,190	6.7	4.5
Red-tailed hawk	925	6.2	3.5
Coot	550	9.5	5.1
Pigeon	310	9.2	4.4
Quail	98	7.4	4.7

SOURCE: Adapted from P.D. Sturkie, ed., *Avian Physiology*, 4th ed. (New York: Springer-Verlag, 1986).

APPROXIMATE ERYTHROCYTE (RED CORPUSCLE) NUMBERS IN SELECTED BIRD SPECIES (MILLIONS PER CUBIC MILLIMETER)

	Red Corpuscles (Millions per Cubic Millimeter)
Blackbird	6.4
Dabbling duck	3.6
Dark-eyed junco	6.2
Diving duck	3.2
Great horned owl	2.2
Guinea fowl	2.8
Jackdaw	4.5
Ostrich	1.8
Peacock	2.0
Pigeon	3.0
Red-tailed hawk	3.2
Red-throated loon	3.1
Ring-necked pheasant	3.2
Rock partridge	2.6
Ruby topaz hummingbird	6.7

SOURCES: Adapted from P.D. Sturkie, ed., *Avian Physiology*, 4th ed. (New York: Springer-Verlag, 1986); J. Dorst, *The Life of Birds*, Vol. 1 (New York: Columbia University Press, 1974).

APPROXIMATE TOTAL PLASMA (OR SERUM) PROTEINS, "ALBUMINS," "GLOBULINS," AND "A/G" RATIO IN VARIOUS SPECIES OF BIRDS

	Total protein (g/100 ml)	"Alb" (g/100 ml)	"Glob" (g/100 ml)	A/G
Bankiva	4.43	1.95	2.47	0.79
Crow	4.40	1.30	2.80	0.46
Guan	3.69	2.03	1.60	1.22
Guinea fowl	3.52	1.45	1.98	0.73
Jackdaw	4.60	1.20	2.80	0.43
Jay	4.80	1.12	3.16	0.35
Magpie	4.30	1.00	2.50	0.40
Peacock	4.36	2.41	1.94	1.24
Pheasant	4.90	2.29	2.62	0.87
Rock partridge	4.66	1.66	2.98	0.56
Rook	4.10	0.81	2.69	0.30

SOURCE: Adapted from P.D. Sturkie, ed., *Avian Physiology*, 4th ed. (New York: Springer-Verlag, 1986).

APPROXIMATE NUMBER OF LEUKOCYTES AND THROMBOCYTES IN BIRD BLOOD

	Number ($\times$ 10^3/mm^3)	
	Leukocytes	Thrombocytes
Canada goose	–	–
Ostrich	21.0	10.5
Pigeon	13.0	–
Quail	23.1	132.0
Red-winged blackbird	–	–
Ring-necked pheasant	–	–

Source: Adapted from P.D. Sturkie, ed., *Avian Physiology*, 4th ed. (New York: Springer-Verlag, 1986).

	Differential count (%)				
	Lymphocytes	Heterophils	Eosinophils	Basophils	Monocytes
Canada goose	46.0	39.0	7.0	2.0	6.0
Ostrich	26.8	59.1	6.3	4.7	3.0
Pigeon	65.6	23.0	2.2	2.6	6.6
Quail	71.6	21.8	4.3	0.2	2.1
Red-winged blackbird	55.0	30.0	3.0	2.5	8.0
Ring-necked pheasant	34.0	48.0	1.0	10.0	8.0

Source: Adapted from P.D. Sturkie, ed., *Avian Physiology*, 4th ed. (New York: Springer-Verlag, 1986).

Digestive System

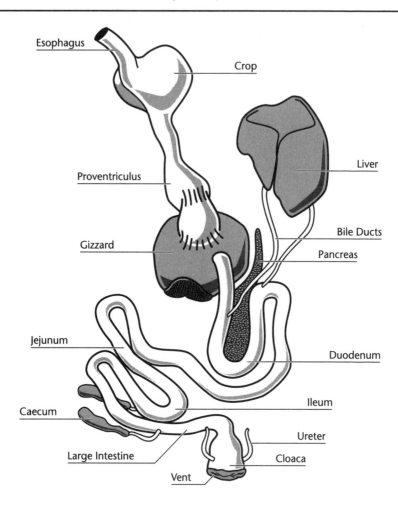

Esophagus

Crop

Liver

Proventriculus

Bile Ducts

Pancreas

Gizzard

Jejunum

Duodenum

Ileum

Caecum

Ureter

Large Intestine

Cloaca

Vent

Respiratory System

APPROXIMATE BREATHING RATES OF RESTING BIRDS RELATIVE TO BODY WEIGHT

Approximate	Breathing Rate Weight (g)	(Breaths per minute)
ostrich	100,000	5
swan	10,000	10
pheasant	1,000	16
kestrel	100	28
wren	10	100
hummingbird	3	250

SOURCE: Adapted from J.C. Welty and L. Baptista, *The Life of Birds*, 4th ed. (Orlando, FL: Harcourt Brace Jovanovich College Publishers, 1990).

AIR SACS

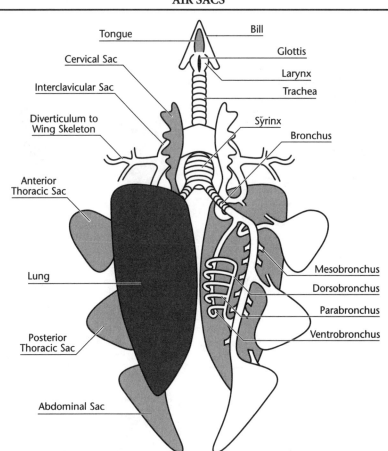

APPROXIMATE TOTAL BODY WATER OF SOME SELECTED BIRD SPECIES RELATIVE TO BODY WEIGHT

	Body weight (g)	% Body Weight in Water
Emu	32,700	63
Ducks	3,090	69
Pigeon	360	64
Japanese quail	105	67
Zebra finch	13	63

SOURCE: Adapted from P.D. Sturkie, ed., *Avian Physiology*, 4th ed. (New York: Springer-Verlag, 1986).

Urogenital System

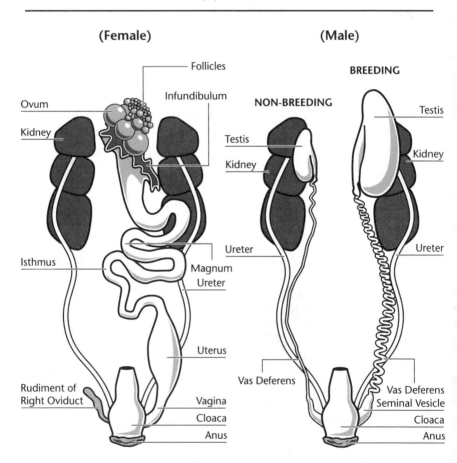

RELATIVE RESPIRATORY VOLUMES IN THE CHICKEN

Air Spaces	Volume (ml)
Cervical (both)	20
Clavicular (single)	55
Cranial thoracic (both)	50
Caudal thoracic (both)	24
Abdominal (both)	110
Lungs (both)	35
Skeletal air space	4
Total respiratory volume	298

SOURCE: A.S. King, Structural and functional aspects of the avian lungs and air sacs. *International Review of General and Experimental Zoology* 2 (1986): 171.

Metabolism and Thermoregulation

METABOLIC RATES OF SELECTED BIRD SPECIES RELATIVE TO BODY WEIGHT

	Weight (g)	Kcal/kg/24h	Kcal/24h
Bennett's cassowary	17,600	29.3	516
Trumpeter swan	8,880	47.1	418
Brown pelican	3,510	75.2	264
Golden eagle	3,000	34	102
Great blue heron	1,870	68.4	128
Raven	850	108	92
Domestic pigeon	311	105.9	32.9
Wood pigeon	150	113	17.0
Kestrel	108	157	17.0
Quail	97	235	23
White-crowned sparrow	26.4	324	8.55
Yellowhammer	26.4	354	9.35
House sparrow	24.3	449	10.90
Great tit	18.5	451	8.36
House wren	10.8	589	6.36
Anna's hummingbird	4.07	1,410	5.83
Rufous hummingbird	3.53	1,601	5.67

SOURCE: J. Dorst, *The Life of Birds*, Vol. 1 (New York: Columbia University Press, 1974).

DEEP-BODY TEMPERATURE OF SELECTED BIRD SPECIES
RELATIVE TO BODY WEIGHT*

	Body mass (g)	Deep-body temp. (°C)
Ostrich	1,000,000	38.3
Emu	38,300	38.1
Rhea	21,700	39.7
Mute swan	8,300	39.5
Domestic goose	5,000	41.0
Gentoo penguin	4,900	38.3
Peruvian penguin	3,900	39.0
Adelie penguin	3,500	38.5
Chinstrap penguin	3,100	39.4
Brown pelican	3,100	40.3
Domestic pigeon	3,000	42.2
Little penguin	900	38.4
Brown-necked raven	610	39.9
Willow ptarmigan	573	39.9
California quail	139	41.3
Mourning dove	120	42.7
American kestrel	119	39.3
Evening grosbeak	60	41.0
Speckled mousebird	53	39.0
Common redpoll	15	40.1
Zebra finch	12	40.3
Ruby-throated hummingbird	3	38.9

*At rest, under thermoneutral conditions

SOURCES: P.D. Sturkie, ed., *Avian Physiology*, 4th ed. (New York: Springer-Verlag, 1986); J. Dorst, *The Life of Birds*, Vol. 1 (New York: Columbia University Press, 1974).

Senses

BRAIN

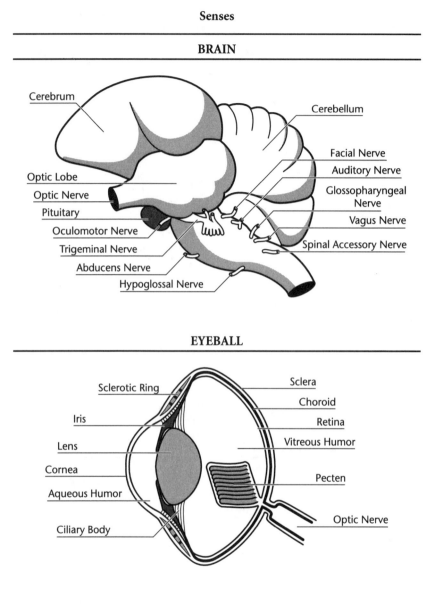

Cerebrum

Cerebellum

Optic Lobe

Facial Nerve

Auditory Nerve

Optic Nerve

Glossopharyngeal
Nerve

Pituitary

Oculomotor Nerve

Vagus Nerve

Trigeminal Nerve

Spinal Accessory Nerve

Abducens Nerve

Hypoglossal Nerve

EYEBALL

Sclerotic Ring

Sclera

Choroid

Iris

Retina

Lens

Vitreous Humor

Cornea

Aqueous Humor

Pecten

Ciliary Body

Optic Nerve

APPROXIMATE HEARING RANGE OF VARIOUS BIRD SPECIES

	Lower Limit (Hz)	Highest Sensitivity (Hz)	Upper Limit (Hz)
American kestrel	300	2,000	10,000
Black-billed magpie	100	800–1,600	21,000
Budgerigar	40	2,000	14,000
Bullfinch	200	3,200	20,000–25,000
Canary	250	2,800	10,000
Canvasback	190		5,200
Cape penguin	100	600–4,000	15,000
Chaffinch	200	3,200	29,000
Crow	300	1,000–2,000	8,000
Eagle owl	60	1,000	8,000
Great horned owl	60	7,000	
Greenfinch		20,000	
House sparrow			18,000
Long-eared owl	100	6,000	18,000
Mallard	300	2,000–3,000	8,000
Pigeon	50	1,800–2,400	11,500
Prairie horned lark	350	7,600	
Red crossbill		20,000	
Ring-billed gull	100	500–800	3,000
Ring-necked pheasant	250	10,500	
Robin		21,000	
Snow bunting	400	7,200	
Starling	700	15,000	
Tawny owl	100	3,000–6,000	21,000

SOURCE: Adapted from P.D. Sturkie, ed., *Avian Physiology*, 4th ed. (New York: Springer-Verlag, 1986).

FREQUENCY RANGES OF SONG SIGNALS IN SELECTED BIRD SPECIES

	Frequency Range of Signal (kHz)	Frequency Range of Maximal Acoustic Energy (kHz)
Bittern	1	0.5
Bonelli's warbler	2.7–7.0	3.5–6.0
Chipping sparrow	2.4–7.0	
Cuckoo	0.2–1.7	0.25–0.5
Nightingale	1–9	
Robin	1.5–11.0	4–7
Song sparrow	2.5–6.7	
White-crowned sparrow	2.2–6.8	
Willow warbler	2–7	
Wood warbler	2.8–9.0	4.5–8.0
Wren	2.5–10.0	

SOURCE: Adapted from J. Dorst, *The Life of Birds*, Vol. 1 (New York: Columbia University Press, 1974).

SIZES OF TYMPANIC MEMBRANES AND COLUMELLAS IN SELECTED BIRD SPECIES RELATIVE TO BODY AREA

	Body area (= weight ⅔) (cm²)	Tympanic membrane (cm²)	Columella base area (cm²)
Cliffchaff	4.0	0.078	0.0036
Willow warbler	4.5	0.004	0.0034
Common tit	5.0	0.089	0.0039
Blue tit	5.1	0.084	0.0032
Icterine warbler	5.7	0.086	0.0030
Black-cap warbler	6.6	0.126	0.0044
Barn swallow	7.4	0.171	0.0038
Chaffinch	7.9	0.114	0.0041
Great tit	7.9	0.104	0.0042
Common bullfinch	9.0	0.117	0.0048
House sparrow	9.6	0.091	0.0042
Blackbird	20.9	0.160	0.0073
Black-billed magpie	35.5	0.265	0.0116
Common gallinule	41.7	0.132	0.0078
Long-eared owl	44.9	0.480	0.0120
Pigeon	46.8	0.204	0.0116
Carrion crow	65.5	0.347	0.0151
Tawny owl	66.4	0.594	0.0198
Mallard	82.5	0.285	0.0109
Common coot	84.0	0.209	0.0106
Great crested grebe	86.0	0.140	0.0095
Common buzzard	86.1	0.330	0.0180
Ring-necked pheasant	113.0	0.368	0.0133
Common crane	245.0	0.418	0.0169

SOURCE: Adapted from P.D. Sturkie, ed., *Avian Physiology*, 4th ed. (New York: Springer-Verlag, 1986).

APPROXIMATE NUMBERS OF TASTE BUDS IN SELECTED BIRD SPECIES

Blue tit	24
Pigeon	37–75
Bullfinch	46
Barbary dove	54
Japanese quail	62
Starling	200
Chicken	250–350
Duck	375
Parrot	300–400

SOURCE: Adapted from P.D. Sturkie, ed., *Avian Physiology*, 4th ed. (New York: Springer-Verlag, 1986).

Flight

WING

(Dorsal View)

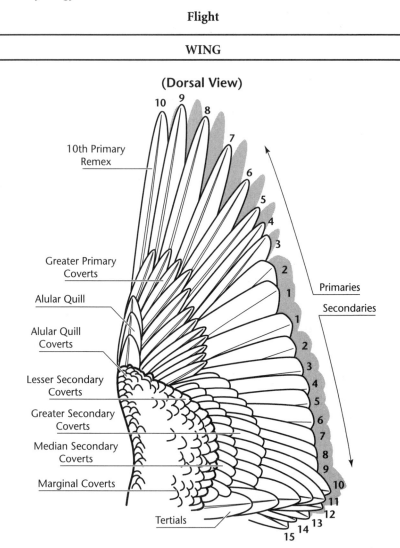

10th Primary
Remex

Greater Primary
Coverts

Alular Quill

Alular Quill
Coverts

Lesser Secondary
Coverts

Greater Secondary
Coverts

Median Secondary
Coverts

Marginal Coverts

Tertials

Primaries

Secondaries

FEATHER

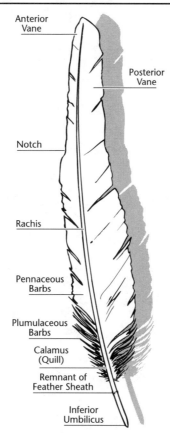

Anterior Vane

Posterior Vane

Notch

Rachis

Pennaceous Barbs

Plumulaceous Barbs

Calamus (Quill)

Remnant of Feather Sheath

Inferior Umbilicus

MAJOR ADAPTATIONS OF BIRDS FOR FLIGHT

Weight Reductions

1) thin, hollow bones
2) fusion of bones in the pectoral and pelvic girdles and spinal column
3) no teeth or heavy jaws
4) absence of tail vertebrae
5) reduced number of digits
6) light feathers
7) air sacs
8) few skin glands
9) laying of eggs
10) reduced gonads in non-breeding season

Power Increases

1) warm-bloodedness
2) insulative coat of feathers
3) energy-rich diet
4) rapid and efficient digestion
5) high glucose levels in the blood
6) high metabolic rate
7) four-chambered heart for double circulation
8) rapid, high-pressure circulation
9) highly efficient respiratory system
10) synchronization of respiratory movements with wing beats

SOURCE: Adapted from J.C. Welty and L. Baptista, *The Life of Birds*, 4th ed. (Orlando, FL: Harcourt Brace Jovanovich College Publishers, 1990).

FEATHER TRACTS

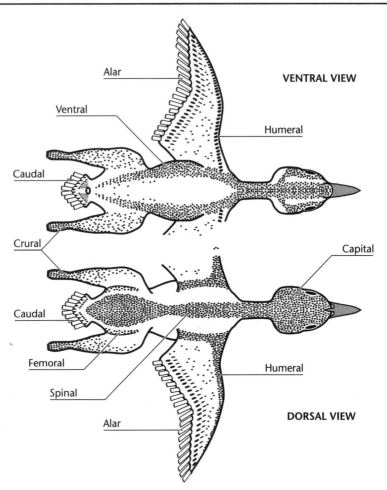

GENERALIZED FLIGHT FEATHER COUNTS
OF SELECTED BIRD GROUPS

	Primary	Secondary	Tail
Quail, pheasants	10	10–18	12–18
Ducks, geese, swans	11	15–24	12–24
Woodpeckers	10	11	12
Trogons	10	11	12
Kingfishers	10–11	11–14	12
Cuckoos	10	11	8–10
Parrots, macaws	10	8–14	12
Swifts	10	8–11	10
Hummingbirds	10	6–7	10
Owls	10	11–19	12
Nighthawks	10	12–15	10
Pigeons, doves	10	11–15	12
Cranes	11	~16	12
Rails, gallinules	10–11	~15	8–14
Sandpipers	10	11	12
Plovers	10	11	12
Gulls, terns, alcids	11	11	12
Hawks, eagles, osprey	10	15–20	12–14
Falcons, caracaras	10	16	12–14
Grebes	12	~22	–
Cormorants	11	~20	12–14
Herons	11	23	8–12
Pelicans	11	20	22–24
New World vultures	10	18–25	12–14
Loons	11	22–23	16–20
Songbirds	9–10	9–11	12

SOURCE: Adapted from N.S. Proctor and P.J. Lynch, *Manual of Ornithology: Avian Structure and Function* (New Haven, CT: Yale University Press, 1993).

PLUMAGES AND MOLTS

Plumage		Molt		
Traditional (Dwight)	**Humphrey & Parks**	**Traditional (Dwight)**	**Extent**	**Humphrey & Parks**
Natal down	Natal down	Postnatal molt	complete	Prejuvenal molt
Juvenal plumage	Juvenal plumage	Postjuvenal molt	partial	1st prebasic molt
1st winter plumage	1st basic plumage	1st prenuptial molt	partial	1st prealternate molt
1st nuptial plumage	1st alternate plumage	1st postnuptial molt	complete	2nd prebasic molt
2nd winter plumage	2nd basic plumage	Prenuptial molt	partial	2nd prealternate molt
2nd nuptial plumage	2nd alternate plumage	2nd postnuptial molt	complete	2nd prebasic molt

SOURCES: J. Dwight, Jr., *Ann. N.Y. Acad. Sci.* 13 (1900): 73–360; P.S. Humphrey and K.C. Parkes, *Auk* 76 (1959): 1–31.

APPROXIMATE WING-BEATS PER SECOND IN SELECTED BIRD SPECIES

	Beats per second		**Beats per second**
Amethyst woodstar hummingbird	78	Mallard	5.0
Ruby-throated hummingbird	70	Capercaillie	4.6
Blue-tailed hummingbird	41.5	Peregrine falcon	4.3
Black jacobin hummingbird	25	Wood pigeon	4.0
Swallow-tailed hummingbird	22	Turnstone	4.0
Pheasant	9.0	Cormorant	3.9
Black guillemot	8.0	Magpie	3.0
Great crested grebe	6.3	Black kite	2.8
Coot	5.8	Herring gull	2.8
Puffin	5.7	Mute swan	2.7
Blackbird	5.6	Heron	2.5
Ringed plover	5.3	Mourning dove	2.5
Wigeon	5.1	Belted kingfisher	2.4
Starling	5.1	Lapwing	2.3
		Rook	2.3

SOURCE: J. Dorst, *The Life of Birds*, Vol. 1 (New York: Columbia University Press, 1974).

WING LOADING IN SELECTED BIRD SPECIES

	Weight (g)	Wing Area (cm²)	Wing Area (cm²/g)
Ruby-throated hummingbird	3.0	12.4	4.2
House wren	11.0	48.4	4.4
Black-capped chickadee	12.5	76.0	6.1
Barn swallow	17.0	118.5	7.0
Chimney swift	17.3	104.0	6.0
Swallow	18.3	135.0	7.3
Whitethroat	18.6	87.1	4.7
Chaffinch	21.1	102.0	4.8
Great tit	21.4	102.0	4.7
Song sparrow	22.0	86.5	3.9
Leach's petrel	26.5	251.0	9.5
Swift	36.2	165.0	4.5
Purple martin	43.0	185.5	4.3
Dunlin	44.0	126.0	2.8
Red-winged blackbird	70.0	245.0	3.5
Greater spotted woodpecker	73.0	238.0	3.3
European starling	84.0	190.3	2.2
Blackbird	91.5	260.0	2.8
Snipe	95.5	244.0	2.5
Common tern	118.0	563.0	4.8
Mourning dove	130.0	357.0	2.7
Magpie	214.0	640.0	3.0
Kestrel	245.0	708.0	2.9
Pied-billed grebe	343.5	291.0	0.8
Partridge	387.0	433.0	1.1
Carrion crow	470.0	1,058.0	2.2
Common barn owl	505.0	1,683.0	3.4
American crow	552.0	1,344.0	2.4
Herring gull	850.0	2,006.0	2.4
Buzzard	1,072.0	2,691.0	2.5
Peregrine falcon	1,222.5	1,342.0	1.1
Mallard	1,408.0	1,029.0	0.7
Black vulture	1,702.0	3,012.0	1.8
Great blue heron	1,905.0	4,436.0	2.3
Common loon	2,425.0	1,358.0	0.6
Greylag goose	3,065.0	2,697.0	0.9
White stork	3,438.0	4,951.0	1.4
Crane	4,175.0	5,553.0	1.3
Golden eagle	4,664.0	6,520.0	1.4
Canada goose	5,662.0	2,820.0	0.5
Whooper swan	5,925.0	3,377.0	0.6
Griffon vulture	7,269.0	10,540.0	1.4
Great bustard	8,950.0	5,728.0	0.6
Mute swan	11,602.0	6,808.0	0.6

SOURCES: J.C. Welty and L. Baptista, *The Life of Birds*, 4th ed. (Orlando, FL: Harcourt Brace Jovanovich College Publishers, 1990); J. Dorst, *The Life of Birds*, Vol. 1 (New York: Columbia University Press, 1974).

SUGGESTED WEIGHT-CARRYING CAPACITIES
OF SELECTED BIRD SPECIES

	Approx. Body Weight (g)[*]	Item Carried	Approx. Weight of Item (g)[**]	Percent of Body Weight
Calliope hummingbird	2.5	mate	2.9	116
Chestnut-collared longspur	20	nestling	14	70
House finch	21	cloth rag	5	23
American kestrel	165	rat	240	145
Osprey	1,800	fish	1,800	100
Pallas's fish-eagle	3,700	carp	5,900	160
Golden eagle	4,309	UID prey item	900	21
Bald eagle	6,300	mule deer	6,800	108
Steller's sea-eagle	8,600	seal	9,100	105
Harpy eagle	9,000	sloth	5,900	65

[*]In all cases, a maximum weight was assigned based on the literature
[**]Low estimated weight indicates either a young animal or partial carcass

SOURCES: B.P. Martin, *World Birds* (Enfield, Middlesex: Guinness Books, 1987); J. Terres, ed., *The Audubon Society Encyclopedia of North American Birds* (New York: Alfred A. Knopf, 1987).

FLIGHT MORPHOLOGY OF SELECTED SPECIES OF SOARING BIRDS

	Mass (g)	Span (m)	Wing Area (m²)	Wing Load (Newtons/m²)	Aspect Ratio
Sharp-shinned hawk	140	0.51	0.057	24.05	4.57
Rock dove	400	0.67	0.063	52.20	6.50
Broad-winged hawk	460	0.81	0.118	35.42	5.61
Lanner falcon	570	1.01	0.132	42.39	7.72
Fulmar	730	1.10	0.121	58.93	10.02
Red-tailed hawk	1,360	1.08	0.222	49.68	5.20
Osprey	1,680	1.49	0.297	54.75	7.20
Black vulture	1,800	1.38	0.331	53.45	5.70
White-backed vulture	5,390	2.18	0.690	76.50	6.90
Common crane	5,500	2.40	0.720	80.00	8.00
Andean condor	10,050	2.88	1.050	93.50	7.90

SOURCE: Adapted from P. Kerlinger, *Flight Strategies of Migrating Hawks* (Chicago: University of Chicago Press, 1989).

FLIGHT SPEEDS FOR SELECTED BIRD SPECIES RELATIVE TO MASS, ASPECT RATIO, AND WING LOADING

	Mass (g)	Aspect ratio[*]	Wing loading[**]	Speed (m/s)	Speed (km/h)
Blue tit	10	6.8	16.8	8	29
Swallow	22	8	16.1	9	32
Chaffinch	22	5.9	20.2	10–14	36–50
House sparrow	28	5.5	26.4	8–11	29–40
Wilson's petrel	38	8	19.4	11	40
Swift	42	10.5	29.1	6.5	23
Dunlin	45	8.6	29.8	13	47
Starling	76	7.2	36.6	9–10	32–36
Common tern	121	13.2	24.5	9–12	32–43
Sparrowhawk	188	6.5	28.1	12	43
Kestrel	200	7.9	30.7	9	32
Oystercatcher	420	9.7	64	14–16	50–58
Crow	460	6.8	36.7	14	50
Wood pigeon	461	6.6	57.5	17	61
Red-throated diver	960	12.1	106	17	61
Herring gull	1,000	10	49.9	10–11	36–40
Mallard	1,010	9.1	113	18	65
Osprey	1,100	8.9	38.5	13	47
Barnacle goose	1,150	10.1	98	19	68
Pheasant	1,200	5.5	123	15	54
Grey heron	1,320	7.8	39.8	12	43
White-fronted goose	1,720	10.8	92	15	54
Eider	2,180	8.4	194	21	76
Crane	4,800	7.3	85	19	68
Bewick's swan	6,200	9.2	147	20	72
Wandering albatross	8,700	15	140	15	54

[*] Wing span squared, divided by area
[**] Weight supported by unit wing area

SOURCE: B. Campbell and E. Lack, *A Dictionary of Birds* (Vermillion, SD: Buteo Books, 1985).

MINIMUM DAILY FLIGHT DISTANCE OF SELECTED MIGRATING RAPTORS

	Total Migration Distance (km)	Days	Minimum Daily Distance (km)
Sharp-shinned hawk	2,000	30	67
Broad-winged hawk	6,000	40	150
Swainson's hawk	8,000	50	160
Lesser spotted eagle	6,000	40	150
Bald eagle	2,500	35	74
Eleonora's falcon	7,000	50	140

SOURCE: Adapted from P. Kerlinger, *Flight Strategies of Migrating Hawks* (Chicago: University of Chicago Press, 1989).

FLIGHT SPEEDS OF BANDED WILD BIRDS
DURING MIGRATION BETWEEN TWO LOCATIONS

	Distance Displaced (km)	Elapsed Time of Flight (days)	Kilometers per Day
Arctic tern	14,000	114	123
Barn swallow	8,800	35	250
Blue-winged teal	4,800	35	140
Great tit	1,200	21	57
Lesser kestrel	8,785	61	144
Lesser yellowlegs	3,100	7	444
Mallard	890	2	445
Manx shearwater	9,500	17	650
Peregrine falcon	1,600	21	76
Red-winged blackbird	2,400	4	600
Ruddy turnstone	4,655	4	1,045
White-crowned sparrow	500	0.5	1,000
Yellow-rumped warbler	725	2	362

SOURCE: J.C. Welty and L. Baptista, *The Life of Birds*, 4th ed. (Orlando, FL: Harcourt Brace Jovanovich College Publishers, 1990).

AVERAGE FLIGHT SPEEDS (M/SEC) OF SELECTED BIRD SPECIES
DURING DAYTIME AND EVENING, MEASURED BY DOPPLER RADAR

	Midday	Evening
American robin	7.2	10.4
Chimney swift	10.3	12.3
Cliff swallow	9.9	8.7
Common grackle	10.2	11.7
Eastern meadowlark	8.4	12.0
European starling	10.0	12.7
House sparrow	10.2	12.3
Mourning dove	9.9	12.0
Northern mockingbird	10.0	9.3
Purple martin	8.5	11.1
Red-winged blackbird	10.0	11.3
Tree swallow	10.0	9.2

SOURCE: T.R. Evans and L.C. Drickamer, *Wilson Bull.* 106/1 (1994): 156–62.

ABILITIES OF BIRDS TO RETURN TO THE SITE OF CAPTURE AFTER TRANSPORT TO A DISTANT, UNFAMILIAR RELEASE SITE

	Number of Birds	Distance (km)	Return (%)	Speed (km/day)
Barn swallow	21	444–574	52	278
Common tern	44	422–748	43	231
European starling	68	370–815	46	46
Herring gull	109	396–1615	90	112
Laysan albatross	11	3,083–7,630	82	370
Leach's storm-petrel	61	250–870	67	56
Manx shearwater	42	491–768	90	370
Northern gannet	18	394	63	185

SOURCE: F.B. Gill, *Ornithology* (New York: W.H. Freeman and Co., 1990).

AVERAGE AIR SPEEDS AND GROUND SPEEDS OF SOME SPECIES OF MIGRATING HAWKS

	Air Speed (mps)		Ground Speed (mps)	
	Stopwatch	Radar	Stopwatch	Radar
American kestrel	14.4	–	10.8	–
Broad-winged hawk	13.7	24.2	11.1	23.7
Cooper's hawk	16.6	21.3	13.1	20.6
Goshawk	–	22.5	–	20.7
Northern harrier	12.9	18.7	10.8	19.4
Osprey	16.2	24.9	13.8	23.7
Red-shouldered hawk	12.2	21.8	15.5	21.6
Red-tailed hawk	16.6	23.9	13.1	24.4
Sharp-shinned hawk	14.2	22.5	10.8	22.7

SOURCE: Adapted from P. Kerlinger, *Flight Strategies of Migrating Hawks* (Chicago: University of Chicago Press, 1989).

MEAN ALTITUDES (M) FLOWN BY MIGRATING RAPTORS IN AUTUMN

	Method of Detection	
	Motor Glider	Radar
American kestrel	640	746
Broad-winged hawk	855	791
Cooper's hawk	–	792
Goshawk	–	803
Merlin	457	–
Northern harrier	–	774
Osprey	818	831
Red-shouldered hawk	–	749
Red-tailed hawk	457	839
Sharp-shinned hawk	610	755

SOURCE: P. Kerlinger, *Flight Strategies of Migrating Hawks* (Chicago: University of Chicago Press, 1989).

CIRCLING PERFORMANCE OF SELECTED BIRD SPECIES

	Circling Radius (m)	Bank Angle	Circle Time (sec)	Air Speed (mps)
Black vulture	17.1	24.7	12.5	8.8
	24.4	20–30	14.1	10.9
Broad-winged hawk	15.4	24.5	13.9	7.0
Brown pelican	18.0	22.9	13.3	8.6
Indian white-backed vulture	40–50	?	13–16	10.0
Kite (*Milvus sp.*)	12.0	?	7–9	5.0
Lappet-faced vulture	15.0	35.0	9.4	10.0
Magnificent frigatebird	12.0	23.7	10.6	7.2
	12.5	20–30	10.1	7.8
Sharp-shinned hawk	5.7–11.5	?	9–12	6.0
Turkey vulture	12.5	20–30	10.1	7.8

SOURCE: P. Kerlinger, *Flight Strategies of Migrating Hawks* (Chicago: University of Chicago Press, 1989).

Reproduction

Territory

RELATIVE TERRITORY SIZES (HECTARES) IN SELECTED BIRD SPECIES*

Black-headed gull	.00003	Prothonotary warbler	1.7
King penguin	.00005	Yellow-bellied sapsucker	2.1
Least flycatcher	.07	Downy woodpecker	2.6
European blackbird	.12	Hairy woodpecker	2.8
American robin	.12	Hazel grouse	4.0
Willow warbler	.15	Song thrush	4.0
Snow bunting	.24	Black-capped chickadee	5.3
Red-winged blackbird	.30	Western meadowlark	9.0
Mockingbird	.32	Great horned owl	50
Coot	.40	Mistle thrush	50
House wren	.40	Red-tailed hawk	130
American redstart	.40	Bald eagle	250
Chaffinch	.40	Crowned hornbill	520
Song sparrow	.40	Ivory-billed woodpecker	700
European robin	.60	Powerful owl	1,000
Chestnut-collared longspur	.60	Golden eagle	9,300
Red-eyed vireo	.84	Bearded vulture	20,000
Ovenbird	1.0		

* Will vary according to many factors, e.g., year, locality, season, and food availability.

INITIATION OF SINGING BEFORE SUNRISE (MIN.) IN SELECTED BIRD SPECIES

Blackbird	44	Wren	22
Song thrush	43	Great tit	17
Eurasian robin	34	Chaffinch	9
Turtle dove	27	Whitethroat	7
Willow warbler	22		

SOURCE: Adapted from J. Dorst, *The Life of Birds*, Vol. 1 (New York: Columbia University Press, 1974).

SONG-TYPE REPERTOIRE SIZES IN SELECTED SPECIES OF SONGBIRDS

	Repertoire size		Repertoire size
Ovenbird	1	Western meadowlark	3–12
White-crowned sparrow	1	Cardinal	8–12
Chingolo sparrow	1	Starling	21–67
European redwing	1	Red-eyed vireo	12–117
Splendid sunbird	1	European blackbird	22–48
Chaffinch	1–6	Marsh wren	33–162
Ring ousel	2–4	Mockingbird	53–150
Great tit	2–8	Nightingale	100–300
Dark-eyed junco	3–7	Song thrush	138–219
		Five-striped sparrow	159–237
		Brown thrasher	2,000+

SOURCE: C.K. Catchpole and P.J.B. Slater, *Bird Song: Biological Themes and Variations* (Cambridge: Cambridge University Press, 1995).

Classifications of Nest Type

platform: Floor of loosely assembled plant materials with a shallow depression for eggs located on ground, in tree, on cliff, or on human-made structure; e.g., osprey

ground: Scraped-out depression or platform of plant materials, e.g., loon

floating: Platform of plant materials lying on surface of water, e.g., grebe

cavity: Burrow in ground (e.g. burrowing owl), as well as hole in tree, cliff, bank, or human-made structure (e.g., kestrel)

cupped: Nest with true structure consisting of materials arranged and compacted for the bottom and sides as well as softer materials for inside lining, e.g., many songbirds

statant: Cupped nest supported mainly from below with rims standing firmly upright, e.g., hummingbird

domed: Statant nest with sides extended to form an arched roof, e.g., magpie

pensile: Cupped nest suspended from branches by stiffly woven rims and sides, e.g., vireos

pendulous: Deeply cupped nest swinging freely from branches by rims and flexibly woven sides, e.g., orioles

adherent: Cupped nests built with adhesive substances to attach to cliffs and other vertical surfaces (e.g., swallows) or built on the ground (e.g., larks) or in preformed cavities (e.g., titmice) or in excavated cavities (e.g., bank swallow)

half-cupped adherent: Half of a cup using saliva to stick nest materials together, e.g., swift

pit or mound: Pile of rotting vegetable matter placed over eggs to warm and incubate them, e.g., megapodes

Gametes

SPERMATOZOA

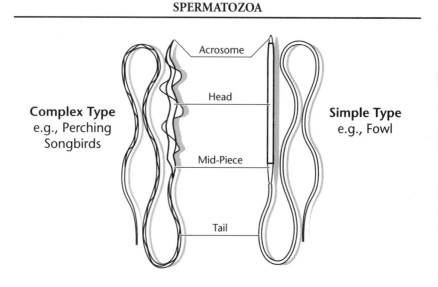

Complex Type
e.g., Perching Songbirds

Simple Type
e.g., Fowl

Acrosome

Head

Mid-Piece

Tail

APPROXIMATE NUMBER OF SPERM-STORAGE TUBULES
IN SELECTED BIRD SPECIES

	Total No. of Sperm-Storage Tubules	Total No. of Branches
Bengalese finch	1,511	1,926
Budgerigar	512	522
Chicken	13,533	13,533
Goose	7,030	7,683
Japanese quail	3,467	3,467
Mallard	1,467	1,491
Pheasant	3,864	4,101
Pigeon	2,310	3,301
Ring dove	5,067	20,621
Turkey	20,000	20,000
Zebra finch	1,499	1,750

SOURCE: Adapted from T.R. Birkhead and A.P. Møller, *Sperm Competition in Birds* (London: Academic Press, 1992).

SPERM-STORAGE DURATION, SPERM NUMBER, CLUTCH SIZE,
AND SPREAD OF LAYING IN SELECTED BIRD SPECIES

	Sperm Storage Duration (days)	Sperm Number ($\times 10^6$) Per Ejaculate	Clutch Size	Spread of Laying (days)
American kestrel	8.1	0.53	4.6	9
Bengalese finch	8.0	–	6	6
Bobwhite quail	8.3	–	14	19
Budgerigar	11.0	10	6	12
Capercaillie	24.0	–	7	9
Chicken	12.0	773	12	12
Domestic duck	10.3	–	17	17
Goose	9.7	0.093	12	12
Guineafowl	7.0	67.3	14	14
Japanese quail	6.3	157	8	10
Mallard	9.9	1,020	11	11
Pheasant	21.0	150	11.8	16.5
Pigeon	8.0	5.6	2	3
Ring dove	8.0	–	2	3
Turkey	42.0	1,577	17	25
Willow ptarmigan	7.8	–	7.5	8
Zebra finch	10.0	–	6	6

SOURCE: Adapted from T.R. Birkhead and A.P. Møller, *Sperm Competition in Birds* (London: Academic Press, 1992).

EGG

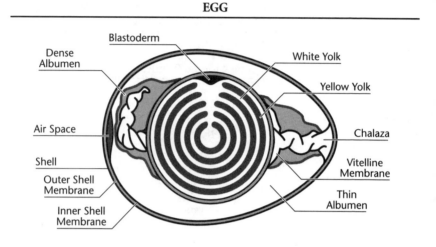

NUTRITIONAL COMPOSITION OF A CHICKEN EGG

	Yolk	Albumen	Shell
Proteins (%)	16.6	10.6	3.3
Carbohydrates (%)	1.0	0.9	–
Fats (%)	32.6	Trace	0.03
Minerals (%)	1.1	0.6	95.10

SOURCE: A.L. Romanoff and A.J. Romanoff, *The Avian Egg* (New York: John Wiley and Sons, 1949).

Egg-Laying

APPROXIMATE EGG-LAYING INTERVALS IN SOME BIRDS[*]

24 hours	songbirds, most ducks, geese, woodpeckers, small shorebirds and grebes, turkeys
38 to 48 hours	ostriches, rheas, large shorebirds and grebes, gulls, ducks, swans, herons, bitterns, storks, cranes, pigeons and doves, falcons, small hawks, owls, cuckoos, hummingbirds, swifts, kingfishers, ravens
62 hours	cuckoos, goatsuckers
3 days	emus, cassowaries, penguins
3 to 5 days	large raptors
5 days	condors, kiwis
5 to 7 days	boobies, hornbills
4 to 8 days	mound-builders

[*] There are exceptions in almost every bird group.

SOURCE: Adapted from J.C. Welty and L. Baptista, *The Life of Birds*, 4th ed., (Orlando, FL: Harcourt Brace Jovanovich College Publishers, 1990).

EGG PATTERNS

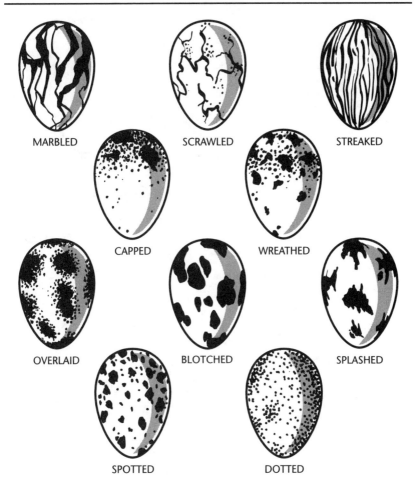

MARBLED   SCRAWLED   STREAKED

CAPPED   WREATHED

OVERLAID   BLOTCHED   SPLASHED

SPOTTED   DOTTED

EGG SHAPES

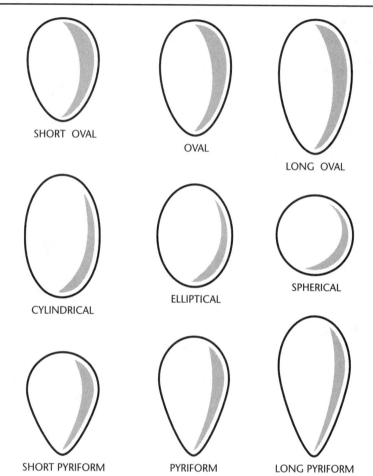

SHORT OVAL

OVAL

LONG OVAL

CYLINDRICAL

ELLIPTICAL

SPHERICAL

SHORT PYRIFORM

PYRIFORM

LONG PYRIFORM

EGG WEIGHT AS A PROPORTION OF FEMALE BODY WEIGHT

	Adult Female Body Weight (g)	Egg Weight (g)	Egg Weight/ Body Weight (%)
Ostrich	90,000	1,600	1.8
Emperor penguin	30,000	450	1.5
Mute swan	9,000	340	3.8
Snowy owl	2,000	83	4.1
Little spotted kiwi	1,200	310	26.0
Peregrine falcon	1,100	52	4.7
Mallard	1,000	54	5.4
Herring gull	895	82	9.2
Puffin	500	65	13.0
American crow	450	34	7.6
Gray partridge	390	26	6.7
Northern bobwhite	180	18	10
American robin	100	8	8.0
Northern cardinal	45	8.6	19.1
Snow bunting	42	6.3	15.0
House sparrow	30	3	10.0
American goldfinch	13	2.3	17.7
House wren	9	1.3	13.7
Vervain hummingbird	2	0.2	10.0

SOURCES: J. Faaborg, *Ornithology: An Ecological Approach* (Englewood Cliffs, NJ: Prentice-Hall, 1988); J.K. Terres, *The Audubon Society Encyclopedia of North American Birds* (New York: Alfred A. Knopf, 1987).

DURATION OF INCUBATION OF SELECTED BIRD SPECIES

Barn owl	30–32	Mallard	22–28
Black-headed gull	23–24	Manx shearwater	51–53
Brown kiwi	75–80	Ostrich	42
Common buzzard	28–31	Ovenbird	12
Cormorant	23–25	Partridge	21–25
Eagle owl	33–36	Pheasant	23–25
Eastern phoebe	16	Pied white wagtail	12–14
Emperor penguin	62–66	Quail	17–20
Emu	56–60	Redshank	23–25
Gannet	43–45	Robin	12–14
Garden warbler	12–13	Rock dove	17–19
Great crested grebe	26–29	Rook	16–18
Great spotted woodpecker	12–13	Silvery-cheeked hornbill	40
Great tit	11–15	Skylark	11–12
Greylag goose	27–29	Sparrow hawk	35–38
Heron	25–26	Starling	12–13
Herring gull	25–27	Swallow	12–14
House sparrow	12–13	Swift	17–22
Hummingbird	11–23	Wren	13–20
Lammergeyer	52	Yellow-nosed albatross	78
Magpie	17–18		

SOURCE: J. Dorst, *The Life of Birds*, Vol. 1 (New York: Columbia University Press, 1974).

ESTIMATED CLUTCH SIZES, INCUBATION PERIODS, AND AGES AT FLEDGING IN SELECTED GROUPS OF BIRDS

	Clutch Size	Incubation Period (in days)	Age at First Flight (In days)
loons	2	28–30	70–80
grebes	3–5	20–25	?
albatrosses	1	64–65	140–165
shearwaters, petrels, fulmars	1	51–53	70–97
storm-petrels	1	41–42	63–70
tropic-birds	1	41–42	70–80
pelicans	2–3	28–36	60–65
gannets	1	43–45	95–107
cormorants	3–6	28–31	46–53
anhingas	3–4	25–28	?
frigatebirds	1	44–55	170–190
herons, bitterns	3–5	17–28	30–60
storks	3–4	28–32	50–55
ibises, spoonbills	2–4	21–24	50–56
flamingos	1–2	28–32	75–78
ducks, geese	3–14	22–31	34–77
swans	5–6	33–37	100–108
New World vultures	2	38–41	70–80
hawks, kites	2–5	28–38	23–45
eagles	2	43–45	70–84
osprey	2–3	32–35	51–59
falcons	2–5	28–32	25–42
grouse, ptarmigan, prairie chickens	9–12	22–24	7–10
quail	10–15	22–23	10–18
pheasants	7–10	23–25	7–8
turkeys	11–13	27–29	11–17
cranes	2	28–36	60–70
limpkin	5–7	?	?
rails, coots	5–12	18–24	?
oystercatchers	3	24–27	34–37
plovers, lapwings	3 or 4	21–27	27–40
sandpipers, turnstones	4	17–28	14–21
stilts, avocets	3–5	22–25	25–28?
phalaropes	4	18–20	?
skuas, jaegers	2 or 2–3	25–28	35–45
gulls	1–5	20–29	35–50
terns	1–3	20–25	28–35
skimmers	4–5	30–32	38–42

ESTIMATED CLUTCH SIZES, INCUBATION PERIODS, AND AGES AT FLEDGING IN SELECTED GROUPS OF BIRDS (CONTINUED)

	Clutch Size	Incubation Period (in days)	Age at First Flight (In days)
auks	1 or 2	21–39	38–40
pigeons, doves	1 or 2	13–19	14–28
cuckoos	2–5	14–18	15–16?
barn owls	5–7	32–34	42–50
owls	2–8	21–34?	23–60
nightjars	2	19–20	20–25
swifts	4–5	19–21	29–31
hummingbirds	2	16–17	19–22
kingfishers	5–7	23–24	29–35?
woodpeckers	3–10	11–14	24–28
flycatchers	3–5	12–16	13–16
larks	3–5	11–14	10–12
swallows	4–6	12–16	18–26
crows, jays, magpies	4–6	16–21	26–40
nutcrackers	2–3	17–18	24–28
tits	4–8	11–15	14–18
nuthatches	5–8	12–16	18–21
treecreepers	5–6	14–15	14–15
dippers	4–5	15–17	24–25
wrens	5–8	12–16	13–22
mimic thrushes	3–5	12–15	11–18
thrushes	3–6	11–16	11–18
Old World warblers, kinglets, gnatcatchers	4–9	13–15	10–14
wagtails, pipits	4–5	13–14	12–13
waxwings	3–6	12–16	14–18
silky flycatchers	2–3	14–16	18–19
shrikes	4–6	11–16	19–20
starlings, mynas	4–6	11–13	19–22
vireos	4	12–14	11–12
New World warblers	3–6	11–14	8–12
weavers	4–6	11–14	12–15
New World blackbirds, meadowlarks	3–5	11–14	9–20
tanagers	4–5	13–14	10–12
siskins, crossbills	3–5	11–15	9–14
sparrows	3–5	11–15	9–14

SOURCE: Adapted from O.S. Pettingill, Jr., *Ornithology in Laboratory and Field* (Minneapolis, MN: Burgess Publ. Co., 1970).

AVERAGE PERIODS ON AND OFF THE NEST FOR TEN SPECIES OF INCUBATING FEMALE SONGBIRDS

	Avg. Off (min.)	Avg. On (min.)	% Time On Nest
Song sparrow	8.8	28.5	75
Marsh tit	7.1	37.9	84
European dipper	8.1	30.9	78
Chiffchaff	8.2	34.3	77
Becard	8.5	12.0	60
Sulfur-bellied flycatcher	8.5	17.0	67
Scarlet finch	9.2	48.5	84
American robin	11.0	44.0	80
European nuthatch	11.3	31.1	73
Hedge sparrow	14.6	29.7	66

SOURCE: M.M. Nice, *Studies in the Life History of the Song Sparrow*, Volume II. (New York, NY: Dover Publications, 1943).

Hatching

MATURITY OF YOUNG BIRDS AT HATCHING

Precocial –
Eyes open, down-covered, leave nest first day or two

1. Completely independent of parents —megapodes
2. Follow parents but find own food —ducks, shorebirds
3. Follow parents and are shown food —quail, chickens
4. Follow parents and are fed by them —grebes, rails

Semiprecocial –
Eyes open, down-covered, stay at nest although able to walk, fed by parents

—gulls, terns

Semialtricial –
Down-covered, unable to leave nest, fed by parents

1. Eyes open —herons, hawks
2. Eyes closed —owls

Altricial –
Eyes closed, little or no down, unable to leave nest, fed by parents

—passerines

SOURCE: J.C. Welty and L. Baptista, *The Life of Birds*, 4th ed. (Orlando, FL: Harcourt Brace Jovanovich College Publishers, 1990).

EMBRYONIC DEVELOPMENT (FOWL)

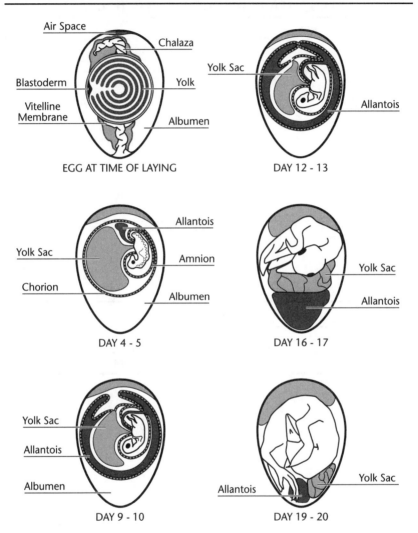

EGG AT TIME OF LAYING

DAY 12 - 13

DAY 4 - 5

DAY 16 - 17

DAY 9 - 10

DAY 19 - 20

A COMPARISON OF ORGANS OF PRECOCIAL
AND ALTRICAL YOUNG BIRDS AT HATCHING

	Percentages of Total Body Weight		
	Eyes	Brain	Intestines
Precocial young			
Japanese quail	5.5	6.2	9.7
Ring-necked pheasant	4.2	4.2	6.5
Snowy plover	10.7	7.2	6.6
Water rail	4.5	6.2	10.5
Altricial young			
Alpine swift	6.1	3.1	14.6
English starling	4.0	3.2	14.1
Jackdaw	5.5	3.6	13.1
Pigeon	4.9	2.9	10.3

SOURCE: Adapted from J.C. Welty and L. Baptista, *The Life of Birds*, 4th ed. (Orlando, FL: Harcourt Brace Jovanovich College Publishers, 1990).

Sex Ratios

SAMPLE SEX RATIOS IN SELECTED SPECIES OF ADULT WILD BIRDS

	Total Number of Birds	Percent Males	Percent Females
American crow	1,000	53	47
Blue-winged teal	5,090	59	41
Boat-tailed grackle	5,333	33	67
Bob-white	45,452	53	47
Brown-headed cowbird	4,281	74	26
House sparrow	20,931	55	45
Mallard	21,723	52	48
Pintail	5,707	66	34
Purple finch	1,380	57	43
Red-winged blackbird	6,480	84	26

SOURCE: J.C. Welty and L. Baptista, *The Life of Birds*, 4th ed. (Orlando, FL: Harcourt Brace Jovanovich College Publishers, 1990).

Mortality

Longevity

LONGEVITY RECORDS FOR WILD BIRDS*

	Maximum Age (yrs)		Maximum Age (yrs)
American crow	15	Gannet	25
American robin	14	Goldcrest	7
Arctic skua	18	Golden eagle	25
Arctic tern	34	Golden oriole	15
Atlantic puffin	21	Grasshopper sparrow	7
Bald eagle	28	Gray catbird	11
Barn owl	18	Great crested flycatcher	14
Barn swallow	16	Great frigate-bird	34
Bay-backed shrike	8	Great tit	15
Black and white warbler	11	Guillemot	32
Blackbird	20	Heron	24
Black-capped chickadee	12	Herring gull	32
Black-footed albatross	43	Honey buzzard	29
Black-headed gull	32	House sparrow	13
Black-throated diver	27	House wren	7
Black vulture	11	Kea	14
Blue-faced booby	23	Kite	26
Blue-gray tanager	9	Kookaburra	12
Blue jay	18	Lapwing	25
Bristle-thighed curlew	24	Laysan albatross	53
Brown-headed cowbird	16	Leach's petrel	20
Brown pelican	31	Little blue penguin	19
Brown-throated sunbird	12	Little grebe	13
Bullfinch	18	Long-eared owl	28
Bulwer's petrel	24	Long-tailed tit	8
Buzzard	24	Mallard	29
Canada goose	23	Manx shearwater	26
Capercaillie	9	Mourning dove	19
Chinstrap penguin	11	Mute swan	22
Common grackle	20	Northern cardinal	16
Coot	19	Northern fulmar	23
Cormorant	17	Olive-winged bulbul	12
Cuckoo	13	Osprey	32
Dark-eyed junco	11	Oystercatcher	36
Dipper	8	Peregrine falcon	14
Double-crested cormorant	23	Pied flycatcher	9
Dunnock	9	Pied wagtail	10
Eider	23	Pink-footed goose	22
Eurasian curlew	31	Purple heron	25
European jay	16	Quail	8
European kestrel	16	Red-bellied woodpecker	20

	Maximum Age (yrs)		Maximum Age (yrs)
Red-throated loon	23	Teal	20
Red-winged blackbird	16	Treecreeper	7
Reed warbler	12	Trumpeter swan	24
Robin	13	Warbling vireo	13
Rook	20	Waved albatross	38
Royal albatross	58	Waxwing	13
Ruby-throated hummingbird	6	White-breasted nuthatch	10
Scarlet tanager	10	White-browed babbler	12
Shag	21	White-crowned sparrow	13
Short-tailed shearwater	30	White pelican	16
Silvereye	11	White stork	26
Skylark	10	Wild turkey	15
Song sparrow	10	Willow tit	9
Spoonbill	28	Woodcock	21
Starling	20	Wood thrush	9
Swift	21	Yellow-eyed penguin	18

* Unofficial, i.e., based on the literature.

POTENTIAL AVERAGE LONGEVITY OF SONGBIRDS SEEN IN NORTH AMERICAN BACKYARDS

	Years		Years
American kestrel	2–4	Mockingbird	4–12
Blackbirds, grackles	4–16	Nuthatches	5–9
Bluebirds	3–6	Orioles	6–8
Brown creeper	3–5	Purple martin	4–8
Brown-headed cowbird	5–13	Quail	4–8
Cardinal	4–13	Screech owl	6–13
Chickadees, titmice	3–12	Sparrows	2–3
Common crow	6–14	Starling	5–20
Doves and pigeons	6–17	Swallows	4–16
Finches	4–12	Tanagers	3–9
Flycatchers	6–11	Thrushes	3–12
Gray catbird	4–10	Towhees	4–14
Grosbeaks	4–13	Waxwings	3–7
Hummingbirds	5–12	Woodpeckers, flickers	4–20
Jays	5–15	Wrens	3–7
Juncos	3–11		

SOURCE: Adapted from J.K. Terres, *The Audubon Society Encyclopedia of North American Birds* (New York: Alfred A. Knopf, 1987).

MAXIMUM KNOWN AGES OF SELECTED SPECIES OF CAPTIVE BIRDS

	Maximum age recorded (years)		Maximum age recorded (years)
Andean condor	77	House sparrow	23
Bateleur eagle	55	Northern cardinal	22
Canada goose	33	Raven	24
Common caracara	55	Siberian white crane	62
Eagle owl	68	Starling	17
Garden warbler	24	Sulfur-crested cockatoo	80
Herring gull	44	White pelican	52

SOURCE: J. Dorst, *The Life of Birds*, Vol. 1 (New York: Columbia University Press, 1974).

ANNUAL ADULT SURVIVAL IN SELECTED BIRD SPECIES

	Mean Annual Adult Mortality (%)	Mean Further Life Expectancy (yrs.)
Royal albatross	3	ca. 36
Fulmar	6	16.2
Sooty shearwater	9	10.2
Yellow-eyed penguin	10	9.5
White-bearded manakin	11	8.6
Canada goose	16	5.6
Common swift	18	5.6
Rook	25	3.5
Band-tailed pigeon	29	3.0
Night heron	30	2.8
Herring gull	30	2.8
Wryneck	33	2.5
Skylark	33	2.5
Blue jay	45	1.7
American robin	48	1.6
California quail	50	1.5
Turtle dove	50	1.5
Starling	53	1.4
American coot	60	1.2
European robin	62	1.1
Song sparrow	70	0.9

SOURCE: Adapted from J.C. Welty and L. Baptista, *The Life of Birds*, 4th ed. (Orlando, FL: Harcourt Brace Jovanovich College Publishers, 1990).

ESTIMATED ANNUAL MORTALITY RATE OF SELECTED BIRD SPECIES

	Estimated Annual Mortality Rate (%)		Estimated Annual Mortality Rate (%)
American robin	48	Pintado petrel	5–6
Blackbird	42	Red-billed firefinch	70–75
Blue tit	41–73	Redshank	25
Bobwhite quail	87	Redstart	56
Buzzard	19	Ringed plover	25–30
Common tern	30	Robin	57–66
Great tit	46	Snow petrel	4–7
Heron	31	Song sparrow	44
Herring gull	30	Sooty shearwater	7
Mallard	40–64	Starling	50–63
Manx shearwater	5	Swallow	63
Mourning dove	69	Swift	18
Mute swan	38	White-bearded manakin	11
Pheasant	72	Yellow-eyed penguin	10

SOURCE: J. Dorst, *The Life of Birds*, Vol. 1 (New York: Columbia University Press, 1974).

RELATIVE ANNUAL HUMAN-RELATED MORTALITY OF BIRDS IN THE UNITED STATES

Cause	Annual Mortality (millions)
Hunting	120
Pest control	2
Scientific research	0.02
Other direct	3.5
Pollution and poisoning	3.5
Collision	
Road kills	57
TV towers	1.2
Windows	80
Cats	500*
Other indirect	3.5

* Assuming that a housecat kills on average 5 birds per year.

SOURCES: R.C. Banks, *Human-related Mortality of Birds in the United States.* Special Scientific Report – Wildlife No. 215. U.S. Dept. Interior (Washington, DC: U.S. Dept. Interior, 1979); F.B. Gill, *Ornithology: An Ecological Approach* (Englewood Cliffs, NJ: Prentice-Hall, 1990); D.A. Klem, *Biology of collisions between birds and windows.* Ph.D. thesis, Southern Illinois University, 1979; J.S. Coleman, S.A. Temple, and S.R. Craven, *Cats and Wildlife: A Conservation Dilemma* (Madison, WI: Cooperative Extension Publ., 1997).

Frequency of Diseases in Wild Birds

RELATIVE OCCURRENCE OF ASPERGILLOSIS IN WILD BIRDS IN NORTH AMERICA

Type of Bird	Frequency of Occurrence
Waterfowl	4
Herons	2
Shorebirds	1
Gulls	4
Raptors (free-living/captive)	2/4
Upland game birds	3
Crows, ravens	4
Blackbirds, cowbirds, grackles	3
Songbirds	3

1	Rare or not reported	3	Occasional
2	Infrequent	4	Frequent

RELATIVE OCCURRENCE OF AVIAN CHOLERA IN WILD BIRDS

Type of Bird	Frequency
Waterfowl	4
Coots	3
Wading birds	1
Cranes	2
Shorebirds	2
Gulls	3
Raptors	1
Upland game birds	1
Crows	3
Songbirds	2

1　Infrequent, rare, or not reported
2　Small number of reports, generally involving individual or small numbers of birds
3　Frequent occurrence, including occasional major die-offs
4　Common occurrence, major die-offs occur almost yearly

REPORTED OCCURRENCE OF AVIAN POX IN WILD BIRDS IN NORTH AMERICA

Type of Bird	Frequency of Reports
Waterfowl	2
Wading birds	1
Shorebirds	1
Marine Birds	4
Raptors	3
Upland game birds	4
Songbirds	4

1　Rare or not reported
2　Small number of reports, generally involving individual birds
3　Occasional; reports tend to involve individual birds rather than groups of birds
4　Multiple; reports often involve a number of birds in a single event

FREQUENCY OF BOTULISM IN MAJOR GROUPS OF WILD BIRDS

Type of Bird	Type C*	Type E*
Waterfowl	5	2
Loons	1	4
Herons	3	1
Shorebirds	5	1
Gulls	4	4
Raptors	2	1
Gallinaceous	2	1
Songbirds	2	1

* Toxins synthesized by Clostridium bacteria.

1　Not reported
2　Infrequent
3　Occasional
4　Frequent
5　Common, die-offs occur almost yearly

RELATIVE OCCURRENCE OF CHLAMYDIAL INFECTIONS IN WILD BIRDS IN NORTH AMERICA

Type of Bird	Frequency of Occurrence
Waterfowl	4
Cranes	1
Herons, egrets, ibises	4
Shorebirds	2
Gulls, terns	3
Raptors	1
Upland game birds	2
Feral pigeons	5
Songbirds	2

1　Rare or not reported
2　Infrequent
3　Occasional
4　Frequent
5　Common

COMPARATIVE SUSCEPTIBILITY OF EIGHT
WATERFOWL SPECIES TO DUCK PLAGUE

Type of Bird	Relative Susceptibility
Mallard	2
Pintail	1
Gadwall	2
Wood duck	3
Blue-winged teal	3
Muscovy	2
Redhead	3
Canada goose	2

1   Slightly susceptible   2   Moderately susceptible   3   Highly susceptible

RELATIVE FREQUENCY OF NASAL LEECH INFESTATIONS IN
SELECTED GROUPS OF MIGRATORY BIRDS

Type of Bird	Relative Frequency
Puddle ducks	3
Diving ducks	2
Mergansers	1
Sea ducks	1
Geese	1
Swans	3
Grebes and loons	1

1   Occasional   2   Often   3   Frequent

RELATIVE OCCURRENCE OF THREE TYPES
OF SALMONELLOSIS IN SELECTED BIRD SPECIES

Species Affected	Pullorum Disease	Fowl Typhoid	Paratyphoid Infection
Ducks/geese/swans	3	a	4
Cranes	1	1	3
Gulls	1	1	4
Pheasants/quail/grouse/turkeys	3	4	4
Common peafowl, guinea fowl	3	4	3
Doves/pigeons	1	b	4
Songbirds	3	3	4
Hawks/owls	1	2	3
Penguins	1	1	3
Canaries/parrots/parakeets	3	2	4

a   Ducklings are susceptible, but the disease   b   Pigeons are highly resistant to this disease
    rarely occurs; geese are not susceptible
1   Not reported   3   Occasional
2   Infrequent   4   Frequent

RELATIVE FREQUENCY OF GROSSLY VISIBLE FORMS OF SARCOCYSTIS IN SELECTED GROUPS OF NORTH AMERICAN MIGRATORY BIRDS

Type of Bird	Expected Occurrence
Puddle ducks	4
Diving ducks	2
Mergansers	2
Sea ducks	2
Geese	2
Swans	2
Wading birds (herons, egrets, ibis)	1

1	Rare or not reported	2	Occasional	3	Often	4	Frequent

RELATIVE FREQUENCY OF TRICHOSTRONGYLID NEMATODES IN THE GIZZARDS OF SELECTED GROUPS OF NORTH AMERICAN MIGRATORY BIRDS

Type of Bird	Expected Occurrence
Puddle ducks	2
Diving ducks	2
Sea ducks	2
Geese	4
Swans	3
Coots	3
Wading birds	1
Shorebirds	1
Gulls and terns	1
Pelicans	1
Raptors	1

1	Rare or not reported	2	Occasional	3	Often	4	Frequent

SUSCEPTIBILITY TO OILING IN MAJOR GROUPS OF WILD BIRDS

Type of Bird	Relative Susceptibility
Ducks, geese, and swans	3
Sea and bay ducks	3
Grebes	3
Loons	3
Cormorants	2
Cranes	1
Waders (herons, egrets, bitterns)	2
Plovers, sandpipers	1
Gulls	2
Pelicans	3

1	Low susceptibility	2	Medium susceptibility	3	High susceptibility

SOURCE: M. Friend, ed., *Field Guide to Wildlife Diseases*, U.S. Department of the Interior Fish and Wildlife Service, Resource Publication 167 (Washington, D.C., 1987).

Threatened and Endangered Bird Species

Canada as of 1997/98

Extinct (3)
Great auk
Labrador duck
Passenger pigeon

Extirpated (2)
Greater prairie chicken
Sage grouse (B.C. population)

Endangered (16)
Acadian flycatcher
Burrowing owl
Eskimo curlew
Harlequin duck (eastern population)
Henslow's sparrow
King rail
Kirtland's warbler
Loggerhead shrike (eastern population)
Mountain plover
Northern bobwhite
Peregrine falcon (subspecies *anatum*)
Piping plover
Prothotonary warbler
Sage thrasher
Spotted owl
Whooping crane

Threatened (7)
Hooded warbler
Loggerhead shrike (western population)

Marbled murrelet
Roseate tern
Sage grouse (prairie population)
White-headed woodpecker
Yellow-breasted chat (B.C. population)

Vulnerable (21)
Ancient murrelet
Barn owl
Caspian tern
Cerulean warbler
Ferruginous hawk
Flammulated owl
Great blue heron (B.C. population)
Ipswich sparrow
Ivory gull
Least bittern
Long-billed curlew
Louisiana waterthrush
Northern goshawk (Queen Charlotte
  population)
Peregrine falcon (subspecies *pealei*)
Peregrine falcon (subspecies *tundrius*)
Prairie warbler
Red-headed woodpecker
Red-shouldered hawk
Ross's gull
Short-eared owl
Yellow-breasted chat (Ontario population)

SOURCE: Committee on the Status of Endangered Wildlife in Canada.

United States as of 1997/98**

Endangered (78)
Akepa
Akialoa kauai
Akiapolaau
American peregrine falcon
Attwater's greater prairie-chicken
Audubon's crested caracara*
Bachman's warbler
Black-capped vireo
Bridled white-eye

Brown pelican
Cactus ferruginous pygmy-owl
California condor
California clapper rail
California least tern
Cape Sable seaside sparrow
Crested honeycreeper
Eskimo curlew
Everglade snail kite
Florida grasshopper sparrow

Golden-cheeked warbler
Guam broadbill
Guam micronesian kingfisher
Guam rail
Hawaiian common moorhen
Hawaiian coot
Hawaiian creeper
Hawaiian crow
Hawaiian dark-rumped petrel
Hawaiian duck
Hawaiian goose
Hawaiian hawk
Hawaiian stilt
Ivory-billed woodpecker
Kauai o'o
Kirtland's warbler
Large kauai thrush
Laysan duck
Laysan finch
Least Bell's vireo
Least tern
Light-footed clapper rail
Mariana common moorhen
Mariana crow
Mariana gray swiftlet
Mariana mallard
Masked bobwhite
Maui akepa
Maui parrotbill
Micronesian megapode
Mississippi sandhill crane
Molokai creeper
Molokai thrush
Nihoa finch
Nihoa millerbird
Northern aplomado falcon
Nukupu'u
Oahu creeper
O'u

Palila
Piping plover*
Po'ouli
Puerto Rican broad-winged hawk
Puerto Rican nightjar
Puerto Rican parrot
Puerto Rican plain pigeon
Puerto Rican sharp-shinned hawk
Red-cockaded woodpecker
Reed nightingale warbler
Roseate tern*
San Clemente loggerhead shrike
Small kauai thrush
Southwestern willow flycatcher
Whooping crane
Wood stork
Yellow-shouldered blackbird
Yuma clapper rail

Threatened (17 species)
Aleutian Canada goose
Audubon's crested caracara*
Bald eagle
Coastal California gnatcatcher
Florida scrub-jay
Inyo California towhee
Marbled murrelet
Mexican spotted owl
Newell's Townsend's shearwater (formerly Manx's)
Northern spotted owl
Piping plover*
Roseate tern*
San Clemente sage sparrow
Spectacled eider
Steller's eider
Tinian monarch
Western snowy plover

* Endangered in some regions and threatened in others.
** Includes Guam and Puerto Rico.

SOURCE: U.S. Fish and Wildlife Service   http://www.fws.gov/r9endspp.html

Birds of Conservation Importance in the United Kingdom*

IUCN Globally Threatened Species
Aquatic warbler
Corncrake
Scottish crossbill

Uncommon and, Rapidly or Historically, Declining British Breeding Birds
Bittern
Black grouse
Black-tailed godwit
Capercaillie
Chough
Cirl bunting
Corn bunting
Dartford warbler
Hen harrier
Marsh harrier
Marsh warbler
Merlin
Nightjar
Osprey
Quail
Red kite
Red-backed shrike
Red-necked phalarope
Roseate tern
Stone curlew
Turtle dove
White-tailed eagle
Woodlark
Wryneck

Rapidly Declining, But Common, British Breeding Birds
Bullfinch
Grey partridge
Linnet
Reed bunting
Skylark
Song thrush
Spotted flycatcher
Tree sparrow

Moderately Declining, Historically Declining But Common, Internationally Important
Avocet
Barnacle goose
Barn owl
Bar-tailed godwit
Bean goose
Bearded tit
Bewick's swan
Blackbird
Black guillemot
Black-necked grebe
Black redstart
Black-throated diver
Black-winged stilt
Brent goose
Cetti's warbler
Common gull
Common scoter
Crane
Crested tit
Curlew
Dotterel
Dunlin
Dunnock
Eider
Fieldfare
Firecrest
Gadwall
Gannet
Garganey
Golden eagle
Goldeneye
Golden plover
Golden oriole

* Based on Avery *et al. Ibis* 137 (Suppl; 1995): 232–39

Goldfinch
Goshawk
Grasshopper warbler
Great northern diver
Great skua
Greenshank
Green woodpecker
Grey plover
Greylag goose
Guillemot
Hawfinch
Herring gull
Honey buzzard
Jack snipe
Kestrel
Kingfisher
Knot
Lapwing
Leach's petrel
Lesser black-backed gull
Little gull
Little tern
Manx shearwater
Marsh tit
Mediterranean gull
Montagu's harrier
Nightingale
Oystercatcher
Parrot crossbill
Peregrine falcon
Pink-footed goose
Pintail
Pochard
Puffin
Purple sandpiper
Razorbill
Red-necked grebe

Redshank
Red-throated diver
Redstart
Redwing
Ringed plover
Ring ouzel
Ruff
Sand martin
Sandwich tern
Savi's warbler
Scarlet rosefinch
Scaup
Shag
Shelduck
Short-eared owl
Shoveler
Slavonian grebe
Snow bunting
Spotted crake
Starling
Stock dove
Stonechat
Storm petrel
Swallow
Teal
Temminck's stint
Turnstone
Twite
Velvet scoter
Water rail
Whimbrel
White-fronted goose
Whooper swan
Wigeon
Willow tit
Wood sandpiper
Woodcock

SOURCE: Joint Nature Conservation Committee, Monkstone House, City Road, Peterborough PE1 1JY, United Kingdom Tel: 07133 62626; Fax: 01733 55948

Mascot Birds

National Birds

Australia	Emu
Chile	Andean condor
Costa Rica	Clay-colored robin
Germany	Eagle
Guatemala	Quetzel
Monserrat	Monserrat oriole
New Zealand	Kiwi
Nicaragua	Turquoise-browned motmot
Panama	Harpy eagle
South Africa	Blue or Stanley's crane
United States of America	Bald eagle

Canadian Provincial Birds

British Columbia: Stellers jay   **Quebec:** Snowy owl
Alberta: Great horned owl   **New Brunswick:** Black-capped chickadee
Saskatchewan: Sharp-tailed grouse   **Nova Scotia:** Osprey
Manitoba: Great grey owl   **Prince Edward Island:** Blue jay
Ontario: Common loon   **Newfoundland:** Atlantic puffin

SOURCE: *Birding in Canada*   http://www.interlog.com/~gallantg/canada/provbird.html

State Birds (United States)

Alabama	Northern flicker
Alaska	Willow ptarmigan
Arizona	Cactus wren
Arkansas	Northern mockingbird
California	California quail
Colorado	Lark bunting
Connecticut	American robin
Delaware	Blue hen chicken
District of Columbia	Wood thrush
Florida	Northern mockingbird
Georgia	Brown thrasher
Hawaii	Nene
Idaho	Mountain bluebird
Illinois	Northern cardinal
Indiana	Northern cardinal
Iowa	American goldfinch
Kansas	Western meadowlark
Kentucky	Northern cardinal
Louisiana	Brown pelican
Maine	Black-capped chickadee

Maryland	Baltimore oriole
Massachusetts	Black-capped chickadee
Michigan	American robin
Minnesota	Common loon
Mississippi	Northern mockingbird
Missouri	Eastern bluebird
Montana	Western meadowlark
Nebraska	Western meadowlark
Nevada	Mountain bluebird
New Hampshire	Purple finch
New Jersey	American goldfinch
New Mexico	Greater roadrunner
New York	Eastern bluebird
North Carolina	Northern cardinal
North Dakota	Western meadowlark
Ohio	Northern cardinal
Oklahoma	Scissor-tailed flycatcher
Oregon	Western meadowlark
Pennsylvania	Ruffed grouse
Rhode Island	Rhode Island red chicken
South Carolina	Carolina wren
South Dakota	Ring-necked pheasant
Tennessee	Northern mockingbird
Texas	Northern mockingbird
Utah	California gull
Vermont	Hermit thrush
Virginia	Northern cardinal
Washington	America goldfinch
West Virginia	Northern cardinal
Wisconsin	American robin
Wyoming	Western meadowlark

Assemblages of Birds

Bouquet or nye of pheasants
Building of rooks
Cast of hawks
Charm of finches
Chattering of starlings
Clamor of rooks
Cluster of knots
Commotion or covert of coots
Company of wigeon
Congregation of plovers
Convocation of eagles
Covey of quails, partridges
Deceit or desert of lapwings
Descent of woodpeckers
Dissimulation of birds
Dule of doves
Exaltation of larks

Fall of woodcocks
Flight of swallows
Gaggle or skein of geese
Gulp of cormorants
Herd of swans or cranes
Host of sparrows
Kettle or screw of hawks
Murder of crows
Murmuration of starlings
Mustering of storks
Nye of pheasants
Ostentation of peacocks
Pack of grouse
Paddling of ducks
Parliament of owls
Peep of chickens
Pitying of turtle doves

Plump of waterfowl
Pod of pelicans
Raft of ducks
Rafter of turkeys
Richness of martins
Siege of herons
Spring of teal
Stand of flamingos
Strand of silky flycatchers
Tiding(s) of magpies
Unkindness of ravens
Walk or wisp of snipe
Watch of nightingales
Wings of plovers
Wreck of seabirds

Records in the Bird World

Anatomy

heaviest and tallest bird: ostrich at maximum 156 kg (345 lb) and 2.7 m (9 ft)

heaviest flying bird: great bustard at maximum 21 kg (46.3 lb)

largest extinct bird: Dromornis stirtoni of Australia at 454 kg (1,000 lb) and 3 m (10 ft) tall

tallest extinct bird: giant moa of New Zealand at 3.7 m (12 ft)

greatest wingspan: wandering albatross at up to 3.63 m (11 ft 11 in)

greatest wingspan of landbirds: Andean condor and marabou stork tied at 3.2 m (10.5 ft)

smallest bird: bee hummingbird at 5.7 cm (2.24 in) and 1.6 g (0.056 oz)

smallest flightless bird: inaccessible island rail at 12.5 cm (5 in) and 34.7 g (1.2 oz)

longest legs: ostrich

longest legs relative to body length: black-winged stilt at 23 cm (9 in), or 60% of its height

tallest bird: greater flamingo at 145 cm (57 in)

absolute shortest legs: virtually non-existent in swifts (*Apodidae*)

longest toes relative to body length: northern jacana at 10 cm (4 in)

longest bill relative to body length: sword-tailed hummingbird at 10.5 cm (4.13 in)

absolute longest bill: Australian pelican at 47 cm (18.5 in)

absolute shortest bill: glossy swiftlet at just a few mm

largest and fleshiest tongue: flamingo

longest tongue relative to body size: wryneck at two-thirds of its body length excluding the tail

smallest hearts relative to body size: Central and South American tinamous at 1.6–3.1% of body weight

longest feathers: onagadori, a domestic strain of red jungle fowl, at 10.59 m (34.75 ft)

longest tail feathers: crested argus pheasant at 173 cm (5.7 ft)

longest tail coverts: Indian and green peafowl at 160 cm (5.24 ft)

widest tail feathers: crested argus pheasant at 13 cm (5.1 in)

longest tail feathers relative to body length: fork-tailed flycatcher at 27 cm (10.75 in)

longest primary feathers relative to body length: pennant-winged nightjar at 60 cm (2 ft)

shortest tails: virtually non-existent in kiwis, emus, rheas, cassowaries

greatest number of feathers: whistling swan at 25,216

lowest number of feathers: ruby-throated hummingbird at 940

most secondary flight feathers: wandering and royal albatrosses with 40 secondaries and 11 primaries on each wing

largest eyeball: ostrich with a diameter of 5 cm (2 in)

Locomotion

fastest-moving bird: diving peregrine falcon at 188 km/h (117 mph)

fastest flapping flight: white-throated needle-tailed swift at 170 km/h (106 mph)

fastest level-flight: red-breasted merganser at 161 km/h (100 mph)

fastest-moving racing pigeon: 177 km/h (110 mph)

slowest-flying bird: American woodcock at 8 km/h (5 mph)

fastest wingbeat: hummingbirds, e.g., amethyst woodstar and horned sungem, at 90/sec *slowest wingbeat:* vultures at 1/sec

longest soaring bird: albatrosses and condors

smallest soaring bird: swift

highest flying bird: Ruppell's griffon vulture at 11,274 m (7 mi)

most aerial bird: sooty terns at 3 to 10 years without landing

most aerial landbird: common swift at 3 years without landing

longest two-way migration: Arctic tern at 40,200 km (25,000 miles)

longest migration (assuming a coastal route): common tern at 26,000 km (16,210 miles) in January 1997

most aquatic bird: penguins with 75% of their lives spend in the sea

fastest running bird: ostrich at 97.5 km/h (60 mph)

fastest running flying bird: greater road-runner at 42 km/h (26 mph)

fastest underwater swimming bird: gentoo penguin at 36 km/h (22.3 mph)

deepest dive for non-flying bird: emperor penguin at 540 m (1,772 ft)

deepest dive for a flying bird: thick-billed murre at 210 m (689 ft)

deepest dive for a flying bird under 210 g: Peruvian diving petrel at 83 m (272 ft)

longest submerged: emperor penguin at 18 min

greatest weight-carrying capacity: bald eagle lifting a 6.8 kg (15 lb) mule deer

Physiology

keenest sense of smell: kiwis

keenest sense of hearing: barn owl

keenest eyesight: diurnal raptors with 1 million cones per sq. mm in the retinal fovea

best light-gathering capacity at night: owls, e.g., tawny owl

greatest G-force (acceleration due to gravity): beak of red-headed woodpecker hitting bark at 20.9 km/h (13 mph)

highest daily frequency of pecking: 12,000 times by black woodpecker

most intelligent bird: African gray parrot, crows, "bait-fishing" green and striated herons

most talkative bird: African gray parrot with a vocabulary of 800 words

birds that use echolocation: cave swiftlets and oilbirds

greatest hibernator: poorwill with body temperature lowered to 18–20 degrees C (64.4–68 degrees F)

greatest bird mimic: marsh warbler with up to 84 songs

most songs sung per unit time: 22,197 in 10 hours by a red-eyed vireo

coldest temperature regularly endured by a bird: average temperatures of –45.6 degrees C (–50 degress F) for emperor penguins

coldest temperature endured by a bird: –62.5 degrees C (–80.5 degrees F) by snowy owl

coldest temperature of land where a bird has been recorded: –89.6 degrees C (–129 degrees F) in Vostok, Russia for south polar skua

warmest temperature regularly endured by a bird: larks and wheatears at 44–45 degrees C (111–113 degrees F)

Reproduction

largest recorded nesting bird colony: 136 million passenger pigeon nesting in an area in Wisconsin covering 1,942 sq km (750 sq mi)

most abundant bird: red-billed quelea at up to 10 billion

lowest altitude for nesting: little green bee-eater at 400 m (1,307 ft) below sea-level in the Dead Sea *longest fasting period:* 134 days for incubating male emperor penguins

most northerly nesting bird: ivory gull at edge of pack ice in Arctic Circle

largest ground nest: dusky scrubfowl nest at 11 m (36 ft) wide and 4.9 m (16 ft) high with over 2,700 kg (300 tons) of forest floor litter

largest tree nest: bald eagle in Florida at 6.1 m (20 ft) deep, 2.9 m (9.5 ft) wide, and weighing 2,722 kg (almost 3 tons)

largest social nest: African social weavers with a 100-chamber nest structure 8.2 m (27 ft) in length and 1.8 m (6 ft) high

largest roofed nest: hamerkop at 2 m (6.5 ft) wide and 2 m (6.5 ft) deep

longest nest burrow: rhinoceros auklet at 8 m (26 ft)

highest tree nest: marbled murrelet at 45 m (148 ft)

smallest nest: Cuban bee and vervain hummingbirds at 1.98 cm (0.78 in) in breadth and 1.98 – 3.0 cm (0.78 – 1.2 in) deep

foulest smelling nest: Eurasian hoopoe

greatest number of sperm storage tubules: turkey at 20,000

greatest longevity of sperm inside a female: turkey at 42 days

largest egg: ostrich measuring 17.8 by 14 cm (7 by 4.5 in)

largest egg laid by a passerine: 57 g (2 oz) by Australian lyrebirds

largest egg laid relative to body weight: little spotted kiwi at 26%

smallest egg laid relative to body weight: ostrich egg at 1–1.5%

smallest egg: West Indian vervain humming-

bird at 10 mm (0.39 in) in length and 0.375 g (0.0132 oz)

roundest eggs: owls, tinamous

longest interval between eggs laid: maleo at 10–12 day intervals

largest clutch laid by a nidicolous species: 19 eggs laid by a European blue tit

largest clutch laid by a nidifugous species: 28 by a bobwhite quail

largest average clutch size: 15–19 by a gray partridge

smallest clutch size: 1 egg laid every 2 years by albatrosses

greatest number of eggs laid consecutively: 146 by a mallard

longest uninterrupted incubation period: emperor penguin at 64–67 days

longest interrupted incubation period: wandering albatross and brown kiwi at 85 days

longest incubation period by a passerine species: 50 days for Australian lyrebird

shortest incubation period: 11 days by small passerines

longest fledging period of flying birds: wandering albatross at 278 days

greatest number of broods raised in one year: 21 by zebra finch pair

fastest to breeding maturity: common quail at 5 weeks

slowest to breeding maturity: royal and wandering albatrosses at 6–10 years

longest-lived wild bird: royal albatross at over 58 years

longest-lived captive bird: sulfur-crested cockatoo at over 80 years

Human Related

largest collection of bird skins: British Museum of Natural History with 1.25 million

most valuable bird: 8 billion domestic chickens produce 562 billion eggs annually

most valuable nest: gray-rumped swiftlet for bird's nest soup

largest domesticated bird: ostrich

earliest domesticated bird: jungle fowl at 3200 BC

heaviest domestic turkey: 37 kg (81 lb)

country with the most endangered birds: Indonesia with 126 (Brazil second with 121) *country with the highest percentage of its bird species endangered:* New Zealand with 30%

country with the most introduced species: United States (Hawaii) with 68

most recent species of bird to be declared extinct: flightless Atitlan grebe of Guatemala in 1984

most recent North American bird to be declared extinct: dusky seaside sparrow, a race of seaside sparrow, in 1987

rarest bird in the world: ivory-billed woodpecker, Jerdon's courser

highest price paid for a bird book: $3.96 million (U.S.) for a set of John James Audubon's *The Birds of America* in 1989

highest price paid for a mounted bird: £9,000 for an extinct great auk by the Natural History Museum of Iceland on 1971

highest price paid for a live bird: £41,000 for a racing pigeon named Peter Pau in 1986

highest price paid for a cage bird: £5,000 for a hyacinth macaw

highest price paid for an egg: £1,000 for an egg of extinct *Aepyornis maximus*

first bird featured on a U.S. postage stamp: bald eagle

SOURCES: B.P. Martin. *World Birds* (Enfield, Middlesex: Guinness Superlatives Ltd., 1987) and many others.

History of Who's Who in Bird Biology and Conservation

Abert, James William (1820–1897): While collecting birds for Spencer F. Baird, discovered a towhee which was later given the scientific name *Pipilo aberti*.

Adams, Edward, MD (1824–1856): British surgeon, naturalist, and collector; involved in two polar expeditions to N. America; the yellow-billed loon species name *adamsii* honors him.

Aiken, Charles Edward Howard (1850–1936): Ornithologist, taxidermist, and traveler; discovered two birds: the white-winged junco, *Junco aikeni*, and a subspecies of the screech owl, *Otus asio aikeni*.

Aldrich, John Warren (1906–1995): Curator of ornithology at the Cleveland Museum of Natural History; chief of the Section of Distribution and Migration of Birds of the U.S. Fish and Wildlife Service; editor of *Audubon Field Notes*; research associate of the Smithsonian Institution; helped form the Buffalo Ornithological Society; member of many organizations, including serving as president of the American Ornithologists' Union.

Alexander, Christopher (1887–1917): Interest in natural history; originated a method to count breeding birds and map territories; acknowledged that different birds occupied different altitudes in mountain areas.

Alexander, Horace Gundry (1889–1989): Interest in birds, especially leaf warblers; contributed to the *Handbook of British Birds* by writing about song periods and identification; authored *Some Notes on Asian Leaf Warblers* and *Seventy Years of Birdwatching*.

Alexandre, Wilfred Backhouse (1885–1965): Research officer; director of the library at the Edward Grey Institute; author of *Birds of the Ocean*.

Ali, Salim (1896–1987): Indian ornithologist who fought for environmental awareness; considered the father of Asian ecological understanding; honorary fellow of the American Ornithologists' Union; published *Handbook of the Birds of India and Pakistan*; recipient of several awards, including the Gold Medal of the British Ornithologists' Union.

Allen, Arthur Augustus (1885–1964): Educator, research scientist, writer, lecturer, bird photographer, and fellow of the American Ornithologists' Union; first in America to bear the title Professor of Ornithology; taught at Cornell University where he remained for more than 50 years; co-founder of the Cornell Laboratory of Ornithology; pioneered in recording wild bird songs and calls; author of several books, including *The Book of Bird Life* and *Stalking Birds with Color Camera*; a medal bears his name to indicate scientific excellence.

Allen, Charles Andrew (1841–1930): Bird collector; memorialized by Allen's hummingbird.

Allen, Joel Asaph (1838–1921): The first curator of birds at Harvard's Museum of Comparative Zoology; a founder of the Nuttall Ornithological Club in Cambridge in 1873 and the American Ornithologists' Union (AOU) in 1883; the first president of the AOU, and the first editor of its journal, *The Auk*; studied geographic variation in birds and devised Allen's Rule.

Allen, Robert Porter (1905–1963): Ornithologist; National Audubon Society conservationist; interest in raptor migration; author of several studies on N. American wading birds; wrote *On the Trail of Vanishing Species*.

Arbib, Robert S., Jr. (1915–1987): Ornithologist; editor of the *Linnaean Newsletter* and *American Birds*; president of the Federation of New York State Bird Clubs and the Linnaean Society of New York; elective member of the American Ornithologists' Union; helped initiate the Hawk Migration Association of North America; co-authored *The Hungry Bird Book* and *Enjoying Birds Around New York City*; recipient of the Burroughs Medal.

Archbold, Richard (1907–1976): Naturalist; member of several expeditions; collected in New Guinea; established the Archbold Biological Station in Florida.

Arminjon, Vittorio (1830–1897): Captain and commander of the first Italian vessel to sail around the world; on this voyage the South Trinidad petrel was discovered and named *Pterodroma arminjoniana* in his honor.

Armstrong, Edward Allworthy (1900–1978): Irish naturalist; studied the wren; corresponding fellow of the American Ornithologists' Union; vice-president of the British Ornithologists' Union; published several books, including *Birds of the Grey Wind*, which received the Burroughs Medal, *Bird Display and Behaviour*, and *The Way Birds Live*.

Armstrong, Rev. Edward Allworthy (1900–1978?): Irish naturalist; wrote *Bird Display: An Introduction to the Study of Bird Psychology* in 1942; co-wrote *The Wren* in 1955; and wrote *The Study of Bird Song* in 1963, as well as many other books on nature and other subjects; given several awards.

Audubon, John James (1785–1851): Formally trained as an artist in France and then migrated to the United States in 1803; traveled widely throughout North America east of the Rockies, observing, shooting, and painting life-sized watercolors of birds; besides being responsible for the famous Elephant Folio prints, Audubon also published a multi-volume *Ornithological Biography, or an Account of the Habits of the Birds of the United States*; widely regarded as a great pioneering student of bird biology and the artistic father of American ornithology.

Austin, Oliver L., Jr. (1903–1988): Professor of zoology; Curator in Ornithology at the Florida Museum of Natural History; introduced the Japanese mist net to the U.S.; a founder and director of the Austin Ornithological Research Station at Wellfleet; fellow of the American Ornithologists' Union; editor of *The Auk*; published *The Birds of Korea* and *Birds of the World*.

Axtell, Harold H. (1904–1992): Naturalist, biologist; curator of biology in the Buffalo Museum of Science; devoted his time to field identification of birds; elective member of the American Ornithologists' Union; fellow of the Buffalo Ornithological Society.

Bachman, Rev. John (1790–1874): Naturalist and clergyman associated with Audubon; co-author of *The Viviparous Quadrupeds of North America*; memorialized by the black oystercatcher, *Haematopus bachmani*, Bachman's sparrow, and Bachman's warbler.

Bailey, Florence Merriam (1863–1948): Ornithologist, writer; promoter of nature education; first woman to be elected a fellow of the American Ornithologists' Union; associated with the United States Biological Survey; participated in the foundation of the Audubon Society of the District of Columbia; member of several expeditions in company of her husband; authored several books, including *Birds through an Opera Glass*; published *Handbook of Birds of the Western United States, Birds of New Mexico*; awarded the Brewster Medal by the American Ornithologists' Union.

Baillie, James L. (1904–1970): Canadian ornithologist; wrote a weekly bird column in the *Toronto Telegram*; assistant curator in the Royal Ontario Museum; participated in the provincial Faunal Survey trips; elective member of the American Ornithologists' Union; president of the Toronto Field Naturalists Club; a founder of the Toronto Ornithological Club; director of the Federation of Ontario Naturalists; secretary-treasurer of the Canadian Audubon Society; published more than 300 papers and articles; life member and recipient of the Ontario Conservation Trophy from the Federation of Ontario Naturalists; recipient of the Centennial Medal; honored by the Baillie Birdathon in Ontario.

Baird, Spencer Fullerton (1823–1887): Participated in the establishment of the Smithsonian Institution which became a major scientific center; in part, helped expand the museum's bird collection; co-authored, with Thomas Brewer and Robert Ridgway, *A History of North American Birds*; influential zoologist who founded the "Baird School" of ornithology; named Lucy's warbler, Grace's warbler, and Virginia's warbler after female acquaintances; memorialized by Baird's sandpiper and Baird's sparrow.

Balph, David Finley (1931–1990): Teacher of animal behavior at Utah State University; studied social behavior and feeding strategies of birds; elective member of the American Ornithologists' Union.

Bannerman, David Armitage (1886–1979): British ornithologist; chairman of the British Ornithologists' Club; worked for the British Museum (Natural History); published many papers on birds of many countries, primarily in Africa; wrote 8 volumes of *The Birds of Tropical West Africa*, 12 volumes of *The Birds of the British Isles*, as well as many other books on birds; received many honors.

Barrow, Sir John (1764–1848): Chief founder of the Royal Geographical Society; remembered for his Arctic travels; commemorated in Barrow's goldeneye and a subspecies of the glaucous gull.

Barth, Edvard K. (1913–1996): Norwegian ornithologist; field zoologist; photographer and writer; curator of birds at Zoological Museum in Oslo; author of more than 200 publications; interest in systematics of the Laridae.

Bartram, Sir John (1699–1777): Quaker botanist; explorer; sent specimens to his friend Linnaeus; memorialized by *Bartramia longicauda*.

Bartram, William (1739–1823): Known as the grandfather of ornithology; described various aspects of bird biology in *Travels through North and South Carolina, Georgia, East and West Florida*, which contained information on various aspects, including nesting and migration; an inspiration to Wilson; honored by Bartram's sandpiper.

Baumgartner, Frederick M. (1910–1996): Teacher at Wisconsin State University at Stevens Point; several areas of study, including owls, bobwhite quail, and birds of prey; elective member of the American Ornithologists' Union; editor of *Audubon Field Notes*; president of the Oklahoma Ornithological Society; co-authored *Oklahoma Bird Life*.

Beebe, C. William (1877–1962): Professional ornithologist; one of the pioneers in the early conservation movement in the U.S.; interest in coloration of birds, e.g., the dichromatism in birds such as snow geese, murres, and peacocks; wrote *The Bird, Its Form and Function*.

Bell, John Graham (1812–1889): Naturalist and pioneer taxidermist; friend of early American ornithologists; gave lessons to U.S. president Theodore Roosevelt; Bell's vireo and the sage sparrow, *Amphispiza belli*, honor his name.

Bendire, Charles (1836–1897): A German immigrant and surgical assistant who received medals for bravery in both the Civil and Indian wars; fascinated with eggs, became curator of Oology at the United States Museum; authored *Life Histories of North American Birds, with Special Reference to Their Breeding Habits and Eggs*; memorialized by Bendire's thrasher.

Benson, Constantine ("Con") Walter (1909–1982): Sportsman; ornithologist; head of Cambridge Bird Club; studied birds of Malawi; made major contributions to African ornithology; author of more than 350 articles; sorted out collection of Museum of Zoology in Cambridge; described 7 new species and several races; approximately 400 titles, including *A Check List of the Birds of Nyasaland* and *The Birds of the Comoro Islands*; awarded the Order of the British Empire; given the Union Medal by the British Ornithologists' Union and the Gill Memorial Medal by the South African Ornithological Society.

Bent, Arthur Cleveland (1866–1954): A businessman and amateur ornithologist; made many contributions to *The Auk* regarding distribution and nesting habits of a wide variety of bird species; is recognized today as having spent a great deal of time editing and, in most part, writing the 26-volume series *Life Histories of North American Birds* which had been started by Bendire.

Berger, Andrew J. (1915–1995): Instructor of anatomy; conservationist; studied avian musculature; fellow of the American Ornithologists' Union and the American Association for the Advancement of Science; authored *Hawaiian Birdlife* and two ornithology textbooks; participated in *Fundamentals of Ornithology*.

Bewick, Thomas (1753–1828): English artist and wood engraver; authored and illustrated *A History of British Birds*; memorialized by Bewick's wren.

Blackburne, Anna (1726–1793): English botanist; maintained a bird museum at her home which was later used in Pennant's *Arctic Zoology* book; honored by the Blackburnian warbler.

Blair, Hugh Moray Sutherland (1901?–1986): British ornithologist; oologist; interest in waders and birds in Scandinavia; major contributor to the 12 volumes of *Birds of the British Isles*.

Bleitz, Donald Louis (1915–1986): Bird photographer; elective member of the American Ornithologists' Union; member of the Eastern and Western Bird Banding Association; founder of the Bleitz Wildife Foundation; over 600 photographs of North American birds; life member of the Cooper Ornithological Society and the Wilson Ornithological Club.

Bonaparte, Charles Lucien (1803–1857): Napoleon's brother; made systemic and zoogeographical contributions in supplemental volumes of Wilson's *American Ornithology*; for his work in Conspectus Generum Avium, has been known as the father of systemic ornithology; commemorated by Bonaparte's gull.

Bond, James (1900–1989): Ornithologist, naturalist; specialist in the birds of the West Indies; published more than 100 papers; authored the *Checklist of the Birds of the West Indies*; recipient of the Brewster Medal from the American Ornithologists' Union; Ian Fleming's fictional superhero named after him.

Bonelli, Franco Andrea (1784–1830): Italian entomologist, zoologist, and naturalist; professor; founded the Turin Museum in 1811, which contributed greatly to ornithology in Italy; memorialized by Bonelli's eagle and Bonelli's warbler (*Phylloscopus bonelli*).

Borror, Donald J. (1907–1988): Entomologist interested in bird songs; pioneer of bioacoustics; fellow of the American Ornithologists' Union; 15,000 recordings; more than 50 publications on avian communication, most of which concentrate on North American bird species.

Botteri, Signor Matteo (1808–1877): Dalmatian botanist; collector; professor of natural history in Veracruz, Mexico; collected Botteri's sparrow, which was named after him.

Boulton, W. Rudyerd (?–1983): Ornithologist in Africa; elective member of the American Ornithologists' Union; founded the Atlantica Foundation; worked for the American Museum of Natural History, the Carnegie Museum, and the Field Museum of Natural History.

Bourlière, François (1913–1993): French ecologist and gerontologist; promoter of conservation; editor-in-chief of *Revue d'écologie*; corresponding fellow of the American Ornithologists' Union; president of the International Union for Conservation of Nature and Natural Resources; president of the Société Nationale de la Protection de la Nature; recipient of several honors, including the Dutch Royal Order of the Golden Ark.

Brandt, Johann Friedrich (1802–1879): German zoologist; director of the Zoological Museum in St. Petersburg; published more than 300 papers; described several mammals and birds, such as Brandt's cormorant.

Brewer, Thomas (1814–1880): A physician who became a dedicated birder; helped, like Spencer Fullerton Baird, connect the early and modern era of ornithology; is known not only for his book on bird eggs, *North American Oology*, but also for his defense of the house sparrow when it was introduced in the United States; co-author of *A History of North American Birds*; memorialized by Brewer's blackbird and Brewer's sparrow.

Brewster, William (1851–1919): Conservationist, ornithologist; one of the founders and presidents of the American Ornithologist's Union and the Nuttall Ornithological Club of Cambridge; author of more than 300 papers; author of *October Farm* and *Concord River*; honored by Brewster's warbler; a medal named in his honor by the American Ornithologists' Union.

Brodkorb, Pierce (1908–1992): Bird collector; professor at the University of Florida in Gainesville; studied paleontology and osteology; went on several expeditions; compiled the *Catalogue of Fossil Birds*; fellow of the American Orntihologists' Union; recipient of the Brewster Medal.

Broley, Charles Lavelle (1879–1959): Amateur ornithologist especially known for his bald eagle banding project in Florida; wrote *Eagle Man*.

Broun, Maurice (1906–1979): Earliest protector and eventual Curator Emeritus of Hawk Mountain Sanctuary; involved in conservation of raptors; elective member of the American Ornithologists' Union; more than 100 publications; author of *Hawks Aloft: The Story of Hawk Mountain*.

Brown, Leslie (1917–1980): Agriculturist, ecologist, and ornithologist; prolific writer with more than a dozen books; specialist on birds of prey, especially African species; co-authored *Eagles, Hawks and Falcons of the World*; awarded an Union Medal by the British Ornithologists' Union.

Browne, Thomas (1605–1682): British naturalist; put forward the possibility that birds migrated to warmer climates; using dissections, contributed to our comprehension of the anatomy and physiology of birds and mammals.

Buller, Sir Walter Lawry (1838–1906): New Zealand lawyer with an interest in ornithology; collected and studied New Zealand birds; author of *History of Birds of New Zealand* and *Manual of Birds of New Zealand*; fellow of the Royal Society; knighted in 1886; commemorated by Buller's shearwater, *Puffinis bulleri*.

Bullock, William (1775–?): English traveler; proprietor of Bullock's Museum in London; collected several new species of birds in Mexico; memorialized by Bullock's oriole.

Bulwer, James (1794–1879): Diplomat and ambassador to Washington, DC; memorialized by genus *Bulweria* and especially Bulwer's petrel (*Bulweria bulwerii*).

Burkitt, James Parson (1870–1959): Revolutionized the study of bird movement by placing metal bands on legs of robins; specialized in territorial behavior and songs.

Burroughs, John (1837–1921): Popularized the study of nature in America; known as the Hudson River naturalist, wrote 25 books, including *Wake Robin*; innate ability to recognize bird songs; participated in a trip to Yellowstone Park with Theodore Roosevelt; awarded honorary degrees from Yale, Colgate, and the University of Georgia.

Buxton, John (1912–1989): University teacher; ornithologist; carried out bird observations as a POW in Nazi Germany and later published them; first person to bring a mist net into the U.K.

Campbell, Bruce (1912–1993): Naturalist; ornithologist; conducted long-term nestbox study of pied flycatchers; secretary of the British Trust for Ornithology; co-edited *A Dictionary of Birds*; awarded many medals for his work.

Carnes, Betty (1905–1987): Bird photographer; banded many birds; first woman to band a peregrine falcon; president of the New Jersey State Garden Club and the New Jersey Audubon Society; first woman to be elected a member of the American Ornithologists' Union; later became a patron; a scholarship bears her name.

Carson, Rachel (1907–1964): While a marine biologist and having never studied birds, used her considerable writing skills to present the whole story of the misuse of pesticides, e.g., DDT, in a readable fashion in a book entitled *Silent Spring* in 1962.

Cassin, John (1813–1869): Curator of ornithology at the Academy of Natural Sciences of Philadelphia; described and named 193 species of birds; only American in his time to be recognized as an ornithologist; published *Illustrations of the Birds of California, Texas, Oregon, British and Russian America, 1853 to 1855*; Cassin's sparrow and Cassin's finch honor his name.

Catesby, Mark (1682–1749?): Regarded as the first real American naturalist; the founder of American ornithology; fellow of the Royal Society; authored and illustrated *Natural History of Carolina, Florida, and the Bahama Islands*.

Cettis, François (1726–1780): Italian jesuit; zoologist; published *Natural History of Sardinia*; memorialized by Cettis warbler.

Chance, Edgar (1881–1955): Amateur naturalist who specialized in cuckoo behavior; known for his remarkable field observations; authored *The Cuckoo's Secret* and *The Truth about the Cuckoo*.

Chapman, Frank Michler (1864–1945): Popularizer; collected in Florida; research specialized on neo-tropical birds; assistant to the director of the American Museum in New York; curator of the Department of Birds; authored 17 books and 225 articles, including *Handbook of Birds of Eastern North America*; honored by an award from American Museum of Natural History.

Chesterfield, Norman (?–1996): Canadian birder; held the top Canadian bird species list since 1977 and was once the world record holder.

Clark, William (1770–1838): Captain of the famous expedition across the continent; published *History of the Expedition under the Commands of Captain Lewis and Captain Clark*; memorialized by Clark's nutcracker (formerly Clark's crow), which he discovered in Idaho.

Clarke, Eagle (1858–1938): Keeper of Natural History in the Royal Scottish Museum; specialized in migration and faunistics; served on the Committee of the British Association for the Advancement of Science; editor of the *Annals of Scottish Natural History* and *Scottish Naturalist*; president of the British Ornithologists' Union; authored *Studies in Bird Migration*; awarded the Godman-Salvin Medal by the British Ornithologists' Union.

Coffey, Ben B., Jr. (1904–1993): Interest in mid-South bird distribution patterns and the phenology of migration and nesting; recorded bird songs; fellow of the American Ornithologists' Union; member of the Wilson Ornithological Society and the Inland and Northeastern Bird Banding Associations; president of the Tennessee Ornithological Society; editor of *The Migrant*.

Cooper, James Graham (1830–1902): Surgeon, naturalist, ornithologist, and bird collector; published *Ornithology in California*; honored by the Cooper Ornithological Society.

Cooper, William (1798?–1864): One of the founders and secretary of the New York Lyceum of Natural History; first American to become a member of the London Zoological Society; named and described the evening grosbeak; collected Cooper's hawk, which was later named after him; father of James G. Cooper.

Cory, Charles Barney (1857–1921): One of the founders and presidents of the American Ornithologists' Union; bird curator at the Field Museum of Natural History; leading authority on W. Indian birds; authored *A Naturalist in the Magdalen Islands*; Cory's shearwater bears his name.

Costa, Louis Marie Pantaleon (1806–1864): French collector of hummingbirds; honored by Costa's hummingbird, *Calypte costae.*

Cottam, Clarence (1899–1974): Professor; worked for the U.S. Fish and Wildlife Service; studied food habits of birds; fought against pesticide use; first director of the Rob and Bessie Welder Wildlife Foundation; president of The Wildlife Society, Texas Ornithological Society, National Parks Association, and the Council of Southwest Foundations; more than 250 publications; recipient of many awards.

Coues, Elliot (1842–1899): An army officer who collected bird specimens for observations; one of the founders of the American Ornithologists' Union; authored *Birds of the Northwest, Birds of the Colorado Valley*; made a major contribution to ornithology by publishing the *Key to North American Birds*; honored by an award for the American Ornithologists' Union.

Coward, Thomas Alfred (1867–1933): Popularizer who broadcasted on natural history; co-authored *The Vertebrate Fauna of Cheshire and Liverpool Bay*; authored *Birds of the British Isles and Their Eggs.*

Cramp, Stanley (1913–1987): British ornithologist; chief editor of the 7 volumes of the handbook *The Birds of the Western Palearctic*; senior editor of journal *British Birds*; co-authored *The Seabirds of Britain and Ireland*; president and Union Medallist of the British Ornithologists' Union; several other awards as well.

Crandall, Lee Saunders (1887–1969): General Curator Emeritus of the New York Zoological Society; known as "the zoo man"; member of several expeditions; fellow of the American Ornithologists' Union; served on several committees; published 250 articles and four books; recipient of the Everly Gold Medal of the American Association of Zoological Parks and Aquariums.

Craveri, Frederico (1815–1890): Italian professor of chemistry who collected birds for the Turin Academy of Science; collected Craveri's murrelet, which bears his name.

Cruickshank, Helen Gere (1907–1995): Educator, traveler, photographer; authored several books, including *Bird Islands Down East*, and *Flight into Sunshine*, which was awarded the John Burroughs Medal by the American Ornithologists' Union.

Curry-Lindahl, Kai (1917–1990): Swedish zoologist, conservationist, and naturalist; lecturer at the University of Stockholm; editor of *Acta Vertibratica*; honorary fellow of the American Ornithologists' Union; participated in committees and organizations related to ornithology and conservation including the International Council for Bird Preservation and the World Wildlife Fund; over 600 papers and 100 books.

Darwin, Charles (1809–1882): Put foward the theory of evolution by natural selection; the most important scientist in the history of biology; a naturalist; traveled on the H.M.S. *Beagle* in an exploratory journey around the globe; particular interrest in the Galapagós finches; wrote the famous book *On the Origin of Species by Means of Natural Selection or the Preservation of Favored Races in the Struggle for Life*, as well as many other important books on biology.

Dathe, Heinrich (1910–1991): East German ornithologist who influenced Saxony ornithology; founded and developed the Tierpark Berlin; founder and editor of *Beiträge zur Vogelkunde*; corresponding fellow of the American Ornithologists' Union.

Dawson, William Leon (1873–1928): Photographer of birds; author of *Birds of Ohio, Birds of Washington*, and *Birds of California*.

Dear, Colonel L.S. (1883–1959): Naturalist, conservationist; first president of the Thunder Bay Field Naturalists' Club; later named honorary president; published *The Breeding Birds of the Region of Thunder Bay*.

Degland, Côme Damien (1787–1856): Director of the Musée d'Histoire Naturelle, located in Lille, France; known for his work on European birds; the author of *Ornithologie européene*; the white-winged scoter, *Melanitta fusca deglandi*, bears his name.

Delacour, Jean (1890–1985): Ornithologist; familiar with birds of all faunistic regions; promoted international conservation; collector of rare living birds; owned a private zoo; founder and editor of *L'Oiseau*; several tropical expeditions; discovered several new species; founder and president of the International Council for Bird Preservation; author of several books, including *Pheasants of the World* and *Wild Pigeons and Doves*.

Dexter, Ralph Warren (1912–1991): Teacher at Kent State University; long-term study of chimney swifts; fellow of the American Association for the Advancement of Science; president of the Ohio Academy of Sciences; elective member of the American Ornithologists' Union.

Diaz, Augustin (1829–1893): Mexican soldier; engineer; geographer who helped establish U.S.–Mexican border; mapped out Mexico for his government; honored by Mexican duck (*Anas diazi*).

Doubleday, Neltje Blanchan (1865–1918): Woman birdwatcher; published *Bird Neighbors, Birds That Hunt and Are Hunted, How to Attract the Birds*, and *Birds Worth Knowing*.

Dresser, Henry Eeles (1838–1915): Egg collector; secretary of the Britist Ornithologists' Union; author of *Eggs of the Birds of Europe* and *A History of the Birds of Europe*.

Drury, William Holland (1921–1992): Professor at the College of the Atlantic; conservationist, artist; first director of the Hatheway School of Conservation Education; first to identify the transoceanic migration of the blackpoll warbler; studied herring gulls; fellow of the American Ornithologists' Union.

Duncan, Sir Arthur Bryce (1928–1984): Scottish ornithologist; helped form the Cambridge Bird Club; first chairman of the Scottish Ornithologists' Club; chairman of the Nature Conservancy in the U.K.

Dunnet, George Mackenzie (1928–1995): Scottish ornithologist; ecologist; created Culterty Field Station at Aberdeen University; interested in seabirds; first chairman of the Seabird Group; leading authority of fleas as parasites of birds in Australia and Antarctic; president of the British Ecological Society; awarded the Godman-Salvin Medal by the British Ornithologists' Union.

Durrell, G. (1925–1995): Writer and television raconteur; zoo collector; conservationist; founded the Jersey Wildlife Preservation Trust; wrote many popular books on wildlife; honored by the Durrell Institute of Conservation by the University of Kent.

Dwight, Jonathan, Jr., MD (1858–1929): Fellow, treasurer, and president of the American Ornithologists' Union; studied bird plumages; author of *Sequence of Plumage and Moults of the Passerine Birds of New York.*

Eckstorm, Fannie Hardy (1865–1946): Went on several expeditions with her father; founded a College Audubon Society in Smith College; authored *The Bird Book* and *Woodpeckers.*

Eisenmann, Eugene (1906–1981): Lawyer with interest in birds; research associate of the American Museum of Natural History; president of the Linnean Society of New York; member of the International Commission on Zoological Nomenclature; vice-president of the American Ornithologists' Union; editor of *The Auk*; vice-chairman of the Pan-American Section of the International Council for Bird Preservation; authored *The Species of Middle American Birds.*

Elliott, Sir Hugh (1913–1989): Collector; ornithologist; studied birdlife in Tanganyika; made important contributions to wildlife conservation there; co-wrote *Herons of the World*; president of the British Ornithologists' Union.

Elliott, Daniel Giraud (1835–1915): One of the founders and presidents of the American Ornithologists' Union; representative of the American Museum; curator at the Field Museum in Chicago; worked on monographs concerning different groups of birds; authored and illustrated the 2-volume *Birds of North America.*

Etchécopar, Robert Daniel (1905–1990): Honorary fellow of the American Ornithologists' Union; secretary-general of the Société Ornithologique de France; director of the banding center in the Paris Museum; founder and president of Euring.

Falla, Sir Robert (1901–1979): New Zealand ornithologist; interest in petrels and moas; named several petrel species; president of the Royal Society of New Zealand and the Royal Australian Ornithologists' Union; awarded the Polar Medal for his Antarctic work.

Farner, Donald S. (1915–1988): Professor of Zoology at Washington State University; interest in photoregulation, reproductive biology, and endocrinology; president of the American Ornithologists' Union and the International Union of Biological Sciences; honorary member of the Cooper Ornithological Society; editor of *The Auk*; 260 publications; recipient of the Brewster Medal.

Farrand, John, Jr. (1937–1994): Zoologist at the Smithsonian Institution; curatorial assistant in Ornithology at the American Museum of Natural History; editor-in-chief of *American Birds*; elective member of the American Ornithologists' Union; president of the Linnean Society of New York; author of several books, including *The Audubon Society Master Guide to Birding* and *Master-pieces of Bird Art*; a Pliocene lily-trotter, *Jacana farrandi*, honors his name.

Fischer, Johann Gotthelf, Von Waldheim (1771–1853): German professor of zoology in Moscow; doctor and geologist; remembered for his work in Russia on natural history; memorialized by the species name of the spectacled eider, *Somateria fischeri.*

Fisher, James Maxwell McConnell (1912–1970): Helped popularize interest in natural history; assistant curator of the Zoological Society of London; interest in seabirds; several books and papers, including *Wild America*, which he wrote with Peterson; awarded the Union Medal by the British Ornithologists' Union, the Tucker Medal, Arthur Allen Medal by the American Ornithologists' Union, and the Gold Medal by the Royal Society for the Protection of Birds.

Fisher, Harvey Irvin (1916–1994): Professor and chair of the Zoology Department at the University of Illinois; studied the laysan albatross; interest in the functional anatomy of birds; studied footedness in birds; fellow of the American Ornithologists' Union; editor of *The Auk*; founding editor of *Pacific Science*.

Fisher, Albert Kenrick, MD (1856–1948): One of the founders and presidents of the American Ornithologists' Union; helped found an economic ornithology branch in the federal Division of Entomology; ornithologist on a few expeditions notably to the Southwest, Alaska, and the Pinchot South Seas; wrote *The Hawks and Owls of the United States and Their Relation to Agriculture*.

Fleming, James Henry (1872–1940): Ontario bird collector; self-taught ornithologist; member of the Great Lakes Ornithological Club; member of the Brodie Club; president of the American Ornithologists' Union; published over 40 papers; authored *Birds of Toronto*; Honorary Curator of Ornithology at the National Museum of Canada and the Royal Ontario Museum.

Fleming, Sir Charles (1916–1987): Studied birds of New Zealand and the surrounding areas; participated in the formation of the Ornithological Society of New Zealand; member of the Royal Society of New Zealand.

Forbush, Edward Howe (1858–1929): Ornithologist, writer, lecturer, and conservationist of New England; fellow of the American Ornithologists' Union; past president of the Massachusetts Audubon Society; also presided over the New England Bird Banding Association and the Federation of Bird Clubs of New England; State Ornithologist of Massachusetts for eight years; author of the classic book *The Birds of Massachusetts and Other New England States*; also authored *Useful Birds and Their Protection* and *A History of Game Birds, WildFowl and Shorebirds of Massachusetts and Adjacent States*.

Ford, Julian R. (1932–1987): Australian expert on geographic variation and hybrid zones in birds; corresponding fellow of the American Ornithologists' Union; recipient of many awards and grants.

Forster, Johann Reinhold (1729–1798): German naturalist; accompanied Cook on his second voyage around the world; authored the first book that attempted to cover N. American fauna: *A Catalogue of Animals of North America*; collected and described several new bird species; honored by Forster's tern, *Sterna forsteri*.

Foster, William (1852–1924): Bird illustrator; member of the Watercolor Society; illustrated *Game Birds of India*.

Franklin, Sir John (1786–1847): English navigator and explorer who collected birds; died while seeking the Northwest Passage in the Canadian Arctic; his name is preserved in Franklin's gull.

Friedmann, Herbert (1900–1987): Studied parasitic birds, especially cowbirds; head curator of zoology at the Smithsonian Institution; president of the American Ornithologists' Union; elective member of the National Academy of Sciences; author of 17 books and 315 papers, articles, including "The Cowbirds: A Study in the Biology of Social Parasitism"; recipient of the Elliot Medal from the National Academy of Sciences; also awarded the Leidy Medal.

Frohawk, Frederick William (1861–1946): Bird illustrator; fellow of the Entomological Society; contributed to *Encyclopaedia Britannica*; more than 1,000 drawings in books about birds.

Fuertes, Louis Agassiz (1874–1927): Great American bird painter considered to be the father of modern bird art; birder; lecturer at Cornell University; illustrated many books.

Fuggles-Couchman, Robin (?): Ornithologist and bird collector in Africa; life member of the British Ornithologists' Union; memorialized in two subspecies of birds, a bush warbler and a flycatcher.

Gambel, William (1819?–1849): Ornithologist and protégé of Thomas Nuttall; bird collector; name preserved in Gambel's quail and the mountain chickadee, *Parus gambeli*.

Godman, Frederick Du Cane (1834–1919): Associated with Osbert Salvin; went on an expedition to Jamaica and wrote *Biologia Centrali-Americana*; helped found the British Ornithologists' Union, where he was secretary and later president; author of *A Monograph of the Petrels*; awarded the Gold Medal by the British Ornithologists' Union; honored by Godman-Salvin Award.

Gould, John (1804–1881): Curator and preserver of the Zoological Society of London Museum and later elected a fellow; concentrated on lithography and sketching of birds which followed the production of *Birds of Europe, Birds of Australia, Birds of Asia, Birds of Great Britain*; explored and collected in Australia; honored by the Gould League of Bird Lovers, formed to help protect Australian birds.

Greenewalt, Crawford H. (1902–1993): Helped develop high-speed photography capable of "freezing"; studied flight; elective member of the American Ornithologists' Union; life member of the Cooper Ornithological Society and the Wilson Ornithological Society; author of *Hummingbirds and Dimensional Relationships for Flying Animals*.

Greenway, James C., Jr. (1903–1989): Conservationist; worked for the Museum of Comparative Zoology and the American Museum of Natural History; member of several expeditions; fellow of the American Ornithologists' Union; participated in the American Committee for International Wildlife Protection and the International Council for Bird Preservation; published *Extinct and Vanishing Birds of the World*.

Grimes, Samuel A. (1906–1996): Ornithologist, bird photographer; photographs appear in many books and journals; elective member of the American Ornithologists' Union; first honorary member of the Florida Ornithological Society; President Emeritus of the Tall Timbers Research Station.

Grinnell, Joseph (1877–1939): Ornithologist; director of Museum of Vertebrate Zoology at University of California in Berkeley; editor of *The Condor*; interest in avifauna of California; elected the youngest fellow of the American Ornithologists' Union, and later its president; over 500 publications; honored by Grinnell's waterthrush and *Lanius ludovicianus grinnelli*.

Griscom, Ludlow (1890–1959): Ornithologist at American Museum of Natural History; patron saint of modern bird-watching; interest in Mexican and Central American birdlife; extensive writings; many protégés; chief contribution was to show that shooting was not necessary to identify birds.

Gronvold, Henrik (1858–1940): Bird illustrator known for his egg drawings; illustrated *Birds of Australia* and *The British Warblers*.

Gudmundsson, Finnur (1909–1979): Icelandic ornithologist; conservationist; limnologist; studied status of many Icelandic bird species; worked at the Natural History Museum of Iceland; interest in ptarmigan; translated *Field Guide to the Birds of Britain and Europe* for use in Iceland.

Gullion, Gordon W. (1923–1991): Professor at the University of Minnesota; long-term study of ruffed grouse; more than 160 articles; recipient of many awards.

Gunn, William Walker Hamilton (1913–1984): Known for his bird sound recordings, his research on bird migration, and the application of radar use to prevent avian-aircraft collisions; executive director of the Federation of Ontario Naturalists; president of the Wilson Ornithological Society; recipient of the Arthur A. Allen Award by Cornell University and the Douglas H. Pimlott Conservation Award by the Canadian Nature Federation.

Hagar, Joseph Archibald (1896–1989): Ecologist, biologist; studied raptors and birds of the northeast wetlands; first to associate eggshell thinning to the reduction in population numbers of the peregrine falcon; elective member of the American Ornithologists' Union.

Hamerstrom, Frederick Nathan (1909–1990): Project leader of the Prairie Grouse Management Research Unit in Wisconsin which concentrated on the prairie chicken and the sharp-tailed grouse; interested also in hawks and owls; fellow of the American Ornithologists' Union; president of the Wisconsin Society of Ornithology; vice-president of the Wisconsin Academy of Science, Letters and Arts; received many awards in addition to being twice recipient of the Wildlife Society's Award for his publications; honored along with his wife, Fran, by an award of the Raptor Research Foundation.

Hammond, William Alexander, MD (1829–1900): Collected birds; Hammond's flycatcher bears his name.

Harcourt, Edwin William Vernon (1825–1891): English traveler and writer who described Harcourt's petrel; author of *Sketch of Madeira*.

Harlan, Richard, MD (1796–1843): Physician and naturalist; authored *Fauna Americana*; honored by Harlan's hawk.

Harris, Edward (1799–1863): Member of the Yellowstone expedition with Audubon; commemorated by Harris's hawk and Harris's sparrow.

Hartert, Ernst Johannes Otto (1859–1933): Director of the Tring Museum; authored an important taxonomical work: *Die Vogel der Palaarktischen Fauna*; recognized that birds had geographical forms; established the trinomial system; participated in *The Catalogue of Birds* of the British Museum.

Harting, James Edmund (1841–1928): Helped establish the library at the British Museum of Natural History; editor of *The Field* and *The Zoologist*; founded the New Hawking Club; librarian and assistant secretary at the Linnean Society; authored several books, including *Habits and Mangement of Hawks* and *Our Summer Migrants*.

Haverschmidt, François (1906–1987): Ornithologist of the Netherlands; interest in meadow birds; active in conservation; corresponding member of the American Ornithologists' Union; authored *Birds of Surinam*; 350 papers and 6 books; received several honors.

Heermann, Adolphus Lewis, MD (1827?–1865): Collected birds and their eggs for Spencer F. Baird; attached to the Pacific Railroad Surveys; honored by Heermann's gull.

Henshaw, Henry Wetherbee (1850–1930): Ornithologist and naturalist; a founder of the American Ornithologists' Union; Chief, U.S. Biological Survey; discovered that the male and female Williamson's sapsucker were of the same species; known for his rapid preparation of bird skins.

Henslow, John Stevens (1796–1861): Professor of botany who taught Charles Darwin in England; friend of Audubon; honored by Henslow's sparrow.

Herrick, Francis Hobart (1858–1940): Biologist and bird photographer; fellow of the American Ornithologists' Union; studied bald eagles, which led to articles in *The Auk* and a book: *The American Eagle*; authored the first Audubon biography (*Audubon: The Naturalist*); wrote *The Home Life of Wild Birds*.

Hickey, Joseph J. (1907–1993): Ornithologist, conservationist; professor at the University of Wisconsin; researched the effects of pesticides; helped discover the cause of the declining peregrine falcon population; founder and secretary of the Nature Conservancy; editor of several journals, such as *Journal of Wildlife Management*; president of the American Ornithologists' Union; author of *A Guide to Bird Watching*; recipient of many awards, including the Aldo Leopold Medal, the Arthur A. Allen Medal, and the Elliott Coues Award.

Hochbaum, Hans Albert (1911–1988): Director of the Delta Waterfowl Research Station; artist; fellow of the American Ornithologists' Union; authored *The Canvasback on a Prairie Marsh*, for which he received a Literary Award and the Brewster Medal; also received a Literary Award for *Travels and Traditions of Waterfowl*; recipient of several other awards.

Höhn, Emil Otto (1919–1997): Canadian zoologist; naturalist; ornithologist; physiologist; specialist in avian endocrinology; interest in Arctic wildlife; wrote several books on nature.

Holboell, Carl Peter (1795–1856): Governor of South Greenland with an interest in natural history; named and described several species of birds; memorialized in a subspecies of the red-necked grebe, formerly known as Holboell's grebe.

Holgersen, Holger (1914–1996): Norwegian ornithologist; director of the Stavanger Museum; participated in the ringing schemes of Norway and Europe; editor of *Sterna*; honorary member of the Norwegian Ornithological Society; corresponding fellow of the American Ornithologists' Union; published about 200 articles.

Hoogstraal, Harry (1917–1986): Entomologist and ornithologist; Egyptologist; compiled a major bibliography on ticks and tick-borne diseases in migratory birds; honored by the Hoogstraal Collection and Tick Study Center in Washington, DC.

Hope, Clifford (1910–1953): Canadian bird collector; worked for the Royal Ontario Museum of Zoology, where he became Chief Preparator in the Division of Ornithology; participated in several expeditions; studied the effects of DDT and budworm on birds.

Hornemann, Jens Wilkin (1770–1841): Danish professor of botany; honored by the species name of the hoary redpoll, *Acanthis hornemanni*.

Howard, Eliot (1873–1940): Amateur naturalist who specialized on warblers; authored *The British Warblers* and *Introduction to the Study of Bird Behaviour*; vice-president of the British Ornithologists' Union.

Hudson, William Henry (1841–1922): Ornithologist, writer; interest in wildlife of the Pampas; co-authored *Argentine Ornithology*; promoted bird protection and was a member of the first committee of the Royal Society for the Protection of Birds.

Hutchins, Thomas (1730–1790): English naturalist and surgeon; observed and collected birds and mammals while working for the Hudson's Bay Company in Canada.

Hutton, William (?): Collector of birds around Washington, DC; discovered Hutton's vireo, which was later named in his honor.

Huxley, Sir Julian (1887–1975): Zoologist, professor; specialized in bird courtship; member of the British Ornithologists' Union; fellow of the Royal Society; secretary of the Zoological Society of London; secretary-general of UNESCO; authored books on different subjects; recipient of an Oscar for a film on the gannet.

Immelmann, Klaus (1935–1987): Professor of biology; director of the Institute of Ethology at the University of Bielefeld; studied the ontogeny behavior of birds and mammals; honorary fellow of the American Ornithologists' Union; president of the German Ornithological Society and the German Zoological Society; more than 100 publications, including many books.

Ingram, Captain Collingwood (1880–1981): British ornithologist; horticulturist; a member of the British Ornithologists' Union for 80 years; interest in Japanese birds; wrote *The Birds of the Riviera*.

Ivor, Hance Roy (1880–1979): Self-trained ornithologist; among first to realize importance of studying comparative behavior of semi-tame and wild birds; pioneered "anting" behavior.

Jacques, Florence Page (1890–1972): Author of natural history travelogs such as *Canoe Country, The Geese Can Fly, As Far as the Yukon, Birds Across the Sky, Snow Shoe Country*; was awarded the John Burroughs Medal from the American Ornithologists' Union.

Johansen, Hans Christian (1897–1973): Zoologist, teacher; worked at the Zoological Museum of Copenhagen University; studied waders; corresponding fellow of the American Ornithologists' Union; recipient of a Danish Royal Medal.

Johnson, Alfred W. (1894–1979): Chilean ornithologist; early interest in the Humboldt penguin; wrote *The Birds of Chile and Adjacent Regions of Argentina, Bolivia and Peru* and *Las Aves de Chile*; several awards, including the Brewster Award from the American Ornithologists' Union.

Jones, Lynds (1865–1951): Started his career as teacher of ecology; professor of zoology at Oberlin College who taught the first ever ornithology course in an American college or university; interest in bird migration; a founder and later president of the Wilson Ornithological Society for 13 years; editor of *Wilson Bulletin*; fellow of the American Ornithologists' Union.

Jourdain, Francis Charles Robert (1865–1940): Traveler, egg collector; part of an expedition to Spitsbergen; authority on Western Palearctic birds; editor of *British Birds*; vice-president of the British Ornithologists' Union.

Kale, Herbert W., II (1931–1995): Ornithologist; vice-president of ornithology at the Florida Audubon Society; organized and directed the Florida Breeding Bird Atlas project; fought for the protection of Florida birds; fellow of the American Ornithologists' Union; founder and president of the Florida Ornithological Society and the Colonial Waterbird Society; associate editor of *The Auk*; editor of *Colonial Waterbirds*.

Keeton, William (1933–1980): Entomologist; professor at Cornell University who influenced many students of biology; pioneer and world authority in avian navigation; interest in homing pigeons; fellow of the American Ornithologists' Union; many awards.

Kendeigh, Samuel Charles (1904–1986): Professor Emeritus of Zoology at the University of Illinois; studied the ecology and physiology of birds; editor of *The Ecology of North America*; helped found the Illinois Nature Preserves Commission, the Nature Conservancy, and the Animal Behavior Society; president of the Wilson Ornithological Society and the Ecological Society of America; vice-president of the American Ornithologists' Union; president of the Champaign County Audubon Society; author of *Physiology of the Temperature of Birds*; over 90 publications; recipient of the Brewster Award from the American Ornithologists' Union and the Eminent Ecologist Award from the Ecological Society of America.

Keulemans, John Gerrard (1842–1912): Illustrator with special interest in natural history; many autolithographs; author of *Natural History of Cage Birds*.

Keve, Andrew (1909–1984): Hungarian ornithologist; researcher at the Hungarian Institute of Ornithology; worked on birds in the Carpathian Basin; fellow of the Natural History Museum of Vienna, Austria, and Hungary; corresponding member of the British Ornithologists' Union and the American Ornithologists' Union.

King, James R. (1927–1991): Professor of zoophysiology at Washington State University; studied avian biology and environmental physiology; president of the American Ornithologists' Union and the Council of the Cooper Ornithological Society; editor of *The Condor*; co-editor of *Avian Biology*; recipient of the Brewster Medal.

Kirtland, Jared Potter (1793–1877): Physician, teacher, horticulturist, and naturalist especially involved with fishes of Ohio; honored by Kirtland's warbler, which he collected.

Kittlitz, Friedrich Heinrich (1779–1874): German explorer-naturalist; member of an expedition to Kamchatka; memorialized by Kittlitz's murrelet.

Koplin, James R. (1934–1987): Zoologist, educator who influenced many students despite a short life; studied woodpecker predation; improved our knowledge of raptors; elective member of the American Ornithologists' Union.

Kortright, Francis Herbert (1887–1972): President of the Canadian National Sportsmen' Show, the Conservation Council of Ontario, and the Toronto Anglers' and Hunters' Association; recipient of the Brewster Medal for his book on North American waterfowl; received several other awards; a waterfowl park, a nature centre, a lake in the Ontario region bear his name.

Lack, David Lambert (1910–1973): Helped develop radar during World War II; studied bird migration; a major part of his career was spent as director of the Edward Grey Institute of Field Ornithology at Oxford; his work consisted mostly of island bird faunas, especially that of Darwin's Galapágos finches; published *The Natural Regulation of Animal Numbers* and *Population Studies of Birds*, among others.

Laing, Hamilton Mack (1883–1982): Worked for the Museum of Canada and the Royal British Columbia Museum; elective member of the American Ornithologists' Union; author of 900 articles; a subspecies of the northern goshawk, *Accipiter gentilis laingi*, bears his name.

Lawrence, George Newbold (1806–1895): One of the founders of the American Ornithologists' Union; worked with birds of tropical America; author of *Catalogue of Birds Observed in New York*; participated as author in the vol. IX of Spencer F. Baird's *Reports of Exploration and Surveys for a Railroad Route from the Mississippi River to the Pacific Ocean*; honored by Lawrence's goldfinch.

Lawrence, Louise de Kiriline (1894–1992): Studied ornithology; authored *A Comparative Life History of Four Species of Woodpeckers*; her book *The Lovely and the Wild* awarded the John Burroughs Medal by the American Ornithologists' Union; regarded by Ernst Mayr as one of the best life-history researchers in North America.

Lawrence, Newbold Trotter (1855–1928): Amateur ornithologist; Lawrence's warbler named after him but later discovered to be a hybrid.

Leach, William Elford (1790–1836): Zoologist at the British Museum in London; authority on crustaceans; Leach's storm-petrel honors his name.

Lear, Edward (1812–1888): Bird illustrator; specialized in members of the parrot family; associated with the Linnean Society; first to portray all the members of one family: *Illustrations of the Family Psittacidae or Parrots*.

Le Conte, John Lawrence, MD (1825–1883): Entomologist; honored by Le Conte's sparrow, *Ammodramus leconteii*; also memorialized by Le Conte's sharp-tailed bunting and Le Conte's thrasher.

Lekagul, Boonsong (1907–1992): Artist, biologist, conservationist of Thailand; started the Bangkok Bird Club; participated in the International Committee for Bird Protection and the World Wildlife Fund; corresponding fellow of the American Ornithologists' Union; author of *Bird Guide of Thailand*; recipient of the Getty Award.

Leopold, Aldo (1886–1948): Professor of University of Wisconsin who influenced many students in ornithology; pioneer in wildlife conservation; developed the theory of game management; wrote *A Sand County Almanac* and *Sketches Here and There*, as well as many other publications and books on wildlife management.

Leopold, A. Starker (1913–1983): Wildlife biologist, naturalist, conservationist; professor of zoology at the University of California; director of the Museum of Vertebrate Zoology; interest in Mexico and game birds; elected to the Academy of Sciences; fellow of the American Ornithologists' Union; president of the Board of Governors in the Cooper Ornithological Society; president and honorary member of the Wildlife Society; author of *Wildlife of Mexico: The Game Birds and Mammals*; recipient of the Wildlife Publication Award for his book *The California Quail*; many other awards, including the Aldo Leopold medal.

Lesson, René Primivère (1794–1849): French naturalist; collected and described several bird species; gave the species name, *clemenciae*, to the blue-throated hummingbird to honor his wife.

Lewis, Meriwether (1774–1809): Secretary of Thomas Jefferson; commanded an exploring expedition, the Lewis and Clark expedition, to the Pacific Ocean; discovered Lewis's woodpecker, later named after him.

Lichtenstein, M. Heinrich (1780–1857): Director of zoology at the Berlin Museum; commemorated by Lichtenstein's oriole.

Lincoln, Thomas (1812–1833): Accompanied Audubon on his Labrador expedition, where he collected Lincoln's sparrow, which was later named after him.

Linnaeus, Carolus (1707–1778): A botanist and bird biologist; became known as the father of biological taxonomy; professor of medicine and botany at Uppsala University; developed the Linnaean system of binomial nomenclature which is still widely used today; described and gave scientific names to a large number of birds that live in North America; *Systema Naturae* considered to be the starting point of zoological nomenclature.

Lloyd, Hoyes (1888–1978): Ornithologist, conservationist; helped create a number of sanctuaries; head of the Migratory Birds Unit, later named superintendent of Wild Life Protection; president of the American Ornithologists' Union; president of the Ottawa Field-Naturalists' Club; served on many other committees, organizations and congresses; honorary member of the Ottawa Field-Naturalists' Club and, along with his wife, the Wildlife Society; recipient of the Aldo Leopold Memorial Medal from the Wildlife Society and the Seth Gordon Award of the International Association of Game, Fish, and Conservation Commissioners.

Lodge, George Edward (1860–1953): Bird illustrator, taxidermist; special interest for birds of prey; falconer; his garden was a bird sanctuary.

Lorenz, Konrad (1903–1989): Influenced the study of animal behavior; imprinted graylag goose on himself; studied social corvids; honorary fellow of the American Ornithologists' Union; recipient of many honors, including the Nobel Prize.

Lowery, George H., Jr. (1913–1978): Boyd Professor of Zoology at the Louisiana State University; director of the Louisiana State University Museum of Natural Science; president of the American Ornithologists' Union; studied the nocturnal migration of birds, for which he received a Brewster Award; recipient of an Outstanding Conservationist Award of the Year from the Outdoor Writers Association and Conservation Educator of the Year by the Louisiana Wildlife Federation; memorialized by a species of owl, *Xenoglaux loweryi.*

MacArthur, Robert (1930–1972): A major force in changing how ecologists think about the world; brought mathematical theory into ecology; his work focused on competition in birds; co-founded concept of island biogeography.

MacGillivray, William (1796–1852): Scottish ornithologist, lecturer, and professor who participated in *Audubon's Ornithological Biography*; authored *History of British Birds*; honored by MacGillivray's warbler.

Macoun, James Melville (1862–1920): Canadian naturalist; president of the Ottawa Field-Naturalists' Club; editor of *The Ottawa Naturalist*; memorialized by *Papaver macounii*, a pepper.

Marshall, Alan John "Jock" (1911–1967): Australian field zoologist; professor and dean; avian physiologist; interest in seasonal cycles of birds; pioneer of ecological endocrinology; wrote *Bower-birds: Their Display and Breeding Cycles, Biology and Comparative Physiology of Birds* as well as several other books; memorialized by dedication in Avian Biology series and the Jock Marshall Zoology Reserve at Monash University.

Marshall, W.H. (1912–1996): Professor of wildlife management at University of Minnesota; interest in coots and biota of native prairie; elective member of American Ornithologists' Union.

Mathews, Gregory Macalister (1876–1949): Interest in Australian birds; published *Birds of Australia*; co-authored *The Manual of Australian Birds*; compiled *Systema Avium Australasinarum*.

Mauri, Ernesto (1791–1836): Italian botanist; director of the Botanical Gardens of Rome; helped produce *Iconografia della Fauna Italica*; honored by the western sandpiper, *Calidris mauri*.

Mayaud, Noël (1899–1989): Studied France avifauna; a founder and editor/coeditor of *Alauda*; research associate at the Centre National de la Recherche Scientifique; honorary fellow of the American Ornithologists' Union; published *Inventaire des oiseaux de France*.

Maynard, Charles Johnson (1845–1929): Naturalist and traveler who collected birds; a Florida subspecies of the mangrove cuckoo, Maynard's cuckoo, and a subspecies of the white-eyed vireo, *Vireo griseus maynardi*, are named after him.

McAtee, Waldo Lee (1883–1962): The leading economic ornithologist in the nation; became an expert on the food habits of birds and other vertebrates; his work includes more than 1,200 books, articles, reviews, and letters.

McCabe, Robert A. (1914–1995): Wildlife scientist; chairman of the Department of Wildlife Management at the University of Wisconsin; first to use egg-white electrophoresis, the precursor to DNA/RNA analyses, to study phylogenetic relationships among birds; one of the first to use radio isotopes to study movement and distribution and also one of the first to use infrared light for night observation; built North America's first duck decoy trap; fellow of the American Ornithologists' Union; president of the Wildlife Society and the Wisconsin Society for Ornithology; recipient of several awards, including the Aldo Leopold Medal.

McCown, John (1815?–1879): Collected birds while on military service; honored by McCown's longspur, which he collected.

McGregor, Richard Crittenden (1871–1936): Australian fellow of the American Ornithologists' Union; published *Index to the Genera of Birds of the World*; a subspecies of the house finch, McGregor's house finch, was named after him.

McIlwraith, Thomas (1824–1903): Collector of birds; sent specimens to the Smithsonian Institution; Superintendent of the Committee of Migration of birds for Ontario; a founder of the American Ornithologists' Union; published *Birds of Ontario*.

McKay, Charles Leslie (?–1883): Collector of birds for the U.S. National Museum; memorialized by McKay's bunting.

Mengel, Robert M. (1921–1990): Professor at the University of Kansas; diverse interests; bird painter; fellow of the American Ornithologists' Union; editor of *The Auk*; editor of the AOU monographs; wrote *Birds of Kentucky*.

Merriam, Clinton Hart (1855–1942): Zoologist and naturalist; first director of Biological Survey; president of American Ornithologists' Union; brother of Florence Merriam Bailey.

Mewaldt, Leonard Richard (1917–1990): Professor of zoology at San Jose State University; studied nutcrackers and *Zonotrichia* sparrows; involved with bird research stations and observatories; fellow of the American Ornithologists' Union; president and honorary member of the Cooper Ornithological Society; president of the Western Bird Banding Association.

Meyer de Schauensee, Rudolphe (1901–1984): Ornithologist; worked at the Academy of Natural Sciences; more than 120 publications; author of *The Species of Birds of South America*, *The Birds of China*, and other books; recipient of the Brewster Medal from the American Ornithologists' Union.

Middendorff, Alexander Von (1815–1894): German scientist who explored Russia; first to suggest that birds could detect the magnetic poles; described and named Middendorff's grasshopper warbler.

Miller, Olive Thorne (1831–1918): Bird-watcher and bird writer; author of 11 books on birds, including *A Bird Lover in the West* and *With the Birds in Maine*.

Miller, Alden H. (1906–1965): A leader in the field of bird ecology, behavior, and physiology during the 1930s through the 1950s; professor at the University of California at Berkeley and, for some time, director of its Museum of Vertebrate Zoology; published several hundred papers; supervised Ph.D. theses of many important ornithologists.

Miner, John Thomas (1865–1944): Dedicated to conservation education; one of the pioneer banders; founder of Jack Minor Bird Sanctuary on Lake Erie; National Wildlife Week, in the month of April, honors him.

Mitchell, Margaret Howell (1901–1988): Canada's first woman ornithologist of international repute; volunteered in the bird department of the Royal Ontario Museum, where she worked on the Passenger Pigeon inquiry; published *The Passenger Pigeon in Ontario*; elective member of the American Ornithologists' Union.

Monroe, Burt L., Jr. (1930–1994): Expert on the systematics and distribution of the world's birds; learned the Latin names of N. American birds; a president of the American Ornithologists' Union; co-authored *Distribution and Taxonomy of the Birds of the World*; compiled the *Ten-Year Index to "The Auk"*; known as the "keeper" of Kentucky ornithology; served on many boards and committees.

Moltoni, Edgardo (1896–1980): Italian ornithologist; worked mostly at the Civic Museum of Natural History in Milan; studied avifauna of Italy; principal editor of *Rivista Italiana di ornitologia*; author of over 450 publications.

Montagu, George (1751–1817): Author of *Ornithological Dictionary*, which was the best handbook at the time; described the roseate tern.

Moreau, Reginald Ernest (1897–1970): Specialized in African ornithology and in the ecology of tropical forests and savannahs; editor of *The Ibis*; president of the British Ornithologists' Union; authored *The Palaearctic-African Bird Migration Systems*; recipient of the Godman-Salvin Medal.

Mousely, William Henry (1865–1949): Civil engineer; best all-round naturalist-ornithologist in Canada in first half of 20th century; interest in nesting behavior of shorebirds and warblers; proponent of "territory theory."

Murphy, Joseph Robison (1925–1992): Ecologist; professor at Brigham Young University; interest in raptors; president of the Raptor Research Foundation; editor of the *Journal of Raptor Research*; elective member of the American Ornithologists' Union.

Murphy, Robert Cushman (1887–1973): A naturalist; prominent American ornithologist; undertook a voyage on the Antarctic waters, where he became the expert on marine birds; a junior colleague of Chapman's; wrote the classic *Oceanic Birds of South America*.

Murton, Ron (1932–1978): British ornithologist; wrote *The Woodpigeon* and *Man and Birds*; studied circadian rhythms in birds; wrote *Avian Breeding Cycles*.

M'Dougall, Patrick (1770–1817?): Doctor; credited with shooting the type specimen of the roseate tern; memorialized by *Sterna dougallii*.

Naik, Ramesh Maganbhai (1931–1991): Head of the Department of Biosciences at India's Saurashtra University; studied structure and physiology of avian flight muscles; interested also in the house swift; helped develop the study of ornithology in India; corresponding fellow of the American Ornithologists' Union; a founder and editor of *Pava*.

Naumann, Johann Andreas (1744–1826): German naturalist; wrote authoritative treatises on birds; memorialized by Naumann's thrush and *Falco naumanni*.

Neboux, Adolphe Simon (?): The blue-footed booby, *Sula nebouxii*, was named in his honor after he collected it from an expedition around the world.

Nethersole-Thompson, Desmond (1908–1989): British egg-collector; ornithologist; author of *The Greenshank*, four monographs on snow buntings, dotterels, pine crossbills, and greenshanks; *Waders: Their Breeding Haunts and Watchers*; and *Highland Birds*.

Newton, Alfred (1829–1907): Doyen of British ornithologists; zoology professor at Cambridge; helped found the British Ornithologists' Union and *The Ibis*; supported the Protection of Birds Act; author of *The Dictionary of Birds*; received the Gold Medal from the Royal Society.

Nice, Margaret Morse (1883–1974): To date the most scholarly important woman in the history of ornithology; intensively studied birds out of her house and authored more than 60 articles on various aspects of avian ecology and behavior, especially the role of territoriality and the development of precocial birds; her autobiography was entitled *Research is a Passion with Me*; her most enduring work was an eight-year study of colour-banded song sparrows in Ohio; could search the ornithological literature in seven languages.

Nordmann, Alexander V. (1803–1866): Russian zoologist; memorialized by *Glareola nordmanni*.

Nuttall, Thomas (1786–1859): A self-taught naturalist; he authored the first "field guide" to the birds of North America entitled *A Manual of the Ornithology of the United States and Canada*; honored by Nuttall's woodpecker and Nuttall Ornithological Club.

Nutting, Charles Cleveland (1858–1927): Professor of zoology at the University of Iowa; collector for museums; honored by Nutting's flycatcher, which he collected.

Oberholser, Harry Church (1870–1963): Biologist of the U.S. Fish and Wildlife Service; expert in bird identification; published more than 900 papers on ornithology and *Bird Life of Louisiana*; author of *The Bird Life of Texas*; memorialized by the dusky flycatcher, *Empidonax oberholseri*, and a subspecies of the curve-billed thrasher.

Olendorff, Richard R. (1943–1994): Raptor biologist and conservationist; Endangered Species Coordinator of the Bureau of Land Management; participated in the recovery programs of the California condor, bald eagle, and peregrine falcon; established the Raptor Research and Technical Assistance Center in Idaho; elective member of the American Ornithologists' Union;

help found the American Falconers Association; president of the Raptor Research Foundation, which honored him with the President's Award.

Olrog, Claes Christian (1912–1985): Neotropical ornithologist; studied birds in Argentina, Bolivia, and Brazil; member of several expeditions; more than 100 publications; author of *Las Aves Argentinas*, a field guide.

Ord, George (1781–1866): Early American naturalist; editor and biographer for Alexander Wilson.

Owre, Oscar T. (1917–1990): Teacher of ornithology; founder of the University of Miami bird reference collection; president of the Tropical Audubon Society which has a fund named after him; helped found the Biscayne National Park; elective member of the American Ornithologists' Union.

Pallas, Peter Simon (1741–1811): Professor; German zoologist and explorer; participated in many expeditions, especially in Russia; responsible for describing many new bird species; *Zoographia Rosso-Asiatica* published posthumously; memorialized by Pallas's reed bunting and Pallas's sea-eagle.

Palmgren, Pontus (1907–1993): Finnish biologist; studied the autoecology of bird species and other subjects, including the anatomy of bird legs and zugunruhe with respect to meteorological factors; honorary fellow of the American Ornithologists' Union; secretary of the Finnish Society of Sciences; editor of *Ornis Fennica*.

Parker, Theodore A. III (1953–1993): Major contributor to neotropical ornithology; interest in vocalization; elective member of the American Ornithologists' Union.

Pennant, Thomas (1726–1798): Gave the bean goose its name because he liked beans.

Peterson, Roger Tory (1908–1996): Educator, artist, writer, photographer, filmmaker, conservationist; inventor of the modern field guides; produced the first pocket-sized bird guide, *A Field Guide to the Birds*, which enables users to pinpoint species characteristics; popularized birdwatching like no one before him; director and senior lecturer of education for the National Audubon Society; recipient of many awards; memorialized by the species name of the cinnamon screech owl, *Otus petersoni*.

Pettingill, Eleanor Rice (1908–1977): Free-lance ornithologist and photographer; went on a photographic expedition to film penguins in the Falkland Islands; author of *Penguin Summer*.

Phelps, William H., Jr. (1902–1988): Venezuelan ornithologist who explored his country; helped develop neotropical ornithology; built the Coleccion Ornithologica Phelps, the largest bird collection in Latin America; honorary fellow of the American Ornithologists' Union; a founder and president of Sociedad Venezolana de Ciencias Naturales; more than 65 papers and books; recipient of the Explorers' Club Medal and the David Livingstone Centennial Medal.

Phillips, Allan R. (1914–1996): American ornithologist; more than 170 publications, including 4 books; wrote *The Known Birds of North and Middle America*; mentor of many students of ornithology; specialist in alpha taxonomy of birds; named or renamed 160 avian taxa.

Porter, Gene Statton (1863–1924): Woman bird photographer and writer; authored *The Song of the Cardinal*.

Powys, Thomas Lyttleton (Lord Lilford) (1833–1896): Interest in birds, especially birds of prey; traveled around the Mediterranean; author of *The Coloured Figures of the Birds of the British Islands.*

Prestt, Ian (1929–1995): Zoologist; studied toxic chemicals in British birds, mainly raptors; director and later the president of the Royal Society for the Protection of Birds; became first Member of Honour for BirdLife International.

Prigogine, Alexandre (1913–1991): Explorer; collector of more than 20,000 bird specimens from the Congo; first to apply concept of para- and allospecies to bird taxonomy in central Africa; described five bird species and many races; memorialized by four bird species in the genera *Pholidus, Caprimulgus, Chlorocichlia* and *Nectarinia.*

Quay, Wilbur Brooks (1927–1994): Mammalogist, teacher; studied the pineal gland and avian reproduction; pioneered technique of cloacal lavages; helped found and edit the *Journal of Pineal Research*; life member of the American Ornithologists' Union, the Cooper Ornithological Society and the Wilson Ornithological Society; president of the Western Bird Banding Association; more than 400 publications.

Rahn, Hermann (1912–1990): Physiology professor; studied the respiratory physiology of avian eggs; elective member of the American Ornithologists' Union; more than 225 publications; elected to the National Academy of Sciences; recipient of many awards including the Elliott Coues Award.

Rand, Austin L. (1905–1982): Ornithologist; acting chief of the Biological Division of the National Museum of Canada; chief curator of zoology at the Field Museum of Natural History; president of the American Ornithologists' Union; elective member of the International Ornithological Committee; published 103 papers on a variety of subjects; author of four books, including *Ornithology: An Introduction.*

Raveling, Dennis G. (1939–1991): Faculty member of the University of California; studied the nestling ecology of Canada geese; researched the Arctic-nesting geese in the Pacific Flyway; fellow of the American Ornithologists' Union and the American Association for the Advancement of Science; president of the California Wetlands Foundation; recipient of several awards for his contributions to wetland and waterfowl conservation.

Richdale, Lancelot Eric (1900–1983): New Zealand ornithologist; interest in seabirds; corresponding fellow of the American Ornithologists' Union; wrote two books on penguins; several awards; memorialized by the Richdale Observatory at Taiaroa Head.

Richmond, Charles W. (1868–1932): Scholar; bibliographer; helped Ridgway with *The Birds of North and Middle America*; created card catalogue of bird collection at the National Museum; was memorialized by *Richmondena cardinalis.*

Ridgway, Robert (1850–1929): Curator at the Smithsonian Institution and then at the U.S. National Museum; one of the founders and presidents of the American Ornithologists' Union; co-authored *A History of North American Birds*; a leading American ornithologist of his generation; helped produce the first *Checklist of North American Birds*; hundreds of publications and 8 volumes of *Birds of North and Middle America*; memorialized by the species name of the buff-collared nightjar, *Caprimulgus ridwayi*, and a few subspecies of North American birds.

Ross, Bernard Rogan (1827–1874): Chief Factor of the Hudson's Bay Company and correspondent with the Smithsonian Institution; contributed a fair number of bird specimens; Ross's goose is named after him.

Ross, Sir James Clark (1800–1862): British explorer; navigated in the Arctic on five expeditions, one of which was to find and rescue Sir John Franklin; honored by Ross's gull.

Rothschild, Lord Walter (1868–1937): Bird collector who maintained a museum at Tring; authored several books, including *Novitates Zoological*, *Extinct Birds* and *A Monograph of the Genus Casuarius*.

Rowan, William (1891–1957): Important Canadian ornithologist; worked on bird migration; studied gonads of juncos; initiated the study of breeding seasons, daylength, and avian reproductive physiology, as well as the physiological basis of migration.

Ruschi, Augusto (1915–1986): Brazilian who studied Atlantic coastal rain forest fauna and flora; promoted the conservation of the rain forest; founder and director of the Museu Biologia Prof. in Santa Teresa; corresponding fellow of the American Ornithologists' Union; author of *Aves do Brasil*; published more than 400 papers.

Sabine, Joseph (1770–1837): Older brother of Sir Edward; member of an Arctic expedition; honored by a subspecies of the ruffed grouse, *Bonasa umbellus sabini*.

Sabine, Sir Edward (1788–1883): British astronomer and physicist; member of an Arctic expedition; honored by Sabine's gull.

Salmon, H. Morrey (1892?–1985): Ornithologist; conservationist; father of British bird/nature photography; used it to count seabirds in colonies and pioneered use of flash on nocturnal species; wrote *Birds in Britain Today*; awarded the Gold Medal from the British Ornithologists' Union.

Salomonsen, Finn (1909–1983): Contributed to Greenland ornithology; chief curator of the Zoological Museum in Copenhagen; corresponding fellow of the American Ornithologists' Union; president and editor of the journal of the Danish Ornithological Society; more than 200 publications.

Salvin, Osbert (1835–1898): Associated with Frederick Godman; interest in neotropical birds; editor of *The Ibis*, where he co-authored the first paper in the first issue; one of the founding members of the British Ornithologists' Union and its treasurer; contributed to *The Catalogue of Birds* in the British Museum; awarded the Gold Medal by the British Ornithologists' Union; honored by Godman-Salvin Award.

Sauer, Edgar Gustav Franz (1925–1979): Zoologist; professor at the University of Florida; studied stellar orientation in birds; interest in plovers, bobolinks, and ostriches; fellow of the American Ornithologists' Union; director of the Zoologishes Forschungsinstitute und Museum Alexander Koenig in Bonn.

Saunders, Aretas Andrews (1884–1970): Naturalist; teacher; observed birds in Montana, New York, and the Adirondacks; studied bird songs; fellow of the American Ornithologists' Union; authored *Birds of Montana*, *Guide to Bird Song*, and *The Lives of Wild Birds*; a memorial fund honors his name.

Saunders, Howard (1835–1907): Amateur ornithologist; specialized in gulls and terns as well as the birds of Spain; vice-president of the Zoological Society and the Linnean Society; secretary of the British Ornithologists' Union; contributed to *The Catalogue of Birds* in the British Museum; published *An Illustrated Manual of British Birds*.

Saunders, William Edwin (1861–1943): Pharmacist; ornithologist, conservationist, naturalist; president of the Wilson Ornithological Club; helped found and presided over the Ornithological Section of the Entomological Society of Ontario and the Federation of Ontario Naturalists.

Say, Thomas (1787–1834): Entomologist who went on a expedition to the Rocky Mountains to report on birds observed; memorialized by Say's phoebe, *Sayornis saya*, as well as the genus name of the phoebes, *Sayornis*.

Schlegel, Gustav (1840–1903): Eminent sinologist and naturalist; memorialized by *Anthus gustavi*.

Schorger, Arlie William (1884–1972): Interest in birds and natural history; bird and mammal collector; fellow of the American Ornithologists' Union; author of *Handbook of the Birds of Eastern North America* and *The Wild Turkey: Its History and Domestication*; received the Brewster Award for *The Passenger Pigeon: Its History and Domestication*.

Schreiber, Ralph W. (1942–1988): Scientist, curator; world authority on seabirds, with more than 100 publications; head of the Section of Birds and Mammals at the Natural History Museum of Los Angeles County; conservationist; was active in the International Council for Bird Preservation; awarded the Elliot Coues Award by the American Ornithologists' Union.

Schüz, Ernst (1901–1990): German ornithologist; headed the Vogelwarte Rossitten, a world-famous bird ringing and research station; a leading authority of bird migration research; wrote the *Grundriss der Vogelzugskunde*; co-founded Der Vogelzug; honorary fellow of the American Ornithologists' Union; published *Atlas of Bird Migration*; more than 100 papers.

Sclater, Philip Lutley (1829–1913): British ornithologist and zoogeographer; interest in neotropical birds; editor of *The Ibis*; fellow of the Royal Society; secretary of the Zoological Society of London; one of the founders of the British Ornithologists' Union; author of *The Geographic Distribution of the Members of the Class Aves*; 1,300 articles and books; honored by the Mexican chickadee, *Parus sclateri*.

Scott, Sir Peter Markham (1909–1989): Author, illustrator, conservationist; life fellow of the Zoological Society of London; interest in wildfowl; help to found the World Wildlife Fund; authored and illustrated *A Coloured Key to the Wildfowl of the World*; illustrated *The Waterfowl of the World*; author of *Wild Geese and Eskimos* and co-author of *A Thousand Geese*.

Scott, Winfield (1786–1866): Great American general and war hero; memorialized by Scott's oriole.

Seebohm, Henry (1832–1895): Amateur ornithologist; authored *The Geographical Distribution of the Family Charadriidae, or the Plovers, Sandpipers, Snipes and Their Allies*; also authored *A Monograph of the Turdidae, or Family of Thrushes*.

Selby, Prideaux John (1788–1867): Published *Illustrations of British Ornithology*; editor of the *Magazine of Zoology and Botany*.

Selous, Edmund (1858–1934): Considered to be the founder of modern studies of behavior; author of *Realities of Bird Life*; also authored *The Birdwatcher in the Shetlands*, *Thought Transference in Birds*, *Bird Life Glimpses*, and *Evolution of Habit in Birds*.

Serle, William (1912–1992): Minister; ornithologist; collector of bird skins and eggs; interest in Scottish and African birds; wrote *The Collins Field Guide to the Birds of West Africa*.

Serventy, Dominic Louis (1904–1988): Australian ornithologist; studied the short-tailed shearwater; honorary fellow of the American Ornithologists' Union; hundreds of publications.

Seton, Ernest Thompson (1860–1946): Scientist, artist; editor of the *Proceedings of the Ornithological Subsection of the Biological Section of the Canadian Institute*; author of numerous books including a monograph on the birds of Manitoba; parks in the Toronto and Manitoba region honor his name; recipient of several awards.

Sharpe, Richard Bowdler (1847–1909): Headed the bird section of the British Museum of Natural History; member of the Yarkand Mission; founder of the British Ornithologists Club; numerous articles, papers and books; contributed largely to *The Catalogue of Birds in the British Museum*.

Sherman, Althea (1853–1943): Amateur ornithologist; author of many articles and essays in ornithological journals; remembered for having built a swift observation tower at her home.

Shortt, Terrence (1910–1986): Canadian artist; ornithologist; naturalist; worked at the Royal Ontario Museum for 45 years; participated in 36 field expeditions; elective member of the American Ornithologists' Union; author of *Not as the Crow Flies* and more than 30 papers on birds; many paintings and illustrations.

Sick, Helmut (1910–1991): German ornithologist who specialized in Brazilian birdlife; more than 200 publications; wrote *Ornitologia Brasileira, uma Introdução*; pioneered the establishment of modern ornithology in Brazil.

Singer, Arthur Bernard (1917–1990): Wildlife artist; his paintings can be seen in *Birds of the World*, the popular field guide, *Birds of North America*, as well as in several other books; designed a series of stamps; elective member of the American Ornithologists' Union; recipient of the Augustus St. Gaudens Medal by the Cooper Union and the Hal Borland Medal by the National Audubon Society.

Smith, Gideon B. (1793–1867): Baltimore physician; friend and correspondent of Audubon's; Smith's longspur bears his name.

Smith, Joseph (1836–1929): Bird illustrator; illustrations in *Exotic Ornithology*; contributed to *The Catalogue of Birds in the British Museum*.

Smith, Phyllis Barclay (?–1980): British ornithologist; linguist; served as secretary to numerous ornithological bodies; later became secretary-general and a main builder of the International Council for Bird Preservation; editor of *Avicultural Magazine*; wrote several books on birds; awarded many medals in several countries.

Snyder, Lester L. (1894–1968): Canadian conservationist; curator of birds and later associate director in the Royal Ontario Museum of Zoology; headed field expeditions in the province; fellow of the American Ornithologists' Union; founded the Brodie Club; helped organize the Toronto Field-Naturalists and the Federation of Ontario Naturalists, which he directed.

Southern, Harry Neville "Mick" (1909?–1986): British naturalist; bird photographer; mammalogist; known for work on predator–prey relationships involving owls; editor of *Bird Study* and *Journal of Animal Ecology*; awarded the Union Medal by the British Ornithologists' Union, as well as others.

Speirs, Doris Louise Huestis (1894–1989): Founder of the Margaret Nice Ornithological Club; edited Margaret Nice's autobiography; helped found the Pickering Naturalists' Club; interest in the evening grosbeak; an award of the Society of Canadian Ornithologists bears her name.

Spencer, Robert (1923–1994): British ornithologist; head of the National Bird Ringing Scheme for 29 years; served on staff of British Trust for Ornithology; contributed immensely to bird ringing; pioneered the movement for bird observatories; helped found EURING; principal editor of *The New Atlas of Breeding Birds in Britain and Ireland: 1988–1991*; awarded several medals.

Spofford, Walter (1908–1995): Teacher; falconer; passion for birds of prey, especially peregrine falcons and golden eagles.

Sprague, Isaac (1811–1895): Botanical artist who became interested in birds which led him to accompany Audubon on the Missouri R. expedition; honored by Sprague's pipit, *Anthus spragueii*.

Sprunt, Alexander, Jr. (1898–1973): Contributed to the ornithology of South Carolina; participated in the second supplement to Arthur T. Waynes's *Birds of South Carolina*; fellow of the American Ornithologists' Union; nature columnist for a local newspaper; a bird sanctuary is named after him.

Stanwood, Cordelia (1865–1958): Interest in birds; photographer; specialized in the nesting behavior of woodland species; her home is now a nature center; her photographs are preserved by the Wildlife Foundation which bears her name.

Steller, Georg Wilhelm (1709–1746 or 1769?): German zoologist and traveler; ship surgeon and mineralogist of the Arctic expedition on the *St. Peter*; first European to set foot in Alaska; collected Steller's crow, which bears his name and the species name *Stelleri*; honored also by Steller's sea eagle and Steller's eider; only naturalist to see the spectacled cormorant alive.

Stewart, Paul A. (1909–1994): Elective member of the American Ornithologists' Union; studied the ecology and management of the wood duck; interest in blackbird roosts and black vultures; published 130 papers.

Stewart, Robert Earl, Sr. (1913–1993): Wildlife research biologist; studied waterfowl in the Chesapeake Bay; initiated the Audubon Winter Bird Population Study; fellow of the American Ornithologists' Union; author of *Waterfowl Populations in the Upper Chesapeake Region*.

Stirrett, George Milton (1899–1982): Wildlife biologist with the Canadian Wildlife Service; worked with waterfowl; participated in the formation of the Federation of Ontario Naturalists; Chief Parks Naturalist of National Parks of Canada; recipient of a Heritage Canada Foundation Award and a Paul Harris Fellow Award.

Stoddard, Herbert Lee (1889–1968): Ornithologist, naturalist; fellow of the American Ornithologists' Union; author of *The Bobwhite Quail*; awarded the Brewster Medal.

Stone, Witmer (1866–1939): Ornithologist, naturalist; worked at the Academy of Natural Sciences for 50 years; special interest in migration, molts, and plumages; helped found the Delaware Valley Ornithological Club; president of the American Ornithologists' Union, the Pennsylvania Audubon Society, and the National Association of Audubon Societies; editor of *The Auk*.

Streseman, Erwin (1889–1972): German ornithologist; teacher; explorer; collector; curator of birds at Berlin Zoological Museum; many important contributions to avian taxonomy; interest in molts and plumages; wrote *Aves*, a monumental 900-page handbook on ornithology; editor of *Journal für Ornithologie*.

Stroud, Robert (?–1963): Life prisoner in the U.S. for 54 years; self-trained pathologist specializing in bird diseases; wrote *Stroud's Digest on the Diseases of Birds*; known widely as the "Birdman of Alcatraz."

Sutton, George Miksch (1898–1982): One of the most beloved ornithologists of this century; artist; wrote dozens of books, including *Eskimo Year*, hundreds of papers, and produced hundreds of paintings and drawings of birds; spent part of his life as curator of birds at Cornell University, later at the Museum of Zoology at the University of Michigan at Ann Arbor.

Swainson, William (1789–1855): English naturalist, ornithologist, traveler, writer, and illustrator in zoology; fellow of the Linnaean Society; fellow of the Royal Society; named and described more than 20 species of N. American birds; many publications, including *Fauna Boreali-Americana* and *Zoological Illustrations*; memorialized by Swainson's hawk, Swainson's warbler, and Swainson's thrush.

Swanson, Gustav A. (1910–1995): Professor; head of the Department of Conservation at Cornell University; head of the Department of Fisheries and Wildlife Biology at Colorado State University; fellow of the American Ornithologists' Union; founding member of the Minnesota Bird Club and the Minnesota Ornithologists' Union; founder and president of the Wildlife Society; editor of *Journal of Wildlife Management*.

Tanner, James T. (1914–1991): Studied the ivory-billed woodpecker; elective member of the American Ornithologists' Union; founder of the ecology program at the University of Tennessee; president and curator of the Tennessee Ornithological Society; editor of *The Migrant*; recipient of the Distinguished Service Award.

Taverner, Percy Algernon (1875–1947): Originator of the first co-operative banding scheme in North America; conservationist who helped create the Point Pelee National Park and Bonaventure Island Bird Sanctuary; worked for the National Museum of Canada; president of the Ottawa Field-Naturalists' Club; several books, including *Birds of Canada*.

Temminck, Coenraad Jacob (1778–1858): Dutch zoologist; memorialized by Temminck's stint (*Calidris temminckii*).

Thaxter, Celia Leighton (1835–1894): Participated in nature education for children by writing poems which were mostly about birds; wrote an influential anti–plume-hunting essay.

Thayer, John Eliot (1862–1933): Ornithologist; established the Thayer Museum in Lancaster, MA, which contained a large private collection of birds and an ornithological library; honored by Thayer's gull, *Larus thayeri*.

Thomson, Arthur Landsborough (1890–1977): Specialized in bird migration; help organize bird ringing in Britain; edited *The New Dictionary of Birds*; president of the British Ornithologists' Union; promoted the protection of birds; authored several books, including *Problems of Bird Migration*; recipient of several medals: Buchanan Medal, Godman-Salvin Medal, and Bernard Tucker Medal.

Thorburn, Archibald (1860–1935): Bird illustrator; illustrated plates for *The Coloured Figures of the Birds of the British Museum*; published *British Birds* and illustrated many other books.

Thorpe, William Homan (1902–1986): Entomologist; ornithologist; widely acclaimed expert on bird song; interest in learning and imprinting in birds; wrote *Learning and Instinct in Animals* as well as two major books on bird song; interest in duetting in birds; president of the British Ornithologists' Union and later received the Godman-Salvin Medal from them.

Tinbergen, Nikolaas (1907–1988): Biologist; helped found ethology; professor of Animal Behaviour at Oxford University; concentrated his work on a variety of animals with his most remarkable work on herring gulls; a Nobel Prize winner; authored several books, including *Study of Instinct and Social Behaviour of Animals*.

Todd, Walter Edmond Clyde (1874–1969): Curator Emeritus of the Carnegie Museum in Pittsburgh; studied the birds of southern Saskatchewan and Labrador; only person to be twice recipient of the Brewster Medal; three bird taxa honor his name.

Tolmie, William (1812–1886): Scottish physician; head of Hudson's Bay Company; memorialized by *Oporornis tolmiei*.

Townsend, John Kirk (1809–1851): Ornithologist known for his "Narrative of a Journey Across the Rocky Mountains"; bird collector and member of the Academy of Natural Sciences in Philadelphia; became a curator in 1837; was later hired by the National Institute of Washington, DC; commemorated by Townsend's solitaire, which he collected; also honored by Townsend's warbler and in a subspecies of the dark-eyed junco, rock ptarmigan, fox sparrow, and snow bunting.

Townsend, Charles Haskins (1859–1944): Worked for the U.S Fish Commission, where he was chief of the Division of Fisheries; director of the New York Aquarium; described several species of birds, including Townsend's shearwater, which honors his name.

Traill, Thomas Stewart, MD (1781–1862): Scottish naturalist; a founder of the Royal Institution of Liverpool; professor of medical jurisprudence who edited *Encyclopaedia Britannica*'s 8th edition; memorialized by Traill's flycatcher.

Tristram, Canon Henry Baker (1822–1906): Bird collector; specialized in birds of North Africa and the Middle East; author of *Fauna and Flora of Palestine*; memorialized by Tristram's grackle and Tristram's warbler.

Trudeau, James De Bertz (1817–1887): Physician; he collected Trudeau's tern, which bears his name.

Tuck, Leslie Mills (1911–1979): Canadian naturalist, nature photographer; Newfoundland Dominion Wildlife Officer; studied the reproductive biology of murres; interest in the Wilson's snipe; founded the Newfoundland Natural History; helped in the protection of Funk Island by having it declared a sanctuary; fellow of the American Ornithologists' Union; twice recipient of the Wildlife Society's Outstanding Publication of the Year Award with his books *The Murres: Their Distribution, Populations and Biology* and *The Snipes*.

Tucker, Bernard William (1901–1950): Central figure of British ornithology; professionnal zoologist; reader of ornithology at Oxford University; editor of *British Birds*; vice-president British Ornithologists' Union; president of the Oxford Ornithological Society; participated in the foundation of the British Trust for Ornithology and the Edward Grey Institute of Field Ornithology; corresponding fellow of the American Ornithologists' Union.

Vallisnieri, Antonio (1661–1730): Italian naturalist and professor of medicine; the species name of the canvasback duck, *Aythya valisineria* (which is misspelled), honors him because he named the genus of the plant that the duck is fond of.

Van Tyne, Josselyn (1902–1957): Important ornithologist in North America; president of the American Ornithologists' Union and the Wilson Ornithological Society; editor of the *Wilson Bulletin*; studied birds in Michigan and tropical America; senior author of an ornithological textbook.

Vaurie, Charles (1906–1975): Taxonomist; curator at the American Museum of Natural History; author of more than 150 papers and *Birds of the Palearctic Fauna* and *Tibet and Its Birds*.

Vaux, William Sansom (1811–1882): Vice-president of the Philadelphia Academy of Natural Sciences; honored by Vaux's swift.

Verreaux, Jules Pierre (1807–1873): French explorer and collector; directed, along with his brother, the most important shop in the world dealing in natural history; collected exotic specimens; honored by the species name of the white-fronted dove, *Leptotila verreauxi*.

Viellot, Louis Jean Pierre (1748–1831): Master taxonomist in France; named 26 genera and 32 species of North American birds; wrote books on birds of North America, tropical birds, ornithology in France.

Wagler, Johann Georg (1800–1832): German systematist; professor of zoology at the newly founded University of Munich; director of its museum; published *Systema Avium*; memorialized by Wagler's oriole, *Icterus wagleri*, which is now called the black-vented oriole.

Ward, Peter (1934–1979): British ornithologist; renowned expert on ecology of red-billed queleas, especially their control as a crop pest in Africa.

Welty, Joel Carl (1901–1986): Ornithologist, teacher; elective member of the American Ornithologists' Union; remembered for his textbook *The Life of Birds*, which has undergone several editions and received the Borzoi Book Award.

Wetmore, Alexander (1886–1978): The sixth secretary of the Smithsonian Institution and the second ornithologist to hold that position; president and honorary president of the American Ornithologists' Union; described 189 new species and subspecies; his publications include work on bird migration, taxonomy, biogeography, and paleontology; by involving many scientific organizations; promoted the study of bird biology; replaced Ridgway as the leading ornithologist in North America; a glacier in Antarctica is named after him.

White, Charles Matthew Newton (1914–1978): Ornithologist; anthropologist; naturalist; studied African birds, especially in Northern Rhodesia; interest in systematics.

White, Gilbert (1720–1793): Naturalist and author of *The Natural History of Selborne*; interested in the migration of birds.

Whitney, Josiah Dwight (1819–1896): State geologist; director of the Geological Survey of California; Sturgis Hooper professor of geology at Harvard University; honored by the species name of the elf owl, *Whitneyi.*

Wied, Alexander Phillip Maximilian (1782–1867): German traveler and naturalist; discovered and described a subspecies of the turkey vulture, and the pinon jay (also known to some as Maximilian's jay); memorialized by Wied's crested flycatcher.

Wilkinson, William Henry Nairn (1932–1996): Game hunter; British ornithologist; interest in the white-fronted goose; helped found Ornithological Society of Turkey, which later evolved into the Ornithological Society of the Middle East.

Williamson, Robert Stockton (1824–1882): Headed one of the Pacific Railroad exploratory expeditions to the Far West; during this expedition, Williamson's sapsucker was collected.

Wilson, Alexander (1766–1813): Considered as the scientific father of American ornithology; traveled through the eastern states collecting bird specimens for later observations; drew and painted birds; the author of the 9-volume great classic book *American Ornithology or the Natural History of the Birds of the United States*; memorialized by Wilson's storm-petrel, Wilson's phalarope, Wilson's snipe, Wilson's plover, Wilson's warbler, and in the genus name of several North American wood warblers.

Wilson, Edward (1872–1912): Studied the fluctuation in population numbers of a bird species; specialized in the red grouse; co-authored *The Grouse in Health and Disease.*

Witherby, Harry Forbes (1873–1944): British amateur zoologist; joined the family publishing firm H.F.& G. Witherby, which published many important British ornithology books; founder of the national ringing scheme; founded and edited *British Birds Magazine*; edited and contributed to the writing of *The Practical Handbook of British Birds*; president of the British Ornithologists' Union; honorary treasurer and secretary of the British Ornithologists' Club; awarded the Godman-Salvin Medal.

Wolf, Josef (1820–1899): Bird illustrator; first to make a lifetime career as an illustrator of wildlife; focused on birds in motion; worked for the Zoological Society in London; illustrated *Genera of Birds* and other books.

Wolters, Hans Edmund (1915–1991): Head of the Department of Ornithology at the Alexander Koenig Zoological Research Institute and Museum; editor of *Bonner zoologische Beiträge and Bonner zoologische Monographien*; concentrated his studies on the systematics of families in the Passeriformes; one of the first to use cladistic principles to reconstruct the avian phylogeny; honorary member of the German Ornithological Society; honorary fellow of the American Ornithologists' Union.

Wood, Merrill (1908–1992): Instructor of zoology and ornithology at Penn State; organizer and vice president of the Eastern Bird Banding Association; treasurer of the Wilson Ornithological Society; patron of the American Ornithologists' Union; published *Birds of Pennsylvania* and *A Bander's Guide to Determining the Age and Sex of Birds*; recipient of the Distinguished Service Award from the College Alumni Society of Penn State.

Worthen, Charles Kimball (1850–1909): Naturalist located in New Mexico who collected and sold natural history specimens; honored by Worthen's sparrow, *Spizella wortheni.*

Wright, Charles (1811–1885): Botanist and field collector of plants and birds; made important contributions to the botany of Texas; collected the gray flycatcher, *Empidonas wrightii*, which was named after him.

Wright, Mabel Osgood (1859–1934): Conservationist; associate editor of *Bird Lore*; founded and headed the Connecticut Audubon Society; director of the National Audubon Society; author of several books, such as *Birdcraft*; developed the Birdcraft Museum and Sanctuary.

Wyatt, Claude Wilmott (1842–1900): Traveler, collector, illustrator; ornithologist on the Sinai expedition; published and illustrated *British Birds*.

Wynne-Edwards, Vero Copner (1906–1997): British marine zoologist; botanist; ornithologist; early interest in seabirds, especially transatlantic movements; pioneer of marine ornithology; wrote *Animal Dispersion in Relation to Social Behaviour*; championed controversial "group selection" mechanism; co-editor of *Journal of Applied Ecology*; many honorary memberships in ornithological societies; president of British Ornithologists' Union; awarded many prizes and medals.

Xantus, John (1825–1894): Hungarian bird collector who described several new species of birds such as Hammond's flycatcher, the spotted owl, and a subspecies of the solitary vireo; honored by Xantus's hummingbird and Xantus's murrelet, both of which he collected.

Yamashina, Yoshimaro (1900–1989): Japanese ornithologist; studied cytology, systematics and distribution of birds; founder and Marquis of the Yamashina Institute for Ornithology; described a new species of flightless rail; honorary fellow of the American Ornithologists' Union; author of *Birds of Japan*; recipient of the Jean Delacour Prize and the Golden Ark Award.

Yarrell, William (1784–1856): Founder of the Entomological Society; fellow of the Linnean Society; vice-president of the Zoological Society; author of *A History of British Birds*.

Zénaide, Princess Zénaide Charlotte Julie Bonaparte (1804–1854): Eldest daughter of the King of Spain, cousin and wife of Charles Lucien Bonaparte; honored by *Zenaida* the generic name of several dove species.

Presidents of Major Ornithological Societies

Canada

SOCIETY OF CANADIAN ORNITHOLOGISTS
(founded in 1982; 275 members)

1982–85	M.R. Lein	1992–93	J.B. Falls
1986–87	S.G. Sealy	1994–95	H.R. Ouellet
1988–89	E.H. Dunn	1996–97	D.N. Nettleship
1990–91	J.C. Barlow	1998–??	T. Diamond

United States

AMERICAN ORNITHOLOGISTS' UNION
(founded in 1883; 4,000 members)

1883–89	J.A. Allen	1951–53	J. Van Tyne
1890–91	D.G. Elliot	1953–56	A.H. Miller
1892–94	E. Coues	1957–59	E. Mayr
1895–97	W. Brewster	1959–62	G.H. Lowery Jr.
1898–99	R. Ridgway	1962–64	A.L. Rand
1900–03	C.H. Merriam	1964–66	D. Amadon
1903–04	C.B. Corey	1966–68	H.F. Mayfield
1905–08	C.F. Batchelder	1968–70	J. Aldrich
1908–10	E.W. Nelson	1970–72	R.W. Storer
1911–13	F.M. Chapman	1972–73	J.J. Hickey
1914–16	A.K. Fischer	1973–75	D.S. Farner
1917–19	J.H. Sage	1975–76	J.T. Emlen
1920–22	W. Stone	1976–78	W.E. Lanyon
1923–25	J. Dwight	1978–80	H.B. Tordoff
1926–29	A. Wetmore	1982–84	T.R. Howell
1929–31	J. Grinnell	1984–86	F.C. James
1932–33	J.H. Fleming	1986–88	C.G. Sibley
1935–37	A.C. Bent	1988–90	G.E. Woolfenden
1937–39	H. Friedmann	1990–92	B. Munroe Jr.
1939–42	J.P. Chapin	1992–94	B. Kessel
1942–45	J.L. Peters	1994–96	R.C. Banks
1945–48	H. Lloyd	1996–98	N.K. Johnson
1948–50	R.C. Murphy		

COOPER ORNITHOLOGICAL SOCIETY
(founded in 1893, incorporated in 1944; 2,700 members)

1942–48	H. Robertson	1963–64	E.N. Harrison
1948–51	A. Miller	1964–66	T.R. Howell
1952–59	J.R. Pemberton	1967–69	R.T. Orr
1960–63	W.J. Sheffler	1970–71	L.R. Mewaldt

1972–73	W.H. Behle		1987–89	R.P. Balda
1974–75	H.F. Mayfield		1989–91	J. Verner
1976–77	S. Russell		1991–93	M.L. Morton
1978–80	D.M. Power		1993–95	L.F. Kiff
1981–83	N.K. Johnson		1995–97	S.A. Mahoney
1983–85	R.W. Schreiber		1997–99	J.M. Scott
1985–87	C.J. Ralph			

WILSON ORNITHOLOGICAL SOCIETY
(founded in 1888; 2,600 members)

1888–89	J.B. Richards		1952–54	W.J. Breckenridge
1890–93	L. Jones		1954–56	B.L. Monroe Sr.
1894	W.N. Clute		1956–58	J.T. Emlen Jr.
1894–01	R.M. Strong		1958–60	L.H. Walkinshaw
1902–08	L. Jones		1960–62	H.F. Mayfield
1909–11	F.L. Burns		1962–64	P.B. Street
1912–13	W.E. Saunders		1964–66	R.T. Peterson
1914–16	T.C. Stephens		1966–68	A.M. Bagg
1917	W.F. Henninger		1968–69	H.L. Batts Jr.
1918–19	M.H. Swenk		1969–71	W.W.H. Gunn
1920–21	R.M. Strong		1971–73	P.B. Hofslund
1922–23	T.L. Hankinson		1973–75	K.C. Parkes
1924–26	A.F. Ganier		1975–77	A.J. Berger
1927–29	L. Jones		1977–79	D.A. James
1930–31	J.W. Stack		1979–81	G.A. Hall
1932–34	J.M. Shaver		1981–83	A.B. Gaunt
1935–37	J. Van Tyne		1983–85	J.A. Jackson
1938–39	M.M. Nice		1985–87	C.E. Braun
1940–41	L.E. Hicks		1987–89	M.H. Clench
1942–43	G.M. Sutton		1989–91	J.C. Barlow
1943–45	S.C. Kendeigh		1991–93	R.C. Banks
1946–47	G.M. Sutton		1993–95	R.N. Conner
1948–50	O.S. Pettingill		1995–97	K.L. Bildstein
1950–52	M. Brooks		1997–??	E.H. Burtt Jr.

ASSOCIATION OF FIELD ORNITHOLOGISTS
(founded in 1922; 2,000 members)

1982–84	G.A. Clark Jr.		1990–92	E.H. Burtt Jr.
1984–86	J. Kricher		1992–94	G. Butcher
1986–88	W.E. Davis		1994–96	E. Landre
1988–90	P. Cannell		1996–98	C. Duncan

RAPTOR RESEARCH FOUNDATION, INC.
(founded in 1966; 1,200 members)

1966–74	B.E. Harrell		1990–93	R. Clark
1975–77	J.R. Murphy		1994–95	M. Collopy
1977–81	R.R. Olendorff		1996–97	D.M. Bird
1981–87	J.L. Lincer		1998–??	M. Kochert
1988–89	G.E. Duke			

THE COLONIAL WATERBIRD SOCIETY
(founded in 1976; 650 members)

1978–79	J.C. Ogden	1990–91	H.W. Kale II
1980–81	P.A. Buckley	1992–93	K.L. Bildstein
1982–83	J. Burger	1994–95	D.N. Nettleship
1984–85	R.M. Erwin	1996–97	J.A. Kushlan
1986–87	W.E. Southern	1998–99	I.C.T. Nisbet
1988–89	D.A. McCrimmon Jr.		

United Kingdom

BRITISH ORNITHOLOGISTS' UNION
(founded in 1858; 2,000 members)

1859–67	Col. H.M. Drummond-Hay	1948–55	Sir A.L. Thomson
1867–96	Lord Lilford	1955–60	W.H. Thorpe
1896–13	F. Du C. Godman	1960–65	R.E. Moreau
1913–18	Col. R.G. Wardlaw-Ramsay	1965–70	V.C. Wynne-Edwards
1918–21	W.E. Clarke	1970–75	G. Mountfort
1921–22	H.J. Elwes	1975–79	Sir H. Elliott
1923–28	Lord Rothschild	1979–83	S. Cramp
1928–33	W.L. Sclater	1983–87	J.F. Monk
1933–38	H.F. Witherby	1987–90	D.W. Snow
1938–43	P.R. Lowe	1990–94	J. Kear
1943–48	Sir N.B. Kinnear		

Presidents of Major Bird-Watching Societies

United States

AMERICAN BIRDING ASSOCIATION
(founded in 1969; 20,500 members)

1970–76	G.S. Keith	1989–93	A.R. Keith
1976–79	A. Small	1993–97	D.T. Williams Jr.
1979–83	J.W. Taylor	1997–??	A.R. Keith
1983–89	L.G. Balch		

United Kingdom

ROYAL SOCIETY FOR THE PROTECTION OF BIRDS
(founded in 1889; 1,010,000 members)

1949–54	Duchess of Portland	1980–85	E.M. Nicholson
1955–61	Lord Forester	1985–90	M. Magnusson
1961–66	Lord Hurcomb	1990–91	Sir Derek Barber
1966–70	Sir Tufton Beamish	1991–94	I. Prestt
1970–75	R. Dougall	1994–??	Julian Pettifer
1975–80	Lord Donaldson		

Distinguished Awards Won by Ornithologists

Society of Canadian Ornithologists

DORIS HUESTIS SPEIRS AWARD
(awarded for outstanding contributions to Canadian ornithology)

1986	W.E. Godfrey	1992	T.H. Manning
1987	F.G. Cooch	1993	F. Cooke
1988	H.A. Hochbaum	1994	A.J. Erskine
1989	C.S. Houston	1995	R.W. Nero
1990	J.B. Falls	1996	J. Murray
1991	L. de K. Lawrence	1997	H.J. Boyd

SOURCE: Canadian Society of Ornithologists, Dept. of Biological Sciences, University College of the Cariboo, 900 McGill Rd. (Box 3010), Kamloops, BC V2C 5N3

American Ornithologists' Union

WILLIAM BREWSTER MEMORIAL AWARD
(awarded to the author or co-authors of the most meritorious body of work on birds of the Western Hemisphere published during the ten calendar years preceding a given AOU meeting)

1921	R. Ridgway	1955	W.H. Phelps Sr.
1923	A.C. Bent	1956	G.H. Lowery
1925	M.A. Carriker Jr.	1957	A.A. Allen
	J.C. Phillips	1958	A.W. Schorger
	W.E.C. Todd	1959	A. Wetmore
1929	C.E. Hellmayr	1960	D.S. Farner
1931	A.M. Bailey	1961	H. Mayfield
1933	F.M. Chapman	1962	A. Wolfson
1935	H.E. Stoddard	1963	R.S. Palmer
1937	R.C. Murphy	1964	H. Friedmann
1938	T.S. Roberts	1965	E. Mayr
1939	W. Stone	1966	G.A. Bartholomew
1940	J.L. Peters	1967	W.E.C. Todd
1941	D.R. Dickey	1968	W.E. Lanyon
	A.J. Van Rossem	1971	C. Sibley
1942	M.M. Nice	1972	B. Snow
1943	A.H. Miller		D.W. Snow
1944	R.T. Peterson	1973	A.W. Johnson
1945	H.A. Hochbaum		R.A. Phillipi
1947	F.H. Kortright	1974	J.R. King
1948	D. Lack	1975	J. Haffer
1950	A.F. Skutch	1976	G.H. Orians
1951	S.C. Kendeigh	1977	R. Meyer de Schauensee
1952	J.T. Zimmer	1978	P. Brodkorb
1953	T.E. Howard	1979	W. Dawson
1954	J. Bond	1980	F. Pitelka

1981	W.A. Keeton	1990	F. Cooke
1982	R. Ricklefs	1991	L. Oring
1983	P.R. Grant	1992	N.K. Johnson
1984	S.T. Emlen	1993	R.T. Holmes
1985	J. Fitzpatrick	1994	F. McKinney
	G. Woolfenden	1995	E.S. Morton
1986	V. Nolan	1996	K. Able
1987	J. Brown	1997	J.C. Avise
1988	R.B. Payne	1998	F. Gill
1989	N. Snyder		

ELLIOTT COUES AWARD
(awarded for contributions that have had an important impact on the study of birds within the Western Hemisphere)

1972	N. Tinbergen	1983	M. Konishi
	A. Wetmore	1984	T.J. Cade
1973	J.T. Emlen	1985	T.R. Howell
1974	R.H. MacArthur	1986	F. Nottebohm
1975	W.J. Bock	1987	J. Wingfield
	R.F. Johnston	1988	R. Schreiber
	R.K. Selander	1989	P. Berthold
1976	P. Marler	1991	J. Wiens
1977	J. Delacour	1992	F.C. James
	E. Mayr	1993	J. Cracraft
1978	J.J. Hickey	1994	W. Wiltschko
1980	E. Collias	1995	I. Newton
	N. Collias	1996	E.D. Ketterson
1981	A. Ar	1997	C.H. Robbins
	C. Paganelli	1998	J. Diamond
	H. Rahn		

SOURCE: American Ornithologists' Union, P.O. Box 1897, Lawrence, Kansas 66044-8897

British Ornithologists' Union

FOUNDERS' GOLD MEDAL
(presented to the four original members at the Jubilee Celebration, December 9, 1908)

F.D. Godman	W.H. Hudleston
P.S. Godman	P.L. Sclater

UNION MEDAL
(may be awarded by Council to any member in recognition of eminent services to ornithology and to the Union)

1912	W. Goodfellow	1948	W.P. Lowe
	C.H.B. Grant	1953	A.W. Boyd
	G.C. Shortridge	1959	W.B. Alexander
	A.F.R. Wollaston		E.A. Armstrong

1959	D.A. Bannerman	1976	K. Williamson
	E.V. Baxter	1979	K.E.L. Simmons
	P.M. Scott	1980	G.V.T. Matthews
1960	C.W. Benson	1984	S. Cramp
1967	Salim Ali		P.A.D. Hollom
1968	J.M.M. Fisher		G. Mountfort
	C.R.S. Pitman	1987	I. Newton
1969	C.W. Mackworth-Praed	1988	J.F. Monk
1970	L.H. Brown	1989	R. Spencer
1971	S. Marchant	1991	F.B.M. Campbell
	H.N. Southern	1992	M.P. Harris
	B. Stonehouse	1993	R.M. Lockley
1972	D. Goodwin	1995	R. Tory Peterson
	N.W. Moore	1996	C.J. Mead
1973	B.P. Hall		R.A.F. Gillmor
1975	K.H. Voous	1997	J.S. Ash

GODMAN-SALVIN MEDAL

*(may be awarded by Council to any person as a signal honor for
distinguished ornithological work)*

1922	W.E. Clarke	1968	W.H. Thorpe
1929	E. Hartert	1969	N. Tinbergen
1930	W.L. Sclater	1973	Sir Julian S. Huxley
1946	P.R. Lowe	1977	V.C. Wynne-Edwards
1938	H.F. Witherby	1982	D.W. Snow
1946	P.R. Lowe	1988	C.M. Perrins
1951	R. Melnertzhagen	1990	G.H. Dunnet
1959	D.L. Lack	1991	D.A. Ratcliffe
	Sir A. Landsborough Thomson	1992	J.C. Coulson
1962	E.M. Nicholson	1995	E. Mayr
1966	R.B. Moreau	1996	P.R. Evans

SOURCE: British Ornithologists' Union, c/o The Natural History Museum, Akeman Street, Tring
Hertfordshire HP23 6AP

Bird-Watching Record Holders

World 7000 Club

8040	P. Snetinger	7135	P. Kaestner
7324	J.D. Danzenbaker	7075	C. Pollard
7294	H. Gilston	7006	J. Clemens
7155	P. Winter		

SOURCE: Blake Maybank, *ABA Big Day & Listing Report* Editor, American Birding Association

Top 500+ Birdwatchers in the U.K. and Ireland

R. Johns	516	E. Welland	501
S. Webb	510	R. Millington	501
C. Heard	506	J. Hewitt	500
S. Gantlett	505	D. Holman	499
S. Whitehouse	503	P. Flint	499
D. Filby	502	L. Evans	498

SOURCE: *U.K. 400 – Rare Birds Magazine* as of January 1, 1998

American Birding Association Area 800 Club

836	M. Smith	809	P. Sykes
835	B. Basham	805	J. Huntington
824	T. Koundakjian	802	W. Rydell
819	C. Koundakjian	800	S. Komito
811	D. Lee	800	P. DuMont

SOURCE: Blake Maybank, *ABA Big Day & Listing Report* Editor, American Birding Association

Canada 475 Club

523	N. Chesterfield	482	T. Plath
505	A. Gray	481	G. Bennett
504	J.A. MacKenzie	477	B. Maybank
503	H. Mackenzie	476	D. Stirling
502	P. Hamel	475	E. Tull
500	R. Foxall		

SOURCE: Blake Maybank, *ABA Big Day & Listing Report* Editor, American Birding Association

New Jersey Audubon Society's World Series of Birding

Urner-Stone Cup Award Recipients

Year	Total Species	Team	Team Members
1998	200	Phillipsburg Riverview Org.	D. Dunlap, M. King, M. Yoo, R. Johnson
1997	217	Kowa Optimed	T. Hince, G. Gervais, P. Pratt, B. DiLabio
1996	229	Birders World Magazine	D. Wormer, C. Aquila, D. Dendler
1995	221	Kowa Optimed	T. Hince, G. Gervais, P. Pratt, B. DiLabio
1994	218	Birders World Magazine	D. Wormer, C. Aquila, D. Dendler
1993	215	Kowa Optimed	T. Hince, P. Pratt, B. DiLabio, G. Gervais
1992	205	Minolta Corp	D. Miranda, R. Crossley, S. Angus, J. Panzinger, J. Faber

Year	Total Species	Team	Team Members
1991	199	Bausch & Lomb	G. Hanisek, J. Dowdell, J. Zamos, J. DeMarrais
1990	210	Zeiss Optics	P. Dunne, L. Dunne, P. Bacinski, R. Radis, D. Freiday
1989	201	Bausch & Lomb	G. Hanisek, J. Dowdell, J. Zamos, J. DeMarrais
1988	200	Zeiss Optics	P. Dunne, P. Bacinski, M. Gustafson, B. Peterjohn
1987	205	Bausch & Lomb	G. Hanisek, J. Dowdell, J. Zamos, J. DeMarrais
1986	199	Bausch & Lomb	G. Hanisek, J. Dowdell, J. Zamos, J. DeMarrais
(tie)			
1986	199	Leica	R. Kane, A. Keith, P. Buckley, W. Wander, D. Harrison
1985	182	D.V.O.C.	A. Brady, C. Danzenbaker, A. Hill, M. Danzenbaker, K. Brethwaite
1984	201	Zeiss Optics	R.T. Peterson, P. Dunne, L. Dunne, D. Sibley, P. Bacinski, W. Boyle

SOURCE: Cape May Bird Observatory, Northwood Center, 701 East Lake Drive, P.O. Box 3, Cape May Point, NJ 08212 (609-884-2736)

Ward World Bird-Carving Champions

Year	Category	Artist	Work
1971	Decorative Lifesize	Jules Iski	Old Squaws
	Decorative Decoy Pair	J.B. Garton	Blue-winged Teals
1972	Decorative Lifesize	John Scheeler	American Kestrels
	Decorative Decoy Pair	John Scheeler	Red-breasted Mergansers
1973	Decorative Lifesize	John Scheeler	Peregrine Falcon w/ Green Wing Teal
	Decorative Decoy Pair	Jim Foote	Gadwalls
1974	Decorative Lifesize	Wm. Koelpin	White Fronted Goose w/ Teal
	Decorative Decoy Pair	Paul Burdette	Redheads
1975	Decorative Lifesize	John Scheeler	Prairie Falcon w/ Dove
	Decorative Decoy Pair	Jim Foote	Wigeons
1976	Decorative Lifesize	John Scheeler	Long-eared Owl and Mouse
	Decorative Decoy Pair	Pat Godin	Goldeneyes
1977	Decorative Lifesize	Wm. Schultz	Bittern w/ Marsh Wren
	Decorative Decoy Pair	Tan Brunet	Pintails
1978	Decorative Lifesize	A.J. Rudisill	Clapper Rails w/ Snail
	Decorative Decoy Pair	Tan Brunet	Mallards

Year	Category	Artist	Work
1979	Decorative Lifesize	Lynn Forehand	Red Jungle Fowl
	Decorative Decoy Pair	Randy Tull	Buffleheads
	Decorative Miniature	E. Muehlmatt	Woodcocks
1980	Decorative Lifesize	John Scheeler	Ruffed Grouse
	Decorative Decoy Pair	Pat Godin	Black Ducks
	Decorative Miniature	Gary Yoder	Pheasants
1981	Decorative Lifesize	John Scheeler	Goshawk & Crow
	Decorative Decoy Pair	Tan Brunet	Canvasbacks
	Decorative Miniature	E. Muehlmatt	Least Bittern
1982	Decorative Lifesize	Pat Godin	Along the Grand – Black Ducks and Muskrat
	DecorativeDecoy Pair	Tan Brunet	Green-winged Teals
	Decorative Miniature	Gary Yoder	Mallards in Flight
1983	Decorative Lifesize	A.J. Rudisill	Black-crowned Night Heron
	Decorative Decoy Pair	Tan Brunet	Redheads
	Decorative Miniature	Bob Ptashnik	Avocets
1984	Decorative Lifesize	E. Muelmatt	Bob-white Quail
	Decorative Decoy Pair	Pat Godin	Wigeons
	Decorative Miniature	Robert Guge	Mourning Dove
1985	Decorative Lifesize	Larry Barth	Snowy Owl & Bonaparte's Gull
	Decorative Decoy Pair	Jett Brunet	Ruddy Ducks
	Decorative Miniature	Gary Yoder	Cooper's Hawk & Flicker
1986	Decorative Lifesize	Larry Barth	Terns In Flight
	Decorative Decoy Pair	Marcus Schultz	Cinnamon Teals
	Decorative Miniature	Robert Guge	Puffins
1987	Decorative Lifesize	Gordon Hare	Bluejays
	Decorative Decoy Pair	Jett Brunet	Scaups
	Decorative Miniature	Bob Guge	Eastern Bluebirds
	Natural Finish	Martin Gates	Snowy Egret "Snowy Essence"
1988	Decorative Lifesize	Gordon Hare	Kestrel
	Decorative Decoy Pair	Kent Duff	Wood Ducks
	Decorative Miniature	Peter Kaune	Robins
	Natural Finish	John Sharp	3 Goldeneyes
1989	Decorative Lifesize	Gary Yoder	Robins
	Decorative Decoy Pair	Chris Bonner	American Mergansers
	Decorative Miniature	Philip Galatas	Peregrine Falcon "Watch On"
	Interpretive	Leo & Lee Osborne	Goose Sleeping "Gentle Rest"
1990	Decorative Lifesize	Todd Wohlt	Black Duck and Pied-billed Grebe "Dive"
	Decorative Decoy Pair	D. Schroeder	Shovelers
	Decorative Miniature	Philip Galatas	Red-tailed Hawk
	Interpretive	Vankeuren Marshall	"Courting Kestrels"

Year	Category	Artist	Work
1991	Decorative Lifesize	Larry Barth	Loggerhead Shrike & Hawthorn "Vantage Point"
	Decorative Decoy Pair	D. Scroeder	Oldsquaws
1991	Decorative Miniature	Bob Guge	Cardinal
	Interpretive	John Sharp	Cormorants
1992	Decorative Lifesize	Greg Woodard	Preening Kestrel on cactus "Cactus Flower"
	Decorative Decoy Pair	Victor Paroyan	Blue-winged teals
	Decorative Miniature	Pete Zaluzec	Yellow rails
	Interpretive	John Sharp	Canada Geese
1993	Decorative Lifesize	Larry Barth	Least Bittern and Marsh Wren "In the Cattails"
	Decorative Decoy Pair	Jude Brunet	Ringnecks
	Decorative Miniature	Pete Zaluzec	Plate Billed Mountain Toucan
	Interpretive	John Sharp	Road Kill Pheasant
	Shootin' Rig	Tom Christie	Mallard Pair and Wigeon
1994	Decorative Lifesize	Glenn Ladenberger	Male Northern Goshawk
	Decorative Decoy Pair	Jon Jones	Emperor Goose
	Decorative Miniature	Pete Zaluzec	Bateleur
	Interpretive	John Sharp	City Pigeons
	Shootin' Rig	Keith Mueller	Black Duck Pair & Mallard
1995	Decorative Lifesize	Pat Godin	American Woodcock "Descent Through the Alders"
	Decorative Decoy Pair	Jude Brunet	Gadwalls
	Decorative Miniature	Gary Yoder	Stellar Sea Eagle
	Interpretive	Jeff Muhs	Anhinga "Sun Worshiper"
	Shootin' Rig	Mike Harde	Common Eiders
1996	Decorative Lifesize	Todd Wohlt	Kestrel
	Decorative Decoy Pair	Keith Mueller	Common Eiders
	Decorative Miniature	Michael Arthurs	Roseate Spoonbills "Evening Flight"
	Interpretive	Jeff Muhs	Barn Owl and Crows "Moonlight Run"
	Shootin' Rig	Alan Bell	Redheads (2 hens, drake)
1997	Decorative Lifesize	Larry Barth	Great Reed Warbler
	Decorative Decoy Pair	Victor Paroyan	Pintails
	Decorative Miniature	Todd Wohlt	Indigo Bunting
	Interpretive	John Sharp	Bird Watching
	Shootin' Rig	Weldon Bordelon, Jr.	Gadwalls (2 hens, drake)

SOURCE: Ward Museum, 909 S. Schuumaker Dr., Salisbury, MD 21804 Tel: (410) 742-4988

United States Federal Duck Stamp Artists

1934–35	J.N. "Ding" Darling	mallard pair landing
1935–36	Frank W. Benson	three canvasbacks in flight
1936–37	Richard E. Bishop	three Canada geese in flight
1937–38	Joseph D. Knap	three Canada geese in flight
1938–39	Roland H. Clark	pintail pair landing
1939–40	Lynn Bogue Hunt	resting green-winged teal pair
1940–41	Francis Lee Jacques	two black ducks in flight
1941–42	Edwin R. Kalmbach	ruddy ducks with young
1942–43	Alden L. Ripley	flock of American wigeon
1943–44	Walter H. Bohl	wood duck pair in flight
1944–45	Walter A. Weber	three white-fronted geese landing
1945–46	Owen J. Gromme	three shovelers in flight
1946–47	Robert W. Hines	male redhead landing
1947–48	Jack Murray	two flying snow geese
1948–49	Maynard Reece	three buffleheads in flight
1949–50	Roger E. Preuss	pair of goldeneyes descending
1950–51	Walter A. Weber	two trumpeter swans flying
1951–52	Maynard Reece	two gadwall leaping into flight
1952–53	John H. Dick	pair of harlequin ducks in flight
1953–54	Clayton B. Seager	flock of blue-winged teal
1954–55	Harvey D. Sandstrom	two ring-necked ducks landing
1955–56	Stanley Stearns	three "blue" phase snow geese climbing into the air
1956–57	Edward J. Bierly	two American mergansers in flight along river
1957–58	Jackson Miles Abbott	two drake eiders flying above breaking surf
1958–59	Leslie C. Kouba	three Canada geese in a cornfield
1959–60	Maynard Reece	a Labrador retriever shown holding a dead mallard
1960–61	John A. Ruthven	male and female redhead with chicks
1961–62	Edward A. Morris	hen mallard with chicks
1962–63	Edward A. Morris	two pintail drakes landing on a marsh
1963–64	Edward J. Bierly	two brant descend on coastal waters
1964–65	Stanley Stearns	two Hawaiian geese grazing on grass
1965–66	Ron Jenkins	three drake canvasbacks skimming rough water
1966–67	Stanley Stearns	two tundra swans flying
1967–68	Leslie C. Kouba	pair of oldsquaw sitting on ice floe
1968–69	Claremont Gale Prichard	pair of hooded mergansers sitting on a fallen log
1969–70	Maynard Reece	pair of white-winged scoters running
1970–71	Edward J. Bierly	two Ross's geese
1971–72	Maynard Reece	three cinnamon teal dropping in for a landing
1972–73	Arthur M. Cook	two adult emperor geese landing
1973–74	Lee LeBlanc	pair of Steller's eiders standing along rocky shore
1974–75	David Maass	two wood ducks rising in front of dead tree
1975–76	James P. Fisher	weathered canvasback decoy
1976–77	Alderson Magee	pair of Canada geese guard their four goslings
1977–78	Martin R. Murk	two Ross's geese in flight
1978–79	Albert Earl Gilbert	drake hooded merganser gliding
1979–80	Ken Michaelson	pair of green-winged teal
1980–81	Richard W. Plasschaert	pair of mallards flying over cattail marsh

1981–82	John S. Wilson	pair of ruddy ducks sitting on quiet water
1982–83	David Maass	three canvasbacks landing on a windy lake
1983–84	Phil V. Scholer	pair of pintails
1984–85	William C. Morris	pair of American wigeon swimming
1985–86	Gerald Mobley	single drake cinnamon teal
1986–87	Burton E. Moore Jr.	single fulvous whistling duck swimming
1987–88	Arthur G. Anderson	two drake redheads and a single hen
1988–89	Daniel Smith	single adult snow goose flying
1989–90	Neal R. Anderson	two lesser scaup swimming among reeds
1990–91	James Hautman	black-bellied whistling ducks
1991–92	Nancy Howe	king eiders
1992–93	Joseph Hautman	spectacled eider
1993–94	Bruce Miller	canvasbacks
1994–95	Neal R. Anderson	red-breasted mergansers
1995–96	James Hautman	mallards
1996–97	Wilhelm Goebel	surf scoters
1997–98	Robert Hautman	Canada goose

SOURCE: S. Weidensaul, *Duck Stamps – Art in the Service of Conservation* (New York: Gallery Books, 1989); U.S. Fish and Wildlife Service http://www.fws.gov/~r9dso/dkhome.html.

Bird-Watching

American Birding Association

CODE OF BIRDING ETHICS

1. Promote the welfare of birds and their environment.

1a) Support the protection of important bird habitat.

1b) To avoid stressing birds or exposing them to danger, exercise restraint and caution during observation, photography, sound recording, or filming.

Limit the use of recordings and other methods of attracting birds, and never use such methods in heavily birded areas, or for attracting any species that is Threatened, Endangered, or of Special Concern, or is rare in your local area.

Keep well back from nests and nesting colonies, roosts, display areas, and important feeding sites. In such sensitive areas, if there is a need for extended observation, photography, filming, or recording, try to use a blind or hide, and take advantage of natural cover.

Use artificial lighting sparingly for filming or photography, especially close-ups.

1c) Before advertising the presence of a rare bird, evaluate the potential for disturbance to the bird, its surroundings, and other people in the area, and proceed only if access can be controlled, disturbance minimized, and permission has been obtained from private land-owners. The sites of rare nesting birds should be divulged only to the proper conservation authorities.

1d) Stay on roads, trails, and paths where they exist; otherwise keep habitat disturbance to a minimum.

2. Respect the law and the rights of others.

2a) Do not enter private property without the owner's explicit permission.

2b) Follow all laws, rules, and regulations governing use of roads and public areas, both at home and abroad.

2c) Practice common courtesy in contacts with other people. Your exemplary behavior will generate goodwill with birders and non-birders alike.

3. Ensure that feeders, nest structures, and other artificial bird environments are safe.

3a) Keep dispensers, water, and food clean and free of decay or disease. It is important to feed birds continually during harsh weather.

3b) Maintain and clean nest structures regularly.

3c) If you are attracting birds to an area, ensure the birds are not exposed to predation from cats and other domestic animals, or dangers posed by artificial hazards.

4. Group birding, whether organized or impromptu, requires special care.

Each individual in the group, in addition to the obligations spelled out in Items #1 and #2, has responsibilities as a Group Member.

4a) Respect the interests, rights, and skills of fellow birders, as well as people participating in other legitimate outdoor activities. Freely share your knowledge and experience, except where code c) applies. Be especially helpful to beginning birders.

4b) If you witness unethical birding behavior, assess the situation, and intervene if you think it prudent. When interceding, inform the person(s) of the inappropriate action, and attempt, within reason, to have it stopped. If the behavior continues, document it, and notify appropriate individuals or organizations.

Group Leader Responsibilities [amateur and professional trips and tours]

4c) Be an exemplary ethical role model for the group. Teach through word and example.

4d) Keep groups to a size that limits impact on the environment, and does not interfere with others using the same area.

4e) Ensure everyone in the group knows of and practices this code.

4f) Learn and inform the group of any special circumstances applicable to the areas being visited (e.g., no tape recordings allowed).

4g) Acknowledge that professional tour companies bear a special responsibility to place the welfare of birds and the benefits of public knowledge ahead of the company's commercial interests. Ideally, leaders should keep track of tour sightings, document unusual occurrences, and submit records to appropriate organizations.

SOURCE: American Birding Association, P.O. Box 6599, Colorado Springs, CO 80934-6599; (800) 850-2473 or (719) 578-1614, fax: (800) 247-3329 or (719) 578-1480, e-mail: member@aba.org

Royal Society for the Protection of Birds

BIRDWATCHERS' CODE OF CONDUCT

Today's birdwatchers are a powerful force for nature conservation. The number of those of us interested in birds rises continually and it is vital that we take seriously our responsibility to avoid any harm to birds. We must also present a responsible image to non-birdwatchers who may be affected by our activities and particularly those on whose sympathy and support the future of birds may rest. There are 10 points to bear in mind.

1. Welfare of birds must come first. Whether your particular interest is photography, ringing, sound recording, scientific study or just bird-watching, remember that the welfare of the bird must always come first.

2. Habitat protection. Its habitat is vital to a bird and therefore we must ensure that our activities do not cause damage.

3. Keep disturbance to a minimum. Birds' tolerance of disturbance varies between species and seasons. Therefore, it is safer to keep all disturbance to a minimum. No birds should be disturbed from their nest in case opportunities for predators to take eggs or young are increased. In very cold weather disturbance to birds may cause them to use vital energy at a time when food is difficult to find. Wildfowlers already impose bans during cold weather; birdwatchers should exercise similar discretion.

4. Rare breeding birds. If you discover a rare bird breeding and feel that protection is necessary, inform the appropriate RSPB Regional Office, or the Species Protection Department at the Lodge. Otherwise it is best in almost all circumstances to keep the record strictly secret in order to avoid disturbance by other birdwatchers and attacks by egg-collectors. Never visit known sites of rare breeding birds unless they are adequately protected. Even your presence may give away the site to others and cause so many other visitors that the birds may fail to breed successfully. Disturbance at or near the nest of species listed on the First Schedule of the Wildlife and Countryside Act 1981 is a criminal offence.

5. Rare migrants. Rare migrants or vagrants must not be harassed. If you discover one, consider the circumstances carefully before telling anyone. Will an influx of birdwatchers disturb the bird or others in the area? Will the habitat be damaged? Will problems be caused with the landowner?

6. The Law. The bird protection laws, as now embodied in the Wildlife and Countryside Act 1981, are the result of hard campaigning by previous generations of birdwatchers. As birdwatchers we must abide by them at all times and not allow them to fall in disrepute.

7. Respect the rights of landowners. The wishes of landowners and occupiers of land must be respected. Do not enter land without permission. Comply with permit schemes. If you are leading a group, do give advance notice of the visit, even if a formal permit scheme is not in operation. Always obey the Country Code.

8. Respect the rights of other people. Have proper consideration for other birdwatchers. Try not to disrupt their activities or scare the birds they are watching. There are many other people who also use the countryside. Do not interfere with their activities and, if it is seems that what they are doing is causing unnecessary disturbance to birds, do try to take a balanced view. Flushing gulls when walking a dog on a beach may do little harm, while

the same dog might be a serious disturbance at a tern colony. When pointing this out to a non-birdwatcher be courteous, but firm. The non-birdwatchers' goodwill towards birds must not be destroyed by the attitudes of birdwatchers.

9. Keeping records. Much of today's knowledge about birds in the result of meticulous record keeping by our predecessors. Make sure you help to add to tomorrow's knowledge by sending records to your country bird recorder.

10. Birdwatching abroad. Behave abroad as you would at home. This code should be firmly adhered to when abroad (whatever the local laws). Well-behaved birdwatchers can be important ambassadors for bird protection.

This code has been drafted after consultation between the British Ornithologists' Union, British Trust for Ornithology, the Royal Society for the Protection of Birds, the Scottish Ornithologists' Club, the Wildfowl and Wetlands Trust, and the editors of *British Birds*.

SOURCE: J.E. Pemberton, ed. *The Birdwatcher's Yearbook and Diary 1998* (Buckingham Press, 25 Manor Park, Maids Moreton, Buckingham MK18 1QX England, 1997)

Checklist of Birding Gear

- Alarm clock/watch
- Binoculars
- Bird checklist for the region/state/ province/country
- Bird guide(s)
- Bottled water
- Copy of your itinerary (leave one with family or friend for emergencies)
- Customs certificates for binoculars, cameras, lenses to indicate ownership
- Extra plastic bags of all sizes for protection of equipment from sand, saltwater, etc.
- Film
- First-aid kit: Band-Aids, antacid pills, pain-relief pills, laxative, Lomotil, water-purifying tablets, cortisone cream, Gravol, eye and ear drops, vitamins, snakebite kit, lip balm, malaria pills
- Flashlight with extra batteries
- Hat
- Insect repellent

- Items of personal hygiene
- Maps
- Notebooks
- Passport and spare copy of passport
- Pencils and pens
- Pocket camera
- Poncho
- Scarf/bandana
- Spare pair of mini-binoculars
- Spare eyeglasses and prescription for them
- Sunglasses
- Sunscreen
- Survival whistle
- Survival kit: nylon cord, super-glue, rubber bands, needle and thread, safety pins
- Swiss army knife
- Telescope and tripod
- Toilet paper roll
- Vaccination booklet

Optical Equipment

TWENTY TIPS FOR CHOOSING BINOCULARS

---

1. Always buy the best you can afford.

2. Buy them to best suit the kind of birding you will mostly use them for, e.g., rugged, backyard, or marine.

3. Ensure that they feel good in your hands, whether mini- or regular-sized.

4. Roof-prism binoculars are more expensive, easier to hold, and more rugged than porro-prism versions.

5. Binoculars weighing more than a pound and a half can get heavy after a while.

6. For rugged use, armored binoculars are better.

7. High-quality optics are denser and heavier than low-quality ones, but preferred for a sharper image.

8. Fast-focusing binoculars are invaluable for fast-moving birds.

9. Focus wheels are superior to flat levers because the latter require two hands and are less durable.

10. Non-focusing binoculars will not permit close focusing; close-focusing binoculars are very useful in woodland birding.

11. Magnification between 7 to 10 times is preferable, as higher magnifications can magnify hand-shake and provide a smaller field of view, a darker image, and a shallower depth of field.

12. Zoom binoculars offer inferior optics and a lower field of view.

13. "Fully multi-coated" optics cut glare and reduce light loss.

14. A wide field of view is preferable for fast-flying birds, scanning a vista quickly, and locating small birds in thick cover.

15. A generous depth of field minimizes the need to continually focus on birds moving closer or farther away.

16. Eyeglass-wearers need binoculars with a minimum of 15 mm of eye relief.

17. Well-sealed binoculars with internal focusing will minimize entry of dust, pollen, and moisture; fully waterproof binoculars are usually heavier and more expensive.

18. Custom-fitted rain guards to protect the lens, and adjustable, wide leather straps are recommended.

19. When shopping for binoculars, insist on taking them outside for a quick try-out.

20. A lifetime warranty will ensure that your binoculars last you . . . a lifetime.

OPTICAL TERMINOLOGY

alignment: the precise coordination of mechanical and optical elements with one another

armored: covered with shock-absorbing rubber or polyurethane to protect internal elements

automatic-focus: having a mechanism that sets the focus on the object in view

brightness: amount of light admitted by the binoculars, which is a function of the power and diameter of the objective lens

center-focusing: both barrels of the binocular are adjusted simultaneously by wheel or lever

close-focus: binoculars that allow focusing on objects that appear within 3 meters

coated optics: coating of all optical surfaces with a transparent chemical (e.g., magnesium fluoride) to reduce glare

de-alignment: a shift in the position of the lenses due to blows or jarring

depth of view: span of distance in front of and beyond an object in which the object remains in focus

dioptic correction: the adjustment of the optical instrument to the varying visual acuity of one's eyes

exit pupil: circle of light seen in the eye-piece from a distance of about 25 cm

eye relief: distance between the ocular lens and the human eye measured in mm, e.g., important to eyeglass-wearers

eye-cups: rubber rings covering each ocular lens which can be rolled down to accommodate eyeglass-wearers

field of view: the breadth of the view at a standard distance, e.g., a breadth of 100 m at a distance of 1,000 m

focusing wheel: round knob used to adjust the focus on an object

individual ocular adjustment: each eyepiece can be adjusted separately

interior focusing: exterior objective and ocular elements do not move, and thus, no air, dust, or moisture is drawn into the system while focusing

objective lens: larger lens (larger end) whose diameter is measured in millimeters by the second part of the numerical formula engraved on the binoculars, e.g., 7 × 35 mm, 8 × 40 mm

ocular lens: smaller lens (smaller end) to which one places the eyes

optical quality: high-quality, generally made from barium crown glass, and low quality, from less expensive boro-silicate glass

permanent-focus: non-focusing binoculars used for spotting objects more than 15 meters away

porro prism: wide-bodied binoculars where the objective lens and the ocular lens are offset, e.g., not aligned along a vertical axis

power: amount of magnification expressed in first part of the numerical formula engraved on binoculars, e.g., 7 (times) × 35, 8 (times) × 40

quick-focusing: flat lever operated by a finger on each hand holding the binoculars to fast-focus on an object

roof prism: longer, sleeker binoculars in which the objective and ocular lens are aligned along the same tube

water-resistant binoculars: well-sealed optics that keep out water from splashes or light rainfall, but not immersion, heavy rainfall, or exceptionally high humidity

waterproof binoculars: optics that are able to stay completely dry inside when completely immersed in water

zoom binoculars: optics that offer the capability of quickly increasing the power from one level to a much higher one, e.g., 7 to 15 times

Attracting Birds to the Backyard

Housing

SPECIFICATIONS FOR NESTBOXES FOR CAVITY-NESTING BIRDS

	Interior Floor Size of Box (in.)	Interior Height of Box (in.)	Entrance Hole Diameter (in.)	Mount Box This High (ft.)
Chickadees	4 × 4	9–12	$1\frac{1}{8} × 1\frac{1}{2}$	5–15
Prothonotary & Lucy's warbler	4 × 4	12	$1\frac{1}{4}$	5–12
Titmice	4 × 4	12	$1\frac{1}{2}$	5–12
White-breasted nuthatch	4 × 4	12	$1\frac{1}{2}$	5–12
Carolina wren	4 × 4	9–12	$1–1\frac{1}{2}$	5–10
House wren	4 × 4	6–8	$1–1\frac{1}{4}$	6–10
Winter wren	4 × 4	6–8	$1–1\frac{1}{4}$	6–10
Eastern bluebird	4 × 4	12	$1\frac{1}{2}$	5–6
Western bluebird	5 × 5	12	$1\frac{1}{2}–1\frac{9}{16}$	5–6
Mountain bluebird	5 × 5	12	$1\frac{9}{16}$	5–6
Tree swallow	5 × 5	10–12	$1\frac{1}{2}$	5–10
Violet-green swallow	5 × 5	10–12	$1\frac{1}{2}$	5–10
Purple martin	6 × 6	6	2 1/8	15–25
Great-crested flycatcher	6 × 6	12	$1\frac{3}{4}–2$	6–20
Ash-throated flycatcher	6 × 6	12	$1\frac{3}{4}–2$	6–20
House finch	5 × 5	10	$1\frac{1}{2}$	5–10
Downy woodpecker	4 × 4	12	$1\frac{1}{2}$	5–20
Hairy woodpecker	6 × 6	14	$1\frac{1}{2}$	8–20
Red-bellied woodpecker	6 × 6	14	2	8–20
Golden-fronted woodpecker	6 × 6	14	2	8–20
Red-headed woodpecker	6 × 6	14	2	8–20
Northern flicker	7 × 7	16–24	$2\frac{1}{2}$	10–20
Pileated woodpecker	12 × 12	24	4	15–25
Bufflehead	7 × 7	17	3	5–15
Wood duck	12 × 12	24	3 × 4	5–20
Hooded merganser	12 × 12	24	3 × 4	5–30
Goldeneye	12 × 12	24	$3\frac{1}{4} × 4\frac{1}{4}$	15–20
Common merganser	12 × 12	24	5 × 6	8–20
Saw-whet owl	7 × 7	12	$2\frac{1}{2}$	8–20
Screech-owl	8 × 8	18	3	8–30
Boreal owl	8 × 8	18	3	8–30
Barred owl	14 × 14	28	8	15–30
Barn owl	12 × 36	16	6 × 7	15–30
American kestrel	9 × 9	16–18	3	12–30

SOURCE: Adapted from S. Shalaway, *A Guide to Bird Homes* (Marietta, OH: Bird Watcher's Digest, 1995).

DIMENSIONS OF NESTING SHELVES

	Floor of Shelf (in.)	Depth of Shelf (in.)	Mount Shelf this High (ft.)
Song sparrow	6 × 6	6	1–3
Eastern phoebe	6 × 6	6	8–12
Barn swallow	6 × 6	6	8–12
American robin	6 × 8	8	6–15

TEN TIPS FOR INSTALLING A PURPLE MARTIN HOUSE

1. Select the right location, i.e., 15 feet away from obstructions, but near your house; water body within a mile or two.

2. Height above ground should be 12 to 20 feet; hole diameters $1\frac{3}{4}$ to $2\frac{1}{2}$ inches; cavity space 6 by 6 by 6 inches.

3. Choose light colors to reflect hot sun.

4. Ensure plenty of ventilation.

5. The house should be rain-proof and should drain well.

6. Railings on ledges will prevent falling youngsters.

7. Light interiors in compartments will discourage starlings.

8. Easy access will facilitate annual cleaning and removal of sparrow nests.

9. Both metal and wooden houses are suitable if they are durable.

10. Predator guards should keep out snakes, raccoons, hawks, and owls.

NEST MATERIAL OFFERINGS FOR BIRDS

Bulrush	Furniture stuffing	Soft cloth strips*
Burlap threads*	Horsehair	Spanish moss
Cedar bark	Human hair	String*
Cotton batting	Mud	Strips of paper
Cotton gauze*	Paintbrush bristles	Thread*
Dental floss*	Pet hair	Wood shavings
Dried grass	Pillow feathers	Wool
Dried moss	Poultry farm feathers	Yarn*
Excelsior	Rootlets	
Fine twigs	Rope threads*	

* Keep less than 6 inches long to avoid entanglement and strangulation.

Plants

FRUIT-BEARING PLANTS FOR NORTH AMERICAN BIRDS

Arrowwood	Firethorn	Pincherry
Barberry	Hackberry	Plum
Bayberry	Hawthorn	Pyracantha
Blackberry	Highbush blueberry	Raspberry
Coralberry	Highbush cranberry	Russian olive
Cotoneaster	Holly	Serviceberry
Crabapple	Honeysuckle	Snowberry
Currant	Mountain ash	Staghorn sumac
Dogwood	Mulberry	Sweet cherry
Elderberry	Nannyberry	Viburnum

GARDEN FLOWERS FOR NORTH AMERICAN BIRDS

Aster	Cornflower	Prince's plumes
Bachelor's button	Cosmos	Rock purslane
Basket flower	Dandelion	Royal sweet sultan
Bluebell	Dayflower	Silene
Calendula	Dusty miller	Sunflower
California poppy	Love-lies-bleeding	Sweet scabious
China aster	Marigold	Tarweed
Chrysanthemum	Phlox	Thistle
Coneflower	Portulaca	Verbena
Coreopsis	Prince's feather	Zinnia

TYPICAL CHARACTERISTICS OF FLOWERS POLLINATED BY HUMMINGBIRDS

Flowering time:	diurnal
Flower shape:	weakly zygomorphic or radial
Blossom color:	vivid, often red
Odor:	none
Nectar:	very abundant in broad tubes
Flower position:	horizontal or hanging
Petal position:	often recurved

SOURCE; Adapted from P.A. Johnsgard, *The Hummingbirds of North America* (Washington, DC: Smithsonian Institution Press, 1983).

FLOWERING PLANTS FOR HUMMINGBIRDS*

Azalea
Amaryllis
Bee balm
Bergamot (wild, scarlet)
Blazing star
Bleeding heart
Bugleweed
Butterfly milkweed
Cardinal flower
Citrus tree
Clematis
Columbine
Coral bells
Coralberry
Dahlia
Daylily
Delphinium
Evening primrose
Fire pink
Fireweed

Flowering tobacco
Four o'clock
Foxglove
Fuschia
Gay-feather
Gladiolus
Hibiscus
Hollyhock
Horse chestnut
Hosta
Impatiens
Indian paintbrush
Jewelweed
Larkspur
Limber honeysuckle
Madrone
Manzanitas
Mimosa tree
Morning glory
Nasturtium

Northern catalpa
Ohio buckeye
Orange honeysuckle
Paintbrush
Petunia
Phlox
Red-hot poker
Scarlet gila
Scarlet runner bean
Scarlet sage
Siberian pea tree
Snapdragon
Spider flower
Sweet William
Tartarian honeysuckle
Tiger lily
Trumpet honeysuckle
Trumpet vine
Weigela
Zinnia

* Check local nursery for proper regional growing conditions

SHRUBS AND TREES FOR NORTH AMERICAN BIRDS

Northeast
American elder
American holly
American mountain ash
Amur honeysuckle
Black cherry
Black tupelo
Brambles
Cardinal autumn olive
Downy serviceberry
Eastern red cedar
Eastern white pine
Flowering crabapples
Flowering dogwood
Hawthorns
Highbush cranberry
Red mulberry
Red-osier dogwood
Russian olive
Staghorn sumac

Tatarian honeysuckle
Virginia creeper
White oak
Wild grapes

Southeast
American beautyberry
Common greenbrier
Cabbage palmetto
Common persimmon
Live oak
Loblolly pine
Scarlet firethorn
Shagbark hickory
Sugar hackberry
Yaupon holly

Prairies and Plains
Amur maple
Buffalo currant

Burr oak
Common chokecherry
Common hackberry
Ponderosa pine
Saskatoon serviceberry
Skunkbush
Snowberry
White mulberry

Mountains and Deserts
Blueberry elder
Canyon grape
Cascara buckthorn
Colorado blue spruce
Douglas hawthorn
Golden currant
Green mountain ash
Grouseberry
Mesquite

Prickly pear cactus	California pepper tree	Pacific wax myrtle
Quaking aspen	Common fig	Shore pine
Western thimbleberry	Four-wing saltbush	Tall red huckleberry
	Holly-leaved buckthorn	
Pacific coast	Holly-leaved cherry	
California live oak	Pacific dogwood	

* For more information and lists of other recommended species, see S.W. Kress, *The Audubon Society Guide to Attracting Birds* (New York: Charles Scribner's Sons, 1985).

CHARACTERISTICS OF PREFERRED NESTING TREES OF SOME NORTH AMERICAN WOODPECKERS

	When Using Territory	Territory Size (hectares)	Minimum No. of Snags Used/Pair	Average dbh of Nest Trees (cm)	Average Height of Nest Trees (m)	Maximum Pairs per 40 Hectares	Snags Needed per 40 Hectares to Maintain 100% of Cavity Nesters
Downy woodpecker	All year	4	4	20	6	10	400
Hairy woodpecker	All year	8	4	30	9	5	200
Pileated woodpecker	All year	70	4	56	18	0.6	24
Common flicker	Breeding	16	2	38	9	2.5	150
Red-bellied woodpecker	All year	6	4	46	12	6.7	270
Red-headed woodpecker	Breeding	4	2	50	12	10	200
Black-backed three-toed woodpecker	All year	30	4	38	9	1.3	52
Northern three-toed woodpecker	All year	30	4	35	9	1.3	52
Yellow-bellied sapsucker	Breeding	4	1	30	9	10	100

SOURCE: Adapted from K.E. Evans and R.N. Connor, U.S. Dept. Agriculture Forest Service publication GTR NC-51 (Washington, DC, 1979).

Feeding

TWENTY TIPS FOR SETTING UP A BACKYARD PROGRAM

---

1. The bird table or platform feeder should have raised borders to prevent seed from blowing off, kept free of built-up droppings, and be well drained.

2. Hanging feeders best keep seed clean, dry, and available in heavy snowfall.

3. Box-shaped hopper feeders set on a post and equipped with a seed catch tray and shelf perches are most attractive to ground-feeding birds.

4. Long, cylindrical tube feeders which are hung or placed on a pole and which have multiple feeding ports, each with a stick perch, are preferred by finches, chickadees, and titmice.

5. All feeders should be easily filled and cleaned and made of durable plastic or wood (weather-resistant cedar).

6. Birds will not freeze to the metal parts of feeders.

7. Feed year-round to enjoy the different varieties frequenting the neighborhood and watch parents bring their young to the feeder.

8. Locate your feeder near enough cover to provide shelter from weather, but not enough to hide lurking predators like cats and hawks; feeders near windows should be installed close enough to prevent startled birds from striking the glass with serious impact.

9. While some consistency in feeding is recommended, especially in prolonged harsh weather, birds do not become totally dependent on feeders, especially if there are other feeders in the neighborhood.

10. The best ways to keep squirrels out of feeders by installing suitably sized baffles above or below, covering feeders in coated metal mesh, using a squirrel-proof hopper feeder with a weight-sensitive perch, offering the squirrels alternative food sources, or substituting safflower for sunflower seed.

11. Buy fresh seeds that are well filled and free of insects.

12. The best all-round seed accepted by the greatest variety of birds is black-oil sunflower with its thinner shell, more meat, and higher fat content; the best all-round seed for small finches, siskins, and redpolls is niger; the best all-round hulled foods are sunflower and non-salted peanuts; and the best all-round mix is black-oil sunflower seed, white millet, and cracked corn.

13. To minimize feeding by pigeons, doves, and house sparrows, do not offer cracked corn or white millet; to dissuade grackles, use safflower instead of sunflower.

14. Clean feeders regularly by removing old, moldy seed and by soaking in a light bleach solution (9 parts water to 1 part bleach).

15. Rendered beef or mutton suet offered year-round in a log drilled with wide holes, an onionskin bag, or wire cage will attract woodpeckers, nuthatches, and dozens of other backyard species.

16. Whether peanut butter offered in its pure form causes small birds to choke to death is controversial.

17. Offering grit in the form of coarse builder's sand or chicken grit will help seed-eaters grind their digested seeds.

18. Crushed oyster shells or dried, broken eggshells serve as calcium and mineral supplements for birds, especially laying females.

19. Halved oranges impaled on large spikes, and sugar solutions, are attractive to orioles and other nectar feeders.

20. Birds of prey that sometimes hunt feeder birds are protected by law and are a part of nature.

FEEDER PREFERENCES FOR SOME NORTH AMERICAN BACKYARD BIRDS

	Ground Feeders	Raised Feeders (Low)	Raised Feeders (High)	Hanging Feeders	Suet Feeders
American goldfinch		X	X	X	
American tree sparrow	X	X			
Black-capped chickadee	X	X	X	X	X
Blue jay		X	X		
Carolina wren		X			
Common grackle	X	X			
Dark-eyed junco	X	X			
Evening grosbeak			X		
House finch		X	X	X	
House sparrow	X	X	X		
Mourning dove	X	X			
Northern cardinal		X	X		
Northern flicker	X	X			X
Northern mockingbird		X			
Pine siskin		X	X	X	
Purple finch			X	X	
Downy woodpecker		X	X		X
Red-bellied woodpecker	X	X			X
Red-breasted nuthatch	X	X			X
Red-headed woodpecker	X	X			X
Yellow-bellied sapsucker		X			X
Red-winged blackbird	X	X	X	X	
Song sparrow	X	X			
Starling	X	X		X	X
Tufted titmouse		X		X	
White-breasted nuthatch		X			X
White-crowned sparrow	X	X			
White-throated sparrow	X	X			

SOURCE: Adapted from K. Burke, ed., *How to Attract Birds* (San Francisco, CA: Ortho Books, 1983).

MOST WIDELY RECOMMENDED SEED TYPES
(In Rough Order of Popularity)

Black sunflower	Peanut hearts	Golden millet
Black-striped sunflower	White millet	Canary seed
Gray-striped sunflower	Cracked corn	Safflower
Hulled sunflower	Niger	Rapeseed
Peanut kernels	Red millet	

ALTERNATIVE SEED-NUT OFFERINGS

Apple seeds	Alfalfa meal	Hulled oats
Pecan meats	Barley	Butternut
Cooked rice	Black walnut	Whole kernel corn
Melon seeds (ground)	Wheat	English walnut
Pumpkin seeds (ground)	Whole oats	Hickory nut
Squash seeds (broken)	Sorghum	Hempseed
Almonds (chopped)	Flaxseed	Rye

MOST WIDELY RECOMMENDED NON-SEED FOODS

American cheese	Cracker crumbs	Raisins
Baked apple	Cranberries	Strawberries
Raw apple	Cooked currants	Watermelon
Bananas	Cooked eggs	Cooked sweet potatoes
Bayberries	Crushed eggshells	Tomatoes
Blueberry	Grape jelly	Cooked potatoes
Biscuits	Grapes	Figs
Dog biscuits	Rolled oats	Salt
Baked goods	Mealworms	Beef suet
Cottage cheese	Meat scraps	Mutton suet
Cream cheese	Orange halves	Pokeberries
Cherries	Oyster shell	Peaches
Coconut	Pear halves	
Corn bread	Pie crust	

FOOD PREFERENCES OF COMMON FEEDER BIRDS
OF NORTH AMERICA

Species	Preferred Foods
Blackbirds, starlings	Cracked corn, milo, wheat, table scraps, baked goods, suet
Cardinals, grosbeaks, pyrrhuloxias	Sunflower, safflower, cracked corn, millet, fruit
Crows, magpies, and nutcrackers	Meat scraps, suet, cracked corn, peanuts, baked goods, leftovers, dog food
Finches, siskins	Thistle (niger), sunflower hearts, black-oil sunflower seed, millet, canary seed, fruits, peanut kernels, suet mixes
Hummingbirds	Plant nectar, small insects, sugar solution
Jays	Peanuts, sunflower, suet, meat scraps, cracked corn, baked goods
Kinglets	Suet, suet mixes, baked goods
Mockingbirds, thrashers, catbirds	Halved apple, chopped fruits, baked goods, suet, nut-meats, millet (thrashers), soaked raisins, currants, sunflower hearts
Nuthatches	Suet, suet mixes, sunflower hearts and seed, peanut kernels, peanut butter
Orioles	Halved oranges, apples, berries, sugar solution, grape jelly, suet, suet mixes, soaked raisins and currants
Pigeons, doves	Millet, cracked corn, wheat, milo, niger, buckwheat, sunflower, baked goods
Quail, pheasants	Cracked corn, millet, wheat milo
Roadrunners	Meat scraps, hamburger, suet
Robins, bluebirds, other thrushes	Suet, suet mixes, mealworms, berries, baked goods, chopped fruits, soaked raisins, currants, nutmeats, sunflower hearts
Sparrows, buntings	Millet, sunflower hearts, black-oil sunflower, cracked corn, baked goods
Tanagers	Suet, fruits, sugar solution, mealworms, baked goods
Titmice, chickadees	Peanut kernels, sunflower, suet, peanut butter
Towhees, juncos	Millet, sunflower, cracked corn, peanuts, baked goods, nutmeats
Warblers	Suet, suet mixes, fruit, baked goods, sugar solution, chopped nutmeats
Waxwings	Berries, chopped fruits, canned peas, currants, raisins
Woodpeckers	Suet, meat scraps, sunflower hearts/seed, cracked corn, peanuts, fruits, sugar solution
Wrens, creepers	Suet, suet mixes, peanut butter, peanut kernels, bread, fruit, millet (wrens)

SOURCE: J. Zickefoose, *Enjoying Bird Feeding More* (Marietta, Ohio: Bird Watcher's Digest, 1994).

TEN TIPS FOR SETTING UP A HUMMINGBIRD FEEDER

1. Choose a feeder that is attractive to hummingbirds (with some red parts), easy to clean (dishwasher-safe), functional on windy days, and equipped with insect guards.

2. Choose a feeder size that is large enough to prevent constant refilling but small enough to keep the solution from fermenting or going sour.

3. Hang your feeder near blossoming, bright flowers, especially red ones, out of direct sunlight and heavy wind, and close enough to enjoy the birds.

4. Feeders near windows should be hung close to the glass to prevent spooked hummingbirds from colliding with the glass at high speed.

5. To make a sugar solution, bring to a boil one part white sugar (do *not* use honey) and four parts water, let sit, and store in fridge.

6. It is not necessary to add red food coloring to attract the birds; the red parts of the feeder will suffice.

7. Hang the feeder with an easily visible string or wire to prevent collisions.

8. Put your feeder up in early spring and keep your feeder up as long as possible in the fall, as it will not keep hummingbirds from migrating and may provide food for stray migrants.

9. If there are several hummingbirds frequenting the yard, put up several feeders to minimize fighting.

10. Most important, wash the feeder with a warm, soapy solution every time it is filled.

FAVORITE RECIPES FOR THE BIRDS

1. Marvel Meal

1   cup peanut butter
1   cup vegetable shortening, melted beef
    suet, or bacon drippings
4   cups cornmeal (yellow is higher in Vitamin A)
1   cup white flour

This makes a soft, doughy food that can be offered in hardware cloth cages, smeared on the bark of trees, or pressed into holes in a suet log.

2. Miracle Meal

4   cups yellow corn meal
1   cup all-purpose flour
1   cup lard or melted suet
1   teaspoon corn oil

Plus sunflower hearts, peanut hearts, chopped soaked raisins

Melt lard and stir in other ingredients. Spike with sunflower hearts, peanut hearts, orr chopped soaked raisins, as desired. Let set, cut into chunks, feed as suet. Mainly for bluebirds, but other birds like it too.

3. Bluebird Food

5   parts oatmeal
1   part corn syrup
1   part peanut butter
1   part bacon grease or lard

Mix well and push into holes in a feeder log. Other birds like it too.

SOURCES:
Recipe 1: J.K. Terres *in* J. Zickefoose. *Enjoying Bird Feeding More* (Marietta, OH: Bird Watcher's Digest, 1986)
Recipe 2: J. Zickefoose. *Enjoying Bluebirds More* (Marietta, OH: Bird Watcher's Digest, 1993)
Recipe 3: O.W. Watkins in *Bird Watcher's Digest*, Jan./Feb. Issue (Marietta, OH: Bird Watcher's Digest, 1998)

TEN TIPS FOR INSTALLING A BIRD BATH

1. Most commercially available, household, and natural receptacles will work as long as they are shallow, i.e., one to two inches deep.

2. It should be placed reasonably close to perches for both drying off and for cover against sudden attack by cats, hawks, etc.

3. It should be within easy reach of a garden hose.

4. A plastic scrub brush should be used to clean it during each filling.

5. A weak bleach solution and/or bath placement in the shade helps deter algae.

6. A rough bottom should facilitate birds' proper footing.

7. Overhanging branches should be trimmed to avoid contamination from birds perching above.

8. Addition of moving water like a drip or a spray to make noise will be more attractive.

9. Addition of hot water or use of submersible heaters to keep the bath open year-round should be used with caution in exceptionally cold weather; adding anti-freeze or glycerine is not recommended.

10. Hummingbirds and swallows like to fly through a fine mist.

DIMENSIONS OF NESTING SHELVES

	Floor of Shelf (in.)	Depth of Shelf (in.)	Mount Shelf This High (ft.)
Song Sparrow	6 × 6	6	1–3
Eastern phoebe	6 × 6	6	8–12
Barn swallow	6 × 6	6	8–12
American robin	6 × 6	8	6–15

TEN TIPS FOR INSTALLING A PURPLE MARTIN HOUSE

1. Select the right location, i.e., 15 feet away from obstructions, but near your house; water body within a mile or two.

2. Height above ground should be 12 to 20 feet; hole diameters 1¾ to 2½ inches; cavity space 6 by 6 by 6 inches.

3. Choose light colors to reflect hot sun.

4. Ensure plenty of ventilation.

5. The house should be rain-proof and should drain well.

6. Railings on ledges will prevent falling youngsters.

7. Light interiors in compartments will discourage starlings.

8. Easy access will facilitate annual cleaning and removal of sparrow nests.

9. Both metal and wooden houses are suitable if they are durable.

10. Predator guards should keep out snakes, raccoons, hawks, and owls.

NEST MATERIAL OFFERINGS FOR BIRDS

Bulrush	Furniture stuffing	Soft cloth strips*
Burlap threads*	Horsehair	Spanish moss
Cedar bark	Human hair	String*
Cotton batting	Mud	Strips of paper
Cotton gauze*	Paintbrush bristles	Thread*
Dental floss*	Pet hair	Wood shavings
Dried grass	Pillow feathers	Wool
Dried moss	Poultry farm feathers	Yarn*
Excelsior	Rootlets	
Fine twigs	Rope threads*	

*Keep less than 6 inches long to avoid entanglement and strangulation.

Resources for Bird Lovers

Ornithological and Bird-Watching Organizations

WORLD

BirdLife International
Wellbrook Court, Girton Road, Cambridge
CB3 0NA, England
Tel: +41 (0)1223 277318

Colonial Waterbird Society
Oakland University, Rochester, MI 48309-
4401, USA
Email: mccrimmon@oakland.edu
http://www.nmnh.si.edu/BIRDNET/CWS/

European Ornithological Union
Instituto Nazional per la Fauna Selvatica,
via Ca'Fornacetta 9, 40061 Ozzano Emilia
(BO), Italy

International Birdwatching Center (Israel)
P.O. Box 774, Eilat 88106

International Crane Foundation
E-11376, Shady Lane Road, Baraboo, WI
53913
Tel: (608) 356-9462

The International Osprey Foundation, Inc.
P.O. Box 250, Sanibel, FL 33957, USA
Tel: (813) 472-5218

Oriental Bird Club
c/o Dr. Robert S. Kennedy, Cincinnati
Museum of Natural History,
1720 Gilbert Avenue,
Cincinnati, OH 45202-1401, USA
Email: kennedrt@ucbeh.san.uc.edu.
http://www.netlink.co.uk/users/aw/obchome.
html

The Peregrine Fund
566 West Flying Hawk Lane, Boise, ID
83709, USA
Tel: (208) 362-3716 Fax: (208) 362-2376
Email: tpf@peregrinefund.org
http://www.peregrinefund.org/

Raptor Research Foundation
http://www.weber.edu/rrf/Default.html

**RARE Center for Tropical Bird
Conservation**
1529 Walnut Street, Philadelphia, PA 19102,
USA
Tel: (215) 568-0516

World Owl Trust
The Owl Centre, Muncaster Castle,
Ravenglass, Cumbria CA18 1RQ, England
Tel: +41 (0)1229 717393

World Pheasant Association
P.O. Box 5, Lower Basildon, Reading
RG8 9PF, England
Tel: +41 (0)1734 845140

**World Working Group on Birds of Prey
and Owls**
Wangenheimstrasse 32, Berlin D-14193,
Germany
Email: wwgbp@aol.com

AFRICA

African Bird Club
c/o BirdLife International, Wellbrook
Court, Girton Road, Cambridge CB3 0NA,
England
Email:aw@pobox.com.
http://www.africanbirdclub.org/

BirdLife South Africa
P.O. Box 84394, Greenside 2034, RSA
Tel: 27 11 789-1122 Fax: 27 11 789-5188
Email: info@birdlife.org.za
http://www.birdlife.org.za/

Botswana Birdwatching Club
P.O. Box 71, Gaborone, Botswana

Cape Bird Club (South Africa)
P.O. Box 5022 Cape Town 8000, RSA
Tel: 021 686 8795
Email: divaluce@iafrica.com
http://users.iafrica.com/d/di/divaluce/cbc.html

Centrale ornithologique Marocaone
Inst. Scientific, Départemnt de Zoologie,
Avenue IBN Batouta, BP 703, Rabat

Gambia Ornithologists' Society
P.O. Box 757, Banjul, Gambia

GOAEP
Laboratoire d'Ornithologie, Parc
Zoologique et des Loisirs d'Alger,
Departement de Zoologie, Route de
Kaddous, Alger

Grupo Ornithologico Canario
(Canary Islands)
Nueva de Duggi 20, 1 Santa Cruz, Tenerife

Natal Bird Club
P.O. Box 1218, Durban 4000, RSA
http://www.durban.org.za/mph/birdc/

Ornithological Association of Zimbabwe
P.O. Box CY 161 Causeway, Zimbabwe
Tel: 263 4 794614 Fax: 263 4 794611
Email: birds@harare.iafrica.com
http://users.harare.iafrica.com/~birds/

Raptor Conservation Group
P.O. Box 72155, Parkview 2122, RSA
Tel: 011-646-4629 Fax: 011-646-4631

Vulture Study Group
P.O. Box 72334, Parkview 2122,
Johannesburg, RSA
Tel: (011) 646-8617

West African Ornithological Society
c/o 1 Fisher's Heron, East Mills,
Fordingbridge, Hants SP6 2JR, England

Wesvaal Bird Club
P.O. Box 2413, Potchefstroom 2520, RSA
http://www.geocities.com/rainforest/vines/2
022/index.html

Zambian Ornithological Society
c/o Kafue Fisheries, P.O. Box 31522, Lusaka,
Zambia
Fax: 260 32 30707

ASIA

Bird Conservation Nepal
P.O. Box 12465, Kamaladi, Kathmandu
Tel: +977 1 224487 Fax: +977 1 243250

Bird Conservation Society of Thailand
69/12 Soi Ramintha 24, Ramintha Rd.,
Ladprao, Bangkok 10230
Tel/Fax: +66 2 510 5921

BirdLife Asia
http://www.kt.rim.or.jp/~birdinfo/
Email: marutani@st.rim.or.jp

BirdLife International – Indonesia Programme
Jl. A. Yani 11, Bogor 16161, Indonesia
or P.O. Box 310/Boo, Bogor 16003, Indonesia
Tel: 62 – 251 – 333234
Email: birdlife@server.indo.net.id
http://www.kt.rim.or.jp/~birdinfo/
indonesia/index.html

Ceylon Bird Club
P.O. Box 11, Colombo, Sri Lanka

Chinese Wild Bird Federation
2F, No 6, Alley 13, Lane 295, Sec 1,
Fu-Shin Road 106, Taipei
Tel: +886 2 706 7219 Fax: +886 2 754 8009

Hong Kong Bird Watching Society
GPO B ox 12460, Hong Kong
Email: hkbws@hkstar.com
http://home.hkstar.com/~hkbws/

Japan Alcid Society
http://www2.gol.com/users/kojiono/
Email: kojiono@gol.com

Japanese Association for the Preservation of Birds
8-20 Nampeidai-machi, Toyko 150

Japanese Seabird Conservation Commitee
Email: kojiono@gol.com

Ornithological Society of Japan
c/o Natural Science Museum, Hyakunin-cho
3-23-1, Shinjuku-ku, Toyko 160

Philippine Eagle Conservation Program
P.O. Box 246, Davao City 9501, Mindanao, Philippines

Society for the Research of Golden Eagle (SRGE)
Yukihata 482-57, Yasu, Shiga 520-23, Japan

Wild Bird Society of Japan
2-35-2 Minamidaira, Hino City, Toyko 191

Wild Bird Society of Taipei
6, Alley 13, Lane 295, Fu-Shin South Rd.,
Section 1, Taipei, Taiwan
Tel: 886-2-325-9190

Wild Bird Society of Taiwan
http://com5.iis.sinica.edu.tw:8000/~cwbf/
Email: cwbf@tpts1.seed.net.tw

India

Bombay Natural History Society
Hornbill House
Opposite Lion's Gate
Shahid Bhagar Singh Road
Bombay, 400 023, India

Raptor Research Centre
P.O. P & T Colony, 7-1, Chaitanyapuri,
Hyderabad 500 660, Andhra Pradesh, India

Middle East

Ornithological Society of Egypt
4 Ismail El Mazni Street, Flat 8,
Heliopolis, Cairo
Fax: + 20 2 3457234

The National Avian Research Center (NARC) (United Arab Emerites)
Maqtaa Bridge Main Site, P.O. Box 45553,
Abu Dhabi, United Arab Emirates
Tel: ++ 971 (2) 414441 Fax: ++ 971 (2) 414131
Email: erwda@emirates.net.ae
http://www.erwda.gov.ae/narc.htm

Oman Bird Group
Oman Natural History Museum,
P.O. Box 668, Muscat 113
Tel: +968 605400 Fax: +968 602735

Ornithological Society of the Middle East
c/o RSPB., The Lodge, Sandy, Bedfordshire
SG19 2DL, England
Tel (Fax) +44.1405.704665
Email: ag@netlink.co.uk
http://www.netlink.co.uk/users/ag/osme/
osmehome.html

Pakistan Ornithology Trust
L28 Sobra City, Tarbela, West Pakistan

EUROPE

Albania

Albanian Society for the Protection and Preservation of Birds and Mammals
Faculty of Natural Sciences, Tirana University, Al-Tirana, Albania
Tel/Fax: +355 42 29 028

Austria

BirdLife Austria
Mueumsplatz 1/10/8, A-1070 Wien, Austria
Tel: +43 1 523 4651 Fax: +43 1 524 7040

Belarus

Bielorussian Ornithological Society
Institute of Zoology, Belarus Academy of Sciences, F. Skoriny st. 27, BY-Minsk 220072, Belarus

Belgium

Aves asbl – Société d' études Ornithologiques
http://www.biol.ucl.ac.be/ecol.html/Organis/
FBDB/AVES/AVES.Intro. html
http://www.rw.be/mrw/dgrne/sibw/
organisations/aves/HOME.HTM
Email: aves-coa@infonie.be

Grup Balear d' Ornitologia i Defensa de a Naturalesa (Balearic Group of Ornithology and Defence of Nature)
Servei d'Educació Ambiental, GOB, Verí, 1, 3r – 07001 Palma
Tel. 72 11 05 – Fax. 71 13 75
Email: gob@ocea.es
http://www.ocea.es/gob/home.htm

Brussels, Ornithological Working Group
Mensenrechtenlaan 22, 1070 Brussels
Tel.: (02) 524.28.52
Email: erik.toorman@bwk.kuleuven.ac.be
http://sun-hydr-01.bwk.kuleuven.ac.be/
hydraulics/EToorman/avib.ht ml

Ligue Royal Belge pour la Protection des Oiseaux (LBPO)
Rue de Veeweyde 43, B-1070 Brussels

Bulgaria

Bulgarian Society for the Protection of Birds
P.O. Box 114, Diana Bad/Izgrev, BG-1172 Sofia, Bulgaria
Tel/Fax: +359 2 689413

Croatia

Croatian Society for Bird and Nature Protection
Ilirski Trg 9, HR-10000, Zagreb, Croatia
Tel/Fax: +385 1 345 445

Denmark

Danish Bird Association
Vesterbrogade 140, DK-1620 Copenhagen V, Denmark
Tel: 45-31-31-4404

Dansk Ornithologisk Forening (DOF)
Fuglenes Hus, Vesterbrogade 140, DK-1620, Copenhagen V, Denmark
Tel: +45 31 312435

Estonia

The Estonian Ornithological Society (EOS)
P.O. Box 227, Struve St 2, Tartu, Estonia
Tel/Fax: 327 7 430 198
Email: jaanus@linnu.tartu.ee
http://www.loodus.ee/eoy/eindex.html

Finland

Birdlife Finland
P.O. Box 1285, FIN-00101 Helsinki, Finland
Tel: 09 6854700 Fax: 09 6854722
Email: birdlife@surfnet.fi
http://www.surfnet.fi/birdlife/

Association of Ornithological Societies in Finland
PL 17, FIN-18101, Heinola

Finnish Ornithological Society (OF)
P. Rautatiekatu 13, SF-00100, Helsinki 10

France

Ligue Pour la Protection des Oiseaux (LPO)
La Corderie Royale, BP 263, F-17305 Rochefort, CEDEX
Tel:33 5 46 821234 Fax: +33 5 46 839956

Societe d'Etudes Ornithologiques de France
Museum National d'Histoire Naturelle, 4, Avenue du Petit Château, 91800 Brunoy, France

Germany

Dachverband Deutscher Avifaunisten (DDA)
am Schafberg 31, D-96476 Rodach

Deutsche Ornithologen-Gesellschaft
Deutsche Bank, Postfach 106013, D-70049, Stuttgart

NABU
OT Meissendorf, D-29308 Winsen/Aller
Tel: 49-(0)5056-97010
Fax: 49-(0)-5056-970197
Email: nabu.akademie@t-online.de
http://www.NABU.de/

Saarland, Working Group for Ornithology
http://www.coli.uni-sb.de/~bos/obs-eng.html

Greece

Hellenic Ornithological Society
Emm.Benaki 53, GR 106 81 Athens, Greece
Tel/Fax:++301 3811 271
http://www.nature.ariadne-t.gr/nature/ornithology/ornithology.htm l

Hungary

Hungarian Ornithological and Nature Conservation
Költö u. 21, Pf 391, H-1536, Budapest
Tel/Fax: +36 1 175 8327
http://agy.bgytf.hu/~nzept/natcon.html

Iceland

Icelandic Society for the Protection of Birds
P.O. Box 5069, IS-125, Reykjavik

Ireland

Birdwatch Ireland
Ruttledge House, 8 Longford Place, Monkstown, Co Dublin, Ireland
Tel: (01) 28004322

Northern Ireland Birdwatchers' Association
Larches, 12 Belvoir Close, Belvoir Park, Belfast BT8 4PL, Ireland
Tel: 01232 693232

Northern Ireland Ornithologists' Club
The Roost, 139 Windmill Road, Hillsborough, Co Down BT26 6NP, Ireland
Tel: 01846 639254

Italy

Capinera
Email: almasi@mbox.vol.it
http://www.symbolic.pr.it/capinera/

Centro Italiano Studi Ornitologici – CISO
Dipartimento di Scienze del Comportamento Animale (DI.S.C.A.U.), via Volta 6 – I –
56126 Pisa, Italy
Tel: 39 (0)50-20255 Fax: 39 (0)50-24653.
Email: bedini@discau.unipi.it
http://www.unipv.it/~webbio/ciso/ciso.htm

Comitato Italiano per la Protezione Dei Rapaci (CIPR)
Via Degli Estensi 165, Roma 00164, Italy

LIPU
Via Trento, 49 – 43100 Parma (PR), Italy
Tel: (+39) 0521/27.30.43 Fax: (+39)
0521/27.34.19
http://www.italnet.it/lipu/index.htm

Societa Ornitologica Italiana (SOI)
Via de Roma 13, Ravenna, Logetta
Lombardesca

Latvia

Latvian Ornithological Society (LOB)
AK 10, LV-1047 Riga
Tel/Fax: +371 7221 580

Lithuania

Lithuanian Ornithological Society (LOD)
Akademijos-2, LT-2600, Vilnius
Tel: +370 2 729 253 Fax: +370 2 729 255

Luxembourg

**Ligue Luxembourgeoise pour la Protection
de la Nature et des Oiseaux**
Kräizhaff, Rue de Luxembourg, L-1899
Kockelscheuer
Tel: +352 290 404 Fax: +352 290 504

Macedonia

**Bird Study and Protection Society of
Macedonia**
Institute of Biology, Faculty of Sciences,
MAC-91000 Skopje
Tel/Fax: +389 91 117055 ext. 614

Malta

BirdLife Malta
P.O. Box 498, Valletta CMR01, Malta
Email: merill@geocities.com
http://www.geocities.com/RainForest/3211/

Netherlands

Dutch Birding Association
Dutch Birding, C/O Jeannette Admiraal,
Iepenlaan 11, 1901 ST, Castricum
The Netherlands
Email: meijerpc@worldonline.nl
http://www.mebweb.nl/DutchBirding/

**Dutch Seabird Group / Nederlandse
Zeevogelgroep (NZG)**
Netherlands Institute for Sea Research,
P.O. Box 59, 1790 AB Den Burg, Texel,
The Netherlands
Tel: +31.2223.69488 Fax: +31222319674
E-mail: camphuys@nioz.nl

Netherlands Ornithologists Union (NOU)
C.J. Camphuysen, c/o Netherlands Institute
for Sea Research, P.O. Box 59, 1790 AB Den
Burg, Texel, The Netherlands
Tel: +31.2223.69488 Fax: +31222319674
Email: camphuysen@pi.net

Vogelbescherming Nederland
Driebergseweg 16c, 3708 JB Zeist,
Nederland
Tel: +31 30 69 37700 Fax: 31 30 69 18844

Norway

Norsk Ornitologisk Forening (NOF)
Seminarplassen 5, N-7060 Klaebu
Tel: +47 72 831166 Fax: +47 72 831255

Poland

**Ogólnopolskie Towarzystwo Ochrony
Ptakow (OTOP)**
P.O. Box 335, PL-80-958 Gdansk 50
Tel/Fax: +48 58 412693

Polish Society for the Protection of Birds
32 Cambridge Road, Girton, Cambridge
CB3 0PJ, England
Tel: 0223 277318

Portugal

CEAI – Centro de Estudos da Avifauna Iberica
Prolongamento da Av. Infante D. Henrique, Talhão 7 r/c, 7000 Évora, Portugal
Tel: 351-66-746102
Email: ceai@geocities.com
http://www.geocities.com/RainForest/5626/

The Portuguese Society for the Study of Birds (SPEA)
SPEA, Rua da Vitoria, 53, 2-Dto, 1100 Lisboa, Portugal
Tel/Fax: +351.1.3431847

Associaçao Cientifica para a Conservaçao das Aves de Rapina
Apto. 105, 2775 Carcavelos, Portugal

Romania

Societatea Ornitologica Romana (SOR)
Str Gheorghe Dima 49/2, RO-3400 Cluj
Tel/Fax: +40 64 438086

Slovenia

Ixobrychus, Ornithological Society
http://stenar.arnes.si/guest/kpornitold1/index.html

Spain

CCO (Catalan centre of ornithology)
c/o Montserrat 125, 08915 Badalona (Barcelonès)
Tel/Fax: (93) 3983572
Email: cco@mx3.redestb.es

CCO-P (Catalan center of ornithology-West)
Oficina de correus 25185 La Granja d'Escarp (Segrià)
Tel: (909) 410334
Email: cco.ponent@gratismail.com

Ornithological Station of Baix Cinca
Mas Moixons s/n, 50170 Mequinensa (Baix Cinca)
Tel: (909) 410334
Email: natura.baixcinca@bcn.servicom.es

Spanish Society of Ornithology
Dr. Mario Diaz Esteban, Departamento de Ecologia, Facultad de Biologia, Universidad Complutense, E-28040 Madrid, Spain
Tel: +1 394 50 84 Fax: +1 394 50 81
Email: mdiazbio@eucmax.sim.ucm.es

SVO (Valencian society of ornithology)
Gran via marquès del Turia 28, 46005 Valencia, Valencien Country

Sweden

Club 300
Email: tommy.eriksson@calliope.se
http://www.club300.se/

Ornitologiska Förening Conservation, Göteborgs
Box 166, 421 22 Västra Frölunda, Sweden
http://www.tripnet.se/gof/
Email: skoog@tripnet.se

Scandinavian Ornithological Society
Erik Hirschfeld, Södra Förstdsgatan 62, 211 43 Malmö
Tel/Fax: 040-23 74 35
Email:e.hirschfeld@swipnet.se
http://www.skof.se/

Scandinavian Ornithologists' Union
Dept. Animal Ecology, Ecology Building, S-223 62 Lund, Sweden

Skåne's Ornithological Society, SKOF
http://www.algonet.se/~skof/eindex.htm

Swedish Bird Association (Sveriges Ornitologiska Forening)
Skeppargatan 19, Box 14219, S-104 40, Stockholm, Sweden
Tel: 86-62-6434

Switzerland

La Societe Romande pour l'Etude et la Protection des Oiseaux
Claude Guex, rue des Eaux-Vives 78,
CH-1207 Geneva, Switzerland

Turkey

Raptor Research Group Turkey (YIKAT/RRGT)
http://www.geocities.com/Rain Forest/Vines/7047/index.html

United Kingdom

Army Ornithological Society
Rose Cottage, Bottesford, Pewsey, Wilts
SN9 6LU, England
Tel: 01252 349466

Aviornis
Bucephala, Lapwater Lane, Holbeach St.
Marks, Spalding, Lincs PE12 8EX, England
Tel: 01406 701420

Barn Owl Trust
Waterleat, Ashburton, Devon TQ13 7HU,
England
Tel: 01364 653026

Bird Stamp Society
9 Cowley Dr., Worthy Down, Winchester,
Hants SO21 2QW, England
Fax: 01962 887423

British Falconers' Club
Home Farm, Hints, Tamworth, Staffs
B78 3DW, England
Tel: –1543 481737

British Ornithologists' Club
Dene Cottage, West Harting, Petersfield,
Hants GU13 5PA, England
Tel: 01730 825280

British Ornithologists' Union
The Natural History Museum, Tring,
Hertfordshire HP23 6AP, England
Tel: 01442 890080 Fax: 01442 890693
http://www.bou.org.uk/

British Trust for Ornithology
The Nannery, Nannery Place, Thetford,
Norfolk IP24 2P4, England
Tel: 0842 750050

British Waterfowl Association
Gill Cottage, New Gill, Bishopdale,
Leyburn, N Yorks DL8 3TQ, England
Tel: 01969 663693

Edward Grey Institute of Field Ornithology
Dept. of Zoology, South Parks Road, Oxford
OX1 3PS, England
Tel: 01865 271275

Gibraltar Ornithological & Natural History Society
Gibraltar Natural History Field Centre,
Jews' Gate, Upper Rock Nature Reserve,
P.O. Box 843, Gibraltar
Tel: (+350) 72639 – Fax: (+350) 74022
Email: gonhs@gibnet.gi
http://gibnet.gi/~gonhs/

Golden Oriole Group
5 Bury Lane, Haddenham, Ely, Cambs
CB6 3PR, England
Tel: 01353 740540

Hawk and Owl Trust
c/o Birds of Prey Section, London Zoo,
Regent's Park, London NW1 4RY, England
Tel: 71 722 3333

Knutsford Ornithological Society
Email: tony@usher.u-net.com
http://www.usher.u-net.com/

Manx Ornithological Society
Water Edge, Lime Street, Port St. Mary,
Isle of Man IM9 5EF
Tel: 01624 834015

National Birds of Prey Centre
Newent, Glos GL18 1JJ, England
Tel: 01531 820286

Northwest Raptor Protection Group
Email: conservation@raptor.uk.com
http://www.information-
bureau.uk.com/nwrpg/

Royal Air Force Ornithological Society
RAFOS, MOD DEO (L) Conservation,
Blandford House, Farnborough Road,
Aldershot, Hants GU11 2HA, England

Royal Naval Birdwatching Society
19 Downlands Way, South Wonston,
Winchester, Hants SO21 3HS, England
Tel: 01962 885258

Royal Society for the Protection of Birds
The Lodge, SANDY, Bedfordshire,
SG19 2DL, England
Tel: (44) (0)1767 680551
Email: bfisk@aol.com
http://members.aol.com/bfisk/rspb.htm

Scottish Ornithologists' Club
21 Regent Terrace, Edinburgh
EH7 5B2, Scotland
Tel: 0131 556 6042

Seabird Group
SNH, Ground Floor, Stewart Buildings,
Alexandra Wharf, Lerwick, Shetland ZE1 0LL

Sheffield Bird Study Group
Email: a.j.morris@sheffield.ac.uk
http://www.shef.ac.uk/uni/projects/sbsg/

UK400 Club
8 Sandycroft Rd., Little Chalfont,
Amersham, Bucks HP6 6QL, England
01494 763 0101
webman@uk400.demon.co.uk

Wader Study Group
c/o BTO, The Nunnery, Thetford, Norfolk
IP24 2PU, England
Email: rodwest@thenet.co.uk

Welsh Ornithological Society
Crud yr Awel, Bowls Rd., Blaenporth,
Ceredigion SA43 2AR, Wales
Tel: 01239 811561

Wildfowl & Wetlands Trust
Slimbridge, Gloucester GL2 7B2, England
Tel: 01453 890333

NORTH AMERICA

Canada

Association des amateurs d'hirondelles du Québec
714 chemin Authier, Ste. Hilaire, QC
J3G 4S6, Canada
Tel: 514-464-6094
Fax: 514-464-5441
Email: hironbec@microtec.net
http://www.ivic.qc.ca/~dcampbel/aahq

Avian Science and Conservation Centre
Macdonald Campus of McGill University,
21,111 Lakeshore Road, Ste. Anne de
Bellevue, QC H9X 3V9, Canada
Tel: 514-398-7760
Fax: 514-398-7990
Email: bird@nrs.mcgill.ca

Bird Studies Canada
P.O. Box 160, Port Rowan, ON N0E 1M0
Tel: (519) 586 3531 Fax: (519) 586 3532
Email: bsc@nornet.on.ca mswb@mail.
nornet.on.ca iba@nornet.on.ca

British Columbia Field Ornithologists
P.O. Box 8059, Victoria, BC, Canada
V8W 3R7
Email: ambuhler@coastnet.com
Tel: (250) 744-2521 Fax: (250) 952-2180

British Columbia Waterfowl Society
5191 Robertson Road, Delta, BC V4K 3N2
Tel: (604) 946-6980

The Canadian World Parrot Trust
P.O. Box 29, Mount Hope, ON, Canada,
L0R 1W0
Email: cwparrot@worldchat.com
http://wchat.on.ca/parrot/cwparrot.htm

Club des ornithologues de Québec
http://www.mediom.qc.ca:80/coq/home.html

Ducks Unlimited Canada
1190 Waverley Street, Winnipeg, MN
R3T 2E2
Tel: (204) 477-1760

Edmonton Bird Club
Box 1111, Edmonton, AB T5J 2M1

**Étude des Populations d'Oiseaux du
Québec (EPOQ)**
194 Ouellet, Rimouski, PQ, G5L 4R5
Tel: (418) 723-1880

The Greater Toronto Raptor Watch
P.O. Box 14555, 75 Bayly Street West, Ajax,
ON, L1S 7L4

Le club des bécassiers du Québec
789-24ième ave., Lachine, QC H8S 3W4,
Canada
Tel: 514-637-8445

Manitoba Naturalists Society
MNS Office, 401-63 Albert Street,
Winnipeg, MN R3B 1G4
Tel: (204) 943-9029
Email: cward@pangea.ca
http://www.wilds.mb.ca/mns/birder/index.
html

**Natural History Society of Prince Edward
Island**
Box 2346, Charlottetown, PEI C1A 1R4

New Brunswick Federation of Naturalists
c/o New Brunswick Museum, 277 Douglas
Avenue, Saint John, NB E2K 1E5
Tel: (506) 693-1196

Nova Scotia Bird Society
c/o Nova Scotia Museum of Natural
History, 1747 Summer Street, Halifax, NS
B3H 3A6
Tel: (902) 429-4610
Email: ip-bird@chebucto.ns.ca
http://www.cfn.cs.dal.ca/Recreation/
NS-BirdSoc/nsbsmain.html

Ontario Field Ornithologists
Box 62014, Burlington Mall Postal Outlet,
Burlington, ON L7R 4K2
Email: ofo@interlog.com
http://www.interlog.com/~ofo/

The Owl Foundation
4117 – 21st Street, R.R. 1 Vineland, Station,
ON L0R 2EO, Canada
Tel: 905-562-5986

Partners in Flight – Canada
P.O. Box 79040, Hull, PQ J8Y 6V2

**The Province of Quebec Society for the
Protection of Birds/
La Société Québécoise de Protection des
Oiseaux**
P.O. Box 43, Station B, Montreal, PQ H3B 3J5
Tel: (514) 637-2141

Saskatchewan Natural History Society
Box 414, Raymore, SK S0A 3J0
Tel: (306) 746-4544

Toronto Ornithological Club
560 Blythwood Road, Toronto, ON M4N 1B5

**Union Québécoise de réhabilitation des
oiseaux de proie (UQROP)**
C.P. 246, Ste. Hyacinthe, QC J2S 7B6, Canada
Tel: 514-345-8521
Fax: 514-778-8110

Vancouver Island Birding
http://qb.island.net/~bfest/birder.htm

Vancouver Parks Birding
http://www.gvrd.bc.ca/go/todo/bird.html

The Yukon Bird Club
Box 31054, Whitehorse, YT, Canada Y1A 5P7
Email: ceckert@yknet.yk.ca
http://www.yukonweb.wis.net/
community/ybc/

United States

American Backyard Bird Society
Box 10046, Rockville, MD 20849
Tel: (301) 309-1431

American Bird Conservancy
1250 24th Street NW, Suite 400,
Washington, DC 20037
Tel: (202) 778-9666 Fax: (202) 778-9778
Email: abc@abcbirds.org

American Birding Association
P.O. Box 6599, Colorado Springs, CO 80934
Tel: (719) 578-1614 1 800 835-2473
Fax: (719) 578-1480
Email: member@aba.org
http://www.americanbirding.org/

American Ornithologists' Union
c/o Division of Birds MRC 116,
National Museum of Natural History,
Washington, DC 20560
Tel: (202) 357-1300
Email:aou@sivm.si.edu
http://pica.wru.umt.edu/AOU/AOU.html

Archbold Biological Station
Fred E. Lohrer, P.O. Box 2057,
Old State Road, 8, Lake Placid, FL 33882
Tel: (941) 465-2571 Fax: (941) 699-1927
Email: flohrer@archbold-station.org
Web: www.archbold-station.org

Association of Field Ornithologists, Inc.
C. Ray Chandler, Dept. of Biology, Georgia
Southern Univ., Statesboro, GA 30460
Email: beason@uno.cc.geneseo.edu
http://www.nmnh.si.edu/BIRDNET/AFO/
index.html

Birdlife International (U.S Office)
c/o World Wildlife Fund, 1250 24th Street,
NW, Washington, DC 20037
Tel: (202) 778-9563

The Brooks Bird Club, Inc.
707 Warwood Avenue, Wheeling, WV 26003

The Canvasback Society
Box 101, Gates Mills, OH 44040
Tel: (216) 443-2340

Carolina Raptor Center, Inc.
P.O. Box 16443, Charlotte, NC 28297-6443,
USA

Center for the Study of Tropical Birds
218 Conway, San Antonio, TX 78209
Tel: (512) 828-5306

The Cooper Ornithological Society
Ornithological Societies of North America
(O.S.N.A.), P.O. Box 1897, Lawrence, KS
66044-8897
Tel: (213) 740-2777
Email: rcurry@email.vill.edu
http://www.nmnh.si.edu/BIRDNET/COS/

The Cornell Lab of Ornithology
159 Sapsucker Woods Road, Ithaca, NY
14850
Tel: (607) 254-2473
http://birds.cornell.edu/

Delta Waterfowl Foundation
102Wilmot Road, Suite 410, Deerfield, IL
60015
Tel: (708) 940-7776

Ducks Unlimited, Inc.
One Waterfowl Way, Long Grove, IL 60047
Tel: (708) 438-4300

The Eagle Foundation
300 East Hickory Street, Apple River, IL
61001
Tel: (815) 594-2259

**George Miksch Sutton Avian Research
Center, Inc.**
Box 2007, Bartlesville, OK 74005
Tel: (918) 336-7778

Hawk Migration Association of North America
c/o Secretary, Box 3482, Lynchburg, VA 24503
Tel: (804) 847-7811

Hawk Mountain Sanctuary Association
RD 2, Box 191, Kempton, PA 19529-6961
Tel: (610) 756-6961

HawkWatch International, Inc
Box 660, Salt Lake City, UT 84110
Tel: (801) 254-8511

Inland Bird Banding Association
RD 2, Box 26, Wisner, NE 68791
Tel: (402) 529-6679

International Wild Waterfowl Association
5614 River Styx Road, Medina, OH 44256

Kansas Ornithological Society
1425 S. Wichita, Wichita, KS 67213
Tel: (316) 265-4059
Email: barnowls@juno.com

Migratory Bird Center
Mary Deinlein, Smithsonian Migratory Bird
Center, National Zoo, Washington, DC
20008
Tel: 202-673-4908 Fax: 202-673-4916
Email: ani@erols.com
http://www.si.edu/natzoo/zooview/smbc/s
mbchome.htm

National Audubon Society (Central Bureau)
700 Broadway, New York, NY 10003
Tel: 212 979-3000
Email: expert@list.audubon.org
http://www.audubon.org/

National Audubon Society (Sanctuary Department)
93 West Cornwall Road, Sharon, CT 06069
Tel: (203) 364-0048

National Bird-Feeding Society
2218 Crabtree, Northbrook, IL 60065
Tel: (708) 272-0135

National Flyway Council
Wyoming Game and Fish Department,
5400 Bishop Boulevard, Cheyenne, WY
82006
Tel: (307) 777-7735

National Foundation to Protect America's Eagle
Box 120206, Nashville, TN 37212
Tel: (800) 2-EAGLES (615) 847-4171

The National Wild Turkey Foundation
Wild Turkey Building, Box 530, Edgefield,
SC 29824
Tel: (803) 637-3106

Neotropical Migratory Bird Conservation
The National Fish and Wildlife Foundation,
1120 Connecticut Avenue NW, Suite 900,
Washington, DC 20036
Tel: 202-857-0166 Fax: 202-857-0162
Email: email info@nfwf.org
http://www.nfwf.org/nfwfne.htm

New Mexico Ornithological Society
1108 Columbia Drive NE, Albuquerque,
NM 87106
Email: bneville@unm.edu
http://biology001.unm.edu/~nmos/

North American Crane Working Group
2550 North Diers Avenue, Suite H,
Grand Island, NE 68803
Tel: (308) 384-4633

North American Falconers Association
305 Long Avenue, North Aurora, IL 60542

North American Loon Fund
Six Lily Pond Road, Gilford, NH 03246
Tel: (603) 528-4711

Pacific Seabird Group
Jan Hodder, Oregon Institute of Marine
Biology, University of Oregon, P.O. Box 5389,
Charleston, OR 97420
Email: sspeich@azstarnet.com
http://www.nmnh.si.edu/BIRDNET/PacBirds/

Pheasants Forever, Inc.
Box 75473, St. Paul, MN 55175
Tel: (612) 481-7142

Platte River Whooping Crane Trust
2550 North Diers Avenue, Suite H, Grand
Island, NE 68803
Tel: (308) 384-4633

**Prairie Grouse Technical Council Wildlife
Research Council**
317 West Prospect, Fort Collins, CO 80526
Tel: (303) 484-2836

Purple Martin Conservation Association
Edinboro University of Pennsylvania,
Edinboro, PA 16444
Tel: (814) 734-4420

Quail Unlimited, Inc.
Box 10041, Augusta, GA 30903
Tel: (803) 637-5731

The Raptor Center
University of Minnesota, 1920 Fitch
Avenue, St. Paul, MN 55108

Raptor Education Foundation, Inc.
21901 East Hampden Avenue, Aurora, CO
80013
Tel: (303) 680-8500

**Raptor Society of Metropolitan
Washington**
P.O. Box 482, Annandale, VA 22003, USA

Roger Tory Peterson Institute
110 Marvin Parkway, Jamestown, NY 14701
Tel: (716) 665-BIRD

The Ruffed Grouse Society
451 McCormick Road, Coraopolis, PA 15108
Tel: (412) 262-4044

Society for the Preservation of Birds of Prey
Box 66070, Los Angeles, CA 90066
Tel: (310) 397-8216

The Trumpeter Swan Society
3800 County Road 24, Maple Plain, MN
55359
Tel: (612) 476-4663

The Turkey Vulture Society
Bill Kohlmoos, President, P.O. Box 50300,
Reno, NV 89513
Email: vulture@accutek.com
Web: http:/www.accutek.com/vulture

Watchlist Bird Species at Risk
Email: vmuehter@audubon.org
http://www.audubon.org/bird/watch/

Western Field Ornithologists
300 East University Boulevard, Suite 120,
Tucson, AZ 87505
Tel: (602) 629-0510

**Whooping Crane Conservation
Association, Inc.**
1007 Carmel Avenue, Lafayette, LA 70501
Tel: (318) 234-6339

Wild Bird Feeding Institute
1441 Shermer Road, Northbrook, IL 60062
Tel: (312) 272-0135

Wildfowl Foundation
1101 14th Street NW, Suite 725,
Washington, DC 20005
Tel: (202) 371-1808

The Wildfowl Trust of North America, Inc.
Box 519, Grasonville, MD 21638
Tel: (410) 827-6694

The Wilson Ornithological Society
Museum of Zoology, University of
Michigan, Ann Arbor, MI, 48109-1079
Tel: (202) 357-1970
http://www.ummz.lsa.umich.edu/birds/
wos.html

Women in Ornithology Resource Group
http://www-rci.rutgers.edu/~tsipoura/
worg.html

World Bird Sanctuary
Box 270270, St. Louis, MO 63127
Tel: (314) 398-6193

World Pheasant Association of U.S.A., Inc.
15545 Regaldo Street, Hacienda Heights,
CA 91745
Tel: (602) 455-5522

The Xerces Society
Ten SW Ash Street, Portland, OR 97204
Tel: (503) 222-2788

AUSTRALASIA

The Australasian Wader Studies Group
Brenda Murlis, 34 Centre Road, Vermont,
Victoria 3133, Australia
Email: raou@raou.com.au
http://avoca.vicnet.net.au/~birdsaus/emu/
emu.html

The Australasian Seabird Group
Paul Scofield, ASG Secretary/Treasurer,
RAOU Head Office, 415 Riversdale Road,
Hawthorn East, Victoria 3123, Australia
Email: raou@raou.com.au
http://avoca.vicnet.net.au/~birdsaus/emu/
emu.html

Australasian Raptor Association
Flora's Cottage, Fairy Glen Road,
Collinsvale, Tasmania 7012, Australia
Tel: 039 8822622 Fax: 039 92282677
Email: membership@raou.com.au
http://www.tasweb.com.au/ara/index.htm

Australian Bird Study Association
P.O. Box A313, Sydney South, NSW 2000

Birds Australia (Form.: Royal Australian
Ornithologists' Union)
415 Riversdale Road, Hawthorn East,
Victoria 3123, Australia
Tel: (03) 9 882 2622 Fax: (03) 9 882 2677
International callers: 61 3 9882 2622
Fax: 61 3 9882 2677)
Email: raou@raou.com.au
http://www.vicnet.net.au/~birdsaus

Canberra Ornithology Group
The Secretary, Canberra Ornithologists
Group Inc., P.O. Box 301, Civic Square Act
2608
Email: fennellp@pcug.org.au
http://www.canberrabirds.dynamite.com.au/

New Guinea Bird Society
P.O. Box 1598, Boroko

Ornithological Society of New Zealand
c/o Dominion Museum, Wellington

Raptor Association of New Zealand
62 Menin Road, Onekawa, Napier 434-102,
New Zealand

**Royal Forest and Bird Preservation Society
of New Zealand**
P.O. Box 631, Wellington

Society for the Preservation of Raptors
Avicultural Society of Western Australia,
13 Rangeview Road, High Wycombe 6057,
Western Australia, Australia

Victorian Ornithological Research Group
Arnis Dzedins, P.O. Box 1000, Blind Bight,
Victoria 3980
Email: lec@bom.gov.au
http://www.vicnet.net.au/~vorg/lecvorg.htm

SOUTH AND CENTRAL AMERICA, CARIBBEAN

Asociacion Ornithilogica del Plata
25 de Mayo, 749-2° Piso, oficina 6,
1002 Buenos Aires
Tel/Fax: +54 1 312 8958

Asociacion Audubon de El Salvador
1a C.P. Condominios Montemaria, Edificio
'A' 2da planta No. 2, San Salvador
Tel: +503 2980811 Fax: 503-2749180
Email: harrouch@es.com.sv

The Bahamas National Trust
P.O. Box N-4105, Nassau, Bahamas
Tel: (809) 393 1317 Fax: (809) 393 4978
Email: bnt@bahamas.net.bs
http://flamingo.bahamas.net.bs/environment/

Belize Audubon Society
12 Fort St., P.O. Box 1001, Belize City
Tel: +501 2 77369 Fax: +501 2 34985

BirdLife Quito Office
Casilla postal 17-17-717, Quito, Ecuador
Tel: 593-2-443261
Email: birdlife@ecnet.ec
http://www.latinsynergy.org/birdlife.html

Brazilian Ornithological Society
Caixa Postal 238 – 86870-000 Ivaiporã-PR
–Brasil
Email: salviano@ao.com.br
http://www.ao.com.br/

CIPA-MEX (Mexico)
Depto de Zoologia, Instituto de Biologia,
UNAM AP, 70-153, Mexico DF 04510
Tel: +52 5 622 5704 Fax: +52 5 550 0164
Email: escalant@servidor.unam.mx

Dominican Ornithological Society
Mus. National de Historia Natural, Ave.
Cesar N. Penson, Santa Domingo

Falklands Conservation
http://www.falklands-nature.demon.co.uk

Fundacion Ornitologica del Ecuador
(CECIA)
El Nacional 304 y El Telegrafo,
PO Box 17-17-906, Quito
Tel/Fax: +593 2 433238

Gosse Bird Club (Jamaica)
Email: gosse@infochan.com
http://www.angelfire.com/ga/GosseBirdClub/
index.html

GUPECA
Casilla de Correo 6955, Montevideo, Uruguay
Tel: 598-2-750400 Fax: 598-2-409973
Email: bentos@genetica.edu.uy gual@fcien.
edu.uy

Neotropical Birdclub
c/o The Lodge, Sandy, Bedfordshire,
SG19 2DL, England
Email: balchin@radstone.co.uk
http://www.neotropicalbirdclub.org/

Panama Audubon Society
Box 2026, Balboa-Ancon, Republic of
Panama
Tel: +507 224 4740
Email: audupan@pananet.com
http://www.pananet.com/audubon/
Raptor Group / Grupo Rapaces
Fundacion vida Silvestre Argintina,
L.N.ALEM 968, PB 1001 Capital Federal,
Buenos Aires, Argentina

STINASU
PO Box 436, Paramaribo, Suriname
Tel: 597-271856 Fax: 597-422555

Union de Ornitologos de Chile (Chile)
Casilla 572-11, Santiago
Tel: +56 2 271 2865 ext. 257
Fax: +56 2 272 7363
Email: geotec@huelen.reuna.cl

Bird-Banding Organizations

EUROPE

General

Euring: The European Union for Bird Ringing
Netherlands Institute of Ecology,
P.O. Box 40, NL-6666 ZG Heteren
http://www.aki.ku.dk/zmuc/ver/ringeuri.htm

Belgium

Durme 5 Ringing Group, Belgian Ringing Scheme
Email: Kearsley.Lyndon@ping.be

Denmark

Copenhagen Bird Ringing Centre
Copenhagen Ringing Centre, Zoological Museum, Universitetsparken 15, DK-2100 Copenhagen
http://www.aki.ku.dk/zmuc/ver/ringing.htm

England

Burton & Holder Ringing Group
Phillip Burton
Email: PJKBurton@aol.com

Durham Ringing Group
Robin M. Ward
Email: R.M.Ward@durham.ac.uk

East Yorkshire Ringing Group
Peter J. Dunn
Email: p.dunn@virgin.net

Gordano Valley Ringing Group
Lyndon Roberts
Email: lroberts@dircon.co.uk

Loganhurst Ringing Group
Dr. Steve Christmas
Email: sechris@liverpool.ac.uk

Morcambe Bay Wader Group
Jack Sheldon at Barrow
Email: Wes@cygnus.airtime.co.uk

North-west England Swan Study Group
Wes Halton, 5 Westland Ave, Farnworth, Bolton, Lancs. BL4 9SR
Tel: 01204 709302
Email: Wes@cygnus.airtime.co.uk
http://www.airtime.co.uk/users/cygnus/swanstud.htm

Rye Meads Ringing Group
Paul Roper, 1 Dewhurst Old School, Churchgate, Cheshunt Herts EN8 9WB
Tel: 01992 640388
Email emmens@dial.pipex.com
http://dspace.dial.pipex.com/town/avenue/kbu36/#RMRG

Shorebird Team, University of Durham
Robin M. Ward
Email: R.M.Ward@durham.ac.uk

Tees Ringing Group
Robin M. Ward
Email: R.M.Ward@durham.ac.uk

Finland

Laajalahti Ringing Group
Martin Helin
Email: martin.helin@posti.telebox.fi

Raasio Wader Ringing Station
http://www.jmp.fi/~pslty/raasio/raasio_en.html

Ireland

Cape Clear Bird Observatory
Clive Hutchinson
Email: hutch@indigo.ie

Italy

Dept. of Biology Ringing Group (Univ. of Ferrara)
Contact: Dr. Stefano Volponi Ph.D., Dept. of Biology, Univ. of Ferrara, Via L. Borsari, 46, I-44100 Ferrara
Email: col@dns.unife.it

Isola della Cona
Paul Tout, 1 Dewhurst Old School, Churchgate, Cheshunt, Herts EN8 9WB
Tel: 01992 640388
Email: tout@spin.it
http://www.spin.it/~tout/ENGCONA1.HTM#Bird-ringing

Netherlands

Vogel Ring Groep Schiermonnikoog
VRG Schiermonnikoog, Langestreek 32, NL-9166 LC Schiermonnikoog, The Netherlands
Email: holmer@worldonline.nl
http://www.geocities.com/RainForest/6549/vrgs.htm

Norway

Aust-Agder Ringing Group
c/o Dagfinn Dahl, Vipeveien 12, 4820 Froland

Bergen Ringing Group
c/o Tor Bjarte Reigstad, 5240 Valestrandsfossen

Bodø Ringing Group
c/o Harald Misund, Tyttebærveien 18, 8018 Mørkved

Drammen og Omegn Ringing Group
c/o M. Winness, Underlia 57, 3024 Drammen

Eiker Ringing Group
c/o Anders Hals, Furua 12, 3320 Vestfossen

Elverum Ringing Group
Boks 90, 2401 Elverum

Grenland Ringing Group
Boks 1076, 3704 Skien

Hadsel Ringing Group
c/o Vidar Bjørg, Seljeveien 5, 8490 Melbu

Hemsedal Ringing Group
v/ Bent Fjellheim, 3560 Hemsedal

Hornnes Ringing Group
c/o Lars Breistøl, 4670 Hornnes

Jæren Ringing Group
c/o Magnar Bø, Eskelandssvingene 17, 4028 Stavanger

Jomfruland Bird Observatory
Kragero, SE Norway.
http://www.hit.no/~u941436/jomfeng.htm

Karmøy Ringing Group
v/ Arnt Kvinnesland, Blikshavn, 4280 Skudesneshavn

Kragerø Ringing Group
c/o Øyvind Olsen, Revesnaret 5, 3790 Helle

Kristiansand Ringing Group
Boks 2112, 4601 Kristiansand S

Kvæfjord Ringing Group
c/o Gustav Schwer, Eldaskogveien 1, 9410 Borkenes

Lista Ringing Group
Boks 171, 4560 Vanse

Lofoten Ringing Group
v/Harald Våge, Boks 316, 8370 Leknes

Mandal Ringing Group
Boks 475, 4501 Mandal

Mjøsen Ringing Group
v/Dag Fjeldstad, 2634 Fåvang

Nord-Trøndelag Ringing Group
c/o Knut Krogstad, Feltspatveien 10, 7500 Stjørdal

Odda Ringing Group
Boks 303, 5751 Odda

Os Ringing Group
c/o Jimmy Øvredal, 5200 Os

Oslo & Akershus Ringing Group
v/Tollef Helleren, L. Karstensvei 4,
1064 Oslo

Rana Ringing Group
c/o Kjell A. Meyer, Risegrana 7,
8610 Grubhei

Salten Ringing Group
Postboks 111, 8150 Ørnes

Setesdal Ringing Group
v/ Lars Breistøl, 4670 Hornnes

Sunnmøre Ringing Group
v/ Kjell Mork, Soot, 5060 Hareid

Sveio Ringing Group
c/o Frank Nilsen, 5526 Auklandshamn

Tromsø Ringing Group
c/o Karl Birger Strann, Gneisveien 16,
9022 Krokelvdalen

Trysil Ringing Group
c/o Bjørn E. Foyn, Nystedsvingen 10,
2420 Trysil

Ulefoss Ringing Group
Rune Solvang, Kåsene 27, 3745 Ulefoss

Utsira Ringing Group
Boks 23, 5515 Utsira

Scotland

Aberdeen University Ringing Group
Paul Doyle
Email: p.doyle@aberdeen.ac.uk

Grampian Ringing Group
R. Rae, 11, Millend, Newburgh,
Aberdeenshire

Lothian Ringing Group
Clive Walton
E mail: Clive.Walton@trinity.edin.sch.uk

Spain

**Grup d'Anellament del Grup Balear
d'Ornitologia i Defensa de la Naturalesa
(GOB)**
Pere Garcás
Email: gob@ocea.es

**Grup Catala d'Anellament, Catalan Group
of Ringers**
Ricard Gutierrez
Email: argutbe@correu.gencat.es
Gran Via de les Corts Catalanes,
612-614 2n, E-08007 Barcelona
Fax: +34-3-3046760

Ringing group of Calldetenes-Osona
Plaça 11 de Setembre s/n, 08519
Calldetenes, Catalonia
Contact: Jordi Baucells Colomer,
Tel 8891697

Sweden

Bird station Stora Fjaederaegg
Per Hansson
Email: Per.Hansson@ssko.slu.se

Haparanda Sandskdr Bird Ringing Station
http://peters-mac.adm.luth.se/HSFShem.2

Takern Fieldstation
Tåkerns Fältstation, Box 204595 22, Mjölby
Tel +046142 145 69
Email: lars.gezelius@e.lst.se
http://www.lysator.liu.se/~ngn/tfhome.html

AUSTRALASIA

The Australian Bird & Bat Banding Scheme
Australian Nature Conservation Agency,
GPO Box 8, CANBERRA, ACT, 2601

http://kaos.erin.gov.au/life/species/fauna/
flightlines/flightline s.html

MIDDLE EAST

Israel Bird Ringing Center
Tisch Family Zoological Gardens,
P.O. Box 898, Jerusalem 91008

Tel: +972-2-6430111 Fax: +972-2-6430122
Email: jshamoun@netmedia.net.il

NORTH AMERICA

General

Atlantic Bird Observatory
(Bon Portage Island and Seal Island, NS)
Phil Taylor
Dept. of Biology, Acadia University
Wolfville, NS, B0P 1X0
Tel: 902-585-1287 Fax: 902-585-1059
Email: philip.taylor@acadian.ca

Bird Banding Laboratory
U.S. Geological Survey-Biological Resources
Division, Patuxent Wildlife Research Center
12100 Beech Forest Road, Suite 4037,
Laurel, MD 20708-4037
Tel: 301-497-5790 Fax: 301-497-5717
Email: BBL@nbs.gov
Email for Bird Band Reports only:
Bandreports@patuxent.nbs.gov
http://www.pwrc.nbs.gov/bbljohn.htm

Canada

**Canadian Wildlife Service Bird
Banding Office**
Bird Banding Office
National Wildlife Research Centre
Canadian Wildlife Service
Ottawa, ON, K1A 0H3
Tel: 819-997-4213
Fax: 819-953-6612
Email: Lucie.Metras@ec.gc.ca

Mountsberg Banding Operation,
Mountsberg Conservation Area,
2259 Milborough Line, Campbellville, ON
L0P 1B0
Tel: 905-854-2220 (Ask for Martin Wernaart)
Email: buffalo@worldchat.com

Toronto Bird Observatory
Lori Nicholls
Box 439, 253 College St.
Toronto, ON, M5T 1R5
Tel: 416-604-8843
Email: nkh.sin@netrover.com

Delta Marsh Bird Observatory
Heidi den Haan
Rural Route #1, Box 1,
Portage la Prairie, MB, R1N 3A1
Tel: (204) 239-4287 Fax: (204) 239-5950
Email: hdenhaan@cc.umanitoba.ca
http://www.umanitoba.ca/faculties/science/
delta_marsh/dmbo/dmbo.h tml

Beaverhill Bird Observatory Society (BBO)
P.O. Box 1418, Edmonton, AB, T5J 2N5
Tel: Geoff Holroyd (403)438-1462 Jason
Duxbury (403)430-1694
Email: jduxbury@gpu.srv.ualberta.ca
http://www.connect.ab.ca/~fan/fa02003.htm

Long Point Bird Observatory (Ontario)
Email: generalinfo@bsc-eoc.org
http://www.nornet.on.ca/~bsc/Lpbo.html

United States

Alaska Bird Observatory
Alaska Bird Observatory, P.O. Box 80505,
Fairbanks, AK 99708
Tel: (907) 451-7059
Email: birds@polarnet.com
http://www2.polarnet.com/~birds/

Braddock Bay Bird Observatory
(New York)
http://www.ornith.cornell.edu/Birding/ny/
western/Braddockinfo.htm l

Cape May Bird Observatory
P.O. Box 3, 701 East Lake Drive
Cape May Point, NJ 08210
Tel: 609-861-0700 Fax: 609-861-1651

Colorado Bird Observatory
13401 Piccadilly Road, Brighton, CO 80601
Tel: 303-659-4348 Fax: 303-659-5489
EMmail: COBIRDOB@AOL.COM
http://eelink.umich.edu/GAIN/RM.dir/
html.dir/entry.105.html

Golden Gate Raptor Observatory, (GGRO)
Building 201, Fort Mason, San Francisco,
CA 94123, USA
Tel: 415-331-0730 Fax: 415-331-7521
Email: ggro@ggnpa.org

The Hummer/Bird Study Group
P.O. Box 250, Clay, AL 35048-0250
Tel: 205/681-2888 Fax 205/681-1339
Email: HummerBSG@AOL.com
http://ourworld.compuserve.com/
homepages/Bill_Rogers_AL/humgrp.ht m

Manomet Bird Observatory
P.O. Box 1770 Manomet, MA 02345
Tel: (508) 224-6521 Fax: –9220
http://jasper.stanford.edu/OBFS/OBFS_Stat
ions/MA_Manomet_Bird_Obs erv._.html

Migratory Bird Banding: U.S. Fish and Wildlife Service
http://www.emtc.nbs.gov/http_data/
umr_refuge/umrlax/laxband.html

Monitoring Avian Productivity and Survivorship (MAPS) Program
http://www.im.nbs.gov/birds.html
Email: Sam_Droege@nbs.gov

The Point Reyes Bird Observatory (PRBO)
4990 Shoreline Highway, Stinson Beach,
CA 94970
Tel: 415-868-1221 Fax: 415-868-1946
Email: prbo@prbo.org
http://www.igc.org/prbo/

Rio Grande Valley Bird Observatory
P.O. Box 8125, Weslaco, TX 78599-8125
Tel: 956-969-2475
Email: rgvbo@geocities.com
http://www.geocities.com/RainForest/2240/

Rouge River Bird Observatory
Natural Areas Dept., University of
Michigan-Dearborn, Dearborn, MI 48128
http://www.umd.umich.edu/dept/
rouge_river/index.html

Southeastern Arizona Bird Observatory
P.O. Box 5521, Bisbee, AZ 85603-5521
Tel: (520) 432-1388
Email: sabo@SABO.org
http://www.sabo.org/

WhiteFish Point Bird Observatory
Michigan Audubon Society, P.O. Box 80527,
Lansing, MI 48908-0527
http://www.wpbo.org/home.htm

U.S. Fish and Wildlife Service Migratory Bird Offices:

California, Hawaii, Idaho, Nevada, Oregon
and Washington:
U.S. Fish and Wildlife Service, 911 N.E. 11th
Avenue, Portland OR 97232-4181
Tel: (503) 872-2715 Fax: (503) 231-2364

Arizona, New Mexico, Oklahoma, and Texas:
U.S. Fish and Wildlife Service, Box 709,
Albuquerque, NM 87103-0709
Tel: (505) 248-7882 Fax: (505) 248-7885

Illinois, Indiana, Iowa, Michigan, Minnesota, Missouri, Ohio, and Wisconsin:
U.S. Fish and Wildlife Service, Box 45, Federal Bldg., Ft. Snelling MN 55111-0045
Tel: (612) 725-3776 Fax: (612) 725-3013

Alabama, Arkansas, Florida, Georgia, Kentucky, Louisiana, Mississippi, North Carolina, Puerto Rico, South Carolina, and Tennessee:
U.S. Fish and Wildlife Service, Box 49208, Atlanta, GA 30359
Tel: (404) 679-7070 Fax: (404) 679-7285

Connecticut, Delaware, Maine, Maryland, Massachusetts, New Hampshire, New Jersey, New York, Pennsylvania, Rhode Island, Vermont, Virginia, and West Virginia:

U.S. Fish and Wildlife Service, Box 779, Hadley, MA 01035-0779
Tel: (303) 236-7890 Fax: (303) 236-7901

Colorado, Kansas, Montana, Nebraska, North Dakota, South Dakota, Utah, and Wyoming:
U.S. Fish and Wildlife Service, Box 25486 –DFC(69400), Denver CO 80225-0486
Tel: (907) 786-3300 Fax: (907) 786-3313

Alaska:
U.S. Fish and Wildlife Service, 1011 E. Tudor Rd Room 155, Anchorage, AK 99503-6199
Tel: (907) 786-3300 Fax: (907) 786-3313

Internet Links to Worldwide Birding

Bird Links
http://www.phys.rug.nl/mk/people/wpv/birdlink.html

The Bird Web
http://www.abdn.ac.uk/~nhi019/intro.html

Bird World
http://sdcd.gsfc.nasa.gov/test-bin/Jones.cgi/ISTO/Birdtracks/birdworld2/birdworld2.html

Birding British Columbia
http://www.iceonline.net/home/ianj3/bbc.html

Birding Canada
http://www.interlog.com/~gallantg/canada/index.html

Birding.com
http://www.birder.com/

Birding in Quebec
(Major site for Quebec, World Birders)
http://www.ntic.qc.ca/~nellus/quebangl.html

Birding on the Web
http://www-stat.wharton.upenn.edu/~siler/birding.html

BirdNet
http://www.nmnh.si.edu/BIRDNET/BIRDLINKS.html

Birdsite: The Center of the Bird World on the Web
http://www.birdsite.com/birdsite.html

Electronic Resources on Ornithology
http://www.chebucto.ns.ca/Environment/NHR/bird.html

Euro-BirdNet
http://www.netlink.co.uk/users/ag/ebn index.html

Ontario Birding
http://www.interlog.com/~gallantg/ontario.html

The O.W.L. The Ornithological Web Library
http://www.bright.net/~vfazio/the-owl.htm

Victoria Birding Online
http://www.islandnet.com/~boom/birding/

Discussion Groups

AviMonde
subscription: majordomo@cedep.net
message: subscribe AVIMONDE Your E-mail
posting: avimonde@cedep.net
contact address: Jean Laporte
(jlaporte@microtec.net)

BIRDING-AUS
Email to: majordomo@deakin.edu.au
Leave the Subject: line blank
In the Message: area type: subscribe birding-aus
web page:
http://www.deakin.edu.au/~russwood/

BIRDCHAT – birds, birding and birders
subscription: listserv@listserv.arizona.edu
message: subscribe BIRDCHAT Your Name
posting (semi-moderated) –
birdchat@listserv.arizona.edu

contact address: birdchat-request@listserv.
arizona.edu

BIRDERS of a FEATHER—CHAT "LIVE"
web page: http://www.ols.net/~dl4/

BirdServ ZiNgY Daily Bird Mail Reader
www.nbhc.com/birdmail.htm

ORNITH-L – scientific discussion on
ornithology: systematics, physiology, ecology, conservation, etc.
(not for birding or banding)
subscription: listserv@uafsysb.uark.edu
message: subscribe ORNITH-L Your Name
posting (moderated): address available
upon subscription
contact address: Jeanette Bider
(jbider@comp.uark.edu)

Rare Bird Reports

BIRD_RBA – Rare Bird Alerts
(for rarest records in North America)
subscription: listserv@listserv.arizona.edu
message: subscribe BIRD_RBA Your Name
posting: bird_rba@listserv.arizona.edu
contact address:
bird_rba-request@listserv.arizona.edu

BIRDCNTR – Rare Bird Alerts
(Central USA+CAN)
subscription: listserv@listserv.arizona.edu
message: subscribe BIRDCNTR Your Name
posting (moderated): birdcntr@listserv.
arizona.edu
contact address:
birdcntr-request@listserv.arizona.edu

BIRDEAST – Rare Bird Alerts
(Eastern USA+CAN)
subscription: listserv@listserv.arizona.edu
message: subscribe BIRDEAST Your Name
posting (moderated): birdeast@listserv.
arizona.edu
contact address:
birdeast-request@listserv.arizona.edu

BIRDWEST – Rare Bird Alerts
(Western USA+CAN)
subscription: listserv@listserv.arizona.edu
message: subscribe BIRDWEST Your Name
posting (moderated): birdwest@listserv.
arizona.edu
contact address:
birdwest-request@listserv.arizona.edu)

EBN (EuroBirdNet) –
European bird news and trip reports
send request to Martin Helin
(Martin.Helin@otax.hut.fi)
posting: ebn@otax.tky.hut.fi
web page: http://www.pheromone.ekol.lu.se/
Eurobirdnet.html

Ontario Rare Birds
contact: Gord Gallant
www.interlog.com/~gallantg/recent.html

Quebec Rare Birds
contact: Nelson Roy
www.ntic.qc.ca/~nellus/hotbirds.html

Mailing Lists

REGIONAL

Arbird-L – Arkansas Birds (USA)
subscription: listserv@uafsysb.uark.edu
message: subscribe arbird-l Your Name
contact address: Kimberly Smith
(kgsmith@comp.uark.edu)

AZ-NM CHAT –
Arizona and New Mexico (USA)
subscription: listserv@listserv.arizona.edu
message: subscribe BIRDWG05 Your Name
posting: birdwg05@listserv.arizona.edu
contact address:
birdwg05-request@listserv.arizona.edu
web address: http://compstat.wharton.
upenn.edu:8001/~siler/azfile.html

BIRDING-AUS – Australia
subscription: majordomo@deakin.edu.au
message: subscribe birding-aus
posting: birding-aus@deakin.edu.au
contact address:
majordomo-owner@deakin.edu.au

Bloomington-birds –
Bloomington, Indiana (USA)
subscription: majordomo@ucs.indiana.edu
message: subscribe bloomington-birds

BW – Birdwatching (Turkey)
subscription: listproc@wasp.bio.metu.tr
message: subscribe BW Your Name

CALBIRD – California (USA)
subscription: listserv@pterodroma.kiwi.net
message: subscribe Calbird
posting: calbird@pterodroma.kiwi.net
web page: http://compstat.wharton.upenn.
edu:8001/~siler/calfile.html

BIRDING – Northern California (USA)
subscription: listproc@mail.mother.com
message: subscribe birding Your Name
posting: birding@mother.com

Carolinabirds –
North and South Carolina (USA)
subscription: majordomo@acpub.duke.edu
message: subscribe carolinabirds
posting: carolinabirds@acpub.duke.edu
contact:
Will Cook (cwcook@acpub.duke.edu)

CAYUGABIRDS-L –
Upstate New York (USA)
subscription: listproc@cornell.edu
message:
subscribe cayugabirds-l Your Real Name
posting: cayugabirds-l@cornell.edu
web page: http://compstat.wharton.upenn.
edu:8001/~siler/cayufile.html

COBIRDS – Colorado (USA)
subscription: listproc@lists.colorado.edu
message: subscribe cobirds Your Name
posting: cobirds@lists.colorado.edu
contact: Alan Versaw (btyw@kktc.com)

Genesee Valley Birds –
New York State (USA)
subscription: listproc@listproc.cc.geneseo.edu
message: sub geneseebirds-l Your Name
posting:
geneseebirds-l@listproc.cc.geneseo.edu

HKBWS (Hong Kong Birdwatching Society)
web page: http://home.hkstar.com/~hkbws/
index1.html

LABIRD-L – Louisiana (USA)
subscription: listserv@listserv.lsu.edu
message: subscribe labird-l Your Name
posting: labird-l@listserv.lsu.edu

MARVADEL – Maryland, Virginia,
Delaware, and adjacent regions (USA)
send request to John Tebbutt
(marvadel-request@amazon.ncsl.nist.gov)
posting: marvadel@amazon.ncsl.nist.gov

MassBird –
Massachusetts and New England (USA)
subscription: majordomo@world.std.com
message: subscribe massbird user@address.
here (your name)
posting: massbird@world.std.com
contact: Barbara Volkle
(Barb620@world.std.com)
web page: http://www.mdroid.com/~mikee/
mabird.html

Mex-Bird – Mexico
subscription: listserv@list.audubon.org
message:
subscribe mex-bird firstname lastname
posting: mex-bird@list.audubon.org

MissBird – Mississippi (USA)
subscription: listserv@sunset.backbone.
olemiss.edu
message:
subscribe missbird firstname lastname
posting:
missbird@sunset.backbone.olemiss.edu
contact: Martin Davis
(missbird@sunset.backbone.olemiss.edu)

MnBirdNet – Minnesota (USA)
subscription:
MnBird-request@linux.winona.msus.edu
message:
subscribe (info for more informations)
contact: Carol Schumacher
(wncarols@linux.winona.msus.edu)
web page:
http://linux.winona.msus.edu/mnbird/digest

Montreal Birds
contact: Louise Courtemanche
www.interlog.com/~gallantg/canada/queint.
html

NYSBirds-L – New York State (USA)
subscription: listproc@CORNELL.EDU
message:
subscribe NYSBirds-L your real name
posting: NYSBirds-L@Cornell.edu
web page: http://www.ornith.cornell.edu/
Birding/ny/NYSBirds-L_info.html

Nathistory – (India)
subscription: listproc@lists.princeton.edu
message: subscribe nathistory-india
your_email_address your_name
contact address: Vivek Tiwari
(vivek@ee.princeton.edu)

NatureNB – (New Brunswick) (Canada)
subscription: listserv@listserv.unb.ca
message: subscribe NatureNB your name
posting: naturenb@listserv.unb.ca

NatureNS – (Nova Scotia) (Canada)
subscription: majordomo@chebucto.ns.ca
message:
subscribe NatureNS Your-Email-Address
posting: natureNS@chebucto.ns.ca
contact address: NatureNS Listowner

OBOL (Oregon Birder On-Line) (USA)
subscription: majordomo@mail.orst.edu
message:
subscribe obol Your-Email-Address
posting: OBOL@mail.orst.edu
contact address: Greg Gillson
web page: http://www.cyber-dyne.com/~lb/
subscr.htm

ORNITHO-QC – Québec (Canada)
subscription: listes@endirect.qc.ca
message: subscribe ornitho-qc
posting: ornitho-qc@endirect.qc.ca
contact address: Denis Dumouchel
(dd@mic.qc.ca)
web page: http://mic.qc.ca/ornitho/
ornitho-qc.html

ORNITHOLOGIE – Europe
subscription: Majordomo@union-fin.fr
message: subscribe ornithologie
posting: ornithologie@union-fin.fr
contact address: Gilles Vannier
(vannier@alex.union-fin.fr)

PABirds – Pennsylvania (USA)
subscription: listproc@ship.edu
message: subscribe pabirds Your Name
posting: pabirds@ship.edu
contact address: Don Henise
(deheni@ark.ship.edu)

RiverBird –
States along the Mississippi (USA)
subscription:
riverbird-request@linux.winona.msus.edu
message: subscribe
contact address: Carol Schumacher
(wncarols@linux.winona.msus.edu)

SABirdNet – (South Africa)
subscription: maiser@listserv.und.ac.za
message: subscribe sabirdnet Full Name
(or unsubscribe sabirdnet)
posting: sabirdnet@listserv.und.ac.za
contact: Jenny Norman
(norman@cc.und.ac.za)

San Diego Birds – San Diego and Imperial
Counties (USA)
posting: sdbirds@basiclink.com
contact: Douglas Aguillard
(doug@basiclink.com)

South Dakota subscription
subscription: send a short message to Dan
Tallman (tallmand@wolf.northern.edu)
contact: Dan Tallman
(tallmand@wolf.northern.edu)

TWEETERS – Washington State (USA)
subscription: listproc@u.washington.edu
message: subscribe tweeters Your Real Name
(or unsubscribe tweeters)
posting: tweeters@u.washington.edu
contact:
Dan Victor (dvictor@u.washington.edu)

TEXBIRDS – Texas (USA)
subscription: listserv@list.audubon.org
message: subscribe texbirds Your Name
(or signoff texbirds)
posting: texbirds@list.audubon.org
contact: E.G. White-Swift (egws@flash.net)

Toronto Area Birding Report –
Toronto (Canada)
web address:
http://www.zoo.utoronto.ca/FUN/birds.html

UKBIRDNET – United Kingdom
subscription: ukbirdnet-
request@dcs.bbk.ac.uk
message: subscribe ukbirdnet Your Name
posting: ukbirdnet@dcs.bbk.ac.uk
web address:
http://compstat.wharton.upenn.edu:8001/~
siler/ukfile.html

SUBJECT-ORIENTED

AVIFAUNA – (Spanish)
subscription: listasrcp@rcp.net.pe
message: add Your-Email-Address avifauna
posting: avifauna@rcp.net.pe
contact address: birdlife@cipa.org.ec

BIRDBAND – Bird Banding
subscription: listserv@listserv.arizona.edu
message: subscribe BIRDBAND Your Name
posting: birdband@listserv.arizona.edu
contact address:
birdband-request@listserv.arizona.edu

BIRDFEEDER – Backyard Banding
subscription:
birdfeeder-request@userhome.com
message: subscribe
contact address: Stefanie Wieclawek
(nan@vaxxine.com)

BIRDTRIP – Trip Report
subscription: listserv@listserv.arizona.edu
message: subscribe BIRDTRIP Your Name
posting: birdtrip@listserv.arizona.edu
contact address: birdtrip-
request@listserv.arizona.edu

CAVNET – cavity-nesting bird scientific
discussion list
subscription: listserv@uvvm.uvic.ca
message: subscribe CAVNET your name
posting: cavnet@uvvm.uvic.ca
contact: Eric Walters (ewalters@bio.fsu.edu)
web page:
http://ism.idirect.com/index//ewalters.html
http://cgi.idirect.com/index/.//ewalters.html

EAGLE-NET – Eagle scientific discussion list
subscription: majordomo@unixg.ubc.ca
message: subscribe EAGLE-NET

contact: Greg Howald and Chris Coker
(eaglenet@unixg.ubc.ca)
web page: http://www.interchange.ubc.ca/
eaglenet/eaglenet.html

Cracids Newsletter
subscription: Ecotropics@aol.com
message: Send your Name and E-mail to
receive the Cracid Newsletter regularly

FWS-SHOREBIRDS – Shorebirds Sister
School Program
subscription: majordomo@www.fws.gov
message: subscribe FWS-SHOREBIRDS
contact: Heather Johnson
(heather_johnson@mail.fws.gov)
web address: http://www.wetlands.ca/
exploring/archive/sssp.html

GROUSE – Grouse-Newsgroup
(Capercaillie, Black Grouse, Hazel Grouse, etc.)
contact: Wolfgang Kantner
(h8840785@edv1.boku.ac.at)

HMANA – North American Hawk
Migration Association
subscription: listserv@listserv.arizona.edu
message: subscribe Birdhawk your-name
posting: birdhawk@listserv.arizona.edu
contact address:
birdhawk-request@listserv.arizona.edu
web address: http://www.idbsu.edu/english/
jbattali/raptors/HMANA/westcont. html">
HMANA

HUMMER – Hummingbirds
subscription: mailthing@chattanooga.net
message: subscribe hummer
(or unsubscribe hummer)
web address: http://www.chattanooga.net/
hummer/mailer.html

HUMNET-L – Hummingbirds
subscription: listserv@listserv.lsu.edu
message: subscribe humnet-l Your Name
posting: humnet-l@listserv.lsu.edu

ID-Frontiers – About Bird Identification
subscription: listserv@listserv.arizona.edu
message: subscribe BIRDWG01 Your Name
posting: birdwg01@listserv.arizona.edu
contact address:
birdwg01-request@listserv.arizona.edu

JAYNET – Corvids
posting: jaynet@relay.doit.wisc.edu
contact: jaynet@relay.doit.wisc.edu

**Journey North: A Global Study of Wildlife
Migration**
www.learner.org/jnorth

Raptor Repertoire
web address:
http://www.theriver.com/Public/raptor/

SEABIRD-L – Seabirds
address: seabird-l@utc.ac.za
subscription: listserver@uct.ac.za
message: SUBSCRIBE SEABIRD Your Name
posting: seabird@uct.ac.za
contact: John Cooper
(jcooper@botzoo.uct.ac.za)
web address: http://compstat.wharton.upenn.
edu:8001/~siler/seafile.html

NW-Pelagics – Pelagic Birding from
California to British Columbia
subscription: majordomo@teleport.com
message: subscribe nw_pelagics-L

TITNET – Paridae and Hole-nesting Bird
Discussion List
subscription: listserver@relay.doit.wisc.edu
message: subscribe TitNet (Your Name)
contact: Jack P. Hailman
(jhailman@macc.wisc.edu)

WADERS-L – Charadriidae
subscription: listserver@uct.ac.za
message: subscribe waders-l your name
posting: waders-l@uct.ac.za
contact: Rene Navarro
(trauco@maths.uct.ac.za) or Les Underhill
(lgu@maths.uct.ac.za)
web address:
http://www.wetlands.ca/waders-list/

**World Forum for Acoustic Ecology:
Discussion Group**
Contact: acoustic-ecology@sfu.ca
web address:
http://interact.uoregon.edu/MediaLit/FC/W
FAEDisc.html

Birding Hotlines

CANADA

Alberta:
Calgary (403) 237-8821
Edmonton (403) 433-2473

British Columbia:
Vancouver (604) 737-3074
Victoria (604) 592-3381

New Brunswick:
Provincewide (506) 382-3825
Shediac/Moncton (506) 532-2873 (French)

Nova Scotia:
Provincewide (902) 852-2428

Ontario:
Oshawa (905) 576-2738
Ottawa (613) 825-7444

Sault Ste. Marie (705) 256-2790
Toronto (416) 350-3000, ext. 2293
Windsor/Detroit (810) 477-1360
Windsor/Pt. Pelee (519) 252-2473
Hamilton (905) 648-9537

Quebec:
Eastern Quebec (418) 660-9089 (French)
Sagueny/Lac St. Jean (418) 696-1868 (French)
Bas St. Laurent (418) 725-5118 (French)
W. Quebec (819) 778-0737 (French)
Montreal (514) 989-5076 (English)
Montreal (514) 978-8848 (French) / (514)
990-1506 (Periphery)
Coeur-du-Quebec (819) 370-6720

Saskatchewan:
Regina (306) 949-2505

UNITED STATES

North American Rare Bird (NARB) Alert:
800-458-BIRD

Alabama:
Statewide (205) 987-2730

Alaska:
Statewide (907) 338-2473
Fairbanks (907) 451-9213
Kachemak Bay (907) 235-7337
Seward (907) 224-2325

Arizona:
Phoenix (602) 832-8745
Tucson (520) 798-1005

Arkansas:
Statewide (501) 753-5853

California:
Arcata BIRDBOX (707) 822-5666
Los Angeles (213) 874-1318
Monterey (408) 375-9122
(Updates (408) 375-2577)
Morro Bay (805) 528-7182
N. Cal. (415) 681-7422
Orange County (714) 487-6869
Sacramento (916) 481-0118
San Bernardino (909) 793-5599
San Diego (619) 479-3400
San Joaquin Valley/Southern Sierra (209)
271-9420
Santa Barbara (805) 964-8240
Southern (818) 952-5502

Colorado:
Statewide (303) 424-2144

Connecticut:
Statewide (203) 254-3665
Eastern (860) 599-5195

Delaware:
Statewide (302) 658-2747
DC-Area (301) 652-1088
(Covers MD/DC/N. VA/DE)
Baltimore (410) 467-0653
(Covers MD/DE/E. PA)
Philadelphia (215) 567-2473

District of Columbia:
DC-Area (301) 652-1088
(Covers MD/DC/N. VA/DE)

Florida:
Statewide (561) 340-0079
Miami (305) 667-7337
Lower Keys (305) 294-3438
S. Georgia/N. Florida (912) 244-9190

Georgia:
Statewide (770) 493-8862
S. Georgia/N. Florida (912) 244-9190

Idaho:
Northern (208) 882-6195
Southeast (208) 236-3337
Southwest (208) 368-6096

Illinois:
Central Illinois (217) 785-1083
Chicago (847) 671-1522
DuPage (630) 406-8111
Northwestern (815) 965-3095

Indiana:
Statewide (317) 259-0911

Iowa:
Statewide (319) 338-9881

Kansas:
Statewide (913) 372-5499
Kansas City (913) 342-2473
Wichita (316) 681-2266

Kentucky:
Statewide (502) 894-9538

Louisiana:
Baton Rouge (504) 768-9874
Southeastern (504) 834-2473
Southwest (318) 233-2473

Maine:
Statewide (207) 781-2332

Maryland:
DC-Area (301) 652-1088 (Covers
MD/DC/N. VA/DE)
Baltimore (410) 467-0653 (Covers
MD/DC/N. VA/DE)

Massachusetts:
Boston (617) 259-8805
Cape Cod (508) 349-9464
Nantucket Island (508) 228-8818
Western Mass. (413) 253-2218

Michigan:
Statewide (616) 471-4919
Detroit (810) 477-1360
Sault Ste. Marie (705) 256-2790

Minnesota
Duluth (218) 525-5952
Statewide (612) 780-8890

Missouri:
Kansas City (913) 342-2473
Statewide (573) 445-9115
St. Louis (314) 935-8432

Montana:
Statewide (406) 721-9799
Big Fork (406) 756-5595

Nebraska:
Statewide (402) 292-5325

Nevada:
Southern (702) 649-1516
Northwestern (702) 324-2473

New Hampshire:
Statewide (603) 224-9900

New Jersey:
Cape May (609) 861-0466
Statewide (908) 766-2661

New Mexico:
Statewide (505) 662-2101
New Mexico Ornithological Society Hotline
505-323-9323

New York:
Albany (518) 439-8080
Buffalo (716) 896-1271
Ithaca (607) 254-2429
Lower Hudson Valley (914) 666-6614
New York (212) 979-3070
Rochester (716) 425-4630
Syracuse (315) 668-8000

North Carolina:
Statewide (704) 332-2473

North Dakota:
Statewide (701) 250-4481
(5 pm – 7 am weekdays, 24 hours on
weekends & holidays)

Ohio:
Cincinnati (513) 521-2847
Cleveland (216) 526-2473
Columbus (614) 221-9736
Blendon Woods Park (614) 895-6222
SW Ohio (937) 277-6446
NW Ohio (419) 875-6889
Youngstown (330) 742-6661

Oklahoma:
Oklahoma City (405) 373-4531
Statewide (918) 669-6646

Oregon:
Statewide (503) 292-0661
Northeastern (208) 882-6195

Pennsylvania:
Allentown (610) 252-3455
Central (717) 255-1212, ext. 5761
Philadelphia (215) 567-2473
Reading/Berks County (610) 376-6000,
ext.2473
Western Pennsylvania (412) 963-0560
Wilkes Barre (717) 825-2473

Rhode Island:
Statewide (401) 949-3870 (Reports to
401-949-5454)

South Carolina:
Statewide (704) 332-2473

South Dakota:
Statewide (605) 773-6460

Tennessee:
Statewide (615) 356-7636
Chattanooga (423) 843-2822

Texas:
Statewide (713) 964-5867 (Reports to
281-992-2757)
Abilene (915) 691-8981
Austin (512) 926-8751
Central (817) 662-4390
Corpus Christi (512) 265-0377
Lubbock (806) 797-6690
Northcentral (817) 329-1270
Northeast (903) 234-2473
Lower Rio Grande Valley (210) 969-2731
San Antonio (210) 308-6788

Utah:
Statewide (801) 538-4730

Vermont:
Statewide (802) 457-2779

Virginia:
DC-Area (301) 652-1088 (Covers
MD/DC/N. VA/DE)
Statewide (757) 238-2713

Washington:
Statewide (206) 933-1831
reports to (206) 454-2662
Southeastern (208) 882-6195
Lower Columbia Basin (509) 943-6957

West Virginia:
Statewide (304) 736-3086

Wisconsin:
Statewide (414) 352-3857
Madison (608) 255-2476
Northeast (Green Bay) (414) 434-4207

Wyoming:
Statewide (307) 265-2473

UNITED KINGDOM

Birdline National	0891 700 222	Birdline Midlands	0891 700 247
Birdline Scotland	0891 700 234	Birdline East Anglia	0891 700 245
Birdline Northwest	0891 700 249	Birdline Southeast	0891 700 240
Birdline Northeast	0891 700 246	Birdline Southwest	0891 700 241
Birdline Wales	0891 700 248	Birdline Scilly	0891 700 243

SOURCE: U.K. 400 – Rare Birds Magazine as of January 1, 1998.

Government Organizations

NORTH AMERICA

The North American Breeding Bird Survey
U.S. Department of the Interior Patuxent
Wildlife Research Center, 11410 American
Holly Drive, Laurel, MD, 20708.
http://www.mbr.nbs.gov/bbs/bbs.html

Partners in Flight
Patuxent Wildlife Research Center, 12100
Beech Forest Road, Suite 4039, Laurel,
Maryland 20708-4039 USA
Tel: 970-226-9487 Fax: 970-226-9230
Email: Janet_Ruth@USGS.GOV
http://www.pwrc.nbs.gov/pif/

United States Fish and Wildlife Service
Kathryn L. Bender, Chief, Correspondence
Control Unit, U.S. Fish and Wildlife Service
Tel: 202-208-7535
Email: Web_Reply@mail.fws.gov
http://www.fws.gov/

**U.S. Geological Survey's Biological
Resources Division**
Biological Resources Division – USGS, U.S.
Department of the Interior, Office of Public
Affairs, 12201 Sunrise Valley Drive, Reston,
VA 20192
Email: biologywebteam@usgs.gov
http://www.nbs.gov/

Office of Migratory Bird Management
Kathryn L. Bender, Chief, Correspondence
Control Unit, U.S. Fish and Wildlife Service
Tel: 202-208-7535
Email: Web_Reply@mail.fws.gov
http://www.fws.gov/~r9mbmo/homepg.html

National Wildlife Refuge System
Tel: 1-800-344 WILD
Email: Sean_Furniss@fws.gov
http://bluegoose.arw.r9.fws.gov/

Environment Canada Atlantic
http://www.ns.ec.gc.ca/index.html

Environment Canada
http://www.ec.gc.ca/

The Canadian Wildlife Service
Canadian Wildlife Service, Environment
Canada, Ottawa, Ontario, K1A 0H3
Tel: (819)997-1095
http://www.ec.gc.ca/cws-
scf/cwshom_e.html

UNITED KINGDOM

Countryside Commission
John Dower House, Crescent Place,
Cheltenham, Glos GL50 3RA
Tel: 01242 521381

Countryside Council for Wales
Plas Penrhos, Ffordd Penrhos, Bangor,
Gwynedd LL57 2LQ
Tel: 01248 385500

**Department of the Environment for
Northern Ireland**
Environment and Heritage Service,
Commonwealth House, 35 Castle St.,
Belfast BT1 1GU
Tel: 01232 546521

English Nature
Northminster House, Peterborough PE1 1UA
Tel: 01733 455100

Institute of Terrestrial Ecology
Monks Wood, Abbots Ripton, Huntingdon
PE17 2LS
Tel: 01487 773381

Scottish Natural Heritage
12 Hope Terrace, Edinburgh, EH9 2AS
Tel: 0131 446 2201

Bird Journals and Magazines

AFRICA

Africa: Bird and Birding
(Birdlife South Africa News)
P.O. Box, 582973, Minneapolis, MN
55458-2973.
Tel: 1-800-668-6134
Email: afrimagaz@aol.com

Kenya Birds
Joint Publication of Department of
Ornithology, National Museums of Kenya
and Birdlife Kenya
Dr. L.A.Bennun, Department of
Ornithology, National Museums of Kenya,
Box 40658, Nairobi, Kenya
Tel: + 254-2-742161/2/3/4 EXT 242,
Fax: + 254-2-741049,
Email: KBIRDS@AFRICAONLINE.CO.KE

Lammergeyer (Journal of the Natal Parks
Board)
The Director, P.O. Box 662,
Pietermaritzburb 3200, RSA

Ostrich (Birdlife South Africa)
Secretary, Birdlife South Africa, P.O. Box
84394, Greenside, Johannesburg 2034, RSA
Tel: (011) 8884147 Fax: (011) 7827013
Email: info@birdlife.org.za
http://www.birdlife.org.za/

SCOPUS
Ornithological Sub-Committee of the East
Africa Natural History Society
G.C.Backhurst, Box 15194, Nairobi, Kenya
Tel: + 254-2-7
Email: Graeme@ken.healthnet.org

VULTURE NEWS
Vulture Study Group, P.O. Box 72334,
Parkview 2122, Johannesburg, RSA
Tel: (011) 646-8617

AUSTRALASIA

The Emu
Royal Australasian Ornithologists Union
(RAOU)
415 Riversdale Road, Hawthorn East,
VIC 3123, Australia
Tel: (03) 9 882 2622.
(International callers: +61 3 9882 2622)
Fax: (03) 9 882 2677.
(International callers: +61 3 9882 2677)
Email: raou@raou.com.au
http://avoca.vicnet.net.au/~birdsaus/emu/
emu.html

Flightlines
Australian Bird and Bat Banding Scheme,
Australian Nature Conservation Agency
GPO Box 8, Canberra, Act, 2601, Australia
http://kaos.erin.gov.au/life/species/fauna/
flightlines/flightline s.html

Notornis (Journal of the Ornithological
Society of New Zealand)

P.O. Box 316, Drury, South Auckland,
New Zealand
Tel/Fax: (09) 294 8334

The Stilt
Australasian Wader Studies Group, Royal
Australasian Ornithologists Union (RAOU)
415 Riversdale Road, Hawthorn East,
VIC 3123, Australia
Tel: +61 3 9882 2622 Fax +61 3 9882 2677
Email: raou@raou.com.au
http://www.vicnet.net.au/~raou/raou.html

Wingspan
Royal Australasian Ornithologists Union
(RAOU)
415 Riversdale Road, Hawthorn East, VIC
3123, Australia
Tel: +61 3 9882 2622, Fax +61 3 9882 2677
Email: raou@raou.com.au
http://www.vicnet.net.au/~raou/raou.html

EUROPE

Belgium

L'Homme et L'Oiseau, Rue de
Veeweydestraat, 43-45, 1070 Bruxelles

Bird Census News
European Bird Census Council, EBCC
Dr. A. Anselin, E. Poetoustraat 13,
B-9030 Mariakerke, Belgium
Tel: +32 2 558 18 26, Fax: +32 55818 05
E-mail: anny.anselin@instnat.be

Finland

Alula
Antero Topp, P.O.Box 85, FIN-02271
Espoo, Finland
Tel: +358-9-803 6330
mobile: +358-40-5063544
Fax: +358-9-8036330
Email: antero.topp@ntc.nokia.com

Aureola
The Ornithological Society of Northern
Ostrobotnia, Aureola, PL 388, 90101
Oulu, Finland
Email: teskelin@paju.oulu.fi

Ornis Fennica
The Finnish Ornithological Society, POB 17
(P.Rautatiekatu 13), FIN-00014
Helsinki, Finland
Tel. +358 8 5531 214 Fax. +358 8 5531 227
Email:mmonkkon@cc.oulu.fi

France

Alauda (Revue Trimestrielle de la Société
d'Études Ornithologiques de France)
Musée National d'Histoire Naturelle,
Laboratoire d'Écologie Générale, 4, ave. du
Petit-Château – F-91800 Brunoy, France

Ornithos
Ligue pour la Protection des Oiseaux
(LPO), rue des Champs des Gardes,
F-34230 Vendemian, France
Tel: +33 467 967 790 Fax: +33 467 967 790
Email: duquet@club-internet.fr

Vivre Avec Les Oiseaux, Européenne de
Magazines, 44, ave. George V, 75008
Paris, France

Germany

Journal für ornithologie
Deutschen Ornithologen-besellschaft,
Dr. Einhard Bezzel,
Gsteigstrasse 43, D-82467
Garmisch-Partenkirchen
Fax: 08821/2392

GEO Vögel
http://www.geo.de/wissen/tiere/voegel.html
Email: webmaster@geo.de

Ornis
Johannes Schlegel, Knappensteig 22, 09456
Annaberg-Buchholz, Germany
Email: rschlegel@t-online.de
http://home.t-online.de/home/rschlegel/
ornis.htm

Ornithologische Jahresberichte Helgoland
Ornithologische Arbeitsgemeinschaft
Helgoland, Postfach 869, 27498 Helgoland
Tel: FRG (0)47251338
Fax: FRG (0)47251338
Email: 047251339.0001@t-online.de

Netherlands

ARDEA
Netherlands Ornithologists Union (NOU)
C.J. Camphuysen, c/o Netherlands Institute
for Sea Research, P.O. Box 59, 1790 AB
Den Burg, Texel, The Netherlands
Tel: +31.2223.69488 Fax: +31222319674
Email: camphuys@nioz.nl or kees.
camphuysen@pi.net

Dutch Birding
P.O.Box 116, 2080 AC Santpoort,
The Netherlands
Tel: +31 23 5376749 Fax: +31 348 430216
or +31 348 420394.
Email: meijerpc@worldonline.nl
http://www.mebweb.nl/DutchBirding

SULA
Dutch Seabird Group / Nederlandse
Zeevogelgroep (NZG)
Netherlands Institute for Sea Research,
P.O. Box 59, 1790 AB Den Burg, Texel,
The Netherlands
Tel: +31.2223.69488 Fax: +31222319674
E-mail: camphuys@nioz.nl or kees.
camphuysen@pi.net

Norway

Utsira Bird Observatory's Yearbook
Utsira Bird Observatory, Bjørn O. Tveit.
Postboks 23, 5515 Utsira, Norway
Email: bjorn.tveit@gyldendal.no
http://home.sol.no/bhoeylan/utsira/e_start.
html

Poland

The Ring
Bird Migration Research Station, University
of Gdansk, Przebendowo, 84-210
Choczewo, Poland
Tel: + 48 58 723315 Fax + 48 58 203834
E-mail: biopb@univ.gda.pl

Portugal

Pardela
The Portuguese Society for the Study of
Birds (SPEA), Rua da Vitoria, 53, 2-Dto,
1100 Lisboa, Portugal
Tel/Fax: +351.1.3431847

Spain

Ardeola
Spanish Society of Ornithology, Dr. Mario
Diaz Esteban, Departamento de Ecologia,
Facultad de Biologia, Universidad

Complutense, E-28040 Madrid, Spain
Tel: +1 394 50 84 Fax: +1 394 50 81
Email: MDIAZBIO@EUCMAX.SIM.UCM.ES

Butlleti del Grup Catala d'Anellament
(Catalan Ringers Group Bulletin)
Grup Catala d'Anellament,
Museu de Zoologia, P.O. Box 593, E-08080
Barcelona, Spain

Sweden

ANSER
Scandinavian Ornithological Society,
Lennart Nilsson, Svenska vägen 40,
SE-226 39, Lund or Södra Förstdsgatan
62 211 43 Malmö
Tel: +46 (0)46 141310 Tel/Fax 040-23 74 35
Email: birds@skof.se
http://www.skof.se/

Cinclus Scandinavicus (The international
magazine about the Dipper)
Texasgatan 5, SE-593 41 Västervik
Tel: +46(0)11121682
Email: juhani.vuorinen@facere.se,
http://www.torget.se/users/c/cinclus/
Csinfo.htm

Fåglar I Norrbotten
Norrbottens Ornitologiska Forening,
Box 193, S-971 06 LULEAA, Sweden
Tel: +46 92047481
Email: TGN@on.mobile.telia.se

Faglar i Norrkopingstrakten
Fagelforeningen i Norrkoping,
Juhani Vuorinen, Bergslagsgatan 37,
SE-602 18 Norrkoping
Email: juhani.vuorinen@facere.se
http://www.torget.se/users/c/cinclus/
finkinfo.htm

Journal of Avian Biology
Dr. Hans Källander, Dept of Ecology,
Lund University, Ecology Building, S-223 62
Lund, Sweden
Tel: +46 46 2223793 Fax: +46 46 2223790
Email: JAB@ekol.lu.se
http://oikos.ekol.lu.se/JAB.jrnl.html

Oikos
Dr. Pehr H. Enckell, Dept. of Ecology,
Lund Univ., Ecology Building, S-223 62
Lund, Sweden
Tel: +46 46 2223791 Fax: +46 46 2223790
Email: Oikos@ekol.lu.se
http://oikos.ekol.lu.se/Oikosjrnl.html

Ornis Svecica
Sveriges Ornitologiska Forening,
Ekhagsvagen 3, 104 05 Stockholm

Svenska fageltidskriftspaketet
SOF/Juhani Vuorinen, Bergslagsgatan 37,
SE-602 18 Norrkoping
Tel: +46(0)11-121682
Fax: +46(0)11-121682
Email: juhani.vuorinen@facere.se
http://www.torget.se/users/c/cinclus/
svftpinfo.htm

Vår Fågelvärld
Sodra Forstadsgatan 62, 211 43 Malmo
Tel/Fax: 040 23 74 35
Email: e.hirschfeld@swipnet.se
http://www.ornitologerna.se/

Switzerland

Nos Oiseaux
La Société Romande pour l'Étude et la
Protection des Oiseaux
Claude Guex, rue des Eaux-Vives 78,
CH-1207 Geneva, Switzerland
Tel/Fax: 032/91303976

United Kingdom

Bird Conservation International
Cambridge University Press, The Journals
Department, 40 West 20th Street, New York,
NY 10011-4211, USA.
http://www.cup.cam.ac.uk/ (UK)
http://www.cup.org/ (USA)

Birding World
Hazel Milington, Stonerunner, Coast Road,
Cley-next-the-Sea,Holt, Norfolk
NR25 7RZ, England
Tel: 01263 741139

Bird Study (Journal of the British Trust
for Ornithology [BTO])
British Trust for Ornithology, National
Centre for Ornithology, The Nunnery,
Nunnery Place, Thetford, Norfolk
IP24 2PU, England
Tel: 01865 271158 Fax: 01865 271168,
Email: andrew.gosler@zoo.ox.ac.uk

Birds in the Sheffield Area
(Sheffield Bird Report – Annual)
Sheffield Bird Study Group, 4a Raven Road,
Sheffield S7 1SB, England
Tel: 0114 222 0433 (Office hours)
E-mail: a.j.morris@sheffield.ac.uk
http://www.shef.ac.uk/uni/projects/sbsg/
index.html

British Birds
Fountains, Park Lane, Blunham, Bedford
MK44 3NJ, England
Tel/Fax: (01767) 640025

Birdwatch
Solo Publishing Ltd., Bow House, 153-159,
Bow Road, London E3 2SC, England
Tel: 0181 9831855 Fax: 0181 9830246
http://www.birdwatch.co.uk/

Birdwatching
EMAP Pursuit Publishing Ltd.,
Bretton Court, Bretton, Peterborough
PE3 8DZ, England
Tel: 01733 264666 Fax: 01733 465939
Email: 100655.1672@compuserve.com

Bulletin of the British Ornithologist's Club
M.B. Casement, Dene Cottage,
West Harding, Petersfield, Hants
GU31 5Pa, England

Ibis
BOU, c/o The Natural History Museum,
Akeman St., Tring, Herts
HP23 6AP, England
Tel: 01442 890080 Fax: 01442 890693

Irish Birds
BirdWatch Ireland (formerly the Irish
Wildbird Conservancy), Ruttledge House,
8 Longford Place, Monkstown, Co.
Dublin, Ireland
Tel: +353 1 402 2333 Fax: +353 1 402 2467
E-mail bkavanagh@rcsi.ie
http://infomatique.iol.ie:8080/IrishBirds/

The Magpie
Sheffield Bird Study Group, 4a Raven Road,
Sheffield S7 1SB, England
Tel: 0114 222 0433 (Office hours)
Email: a.j.morris@sheffield.ac.uk
http://www.shef.ac.uk/uni/projects/sbsg/
index.html

Ringing & Migration
British Trust for Ornithology, National
Centre for Ornithology, The Nunnery,
Nunnery Place, Thetford, England
Norfolk IP24 2PU
Email: m.hounsome@man.ac.uk

Birds
Royal Society for the Protection of Birds
The Lodge, Sandy, Bedfordshire,
SG19 2DL, England
Tel: (44) (0)1767 680551
Email: bfisk@aol.com
http://members.aol.com/bfisk/rspb.htm

Wildfowl
The Wildfowl & Wetlands Trust,
Slimbridge, Slimbridge, Glos,
GL2 7BT, England
Tel: (01453) 890333

World Birdwatch
Birdlife International, Wellbrook Court,
Girton Road, Cambridge CB3 0NA, England
Tel: +44 01223 277318
Fax: +44 01233 277200

ASIA

General

Forktail
Oriental Bird Club, Tim Inskipp c/o RSPB,
The Lodge, Sandy, Bedfordshire, England
E-mail: inskipp@wcmc.org.uk
http://www.netlink.co.uk/users/aw/
obchome.html

OBC Bulletin
Oriental Bird Club, Richard Thomas,
59 Coolidge Gardens, Cottenham,
Cambridge CB4 4RQ, England
Tel: (01954) 252807
Email: thomasr@rsc.org
http://www.netlink.co.uk/users/aw/
obchome.html

Russia

The Russian Journal of Ornithology
c/o Eugene Potapow,
Department of Zoology, South Parks Rd.,
Oxford OX1 3PS, England

Hong Kong

Hong Kong Bird Report
Geoff Carey. Flat 11D Block 3, Royal Ascot,
Fo Tan, New Territories, Hong Kong
E-mail: gjc@netvigator.com

Japan

STRIX
The Wild Bird Society of Japan
Email: koita@j-link.or.jp
http://www.j-link.or.jp/~koita/stst14.html
& http://www.jlink.or.jp/~koita/rei300.html

Yamashina Institute for Ornithology
(Journal of)
Konoyama, Abiko, Chiba, 270-11 Japan

NORTH AMERICA

Canada

Bird Trends
Migratory Birds-Conservation
Division/Canadian Wildlife Service, Ottawa,
ON K1A 0H3

Birder's Journal
8 Midtown Dr., Suite 289, Oshawa,
ON Canada L1J 8L2

The Canadian Field Naturalist
Dr. Francis R. Cook, Editor, RR 3,
North Augusta, ON K0G 1R0
Email: ofnc@achilles.net
http://www.achilles.net/ofnc/cfn.htm

Canadian IBA News
Canadian Nature Federation, 1 Nicholas
Street, Suite 520, Ottawa, ON K1N 7B7
Tel: (613) 562-3447 Fax: (613) 562-3371
Email: cschultz@web.net iba@nornet.on.ca

Harmonie
Harmonies d'oiseaux, 573, 2ième Rue,
Suite 2, Laval, PQ, H7V 1H5
Tel: (514) 978-9017
Email: glauz@total.net
http://www.total.net/~glauz/harmonies/

L'Hirondelle
Association des Amateurs d'Hirondelles du
Québec, 228 de la Salle, Mont-Saint-Hilaire,
PQ J3H 3C2

Ontario Field Ornithologists
Ontario Birds and OFO NEWS
Box 62014, Burlington Mall Postal Outlet,
Burlington, ON L7R 4K2

Picoides
Society of Canadian Ornithologists
C/O A.J.Erskine, Editor, Picoides, Canadian
Wildlife Service, P.O.Box 1590, Sackville,
NB E0A 3C0
Tel: (506) 364-5035 Fax: (506)364-5062

Québec Oiseaux
Association Québécoise des Groupes
D'ornithologues (AQGO)
4545, Pierre-de-Coubertin, CP 1000,
Succ. M, Montréal PQ H1V 3R2
Tel: (819) 472-2632
Email: ndavid@netrover.com

Yukon Warbler
Box 31054,Whitehorse, YT Y1A 5P7

United States

Birding
American Birding Association, Inc.
P.O. Box 6599, Colorado Spring, CO 80934
Tel: (800) 850-2473

The Auk
Montana Cooperative Wildlife Research
Unit, University of Montana, Missoula, MT
59812
Email: auk@selway.umt.edu
http://pica.wru.umt.edu/Auk/Auklet.html

Bird Behavior
David B. Miller, Department of Psychology,
University of Connecticut, 406 Babbidge
Road, U-20, Storrs, CT 06269-1020
Email:
MILLERD@UCONNVM.UCONN.EDU
http://www.ucc.uconn.edu/~millerd/
bbframes.html

Birding
American Birding Association, Paul Baicich
(P.O. Box 404, Oxon Hill, MD 02750)
Tel: 800-850-2473
http://www.amereicanbirding.org

Bird Observer
Bird Observer of Eastern Massachusetts,
Inc., P.O. Box 236, Arlington, MA 02174
Tel: 617-641-1769
Email: mpeli74592@aol.com

Birder's World Magazine
Kalmbach Publishing Co., 21027 Crossroads
Circle, P.O. Box 1612,Waukesha, WI
53187-1612
Tel: 1-800-533-6644
Outside the U.S. and Canada:
Tel:414-796-8776 Fax: 414-796-1615
Email: kkammeraad@birdersworld.com
http://www.kalmbach.com/birders/world.html

Bird Watcher's Digest
P.O. Box 110, Marietta, OH 45750
Tel: (800) 879-2473
Email: ReadBWD@aol.com
http://www.petersononline.com/birds/bwd/
index.html

Bird World
850 Park Ave., Monterey, CA 93940

Blue Skies Above (News from the ...)
The Turkey Vulture Society
Bill Kohlmoos, President, P.O. Box 50300,
Reno, NV 89513
Email: vulture@accutek.com
Web: http:/www.accutek.com/vulture

The BWD Skimmer
P.O. Box 110, Marietta, OH 45750
Tel: 1 800 421-9764
Email: ReadBWD@aol.com
http://www.petersononline.com/birds/bwd/
index.html

The Chat (Journal of the Carolina Bird
Club [CBC])
Dennis Forsythe, c/o North Carolina State
Museum of Natural Sciences, 102 N.
Salisbury Street, Raleigh, NC 27603

Colonial Waterbird
Peter Frederick, Dept. of Wildlife, 118
Newins-Ziegler Hall, University of Florida,
Gainesville, FL 32611
Tel: (352) 846 0565

Email: PCF@GNV.IFAS.UFL.edu
http://www.nmnh.si.edu/BIRDNET/CWS

Condor
Ornithological Societies of North America
(OSNA), P.O. Box 1897, Lawrence, KS
66044-8897
Email: rcurry@email.vill.edu
http://www.nmnh.si.edu/BIRDNET/COS/
index.html

Conservation Biology
Reed Noss, Editor, Department of Fisheries
and Wildlife, Oregon State University,
Corvallis, OR 97331

Delmarva Ornithologist
P.O. Box 4247, Greenville, DE 19807

Ducks Unlimited
1 Waterfowl Way, Memphis, TN 38120
Tel: (901) 758-3825

The Euphonic
Kurt Rademacher, Editor, Box 8045, Santa
Monica, CA 93456

Florida Birding
Noel Wamer, 502 East Georgia St.,
Tallahassee, FL 32303

Bird and Conservationists' Gazette, P.O. Box
171227, Salt Lake City, UT 84117

The Journal of Raptor Research
Raptor Research Foundation, Inc., Marc J.
Bechard, Department of Biology, Boise
State University, Boise, ID 83725
http://www.weber.edu/rrf/

KBBW (Kachemak Bay Bird Watch)
Birchside Studio, Box 841, Homer, AK
99603

The Living Bird
The Cornell Lab of Ornithology, 159
Sapsucker Woods Rd., Ithaca, NY 14850
Tel: (607) 254-2473
http://birds.cornell.edu/

Mayland Birds
Maryland Ornithological Society, Inc.,
Cylburn Mansion, 4915 Greenspring Ave.,
Baltimore, MD 21209
Tel: (301) 762-0560

Meadowlark (Journal of the Illinois
Ornithological Society)
Sheryl De Vore, 967 Braeburn, Mundelein, IL
60060
E-mail: sdevore@ais.net

National Audubon Field Notes
American Birding Association, P.O. Box
6599, Colorado Springs, CO 80934

Nature Society News
Purple Martin Junction, Griggsville, IL
62340

North American Bird Bander
c/o Robert Pantle, 35 Logan Hill Rd.,
Candor, NY 13743

Partners in Flight
c/o Peter Stangel, National Fish and Wildlife
Foundation, 1120 Connecticut Ave. NW,
Suite 900, Washington, DC 20036

Purple Martin Update
Purple Martin Conservation Association,
Edinboro University of Pennsylvania,
Edinboro, PA 16444

Refuge Reporter
James and Mildred Clark, Millwood, VA
22646-0156
Tel: (540) 837-2152
Email: refrep@mnsinc.com

South Dakota Bird Notes
South Dakota Ornithologists' Union, NSU
Box 740, Aberdeen, SD 57401
Tel: 605-626-2456 Fax: 605-626-3022
E-mail: tallmand@wolf.northern.edu

Teaming With Wildlife
International Association of Fish and
Wildlife Agencies
444 North Capitol St., NW, Suite 544,
Washington, DC 20001

U.S. Birdwatcher
U.S. Section Office, ICBP-US, c/o World
Wildlife Fund, 1250 24th Street NW,
Washington, DC 20037
Tel: (202) 778-9563

Western Birds
Western Field Ornithologists, Philip Unitt,
San Diego Natural History Museum, P.O.
Box 1390, San Diego, CA 92112-1390
Tel: 213-744-3368
Email: garrett@bcf.usc.edu

WildBird Magazine
Fancy Publications, Inc., P.O. Box 6050,
Mission Viejo, CA 92690
Tel: (714) 855-8822

Wildlife Rehabilitation Today
Coconut Creek Publishing Company, 2201
NW 40th Terrace, Coconut Creek, FL 33066

Wilson Bulletin
Wilson Ornithological Society, Museum of
Zoology, University of Michigan, Ann
Arbor, MI 48109-1079
Email: EHBURTT@CC.OWU.EDU
http://www.ummz.lsa.umich.edu/birds/wos.
html

CENTRAL AMERICA AND THE CARIBBEAN

Jamaica

The Broadsheet
Gosse Bird Club of Jamaica., C/O Catherine
Levy, Editor, The Broadsheet, Gosse Bird

Club, 93 Old Hope Road, Kingston 6,
Jamaica W.I.
Tel: (876) 978-5881 Fax: (876) 978-5881.
E-mail: address mclevy@toj.com
http://www.jatoday.com.jm/gossebird.html

MIDDLE EAST

Sandgrouse
Ornithological Society of the Middle East,
c/o RSPB., The Lodge, Sandy, Bedfordshire
SG19 2DL, England
Tel/Fax: +44.1405.704665
Email: ag@netlink.co.uk
http://www.netlink.co.uk/users/ag/osme/

Israel Bird Ringing Center Newsletter
Israel Bird Ringing Center, Tisch Family
Zoological Gardens, P.O. Box 898, Jerusalem
91008
Tel: +972-2-6430111 Fax: +972-2-6430122.
E-mail: jshamoun@netmedia.net.il

Virtual or Internet Magazines

@vesNews
Online Magazine for Birdwatchers
http://www.surfnet.fi/birdlife/aves/index.html

Bird On!
Jacobi Jayne & Company
Tel: +44 1227 860388 Fax: +44 1227 860521
Email: birdon@birdon.com
http://www.birdcare.com/birdon/

Bird Watch
Fulham House, Goldsworth Road, Woking,
Surrey GU21 1LY, UK
Fax: +44 (0)1483 766201
http://www.birdwatch.co.uk/

InterBirdNet
http://dspace.dial.pipex.com/town/square/
gf09/

The NW Bird Watcher (Pacific Northwest)
Greg Gillson, The Bird Guide, Inc., 311 Park
Street, Banks, OR 97106
Tel: 503-324-0508
Email: guide@teleport.com
http://www.teleport.com/~guide/

The Virtual Birder Magazine
http://www.virtualbirder.com/vbirder/

Bibliographic Services on the Subject of Birds

ABSEARCH, Inc.
Computer Indices and Abstracts for
Professional Journals –Ornithology
2457 West Twin Road, Moscow, ID 83843
Tel: 1-800-867-1877
Fax: (208) 885-3803

**An Annotated Bibliography of Oregon
Bird Literature Published Before 1935**
(George A. Jobanek)
http://qpr.wind98.com/v/research.pl/
qprwind98/0870713965/av/88011
3/key1d/qpremiumj

**Avian Collision and Electrocution: an
annotated bibliography**
http://www.energy.ca.gov/energy/reports/av
ian_bibliography.html

Birds at Risk: Canada
http://nais.com.emr.ca/~medaglia/risk/birds/
ebirds/bibird.html

Chilean Birds Bibliography
http://macul.ciencias.uchile.cl/~andress/aves/
librosaves.html

Connecticut Birds
http://ourworld.compuserve.com/
homepages/jbair/bibliogr.htm

DUCKDATA
http://www.nwrc.nbs.gov/duckdata/about_
dd.html

GooseRef
http//mendel.mbb.sfu.ca/gooseref/

**Golden Eagle Population Study:
Bibliography**
http://www.nrel.gov/wind/ge_ref.html

History of Ornithology (Byron Butler)
http//pluto.njcc.com/~llarson/OrnHistory.
html

Human Disturbances to Waterfowl
http://www.npsc.nbs.gov:80/resource/
literatr/disturb/disturb.htm

Icterinae
gopher://fmppr.fmnh.org:70/11/.fmnh/.acad/.
zoo/.brd/.icterid

Lesser Scaup
http://www.npsc.nbs.gov:80/resource/
literatr/scaupbib/scaupbib.ht m

Northern Pintail
http://www.npsc.nbs.gov:80/resource/
literatr/pintbibl/pintbibl.ht m

Ornithological Literature Search
http//www.ecologynet.stir.ac.uk/home/
information/auk/authent/acce ss.htm

Procellariiformes (John Warham)
http://www.canterbury.ac.nz/zool/jwbib.htm

Quebec Birds
http://www.ntic.qc.ca/~nellus/bibliogr.html

**A List of References on Endangered,
Threatened, and Recently Extinct Birds**
http://www.si.edu/welcome/faq/endsp5.htm

The Raptor Center (Bibliography)
http://www.raptor.cvm.umn.edu/raptor/
biblio.html

Raptor Information Clearinghouse
http://www.charweb.org/organizations/
science/raptorcenter/Clearin gHouse.html

**Raptor Information System, USGS
Biological Resources Division**
http://www.ris.idbsu.edu

The Raven Archive
http://www.rinzai.com/raven/

Red-Cockaded Woodpecker bibliography
gopher://dewey.lib.ncsu.edu:70/00/library/
disciplines/biology/woo dpecker/rcwbib.txt

Rhea Bibliography
http://www.niss.ac.uk/cgi-bin/getipage?1164

**Threatened Fauna in Australia:
a select bibliography**
http://mac-ra26.sci.deakin.edu.au/fauna.html

Videos of Birds

Asia

Kingdom of the Lyrebird
L Erdos and J Erdos
Narrated by Frederick Parslow
54 mins.
Australia

Africa

Birds of the Kruger National Park
250 species found in this South African
National Park. No announcements
(time-indexed bird list)
90 mins.

Okavango Magic (Botswana)
Kenneth Newman
58 mins. approx.

Europe

*BBC-RSPB Video Guide to British Garden
Birds*
With David Attenborough
85 mins.
BBC Video

*Bird Brain of Britain and the Flying
Gourmet's Guide*
BBC Wildlife Special
58 mins.
BBC Video

Birds of Cyprus
Lucas Christophorou
Volumes 1–5

British Waders, Wildfowl and Gulls Series
Narrated by Bill Oddie. 164 mins. total.
3-video set covering 91 species of wader,
swan, geese, duck and gull, including all
commoner and most rarer species
1994

Flamingoes / Flamants Roses
(English Version)
23 mins.
Tour du Valat, France

Gosney in Eastern Europe
(Poland and Hungary)
Dave Gosney
44 min.
BirdGuides

*Kingfisher, Secret Splendour of the Brooks
and Short-Eared Owl*
RSPB Films
55 mins.
BBC Video

Nos Virtuoses
15 species from the U.K. and Europe
singing in their natural habitat, with
accompanying descriptions in the enclosed
booklet. Names are listed in Latin, French,
English, German and Dutch.
51 mins.

Osprey and the Secret Reeds
RSPB Films
78 mins.
BBC Video

The Video Guide to European Birds
J. Flegg
Series: The Video Guide to European Birds
Complete 9-tape set
Still pictures, moving footage, and sound
recordings for over 420 species in taxo-
nomic sequence on 9 videos.

The Video Guide to North European Birds
J. Flegg
324 species shown. Includes color stills,
moving footage, and sounds recordings

from *All the Birdsongs of Europe.*
5-tape set
Series contains the following volumes:
Tape 1 – *Divers to Ducks*
Tape 2 – *Raptors to Waders*
Tape 3 – *Skuas to Woodpeckers*
Tape 4 – *Larks to Flycatchers*
Tape 5 – *Tits to Buntings*

Where Eagles Fly and *The Language of Birds*
RSPB Films
Two films on one video, covering the golden
eagle and other wildlife of the Scottish
Highlands, and birdsong.
73 mins.
BBC Video

North America

Attracting Birds with Water
Avian Aquatics

Attracting Western Birds with Water
Avian Aquatics

A Celebration of Birds (with R.T. Peterson)
Judy Feith and Michael Male
Bullfrog Films, Inc. Olney, PA 19547
Tel: (215) 779 8226

*Audubon Society's Video Guide to Birds of
North America*
5 volumes, including all 505 North
American species
VHS Video Tape (National Audubon Society)
National Audubon Society, 700 Broadway,
New York, NY 10003
Tel: 212 979-3000
Email: expert@list.audubon.org
http://www.audubon.org/

Birding Hotspots in Texas
Karis and Don Herriott
Published 1991; 74-min. VHS videotape

Birding Montana and the Big Sky Country
Karis and Don Herriott
Published 1993; 62-min. VHS videotape

Birding in Southeast Arizona
Terrie and Larry Gates
Published 1993; VHS videotape

Birding Southeastern Arizona
Karis and Don Herriott
Published 1995; 52-min. VHS videotape

Birds of Alaska
Karis and Don Herriott
Published 1994; 105-min. VHS videotape

Bluebirds Up Close
VHS Video Tape (National Audubon Society)
National Audubon Society, 700 Broadway,
New York, NY 10003
Tel: 212 979-3000
Email: expert@list.audubon.org
http://www.audubon.org/

Cardinals Up Close
VHS Video Tape (National Audubon
Society)
National Audubon Society, 700 Broadway,
New York, NY 10003
Tel: 212 979-3000
Email: expert@list.audubon.org
http://www.audubon.org/

Churchill: Birds of the Canadian Arctic
66 mins.

Creating a Bird Water Garden
Avian Aquatics

Feathers
Laura Butscher
VHS format

Feathers 2
Laura Butscher
VHS format

The Great Horned Owl / the Great Gray Owl
Profiles of Nature
Series: Profiles of Nature 501
50 mins.

Hawks Up Close
VHS Video Tape (National Audubon Society)
National Audubon Society, 700 Broadway,
New York, NY 10003
Tel: 212 979-3000
Email: expert@list.audubon.org
http://www.audubon.org/

How to Start Watching Birds
KBRD Video Prod.
P.O. Box 1540, Fairfield, IA 52556
Tel: 800 779-7256

Hummingbirds Up Close
VHS Video Tape (National Audubon
Society)
National Audubon Society, 700 Broadway,
New York, NY 10003
Tel: 212 979-3000
Email: expert@list.audubon.org
http://www.audubon.org/

Hummingbirds / Bluebirds
Profiles of Nature
Series: Profiles of Nature 506
50 mins.

Large Gulls of North America
John Vanderpool
Published 1997, approx. 60 mins., VHS.

Nesting Seabirds of Machias Seal Island
Karis and Don Herriott
Published 1989; 38-min. VHS videotape

Owls Up Close
VHS Video Tape (National Audubon
Society)
National Audubon Society, 700 Broadway,
New York, NY 10003
Tel: 212 979-3000
Email: expert@list.audubon.org
http://www.audubon.org/

Rare Birds of Sanibel
Karis and Don Herriott
Published 1991; 110-min. VHS videotape

The Red-Tailed Hawk
Profiles of Nature
Series: Profiles of Nature 503
50 mins.

Spring Migration at the Dry Tortugas
Karis and Don Herriott
Published 1990; 55-min. VHS videotape

Through the Seasons: An Introduction to the Seabirds and Marine Mammals of Monterey Bay
Les Lieurance and Debi Shearwater
Published 1994; 36-min. VHS videotape

Oceania

Feathered Nomads (Australia)
L Erdos
56 mins.

Kingfishers of Australia
28 mins.
Australia

Pigeons of Australia
The Bronzewings
28 mins.

When Birds Don't Know You're There
L Erdos
Shows Australian songbirds, undisturbed in their natural environment, exhibiting patterns of behavior previously missed in the existing literature.
60 mins. (approxs)

South and Central America

Birds of Costa Rica
Richard Kuehn and Dean Schuler
Released 1997; VHS, 120 mins.

The Flight of the Condor A Wildlife Exploration in the Andes
Michael Andrews
60 mins.

World/General

Dave Gosney Videos
Birdguides, P.O. Box 471, Sheffield, S62VT
Tel (UK): 0800 91 93 91 Tel: 44 114 283
1002 Fax: 44 114 283 1003
Email: dave@birdguides.com
Series includes: *Gosney in Mallorca, Gosney in the Arctic, Gosney in Israel, Gosney in Eastern Europe, Gosney in Morocco, Gosney in Spain,* and *Gosney in Turkey.*

How to Start Watching Birds
Diane Porter
90 mins. VHS

An Identification Guide to the World's Tringa Sandpipers
Andy Butler
54 mins.

Newman's Birds: An Introduction
Kenneth Newman
56 mins.

Parrots – Look Who's Talking!
Paul Reddish
48 mins.

Video Guides to Waders
Edited by Paul Doherty
Shorebirds, Volume 1: Oystercatchers, Stilts, Avocets, Thick-knees, Coursers, Pratincoles and Plovers

Audio Recordings of Birds

Africa

*Bird Calls of the Kruger National Park,
Volume 1*
G.L. Maclean
99 species

Birds of the African Rainforests (Parts 1 and 2)
Stuart Keith
2 cassettes

Birds of the Gambia
R. Thomas and S. Thomas
Home recording of 46 Gambian species.
60 mins.

Bird Recordings from Ethiopia
Steve Smith
Recordings of 67 species
(including 10 endemics).
1996

Bird Recordings from the Gambia
Steve Smith
52 species recorded on a trip in February
1994

Birds of Southern Africa
Guy Gibbon
300 common and garden birds
100 mins.
SA Birding, South Africa

Bird Songs of Zambia
Robert Stjernstedt
Contains songs and calls of 415 species on 3
cassettes.

Birdsong of Zambia
R. Stjernstadt
Songs and calls of 343 species on 3 cassettes.
Home recording, species list.

Common Birds of Central Africa
Robert Stjernstedt
Songs and calls of 104 species on a single
cassette.

LBJ's of Southern Africa
Guy Gibbon
Songs and calls of 92 species of larks,
warblers, cisticolas, prinias, and pipits on a
single cassette.

Moroccan Bird Songs and Calls
Mats Stromberg
76 species recorded
c. 90 mins. Includes booklet.

Rare Birds of Zambia
Robert Stjernstedt
Songs and calls of 95 species on a single
cassette

Southern African Bird Calls
L. Gillard
Songs and calls of 541 species on 3 cassettes.
Cassettes available individually or as
3-cassette set

Southern African Bird Sounds
Guy Gibbon
Published 1991; 6 cassettes, 70-page booklet
Covers 888 of Southern Africa's 915 species,
330 more species than previously available.

Asia

160 Wild Birdsongs of Japan
Boxed set of 4 cassettes or 3 CDs

*An Audio Guide to the Birds of South India,
Part 1*
P.S. Sivaprasad
Single cassette, c. 90 mins., with booklet.
Gives recordings of 66 species, including
8 endemics.
1994

Birds of Indonesia 1990
D. Gibbs
Over 50 species from Sulawesi, Java,
Sumatra. Home recording

Birds of Irian Jaya
Steve Smith
Includes 48 species, including 9 birds of
paradise
1991

Birds of Irian Jaya and Halmahera
R. Thomas and S. Thomas
Home recording. Covers more than 40
species, including 8 birds of paradise

Birds of Java, Bali and Sumatra
Steve Smith
41 species on one cassette
1991

Birds of the Lesser Sundas
Steve Smith
43 species, including 25 Wallacean endemics
1991

Birds of the Moluccas
Steve Smith
42 species, including 19 Wallacean
endemics.
1991.

Birds of Polynesia
Leslie McPherson
56 species on a single cassette, including
species from Pitcairn Island, Cook Islands,
Kiribati, Niue Island, Tonga, Western
Samoa, Fiji, and Rotuma

Bird Recordings from Sri Lanka
Steve Smith
More than 46 species on a single cassette,
recorded on a trip made in January 1995

Birds of Sulawesi
Steve Smith
43 species covered, including 22 Wallacean
endemics, recorded on a trip made in July-
August 1991

Birds of the South Pacific
R. Thomas and S. Thomas
Home recording. Covers 36 species from
New Zealand, Fiji, Western Samoa, and New
Caledonia

Birds of Sabah, Sulawesi and the Lesser Sundas
R. Thomas and S. Thomas
Home recording. Covers 70 species, including
6 pittas. Part of a new series of tapes covering
this region

Birdsongs of the Himalayas
Scott Connop
Published 1995; cassette
Songs and calls of 70 species found in the
Himalayan region. Half the tape covers Old
World flycatchers, warblers, and babblers of
the area. Recording locations and elevations
provided.

Bird Songs of Korea
Lab of Ornithology, Dept. of Biology,
Kyung-Hee University
1996
Email: skylark@nuri.net

Birdsongs of Nepal
Scott Connop
Published 1993; cassette
The sounds of 66 bird species recorded in
Nepal.

*A Field Guide to the Bird Songs of
South East Asia*
Edited by T. White
National Sound Archive
110 mins. approx.
2 cassettes

Soviet Bird Songs
K. Mild
2 cassettes of songs and calls of 122
Soviet birds.
English booklet describing their calls,
location, habitat, and behavior
41 mins.

Europe

*All the Bird Songs and Calls of Britain and
Europe*
Jean C. Roché
Published 1994; 4 CDs or 4-cassette set
A guide to songs and calls of the breeding
and migrant birds of Britain and Western
Europe in systematic order. Each of 396

species has a numbered track for instant access on the CD.
Volume 1: *Falconidae*
Volume 2: *Tetraonidae – Columbidae*
Volume 3: *Cuculidae – Sylvidae*
Volume 4: *Sylvidae – Emberizidae*

Ayrshire's Moorland Birds (Scotland)
Angus Hogg and Ken Jackson
Cassette
1997

Ayrshire's Upland Birds (Scotland)
Angus Hogg and Ken Jackson
Cassette
1997

Birdsong in Britain
G. Sample
1994: c. 74 mins.

British Bird Songs and Calls
Ron Kettle
100 mins. approx.
National Sound Archive

British Bird Sounds on CD
R. Kettle and R. Ranft
Approximately 152 mins.
Boxed 2-CD set with booklet.
British Library

British Wild Birds in Stereo
John Burton

Collins Field Guide: Bird Songs and Calls of Britain and Northern Europe
Geoff Sample
Identifies more than 160 species of bird by their songs and calls.

Garden Bird Sounds
70 common British garden birds
58 mins.

Larks Ascending
J.-C. Roché
Songs of 7 European lark species
65 mins.
France

Larger Thrushes
J.-C. Roché
75 mins.
France

Nocturnal and Diurnal Birds of Prey
J.-C. Roché
40 species of diurnal raptors and owls of Europe
Single cassette

A Nocturne of Nightingales
J.-C. Roché
c. 65 mins.

Our Favourite Garden Birds
J.-C. Roché
99 garden bird species from Britain and Western Europe
75 mins.

The Peterson Field Guide to the Bird Songs of Britain and Europe
J. Boswell and S. Palmer
Vols. 1-4

A Sound Guide to Waders in Britain
John Burton, David Tombs, and Nigel Tucker

Sounds of Migrant and Wintering Birds
(Western European)
C. Chappuis
147 species
2 audio cassettes, 106 mins. (approx)

Sylvia Warblers
Jean C. Roché
Songs of the European warblers
CD or cassette.
61 mins.

Warbler Haunts
Richard Margoschis
16 species of breeding warblers of Britain, including Goldcrest and Firecrest, with announcements
60 mins. Stereo.

Your Favourite Bird Songs
John Burton and David Tombs
Songs of the 12 most popular British wild songbirds selected from a readership poll by *BBC Wildlife* magazine.

Middle East

Bird Songs of Israel and the Middle East
Krister Mild
2 cassettes, mono, dolby B, 84 pp booklet, 16 pp checklist

North America

Alaska Bird Songs
Leonard Peyton
Published 1993; cassette
Recordings of 65 species of birds found throughout Alaska, each singing up to three uninterrupted minutes.

Backyard Bird Song
Richard K. Walton and Robert W. Lawson
Published by Houghton Mifflin Company, 1991
Cassette or CD

Birding by Ear, Eastern/Central
Richard K. Walton and Robert W. Lawson
Published by Houghton Mifflin Company
3 cassettes or CD

Birding by Ear, Western
Richard K. Walton and Robert W. Lawson
Published by Houghton Mifflin Company, 1990
3 cassettes or CD

Birding by Ear: Eastern/Central
Peterson Field Guides
Houghton Mifflin
https://www1.shore.net/wbird/bin/vsc/wbird/audio/audio.htm?E+wbir d

Curious Bird Enticer (Eastern) Audio Tape
PO Box 990~Depoe Bay, OR 97341-0990
Tel: (541) 765-2473 or (888) 345-OWLS
Fax: (541) 765-2195 or 1-800-352-6024

Curious Bird Enticer (Western) Audio Tape
PO Box 990~Depoe Bay, OR 97341-0990
Tel: (541) 765-2473 or (888) 345-OWLS
Fax: (541) 765-2195 or 1-800-352-6024

Know Your Bird Sounds, Volume 1

Know Your Bird Sounds, Volume 2

More Birding by Ear, Eastern/Central
Richard K. Walton and Robert W. Lawson,
Published by Houghton Mifflin Company, 1994
3 cassettes or CD

Peterson Field Guide to Eastern/Central Bird Songs
Cornell Laboratory of Ornithology & Interactive Audio
Houghton Mifflin

Peterson Field Guide to Western Bird Songs
Cornell Laboratory of Ornithology & Interactive Audio
Houghton Mifflin

Stokes Field Guide to Bird Songs: Eastern Region
Lang Elliott with Donald and Lillian Stokes
Published by Little, Brown & Company, 1997
3 cassettes or 3 CDs

Birdsongs of the Pacific States (U.S.A)
Thomas G. Sanders
Recordings of 135 species which frequent the Pacific states, organized by habitat

Bird Songs of California: Selected Bird Songs from the Sierras to the Pacific
Primary songs of 71 species of birds found west of the Sierran watershed
Double audio cassette

Bird Sounds of Canada
Monty Brigham
Sound field guide to Canada's birds
Produced as boxed sets of either 4 cassettes or 2 CD-packs, each containing 32-page booklets. A full set comprising 12 cassettes

or 6 CDs is also available.
Series contains the following volumes:

> Volume 1: *Loons to Woodpeckers*
> Volume 2: *Flycatchers to Vireos*
> Volume 3: *Warblers to Sparrows*

1994

Bird Songs of the Kootenays
John Neville
Published 1996; 1 CD

Birdsongs of the Pacific States
Thomas G. Sander
Published 1995; 2 CDs or 2 cassettes
135 species which frequent the Pacific
states.

*Bird Songs of South Eastern Arizona and
Southern Texas*
Geoffrey A. Keller
Published 1988 Cornell Laboratory of
Ornithology; cassette
93 sought-after species recorded on location.

Bird Songs and Calls of Lake Tahoe
John V. Moore
Published 1995; cassette
Features many vocalizations from each of
45 species commonly found in the northern
Sierra Nevada.

Guide to Bird Sounds
Cornell Laboratory of Ornithology
Published 1985; 2 cassettes or 1 CD
Keyed by page number to the *National
Geographic Field Guide to the Birds of North
America*, both editions.179 species.

Songbirds of the Rocky Mountain Foothills
Kevin J. Colver
Published 1994; CD or cassette
33 species on this recording emphasizes
habitat

Songbirds of the Southwest Canyon Country
Kevin J. Colver
Published 1994; CD or cassette
Songs of 66 species of birds.

Songbirds of Yellowstone and the High Rockies
Kevin J. Colver
Published 1996; CD or cassette
Recordings of 78 species commonly sought
by birders.

Songbirds of Yosemite and the Sierra Nevadas
Kevin J. Colver
Published 1995; CD or cassette
76 bird species found in the Sierra Nevada's
Yosemite region of California.

Sounds of Florida's Birds, 3rd Edition
John William Hardy
Revised 1996; cassette
98 species of birds sing and call, most of
them recorded in Florida.

Voices of Hawaii's Birds
Hawaii Audubon Society
Published 1996; two 60-minute cassettes
Songs of 110 species of birds found in the
Hawaiian Islands.

Warblers of North America
Songs of the warblers of North America
Donald J. Borror and William W.H. Gunn
Published 1985 Cornell Laboratory of
Ornithology; 2 cassettes
281 samples of songs of 57 species, calls of
48 species.

Oceania

Australian Bird Sounds: Vol. I, II, and III
David Stewart
Published 1996; cassettes
Vol. I includes 63 species of non-passerines
from Queensland's Wet Tropics; Vol. II has
61 species of passerines from the same area.
Vol. III has 61 species from Lamington
National Park, including the first-ever
recording of Albert's lyrebird.

Bird Calls of Eastern Australia
Len Gillard
152 species including some from Tasmania.
Single cassette
Birds Australia(formerly RAOU)

Bird Calls of North Queensland Rainforests
A. Griffin and R.J. Swaby
66 species in taxonomic order. Single cassette
Birds Australia(formerly RAOU)

Bird Calls of Tropical Eastern Australia
A. Griffin and R.J. Swaby
86 species in taxonomic order
Birds Australia(formerly RAOU)

Bird Safari in Australia
Laszlo Erdos and J. Erdos
Southern Australia
54 mins.

A Field Guide to Australian Birdsong
Series contains the following volumes:

> Volume 1: *Emu to Striated Heron* Rex Buckingham and Len Jackson

> Volume 2: *Rufous Night Heron to Chestnut Rail* Rex Buckingham and Len Jackson

> Volume 3: *Red-necked Crake to Black-naped Tern* Len Gillard

> Volume 4: *Sooty Tern to Superb Parrot* Len Gillard

> Volume 5: *Regent Parrot to Masked Owl* Len Gillard

> Volume 6: *Eastern Grass Owl to Ground Cuckoo-shrike* R. Buckingham and L. Jackson

> Volume 7: *White-winged Triller to White-breasted Whistler* R. Buckingham

> Volume 8: *Little Shrike-thrush to Hall's Babbler* R. Buckingham and L. Jackson

> Volume 9: *Chestnut-crowned Babbler to Redthroat* R. Buckingham and L. Jackson

> Volume 10: *Calamanthus to Noisy Friarbird* Len Gillard

> Volume 11: *Little Friarbird to Scarlet Honeyeater* R. Buckingham and L. Jackson

Kakadu: World of Waterbirds
Terence Lindsey
52 mins.
Australia

New Zealand Birds: A Sound Guide
Leslie McPherson
7 cassettes. Sold only as a set

New Zealand Songbirds
B. Gill, J. Hawkins, and L. McPherson
Descriptive book, and a cassette recording
of 25 species
56 pages
Godwit, New Zealand

Papua New Guinea Bird Calls: Non-Passerines
H. Crouch
74 species. 1 cassette.

Papua New Guinea Bird Calls: Passerines
H. Crouch
78 species. 1 cassette.

Song Birds of South Australia
H. Crouch and A. Crouch
32 species given. Single cassette.
Birds Australia(formerly RAOU)

Songs and Calls of Tasmanian Birds
Kelsey Aves
64 species. 1 cassette.

South and Central America

The Birds of Cabañas San Isidro, Ecuador
John V. Moore and Mitch Lysinger
Published 1997; 2 cassettes
Vocalizations of 154 species from the mid-elevation montane forests of the eastern slope of the Ecuadorian Andes.

Birds of Eastern Ecuador
Peter H. English and Theodore A. Parker III
Published 1992; cassette
Songs and calls of 99 Ecuadorian species recorded in a variety of locations in South America.

Bird Songs of Belize, Guatemala and Mexico
Dale Delaney
Published 1992; Cornell Lab of Ornithology. 70 species. 1 cassette. A selection of rarities, regional endemics, and distinctive subspecies.

Bird Songs in Cuba
George Reynard
Cornell Laboratory of Ornithology
122 species on a double-LP set.

Bird Songs and Calls from Southeast Peru
Ben B. Coffey, Jr. and Lula C. Coffey
Published 1993; cassette
Songs and calls from 85 species.

Bird Songs in the Dominican Republic
G. Reynard
Cornell Laboratory of Ornithology
100 species on a double-LP set.

Bird Sounds of Trinidad and Tobago
William L. Murphy
Revised 1991; 28-minute cassette
Calls of 39 species.

Birds of Trinidad and Tobago
Terry White
32 species recordings

A Bird Walk at Chan Chich (Belize)
John V. Moore
Revised 1994; 86-minute cassette
Songs of 150 species of birds along the trails
of Chan Chich Lodge.

Brazilian Birds
J.D. Frish
5-CD Set. A collection of rarely heard
Brazilian bird songs.
Dalgas, Brazil

Cantos de Aves do Brasil
1998

*Ecuador: More Bird Vocalisations from the
Lowland Rainforest, Vol 1*
John V. Moore
Published 1994; 58-minute cassette
Vocalizations from 105 species of the low-
land rainforest of Ecuador.

*Ecuador: More Bird Vocalizations from the
Lowland Rain Forest, Vol. 2*
John V. Moore
Published 1996; 90-minute cassette

Songs of 117 species including 250 separate
cuts recorded by the author in the lowland
rainforest of Ecuador.

*Ecuador: More Bird Vocalizations from the
Lowland Rainforest, Vol. 3*
John V. Moore
Published 1997; 90-minute cassette
Vocalizations from 130 species featuring
birds from the lowland rainforest of
Ecuador, most of which have never been
published before.

Songs of Argentine Birds
Roberto Stranek
The calls and songs of over half the
Argentine avifauna.
4 tapes & 8 explanatory booklets (in
Spanish and English)

Songs of Mexican Birds
B. Coffey
1990: 246 species on 2 cassettes.

*A Sound Guide to the Birds of South East
Peru*
S. Grove
93 species. 1 cassette.

Sounds of La Selva (Eastern Ecuador)
John V. Moore
Revised 1994; 80-minute cassette
Vocalizations of over 120 species of birds in
the lowland rainforests of Eastern Ecuador.

Sounds of Nature: Finches
Donald J. Borror and William W.H. Gunn
Series: Sounds of Nature
400 songs from 226 birds of 43 species of
Fringillids of Eastern and Central North
America

*Voices of All Mockingbirds, Thrashers and
Their Allies*
J.W. Hardy, Jon C. Barlow, and Ben B.
Coffey, Jr.
Published 1987; cassette
34 species sing and call, and imitate other
species. Program notes sort them out for you.

Voices of Birds of the Galapagós Islands
John William Hardy
Revised 1991; cassette
Revised and expanded to include the songs
and calls of 37 species, including 12 finches.

Voices of Costa Rican Birds: Caribbean Slope
David L. Ross, Jr. and Bret M. Whitney
Published 1995; 2 cassettes or 2 CDs
A selection of vocalizations from 220
species of the eastern slope of Costa Rica,
produced by the Cornell Lab's LNS.

Voices of Mexican Sparrows
J.W. Hardy and Larry L. Wolf
Published 1993; cassette
Contains vocalizations of eight species.

Voices of Neotropical Birds
John William Hardy
Revised 1983; cassette
Voices of over 50 species of neotropical birds.

Voices of Neotropical Wood Warblers
J.W. Hardy, Ben B. Coffey, Jr. and George B.
Reynard
Published 1994; cassette
Family Emberizidae, subfamily Parulinae,
including the Wrenthrush
Songs and calls of 63 species, including
regional variations if available and appro-
priate. approx. 76 mins.

Voices of New World Owls
J.W. Hardy, B.B. Coffey, Jr., and G.B.
Reynard
Published 1990; cassette
Calls of 61 species

*Voices of the New World Jays, Crows and
Their Allies*
John William Hardy
Revised 1990; cassette
Songs of 48 corvids which breed in the
Western Hemisphere.

Voices of New World Pigeons and Doves
J.W. Hardy, G.B. Reynard, and B.B. Coffey, Jr.
Published 1989; cassette
Sounds of 59 of the 71 species known to
breed in the Western Hemisphere.

Songs of the Vireos and Their Allies
Jon C. Barlow and J.W. Hardy
Revised 1995; cassette
Recordings of all but two of the known
species of vireos and most of their tropical
relatives, the greenlets, peppershrikes, and
shrike-vireos.

Voices of the Peruvian Rainforest
Theodore A. Parker III
Published 1985; cassette
Recordings made at 4 locations feature
songs and calls of representative species.

Voices of New World Cuckoos and Trogons
J.W. Hardy, George B. Reynard, and Ben B.
Coffey, Jr.
Revised 1995; cassette
Eight species of cuckoos, from Canada to
Argentina, and 25 species of trogons are
recorded.

Voices of the New World Quails
J.W. Hardy and Ralph J. Raitt
Published 1995; cassette
Recordings of 26 of the 29 species of quails,
wood-quails, and bobwhites found in the
New World.

Voices of the New World Thrushes
John William Hardy and Theodore A.
Parker III
Published 1992; cassette
Vocalizations of 68 species of thrushes
known to breed in the Western Hemisphere.
Supplementary booklet.

Voices of the Tinamous
J.W. Hardy, Jacques Vielliard, and Roberto
Straneck
Revised 1995; cassette
Contains 34 recordings of members of one
of the most secretive families of birds.

Voices of the Woodcreepers
J.W. Hardy, T.A. Parker III, and Ben B.
Coffey, Jr.
Revised 1995; cassette
Covers 46 species of the neotropical family
Dendrocolaptidae.

Voices of the Wrens, 3rd Edition
John William Hardy
Revised 1995; cassette
Contains songs of all but one of known
forms of wrens.

World/General

World Forum for Acoustic Ecology (WFAE)
Simon Fraser University (SFU)
School of Communication,
Burnaby, BC, Canada, V5A 1S6
Fax: (604) 291-4024
Email: wfae@sfu.ca
http://interact.uoregon.edu/MediaLit/WFA
EHomePage

*Lifesong: Amazing Sounds of Threatened
Birds*
Tape of songs of threatened bird species
from around the world.

National Geographic's Guide to Bird Sounds
Geographic field guide.

New World Sound Guides
Series contains the following volumes:

> *Songs of the Vireos and Their Allies*
>
> *Voices of all the Mockingbirds, Thrashers
> and Their Allies*
>
> *Voices of Neotropical Birds*
>
> *Voices of the New World Cuckoos and
> Trogons*
>
> *Voices of the New World Jays, Crows and
> Their Allies*
>
> *Voices of the New World Nightjars and
> Their Allies*
>
> *Voices of the New World Nightbirds* (NW
> Owls + NW Nightjars & Allies)
>
> *Voices of the New World Owls*
>
> *Voices of the New World Pigeons and Doves*
>
> *Voices of the New World Quails*
>
> *Voices of the New World Thrushes*
>
> *Voices of the Tinamous*
>
> *Voices of the Woodcreepers*
>
> *Voices of the Wrens*

CD-ROMs on Birds

AviSys Version 4.0
Perceptive Systems, PO Box 3530, Silverdale, WA 98383
http://www.mindspring.com/~avisys

BirdArea
Santa Barbara Software Products
1400 Dover Road, Santa Barbara, CA 93103
Phone/Fax: 805 963 4886
Email: sbsp@aol.com
http://members.aol.com/sbsp/index.html

BirdBase with AOU list or with World List
Santa Barbara Software Products
1400 Dover Road, Santa Barbara, CA 93103
Phone/Fax: 805 963 4886
Email: sbsp@aol.com
http://members.aol.com/sbsp/index.html

Bird Brain 4.0
Ideaform Inc.
908 East Briggs Fairfield, IA 52556
Tel: 515-472-7256 1 800 779 7256
http://www.birdwatching.com/index.html

The Bird-Book CD-ROM (Australian Birds)
Ken Simpson
Natural Learning, Australia
Tel: +44(0)1803 865913 Fax: +44(0)1803865280
Email: orders@nhbs.co.uk
http://www.nhbs.co.uk/

Birder's Diary 2.0
(Thayer Software)
ISBN 1-887148-09-4
http://www.birdwatching.com/software.html

Birds of Britain and Europe: The Ultimate Interactive Bird Guide
427 species, 850 col. illus., 500 sound clips, 90 video clips, 427 maps
Tel: +44(0)1803 865913 Fax: +44(0)1803865280
Email: orders@nhbs.co.uk
http://www.nhbs.co.uk

Birds of Europe
Expert Centre for Taxonomic Identification
Series: World Biodiversity Database
Subseries contains the following volumes:
Birds of Europe Uccelli d'Europa Die Vogel Europas
http://science.springer.de/newmedia/lifesci/eti/birds.htm

Birds of North America (Version 2.0)
Thayer Birding Software
Revised 1997; CD-ROM for PC
Pictures and songs of 918 North American birds on CD-ROM. Includes 200 additional images of birds of the world, state bird checklists, binocular and scope ratings, scientific articles. Checklists for 63 states/provinces, direct links to over 30 birding web sites on the Internet, and listings of 1192 bird clubs.
http://www.birdwatching.com/software.html

Bird Song Master (North America or Costa Rica)
(Micro Wizard)
http://www.birdwatching.com/software.html

Bird Sounds of Bolivia
Sjoerd Mayer
Published 1996; CD-ROM for PC
Over 1,060 recordings of 538 species of Bolivian bird are given.
Bird Songs International, Wierengastraat 42, NL-9969 PD, Westernieland, Holland
Fax: 31 595 528629
Email: 101363.650@compuserve.com
http://ourworld.compuserve.com/homepages/bird_songs_international /englisht.htm

Birdstar: A Field Guide to the Birds of North America
LJB Expert Systems, 96 Craig Dr., Kitchener, ON N2B 2J3
Email: lbond@golden.net
http://www.golden.net/~lbond/birdstar.htm

British Birds: An Interactive Multimedia CD-ROM
British Library
Tel: +44(0)1803 865913 Fax:
+44(0)1803865280
Email: orders@nhbs.co.uk
http://www.nhbs.co.uk/

Bruce Flaig's Birds, Vol. 1
Softdisk
PO Box 30008, Shreveport LA 71130-0008
Tel: 1-800-831-2694
http://www.softdisk.com/sd/birding/

Common Birdsongs
R. Wayne Campbell, editor
Published 1994; CD-ROM for PC
120 common, widespread, and distinctively
vocal species are profiled, mainly male birds
in breeding plumage. Includes video clips as
well as animated sonograms depicting each
call on screen.

Corel Birds on CD ROM – 100 High Resolution Images on CD Rom
(Corel Corporation)
Channel MarketMakers, 12 Mortimers
Farm, Paultons Park, Ower, Nr Romsey,
Hampshire, SO51 6AL., England
Tel: 44 (0)1703 814142
Fax: 44 (0)1703 813830.
Email: enquiries@cmm1.com
http://www.cmm1.com/photos/titles/
008000.html

Discover Birds with Ken Newman
(South Africa)
Ken Newman
Tel: +44(0)1803 865913 Fax:
+44(0)1803865280
Email: orders@nhbs.co.uk
http://www.nhbs.co.uk/

Essential Ornithological Abstracts CD ROM – Essential Life Sciences Series (1955–Present)
National Information Services Corporation
NISC USA, Wyman Towers, 3100 St. Paul
Street, Baltimore, MD, 21218
Tel: 1 410-2430797 Fax: 1 410-2430982
Email: sales@nisc.com
http://www.nisc.com

Eyewitness Virtual Reality Bird CD-ROM
http://www.birdwatching.com/software.html
(DK Books)

Guide to All the Birds of Europe, The CD-Rom
Series contains the following volumes:

> CD-ROM Guide to All the Birds of
> Europe (5 CDs)
>
> CD-ROM Guide to the British Birds
>
> CD-ROM Guide to British Birds:
> Birdfile Update
>
> CD-ROM Guide to the Birds of
> Northern Europe, Deluxe Version (5 CDs)

Tel: +44(0)1803 865913 Fax:
+44(0)1803865280
Email: orders@nhbs.co.uk
http://www.nhbs.co.uk/

Guide to British Birds, The CD-ROM
Birdguides
P.O. Box 471, Sheffield, S62VT
Tel (UK): 0800 91 93 91 44 114 283 1002
Fax: 44 114 283 1003
Email: dave@birdguides.com
http://www.birdguides.co.uk/products/
brcd.html

Guide to British Birds, including the Birdfile
Birdguides, P.O. Box 471, Sheffield, S62VT
Tel (UK): 0800 91 93 91
Tel: 44 114 283 1002
Fax: 44 114 283 1003
Email: dave@birdguides.com
http://www.birdguides.co.uk/cdrom/british
cd.html

Guide to All the Birds of Europe
Birdguides, P.O. Box 471, Sheffield, S62VT
Tel (UK): 0800 91 93 91 Tel: 44 114 283
1002 Fax: 44 114 283 1003
Email: dave@birdguides.com
http://www.birdguides.co.uk/cdrom/eurocd
.html

Guide to Common Birds
Birdguides, P.O. Box 471, Sheffield, S62VT
Tel (UK): 0800 91 93 91
Tel: 44 114 283 1002
Fax: 44 114 283 1003
Email: dave@birdguides.com
http://www.birdguides.co.uk/cdrom/british
cd.html

Know Your Owls (Birds of Prey, Vol. 1)
R. Wayne Campbell, editor
Published 1994; CD-ROM for PC
The first disk of a 2-volume set that covers all
North American birds of prey. A comprehensive survey of our 19 nesting species of owls.
ISBN 1-896154-02-6
http://www.axia.com/

Know Your Birds of Prey Vol. 2: Vultures to Falcons
(Axia International, Inc.)
R. Wayne Campbell, editor
Published 1995; CD-ROM for PC
Every species of diurnal raptor in North
America.
ISBN 1-896154-02-6
http://www.axia.com/

Know Your Common Bird Songs CD-ROM
(Axia International, Inc.)
More than 120 common birds identified by
their characteristic sounds: calls and songs.
Each bird characterized by its use of one
or more of 18 distinct habitats, and by
geographic region in North America. Each
sound accompanied by a Song Wave, a
dynamic audiogram.
ISBN 1-896154-07-7
http://www.axia.com/

Know Your Waterfowl CD-ROM
(Axia International, Inc.)
R. Wayne Campbell, editor
Published 1994; CD-ROM for PC
A guide to North America's nesting ducks,
geese, and swans, which includes 500 full-
screen photos, almost one-half hour of
video, and 45 minutes of self-running
introductory programs.
ISBN 1-896154-00-X
http://www.axia.com/

LANIUS Excalibur 1.0
Ornithological Database
Lanius Software, 1470 Creekside Dr., Suite
23, Walnut Creek, CA 94596
Tel: (510) 932 4201
Email: logshrike@compuserve.com
Web: www.glenalpine.com/lanius

Les oiseaux de nos jardins (Belgium)
(Sittelle)
http://www.rw.be/mrw/dgrne/sibw/
organisations/aves

The Multimedia Bird Book – An Interactive Field Guide
ISBN:1-887468-00-5
https://www1.shore.net/wbird/bin/vsc/wbir
d/cdrom/cdrom.htm?L+wbir d+bebm3016

National Audubon Society Interactive CD-ROM Guide to North American Birds
(Random House)
ISBN 0679760164
http://www.randomhouse.com/audubon/

North American Birds by Sight and Sound CD-ROM
NatureWare, 3210 Dudley, Lincoln, NB
68503
Email: clemen@natureware.com
http://www.natureware.com/

100 Birds of Sweden
(Images & Triggers AB)
Masvagen 15B, S-227 33 Lund, Sweden
Email: info@imatri.se
http://www.imatri.se/

Peterson Multimedia Guides: North American Birds Version 1.1
Houghton Mifflin Interactive; Published
1996; CD-ROM for Windows
Hosted by Roger Tory Peterson, this CD-
ROM covers all of the nearly 1,000 North
American bird species. Includes illustrations
and text from the Peterson Eastern and
Western field guides. In addition, birds
songs and calls, photographs, and range
maps are included.
Houghton Mifflin Interactive, 120 Beacon
Street, Somerville, MA 02143
Tel: 617-503-4800 Fax: 617-503-4900

Email: hmi@hmco.com
https://www1.shore.net/wbird/bin/vsc/wbird
/welcome/media.htm?L+wb ird+bebm3016

Raptors: Birds of Prey CD-Rom
(Discerning Nature)
Tel: 1-888-347-DISCERN (2376)
Email: DiscNat@aol.com
http://www.dynrec.com/raptors.html

Roberts' Multimedia Birds of Southern Africa
Southern African Birding, P.O.Box 1438, Westville 3630, Durban, South Africa
Tel/Fax: +27+(0)31 865948
Email: guy@sabirding.co.za
http://www.sabirding.co.za/

Simpson and Day's Birds of Australia – CD ROM, Version 4.0
Ken Simpson and N Day
Natural Learning, Australia
Tel: +44(0)1803 865913 Fax:
+44(0)1803865280
Email: orders@nhbs.co.uk
http://www.nhbs.co.uk/

Yardbirds
Bird Identification Software
(Ramphastos), P.O. Box 310, Dover, NH 03821
Tel: (888) 221-BIRD

Commercial Outlets for Books and Software on Birds

American Birding Association
ABA Sales, Colorado Springs, CO 80934
Tel: (719) 578-0607 (800) 634-7736 (in USA and Canada) / (719) 578-0607 (intern.)
Fax: (800) 590-2473 (in USA and Canada) / (719) 578-9705 (international)
Email: abasales@abasales.com
Web site: http://www.americanbirding.org

The Aviary Bookstore
111 Pullen Road, Rockwall, TX 75087
Tel: (972) 771-7965
Email: webmaster2@theaviary.com
http://theaviary.com

BirdGuides
PO Box 471, Sheffield, S62YT, England
Tel: 0800 91 93 91 Int: 44 114 283 1002
Fax: 44 114 283 1003
Email: dave@birdguides.com
http://www.birdguides.com/

BirdWatcher's Marketplace
Bird Watcher's Marketplace, 3150 Plainfield Ave NE, Grand Rapids, MI
Tel: (800) 981-BIRD (616) 365-1172
Fax: (616) 365-1872
Email: lucy@birdwatchers.com
http://www.birdwatchers.com/

Buteo Books
Route 1, Box 242
Shipman, VA 22971
Tel: 804-263-8671; orders (800) 722-2460
Fax: 804-263-4842

Hancock Wildlife Research Center
1431 Harrison Avenue, Blaine, WA 98230-5005
Tel: 1-800-938-1114 or (604) 538 – 1114
Fax: 1-800-983-2262 or (604) 538 – 2262
Email: sales@hancockwildlife.org
http://www.hancockwildlife.org/index.html

Harrell Books
P.O. Box 425
Friday Harbour, WA 98250
Tel: 360-378-6146

Hi Jolly's Bird Books
700 Main Street, Susanville, CA 96130
Tel: 916/252-1401 Fax: 916/252-1402
Email: hijolly@psln.com
http://www.cascade.net/~hijolly/

High Meadows Natural History Books
1198 Clear Creek Dr., Boise, ID 83709
Tel: 208-323-0328
Email: himeadows@aol.com

NHBS Mailorder Bookstore
2-3 Wills Road, Totnes, Devon, TQ9 5XN, England
Tel: +44(0)1803 865913
Fax: +44(0)1803 865280
Email: nhbs@nhbs.co.uk
Website: http://www.nhbs.com

Pandion Books
884 NW Chipmunk Place, Corvallis, OR 97330
Tel: 541-752-3356 (evenings)

Peacock Bookstore
437 Prince George Street, Williamsburg, VI 23185
Tel: 757-229-7644
Email: miller@tni.net
http://www.wolfpaw.com/princegeorge/books.html

St. Ann's Books
Rectory House, 26, Priory Road,
Great Malvern, Worcestershire, WR14 3DR, England
Tel: 0684-562818
Fax: 0684-566491

T.J. Myers Natural History Books
PO Box 962, Randwick NSW 2031 Australia
Tel: +612 9385 2125 Fax: 9385 2125
Email: p1025511@vmsuser.acsu.unsw.edu.au
http://www.ozemail.com.au/~arenanet/exposure/04005/

Wild Bird Center
1270A Newell Avenue, Walnut Creek, CA 94596
Tel: (510) 937-SEED Fax: (510) 937-6291
Email: joanie@birdware.com
http://www.birdware.com/

Wild Bird General Store
4712 – 99 Street, Edmonton, AB T6E 5H5
Tel: (403)439-7333 Fax: (403)439-7467
1-800-465-5099
Email: wildbird@freenet.edmonton.ab.ca
http://www.freenet.edmonton.ab.ca/wildbird/

Wildbird Emporium
The Wild Bird Emporium, 21 Olde Towne Road, Auburn, NH 03032
Tel: 603 483-5523 Fax: 603 483-8444
Email: info@wbird.com
http://www.wbird.com/

Birding Festivals in North America

January

Bald Eagle Days
Rocky Mountain Arsenal National Wildlife Refuge month-long celebration of 50 or more bald eagles
Tel: 303-289-0232 ext. 150

Quad Cities Bald Eagle Days
Days Rock Island, Illinois
Bald eagle viewing and programs.
Tel: 309-788-5912

Eaglefest
Emory, Texas
With more than 50 bald eagles recorded by Texas Parks and Wildlife on nearby Lakes Fork and Tawakoni, Emory claims to be the "Eagle Capital of Texas." Emory is about 1½ hours from Dallas.
Contact: Eaglefest, Box 695, Emory, TX 75440
Tel: 903-473-3913

Wings Over Willcox
Willcox, Arizona
More than 10,000 Sandhill cranes, wading birds, and winter waterfowl, plus the possibility of up to 20 different raptor species.
Contact: Willcox Chamber of Commerce, 1500 N. Circle 1 Rd., Willcox, AZ 85643
Tel: 800-200-2272

Morro Bay Winter Bird Festival
Morro Bay, California
Up to 230 wintering species, with tufted duck, Allen's hummer, and Pacific golden plover possible.
Tel: 800-231-0592

Keokuk Bald Eagle Appreciation Days
Keokuk, Iowa
Bald eagles along the Mississippi River,
with live eagle demonstrations and
information booths.
Contact: Keokuk Area Convention and
Tourism Bureau, 401 Main St., Keokuk, IA
52632
Tel: 800-383-1219 or 319-524-5055.

Eagles Et Cetera
Bismark, Arkansas
Tel: 501-865-2801

Winter Bird Festival
Albuquerque, NM
Tel: 505-344-7240

Annual Imperial Beach Bird Fest
San Diego, California
Wintering birds and area specialities, field
trips, and seminars.
Tel: 619-282-8687

Winter Wings Weekend
Lake Village, Arkansas
Wintering waterfowl amid the beauty of
Lake Chicot. Contact at 2542 Highway 257,
Lake Village, AR 71653
Tel: 870-265-5480

February

Upper Skagit Bald Eagle Festival
Skagit Valley, Washington
Bald eagle viewing, including by river raft.
Contact: Bald Eagle Festival, Box 571,
Concrete, WA 98237
Tel: 360-853-7009

Annual Trumpeter Swan Festival
Courtenay, British Columbia
Large flocks of trumpeter swans; guided
tours and interpretive programs.
Tel: 604-334-2205

Coot Festival
Golden Shores, Arizona, and Needles,
California
Tel: 760-326-3853

Eagle Days Festival
Pueblo, Colorado
Dozens of wintering bald eagles, plus gulls
and scoters.
Tel: 719-561-4909

Celebration of Tropical Birds
Panama City, Panama
Tel: 800-328-VENT

Weekend for Wildlife
Georgia Dept. of Natural Resources, 205
Butler St. SW, Suite 1258, Atlanta, GA 30334
Tel: 912-994-1438 404-656-0772

California Duck Days
Davis, California
Hundreds of thousands of ducks, geese, and
shorebirds can be seen in this Sacramento
Valley festival.
Contact: California Duck Days, Box 73333,
Davis, CA 95617
Tel: 800-425-5001

Klamath Basin Bald Eagle Conference
Klamath Falls, Oregon
Claims to be the home of the largest
concentration of bald eagles in the lower
48 states.
Contact: Oregon Dept. of Fish and Wildlife,
1850 Miller Island Road West, Klamath Falls,
OR 97603
Tel: 541-883-5732

Salton Sea International Bird Festival
Imperial California
Guided tours in the Imperial Valley and
Northern Baja.
Tel: 760-344-5FLY
http://www.imperialcounty.com/birdfest/
index.html

A Celebration of Whooping Cranes
Port Aransas, Texas
Tel: 512-749-5919

Pella Bald Eagle Day
Pella, Iowa
Tel: 515-828-7522

March

Spring "Wing Ding"
Clay Center, Nebraska
Tel: 402-762-3518

Eagle Watch
Winona, Minnesota
Winona Convention and Visitor Bureau,
Box 870, Winona, MN 55987-0870
Tel: 800-657-4972 or 507-452-2272

Monte Vista Crane Festival
Monte Vista, Colorado
Monte Vista Crane Festival, Box 585,
Monte Vista, CO 81144
Tel: 719-852-3552

Bluebird Festival
Jackson, Michigan
Dahlem's Center, 2111 Emmons Road,
Jackson, MI 49201
Tel: 517-782-3453

Buzzard Sunday
Hinckley Chamber of Commerce,
P.O. Box 354, Hinckley, OH 44233
Tel: 216-351-6300

Wings Over the Platte
Grand Island, Nebraska
The Platte River area is home to thousands
of waterfowl and sandhill cranes, which are
returning home for the spring.
Contact: Grand Island Convention and
Visitor's Bureau, Box 1486, Grand Island,
NE 68802
Tel: 800-658-3178

Attwater's Prairie Chicken Festival
Eagle Lake, Texas
Tours to the Attwater's Prairie Chicken
National Wildlife Refuge to see this
endangered bird, plus migrating species.
Contact: Eagle Lake Chamber of Commerce,
408 E. Main St., Eagle Lake, TX 77434
Tel: 409-234-2780

Fins, Feathers & Flowers
Eufaula NWR, 509 Old Highway 165,
Eufaula, AL 36027
Tel: 334-687-4065

Presqu'ile Waterfowl Festival
Brighton, Ontario
Tel: 613-475-2204

Sand Lake Eagle Day
Columbia, South Dakota
The peak of eagle migration, plus migrating
waterfowl.
Tel: 605-885-6320

April

Lake Erie Wing Watch Weekend
Port Clinton, Ohio
The possibility of seeing more than 300
species, along the southwest coast of Lake
Erie during migration.
Contact: Magee Marsh Wildlife Area, 13229
W. State Route 2, Oak Harbor, OH 43449
Tel: 419-898-0960 or 800-441-1271

Brant Festival
Parksville, British Columbia
Tel: 250-248-4117

John Scharff Migratory Bird Festival
Harney Copunty Chamber of Commerce,
18 West D St., Burns, OR 97720
Tel: 541-573-2636

Texas Tropics Nature Festival
McAllen, Texas
Tel: 800-250-2591

Annual Bluebird Festival
Wills Point, Texas
The highest concentration of bluebirds
in Texas.
Contact: Wills Point Chamber of
Commerce, Box 217, Wills Point, TX 75169
Tel: 903-873-3111 or 800-972-5824

Great Louisiana Bird Fest
Mandeville, Louisiana
Participate in 10 different field trips, spotting
115 species over a three-day weekend.
Tel: 800-634-9443.

Godwit Days
Arcata, California
Shorebirds, raptors, and specialities such as
spotted owl and marbled murrelets.
Tel: 707-822-5953

Walker Lake Loon Festival
Walker Lake, Nevada
Tel: 702-348-2644

Barnsley Gardens Spring Bird Festival
Adairsville, Georgia
Tel: 770-565-9841

Garnet Festival
Wrangell, Alaska
Tel: 800-367-9545

Upper Texas Coast Birding Festival
Galveston, Texas
Tel: 409-737-4031

Kern Valley Bioregions Festival
Kern Valley, California
Contact: Karen Philips, Box 854, Weldon,
CA 93283
Tel: 760-378-3345

Creston Valley Osprey Festival
Creston, British Columbia
Tel: 604-428-3260

Snowgoose Festival
Town of Tofield, Box 30, Tofield, AB T0B 4J0
Tel: 403-662-3269
web address:
http://www.tcnap.tofield.ab.ca/snowgoos/sn
owgoos.htm

Delmarva Birding Weekends
Maryland Department of Natural
Resources, 580 Taylor Ave., Floor E-1,
Annapolis, MD 21401
Tel: 410-974-3195 800-852-0335

Migration Celebration
Lake Jackson, Texas
Tel: 800-938-4853

Gray's Harbor Shorebird Festival
Hoquiam, Washington
Shorebird migration
Gray's Harbour Audobon Society,
P.O. Box 444, Montesano, WA 98563
Tel: 800-321-1924 or 360-532-1924
web address: http://www.wln.com/~dschwick

May

Baillie Birdathon
Bird Studies Canada:
Tel: 519-586-3531 Fax: 519-586-3532
E-mail: brdathon@nornet.on.ca

Point Pelee Festival of Birds
Leamington, Ontario
Tel: 519-322-2365

Buzzard Day
Glendive, Montana
Tel: 406-365-6256

Wings Over the Rockies Bird Festival
Invermere and Radium, British Columbia
Tel: 888-342-3210

Copper River Delta Shorebird Festival
Cordova, Alaska
Contact:Cordova Chamber of Commerce,
Box 99, Cordova, AK 99574
Tel: 907-424-7260

Kachemak Bay Shorebird Festival
Homer, Alaska
Contact: Homer Chamber of Commerce,
Box 541, Homer, AK 99603
Tel: 907-235-7740

Big Stone Bird Festival
Big Stone Lake Area, Ortonville, Minnesota
Tel: 800-568-5722

**Chincoteague NWR International
Migratory Bird Celebration**
Chincoteague, Virginia
Tel: 757-336-6122

Golden Bear Birding Festival
Golden, British Columbia
Tel: 800-622-GOLD

Nest with the Birds
Kelleys Island, Ohio
Tel: 419-746-2258

Cape May Spring Weekend
Cape May, New Jersey
Cape May Bird Observatory, 707 E. Lake Dr.,
Box 3, Cape May Point, NJ 08212
Tel: 609-884-2736

Detroit Lakes Festival of Birds
Rochert, Minnesota
Tel: 800-542-3992 ext. 790

Salmon Arm Grebe Festival
Salmon Arm, British Columbia
Tel: 250-832-5200

Plover and Wildlife Festival
Newburyport, Massachusetts
Returning plovers and songbird species,
boat tours, and birdbanding demonstrations.
Tel: 978-465-5753 ext. 26

Warblers and Whimbrels Weekend
Brighton, Ontario
Tel: 613-475-4324

Prince Edward County Birding Festival
Demorestville, Ohio
Tel: 613-476-5072

Loon and Fish Festival
Seeley Lake, Montana
Tel: 406-677-3276

Kirtland's Warbler Festival
Oscoda County Chamber of Commerce,
Box 670, Mio, MI 48647
Phone: 517-826-3712
or Kirtland Community College
Tel: 517-275-5121 x 347 Fax: 517-275-8210.

Shorebirds' and Friends' Festival
Wadena, Saskatchewan
Tel: 888-338-2145

August

The Loon Festival
Loon Preservation Commitee, P.O. Box 604,
Lee's Mills Road, Moultonborough, NH 03254
Tel: (603) 476-5666

Southwest Wings Birding Festival
Southwest Wings Birding Festival, Box
3432, Sierra Vista, AZ 85636
Tel: 800-946-4777

Annual Monarch and Migrants Weekend
Brighton, Ohio
Tel: 613-475-4324

September

Festival of Hawks
Essex, Ontario
Contact: Essex Region Conservation
Authority, 360 W. Fairview Ave., Essex, ON
N8M 1Y6
Tel: 519-766-5209

Annual Sandhill Crane Days
Hyrum, Utah
Tel: 801-245-6747

Oregon Shorebird Festival
Coos Bay, Oregon
Beautiful scenery combined with pelagic and
shorebird field trips.
Contact: Oregon Shorebird Festival, 1691
Grant St. SE, North Bend, OR 97459
Tel: 503-756-5688

Hummingbird Celebration
Rockport-Fulton Area Chamber of
Commerce, 404 Broadway, Rockport, TX
78382
Tel: 800-242-0071

Wings'n Water Festival
Stone Harbor, New Jersey
Tel: 609-368-1211

Wye Marsh Festival
Midland, Ontario
Tel: 705-526-7809

Barnsley Gardens Fall Bird Festival
Adairsville, Gerogia
Tel: 770-773-7480

Annual Effigy Mounds Hawkwatch
Harpers Ferry, Iowa
Tel: 319-873-3491

Kern Valley Vulture Festival
Kern River Preserve, Box 1662, Weldon, CA 93283
Tel: 760-378-3345

Fall Birding Weekend
Elkins, West Virginia
Tel: 304-637-4082

Midwest Birding Symposium
MBS Information, P.O.Box 110, Marietta, OH 45750
Tel: (888) 844-6330

October

Cape May Autumn Weekend
Cape May Bird Observatory, 707 E. Lake Dr., Box 3, Cape May Point, NJ 08212
Tel: 609-884-2736

Bridger Raptor Festival
Bozeman, Montana
Tel: 406-587-5920

Migration Madness
Campbellville, Ontario
Tel: 905-854-2276

Eastern Shore Birding Festival
Delmarva Peninsula, Virginia
Eastern Shore of Virginia Chamber of Commerce, P.O. Drawer R, Melfa, VA 23410
Tel: 757-787-2460.

National Wildlife Refuge Week at Chincoteague NWR
Chincoteague, Virginia
Tel: 757-336-6122

Buteos on the Beach
Hollywood, Florida
Tel: 954-923-4000

The Bird Show
Cape May, New Jersey
Tel: 609-884-2736

November

Avocet Festival
San Francisco Bay National Wildlife Refuge, P.O. Box Box 524, Newark, CA 94560-0524
Tel: (510) 792-0222

Snow Goose Festival
Delta, British Columbia
Tel: 604-946-6980

Wings Over Water Festival
Manteo, North Carolina
Tel: 800-446-6262

Swan Watch Weekend
Winona, Minnesota
Tel: 800-657-4972

Lodi Crane Festival
Lodi, California
Tel: 800-304-LODI

Rio Grande Valley Birding Festival
Harlingen, Texas
Birds such as the Altamira oriole, brown jay, chachalacas, and other Valley specialities.
The "Bottom Half" of the Great Texas Bird Trail.
Contact: Harlingen Chamber of Commerce, 311 East Tyler, Harlingen, TX 78550
Tel: 800-531-7346

Alaska Bald Eagle Festival
Haines, Alaska
Nearly 4,000 eagles in the area, drawn by the salmon in the Chilkat River Valley.
Contact: Alaska Bald Eagle Festival, Box 1449, Haines, AK 99827
Tel: 907-766-2202 or 800-246-6268.

Space Coast Flyway Festival
Titusville, Florida
Tel: 407-267-3035

Festival of the Cranes
Socorro Chamber of Commerce, Box 743,
Socorro, NM 87801
Tel: 505-835-0424.

Waterfowl Week
Chincoteague, Virginia
Tel: 757-336-6122

December

Squaw Creek Eagle Days
Mound City, Missouri
Tel: 660-442-3187

Swan Days
Mattamuskeet NWR, Route 1, Box N-2,
Swan Quarter, NC 27885
Tel: 919-926-4021

Eagle Watch Weekend
Coeur d'Alene, Idaho
Tel: 208-769-5000

Tour Operators

Guides to Guided Bird Tours
27 Tall Cedar Court, RR 6, Belle Mead, NJ
08502
Tel: (908) 359-2097

Africa

African Adrenalin (Southern Africa)
http://AfricanAdrenalin.co.za/

African Travel Gateway – Focus Tours
Wildnet Africa, P.O.Box 73528, Lynnwood
Ridge 0040, South Africa
Tel: +2712 991-3083 Fax: +2712 991-3851
Email: webmaster@wildnetafrica.com
Internet:
http://africantravel.com/index.html

Bellbird Safaris (Southern Africa)
Box 158, Livermore, CO 80536
Tel: 800/726-0656, 970/498-9888 Fax: 498-
9766
Email: bellbird@jymis.com
Internet: http://york.jymis.com/bellbird/

Lawson's Tours (Southern Africa)
Internet: http://africanadrenalin.com/law-
sons/lawson.htm
Email: lynette@adventures.co.za

Peter Ginn Birding Safaris (Zimbabwe)
P.O. Box 44, Marondera, Zimbabwe
Ph/fax: 179-23411
Int'l Fax/ Tel: +263-79-23411
Internet:
http://www.awod.com/gallery/business/tai/
ginn.html

Rafiki Safaris (Kenya and Tanzania)
45 Rawson Ave., Camden, ME 04843
Tel: 207-236-4244 Fax: 207-236-6253
Email: rafiki@midcoast.com
Internet: http://www.gorp.com/rafiki/

Asia

Kingbird Tours
Box 196, Planatarium Station, New York,
NY 10024
Tel: (212) 866-7923

Kingfisher Tours (Hong Kong)
2 Villa Paloma, Shuen Wan, Tai Po, Hong
Kong
Tel: (852) 2665 8506 Fax: (852) 2665 8190
Email: myrl@kthk.com.hk
Web: www.kthk.com.hk

R. Subaraj (Singapore and W. Malaysia)
Blk 127, Tampines Street 11, #09-444,
Singapore 1852
Tel: 011 65 787 7048 011 65 787 4733

Varuna Travels & Tours (Nepal)
GPO Box: 1728, Thamel, Kathmandu
Tel: 410655, 424889 Fax: 00977 1 220143
Internet: http://webmerchants.com/varuna/

Russia

East-West Discovery
P.O. Box 69, Volcano, HI 96785
Tel: 808-985-8552 Fax:808-967-8525
Email: eastwest@interpac.net
(Specializes in the Russian Far East)

Grus Expeditions (Russian Far East)
53 W. Jackson Blvd., Suite 1350, Chicago, IL 60604
Tel: 312-663-1800 Fax: 312-663-9405
Internet: http://www.grus.com/

K & I Excursions
18201 Evergreen, Villa Park, CA 92667
Tel: 1 800 285-9845

Europe

Avian Adventures (UK)
Three Woodhaven, Wedge Mills, Cannock, WS11 1RE, England
Tel: 922-417102

British Birding Tours (UK)
BBT(3), 3 Eyhorne Cottage, Musket Lane, Hollingbourne, Kent ME17 1UY, England
Tel/Fax: 011 44 1622 880319

Ibis Excursions (Denmark)
Ganløseparken 46, 3660 Stenløse, Denmark
Tel: (45) 48 19 59 40 Fax: (45) 48 19 59 45
Email: jeffprice@ibis-excursions.dk
Internet: http://www.ibis-excursions.dk

Irish Ecology Tours (Ireland)
Richard Mine Road, Suite E8, Wharton, NJ 07885
1 800 242-7020

Lapwing Tours (UK)
2836 Patilla Ave., Vero Beach, FL 32960
Tel: (407) 562-5247

NatuurBeleven (Netherlands)
6, 1184 TV AMSTELVEEN
Tel.: 020-4961620 Fax: 020-4961620
Email: markui@globalxs.nl
Internet: http://www.infoplaza.nl/ natuurbeleven/, Oostermeerkade

Nick Pope (UK)
2/38 Carshalton Grove, Sutton, Surrey SM1 4LZ, England
Tel: 4461-661-0421

Ornitholidays
1-3, Victoria Drive, Bognor Regis, West Sussex PO21 2PW, England
Tel: 011 44 1243 821230 Fax: 011 44 1243 829574

Wessex Bird Tours (UK)
12 Redland Court Road, Bristol BS6 7EQ, Avon, England
Tel: 01144-272-246255

South & Central America

Antshrike
http://www.maxsite.com/antshrike/

Arete Tours (Jamaica)
Box 362, Middleton, WI 53563
Tel: (608) 831-8235

Asa Wright Nature Centre and Lodge
c/o Caligo Ventures, Inc., 156 Bedford Road, Armonk, NY 10504
Tel: 1 800 426-7781

Birdwatch Costa Rica
Apartado 7911, San Jose, Costa Rica
Fax: (011) 506-228-1573

Caligo Ventures Tours and Travel Trinidad & Tobago
Caligo Ventures, Inc, 156 Bedford Road, Armonk, NY 10504
Toll-Free in the U.S. and Canada
1-800-426-7781
Tel: (914) 273-6333 FAX (914) 273-6370
Email: 103465.1047@compuserve.com
Internet: http://www.webcom.com/caligo/

Chan Chich Lodge (Belize)
Box 37, Belize City, Belize
Tel: 1 800 343-8009 (501) 2-75634

Chau Hiix Lodge (Belize)
Tel: 1 800 654-4424

Olga L. Clarke (Costa Rica)
2027 El Arbolita Drive, Glendale, CA 91208
Tel: (818) 249-5537

Clockwork Travel
5210 Pershing Avenue, Fort Worth, TX
76107
Tel: 800 752 6246 or (817) 735 4130 Fax:
(817) 735 8930
Email: kenneth@clockbird.com
Internet: http://www.clockbird.com/

Costa Rica Resources Co.
10031 Fourth Ave., Suite 3G, Bay Bridge,
NY 11209
Tel: (718) 748-2158

Condor Pacific Eco Tours of the Americas
1730 Omie Way, Lawrenceville, GA 30243
Tel: (404) 995-7537

Corobici River Trips (Costa Rica)
Safaris Corobici, S.A. Canas, Guanacaste,
Costa Rica
Tel: 011.506.669.1091
Email: safaris@nicoya.com
Internet: http://www.nicoya.com/

Ecoltravel (Colombia)
ECOLTRAVEL TOUR OPERATORS
Avenida 15 No.114-09 L. 7 Int. 5, Hotel
Dann Norte Santafé de Bogotá, D. C.,
Colombia, South America
Tel: (57-1)215-3333 – Fax: (57-1)619-6181
– Celular Phone: (93)228-3477.
Email: ecoltrav@alephnet.com
Internet: http://www.alephnet.com/ecoltravel/

Ecoturismo Yucatan
Calle 3 No. 235 x 32A y 34 Col. Pensiones,
C.P. 97219 Mérida, Yucatán, México
Tel: (99) 20-2772 & 25-2187 Fax: (99) 25-9047
Email: ecoyuc@minter.cieamer.conacyt.mx
Internet: http://www.imagenet.com.mx/
EcoYuc/Home.html

Flora and Fauna FieldTours
232 Bellair Drive, Bolton, ON L7E 1Z7
(416) 857-2235

Focus Tours
14821 Hillside Lane, No. 25, Burnsville, MN
55306
Tel /Fax: 612-892-7830

Galapagós Travel
P.O. Box 1220, San Juan Bautista, CA
95045-1220
Tel: 800-969-9014 (Toll free from the U.S.
and Canada)
Tel: 408-623-2920 Fax: 408-623-2923
Email: galapagostravel@compuserve.com.
Internet: http://www.galapagostravel.com/
galapagos/

Green Tracks Tropical Tours
10 Town Plaza, Suite 231, Durango, CO 81301
Tel: Free U.S.A. & Canada: (800) 9-MONKEY
Tel. and Fax: 970-247-8378
Email: gnzg54a@prodigy.com
Internet: http://www.greentracks.com/

Grupo Turven (Venezuela)
Calle Real de Sabana Grande, Edf. Union,
Piso 1, Local 13, P.O. Box 6062, Caracas,
Venezuela
Tel: Venezuela Int. Code: ++58/Caracas
Area Code: 2 Tel: 952.6961 Fax: 951.1176
Email: turven@euribia.it
Internet: http://www.euribia.it/host/turven/

Miller Nature Tours (Costa Rica)
RD 1, Box 1152, Maryland, NY 12116
Tel: (607) 432-5767

Neblina Forest Birding Tours
Tel: 1 800 538 2149 Fax: 011 593 2 567 828
Email; mrvaden@pi.pro.ec

Neotropical Bird Tours
38 Brookside Ave., Livingston, NJ 07039
Tel: 1 800 662-4852

OBServ, Inc.
3901 Trimble Road, Nashville, TN 37215
Tel: 615-292-2739 Fax: 615-292-0955
Email: observinc@aol.com

Oraganization for Tropical Studies
(Costa Rica)
Box 90630, Durham, NC 27708
Tel: (919) 684-5774

Osprey Tours
Box 832, West Tisbury, MA 02575
Tel: (508) 645-9049

Peregrine Enterprises (Trinidad & Tobago)
William L. Murphy, 1011 Ann Street,
Parkersburg, WV 26101-4324
Tel:1-304-485-4710
Email: bmurphy@eurekanet.com
Internet: http://members.aol.com/murph3000/

La Posada de la Montana Costa Rica
Box 308, Greenfield, MO 65661
Tel: 1 800 632-3892

Rancho Naturalista
Apartado 364-1002, San José, Costa Rica
Tel: (506) 39-7138

Sacha Lodge
P.O Box 17171212, Quito, Ecuador
Tel: 522 220-508 871 Fax: 011-593-2-508-872

Selva Bananito Lodge
Apdo. 801-1007, San José, Costa Rica
Costa Rica: Tel/Fax (506) 253-8118 / USA:
Tel/Fax (515) 236-3894
Email: costari@netins.net
Internet: http://www.netins.net/showcase/
costarica/index.html

La Selva Jungle Lodge
6 de Diciembre 2816, Quito, Ecuador
Tel: 550-995 554-686

Selva Verde Lodge
c/o Costa Rica Experts, 3540 NW 13th
Street, Gainsville, FL 32609
Tel: 1 800 858-0999

Michael Snow
Apartado 73, 7200 Siquirres, Costa Rica

Solimar
Apdo. 164-3000 Herada, Costa Rica
Tel: (506) 238-3890 Fax: (506) 237-0196

Touring Society of Jamaica
Box 13, Duncans, Jamaica
Tel: 1 800 624-4935 (809) 925-2253

Villa Encantada (Costa Rica)
Glenn McBride
Tel: 1-800-282-3919 Fax: 602-839-8223
(within USA)
International: 602-839-3919 In Costa Rica:
011-506-694-4169
Email: costavla@worldviewsintl.com
Internet:
http://www.worldviewsintl.com/costavla/

Winchester Tours
P.O. Box 706, New London, NH 03257
Tel: 800-391-2473 or 603-526-9270

Oceania

Birdwatching in Australia
Tel: 800-282-7626 (U.S. & Canada),
+1-602-953-1827 Fax+1-602-953-7279
Email: birdwatcher@birdwatch.com
Internet: http://www.birdwatch.com/

Cassowary House
P.O. Box 252, Kuranda, Queensland 4872,
Australia
Tel: 61 70 93 7318

Diomedea Pty. Ltd.
Alan McBride, Box 190, Cremorne
Junction, New South Wales 2090, Australia
Tel: 62-2-953-2546

Emu Tours Australia
P.O. Box 4, Jamberoo, NSW 2533, Australia
Tel: 61 2 4236 0542 Fax: 61 2 4236 0176
Email emutours@ozemail.com.au
Internet: http://www.ozemail.com.au/
~emutours/

Falcon Tours
One Simons Drive, Roleystone, Western
Australia 6111, Australia

Fine Feather Tours (Australia)
P.O. Box 853, Mossman, North Queensland
4873, Australia
Tel /Fax: (070) 983 103

International: 61 70 983 103
Email: fifetour@ozemail.com.au
Internet: http://www.ozemail.com.au/
~fifetour/

Gipsy Point Lodge
Alan Robertson, Gipsy Point, Victoria 3891,
Australia
Tel: 051-58-8205

Inland Bird Tours
94 Hunter Street, Deniliquin, New South
Wales 2710, Australia
Tel: 058-815278

Kimberley Birdwatching
P.O. Box 220, Broome, W. Australia 6725
Tel/Fax: 011 61 8 9192 1246

Kingfisher Park
Box 133, Silkwood, North Queensland
4856, Australia

Kirrama Wildlife Tours (Northern
Australia)
P.O. Box 133, Silkwood, North Queensland
4856, Australia
Tel: (07) 4065 5181 Fax: (07) 4065 5197
International Tel: 61 7 40655 181
International Fax: 61 7 40655 197
Email: kirrama@4kz.com.au
Internet: http://www.gspeak.com.au/kirrama/

Kiwi Wildlife Tours (New Zealand)
Kiwi Wildlife Tours, 24 Polkinghorne Drive,
Manly, Whangaparaoa, North Auckland, NZ
Tel: 64 9 4242505 Fax: 64 9 4280347
Email: info@kiwi-wildlife.co.nz
Internet: http://www.kiwi-
wildlife.co.nz/Sounds/ls_kiwi.au

Lotus Bird Lodge
P.O. Box 187, Clifton Beach, Queensland
4879, Australia
Tel: +61 (07) 40 590 773 I 1 800 674 974
Fax: +61 (07) 40 590 703 (In Australia) In
U.S.A: 1 800 884 2848 I Fax: 1 714 495 5390
Email: cwtappletrvl@earthlink.net
Internet: http://www.cairns.aust.com/
lotusbird/

Philip Maher
94 Hunter Street, Deniliquin, New South
Wales 2710, Australia
Tel: 058-815278

Graham Pizzy
Victoria Valley Road, Dunkeld, Victoria
3191, Australia

North America

Canada

Cape Perce Nature Tours (Nova-Scotia)
c/o Cathy and Allan Murrant, Sand Lake
Rd. RR1, Port Morien, NS B0A 1T0
Tel: (902)737-2684
Email: cmurrant@highlander.cbnet.ns.ca
Internet: http://compu-clone.ns.ca/
~cmurrant/

Churchill Wilderness Encounter
P.O. Box 9, Churchhill, Manitoba R0B 0E0
Tel: 1-800-265-9458 (204) 675-2248
Fax: (204) 675-2045

Eagle-Eye Tours Inc. (Canada)
P.O. Box 94672, Richmond, BC V6Y 4A4
Tel:1-800-373-5678
Email: birdtours@eagle-eye.com

**Expéditions écologiques de la Société de
Biologie de Montréal**
Société de Biologie de Montréal, 4777,
avenue Pierre-de-Coubertin, Montréal, PQ
H1V 1B3
Tel: (514) 868-3278
Email: execo@geocities.com
Internet: http://www.geocities.com/Yosemite/
8104/accueil.html

Toonoonik Sahoonik Tours
Toonoonik Sahoonik Outfitters, Pond Inlet,
NWT X0A 0S0
Tel: (819) 899-8366 or Fax (819) 899-8364
Internet: http://www.pondtour.com/

Whitewolf Adventure Expeditions
(Canada's Far North)
41-1355 Citadel Drive, Port Coquitlam,
BC V3C 5X6

Tel: (604) 944-5500 Fax (604) 944-3131 1-800-661-6659
Email: adventures@wwolf.com
Internet: http://www.wwolf.com/

United States

ALASKA

Arctic Treks
Jim Campbell and Carol Kasza, Box 73452, Fairbanks, AK 99707
Tel: (907) 455-6502 Fax: (907) 455-6522
Email: arctreks@polarnet.com
Internet: http://www.gorp.com/arctreks/

Discovery Voyages
Box 1500, Cordova, AK 99574
Tel: 800-324-7602

Nature Alaska Tours
P.O. Box 10224 ABA, Fairbanks, AK 99710
Tel/Fax: (907) 488 3746
Email: dwetzel@alaska.net

Steller Wildlife & Exploring
403 Lincoln Street, Ste. 234, Sitka, AK 99835
Tel: 907-747-6157 – Fax: 907-747-3462
Email: 71610.3500@compuserve.com

St. Paul Island Tour
1500 West 33rd Ave, Suite 220, Anchorage, AK 99503
Tel:800-544-2248 – Fax:907-278-2316

Wilderness Birding Adventures
P.O. Box 10-3747, Anchorage, AK 99510-3747
Tel /Fax:907-694-7442

ARIZONA

North Star Alaska
Box 1724, Flagstaff, AZ 86002
Tel: 800-258-8434 – Fax: 520-773-9917

Wings
1643 N. Alvernon Way, Suite 105 BD, Tucson, AZ 85712
Tel: (520) 320-9868 Fax: (520) 320-9373
Email: wings@rtd.com
Internet: http://tucson.com/wings/

CALIFORNIA

Inca Floats
1311 63rd St., Emeryville, CA 94608
Tel: 510-420-1550

Jeff Goodwin Birding Adventures
8492 Gravenstein, Suite C139, Cotati, CA 94931
Tel: 707-794-9361 – Fax:707-794-7297

Los Angeles Audubon Society
7377 Santa Monica Blvd., West Hollywood, CA 90046
Tel: 213-876-0202

Shearwater Journeys
P.O. Box 190, Hollister, CA 95024
Tel: 408-637-8527

FLORIDA

Bird Bonanzas, Inc.
P.O. Box 611563, North Miami, FL 33161
Tel: 305-895-0607 Fax: 305-892-1752

Caribbean Conservation Corporation
4424 NW 13th St. Suite #A1, Gainesville, FL 32609
Tel: 352-373-6441 800-678-7853
Email: resprog@ccturtle.org
Internet: http://www.ccturtle.org/program.htm
(Tortugas & Costa Rica)

Explorations, Inc.
27655 Kent Rd., Bonita Springs, FL 33923
Tel: 800-446-9660 Fax: 941-992-7666
(Amazon Basin)

Florida Nature Tours
Box 5643, Winter Park, FL 32793-5643
Tel:407-273-4400
(Dry Tortugas and South Florida)

Focus Nature Tours
P.O. Box 21230, St. Petersburg, FL 33742
Tel: (813) 523-3338

Swampland Bird Tours Florida
Tel: 941-467-4411 Fax: 941-467-9119
Internet: http://www.geocities.com/CapeCanaveral/1020/swampland.html

HAWAII

Hawaii Forest and Trail
P.O. Box 2975, Kailua-Kona, HI 96745
Tel: 808-329-1993

McCandless Ranch Tours
P.O. Box 500, Honaunau, HI 96726
Tel: (808) 328-8246 Fax: (808) 328-8671
Email: hicrow@aloha.net

Terran Tours
PO Box 1018, Wajmea, Kauai, HI 96796
Tel: (808) 335-3313

IDAHO

Tour du Jour
Poo Wright-Pulliam, P.O. Box 581, Sun
Valley, ID 83353
Tel: (208) 788 – 3903
Email: trdjr@micron.net
Internet: http://netnow.micron.net/~trdjr/

ILLINOIS

Attour, Inc.
2027 Partridge Lane, Highland Park, IL 60035
Tel: 1-888-BRD-ATTU or Tel:(708)-831-0207
Fax: 1-847-831-0309 or (708)-831-0309
Internet: http://www.attu.com/

Tropical Birding Adventures, Inc.
PO Box 81888, Chicago, IL 60681
Tel:800-GO-2-BIRD Fax: 312-777-2923

MAINE

Bold Coast
P.O. Box 364, Cutler, ME 04626
Tel: 207-259-4484
Email: afp@maine.com
Internet: http://w3.maine.com/afp/

Marine Atlantic ie the Bluenose Ferry
Box 250, North Sydney, NS B2A 3M3
Tel:800-341-7981 or 902-794-5700
(Maritime Canada & Maine Coast)

Norton Puffin Tours
Captain Barna Norton, RR 1, Box 990,
Jonesport, ME, 04649-9704
Tel: 800-454-5467

Email: paulg@mix-net.net
Internet: http://www.mainebirding.net/puffin/
(Maine)

Sea Bird Watcher Co.
52 West. St., Bar Harbor, ME 04069
Tel: 1-800-247-3794 or 1-207-288-2025
(Puffins)

MARYLAND

Audubon Naturalist Society
8940 Jones Mill Rd., Chevy Chase, MD
20815
Tel:301-652-9188 Fax:301-951-7179

MASSACHUSETTS

Massachusetts Audubon Society
Natural History Travel, Lincoln, MA 01773
Tel:1-800-289-9504 or 617-259-9500
(Pelagic expeditions from Cape Cod)

MICHIGAN

Sault Convention and Visitors Bureau
Whitefish Point Bird Observatory, 2581-I75
Business spur, Sault Ste. Marie, MI 49783
(Guided tours for owls)

MONTANA

Centennial Birding Tours
Tel: 406-683-5592
(Montana and Yellowstone National Park)

Delaney EcoTours, Ltd.
431 Lafayette Center, Ste. 222, Manchester,
MO 63011-3971
Tel: (314) 230-9675

NEW JERSEY

Neotropic Bird Tours
38 Brookside Ave., Livingston, NJ 07039
Tel: 201-716-0828 Fax: 201-884-2211

NEW YORK

Wonder Bird Tours
Box 2015, New York, NY 10159
Tel: 800-BIRDTOUR Fax: 212-736-0965

NORTH CAROLINA

Pterodroma Ptours
303 Dunhagen Place, Cary, NC 27511
Tel: 919-460-0338
(Pelagic trips off the North Carolina coast)

PENNSYLVANIA

Birding Adventures
201 Elm Ave., Swarthmore, PA 19081
Tel: 610-543-8360

Early Bird Nature Tours
63 South Park Ave., Coatesville, PA 19320
Tel:610-383-8840 Fax: 717-548-3327

TEXAS

Field Guides
P.O. Box 160723, Austin, TX, 78716
Tel:1-800-728-4953 1-512-327-4953 Fax:1-512-327-9231
Email: fgileader@aol.com
Internet: http://www.fieldguides.com/

Pinfeathers Tours
Box 38157, Houston, TX 77238-8157

Victor Emanuel Nature Tours
P.O. Box 33008, Austin, TX 78764
Tel:1-800-328-VENT (512) 328-5221 Fax: 512-328-2919
Email: VENTBIRD@aol.com

Whooping Crane Tours
2637 Harbor Cove #10D, Rockport, TX 78362
Tel: 800-782-BIRD or 512-749-5760
(75-ft. catamaran for viewing Whooping cranes, gulls, terns, and shorebirds)

VIRGINIA

Brian Patteson Pelagic Tours
P.O. Box 1135, Amherst, VI 24521
Tel:804-933-8687
Email: Brian@Patteson.com
Internet: http://www.patteson.com/
(Mid-Atlantic seaboard pelagic trips, incl. Australia)

WASHINGTON

Eagle-Eye Tours Inc.
P.O. Box 5010, Point Roberts, WA 98281
Tel:1-800-373-5678 (604) 948-9177 Fax: (604) 948-9085
Email: birdtours@eagle-eye.com

Pacific Catalyst
313 Jackson St., Port Townsend, WA 98368
Tel: 360-385-2793 Fax: 360-385-2793
Email: catalyst@olympus.net

Pandion Nature Tours
14175 Henderson Rd., Bainbridge Island, WA 98110
Tel: 206-842-8138 Fax: 206-842-7106
Email: geopandion@aol.com

Westport Seabirds
3041 Eldridge, Bellingham, WA 98225
Tel: 360-733-8255
(pelagic trips)

WISCONSIN

Ram Associates
1319 Oakwood Ave., Menomonie, WI 54751
Tel: 715-235-5174

Worldwide

Abercrombie and Kent
1520 Kensington Road, Oak Brook, IL 60521-2141
Tel: 1-800-323-7308
http://www.abercrombiekent.com/

American Birding Association Tours (ABA)
P.O.Box 6599, Colorado Springs, CO 80934
Tel: 800-634-7736 Fax: 800-590-2473
(Tours world wide)

Birds and Birders
Box 737, 9700 AS Groningen, Holland

Birdquest
Two Jays, Kemple End, Birdy Brow, Stonyhurst, Lancashire BB6 9QY, England
Tel: 011 44-254-826317 Fax: 011 44 1254 826780
Email: birders@birdquest.co.uk

Bird Treks
115 Peach Bottom Village, Peach Bottom, PA 17563-9716
Tel: 717-548-3303 Fax: 717-548-3327
Email: birdtrek@epix.net
Internet: http://www.wfu.edu/~roystkt4/schutsky/

Borderland Tours
2550 W. Calle Padilla, Tuscon, AZ 85745
Tel: 800-525-7753

Cal Nature Tours
7310 SVL Box Victorville, CA 92392
Tel: (619) 241-2322

Cheeseman's Ecology/Birding Safaris
20800 Kittredge Road, Saratoga, CA 95070
Tel: (800) 527-5330 Locally: (408) 867-1371
Fax: (408) 741-0358
Email: cheesemans@aol.com
Internet: http://www.cheesemans.com/

Clipper Adventure Cruises
7711 Bonhomme Ave., St. Louis, MO 63015
Tel: 1 800 325-0010 (314) 727-6576

Connecticut Audubon
90 Main St., Centerbrook, CT 06409
Email: ctaudubon@aol.com

Destinations
114 Malone Hollow Road, Jonesborough, TN 37659
Tel: (615) 753-7831

Eco-Expeditions
1414 Dexter Ave. North, Suite 327, Seattle, WA 98109
Tel: 1 800 628-8747

Explore Shipping Corporation
1520 Kensington Rd., Suite 201, Oak Brook, IL 60521
Tel: 1 800 323-7308

Focus on Nature Tours
P.O. Box 9021, Wilmington, DE 19809
Tel: (302) 529-1876 Fax (302) 529-1085
Email: FONT@FOCUSONNATURE.COM
FONT@wittnet.com
Internet: http://www.focusonnature.com/

Holbrook Travel Inc.
3540 NW 13th Street, Gainesville, FL 32609
Tel: 1 800 451-7111 (904) 377-7111

International Expeditions Inc.
One Environs Park, Helena, AL 35080
Tel:1-800-633-4734 (205) 429-1700

Martin Travel
5216 Pershing Ave., Fort Worth, TX 76107
Tel: (817) 377-BIRD

National Audubon Society
700 Broadway, New York, NY 10003
Tel: (212) 979-3000

Peregrine Enterprises Inc.
101 Rathbone Terrace, Marrieta, OH 45750
Tel: (614) 373-3966

Princeton Nature Tours Inc.
282 Western Way, Princeton, NJ 08540
Tel: (609) 683-1111

Questers Worldwide Nature Tours
257 Park Ave. South, New York, NY 10010
Tel: 1 800 468-8668

Raptours
P.O. Box 9021, Wilmington, DE 19809
Tel: (302) 529-1876 Fax (302) 529-1085
Email: raptours@focusonnature.com
Internet: http://www.focusonnature.com/

Treks
Route 2, P.O. Box 210, Kempton, PA 19529
Tel: 610-756-4486 Fax: 610-756-4402
Email: NATURECORP@AOL.COM

Voyagers International
Dave Blanton, Box 915, Ithaca, NY 14851
Tel: 1 800 633-0299

Wildgoose Travel
Box 706, Pacifica, CA 94044
Tel: 1 800 432-2391

Woodstar Tours Inc.
908 South Massachusetts Ave., De Land, FL
32724-7022
Tel: 904-736-0327

Zegrahm & Eco Expeditions
1414 Dexter Ave N #327, Seattle, WA 98109
Tel:1-800-628-8747 (206)285-4000 Fax:
(206)285-5037
Email: zoe@zeco.com
zegrahm@accessone.com
Internet: http://www.zeco.com/zeco.html

Hawk-Watching Sites

TOP THIRTY WATCHSITES WITH AT LEAST 10,000 MIGRANT RAPTORS ANNUALLY

North America

Canada

Beamer Conservation Area, ON
Hawk Cliff, ON
Holiday Beach, ON

United States

Braddock Bay, NY
Cape May Point, NJ
Derby Hill, NY
Golden Gate Observatory, CA
Goshute Mountains, NV
Hawk Mountain Sanctuary, PA
Hawk Ridge, MN
Montclair, NJ

Central America

Cerro San Gill, Guatemala
Veracruz Coastal Plain, Mexico
Southern Panama Canal Zone, Panama

South America

Combeima Canyon, Colombia

Europe

Atanassovo Lake, Bulgaria
Organbidexka, France
Tarifa, Strait of Gibraltar, Spain
Gibraltar (United Kingdom), Spain
Falsterbo, Sweden
Bosphorus-Istanbul, Turkey

Africa

Bab-el-Mandeb, Djibouti
Cap Bon, Tunisia

Asia

Bedaihe, China
Arava Valley, Israel
Elat, Israel
Chokpak Pass, Kazakstan
Belen Pass, Turkey

Pacific Islands

Teluk Terima, Indonesia
Sheting, Taiwan

SOURCE: "Hawks Aloft Worldwide" – a Conservation Initiative of Hawk Mountain Sanctuary Association, 1700 Hawk Mountain Rd., Kempton PA 19529-9449, U.S.A. Tel: (610) 756-6961 Fax: (610) 756-4461

HAWK MOUNTAIN SANCTUARY FLIGHT
STATISTICS OVER SIXTY YEARS

	60-yr. Annual Average	10-yr. Annual (1987–1997)	High count (yr.)	
Bald eagle	47	84	136	(1995)
Golden eagle	45	75	101	(1997)
Turkey vulture	76	138	238	(1997)
Black vulture	6	40	54	(1994)
Osprey	342	625	872	(1990)
American kestrel	367	631	839	(1989)
Merlin	33	99	168	(1995)
Peregrine falcon	23	37	60	(1997)
Red-shouldered hawk	245	294	468	(1958)
Broad-winged hawk	8,527	6,209	29,519	(1978)
Red-tailed hawk	3,208	3,844	6,208	(1939)
Rough-legged hawk	9	11	31	(1961)
Sharp-shinned hawk	4,246	6,281	10,612	(1977)
Cooper's hawk	283	603	786	(1989)
Northern goshawk	69	62	347	(1972)
Northern harrier	223	279	475	(1980)

SOURCE: Hawk Mountain Sanctuary Bookstore, 1700 Hawk Mountain Road, Kempton, PA. 19529-9449.
Tel: (610) 756-6961 Fax: (610) 756-4468

GOLDEN GATE RAPTOR OBSERVATORY FLIGHT STATISTICS

	Number of Raptor Sightings	
	89-97 avg.	High count (yr.)
Turkey vulture	5096	9933 (1997)
Osprey	68	112 (1989)
White-tailed kite	38	74 (1994)
Bald eagle	2	4 (1989)
Northern harrier	581	1289 (1997)
Sharp-shinned hawk	3684	5762 (1993)
Cooper's hawk	2005	2746 (1996)
Northern goshawk	1	11 (1988)
Red-shouldered hawk	217	286 (1997)
Broad-winged hawk	104	251 (1991)
Swainson's hawk	3	9 (1990)
Red-tailed hawk	6913	10,627 (1997)
Ferruginous hawk	19	35 (1987)
Rough-legged hawk	7	69 (1988)
Golden eagle	17	39 (1987)
American kestrel	545	762 (1997)
Merlin	93	187 (1994)
Peregrine falcon	77	224 (1997)
Prairie falcon	7	18 (1989)
Unidentified	1660	2217 (1996)

SOURCE: Golden Gate Raptor Observatory (GGRO), Building 201, Fort Mason, San Francisco, CA 94123,
USA. Tel: 415-331-0730 Fax: 415-331-7521

Resources for Ornithologists

Optical Equipment

Bogen Photo Corp.
565 E. Crescent Ave, P.O. Box 506, Ramsey,
NJ 07446-0506, USA
Tel: +1-201-818-9500 Fax: +1-201-818-9177
Email: info@bogenphoto.com
http://www.bogenphoto.com/

The Brunton Company
620 East Monroe Ave., Riverton, WY 82501,
USA
Tel: 1-800-443-4871 +1-307-856-6559
Fax: +1-307-856-1840
Email: support@brunton.com
http://www.brunton.com/

Bushnell Sports Optics Worldwide
9200 Cody Street, Overland Park, KS 66214,
USA
Tel: 1-800-423-3537 +1-913-752-3400 Fax:
+1-913-752-3550

Bushnell Corporation of Canada
45A West Wilmot, Unit 17, Richmond Hill,
ON L4B 2P2, Canada
Tel: 1-800-361-5702 +1-905-771-2980
Fax: +1-905-771-2984

Canon Inc.
http://www.canon.co.jp

Canon USA Inc.
One Canon Plaza, Lake Success, NY 11042,
USA
Tel: +1-516-488-6700
http://www.usa.canon.com/

Carl Zeiss
73446 Oberkochen, Germany
Tel: +49(0)7364 – 20 – 0
Fax: +49(0)7364-6808

Carl Zeiss Optical
1015 Commerce Street, Petersburg, VA
23803, USA
Tel: 1-800-338-2984 +1-804-861-0033

Celestron International
2835 Columbia Street, Torrance, CA 90503,
USA
Tel: +1-310-328-9560 Fax: +1-310-212-5835
http://www.celestron.com

DOCTER-Optic Eisfeld GmbH
Coburger Strasse 71-107, D-98673 Eisfeld,
Germany

DOCTER OPTICS GmbH
Werk Wetzlar/Schwalbach, Industriegebiet,
D-35641 Schöffengrund, Germany
Tel: +49 64 45/609-129 +49 64 45/609-165
Email: sales@docteroptics.com
http://www.docteroptics.com

DOCTER-Optic Technologies, Inc
4685 Boulder Highway, Suite A, Las Vegas,
NV 89121, USA
Tel: 1-800-290-3634 +1-702-898-7161
Fax: +1-702-898-3737
http://www.globalxs.nl/home/r/roskam/
www.htm
http://www.kodiakcom.com/pressroom/
droptic.html

Electro Optics Canada Inc. (distributor)
25 Watline Avenue, G20, Mississauga, ON
L4Z 2Z1, Canada
Tel: +1-905-712-4239 +1-905-712-4238
Email: electro@passport.ca
http://www.electroptics.com/

Fuji Photo Optical Co. Ltd.
1-324 Uetake, Omiya City, Saitama 330, Japan
Tel: +81-048-668-2152
Fax: +81-048-651-8517
http://www.fujinon.co.jp/

Fujinon Inc.
10 High Point Driv, Wayne, NJ 07470, USA
Tel: +1-973-633-5600 +1-973-633-0018

Fujinon (Europe) GmbH
Halskestrasse 4, 47877 Willich, Germany
Tel: (0) 2154-924-0 (0) 2154-924-290 (fax)

Gitzo
Email: helpdesk@gitzo.com
http://www.gitzo.com/

Kinderman Canada Inc.
361 Steelcase Rd. # 3, Markham, ON
L3R 3V8, Canada
Tel: +1-905-940-9262

Kowa-Optimed Inc.
20001 S. Vermont Ave., Torrance, CA 90502,
USA
Tel: 1-800-966-5692 [1-800-966-KOWA]
Tel: +1-310-327-1913 Fax: +1-310-327-4177
Email: sales@kowa-scope.com
http://www.kowa-scope.com/

Leica AG
Poststrasse 28, Postfach 1243, CH-9001
St. Gallen, Switzerland
Tel: +41-(0)71 30 71 11
Fax: +41-(0)71 30 71 55
http://www.leica.com

Leica Camera AG
Oskar-Barnack-Strasse 11, D-35606 Solms,
Germany
Tel: +49-(0)6442 2080
Fax: +49-(0)6442 208333
Email: leica.hagenauer@freeway.de
http://www.leica-camera.com/home_e.htm
(English)

Leica Camera Inc.
156 Ludlow Avenue, Northvale, NJ 07647, USA
Tel: 1-800-222-0118 +1-201-767-7500
Fax: +1-201-767-8666
http://www.leica-camera-usa.com

Leupold & Stevens
P.O. Box 688, Beaverton, OR 97075-0688, USA
Tel: +1-503-526-5196 1-800-929-4949
http://www.leupstv.com/

Manfrotto Trading
Via Livinallongo, 3, I-20139 Milano, Italy
Tel: +39 02/5697041 Fax: +39 02/5393954
Email: trading@manfrotto.it
http://www.manfrotto.it/trading

Manfrotto Nord Srl
Z.I. di Villapaiera, I-32032 Feltre BL, Italy
Tel: +39 +439 89945 Fax: +39 +439 81434
Email: nord@manfrotto.it
Email: helpdesk@manfrotto.com
http://www.manfrotto.com

Meade Instruments Corporation
16542 Millikan Ave., Irvine, CA 92606, USA
Tel: +1-714-756-2291 Fax: +1-714-756-1450
http://www.meade.com

Meopta Prerov, a.s.
Kabelikova 1, Prerov 750 58, Czech
Republic
Tel: +42 641 / 241111 +42 641 / 204 731
Fax: 204 732
Email: meopta@meopta.cz
http://www.meopta.cz

Minolta Corporation
101 William Drive, Ramsey, NJ 07446, USA
Tel: +1-201-825-4000
http://www.minolta.com/
http://www.minoltausa.com/
http://www.minolta.de/

Mirador Optical Corporation
4040-8 Del Rey Avenue, P.O. Box 11614,
Marina del Rey, CA 90295-8854 USA
Tel: +1-310-821-5587 1-800-748-5844

Nikon Corporation
Fuji Building, 2-3, Marunouchi 3-chome,
Chiyoda-ku, Tokyo 100 Japan
Tel: +81-3-3214-5311 Fax: +81-3-3201-5856
http://www.klt.co.jp/Nikon/
http://www.mitsubishi.co.jp/companies/CO
MP40E/08.html

Nikon Inc.
1300 Walt Whitman Road, Melville, NY
11747, USA
Tel: +1-516-547-4200 Fax: +1-516-547-0309
1-800-247-3464 1-800-NIKON-US
(1-800-645-6687)
http://www.nikonusa.com/index.html

Nikon Canada Inc.
1366 Aerowood Drive, Mississauga, ON
L4W 1C1, Canada
Tel: +1-905-625-9910

Nikon U.K. Ltd.
380 Richmond Road, Kingston-upon-Thames, Surrey KT2 5PR, England
Tel: +44-181-541-4440
http://www.nikon.ch/

Olympus Optical Co., Ltd.
P.O. Box 7004, Shinukuk Monolith, 2-3-1 Nishi-Shinjuku, Shinjuku-ku, Tokyo 163-09, Japan
http://www.olympus.co.jp/

Olympus America Inc.
Two Corporate Center Drive, Melville, NY 11747, USA
Tel: 1-800-622-6372 +1-516-844-5000
Fax: +1-516-844-5262
http://www.olympusamerica.com/

Olympus Optical Co. (Europa) GmbH
http://www.olympus-europa.com/

OP/TECH USA
304 Andrea Drive, Belgrade, MT 59714, USA
Tel: 1-800-251-7815 +1-406-388-1377
Fax: +1-406-388-2063

Opticron
P.O. Box 370, Unit 21, Titan Court, Laporte Way, Luton Beds LU4 8YR, UK

Pentax Corporation
35 Inverness Drive East, Englewood, CO 80112, USA
Tel: 1-800-709-2020 +1-303-799-8000
Email: pentax@knightweb.com pentaxmc@rmii.com
http://www.pentax.com/

Pentax Europe N.V.
http://www.pentaxeurope.com/

Pioneer Research, Inc. (distributor)
97 Foster Road, Moorestown, NJ 08057, USA
Tel: 1-800-257-7742 +1-609-866-9191
Fax: +1-609-866-8615
Email: info@pioneer-research.com
http://www.pioneer-research.com/

Questar Corporation
P.O. Box 59, New Hope, PA 18938, USA
Tel: +1-215-862-5277 Fax: +1-215-862-0512

Redfield Inc.
5800 E. Jewell Avenue, Denver, CO 80224, USA
Tel: +1-303-757-6411 Fax: +1-303-756-2338
http://www.redfield.com/

Ricoh Australia Pty Ltd
[Swarovski distributors]
148 Highbury Rd., Burwood, Victoria, Australia
Tel: (03)9888 7722

SCM Corporation (distributor)
P.O. Box 7518, San Diego, CA 92167, USA
Tel: 1-800-225-9407 Fax: +1-619-692-8199

Sigma Binoculars
16 West 36 St., New York, NY 10018, USA
Tel: 1-800-442-6526 Fax: +1-212-947-3559

Simmons Outdoor Corporation
2120 Killearney Way, Tallahassee, FL 32308-3402, USA
Tel: +1-904-878-5100
http://www.blount.com/

Slik Corporation
Email: tahara@slik.com
http://www.slik.com/

Slik Tripod Division, Tocad America, Inc.
300 Webro Rd., Parsippany, NJ 07054-2882, USA
Tel: +1-201-428-9800 Fax: +1-201-887-2438
Email: tocad@specdata.com
http://www.tocad.com/slik.html

Swarovski Optik K.G.
Swarovski Strasse 70, A-6060 Absam, Tirol, Austria
Tel: +43 0 52 23 / 511-0
Fax: +43 0 52 23 / 41860
http://www.swarovskioptik.com/

Swarovski Optik North America Ltd.
One Wholesale Way, Cranston, RI 02920, USA
Tel: 1-800-426-3089 +1-401-942-3380
Fax: +1-401-946-2587

Swift Instruments, Inc.
952 Dorchester Ave., Boston, MA 02125, USA
Tel: 1-800-446-1116 +1-617-436-2960
Email: swift1@tiac.net
http://www.swift-optics.com

Tasco Sales Inc.
7600 NW 26th Street, Miami, FL 33122, USA
Tel: +1-305-591-3670 Fax: +1-305-592-5895

Tiffen Manufacturing Corporation
90 Oser Ave., Hauppauge, NY 11788, USA
Tel: 1-800-645-2522 +1-516-273-2500
Fax: +1-516-273-2557
http://www.tiffen.com

Tele Vue Optics
100 Route 59, Suffern, NY 10901, USA
Tel: +1-914-357-9522

Unitron, Inc.
170-C Wilbur Place, P.O. Box 469, Bohemia,
NY 11716, USA
Tel: +1-516-589-6666 Fax: +1-516-589-6975
http://www.pdcinc.com/unitron/home.htm

Velbon International Corporation
2433 Moreton St., P.O. Box 2927, Torrance,
CA 90505-5393, USA
Tel: 1-800-423-1623 +1-310-530-5446
Fax: +1-310-618-0166
Email: velbon@ix.netcom.com
http://www.velbon.com

Vernonscope & Co.
5 Ithaca Rd., Candor, NY 13743, USA
Tel: +1-607-659-7000 Fax: +1-607-659-4000

Vivitar Corporation
1280 Rancho Conejo Blvd., Newbury Park,
CA 91320, USA
Tel: 1-800-498-7008 Tel: +1-805-498-7008
Fax: +1-805-498-5086
Email: info@vivitar.com
http://www.vivitar.com

Bird Sound Recording and Amplification Devices

BPA Marketing, Inc.
3519 Bigelow Boul., Pittsburgh, PA 15213
Tel: 1 800 221-1196

Marice Stith Recording Services
59 Autumn Ridge Circle, Ithaca, NY 14850
Tel: 607-277-5920 Fax: 607-277-5942

Natural Technology Industries
Box 582, Youngstown, OH 44501
Tel: (216) 742-6206

Nature Sound Research
Box 84, Ithaca, NY 14851

Sonic Technology Products, Inc.
120 Richardson Street, Grass Valley, CA
95945
Tel: 1 800 247-5548

Walker's Game Ear, Inc.
P.O. Box 1069, Media, PA 19063

Bird Nest Recording Equipment

Janos Török, Behavioural Ecology Group
Dept. Syst. Zool. And Ecol.
Eötvös University
H-1088, Budapest

Puskin u. 3., Hungary
Tel: 36-1266 7864
Fax: 36-1266 7884
Email: yeti01@ludens.elte.hu

Netting for Capturing Wild Birds

Avinet, Inc.
P.O. Box 1103, Dryden, NY 13053-1103, USA
Tel: Toll-Free from U.S.A. and Canada (888)
AVI-NETS (284 6387) (607) 844-3277
Fax: (607) 844-3915.
Web: http://www.avinet.com/

Fuhrman Diversified, Inc.
905 South 8th Street, La Porte, TX 77571, USA
Tel: (713) 470-8397

SpiderTech
Jan Nordblad
Email: j.spidertech@dlc.fi
Advanced Telemetry Systems Inc.

Telemetry Gear for Tracking Birders

470 1st Ave. No., Box 398, Isanti, MI 55040
Phone: 612-444-9267 Fax: 612-444-9384
Email: 70743.512@compuserve.com
http://www.biotelem.org/ats/index.htm

Alpha Omega Computer Systems, Inc.
P.O. Box U, 33815 Eastgate Circle, Corvallis,
OR 97333
Tel: (541) 754-1911 Fax: (541) 754-1913
Email: sales@ao.com
http://www.ao.com

AVM Instrument Company, Ltd.
2356 Research Drive, Livermore, CA 94550
Tel: 510-449-2286 Fax: 510-449-3980
Email: avmtelem@ix.netcom.com
http://cccweb.com/avm

Biosonics
3670 Stone Way North, Seattle, WA 98103
Tel: 206-634-0123 Fax: 206-634-0511

Biotrack
52 Furzebrook Road, Wareham, Dorset
BH20 5AX England
Tel: +44.1929.552.992 Fax: +44.1929.554.948
Email: brian@biotrack.demon.co.uk

Custom Electronics of Urbana, Inc.
2009 Silver Ct. W., Urbana, IL 61801
Tel: 217-344-3460 Fax: 217-344-3460
Email: BSZELPAL@aol.com

Custom Telemetry Co.
1050 Industrial Drive, Watkinsville, GA
30677
Tel: 706-769-4024 Fax: 706-769-4026

Environmental Solutions, Inc.
P.O. Box 720698, San Diego, CA 92129
Tel: North America (800) 553-3818
International (619)484-0147
Fax: (619)484-7212
Email: jjohnsto@envsens.com
http://www.envsens.com/

Falcon Telmetrics
The Parsonage, Llanrothal, Monmouth NP
3QJ, UK
Tel: 01600 84300 Fax: 01600 84450

GFT – Gesellschaft fur Telemetriesysteme mbH
Eiderkamp 54, D-24582 Bordesholm
Tel: +49-(0)4322-699669
Fax: +49-(0)4322-699671
Email: RLS.GFTMBH@T-Online.de

Grant Systems Engineering
266 Alex Doner Drive, Newmarket, ON
L3X 1H3
Tel: 905-836-5029 Fax: 905-836-8365
Email: cgrant@grant.ca
http://www.grant.ca/

Holohil Systems Ltd.
112 John Cavanagh Road, Carp, ON K0A 1L0
Tel: +1.613.839.0676 Fax: +1.613.839.0675
Email: coming soon

Lotek Engineering Inc.
115 Pony Drive, Newmarket, ON L3Y 7B5
Tel: +1.905.836.6680 Fax: +1.905.836.6455
Email: telemetry@lotek.com

Mariner Radar Ltd.
Bridleway, Campsheath, Lowestoft, Suffolk
NR32 5DN, England
Tel: +44.1502.567.195 Fax:
+44.1502.567.762

Merlin Systems, Inc.
445 W Ustick Rd, Meridian, ID 83642
Tel:+1.208.884.3308 Fax:+1.208.888.9528
E-Mail: merlin@cyberhighway.net

Metocean
21 Thornhill Drive, Dartmouth, NS B3B 1R9
Tel: 902-468-2505 Fax: 902-468-4442
Email: mfr@metocean.com
http://www.metocean.com/

Microwave Telemetry Inc.
10280 Old Columbia Road, Suite 260,
Columbia, MD 21046
Tel: +1.410.290.8672 Fax: +1.410.290.8847
Email: Microwt@aol.com

Mini-Mitter Co., Inc.
P.O. Box 3386, Sunriver, OR 97707
Tel: +1.503.593.8639 Fax: +1.503.593.5604
Email: rrushmmtr@aol.com

Seimac Limited
271 Brownlow Ave., Dartmouth, NS B3B 1W6
Tel: (902) 468-3007 Fax: (902) 468-3009
Email: info@seimac.com
http://www.seimac.com/

Sirtrack: Tracking and Telemetry Systems
Sirtrack Limited, Goddard Lane, Private
Bag 1403, Havelock North, New Zealand
Tel: +64 6 877 7736 Fax: +64 6 877 5422
Email: wardd@landcare.cri.nz
http://goddess.hb.landcare.cri.nz/sirtrack/
sirtrack.html

Sonotronics
1130 E. Pennsylvania St., Suite 505, Tucson,
AZ 85714
Tel: +1.602.746.3322 Fax: +1.602.294.2040

Telemetry Solutions, Inc.
1130 Burnett Avenue, Suite J, Concord, CA
94520
Tel: (925) 798-2373 Fax: (925) 798-2375
Email: qkermeen@ix.netcom.com
http://www.track-it.com/products.html

Televilt International AB
Box 53, S-711 22 Lindesberg, Sweden
Tel: +46.581.17195 Fax: +46.581.17196

Telonics
932 East Impala Avenue, Mesa, AZ
85204-66990
Tel: +1.602.892.4444 Fax: +1.602.892.9139

Toyocom
20-4, Nishi-Shimbaxhi 3-chome, Minato-ku,
Tokyo 105 Japan
Tel: +03.3459.7320 Fax: +03.3436.1434

Toyocom Chicago
Tel: +1.708.593.8780 Fax: +1708.593.5678

Toyocom LA
Tel: +1.714.668.9081 Fax: +1.714.668.9158

Vemco
3895 Shad Bay, RR#4, Armdale, NS B3L 4J4
Tel: +1.902.852.3047 Fax: +1.902.852.4000
Email: vemco@fox.nstn.ca

Wildlife Materials Inc.
Route 1, Box 427A, Carbondale, IL 62901
Tel: +1.618.549.6330 Fax: +1.618.457.3340

Satellite Tracking Centers for Birds

The Migration Route Satellite-Tracked By ARGOSAT
http://www.wnn.or.jp/wnn-n/migrant/english/

NASA-Satellite Tracking of Endangered Species
http://outside.gsfc.nasa.gov:80/ISTO/satellite_tracking/birds_hom e2.html

Argos-Global Data Telemetry and Geo-positioning Services
North America
Tel: 301-925-4411 Fax: 301-925-8995
Email: useroffice@argosinc.com
World
Tel: (33) 61 394 700 Fax: (33) 61 751 014
Email: USEROFFICE@argos.CNES.FR
http://www.argosinc.com/

DNA Sexing of Birds

Avian Biotech International
Tel: 1-800-514-9672
Outside the U.S. 850-386-1145
Fax 850-386-1146
Email: agt@nettally.com
http://www.nettally.com/agt/

AviGene Services, Inc.
565 Science Dr., Madison, WI 53711
Tel: (608) 238-3405 Fax: 238-3715
Email: avigene@mailbag.com
http://www.mailbag.com/users/avigene/

DNA Avian Services
Concord, CA (Bay Area)
Tel: 510-685-birds (2737)
Email: birdlady@sj.bigger.net

Mutt Hut
3030 East Palmdale, Palmdale, CA 93550
Tel: (805)272-0738
Email: contact@quikpage.com
http://www.quikpage.com/cgi-bin/contact.cgi

National Veterinary Diagnostic Services
23361 El Toro Road, Suite 218, Lake Forest, CA 92630-6921
Tel: 714-859-3648 Fax: 714-859-6537
Email: info@national-vet.com
http://www.national-vet.com

PE AgGen-Davis
1756 Picasso Avenue, Davis, CA 95616 USA
Tel: (800) 995-2473 Within the US/ (530) 297-3000 Outside the US
Fax: (530) 756-5143
Email: aggendavis@peabd.com
http://www2.perkin-elmer.com/ab/aggen/

PE AgGen-SLC
2411 South 1070 West, Salt Lake City, UT 84119 USA
Tel: (800) 545-7357 Within the US/ (801) 975-1188 Outside the US
Fax: (801) 975-1244
Email: aggenslc@peabd.com
http://www2.perkin-elmer.com/ab/aggen/

PE Zoogen
1756 Picasso Avenue, Davis, CA 95616
Tel: 1-800-995-BIRD
Email: pezoogen@perkin-elmer.com
http://www2.perkin-elmer.com/zo/index.htm

Rosgen Ltd
Roslin Institute, Roslin, Midlothian
EH25 9PS UK
Tel: +44 (0)131 527 0300
Fax: +44 (0)131 527 4223
Email: enquiries@rosgen.co.uk
http://www.rosgen.co.uk

University Diagnostics Limited
Southbank Technopark, 90 London Road,
London SE1 6LN
Tel: 0171-401 9898 Fax: 0171-928 9297

Vetgen Europe
P.O. Box 60, Winchester, SO23 9XN, UK
Tel: (44) 01962-886090,
Fax: (44) 01962-881790
http://www.vetark.co.uk/Vetgen%20pages.html

Vita-Tech Canada Inc.
151 Esna Park Drive, Unit 13, Markham, ON
L3R 3B1
Tel: (416) 798-4988 Toll Free(Can & US):
(800) 667-3411
Fax: (905) 475-7309
Email: info@vita-tech.com
http://www.vita-tech.com

Will-Tell Lab
P.O. Box 50 Jefferson, OR 97352
Tel: (541)327-1783
Email: willtell@proaxis.com
http://www.proaxis.com/~willtell

Specialized Video Camera Recorders for Birds

BirdCam
Weather-resistant color video camera for outdoor photography
The Wild Bird Emporium, 21 Olde Towne Road, Auburn, NH 03032
Tel: 603 483-5523 Fax: 603 483-8444
Email: Info@wbird.com

Bird Courses and Volunteer Opportunities Related to Birds

The Bird Course
Avian Science and Conservation Centre
McGill University
21111 Lakeshore Rd.
Ste. Anne de Bellevue, PQ
H9X 3V9
Tel: 514 398 7760
Fax: 514 398 7990
Email: bird@nrs.mcgill.ca

Certificate of Higher Education in Ornithology
The University of Birmingham School of
Continuing Studies
email: Continuing-Studies@Bham.ac.uk
http://www.birmingham.ac.uk/ContStuds/
Ornithol.html

Spring Field Ornithology
Cornell Laboratory of Ornithology
159 Sapsucker Woods Road
Ithaca, NY 14850
Tel: 607-254-2440

Volunteer Opportunities for Birders 1998 Directory
American Birding Association, P.O. Box
6599, Colorado Springs, CO 80934-6599
Tel: 800 850-2473 Fax: 719 578-1480
Email: member@aba.org

Glossary

abdomen: Undersurface of bird's body, from the top of the **sternum**, or breastbone, to the **cloaca**.

aberrant: Abnormal, or different from others of its kind.

abrasion: Wear on tips of **feather vanes**, perhaps changing the appearance of the **plumage**.

accidental: Species occurring in a particular place infrequently and irregularly (AKA **vagrant**).

accipiter: Forest hawk with short, rounded wings and long tails, e.g. goshawk.

acclimation: Process of adjusting to change in environment, usually temperature.

acclimatization: Physical adjustments to seasonal changes in temperature.

acoustic meatus: Short, curved tube with a circular or oval opening that collects sound waves for hearing.

adaptive coloration: Modification of color to promote concealment or to enhance conspicuousness.

adaptive radiation: Branching-out of one species into several to fit into newly available niches.

addled: Describes an **egg** wherein the developing **embryo** has died, usually in its early stage (AKA rotten).

adult: A bird in its final **plumage** and capable of breeding.

adventitious color: **Feather** color, e.g., soiling, caused by a chemical or other matter in a bird's environment.

advertisement behavior: Evolved communication through displays to increase the conspicuousness of an individual, say for territorial purposes.

aerie: *See* **eyrie**.

aerophaneric: Coloration important in aerial display.

aetiology: The study of causation of disease.

afferent: Carrying impulses inward to nerve centers.

afterfeather: Miniature **feather** attached to the underside of a feather at its superior **umbilicus**.

after-hatching year (AHY): Bird in at least its second calendar year of life.

after-second year (ASY): Bird in at least its third calendar year of life.

aftershaft: Axis, or **shaft**, of an **afterfeather**.

after-third year (ATY): Bird in at least its fourth calendar year of life.

aggregation: A grouping of individual birds attracted to a commonly exploited environmental resource, e.g., food, wind currents.

aggression: Threatening and/or attack behavior by means of postures, movements, and/or vocalizations.

agonistic: Describing aggressive behavior between individuals, e.g., attack, escape.

air sacs: Membranous sacs, usually eight, that fill with air and help with oxygen/carbon dioxide exchange and cooling.

alarm: Visual or vocal warning.

albescence: Abnormal condition of **plumage** associated with **albinism** and looseness or hairiness of **feather** structure.

albinism: Refers to a genetically based lack of pigments occurring in various degrees.

albumen: The **egg** white surrounding and protecting the yolk.

allantois: Membranous sac that receives the waste products from and supplies oxygen to the **embryo**.

Allen's Rule: Body appendages tend to be longer in warmer parts of range and shorter in cooler ones.

allometry: Relationship between the rate of growth between different parts of an individual or between different groups or races.

allopatric: Mutually exclusive in a geographic sense.

allopreening: **Preening** of one bird by another, usually its mate.

alternate plumage: **Plumage** worn in breeding season in those **species** that have two plumages a year.

altitudinal distribution: Distribution of bird **species** in accordance with height above sea level in a given area.

altitudinal migration: Vertical **migration** of individuals during different seasons.

altricial: Describes helpless, featherless **nestlings** dependent on adults for food and warmth for first few weeks of life.

altruism: Act of increasing the chance of survival of another individual while decreasing one's own, e.g., a warning call that could attract attention of predator to caller.

alula: Small **feathers** projecting at the **wrist** of a bird's wing and functioning as a wing slot to prevent turbulence and stalling.

ambivalence: Behavioral term referring to the outcome of two or more conflicting tendencies, e.g., approach or avoidance.

ambulatory: Walking or running.

amnion: Fluid-filled sac enclosing the **embryo** inside the eggshell.

amniotic closure: Refers to protective sealing of eyes and ears during first few days of life in some birds.

anal circlet: Double row of **feathers** surrounding the **cloaca**.

anatomy: Body structure or the study of it.

androgen: Male hormone (e.g., testosterone) involved in reproduction.

angulated: Forming a distinct angle.

ankylosis: Stiffening or fixed union of a joint, occurring either naturally or pathologically.

anosmatic: Having no olfactory sense.

antaposematic: Coloration being used to threaten or dominate rivals.

antebrachium: The wing between the elbow and the **wrist**.

anthine: Pipit-like.

anthropomorphism: Describing or interpreting actions of animals in terms of human actions and thoughts.

anting: Comfort behavior of certain **passerine** birds wherein the **plumage** is treated with body fluids of ants, e.g., formic acid, and other mostly pungent substances, likely for **feather** maintenance.

antiphonal singing: Alternate singing of members of a mated **pair** and not necessarily different songs.

anvil: Hard object (e.g., stone) used by some birds to smash snails.

aposematic: Describing protective adaptations, especially dealing with color or pattern.

appendicular skeleton: The **pectoral** and pelvic girdles and the limbs of a bird's skeleton.

apterium: Area of skin devoid of **contour feathers** located between **pterylae**, or **feather** tracts.

aquiline: Eagle-like.

Archaeopteryx: Believed to be the earliest known **fossil** bird, described in 1861.

area-sensitive species: **Species** that respond negatively to decreasing **habitat** patch size.

arena: *See* **lek**.

areolae: Small naked spaces between the scales of birds' feet.

armchair tick: Bird listing due in general to the **taxonomic** splitting of a **species** or reassessment of a record.

arrested molt: Interruption of **molt** within a **feather tract**, usually **flight feathers**.

aspect ratio: Proportion of wing length to breadth.

assembly: Collection of birds of same kind, e.g., flock, flight, party, raft, host, congregation.

asymmetry: Disproportion or disparity in size of body parts, e.g., skull or internal organs.

atlas: Survey of a large geographical area that maps the occurrence or relative abundance of **species**, often restricted to a particular season, e.g., Breeding Bird Atlas.

attenuated: Tapering to a narrow tip.

auriculars: *See* **ear coverts**.

austringer: Falconer who trains and flies accipiters.

autochthonous: Refers to **indigenous species**.

autolycism: Refers to birds' use of humans and human-made objects, as well as other mammals, reptiles, fishes, and birds.

autumnal recrudescence: Reinitiation of nest-building behavior after the mating season in the fall, with reproductive hormone levels dropping from mating levels to pre-mating levels.

Aves: Scientific name of **class** of animals known as birds (plural of Latin *avis*).

aviary: Enclosed area housing captive birds.

aviculture: The keeping and breeding of non-domesticated birds in captivity.

aviculturist: *See* **bird fancier**.

avifauna: The birdlife of an area.

axial skeleton: Skull, vertebral column, ribs, and sternum.

axillaries: **Feathers** in the axilla, or armpits.

band: Distinctive broad bar of color or metal numbered ring placed on birds' legs for identification.

banding: Placing metal numbered rings on birds' legs for identification.

banner-marks: Conspicuous white areas shown during flight used to deflect predators' attacks from vulnerable areas.

barb: Lateral branch of the **rachis** of a **feather**.

barbicel: Process on a **barbule** of a **barb** of a **feather**.

barbule: Lateral branch of a **feather barb** (AKA **radius**).

bare parts: Area of body surface not covered with **feathers**, e.g., **bill**, eyes, legs, feet.

basic plumage: Plumage worn year-round in **species** with only one per year and, in those with two, the dull plumage as opposed to the breeding plumage.

bastard wing: *See* **alula**.

Batesian mimicry: Resemblance of a palatable to a distasteful **species** for a protective purpose.

bating: Falconry term referring to trained, leashed **raptor** jumping off perch or fist.

bazaar: Russian term for an association between nesting seabirds and various nesting predatory land birds, e.g., ravens, falcons, owls.

beak: Same as **bill**.

beard: Bristly appendage growing from breasts of turkeys.

Beau Geste Hypothesis: Territorial male bird uses a repertoire of song variants to simulate the presence of many individuals to dissuade intruders.

begging: Behavior wherein both young and adult birds **display** to another to secure food.

belly-soaking: Wetting of the underside of an incubating bird to assist in heat loss and/or cool the eggs, generally seen in plovers and related **species**.

belt: Broad band across the breast or belly **plumage**.

Bergmann's Rule: Body size tends to be larger in cool parts of a **species'** range and smaller in the warmer parts.

bewit: A leather bracelet to hold bell onto the leg of a falconer's bird.

Big Day: competition in which **birders** attempt to list as many **species** as possible in a 24-hour period.

bilateral symmetry: Refers to condition wherein external parts on the left and right side of the body are counterparts of one another.

bill: Projecting jaws of a bird, including upper and lower **mandibles** and their horny sheaths.

billing: Mated birds touching or caressing each other with the **bill**, or beak.

bimaculation: Occurrence of two spots in facial **plumage** of some duck **species**.

binding to: Seizing and holding the quarry by a falconer's bird.

binocular vision: Seeing an object with both eyes simultaneously to perceive depth.

biochore: Major ecological formation characterized by a general vegetation type, e.g., forest.

biochromes: Refers to pigment colors of birds as opposed to those caused by **feather** structure.

biodiversity: Variety of life forms, their ecological roles, and their genetic diversity.

biogeography: Study of the distribution of living plant and animal life.

biology: The study of life or animate nature.

biomass: The total weight of organisms per unit area of land or the total weight of organisms of a particular kind, e.g., birds.

biome: A major **biotic** community defined by certain environmental features, e.g., tundra, grassland.

biometry: Application of statistics to **biology**.

biota: General term for **flora** and **fauna**.

biotelemetry: Using radiotransmitters to track movements of birds.

biotic: Describing an organic element in the environment.

biotopes: Areas or regions fairly uniform in **flora** and **fauna** and other environmental features.

biotype: Population of same **genotype**.

bipedal: Two-footed, i.e., no use of **forearms**, for walking.

birdathon: Fundraising event whereupon sponsors pay money for each **species** seen by **bird-watchers** in a prescribed period.

bird calls: Sounds made by humans, sometimes mechanically, to attract birds.

bird city: Large concentrations of colonially nesting birds.

birder: General term to describe a more serious **bird-watcher**, eager to improve his or her skills and possibly maintaining a **life list**.

bird fancier: One who keeps and/or breeds birds (AKA aviculturist).

birding: *See* **birder**.

bird lime: Sticky lime substance applied to perches, or even live prey, to capture birds, usually migratory songbirds in Europe (*also see* **guano**).

Birdline: United Kingdom telephone service that provides up-to-date information on rare bird sightings.

Bird Race: Competition in the United Kingdom in which **birders** try to see as many **species** as possible in 24 hours.

bird's nest soup: Asian or Chinese soup made from saliva used by certain swiftlets to cement their nests.

birds of prey: Generally refers to those birds that use hooked **beaks** and strong toes with sharp **talons** to eat their food, e.g., kites, falcons, eagles, hawks, owls (AKA **raptors**).

bird strike: A collision between birds and aircraft.

bird table: Raised platform where food is put out to attract birds.

bird-watcher: General term to describe those who observe birds casually or otherwise.

bird-watching: *See* **bird-watcher**.

blastula: Stage of cell division reached by the fertilized egg while in the **shell gland**.

blind: Compact structure, e.g., small building, tent, wall, from which **bird-watchers** and **ornithologists** view birds up close.

bluebird trail: Series or line of **nest boxes** set up for bluebirds, often along country roads.

bolus: Mass or ball of food swallowed by a bird or, in the case of indigestible material, regurgitated.

booming ground: Term used in North America to describe social **display** ground of greater prairie chickens.

booted: Describes horny covering of the **tarsus**, or refers to a feathered **tarsus**.

brace: As in dead game, describes two birds of the same **species**.

brachium: The wing between the trunk and the elbow.

brailing: Binding the **manus** to the **forearm** to prevent a wing from being unfolded and, hence, to prevent flight in captive birds.

brancher: Juvenile hawk out of the nest and perching on branches, but not yet fully independent.

breastband: Dark band of **feathers** across breast of bird.

Breeding Bird Atlas: *See* **atlas**.

Breeding Bird Census: Census of breeding birds using **spot-mapping** and coordinated by the National Audubon Society.

Breeding Bird Survey: Point counts of birds along roads during **breeding season** coordinated by the U.S. Fish and Wildlife Service and Canadian Wildlife Service.

breeding cycle: Complete sequence of reproduction, from **courtship** to the independence of the young.

breeding range: Geographical area where **species** breed.

breeding season: Time period during which members of a **species** mate, lay **eggs**, and raise their young.

bridling: Facial **plumage** marking resembling a bridle or a **display** seen in black noddies.

bristle: **Feather** with a **shaft** and no **vane**, resembling a stiff hair.

broad-front migration: Movement of migrating birds across a broad geographical area.

broken-wing trick: Feigning a wing injury to draw a predator away from **eggs** or young, e.g., killdeer.

brood: All young hatching from a single **clutch** of **eggs**.

brooding: Sitting on **eggs**, but mostly young, to protect them from hot sun, rain, or predators.

brood nest: A resting place for young, not necessarily where they hatched from, built by one or both of the parents.

brood parasitism: Exploitative deposition of **eggs** by one **species** into another species' nest, occurring in about 1 percent of all bird species.

brood patch: Heavily vascularized area of the skin on the belly put into contact with **eggs** during **incubation**.

brood-reduction: Reducing the number of young in the nest to assure survival of the remaining **nestlings**.

bulla: Bony sound chamber at the base of a windpipe of a male duck.

bursa of Fabricius: Glandular sac in the upper wall of the **cloaca** of young birds believed to produce antibodies to fight disease.

busking: Aggressive **display** toward intruder by male mute swan paddling both feet in unison.

butt: Earthwork erected to conceal hunters waiting to shoot driven red grouse.

butterfly flight: Slow flapping flight used in aerial **displays** of many birds.

cadge: A carrying device used by falconers to carry more than one falcon into the field.

caecum: Blind tube branching from junction of small and large intestines, usually paired but sometimes single or absent.

cage bird: Collective term for birds, mostly psittacine and **passerine** varieties, commonly kept in captivity, and even domesticated.

Cain and Abel Syndrome: Based on biblical story, refers to sibling aggression in **raptors** (mostly eagles), herons, seabirds, etc., leading to weaker one being killed and sometimes eaten.

calamus: Bare, basal part of a feather shaft.

call: Short, distinctive **vocalization**.

cannibalism: Eating of one bird by another of the same **species**.

cannon-net: *See* **rocket net**.

canopy feeding: Behavior describing birds feeding in the crowns of trees or hunting method of black heron whereupon the wings are held forward over the head.

cap: Darker area of **feather** coloration on top of head.

capon: Castrated domestic fowl.

carinate: Having a **keel** on the **sternum**.

carnivorous: Flesh-eating.

carotenoid pigments: *See* **lipochromes**.

carpal: The **wrist** joint on the wing forming the forward-pointing prominence.

carpometacarpus: Three fused bones of the **manus**.

carpus: **Wrist** or jointed part of the wing.

carrier pigeon: Homing or domestic pigeon.

carrying capacity: Maximum number of individuals that can use a given **habitat** without degrading it and leading to population reduction.

caruncle: Conspicuous unfeathered, fleshy growth on birds' heads.

casque: Enlargement on **bill**'s upper surface on the front of the head in hornbills and on top of the head in cassowaries.

cast: Two or more trained hawks or falcons flown at the same time or to regurgitate a **pellet**.

casting: Refers to regurgitating and ejecting a **pellet** of indigestible fur, **feather**, and bone by certain **species**, e.g., owls.

casual visitor: Bird that infrequently visits a region.

catastrophe: Event that causes a sudden, remarkable decrease in a population, even its elimination.

census: Periodic count of the number of individuals in various bird **species** or the variety of species in a given geographical area.

cere: Raised fleshy area at base of upper **mandible** in **birds of prey**.

cerebellum: Part of the hindbrain that controls muscular coordination.

cerebral hemispheres: Two halves of the forebrain that houses sensory perception, instinct, and behavior functions.

cerebrum: *See* **cerebral hemispheres**.

cerophagy: Act of eating wax, e.g., honeyguides.

chalaza: Pair of twisted strands of **albumen** suspending the **yolk** as it proceeds down the **oviduct**.

character displacement: Divergence of characters, e.g., **bill** size, **plumage** markings, of closely related **species** in an area of geographical overlap.

checklist: Systematic and comprehensive list of **species** occurring in a specific geographical area or region.

chick: Vague term given to **nestling** bird in **altricial** species and **hatchlings** up to a few days of age in **precocial** species.

chicken: General name for domestic barnyard fowl.

choana: Paired funnel-shaped olfactory passages or internal **nares** located inside upper mouth.

chorion: Membrane lining the inner shell wall of an **egg**.

chorology: Study of geographical distribution of organisms.

Christmas Bird Count: Annual North American 24-hour censuses of areas 24 km in diameter by tens of thousands of **birdwatchers** between December 20 and January 2; begun in 1899.

chumming: Tossing putrid fish remains over the side of a boat to attract seabirds.

churring: Sustained low trill or reel, e.g., nightjar.

chyme: Semi-fluid, partly digested food passing from the **gizzard** to the **duodenum**.

cilary muscles: Set of muscles at the base of the **iris** that focus the lens for accommodation.

cinereous: Ashen gray.

cinnamomeous: Yellowish or reddish brown color of cinnamon.

circadian: Refers to biological rhythm of roughly 24 hours.

circannual: Refers to biological rhythms of approximately one year.

CITES: Convention on International Trade in Endangered Species signed by many countries to control trade in wildlife.

clade: *See* **cladistics**.

cladistics: Method of biological classification using characters to define relationships among different taxonomic groups, e.g., **species**.

class: A primary taxonomic category, e.g. **Aves**, Reptilia, Mammalia.

classification: Grouping of organisms into categories, or taxa (*see* **systematics**).

clavicles: Paired breast bones that form the **furcula**.

claw: Nail or **talon** at the end of the toe.

cleidoic: Refers to totally enclosed condition of birds' **eggs**, representing a virtually sealed physiological system (except for pores for gaseous exchange).

cleptoparasitism: *See* **kleptoparasitism**.

cline: A geographical gradient in a phenotypic character, e.g., **egg** size, **plumage** color, within the range of a **species**.

clipping: Cutting the primary **feathers** of one wing to render a captive bird incapable of flight.

cloaca: Combined terminal opening of the alimentary (feces), excretory (urine), and reproductive (semen, **eggs**) systems.

cloacal kiss: Male reproductive organ contacting everted **oviduct** of female during copulatory act.

close ringing: Process of slipping an unbroken band or ring over a **nestling** bird's foot for permanent identification.

club: Term for a gathering of non-breeding seabirds on the edge of a breeding colony.

clutch: A complete set of **eggs** laid by a female.

clutch size: A discrete number of **eggs** laid within a **nest**.

cob: Male swan.

cochlea: Part of inner ear designed to transform sound vibrations into nerve impulses.

cock: Male bird.

cock-fighting: Sport of pitting male domestic fowl against each other in combat.

co-evolution: Reciprocal evolutionary change in two or more interacting **species** wherein each species becomes adapted to the interaction, e.g., predator and prey.

cohort: Term for a group of individuals of similar age within a population.

coition: *See* **copulation.**

cold-searching: Finding nests by closely examining the likely **habitat** (*see* **hot-searching**).

collect: Killing a bird or salvaging a dead bird as a specimen.

coloniality: Clumping of **nests** in a spatio-temporal fashion, sometimes with mixed **species.**

colony: *See* **coloniality.**

color phase: *See* **morph.**

columella: Slender bone stretching across the middle ear to connect the **tympanic membrane** to the inner ear.

comb: Fleshy, featherless, and sometimes brightly colored crest adorning the top of a head of some **gallinaceous** birds.

comfort behavior: Refers to a group of basic stereotyped maintenance activities, e.g., **preening**, bathing, dusting, stretching.

commensalism: A relationship wherein one **species** benefits from another species and in which neither loses or gains.

commissural point: Point at the base of a bird's **bill** where the **mandibles** first come together.

commissure: Line along which the upper and lower **mandibles** close.

Common Birds Census: Censusing birds using the **spot-mapping method** and coordinated by the British Trust for Ornithology.

community: A natural assemblage of species, usually within a defined **habitat** type.

competition: Interaction between two or more individuals of either the same or different **species**, using a common resource.

competitive exclusion: The exclusion of one **species** by another, usually in a particular **habitat**, when exploiting a common resource.

compromise behavior: Form of behavior when two opposing drives are aroused simultaneously.

cones: Color-sensitive cells in the retina of birds that promote visual acuity.

congeneric: **Species** belonging to the same **genus.**

conspecific: Belong to the same **species.**

constant-effort mist netting: Capture method standardized over space and time used for counting numbers of birds caught in **mist nets.**

contact call: Noise made by an individual bird to keep in touch with the rest of the **flock.**

contour feather: A main body **feather**, with **vanes** which are somewhat flat and firm.

control: Recovery and release of a bird already marked in some manner or a standard of comparison for checking inferences deduced from experiments.

convergent evolution: Structural and behavioral similarities in otherwise unrelated **species** or **families** of living organisms.

cooperative breeding: Non-breeding birds helping out at the nests of breeding members of their **species**, e.g., **nest-building, incubation,** feeding **nestlings.**

copradeum: Chamber in the **cloaca** into which the large intestine empties.

copulation: Sexual act leading to the fertilization of the female's ova by the male's spermatozoa (AKA coition).

coracoid: Breast bone connecting the **sternum** with the pectoral girdle.

cornea: Transparent membrane protecting the lens and capable of changing its curvature for focusing.

corniplume: Tuft of **feathers** on head of a bird, e.g., horned lark.

corridor: A narrow front traditionally used by migrating birds, e.g., Pacific flyway.

cosmopolitan: Refers to **species** or even higher **taxa** found in virtually all of the zoogeographic regions in the world, e.g., osprey.

cot: Shelter for domesticated birds, e.g., dovecot.

countershading: Contrast between dark upper parts and light under parts of **plumage** to reduce shadowing effect and act as a form of camouflage.

countersinging: Singing in rivalry with another male within hearing (*see* **duetting**).

courtship: Describes a wide range of activities related to attracting a mate and maintaining a **pair bond** and leading to **copulation** and parenting.

courtship feeding: Feeding of one member of an adult **pair** by the other.

covert: Small **feathers** covering the bird's main **flight feathers** on wings and tail.

covey: Group of **game birds**, especially quail.

cranium: Bony structure housing the brain.

creance: Light line or string attached to **jesses** of a **bird of prey** when being trained to fly to the fist.

creche: Assemblage of still dependent young from several **pairs** of a **species**, e.g., merganser, eider.

crepuscular: Describes birds active at twilight.

crest: Tuft on **feathers** on the crown of a head, which can be lowered or raised.

crissum: Undertail **coverts** distinctively colored relative to the rest of the undersurface of the bird.

critical temperatures: Minimum and maximum ambient temperatures delineating the thermoneutral zone in which metabolic heat production is at a minimum.

cronism: Actual or attempted swallowing of dead or sickly young by their parents.

crop: Enlargement of the esophagus to store food and in some cases, digest food.

crop milk: Milky secretion of the esophagus, usually the crop, regurgitated and fed to young by pigeons, flamingos, and penguins.

cross-fostering: Replacement of **eggs** or young of one **species** by those of another species.

crowing area: Territory defended by male pheasant.

crown: Top of the head from the forehead to the nape.

crus: Outermost segment of the leg between the knee and foot.

cryptic: Describing coloration or other characters that afford concealment or disguise for protection from enemies or capture of prey.

culmen: Ridge of upper **mandible** from base to tip.

cursorial: Adapted to running, e.g., roadrunner.

cuticle: Thin waxy layer apparently protecting the eggshell from water evaporation and microbial invasion.

cyanic: Bluish pigments of **eggs** highlighted by suppression of reddish-brown pigments.

cygnet: A young swan.

dancing bird: *See* **lek**.

dark phase: Melanistic **morph** within a **species**.

Darwin's finches: Group of finches on the Galapágos Islands used by Charles Darwin for his theory on the origin of **species**.

dawn chorus: Burst of spring song from many **species** in a rough order beginning before dawn and then dying away abruptly.

decoy: Live or constructed (often carved) forms, generally of waterfowl, to attract free-ranging birds.

definitive plumage: Final **plumage** worn by adults of a **species** which wore differing plumages previously.

deme: A local population that may be considered separately from other populations of the same **species**.

density-dependent: Factors having an influence on individuals in a population related to the degree of crowding.

density-independent: Factors having an influence on individuals in a population not related to the degree of crowding.

dermis: Inner skin layer.

dertrum: Tip of upper **mandible**.

determinate layer: A **species** whose number of **eggs** in its **clutch** cannot be altered by addition or removal of eggs.

dewlap: Fleshy growth on the lower head, e.g., wattle.

diaphragm: System of membranes that partially divide the thoraco-abdominal cavity into lungs and cervical **air sacs** above and the rest of the air sacs below.

diastataxic: Having an unusually large gap between the fourth and sixth **secondary feathers** due to a missing fifth, e.g., waders.

diastema: Gap in wing in a **diastataxic** bird.

dichromatic: Having two distinct types of coloration, one for each sex or one for each of two color **morphs** of a **species**.

differential migration: Migration to different wintering areas by different individuals within a **species** due to size or sex.

digit: Toe or "finger."

digitigrade: Standing on the toes with the heel in the air.

dihedral: The angle at which the wing meets the body, e.g., raised in turkey vultures and harriers, flat in eagles.

dimorphism: Occurrence of two distinct forms, such as size or **plumage**.

directive marks: Bright or contrasting markings inside the mouths of young birds to help parents feed them.

disc: *See* **facial disc**.

disjunct: Refers to a discontinuous range or distribution of a **species**.

dispersal: Movements of non-breeding birds away from areas of high density, e.g., roost, breeding colony, birthplace.

dispersion: Spread of a **species** over all suitable **habitats** within its **range**.

displacement activity: Less relevant behavioral movements undertaken by an individual unable to perform a behavior of a higher priority.

display: Simple and elaborate behavioral activity by a bird to induce a desired behavior in other birds, e.g., **feathers**, flight, especially for **courtship** and territoriality.

disruption: Form of protective coloration wherein bold markings conceal an organism's anatomical shape, e.g., killdeer plover, or conspicuous features, e.g., eyes.

distraction behavior: Active anti-predator strategies used by an individual to deflect a predator or at least divert attention away from **eggs** or young.

distress call: Loud **vocalization** made by birds seized by a predator or human.

distribution: Geographic **range** of a **species** or other taxonomic categories.

diurnal: Active by day.

divergent evolution: Evolution of different anatomical structures in closely related birds, e.g., **Darwin's finches**.

diversity: Relative abundance and composition of **species** within a given area.

DNA: Deoxyribonucleic acid, a double-stranded molecule, used as genetic material for sources of taxonomic data.

DNA fingerprinting: Using drop of blood, **feather** pulp, or other cellular material containing **DNA** to determine the DNA sequence unique to each individual for testing paternity.

DNA–DNA hybridization: Modern biochemical technique using **DNA** that may be revolutionizing avian systematics.

domestication: Breeding and maintenance of a **species** continuously controlled by humans.

dominance: Refers to regular winner in aggressive encounters, including between members of a breeding **pair**.

dominance hierarchy: Order of **dominance** among individuals within a local flock (AKA **peck order**).

double-brooded: Refers to a **species** laying a second **clutch** after raising one **brood**.

double scratch: Motion of jumping forward and backward in leaves and other debris to seek food, e.g., towhees, juncos.

down: **Feathers** characterized by their fluffy **vanes**.

drake: Male duck.

drift: Displacement of a migrant off its flight track, usually by wind or choosing to fly downwind.

droppings: Waste products from excretory (urine) and alimentary systems (feces).

drumming: Loud tapping on objects by woodpeckers to proclaim a territory or the beating of wings by a ruffed grouse to attract females.

drunkenness: Intoxication of birds as a result of eating fermented berries or nectar.

duckling: Young duck not yet full-grown.

Duck Stamp: Special government stamp that duck hunters must purchase to raise money for waterfowl conservation.

ductus deferens: Convoluted tubes running from the **testes** to the **cloaca** through which mature sperm pass.

duetting: Male and female of a **pair** singing or calling somewhat together in a responsive fashion.

dummy nest: Extra **nests**, often incomplete, built by male wrens perhaps for sleeping or for exaggerated **courtship**.

dump nesting: Laying of **eggs** by more than one female of usually the same **species** in one **nest**, e.g., goldeneye.

duodenum: Part of small intestine between the **gizzard** and the **ileum**.

dusky: Dark brownish-black or blackish.

dusting: Behavioral application of fine earth or sand onto **plumage**, perhaps for feather maintenance.

ear coverts: Modified **contour feathers** that cover the outer ear openings.

ear patch: Area below the orbit.

ear tuft: A bunch of long **feathers** found in pairs on the top of the head and used for behavioral communication, e.g., owls (AKA horns).

ecdysis: Annual shedding of **feathers**.

echolocation: Ability to emit sounds and analyze echoes to detect presence of nearby objects, e.g., cave-dwelling oilbirds.

eclipse plumage: Dull post-nuptial **plumage** stage of short duration occurring in male birds undergoing wing-**feather** renewal, notably in waterfowl.

ecogeographical rules: Rules relating geographical variation in size, body parts, color, etc., e.g., **Gloger's**, **Allen's**, **Bergmann's**.

ecological barrier: Ecological factor which prevents **range** expansion of a **species** or which divides its range.

ecological release: Increase in abundance of a **species** or broadening of a species' feeding habits in the absence of a competing species.

ecological succession: Changes in a **habitat** over time due to its modification by former colonists and the arrival of new **species**.

ecology: Study of plants and animals in relation to their environment.

ecosystem: The sum of all the factors that make up a specific environment.

ecotone: Area of transition between adjacent plant associations and the animal communities related to them.

ecotope: Particular kind of **habitat** in a region.

ecotype: Locally adapted population or race with characters derived from selective pressures from its environment.

ectoparasite: Parasites inhabiting the exterior of its host's body, e.g., mites, lice, ticks.

edaphic: Describes environmental factors dependent on conditions of soil or substratum.

edge effect: Increase in diversity of **flora** and **fauna** in a transition area between two **habitat** or community types.

edge species: **Species** preferring **habitat** in a transition area between two habitat or community types.

edible nests: *See* **bird's nest soup**.

efferent: Carrying impulses outward from nerve centers.

egg: End-product of the development of the female reproductive cell, or **ovum**, consisting of **yolk**, **albumen**, membranes, and outer shell.

egg-bound: Unable to lay an **egg** present in the **oviduct** due to obstruction or malformation of the egg.

egg covering: Covering of eggs **by** adult temporarily departing the nest, e.g., grebes, tits.

egg-eating: Consumption of other birds' **eggs** by adult birds and their young.

egger: Person who collects **eggs** of rare birds.

egg mimicry: Form of **nest parasitism** wherein the color of the parasite's **eggs** resembles that of the host's, e.g., cuckoos.

egg recognition: Ability of some **species** to recognize their own **eggs**, especially in colonially nesting birds, e.g., guillemots.

egg retrieval: Behavior wherein **scrape**-nesting species (e.g., terns, gulls) retrieve **eggs** accidentally ejected from the **nest**, but close by.

Egg Rule: Average **clutch** size within a **species** tends to increase, the more northerly the latitude.

eggshell thinning: The laying of abnormally thin-shelled **eggs** as a result of poor nutrition, disease, age, stress, and, notably, organochlorine pesticides such as DDT.

egg tooth: Small, sharp (often hook-like) projection on the tip of the upper **mandible** used by a full-term **embryo** to chip open the **eggshell** during **hatching**.

elbow: Angle or joint on the wing closest to the body.

electrophoresis: A laboratory process to characterize the different proteins in a mixture by their net charge, size, shape, or isoelectric charges to determine genetic relationships.

emargination: Notched or forked appearance of a tail (or a **primary feather**) due to narrowing of the shape of the feather(s).

embryo: Young bird from the beginning of development in the **egg** until **hatching**.

embryology: Study of **embryo** development.

emigration: Movement of individuals from an areà.

endangered: Category assigned to a **species** whose numbers have declined to a some critically low level.

endemic: Restricted to or only found in a particular geographic area.

endogamy: **Mating** within the group.

endoparasite: Parasites that inhabit the interior of a host's body.

endysis: Developing a new coat of **feathers**.

energetics: Term to describe the intake and utilization of energy.

epidiymis: Body of convoluted tubules lying aside each **testes** where **spermatozoa** accumulate before passing down the *vas deferens*.

epigamic: Describes characters or actions, usually a **display**, to promote synchronized reproductive behavior.

episematic: Describes an appearance, e.g., color, or behavior that aids in recognition.

epithema: Horny growth on the **bill**.

epizootic: Epidemic-like disease that kills large numbers of organisms.

erythrism: Obvious presence of reddish pigments in the **plumage**.

escape distance: Distance upon which a bird will depart upon the approach of a human or predator.

escapee: A formerly captive bird that has escaped into the wild.

estrogens: Female sex hormones responsible for reproduction.

ethology: Study of behavior.

etiology: *See* **aetiology**.

euryoecious: Ability to exist in a wide variety of **habitats**.

euryphagous: Ecologically tolerant of a wide range of foods.

eusyanthropic: Living in or on houses of humans, e.g., phoebes.

eutaxic: Refers to wings with a full complement of **secondary feathers**.

evolution: Theory describing the origin of today's diversity of organisms from a lesser diversity by a process of gradual change from generation to generation.

exanthropic: Living apart from humans.

excrement: *See* **droppings**.

exotic: Describes a **species** that is alien to a particular area.

extinct: Describes a **species** or **subspecies** no longer existing.

extinction: The complete disappearance of a **species** from the earth or from an island.

extirpate: Exterminate, eradicate, or eliminate.

extirpation: The elimination of a **species** from an island, local area, or region.

extralimital: Describes **species** occurring outside the boundaries of a given area.

eyass: A nestling falcon or hawk.

eyelash: Bristle that resembles a human eyelash, e.g., seen in hornbills, cuckoos, ostrich, secretary bird.

eyelid: One of two folds of skin above and below the eye to cover it (*see also* **nictitating membrane**).

eye line: Pale mark running above the eye or dark line running through the eye.

eye ring: Area of contrasting **feathers** or skin encircling an eye.

eyespot: *See* **ocella**.

eye stripe: *See* **eye line**.

eyrie: **Nest** of a **bird of prey**.

facial disc: Well-defined, flat, roundish feature of some birds' faces (e.g., owls', harriers') to act as a parabola to collect sound waves.

facultative brood parasite: A **species** that lays **eggs** in the nest of a host species but is not dependent on doing so to raise young.

falcated: Hooked, sickle-shaped.

falconry: Use of trained **birds of prey** to capture game.

fall: Sudden presence of birds, usually during **migration** and along a coast, caused by an interruption of migration by inclement weather (AKA rush).

false wing: *See* **alula**.

false crop: Expansion of crop as a storage place for seeds, e.g., redpoll.

family: Primary taxonomic category indicating a grouping of genera, e.g., falconidae.

fasciated: Striped or banded.

fault bar: Conspicuous streaks in **tail** feathers caused by poor nutrition leading to improper growth of feather hooks.

fauna: Total animal life of a region or area.

feather: A unit of **plumage** that is unique to birds.

feather comb: Pectinated (comb-like) claw on the middle toes of certain birds, e.g., nightjars.

feather cortex: Lightweight, spongy material within the **feather** shaft.

feather sheath: Protective tissue surrounding the developing **feather** tissue.

feather tract: *See* pteryla.

fecal sac: White, gelatinous package of excrement from **nestlings** removed by parents, presumably for **nest** sanitation.

femur: Thighbone.

feral: Describes populations of domesticated **species** that have reverted to a free-ranging existence.

ferruginous: Iron- or rusty-colored.

fertilization: Union of a male **gamete** (i.e., **spermatozoon**) with a female gamete (i.e., **ovum**) in the female's upper **oviduct**.

fibula: Small thin bone below the knee an running parallel to the **tibiotarsus**.

field character: A distinctive feature or trait used to identify a **species** in the wild.

field guide: A pocket-sized book composed of illustrations and accompanying information used to identify birds in the wild.

field mark: Characteristic (e.g., color, shape) used to identify a wild bird.

filoplume: A type of **feather** resembling a fine, thin hair.

filtration feeding: Using the tongue to press mud and water against a filter of stiff hairs and **lamellae** inside the **mandibles**, e.g, flamingos.

first-year bird: Bird in its first 12–16 months.

fitness: The number of offspring left by an individual of a particular kind of organism.

fixation: An abnormal behavioral attachment of one individual to another of a different **species**.

flammulated: Describes **plumage** tinged with **rufous**.

flank: Fleshy part of the side above the proximal end of the leg.

fledging: Acquisition of first true **feathers** by a young bird.

fledging success: Percentage of **hatchings** that fledge or average number of young fledged.

fledgling: Young bird that has just left the nest.

flight: A form of locomotion achieved in birds by use of **flight feathers** and lightness.

flight feathers: **Primary** and **secondary feathers** of the wing.

flightlessness: Having a reduced or absent flight apparatus such that flight is impossible, e.g., ostriches, some grebes.

flight muscles: Collectively the breast muscles to lift and lower the wings.

flight pattern: Distinctive outline or silhouette of certain flying birds, e.g., **raptors**, ducks.

flight song: Habitual singing during flight to pronounce territory in birds nesting in open **habitats**, e.g., grassland, tundra.

flight year: Year in which some northerly species, general non-migratory, head south in large numbers to seek food resources.

flipper: Modified wing of penguins.

floater: Unpaired bird during the breeding season that is capable of breeding.

floating birds: Reserve of non-breeding or non-territorial birds present in breeding or territorial populations.

flock: *See* **assembly**.

flocking: Joining of individuals of same or different **species** into groups for social purposes.

flora: Total plant life of an area or region.

flyway: Broad-front band or pathway used by migrating birds often over prominent geographic features, e.g., coastlines, mountain ranges.

follicle: Highly vascularized layers of tissue that surround the **ovum** until the latter is released or the growth structure from which a **feather** develops.

food chain: Successional flow of energy from one trophic level to another, e.g., seed eaten by a mouse, mouse eaten by a hawk.

food pass: Aerial food pass from a male to a female **raptor** during breeding season.

footedness: Physiological dominance of one foot over another in some birds, e.g., pigeons, raptors, parrots.

foot-paddling: Quick trembling motions of the foot by some shorebirds to stir up invertebrate prey.

foot-stirring: Raking movements of the foot by herons and egrets to flush out small prey in mud flats, shallow water, and meadows.

foot-trembling: *See* **foot-paddling**.

foramen magnum: Opening through which the spinal cord emerges from the skull.

forearm: Antebrachium.

forebrain: Front section of the brain responsible for complex behavioral instincts and instructions, e.g., nest-building.

forest fragmentation: Development of forests (e.g., logging) that leaves the remaining forest stands in varying sizes and degrees of isolation.

form: A taxonomic term referring to a group of birds below the subspecific level (AKA variety).

fossil: Preserved remains, footprints, and feather impressions of members of **class** *Aves*, used by paleontologists.

fossorial: Habit of digging as in burrowing to make a **nest**.

founder population: Founders of a new population or breeding colony containing only a proportion of the genetic variation of the original parent population.

fovea: A point on the retina of the eye facilitating sharper focus.

fratricide: *See* **Cain and Abel Syndrome**.

freezing: Motionless behavior to escape detection.

fright molt: Sudden partial **molt** that occurs outside of the normal molt period, often caused by fear.

frontal: Pertaining to the forehead.

frugivorous: Fruit-eating.

fulvous: Tawny or brownish-yellow.

furcula: Bony structure formed by fusion of right and left clavicles (AKA wishbone).

gall bladder: Reservoir for bile in birds, but not all.

gallinaceous: Resembling a domestic fowl.

game bird: Quarry species, notably grouse, pheasants, turkeys, snipe, woodcock, bustards, hunted by humans.

gamete: A germ cell, i.e., **spermatozoon**, **ovum**.

gamosematic: Describes appearance or behavior that helps **pair** members find one another.

gander: Male goose.

gape: Wide-open mouth (AKA **commissure**).

gaping: Panting with mouth open to shed heat or **nestling** birds opening their mouths widely to stimulate parents to feed them.

Gause's Rule: Ecological rule wherein two species with identical ecological requirements cannot coexist in the same environment.

gene: Unit of inheritance within a chromosome.

gene flow: Exchange of genetic traits between populations.

genera: Plural of **genus**.

genetic drift: Change in the frequency of a gene complex in a population, usually as a result of isolation of a small segment from its main population.

genetics: Study of heredity, i.e., the passing of characters from parents to offspring.

genetic swamping: One species successfully hybridizing with another and eventually incorporating its gene pool into its own, e.g., mallard and gray duck.

genome: Full set of chromosomes.

genotype: Group in which an individual falls due to its genetic makeup.

genus: Taxomomic category representing a group of **species**.

Geographic Information System (GIS): Set of computer software and hardware for analyzing and displaying spatially referenced features with non-geographic attributes, e.g., **species**.

geographical speciation: Gradual formation of a new **species** caused by geographical isolation from the parent species.

germ cell: *See* **gamete**.

germinal spot: Area on the **yolk sac** that develops into the **blastula** and eventually the **embryo**.

gizzard: The grinding muscular stomach present in most birds (AKA ventriculus).

glaucous: Bluish- or silvery-gray.

gleaning: Foraging for insects or similar food from leafy or bark surfaces.

Gloger's Rule: Races of a given **species** in warm, humid areas are likely to be more heavily pigmented than those in cool and dry areas.

glottis: Slit-like entrance to the **trachea** located in the rear of the mouth.

gobbling ground: North American term for social **display** ground of lesser prairie chicken.

gonad: Refers to primary sex organs, i.e., **testes** in males, **ovaries** in females.

gonys: Prominent ridge formed by the junction of the two halves of the lower jaw toward the tip, e.g., gulls.

gorget: Band of color on throat or upper breast in hummingbirds.

gosling: Young goose.

grallatorial: Pertaining to wading.

graminivorous: Grass-eating.

granivorous: Seed-eating.

gregariousness: *See* **flocking**.

grin line: **Plumage** marking along the lower **mandible** that gives a bird the appearance of smiling, e.g., trumpeter swan.

grit: Coarse, small matter (e.g., stones, sand, diatoms, shells) ingested by some birds to acquire minerals and to aid in digestion.

grooming: Maintenance of **feathers**, i.e. orientation, cleanliness, oiling, and water-proofing.

guano: Excreta or **droppings** of seabirds dried into a rough powder often collected by humans for fertilizer.

guild: Two or more **species'** populations exploiting the same type of resources in similar ways.

gular fluttering: Rapid oscillation of floor of mouth and upper throat, generally for cooling, e.g., as in owls.

gular pouch: Enlarged skin sac in the upper throat for panting (cooling), for storage of fish (e.g., pelicans) or for **display** (e.g., frigatebird).

gular sac: *See* **gular pouch**.

gullet: Anterior part of esophagus.

gynandromorphism: Genetic aberration wherein one part of an animal's body is female and another part is male.

habitat: Particular environment (i.e., **flora**, **fauna**, soil, climate) in which a particular organism lives.

habituation: Learned behavior where an organism does not respond to recurring stimuli.

hacking: A procedure used by falconers to release **raptors** back into the wild.

hackle: Long, slender feather on the neck, e.g., Galliformes.

haggard: Raptor caught as an adult and trained by a falconer.

hallux: The first or hind toe, usually pointing backwards and sometimes reduced in size.

hamulus: A hooked **barbicel**.

hand quill: Primary feather.

handedness: Footedness in parrots where the feet are used to handle food.

Harderian glands: Secretory glands found in the eyes of birds for protective purposes.

hatch year: *See* **hatching year**.

hatching: Emergence of developed **chick** from an incubated egg.

hatching success: Percentage of (fertile) **eggs** that hatch.

hatching year (HY): A bird in first basic **plumage** in its first calendar year.

hatchling: A newly hatched bird.

hawking: *See* **falconry**.

heading: Direction in which a bird is flying.

head-scratching: Use of feet to respond to irritations in areas unreachable with the **bill**.

Heligoland trap: Long, funnel-like wire-netting cage with a wide opening at one end and a windowed catching-box at the other end to trap birds.

helmet: Ornament, usually **feather**-like, on top of some birds' heads, e.g., helmet-shrikes.

helpers: *See* **cooperative breeding**.

hen: A female bird.

herbivorous: Plant-eating.

Herbst's corpuscle: Ovoid masses of nerve endings that receive tactile information.

heritability: Proportion of total variation with a genetic basis within a population.

hermaphrodite: Animal with both male and female sex organs.

heronry: Nesting colony of herons.

Hesse's Rule: Forms of warm-blooded animals living in cold regions have relatively higher heart weights than those in warm regions.

heterochroism: Abnormal color differences.

heterogynism: Taxonomic characters that distinguish closely related species being more strongly marked in females than males.

hibernation: Rare in birds, but *see* **torpidity**.

hill: Display ground of the **ruff**.

hindbrain: Rear section of the brain linking spinal cord and peripheral nervous system.

histology: Study of minute structure of tissues.

hoary: Frosty-gray or silver.

holding: Using the feet to hold food and other objects, e.g., parrots.

home range: Area (that may or may not be defended by an individual, a **pair**, or group of birds) to which they restrict most of their usual activities.

homing: Using various directional cues (e.g., landscape, celestial, geomagnetic) to return to a location, e.g., **nest**, loft.

homogeneous: Of the same character or nature.

homosexuality: Pairing of same-sex birds, occurring in populations where the sex ratio is strongly skewed.

homothermous: Warm-blooded.

hood: Area of distinctive color covering large part of head as in **plumage** or leather cap or helmet fitted for the head of a trained **raptor** to exclude light and vision to induce calming.

hooklet: Smallest unit of **barb** structure that holds **feather** shape.

hooting: Refers to distinctive call of some birds, e.g., owls.

hopping: Locomotion of most perching birds when on the ground.

Hotline: *See* **Rare Bird Alert**.

hot-searching: Finding nests by attempting to flush sitting birds from the vegetation.

hovering: Remaining stationary in midair while beating the wings rapidly, e.g., hummingbird, kestrel.

humerus: Upper wing bone.

hunger trace: *See* **fault bar**.

hybrid: Individual produced from a cross of two individuals of dissimilar genetic background, often morphologically different.

hybridization: *See* hybrid.

hyoid apparatus: Bones of the tongue.

hyoptile: Supplemental small feather originating from the base of a **contour feather**.

hyperphagia: Overeating by migrants to store energy.

hypophysis: Pituitary gland.

hyporachis: Shaft of **hyoptile**.

hyporadius: **Barb** of **hyoptile**.

hypotarsus: Protrusion on back of **tarsometatarsus**.

hypothalamus: Part of the forebrain.

ileum: Posterior part of the small intestine.

image-fighting: Territorial attacks of a bird on its own reflection in a window, mirror, etc.

immature: Young fully feathered bird not in adult **plumage** but capable of breeding.

impervious: Refers to closed **nostrils**, e.g., gannet.

imping: Falconry technique for repairing broken **feathers**.

imprinting: An often irreversible behavioral phenomenon where a young bird develops an attachment to its parent and, hence, **species** recognition.

incubation: The transfer of heat from a bird's body (or, in some megapodes, decaying organic matter) to an **egg** to facilitate embryonic development.

incubation patch: *See* **brood patch**.

indeterminate layer: **Species** in which the number of **eggs** in a **clutch** can be altered by addition or removal of eggs.

indicator species: Those species whose presence, due to their ecological requirements, demonstrate the existence of certain environmental conditions.

indigenous: Describes **species** native to an area.

individual distance: Minimum distance at which one individual will tolerate the presence of another.

information center: Theoretically a communal roost wherein birds gathering pass on information about good feeding sites to one another.

infrasound: Very low-frequency sounds detected by birds but not humans, perhaps used in **homing**.

infundibulum: Top of the **oviduct** that receives the released **ovum** and where fertilization takes place.

ingluvies: *See* **crop**.

inheritance: *See* **genetics**.

injury feigning: Behavior of adult wherein it pretends to be injured to draw predator or intruder away from **nest**.

innate behavior: Behavior that an individual is born with and is not learned.

insectivorous: Insect-eating.

instinct: *See* **innate behavior**.

insurance egg: Extra **egg** laid by a **species** that normally raises only one **nestling**.

integument: Skin and organs comprising the protective covering of an organism, e.g., **plumage**.

integumentary structures: Outgrowths from the skin, e.g., **feathers**, spurs, combs, wattles, sacs, pouches.

intention movements: Incomplete initial phases of a behavior pattern.

interbreeding: Mating between two members of different **species** resulting in **hybrid** offspring.

interference: Optical process responsible for irridescence in feathers by waves of light either reinforcing or cancelling one another.

interference competition: Competition in which one **species** prevents another from having access to a limited resource.

intergradation: Cross-breeding of different **subspecies** within a single **species**.

intermewed: Refers to a hawk that has undergone a **molt** in captivity.

interspaces: *See* **areolae**.

interspecific: Refers to an interaction or relationship between two **species**.

interspecific competition: Competition between individuals of different **species**.

intraspecific: Refers to an interaction or relationship between members of the same **species**.

intraspecific competition: Competition between individuals of the same **species**.

introduced species: **Species** found outside its natural **range** due to inadvertent or deliberate introduction by humans, e.g., house sparrow.

introgression: **Gene** flow between genetically divergent populations or occurring only between **species**.

invasion: Expansion of a **species' range** into a new area (but *also see* **irruption**).

iridiscence: **Display** of spectral colors in **feathers** during repositioning in the sun, e.g., grackles.

iris: Pigmented part of the eye surrounding the pupil.

irruption: Irregular mass movement of birds post-breeding to areas beyond normal **range**, usually caused by a sudden super-abundance of food, e.g., crossbills, **raptors**.

Isabelline: grayish-yellow.

island biogeography: Theory in which the number of **species** on an island results from an equilibrium between immigration and extinction.

isochronal lines: Lines drawn on a map between locations reached by migrants of a given **species** on the same date.

isolating mechanism: A difference between **species** or populations thereof that helps to prevent **interbreeding** and maintain reproductive isolation.

isthmus: Part of the **oviduct** where the two shell membranes are laid down on the **egg**.

jejunum: Part of the small intestine.

jesses: Leather straps worn on the legs of a trained **raptor** for restraining purposes.

jizz: Combination of characteristics which identify a bird (or other animal) in the field.

jugging: Sleeping place of partridge.

jugulum: Lower part of the exterior throat.

juvenal: Describes the first postnatal **plumage** of a young bird.

juvenile: Young bird that has not yet reached breeding maturity.

keel: Narrow median process or carina of the **sternum** for the attachment of breast muscles.

Kelso's Rule: Ear openings and skin flaps covering them are larger among northern-nesting populations of owls and smaller in southern ones.

keratin: Main structural protein making up horny parts of skin, scales, **feathers**, and **bills**.

kettle: Used to describe a **flock** of migrating **raptors** sharing a **thermal**.

keystone species: **Species** whose abundance impacts upon the structure and dynamics of an **ecosystem**.

kin selection: A mechanism whereby **natural selection** works indirectly on related individuals who share a proportion of their **genes**.

kleptoparasitism: Interspecific and intraspecific food-stealing behavior widespread in birds.

knee: Femorotibial leg joint.

koilin: Interior lining of the **gizzard** which can be periodically shed or molted.

kronism: *See* **cronism.**

labyrinth: Semicircular canals in inner ear that facilitate equilibrium.

lachrymal glands: Glands secreting substances that help moisten the eye.

lamellae: Fine, hair-like structures lining **bills** of some **species** to facilitate **filtration-feeding** with small particles.

laparotomy: Minor surgical process for assessment of internal organs, generally to determine sex.

lappet: Drooping folds of skin on the head or neck, e.g., turkey, vulture.

larder: Collection of prey items (e.g., mice, birds) impaled on thorns or barbed wire by shrikes and other birds.

larynx: Uppermost part of the **trachea** below the **glottis.**

laying: Act of deposition of an **egg** (AKA oviposition).

LBJs: Bird-watcher's term that refers to "little brown jobs," i.e., small brownish birds that are hard to identify.

leading edge: The forward or front lifting edge of the wing.

leap-frog migration: Movement of a northern breeding population to wintering grounds lying further south than those occupied by a southern breeding population of the same **species,** as well as the reverse.

learning: Production of adaptive changes in individual behavior resulting from experience.

lek: Communal **display** ground where males of a given **species** congregate to attract and court females.

leucism: Abnormal paleness in the **plumage** due to environmental factors, e.g., abnormal diet.

life bird: Bird **species** observed by a **birder** for the first time.

life expectancy: Number of years an individual might survive in the wild.

life list: Record of birds seen by a **birder** in his or her lifetime.

lifer: *See* **life bird.**

life zone: An area defined in terms of humidity and temperature.

light phase: Pale-colored **morph** within a **species.**

Lincoln Index: An equation or formula referring to a mark-recapture method to determine populations of vertebrates.

lipochromes: Naturally occurring pigments (i.e., yellows, oranges, and reds) in the **feathers** and skin.

lister: **Birder** who is willing to travel great distances to record new bird **species.**

listing: Competitive **birding** for the greatest number of **species** within a given area or time period.

long-distance migration: Migratory pattern in which a **species** flies from its breeding area in Arctic or temperate latitudes to tropical or subtropical latitudes where it winters.

longevity: Number of years an individual might survive under any conditions, i.e., wild or captivity.

loomery: **Breeding** colony of guillemots.

loop migration: Circular pattern of **migration** where the fall pathway differs from the one used in the spring.

lore: Small area between the eye and the bill.

lumper: Someone who prefers to combine apparently distinct forms into one, e.g., **subspecies** into **species.**

lure: Imitation prey swung by falconers to recover their birds.

magnum: Part of **oviduct** where **albumen** is added to the **ovum**.

malar stripe: **Plumage** marking on the cheek of a bird.

Malpighian layer: Epidermal cells which grow into the structure of the **feather** proper.

mandible: Upper and lower half of a bird's **bill**.

mantle: **Feathers** of the back, **scapulars**, and upper wing **coverts**.

manus: Bones (i.e., carpometacarpus and phalanges) representing the "hand."

marbled: Irregular marking of **plumage** with spots, speckles, blotches, or streaks.

marginal coverts: Small **feathers** overlying the secondary **coverts** on the shoulder of the wing.

marking: Refers to **banding**, ringing, or otherwise altering a bird for identification.

mating: *See* **copulation**.

mating system: The relationship between the sexes within the social organization, e.g., monogamy.

maturity: Attainment of an age whereupon a bird is capable of breeding.

maxilla: Upper half of the **bill** or paired facial bones that support the bill.

Mayfield method: Method of calculating the rate of nesting success based on the number of days a **nest** was observed.

Mayr's Rule: Races in cooler climates often more strongly migratory than those in more southerly, warmer ones.

mechanical sounds: Non-vocal sounds made by **bills**, tail, or wings.

medulla oblongata: Lower part of hindbrain.

melanism: Excessive amounts of black or dark brown pigments in **plumage** or **eggs**.

merrythought: *See* **furcula**.

mesoptile: Second of two nestling down **plumages**.

metacarpus: *See* **carpometacarpus**.

metapopulation: Set of populations living in unconnected **habitat** patches but linked by movement of individuals between them.

metatarsus: Fused bones of the foot (*see* **tarsometatarsus**).

mews: Holding facilities for **molting** or breeding **raptors** trained by falconers.

microsmatic: Poorly developed olfactory powers.

midbrain: Middle section of the brain regulating vision, muscular coordination and balance, and physiological controls.

migration: Movements of bird populations at predictable times of year, generally fall and spring, to exploit new resources.

migratory restlessness: Unsettled or active behavior of birds just prior to departing on **migration**.

mimicry: Resemblance of one **species** to another for either mutual or one-sided benefit, but rare in birds (but *see* **vocal mimicry**).

mirror: White spot on black wing tip of some gulls.

mist net: A finely woven, almost invisible net hung from poles used to catch flying birds for purposes of measurement and affixing leg bands.

mobbing: Noisy **flocking** of birds, often of several **species**, to drive off a predator.

molt: Periodic shedding and replacement of worn **plumage**, and even epidermal structures like tarsal scales.

molt migration: Regular movement by some birds to and from an area where they **molt**.

Monitoring Avian Productivity and Survivorship (MAPS): Program coordinated by the Institute for Bird Populations which involves constant-effort **mist netting**, **banding**, and intensive point counts during the **breeding season** at a continent-wide network of stations.

monogamy: Mating with one partner only.

monophagous: Restricting the diet to one type of food.

monotypic: Taxonomic category that has a single representative of the next-lowest category, e.g., monotypic order has only one family.

moon watching: Practice of recording birds flying across the moon.

morph: Variation of color, size, or other characteristic of a **species** (AKA phase).

morphology: Study of form or shape, including color and anatomy.

moult: *See* **molt.**

mustachial stripe: A streak running back from the base of a **bill**, as in **plumage.**

mule: Cross between a canary and another **species** of finch.

multi-brooded: Producing more than one **clutch** or **brood** per season.

Murphy's Rule: Island birds have larger **bills** than related mainland birds.

mutes: Raptor droppings.

mutual preening: *See* **allopreening**.

mycosis: Disease caused by fungus.

myology: Study of muscles.

nail: Horny structure found at the tip of the upper **mandible** of all wildfowl **species** or horny tip of a bird claw.

nape: Back part of the neck.

nares: Paired openings comprising the nasal cavities.

narial feathers: Long **feathers** at the base of the upper **bill** that partly cover the **nares.**

natal dispersal: Movement from natal site to first breeding or potential breeding site.

natal down: Initial coat of **feathers** worn by a **nestling** bird.

natatorial: Pertaining to swimming.

natural selection: Those ecological factors or processes that lead to individuals of a **species** passing on advantageous traits to offspring to perpetuate their **genotype**.

naturalized birds: Species that have been introduced directly or indirectly by humans and now breeding regularly as wild birds.

navigation: The use of landmarks, geomagnetism, position of sun and/or stars, etc., to follow a **migration** route.

nectar-feeders: Birds that feed on sugary fluid in flowers or fruit juices.

nectarivorous: *See* **nectar-feeders**.

neontology: Study of geologically recent forms of life as opposed to **paleontology**.

neossology: Study of young birds.

neossoptile: Refers to natal down **plumage**.

neotropical migrant: Migratory bird in the Neotropical fauna region.

nest: Structure made or adopted by a bird in which to lay and incubate its **eggs**.

nestbox: Artificial **nest**, i.e., made by humans.

nest building: Behavior associated with excavating or constructing a **nest**.

nesting association: Group nesting involving two or more bird **species** or a bird and non-avian species.

nestling: A young bird still in the **nest** and dependent on its parents for some resource.

nest parasitism: Rare phenomenon wherein one **species** of bird takes over the nest of another for its own use, e.g., black-billed cuckoo.

nest-robbing: Eating of **eggs** or young **nestlings** by other birds, e.g., magpies.

nest-sharing: Using of a common **nest** by two females, sometimes of different **species**.

niche: Position or role an organism plays in its community.

niche expansion: Increases in places where a **species** feeds or breeds or in type of foods it eats.

nictitating membrane: A third eyelid, usually transparent, for protection and/or lubrication of the avian eye.

nidicolous: Young birds that remain in the **nest** after **hatching**.

nidification: Building of a **nest**.

nidifugous: Young birds that leave the **nest** immediately upon **hatching**.

nocturnal: Active at night.

nomadism: Movements of **species** that do not revisit breeding or non-breeding areas.

nomenclature: Scientific naming of **species**, **subspecies**, **genera**, **families**, etc., for classification purposes.

nominate: The first officially documented **species** in a **genus**.

non-breeder: Individual that does not breed in a given reproductive season.

nostrils: *See* **nares**.

nuptial: Describes **plumage** or **display** in **breeding season**.

obligate brood parasite: A bird **species** that cannot attain full development independent of a host species.

observatory: An establishment often strategically located to promote study of bird **migration** by observation and/or **banding**.

occiput: Back part of the head just above the nape.

oceanic: Describing birds capable of feeding long distances offshore.

ocella: Eye-like pattern on **plumage**, e.g., American kestrel head.

oil gland: *See* **uropygial gland**.

olfactory bulbs: Parts of forebrain dedicated to processing olfactory data.

oligotokous: Producing few **eggs**.

olivaceous: Brownish-green to greenish-brown.

omnivorous: Eating both plant and animal food.

ontogeny: Developmental history of an individual.

oocyte: Cell stage in the formation of an **ovum**.

oology: Study of birds' **eggs**.

operculum: Flap covering the **nares** or the acoustic meatus.

optic lobes: Parts of brain dedicated to processing visual data.

orbit: Cavity in the skull which houses the eyeball or the circular area around the eye on the head.

ornithichnite: Fossilized footprint of a bird.

ornitholite: Bird fossil.

ornithologist: Person, professional or amateur, who studies birds.

ornithology: The study of birds.

ornithomancy: Predicting the future by observing bird behavior.

ornithophilous: Describes plants fertilized with birds serving as intermediates.

ornithosis: *See* **psittacosis**.

ortstreue: German term referring to the tendency of migrants to return to a previous breeding or wintering area.

ossification: Formation of bone.

osteology: Study of bones and bone structure.

ostium: *See* **infundibulum**.

ovary: Female **gonad**.

overshooting: Movement of birds **migrating** in the right direction but beyond their normal destination.

oviduct: Tube through which the **ovum** passes and undergoes development into a hard-shelled **egg**.

oviparity: Refers to the universal practice of birds **laying eggs** in which **embryos** develop outside the female's body.

oviposition: *See* **laying**.

ovotestis: Pertains to the fusion of **germ cells** of the **ovum** and **testis** in the event of the loss of the left **ovary**.

ovulation: Release of the **ovum** from a ruptured follicle in the **ovary**.

ovum: Female **germ cell**.

owlet: **Nestling** owl.

pair: Two adult birds apparently mated.

pair bond: Relationship between members of a breeding couple from **courtship** through **fledging** young from the **nest**.

pair formation: Establishment of a **pair** through an exchange of social signals and responses for the purpose of reproduction.

palaeontology: *See* **paleontology**.

palaeospecies: *See* **paleospecies**.

paleontology: Study of fossilized remains of plants and animals.

paleospecies: **Species** known only from fossil remains.

palate: Roof of the mouth.

pancreas: Lobulated endocrine gland located in the upper intestine and secreting digestive enzymes as well as two hormones for metabolism regulation.

panting: Rapid breathing to dissipate excessive body heat.

parasematic: Describes an appearance or behavior that distracts the attention of a predator away from the more vulnerable body part or individual to one less vulnerable.

paratrepsis: Term encompassing all forms of distraction **display**.

parental care: Protection, feeding, and care of young from **hatching** to independence by one or both parents.

parthenogenesis: Production of an individual from an **egg** not fertilized by a male **gamete**, e.g., turkey.

partial migrant: Species in which some members of its population migrate and some do not.

Partners-In-Flight: A conservation program for neotropical migrants of the Western Hemisphere endorsed by government and non-government organizations.

passage hawk: One-year old hawk or falcon trapped during migration by a falconer for training.

passage migrant: Migrating birds that pass through an area without remaining in summer or winter.

passerine: Member of the order Passeriformes, i.e., perching songbirds.

patagium: Fold of skin in a wing running from the upper arm to the **forearm**.

patristic: Resemblances among **species** or other taxa attributed to a common ancestry rather than due to **convergent evolution**.

peck order: **Dominance hierarchy** among social birds derived from domestic poultry.

pecten: Comb-like nutritional organ feeding the avascular retina of a eye.

pectoral: Pertaining to the breast.

peep: Refers to look-alike shorebirds.

pelagic: Describes birds dwelling near ocean or open sea.

pellet: Bolus of undigested portions of food (e.g., fur, feather, bones) regurgitated by some birds, especially **birds of prey**.

pelvic: Describes the combination of bones at the base of the spinal column that give support to the legs.

pen: Female swan.

penis: Male copulatory organ found in some birds, e.g., ducks.

pennae: **Contour feather** with the **barbs** forming a coherent **vane**.

perching bird: *See* **passerine**.

perforate: Refers to incomplete septum of some birds, e.g., turkey vulture.

peritoneum: Membrane lining the abdominal cavity and coating the internal organs.

permanent resident: Individual or species that breeds and winters in the same region.

pervious: Open **nares** as opposed to closed ones.

pessulus: Bony structure within the **syrinx** employed to make sound.

pesticide: Chemical agent of synthetic or natural origin used by humans to control nuisance organisms, e.g., insecticides, herbicides, fungicides, rodenticidies.

phalanx: **Digit** bones.

phaneric: Refers to coloration or other characters whose purpose is to be conspicuous as opposed to cryptic.

pharynx: Throat cavity leading to the esophagus and **trachea**.

phase: *See* **morph**.

phenology: Study of visible appearances in relation to season or climate, e.g., first arrival of a **migratory species**.

phenotype: Sum of organism's external characteristics (i.e. appearance) as opposed to **genotype**.

philopatry: Fidelity to a home area (*see* **Orstreue**).

phoresy: Passive transport of one organism by another without involving parasitism.

photoperiodism: Daily light–dark cycle used as a source of predictive information for annual events, e.g., breeding, migration.

phylogeny: Evolutionary history of a taxon.

physiology: Study of bodily function.

pigeon's milk: *See* **crop milk**.

pigmentary colors: Pigments widely found in the **bill**, soft parts, and **feathers** of birds, e.g., melanin, carotenoids, hemoglobin, porphyrins.

pigmentation abnormality: Change in the amount and distribution of pigments, particularly the melanins and lipochromes.

pileated: Crested or capped shape of **feathers** on a bird's crown.

pileum: Entire top of the head from forehead to nape.

pinfeather: Newly growing **feather** still in its sheath.

pinion: Outer portion of a bird's wing from which the **flight feathers** arise, or a single flight feather, or collectively, the flight feathers.

pinioning: Cutting one wing at the carpal joint to prevent the **primary feathers** from growing, permanently prohibiting flight in captive birds.

pipping: The act of chipping a hole in the airspace and **eggshell** by the **embryo** in preparation for **hatching**.

piracy: *See* **kleptoparasitism**.

piscivorous: Fish-eating.

pishing: "Shshshsh" sound preceded with a "p" made by humans to attract songbirds in close.

pitch: Height from which a falcon begins its **stooping**.

play: Activity performed by mostly young, but also adult birds of a wide variety of **species**.

pluma: **Contour feather** where the **barbs** are free and do not form a coherent **vane**.

plumage: **Feather** covering of a bird or feathered appearance of a bird in various stages of immaturity in its lifetime.

plumage abnormality: Abnormal colors, changes in **feather** patterning, changes in feather structure due to changes in the amount and distribution of pigments or chemical changes in the pigments themselves.

plumbeous: Lead-colored.

plume: A long **display** feather, e.g., pheasant tail.

plumula: **Down feather**.

plumule: *See* **plumula**.

plunge-diving: Behavior wherein a flying bird dives into the water from the air.

pneumatization: The invasion of **air sacs** into the hollow bones in birds' skeletons.

podotheca: Horny covering of the unfeathered areas of legs and feet.

pogonium: Web of a **feather**.

pollex: Thumb or first **digit** of the hand of the wing.

polyandry: **Mating** system wherein a female regularly mates with two or more males in a single breeding season.

polychromatism: Refers to variations in **plumage** colors worn by individuals within a species, e.g., gyrfalcon.

polygamy: **Mating** system wherein a bird has more than one mate in a single breeding season.

polygyny: **Mating** system wherein a male regularly mates with two or more females in a single breeding season.

polymorphism: Coexistence within an interbreeding population of two or more genetically determined forms or **morphs**.

polytokous: Producing many **eggs**.

polytypic: Taxon with more than one unit in the next lowest category, e.g., **genus** with several **species**.

population: Total number of individuals in a given area.

poryphyrin pigments: Pigments related to hemoglobin and bile and common in red and brown **feathers** of some bird.

postfledging mortality: Death rate of young after leaving the **nest**.

postjuvenal molt: Renewal of **feathers** from **juvenal** plumage to first winter plumage.

postnuptial molt: Renewal of feathers from breeding plumage to winter plumage.

poult: Domestic chicken.

poultry: Refers to birds of domesticated species to be eaten by humans.

powder down: **Feathers** that produce a fine powder for water resistance.

precocial: Refers to young birds that are active and not **nest**-bound right after **hatching**.

predation: Killing of one **species** by another for food.

preen gland: *See* **uropygial gland**.

preening invitation: Bowing of head and ruffling of feathers by one **species** to induce another to **preen** it, e.g., cowbirds.

preening: Act of grasping **feathers** in the **bill** to remove oil, dirt, and ectoparasites.

prejuvenal molt: First complete change of **feathers** from natal down to **juvenal** plumage.

prenuptial molt: Renewal of feathers from winter plumage to breeding plumage.

primary feather: **Flight feathers** borne on the **manus**.

proaposematic: Refers to markings that warn predators of undesirability, e.g., **egg** patterns or colors.

proepisematic: Refers to **plumage** markings that serve to facilitate recognition and help maintain contact among members of **family** or feeding groups, e.g., waders.

prolactin: Hormone secreted by the pituitary gland and involved with broodiness, formation of a **brood patch**, production of **crop milk**, and other forms of sexual behavior.

promiscuity: Indiscriminate, casual sexual relationships, often brief in nature.

pronating: Rotation of the wing's leading edge downward to increase lift.

protoptile: First of two **nestling down plumages**.

proventriculus: The glandular or chemical stomach preceding the **gizzard**.

psilopaedic: Refers to young bird with little or no **down** when **hatched**.

psittacine: Member of the parrot family.

psittacosis: Virus disease affecting parrots and some other birds and communicable to humans.

pteryla: Discrete tract of skin bearing **contour feathers**.

pterylography: Study of arrangement of **feathers** on the skin.

pterylosis: Arrangement of **contour feathers** into orderly groups or tracts.

ptilopaedic: Refers to young bird wearing **down** when **hatched**.

ptilopody: Refers to feathered toes and legs.

ptilosis: *See* **plumage**.

puffinosis: Disease of the manx shearwater similar to **psittacosis**.

pullet: Immature female domestic fowl.

pullus: Age-class name for **nestling** or **chick** prior to **fledging** used by scientists.

pupil: Round opening in the eyeball that contracts or expands to allow the entry of light.

pygostyle: Caudal end bone of the vertebral column.

pyloric stomach: Specialized chamber between the **gizzard** and small intestine with various functions in different bird species.

pylorus: Opening of the **gizzard** into the **duodenum**.

quasi-social: Referring to behavioral adaptations that facilitate aggregation behavior.

quill: Calamus of a **feather** or a feather in general.

race: *See* **subspecies**.

rachis: Shaft of a **feather**.

racing pigeon: Domesticated pigeon bred for its flying ability.

racket: Terminal broadening of a **feather vane**.

racquet: *See* **racket**.

radiation: Geographical spread of a **species** or group of related species from a geographical region where they originally evolved or divergence of forms of common ancestry.

radiotracking: *See* **biotelemetry**.

radius: Slenderer of two bones comprising the **forearm** of the wing.

raft: Dense **flock** of birds (e.g., waterfowl) on the water.

rain-posture: Special stance taken by certain birds in regions of seasonal downpours to shed water while perching.

ramus: **Barb** of a **feather** or one of two lateral halves of the lower **mandible**.

range: Geographic area in which a **species** is found.

raptor: *See* **bird of prey**.

Rare Bird Alert: Telephone service facilitating exchange of information on rare bird sightings among North American **birders**.

rarity: A bird uncommon in a given area, but perhaps common elsewhere.

ratite: Refers to flightless birds not having a **keel**, e.g., kiwi.

recovery plan: Government plan or program set up to restore **endangered** species in North America.

recovery team: Group of specialists assigned to produce and implement a **recovery plan** for an endangered species in North America.

recruitment: Addition of new individuals to a **population** by reproduction.

rectrices: Main tail **feathers**.

rectrix: *See* **rectrices**.

redirection: Directing a behavioral response at something other than what an observer would expect, e.g., hungry bird pecking at inanimate objects.

reeve: A female **ruff**.

refuge: Land set aside for protection of wildlife.

regurgitation: Act of casting up or vomiting partly digested food for **nestlings** or undigestible parts of prey (i.e., fur, feather and bone) or stomach oil in some young seabirds.

releaser: Behavior for a stimulus that signals another organism to perform an appropriate action.

relic population: Isolated **population** that once had a much wider distribution.

remex: *See* **remiges**.

remicle: Small **feather** found on the wing in some birds.

remiges: Main **flight feather**, i.e., primaries, secondaries.

Rensch's Rule: Stomach, intestine, and **caeca** of birds on a mixed diet are relatively smaller in tropical than temperate zone races or wings of races living in a cold climate or high altitudes are relatively longer than those in warmer climates or low altitudes.

reproductive isolation: Refers to those factors that prevent **interbreeding** between closely related **species**.

reserve: Land set aside for wildlife and with restricted use by people.

resident: Non-**migratory** or sedentary individual, **populations, subspecies**, or **species** that remains in a given area throughout the year.

restoration ecology: Study of re-creating a natural or self-sustaining community or **ecosystem**.

retromigration: **Migratory** movement of birds misled by a geographical feature (e.g., coastline) into taking a direction divergent from or even the opposite of their normal desired one.

reverse migration: **Migratory** movement of birds in the opposite direction to which they are expected.

rhamphotheca: Covering of the **bill** that is horny in most birds but soft and leathery in some shorebirds and waterfowl.

rhodopsin: Light-sensitive substance found in the **rods** of the retina.

rictal bristles: Thin, stiff **feathers** growing around the **beak** in some **insectivorous** birds.

rictus: Soft, fleshy part of a bird's **bill** at the angle of the mouth.

ring: Leg band.

ringing: *See* **banding**.

ringing up: Upward circling flight of hunting falcon to get above its avian prey.

rocket net: Large mesh nets propelled by projectiles shot from cannons to catch large numbers of feeding birds at one time.

rod: Light-sensitive cells in the retina of birds, e.g., more plentiful in nocturnal species.

roding: Territorial twilight flights of male Eurasian woodcock.

rookery: Refers to nesting colony of rooks as well as other birds.

roost: Place that **flocking species** (e.g., blackbirds) gather to sleep.

roosting: Sleep or resting behavior in a bird.

rostrum: **Bill** or beak.

Roundup: **Bird-watching** event whereupon a given area is covered as thoroughly as possible by **birding** teams.

rufescent: Somewhat tinged with reddish.

rufous: Appearing orangy-brown to reddish-brown.

rump: Area between lower back and the base of the tail.

ruptive: Refers to patterns or bold markings (e.g., stripes, spots) that serve to break up the body outline.

rush: *See* **fall**.

saddle: Unbroken continuation of color on upper surface of bird's wings.

salt gland: Specialized glands in the orbital area to secrete excess salt, e.g., seabirds.

saltatory: Pertaining to leaping.

sanctuary: Area of land of any size with restricted use by people.

sap-feeding: Using the tongue to eat sap oozing from a hole drilled in the bark of a tree, e.g., sapsucker.

scansorial: Pertaining to climbing on tree trunks.

scapula: Paired shoulder blade.

scapulars: Feathers above the shoulder.

scapus: Whole **feather** stem.

scaring: Refers to using a stimulus to move birds away from an area where they might cause damage.

scavenger: Bird that feeds upon dead animals, garbage, and sewage.

schizochroism: Color abnormality whereby a pigment or several pigments normally in the **plumage** are missing.

sclera: Ring of overlapping bony plates that protect the eye.

scrape: A slightly hollowed out depression in a **nest** substrate, sometimes lined with material, in which a bird lays its **eggs** or European term for an artificially constructed shallow pool to attract wading birds.

scutella: Overlapping horny scales arranged vertically on the **tarsus.**

search image: Fixation on an abundant food source that is learned from past experience.

second-year (SY): Bird in its second calendar year of life.

secondary feather: Flight feather arising on the **forearm** or **ulna.**

sedentary: *See* **resident.**

seed dispersal: The incidental spreading of seeds by plants via birds, especially frugivores, which void intact seeds.

sematic: Describes a color or behavior that serves as a signal for warning or attraction.

semi-altricial: Refers to a **hatchling** born with its eyes open and a coat of **down** that remains in the nest to be cared for by the parents until **fledging.**

semi-precocial: Same as **semi-altricial,** except that this **hatchling** leaves the nest when it can walk while still fed by the parents.

semi-species: Forms that are closely related but totally isolated geographically.

semicircular canals: Specialized organ within the inner ear that serve to maintain a bird's equilibrium.

semiplume: Type of **feather** intermediate between a **contour feather** and **down.**

set: *See* **clutch.**

setose: Having **bristles.**

sex-role reversal: Refers to a **species** wherein the female courts the male and the male **incubates** the **eggs,** e.g., phalarope.

sexual selection: Refers to competition among members of one sex for **mating** opportunities with the opposite sex or a preference by members of one sex for members of the other based on various characteristics, e.g. size, shape.

sexual dimorphism: Differences in the appearance of the male and female of a **species.**

shaft: Midrib of a **feather.**

shank: Refers to all or part of the leg (AKA **tarsus**).

sharming: Refers to grunts and squeals of a water rail.

shell gland: Uterus of an **oviduct** where **eggshell** is laid down.

short-distance migration: Migratory pattern in which a **species** moves within rather between temperate or tropical zones.

siblicide: *See* **Cain and Abel Syndrome.**

sibling species: Two or more closely related **species** that look like one another but do not interbreed.

sickles: Elongated central tail **feathers** in some species.

sight record: Eyewitness recording of a bird **species** in a given area that was not confirmed by a collected specimen, photograph, or tape recording.

sign stimulus: Phenomenon, usually visual, to which organisms can be expected to respond predictably.

sinciput: Area of head comprising the forehead and crown.

single-brooded: Raising only one family of young in a **breeding season**.

singing assembly: Group of two or more territorial males localized in a lek or arena for courtship and singing.

sink habitat: **Habitat** in which reproduction is not sufficient to balance with mortality to maintain **population** levels.

sink population: **Population** that occupies sink **habitat** and that requires emigration of individuals to sustain itself.

sinuated: Describes a **feather** with one edge cut away in a wavy fashion.

site tenacity: Attachment of birds and their succeeding generations to a nesting site.

skin: Study specimen consisting of a dead bird, i.e., preserved skin, **feathers**, legs, skull, and **beak**.

smoke-bathing: Comfort behavior wherein a bird exposes itself to smoke, steam, or the heat of flames to discourage **ectoparasites**.

soaring: Sustained flight without wing-flapping and aided by air movements.

sociobiology: Study of the biological basis of behavior.

soft parts: *See* **bare parts**.

solferino: Bluish-red.

sonagram: Written reproduction of a recorded bird song.

sonagraph: Machine that employs a stylus to transfer pattern of pitch and frequency from recordings of bird song.

song period: Time of year in which a particular **species** sings.

source habitat: **Habitat** that is capable of exporting individuals.

source population: **Population** that occupies source **habitat** in which the output of offspring exceeds the carrying capacity.

specialist: **Species** with narrow food and/or **habitat** preferences.

speciation: Process wherein new **species** are formed as a result of **reproductive isolation**.

species: Group of **interbreeding** natural **populations** that are reproductively isolated from other populations.

species diversity index: Mathematical index which describes the numbers and relative abundance of bird **species** in a given area.

species group: Refers to a collection of closely related **species**.

species pair: Two very closely related and similar-looking **species**.

species-specific: Referring to one particular **species**.

speculum: Distinctive wing patch on the secondaries, especially seen in waterfowl **plumage**.

spermatozoa: Male **germ cells**.

spermatozoid: Male **germ cell** in the free-swimming stage.

spermatozoon: Male **germ cell**.

spishing: *See* **pishing**.

spleen: Reddish-brown, round organ involved in immune response.

splitter: Someone who prefers to separate bird **forms** into smaller **taxonomic** units, e.g., **subspecies**.

spot-mapping method: Census in which individuals seen or heard during a specified period are plotted on a map to estimate territories or **home ranges**.

spur: Sharp, horny growth on the back of the **tarsus**, e.g., pheasant.

squab: Unfledged **nestling**, usually a pigeon or dove.

squeaking: Making mouse-like noises by puckering one's lips or sucking on the back of one's hand to attract songbirds.

stenoecious: Able to exist in one or a few **habitats**.

stenophagous: Restricted to eating only certain foods.

sternum: Breastbone, or **keel**, to which flight muscles are anchored.

stipule: Newly emerging **feather**.

stomach oil: Foul-smelling liquid regurgitated by some seabirds (e.g., fulmar) in self-defense.

stooping: Steep diving, generally by **birds of prey** pursuing quarry.

stragulum: *See* **mantle**.

striated: Streaked.

structural coloration: Color produced when **feather** structure interferes with light waves to absorb parts of the spectrum and reflect others, e.g., blue.

strutting ground: Refers to the social **display** of the sage grouse.

stupefying baits: Chemicals placed in food to render organisms comatose, e.g., alpha chloralose.

sub-adult: Bird not yet in its full adult **plumage**.

subclass: Secondary taxonomic category between **class** and **order**.

subfamily: Secondary taxonomic category between **family** and **genus**.

subgenus: Secondary taxonomic occasionally interposed between **genus** and **species**.

suborder: Secondary taxonomic category between **order** and **family**.

subsong: Song differing from the main characteristic song of a **species**.

subspecies: **Population** that is morphologically, physiologically, or behaviorally distinct from members of other populations of its **species**, but can interbreed when contact is made.

summer visitor: **Species** that spends the warmer months of the year in a given area but breeds elsewhere.

summer resident: **Species** that breeds in a given area but spends the winter elsewhere.

sunbathing: *See* **sunning**.

sunning: Comfort behavior wherein a bird orientates itself or adopts a special posture to capture the sun's warmth.

superciliary: Refers to **plumage** marking above the eye, e.g., stripe, line.

superfamily: Secondary taxonomic category between **suborder** and **family**.

superorder: Secondary taxonomic category between **subclass** and **order**.

superspecies: **Species** ranked below a **genus**, but having no nomenclatural status.

supinating: Rotating leading edge of the wing upward to promote braking.

supraorbital gland: *See* **salt gland**.

surface-diving: Behavior wherein a bird on the surface of the water submerges itself.

symbiosis: Relationship between two organisms which is beneficial to both.

sympatric: Occurring in the same geographical area.

synanthropic: Preferring human-altered **habitat**.

synaposematic: Refers to a warning signal shared with other species.

synchronous hatching: Refers to the simultaneous emergence of young from a **clutch** of **eggs**.

synsacrum: Bone resulting fusion of thoracic, lumbar, and sacral vertebrae.

syringes: Plural of **syrinx**.

syrinx: Organ of voice or song.

systematics: Refers to the use of nomenclature to classify organisms taxonomically.

tail: Collectively refers to the **feathers** or **retrices** and their respective **coverts** used for flight, **display**, and **courtship**.

talon: Sharp, pointed claw on the toe of a **raptor**.

tape lure: Prerecorded calls used to attract birds.

tarsal scale: Horny, keratinous material covering the exterior of the foot and/or leg sometimes in overlapping fashion.

tarsometatarsus: Bone of a bird's leg between the ankle and the toes.

tarsus: Bird's leg between the ankle and the toes.

tawny: Golden-brown.

taxa: Plural of taxon.

taxis: Movement toward or away from a stimulus.

taxon: Category used for classifying and naming biological entities, e.g. kingdom, phylum, class, order, etc.

taxonomy: Science of classification or using nomenclature to name plants and animals.

tectrices: Plural of **tectrix**.

tectrix: *See* **covert**.

telemetry: *See* **biotelemetry**.

teleology: Study of adaptation.

teleoptiles: Various **feathers** of an adult bird.

teratism: Morphological or anatomical abnormality.

territory: Area defended by one or more individuals against other individuals of the same or different **species**.

tertiaries: Feathers arising from the **humerus** which function as additional **flight feathers** instead of just **coverts**.

testes: Paired male **gonads**.

thermal: Columns of warm air rising from the earth.

third-year (TY): Bird in its third calendar year.

thoracic: Pertaining to the **thorax**.

thorax: Chest cavity housing heart and lungs.

tibiotarsus: Leg bone between the knee and the ankle.

tick: New species added to a **birder**'s list.

ticker: *See* **lister**.

tiercel: Male falcon.

tippet: Elongated facial **feathers** of typical grebes.

toboganning: Use of body by penguins to slide down an icy surface, generally to enter the water.

tomia: Plural of **tomium**.

tomial tooth: Toothlike projection on **mandible** of falcons and shrikes.

tomium: Cutting edge of a **mandible** on a **beak**.

tool-using: Using external objects as extensions of the body to attain a goal, e.g., woodpecker finch using a cactus spine to probe for insects.

topography: External areas and features of a bird's **plumage** and **bare parts**.

torpidity: State of dormancy and lowered body temperature undertaken to conserve energy during a period of energy shortage, e.g., poorwills.

trachea: Windpipe arising from **glottis** and subdividing into two bronchi leading to the lungs.

track: Flight path of a bird relative to the earth's surface.

train: Long tail of a peacock or the tail of a falconer's bird.

transient: Refers to migrating birds that are passing through an area, but neither breed nor overwinter there.

traplining: Behavior of hummingbirds wherein they visit a variety of flowers over a regularly traveled route.

trash bird: **Bird-watcher**'s term that refers to birds undesirable for a **bird list** (e.g., feral pigeon) or a locally abundant species that is a top bird elsewhere.

treading: Act of a male bird **copulating** with a female.

trill: Rapid succession of notes.

trituration: Muscular action of **gizzard** to grind or crush into fine particles.

triumph ceremony: **Display** given by a **pair** of birds following a successful aggressive encounter.

trophic: Pertaining to food or nutrition.

trophic level: Position in the food chain based on the number of energy-transfer steps above or below it, e.g., herbivore.

tropism: Tendency to react to a given stimulus in a certain manner.

tubenose: Marine birds like albatrosses, petrels, and shearwaters that pump out excess salt from special glands via a tube on their **beak**.

tunic: One of three membrane layers enclosing the eyeball.

turacin: Copper-based red pigment in **feathers**.

turning down: Releasing captive-bred birds into the wild.

turnover ratio: Number of **species** entering and disappearing from a community.

twitcher: *See* **lister**.

tympanum: Eardrum.

tympanic membrane: Syringeal membranes that vibrate to produce sound.

ulna: Thicker of two bones comprising the **forearm** of the wing.

umbilicus: Opening in a **feather** shaft allowing for nutrition of a growing feather.

uncinate process: Hook-like projections on birds' ribs for tendon attachments.

unguis: Nail at the tip of the upper **mandible** of waterfowl.

uniparous: Laying only one egg, e.g., auk.

urates: Insoluble part of the nitrogenous wastes of a bird.

uric acid: Collective term for nitrogenous wastes excreted by birds.

urine: Water portion of the nitrogenous wastes of a bird.

urodeum: Chamber of the **cloaca** where the uric acid is stored prior to release.

uropygial gland: Secretory gland just above the base of the tail **feathers** that provides oil for **preening**.

uropygium: *See* **rump**.

uterus: *See* **shell gland**.

vagina: Region of the **oviduct** where the **egg** is held prior to **oviposition**.

vagrant: A bird that accidentally or purposely wanders beyond its normal **range**.

vane: Series of **barbs** on each side of a **rachis** of a **feather**.

variegated: With spots or patches of different colors.

variety: *See* **form**.

vas deferens: *See ductus deferens*.

vector: An animal carrier of parasites or infections transmissable to other organisms.

vent: Opening of the **cloaca**.

ventral: Describing the belly side or the lower surface of the body.

ventriculus: *See* **gizzard**.

vermiculated: **Plumage** covered with a dense pattern of irregular fine lines.

vernacular name: Common, popular, or local name for a bird.

vertex: *See* **crown**.

vexillum: *See* **vane**.

vibrissae: Small, **bristle**-like **feathers** found at the base of the **bill** or around the eyes and sensitive to the touch.

vinaceous: Wine-colored.

visitor: Refers to birds present in a given area at a certain time of the year, e.g., summer, winter.

visual acuity: Sharpness of vision or ability to perceive fine detail.

vitelline membrane: Outside layer that encloses the **yolk** of an **egg**.

vitellus: Egg yolk.

vocal mimicry: Imitation by birds of sounds other than their own **vocalizations**.

vocalization: Sound produced by the **syrinx**.

volant: Capable of flight.

wader: Shorebird.

water dance: **Courtship display** on or under water by alcids, loons, and grebes.

waterfowl: Wild aquatic birds.

wattle: *See* **lappet**.

wave: Refers to an abundance of migrant land birds of many species arriving simultaneously in a given area.

web: Fleshy membrane between the toes, usually in waterbirds, or **vane**, or vexillum.

wildfowl: Quarry **species** of birds other than game birds.

window: Seemingly translucent patch on the underside of wings used as an identifying feature in some birds, e.g., red-shouldered hawk.

window-fighting: *See* **image-fighting**.

wing formula: Mathematical description of the shape of the outer portion of a bird's wing.

wing loading: Mathematical formula involving a bird's wing area and body weight.

wing clapping: Producing a loud crack by striking raised wings together.

wingbar: One or two contrasting lines running across a bird's folded wing.

wingspan: Measurement from one wing tip to the other when wings are fully extended.

winnowing: Wavering sound produced by snipe during **courtship** flight.

Winter Bird Population Study: Census coordinated by the National Audubon Society in the U.S. wherein wintering birds are counted and mapped.

wishbone: *See* **furcula**.

world birder: **Birder** intent on seeing birds all over the world.

wreck: Refers to large number of **pelagic** birds incapacitated on land by strong onshore winds during migration.

wrist: Joint of the **forearm** and the **manus**.

xanthochromism: Abnormal dominance of yellow coloration due to absence of normal amounts of darker pigments.

xerophilous: Adapted to living in a dry climate.

yarak: **Falconry** terms that refers to a readiness to hunt in **raptors**.

Year List: A list of the bird species seen in a selected geographical area in one year.

yolk: Yellow-orange mass of protein and fat granules enclosed by a thin transparent membrane.

yolk sac: Membranous pouch containing the **egg yolk** which is provided as food to the developing **embryo**.

zone: Distinctive broad band of color encircling the body.

zoogeography: Study of the distribution of **flora** and **fauna** over large geographic areas.

zoology: Study of animals.

zoonosis: Disease transmitted naturally from animals to humans.

Zugscheide: German term referring to a line or zone whereupon the birds living on either side migrate in different directions, e.g., white stork.

Zugunruhe: *See* **migratory restlessness**.

Zwischenzug: German term referring to nomadic movements by birds between the **breeding season** and **migration**.

zygomatic arch: Facial bones.